Contemporary Readings in Child Psychology

Contemporary Readings in Child Psychology

Second Edition

E. Mavis Hetherington
Department of Psychology
University of Virginia

Ross D. Parke
Department of Psychology
University of Illinois

McGraw-Hill Book Company

New York St. Louis San Francisco Auckland Bogotá Hamburg
Johannesburg London Madrid Mexico Montreal New Delhi Panama
Paris São Paulo Singapore Sydney Tokyo Toronto

This book was set in Times Roman by The Total Book (ECU/BD).
The editors were Patricia S. Nave and Rhona Robbin;
the production supervisor was Phil Galea.
R. R. Donnelley & Sons Company was printer and binder.

CONTEMPORARY READINGS IN CHILD PSYCHOLOGY

2 3 4 5 6 7 8 9 0 DODO 8 9 8 7 6 5 4 3 2 1

See Acknowledgments on pages 417–419. Copyrights included on this page by reference.

Library of Congress Cataloging in Publication Data

Main entry under title:

Contemporary readings in child psychology.

    Includes bibliographies.
    1. Child psychology. I. Hetherington, Eileen
Mavis, date   II. Parke, Ross D.
BF721.C62 1981   155.4   80-24599
ISBN 0-07-028426-1

To John and Sue
and Our Children:
Grant, Eric, and Jason
Gillian, Timothy, and Megan

Contents

2

INFANCY AND EARLY EXPERIENCE

3

EMOTIONAL DEVELOPMENT

4

LANGUAGE AND COMMUNICATION

5

COGNITION AND LEARNING

6

INDIVIDUAL DIFFERENCES IN INTELLIGENCE

Preface

The field of child psychology has undergone radical changes in the past decade and change is still the clearest characteristic of this exciting area of study. The purpose of this volume is to provide students a firsthand opportunity to share some of the recent research findings of child psychologists.

A number of themes run throughout the field of child psychology and we have tried to choose articles that will illustrate these themes. One of the most important themes is our revised view of the child and the important role that the child plays in his or her own development. We recognize that infants and children are more capable, more influential, and more effective at earlier ages than ever before. The shift is best described by the view of the child as "competent." Recent research in infancy illustrates the shift very dramatically. Gone forever is our old view of infants as passive creatures of limited sensory, perceptual, and social capacities, awaiting the imprint of the adult world. Instead we now recognize that infants have much greater capacity to see, learn, and even socialize; the articles on infancy in this volume have helped dispel our earlier myths by demonstrating the wide range of perceptual and social competence that infants display. Infants are more prepared to respond and to interact with their environment than we previously imagined. Part of the shift in our views of infancy can be credited to our revised recognition of the contribution of biological and genetic factors in child development. We have not shifted back to a one-sided biological view of development; rather we now appreciate the important interactions between genetics and environment in shaping the course of development. In this volume, this interaction is illustrated in a host of different ways, including the IQ controversy, the role of nutrition in cognitive development, and the influence of hormones on sex role development.

Nor is it only our views of the *infant's* competence that have changed: children at *all levels of development* are increasingly recognized as competent, active, and influential. In both cognitive and social development, the child is viewed as an active participant. Children are curious, information-seeking, and information-processing organisms and no longer just passive actors in the learning process as the recent research represented in this book on both language and cognition illustrates so well. Similarly in the social sphere, our views of the child have changed. One shift is the recognition of the important relationship between cognitive and social development; the child's cognitive capacities are viewed as playing an influential role in shaping his or her social behavior and vice versa; social skills may play a role in modifying cognitive development.

A most dramatic change concerns our recognition of the child's role in his or her own socialization. Our unidirectional view of development whereby adults influence children but children do not alter adult behavior, is inadequate. Children play an active role in modifying and altering adult behavior—even in early infancy. A bidirectional view of socialization is now widely accepted with children playing an influential part in their own social and cognitive development.

There are other themes as well. A current concern is the study of the child from a developmental perspective so that the age-related changes and transformations in motor, social, and cognitive spheres can be described and understood. In this search, there are two aims: (1) to describe the nature of the child's development and (2) to explain the processes that account for the developmental progression.

These two aims have led to a recognition that a wide variety of methodological strategies are necessary. No single method will suffice. On the one hand child development specialists have been influenced by recent trends in other fields, such as ethology which emphasizes the study of the organism in its natural environment. Under this influence, there has been a renewed interest in describing the behavior of children at different ages in a variety of naturalistic settings, including homes, schools, and playgrounds. It is hoped that this trend will yield important data concerning how children in different cultures and subcultures develop in their own unique real-life environments.

At the same time, researchers continue the important task of understanding the processes of development. To a large extent, the preferred methodology for achieving this goal is the laboratory experiment. Using a well-controlled situation, this method allows the manipulation of relevant variables in order to establish clear cause-effect relationships. Increasingly, developmental psychologists are combining observational and experimental approaches; the observations yield hypotheses or clues concerning possible processes; in turn, these hunches can be systematically assessed in the laboratory. The importance of this trend is that the laboratory experiments are more likely to be testing hypotheses that will be of relevance to the ways in which children develop in their naturalistic environment.

Just as there are multiple methods, there are multiple theories. Although the grand theoretical scheme of Piaget is still influential, child psychologists are increasingly becoming more modest and restricted in the scope of their theories. As the complexity and multifaceted nature of development become apparent, minitheories that aim to explain smaller pieces of the developmental puzzle are becoming more popular. Theories of sex-typing, aggression, memory, and grammar development are more likely than elaborabe theories aimed at explaining all social development or the total range of cognitive-language development.

Finally, child development is recognizing the culture-bound and even time-bound nature of its findings. As a number of articles in this book clearly show, no single picture of development is accurate for all cultures, social classes, or racial and ethnic groups. Children develop different skills and competencies in different cultural milieus; and no sweeping generalizations concerning children's development can be made without careful specification of a child's cultural background. Similarly, much of our knowledge about children is time-bound. Children and families are in a state of transition and change. It is our job not only to constantly monitor these changes, but to be aware of the very temporary nature of many of our "facts" about children.

Another theme of child psychology today is that it is influenced by and influences social policy concerning children. Just as government programs such as Head Start and day care programs alter the lives of children, the findings of child psychologists often give impetus and support to new types of government intervention on behalf of children. A significant shift over the past decade has been the increasing interdependence of child development as a scientific discipline and government policy.

PLAN OF THE BOOK

It is the aim of this volume to illustrate these contemporary themes in child psychology. An understanding of children must take into account both developmental changes that occur over the span of childhood as well as the processes underlying developmental changes and transitions. Therefore, we have organized this volume to reflect this viewpoint. Our topic-oriented organization permits us to achieve both of our goals. Each chapter deals with both the processes of development as well as the ways in which children change over age.

In this second edition we have provided a balance between overviews of recent research and reports of individual research projects using a wide range of methodologies. To complement our text, Hetherington and Parke's *Child Psychology: A Contemporary Viewpoint,* we have organized this second edition of *Contemporary Readings in Child Psychology* to correspond closely to the topical organization of our text. However, we should emphasize that this volume of readings can easily be used with any of the currently available child and developmental psychology textbooks.

In the first chapter, biological influences on development are represented by a wide range of topics including the impact of premature birth, ethnic differences in the bahavior of newborn infants, and the effects of nutrition on development.

The second chapter deals with a topic of continuing interest: infancy and early experience. Recent advances in cognitive, perceptual, and social development are highlighted and the implications of these findings for understanding Sudden Infant Death are discussed in the Lipsitt paper. In the Kagan and Klein selection, the long-term effects of early experience are critically examined.

Chapter 3 addresses the issue of emotional development from a variety of perspectives including the development of emotions in blind infants, fear of strangers, and ways of overcoming fear of hospitalization in young children.

Language, the topic of Chapter 4, is introduced by Jerome Bruner who shows how language learning may originate in early interactions between mother and infant. Other topics include the development of grammar across a wide variety of cultures, the development of language in deaf children, and communication in different settings and subcultures.

To lead off Chapter 5 on cognitive development, an overview of Piaget is provided, followed by Gelman's recent review of preschool thought, and Flavell's analysis of children's understanding of their own memory processes. Articles concerning children's understanding of the spatial environment and the effects of punishment complete this chapter.

The continuing controversy over genetic and environmental determinants of intelligence is one focus of Chapter 6. Others are recent studies of birth order and IQ.

In Chapter 7, a variety of agents that play important roles in childhood socialization are represented. The family remains an influential socialization agency as illustrated by papers on father-infant interaction, child abuse, the impact of divorce, and finally, an overview of alternative childrearing arrangements, including the effects of day care.

In Chapters 8 and 9, peers and the school—two important but often neglected socialization agencies—are recognized. Recent studies of the determinants of friendship, the effects of physical attractiveness, and ways of increasing interaction of socially isolated children are included in the peer chapter. In the school section, a wide range of topics is represented, including the impact of the physical setting, teacher expectancy effects, early educational interventions, and ways of improving classroom cooperation.

In the final section topical issues such as moral development, altruism, achievement, and sex typing are highlighted. The volume closes with an overview of recent studies of the effects of TV on children's behavior.

It is our hope that you will not only learn from these articles some of the recent findings, methods, and theories of child psychology, but that through these articles you will share the excitement of our contemporary efforts to understand children.

STATISTICAL GUIDE

Many students who read this volume will be unfamiliar with the common statistical terms used in research articles. To make the research articles more readable for students we have edited those articles to minimize the number of statistical terms included. In some cases this type of editing has not been possible, but generally the student can understand the hypotheses, methodology, and findings of the study without becoming enmeshed in specific statistical details which may be beyond the student's level of expertise.

In addition, to help students with some of the common statistical terms, we provide a brief discussion of these terms:

Mean and Median: The mean ($\overline{X}$) and median (M) are both measures of central tendency; the mean refers to the *arithmetic average* and so the mean height of children in a classroom would be the sum of the heights of individual children divided by the number of children in the class. The median, on the other hand, refers to the *middle number* when a group of values are arranged from smallest to largest. Therefore, the median height would be the height of the child who is in the middle of the group if all the students lined up from shortest to tallest.

Standard Deviation: (SD) is a measure of the variability or range of the values in a group of scores. For example, if the heights of the children in a class were all within 1 inch of each other, the standard deviation would be small; if the range was 8 inches, the standard deviation would be larger.

Correlation is an index of the relationship between two variables and is expressed in terms of the direction and size of the relationship. Height and weight are related in a positive direction since as height increases, so does weight typically rise. On the other hand, if one factor increases while the other factor decreases, the correlation is a negative one. Finally, if no relationship exists between two factors, such as eye color and IQ, then we speak of a zero order correlation. This means that changes in one factor are not related in any systematic way to changes in another factor.

Statistical Tests: A variety of tests will be found in the selections such as analysis of variance, t-tests, and chi-squares. Each of these represents different ways of determining whether differences among groups of subjects are due to chance factors. For the analysis of variance, a value of F will be given followed by another value that indicates the level of significance; for t-tests, a t value is provided, and for chi-square, a X^2 value is given. The important issue for your understanding the articles is the *level of significance* associated with each of these tests. Next we provide an explanation of this term.

Levels of Statistical Significance: The purpose of statistical tests is to permit the investigator to determine whether the results of his or her investigation were due to chance factors. For example, two groups of subjects may have received different treatments and the results of the statistical test yielded the following: $p < .05$ or $p < .01$. These values mean that the differences between the groups could have occurred by chance alone only 5 times out of 100 ($p < .05$) or 1 time out of 100 ($p < .01$). Most investigators in child psychology accept a finding as reliable and trustworthy if the difference is at the .05 level of significance.

This is a limited survey of common statistical terms, but we trust that it will help in understanding the articles presented in this book.

Thanks are extended to the following reviewers for their comments on the revision: Dr. Jay Belsky, Pennsylvania State University; Dr. Mary Carol Day, University of Houston; Professor Shari Lynn Kuchenbecker, Chapman College; Dr. Robert Miller, Plymouth State College; Professor Katherine J. Van Giffen, University of Denver.

REFERENCE WORKS

We have listed below a series of common reference sources in child psychology. For students who wish to pursue a topic in greater depth, this list will be a helpful guide to the literature.

Achenback, T. M. *Research in developmental psychology: concepts, strategies, methods*. New York: Free Press, 1978.

Advances in child behavior and development. Vol. 1-12. New York: Academic Press, 1963–present.

Caldwell, B. M., and Ricciuti, H. N. (Eds.) *Review of child development research*. Vol. 3. Chicago: University of Chicago Press, 1973.

Flavell, J. *Cognitive development*. Englewood Cliffs, N.J.: Prentice-Hall, 1977.

Hartup, W. W. (Ed.) *The young child: reviews of research*. Vol. II. Washington: National Association for the Education of Young Children, 1972.

Hetherington, E. M. (Ed.) *Review of child development research*. Vol. 5. Chicago: University of Chicago Press, 1975.

Horowitz, F. G. (Ed.) *Review of child development research*. Vol. 4. Chicago: University of Chicago Press, 1975.

Lewis, M., and Rosenblum, L. A. *The origins of behavior series*. Vol. 1-3. New York: Wiley, 1974, 1975, 1976.

Minnesota symposia on child psychology. Vol. 1-10. Minneapolis: University of Minnesota Press. Vol. 11–present. Erlbaum Assoc.

Mussen, P. H. (Ed.) *Carmichael's manual of child psychology*. Vol. 1-2. New York: Wiley, 1970.

Osofsky, J. (Ed.) *Handbook of infant development*. New York: Wiley, 1979.

E. Mavis Hetherington
Ross D. Parke

Contemporary Readings in Child Psychology

Chapter One

The Biological Basis of Behavior

Some concepts, theories, and controversies in developmental psychology appear briefly, stimulate a flurry of research activity, and disappear having made little lasting impact on the field. Other questions continue to provoke psychologists and to be studied in a relatively unmodified and often unproductive form. Still other problems maintain a tenacious hold on the curiosity of developmental psychologists, but the questions asked about the issues change, new methods of studying them become available, the controversies remain in a changed form. The interaction between biological[1] and environmental factors in development is a topic that clearly falls in the last category.

Although the historical antecedents of this problem might be said to go back to the interests of the ancient Chinese and Greeks in the relation between body types and temperament, a more modern and directly relevant antecedent is Galton's book *English Men of Science; Their Nature and Nurture,* published in 1874. Galton reported that there was an unusually high incidence of intellectually and professionally outstanding persons among the relatives of eminent scientists. Until the interest in learning theory starting early in this century, and notably the rise of behaviorism in the 1930s and 1940s, the predominant emphasis was on the role of heredity as the important determinant of development, particularly intellectual development.

In many ways this biological determinism is a philosophy incompatible with American

---

[1]In our discussion the term "biological factors" will subsume both genetic factors and changes in the anatomy or physiology of the child resulting from external agents or events.

social and political thought, which emphasizes equality, social mobility, and the value of education. In a culture imbued with the Horatio Alger story that a poor boy, if he is virtuous and works hard, can be a success, and the notion that any American can grow up to be president, the emphasis on experience and environment by the behaviorists held great appeal. It is interesting to note that in more rigidly socially structured societies such as in Great Britain and some of the European countries the genetic position found a more hospitable milieu and has been maintained more vigorously than in the United States. The following famous statement by John B. Watson, the leader of behaviorism, is more compatible with the American dream than are "folksy" maxims such as "Blood will tell" or "You can't make a silk purse out of a sow's ear":

> Give me a dozen healthy infants, well-formed, and my own specified world to bring them up in, and I'll guarantee to take any one at random and train him to become any type of specialist I might select—doctor, lawyer, artist, merchant-chief and yes, even beggar-man and thief, regardless of his talents, penchants, tendencies, abilities, vocations, race of his ancestors. (Watson, 1959, p. 104)

Such extreme genetic or environmentalist positions led to what was called "the nature-nurture controversy" where proponents on each side of the controversy championed either biological or experiential factors to the exclusion of others. In the past twenty years such irrational extremism has yielded to the view that behavior is determined by the interaction of biological and experiential factors and the question of whether heredity or environment determines a characteristic is no longer being asked. Instead we are asking "how" and "when" genetic and environmental factors and transactions affect development.

These transactions occur throughout the course of development. The expression of the genotype, the biological inheritance of the individual, as a phenotype, the observable characteristics of an individual, is constantly being modified. The impact of the environment in shaping phenotypical expression of the genotype varies with the kind, the amount, and the timing of experiences. In addition some individuals may be genetically predisposed to be more vulnerable to certain environmental factors than are others. Some individuals and some fetuses may be more likely to alter in response to such things as drugs, malnutrition, anoxia, disease, stress, and sensory or social stimulation or deprivation. Some behaviors are also more difficult to modify than are others. Responses such as smiling, babbling, crawling, and walking in infants seem to be strongly genetically programmed. Blind infants smile at about the same time as seeing infants, the emergence of babbling occurs in a similar fashion in deaf and hearing infants, and children who spend much of their time restrained in swaddling clothes or on a cradle board, crawl and walk at about the same time as infants reared under more mobile conditions. Such behaviors where there are fewer possible alternative paths from phenotype to genotype, or where the behavior is difficult to deflect under extreme variations in experience, are said to be highly "canalized" (Waddington, 1966).

At one time psychologists interested in genetic-environmental transactions were concerned with the child only after birth. It is now recognized that some of the most powerful of these transactions may occur prenatally while the infant is developing rapidly in utero and that some of the adverse effects of such transactions can be averted. Innovations in genetics and perinatology and new techniques in the detection and treatment of genetic disorders have led to an increased interest in prenatal development. Many of the papers in this section deal with very recent advances in our understanding of transactions between genetic and environmental factors and also to a considerable extent with the control over these factors. In many the underlying question is whether through genetic engineering or through the manipulation of environments we can develop more competent individuals.

The paper by Albert Rosenfeld presents new findings on sex determination and anticipates parental preselection of the sex of their children. The research presented by Daniel Freedman emphasized the interaction of culture and biology in producing dramatic ethnic differences in temperament and behavior in babies in the first few days of life. This same emphasis on transactions between social, environmental, and biological factors is found in the papers by Ricciuti and Goldberg. It is not just the direct physical and neurological impact of factors such as malnutrition or prematurity that affect development; it is the associated experiential and social factors that modify or sustain their effects. The subtle influence of prematurity and early separation on mother-infant interaction is examined by Goldberg. Ricciuti is concerned with the influences of various social, educational, family, and child-rearing conditions found in the environment of the economically deprived, malnourished child. In none of the papers is the biological or environmental extremism prevalent twenty years ago apparent. All the authors present a transactional model of development which reflects the thinking of contemporary scientists working on human development.

REFERENCES

Galton, F. *English men of science: Their nature and nurture.* London: Macmillan, 1874.
Waddington, C. H. *Principles of development and differentiation.* New York: Macmillan, 1966.
Watson, J. B. *Behaviorism.* Chicago: University of Chicago Press, 1959.

If Oedipus' Parents Had Only Known

Albert Rosenfeld

Monarchs have traditionally wanted a boy first (so, indeed, have most parents), as heir to the throne. But King Laius of Thebes and his queen, Jocasta, really, *really* would have preferred a girl. They had been warned by the oracle that they would have a son who would kill his father and marry his mother. Sure enough, they did go ahead and have Oedipus—as we know from Freud in case we missed Sophocles.

If Laius and Jocasta had known what we know today about sperm and egg, or if they had had the contemporary equivalent of Dr. Landrum B. Shettles of New York to consult . . .

Among the facts we now know about the human sperm cell is that it is a packet of genetic material propelled by the energetic lashings of its tail—which it discards once it has reached and penetrated the egg. In the process of fertilization, it unites its 23 chromosomes with the egg's 23 to make up the 46 required to complete the manual of genetic instructions for the procreation of a human being.

Egg and sperm each carries, among its 23 chromosomes, a specific sex-determining chromosome, designated as X or Y. The egg's is always an X chromosome. An XX combination results in a female offspring; an XY, in a male. Because only the sperm can carry a Y chromosome, it is the sperm that determines the child's gender. An X-carrier is a gynosperm, or female-producer; a Y-carrier is an androsperm, or male-producer.

Dr. Shettles, who now does his research at the New York Fertility Foundation, has been a pioneer investigator in procreative biology. He has particularly sought to distinguish the differences between the two types of sperm—and to use the knowledge to help prospective parents predetermine the sex of their children. Photographs he produced a few years ago were not so clear to other scientists as to him; hence they were controversial and not universally accepted. But these new photographs, especially that below, taken by the scanning electron microscope, distinctly show the differences.

In each picture the sperm with the smaller, rounder head is the male-producing Y-carrier, and the larger, more oval head belongs to the female-producing X-carrier (hereinafter to be called Y and X and referred to as *he* and *she* as a space-saving convenience—though it does seem a bit strange to be calling a sperm *she*). X carries more genetic material; the male apparently gets short-changed genetically. In addition to being lighter, Y has a longer tail. Thus he is speedier. (Shettles has confirmed this difference by racing them.) But X is more durable. If the egg is ready and waiting, Y has a better chance of getting there first. But if ovulation is still a couple of days away, Y is more likely to have used up his energy, switching the odds to X, who, moving at a more stately pace, picks up the prize.

Other factors that favor Y are an alkaline environment and the presence of the secretions that follow female orgasm. X does better when conditions are slightly acidic. She doesn't necessarily *like* the acid—which in fact slows down both X and Y—but X is apparently better equipped to "tough it out." These discoveries are not all Shettles's by any means, but he uses them—as do a few other doctors—to give parents an opportunity to call the shots with claims of 80 to 85 percent accuracy (see box).

Shettles has for years been interested in those families that have all girls or all boys. In the fathers of all-boy families that he investigated, the spermatozoa were almost exclusively Ys, and in the all-girl cases, they were predominantly Xs.

Dr. Shettles's Advice for Improving Nature's Odds

To FAVOR FEMALE OFFSPRING: (1) intercourse ceasing two to three days before ovulation, preceded by an acid douche of water and vinegar; (2) intercourse without female orgasm; (3) shallow penetration by the male at emission.

To FAVOR MALE OFFSPRING: (1) intercourse at the time of ovulation, with prior abstinence during a given cycle, preceded by an alkaline douche of water and baking soda; (2) intercourse with female orgasm; (3) deep penetration at the time of emission.

In normal sperm, by the way, Ys are present in greater quantities. Nature seems to have provided the added quantity to offset the Y's greater fragility. Though Shettles estimates, from a study of the literature, that 160 males are conceived for every 100 females, so many male embryos are spontaneously aborted that only 105 males are actually born for every 100 females. This handicap appears necessary because more males die at almost every age until, toward the end of life, women outnumber men, reversing the original ratio.

Many researchers have sought ways to separate Xs from Ys, and, by using artificial insemination, to ensure the outcome 100 percent. They have tried centrifugation, electrophoresis, and sedimentation, as well as immunologic and other methods to separate Xs from Ys—and with fair success.

Other methods, too, exist for predetermining the sex of offspring, but they cannot be used until *after* conception, which makes them more controversial and less acceptable ethically. Not that tampering with Xs and Ys is free of controversy. Many people feel that this line of research should not be pursued at all, that people should not have this kind of power and choice. Some fear that passing fads and preferences could drastically overbalance the population one way or the other, thus affecting everything from the economy to the crime rate to the incidence of homosexuality. Others favor this option as a population reducer, arguing that most families that might otherwise go on and on "trying for a girl" or boy might be content with two children—a boy and a girl.

Parents do, in general, seem to welcome the opportunity to preselect the sex of their children; and once the choice is available, they will undoubtedly take advantage of it.

Reading 2

Ethnic Differences in Babies

Daniel G. Freedman

The human species comes in an admirable variety of shapes and colors, as a walk through any cosmopolitan city amply demonstrates. Although the speculation has become politically and socially unpopular, it is difficult not to wonder whether the major differences in physical appearances are accompanied by standard differences in temperament or behavior. Recent studies by myself and others of babies only a few hours, days, or weeks old indicate that they are, and that such differences among human beings are biological as well as cultural.

These studies of newborns from different ethnic backgrounds actually had their inception with work on puppies, when I attempted to raise dogs in either an indulged or disciplined fashion in order to test the effects of such rearing on their later behavior.

I spent all my days and evenings with these puppies, and it soon became apparent that the breed of dog would become an important factor in my results. Even as the ears and eyes opened, the breeds differed in behavior. Little beagles were irrepressibly friendly from the moment they could detect me; Shetland sheepdogs were very, very sensitive to a loud voice or the slightest punishment; wire-haired terriers were so tough and aggressive, even as clumsy three-week-olds, that I had to wear gloves while playing with them; and finally, Basenjis, barkless dogs originating in Central Africa, were aloof and independent. To judge by where they spent their time, sniffing and investigating, I was no more important to them than if I were a rubber balloon.

When I later tested the dogs, the breed indeed made a difference in their behavior. I took them, when hungry, into a room with a bowl of meat. For three minutes I kept them from approaching the meat, then left each dog alone with the food. Indulged terriers and beagles waited longer before eating the meat than did disciplined dogs of the same breeds. None of the Shetlands ever ate any of the food, and all of the Basenjis ate as soon as I left.

I later studied 20 sets of identical and fraternal human twins, following them from infancy until they were 10 years old, and I became convinced that both puppies and human babies begin life along developmental pathways established by their genetic inheritance. But I still did not know whether infants of relatively inbred human groups showed differences comparable to the breed differences among puppies that had so impressed me. Clearly, the most direct way to find out was to examine very young infants, preferably newborns, of ethnic groups with widely divergent histories.

Since it was important to avoid projecting my own assumptions onto the babies' behavior, the first step was to develop some sort of objective test of newborn behavior. With T. Berry Brazelton, the Harvard pediatrician, I developed what I called the

Cambridge Behavioral and Neurological Assessment Scales, a group of simple tests of basic human reactions that could be administered to any normal newborn in a hospital nursery.

In the first study, Nina Freedman and I compared Chinese and Caucasian babies. It was no accident that we chose those two groups, since my wife is Chinese, and in the course of learning about each other and our families, we came to believe that some character differences might well be related to differences in our respective gene pools and not just to individual differences.

Armed with our new baby test, Nina and I returned to San Francisco, and to the hospital where she had borne our first child. We examined, alternately, 24 Chinese and 24 Caucasian newborns. To keep things neat, we made sure that all the Chinese were of Cantonese (South Chinese) background, the Caucasians of Northern European origin, that the sexes in both groups were the same, that the mothers were the same age, that they had about the same number of previous children, and that both groups were administered the same drugs in the same amounts. Additionally, all of the families were members of the same health plan, all of the mothers had had approximately the same number of prenatal visits to a doctor, and all were in the same middle-income bracket.

It was almost immediately clear that we had struck pay dirt; Chinese and Caucasian babies indeed behaved like two different breeds. Caucasian babies cried more easily, and once started, they were harder to console. Chinese babies adapted to almost any position in which they were placed; for example, when placed face down in their cribs, they tended to keep their faces buried in the sheets rather than immediately turning to one side, as did the Caucasians. In a similar maneuver (called the "defense reaction" by neurologists), we briefly pressed the baby's nose with a cloth. Most Caucasian and black babies fight this maneuver by immediately turning away or swiping at the cloth with their hands, and this is reported in most Western pediatric textbooks as the normal, expected response. The average Chinese baby in our study, however, simply lay on his back and breathed through his mouth, "accepting" the cloth without a fight. This finding is most impressive on film.

Other subtle differences were equally important, but less dramatic. For example, both Chinese and Caucasian babies started to cry at about the same points in the examination, especially when they were undressed, but the Chinese stopped sooner. When picked up and cuddled, Chinese babies stopped crying immediately, as if a light switch had been flipped, whereas the crying of Caucasian babies only gradually subsided.

In another part of the test, we repeatedly shone a light in the baby's eyes and counted the number of blinks until the baby "adapted" and no longer blinked. It should be no surprise that the Caucasian babies continued to blink long after the Chinese babies had adapted and stopped.

It began to look as if Chinese babies were simply more amenable and adaptable to the machinations of the examiners, and that the Caucasian babies were registering annoyance and complaint. It was as if the old stereotypes of the calm, inscrutable Chinese and the excitable, emotionally changeable Caucasian were appearing spontaneously in the first 48 hours of life. In other words, our hypothesis about human and puppy parallels seemed to be correct.

The results of our Chinese-Caucasian study have been confirmed by a student of ethologist Nick Blurton-Jones who worked in a Chinese community in Malaysia. At the time, however, our single study was hardly enough evidence for so general a conclusion, and we set out to look at other newborns in other places. Norbett Mintz, who was working among the Navaho in Tuba City, Arizona, arranged for us to come to the reservation in the spring of 1969. After two months we had tested 36 Navaho newborns, and the results paralleled the stereotype of the stoical, impassive American Indian. These babies outdid the Chinese, showing even more calmness and adaptability than we found among Oriental babies.

We filmed the babies as they were tested and found reactions in the film we had not noticed. For example, the Moro response was clearly different among Navaho and Caucasians. This reaction occurs in newborns when support for the head and neck suddenly disappears. Tests for the Moro response usually consist of raising and then suddenly dropping the head portion of the bassinet. In most Caucasian newborns, after a four-inch drop the baby reflexively extends both arms and legs, cries, and moves in an agitated manner before he calms down. Among Navaho babies, crying was rare, the limb movements were reduced, and calming was almost immediate.

I have since spent considerable time among the Navaho, and it is clear that the traditional practice of tying the wrapped infant onto a cradle board (now practiced sporadically on the reservation) has in no way induced stoicism in the Navaho. In the halcyon days of anthropological environmentalism, this was a popular conjecture, but the other way around is more likely. Not all Navaho babies take to the cradle board, and those who complain about it are simply taken off. But most Navaho infants calmly accept the board; in fact, many begin to demand it by showing signs of unrest when off. When they are about six months old, however, Navaho babies do start complaining at being tied, and "weaning" from the board begins, with the baby taking the lead. The Navaho are the most "in touch" group of mothers we have yet seen, and the term mother-infant *unit* aptly describes what we saw among them.

James Chisholm of Rutgers University, who has studied infancy among the Navaho over the past several years, reports that his observations are much like my own. In addition, he followed a group of young Caucasian mothers in Flagstaff (some 80 miles south of the reservation) who had decided to use the cradle board. Their babies complained so persistently that they were off the board in a matter of weeks, a result that should not surprise us, given the differences observed at birth.

Assuming, then, that other investigators continue to confirm our findings, to what do we attribute the differences on the one hand, and the similarities on the other? When we first presented the findings on Chinese and Caucasians, attempts were made to explain away the genetic implications by posing differences in prenatal diets as an obvious cause. But once we had completed the Navaho study, that explanation had to be dropped, because the Navaho diet is quite different from the diet of the Chinese, yet newborn behavior was strikingly similar in the two groups.

The point is often still made that the babies had nine months of experience within the uterus before we saw them, so that cultural differences in maternal attitudes and behavior might have been transferred to the unborn offspring via some, as yet unknown, mechanism. Chisholm, for example, thinks differences in maternal blood pressure may be responsible for some of the differences between Navahos and

Caucasians, but the evidence is as yet sparse. Certainly Cantonese-American and Navaho cultures are substantially different and yet the infants are so much alike that such speculation might be dismissed on that score alone. But there is another, hidden issue here, and that involves our own cultural tendency to split apart inherited and acquired characteristics. Americans tend to eschew the inherited and promote the acquired, in a sort of "we are exactly what we make of ourselves" optimism.

My position on this issue is simple: We are totally biological, totally environmental; the two are as inseparable as is an object and its shadow. Or as psychologist Donald O. Hebb has expressed it, we are 100 percent innate, 100 percent acquired. One might add to Hebb's formulation, 100 percent biological, 100 percent cultural. As D. T. Suzuki, the Zen scholar, once told an audience of neuropsychiatrists, "You took heredity and environment apart and now you are stuck with the problem of putting them together again."

Navaho and Chinese newborns may be so much alike because the Navaho were part of a relatively recent emigration from Asia. Their language group is called Athabaskan, after a lake in Canada. Although most of the Athabaskan immigrants from Asia settled along the Pacific coast of Canada, the Navaho and Apache contingents went on to their present location in about 1200 A.D. Even today, a significant number of words in Athabaskan and Chinese appear to have the same meaning, and if one looks back several thousand years into the written records of Sino-Tibetan, the number of similar words makes clear the common origin of these widely separated peoples.

When we say that some differences in human behavior may have a genetic basis, what do we mean? First of all, we are *not* talking about a gene for stoicism or a gene for irritability. If a behavioral trait is at all interesting, for example, smiling, anger, ease of sexual arousal, or altruism, it is most probably polygenic—that is, many genes contribute to its development. Furthermore, there is no way to count the exact number of genes involved in such a polygenic system because, as geneticist James Crow has summarized the situation, biological traits are controlled by one, two, or *many* genes.

Standing height, a polygenic human trait, can be easily measured and is also notoriously open to the

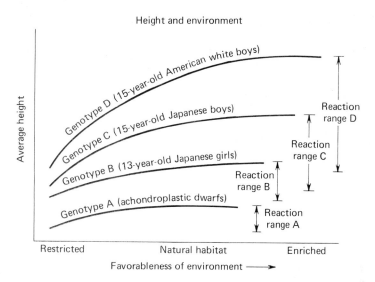

The concept of reaction range shows clearly in this comparison of adolescent groups: the better the environment, the taller the person. Although some groups show considerable overlap in height, no matter how favorable the environment, height cannot exceed the possible reaction range. (© 1974 University of Minnesota Press.)

influence of the environment. For this reason height can serve as a model for behavioral traits, which are genetically influenced but are even more prone to change with changing environment.

There are, however, limits to the way that a given trait responds to the environment, and this range of constraint imposed by the genes is called a *reaction range*. Behavioral geneticist Irving Gottesman has drawn up a series of semihypothetical graphs illustrating how this works with regard to human height; each genotype (the combination of genes that determine a particular trait) represents a relatively inbred human group. Even the most favorable environment produces little change in height for genotype A, whereas for genotype D a vast difference is seen as nutrition improves.

When I speak of potential genetic differences in human behavior, I do so with these notions in mind: There is overlap between most populations and the overlap can become rather complete under changing conditions, as in genotypes D and C. Some genotypes, however, show no overlap and remain remote from the others over the entire reaction range, as in genotype A (actually a group of achondroplastic dwarfs; it is likely that some pygmy groups would exhibit a similarly isolated reaction range with regard to height).

At present we lack the data to construct such reaction-range curves for newborn behavior, but hypothetically there is nothing to prevent us from one day doing so.

The question naturally arises whether the group differences we have found are expressions of richer and poorer environments, rather than of genetically distinguishable groups. The similar performance yet substantial difference in socioeconomic status between Navaho and San Francisco Chinese on the one hand, and the dissimilar performance yet similar socioeconomic status of San Francisco Chinese and Caucasians on the other favors the genetic explanation. Try as one might, it is very difficult, conceptually and actually, to get rid of our biological constraints.

Research among newborns in other cultures shows how environment—in this case, cultural learning—affects reaction range. In Hawaii we met a Honolulu pediatrician who volunteered that he had found striking and consistent differences between Japanese and Polynesian babies in his practice. The Japanese babies consistently reacted more violently to their three-month immunizations than did the Polynesians. On subsequent visits, the Japanese gave every indication of remembering the last visit by crying violently; one mother said that her baby cried each time she drove by the clinic.

We then tested a series of Japanese newborns, and

found that they were indeed more sensitive and irritable than either the Chinese or Navaho babies. In other respects, though, they were much like them, showing a similar response to consolation, and accommodating easily to a light on the eyes or a cloth over the nose. Prior to our work, social anthropologist William Caudill had made an extensive and thorough study of Japanese infants. He made careful observations of Japanese mother-infant pairs in Baltimore, from the third to the twelfth month of life. Having noted that both the Japanese infants and their mothers vocalized much less to one another than did Caucasian pairs, he assumed that the Japanese mothers were conditioning their babies toward quietude from a universal baseline at which all babies start. Caudill, of course, was in the American environmentalist tradition and, until our publication appeared, did not consider the biological alternative. We believe that the mothers and babies he studied were, in all probability, conditioning each other, that the naturally quiet Japanese babies affected their mothers' behavior as much as the mothers affected their babies'.

With this new interactive hypothesis in mind, one of my students, Joan Kuchner, studied mother-infant interactions among 10 Chinese and 10 Caucasian mother-infant pairs over the first three months of life. The study was done in Chicago, and this time the Chinese were of North Chinese rather than South Chinese (Cantonese) ancestry. Kuchner started her study with the birth of the babies and found that the two groups were different from the start, much as in our study of newborns. Further, it soon became apparent that Chinese mothers were less intent on eliciting responses from their infants. By the third month, Chinese infants and mothers rarely engaged in bouts of mutual vocalizing as did the Caucasian pairs. This was exactly what the Caudill studies of Japanese and Caucasians had shown, but we now know that it was based on a developing coalition between mothers and babies and that it was not just a one-way street in which a mother "shapes" her infant's behavior.

Following our work, Caudill and Lois Frost repeated Caudill's original work, but this time they used third-generation Japanese-American mothers and their fourth-generation infants. The mothers had become "super" American and were vocalizing to their infants at almost twice the Caucasian rate of activity, and the infants were responding at an even greater rate of happy vocalization. Assuming that

these are sound and repeatable results, my tendency is to reconcile these and our results in terms of the reaction-range concept. If Japanese height can change as dramatically as it has with emigration to the United States (and with post-World War II diets), it seems plausible that mother-infant behavior can do the same. On a variety of other measures, Caudill and Frost were able to discern continuing similarities to infant and mother pairs in the old country. Fourth-generation Japanese babies, like babies in Japan, sucked their fingers less and were less playful than Caucasian babies were, and the third-generation mothers lulled their babies and held them more than Caucasian American mothers did.

A student and colleague, John Callaghan, has recently completed a study comparing 15 Navaho and 19 Anglo mothers and their young infants (all under six months). Each mother was asked to "get the attention of the baby." When video tapes of the subsequent scene were analyzed, the differences in both babies and mothers were striking. The Navaho babies showed greater passivity than the Caucasian babies. Caucasian mothers "spoke" to their babies continually, using linguistic forms appropriate for someone who understands language; their babies responded by moving their arms and legs. The Navaho mothers were strikingly silent, using their eyes to attract their babies' gaze, and the relatively immobile infants responded by merely gazing back.

Despite their disparate methods, both groups were equally successful in getting their babies' attention. Besides keeping up a stream of chatter, Caucasian mothers tended to shift the baby's position radically, sometimes holding him or her close, sometimes at arm's length, as if experimenting to find the best focal distance for the baby. Most of the silent Navaho mothers used only subtle shifts on the lap, holding the baby at about the same distance throughout. As a result of the intense stimulation by the Caucasian mothers, the babies frequently turned their heads away, as if to moderate the intensity of the encounter. Consequently, eye contact among Caucasian pairs was of shorter duration (half that of the Navaho), but more frequent.

It was clear that the Caucasian mothers sought their babies' attention with verve and excitement, even as their babies tended to react to the stimulation with what can be described as ambivalence: The Caucasian infants turned both toward and away from the mother with far greater frequency than did the Navaho infants. The Navaho mothers and their infants engaged in relatively stoical, quiet, and steady encounters. On viewing the films of these sequences, we had the feeling that we were watching biocultural differences in the making.

Studies of older children bear out the theme of relative unexcitability in Chinese as compared to Anglos. In an independent research project at the University of Chicago, Nova Green studied a number of nursery schools. When she reached one in Chicago's Chinatown, she reported: "Although the majority of the Chinese-American children were in the 'high arousal age,' between three and five, they showed little intense emotional behavior. They ran and hopped, laughed and called to one another, rode bikes and roller-skated just as the children did in the other nursery schools, but the noise level stayed remarkably low, and the emotional atmosphere projected serenity instead of bedlam. The impassive facial expression certainly gave the children an air of dignity and self-possession, but this was only one element effecting the total impression. Physical movements seemed more coordinated, no tripping, falling, bumping, or bruising was observed, no screams, crashes or wailing was heard, not even that common sound in other nurseries, voices raised in highly indignant moralistic dispute! No property disputes were observed, and only the mildest version of 'fighting behavior,' some good-natured wrestling among the older boys. The adults evidently had different expectations about hostile or impulsive behavior; this was the only nursery school where it was observed that children were trusted to duel with sticks. Personal distance spacing seemed to be situational rather than compulsive or patterned, and the children appeared to make no effort to avoid physical contact."

It is ironic that many recent visitors to nursery schools in Red China have returned with ecstatic descriptions of the children, implying that the New Order knows something about child rearing that the West does not. When the *New Yorker* reported a visit to China by a group of developmental psychologists including William Kessen, Urie Bronfenbrenner, Jerome Kagan, and Eleanor Maccoby, they were described as baffled by the behavior of Chinese children: "They were won over by the Chinese children. They speak of an 'attractive mixture of affective spontaneity and an accommodating posture by the children: of the 'remarkable control of young Chinese children'—alert, animated, vigorous, responsive to the words of their elders, yet also unnervingly calm, even during happenings (games, classroom events, neighborhood play) that could create agitation and confusion. The children 'were far less restless, less intense in their motor actions, and displayed less crying and whining than American children in similar situations. We were constantly struck by [their] quiet, gentle, and controlled manner . . . and as constantly frustrated in our desire to understand its origins.' " The report is strikingly similar to Nova Green's description of the nursery school in Chicago's Chinatown. When making these comparisons with "American" nursery schools, the psychologists obviously had in mind classrooms filled with Caucasian or Afro-American children.

As they get older, Chinese and Caucasian children continue to differ in roughly the same behavior that characterizes them in nursery school. Not surprisingly, San Francisco schoolteachers consider assignments in Chinatown as plums—the children are dutiful and studious, and the classrooms are quiet.

A reader might accept these data and observations and yet still have trouble imagining how such differences might have initially come about. The easiest explanation involves a historical accident based on different, small founding populations and at least partial geographic isolation. Peking man, some 500,000 years ago, already had shovel-shaped incisors, as only Orientals and American Indians have today. Modern-looking skulls of about the same age, found in England, lack this grooving on the inside of their upper incisors. Given such evidence, we can surmise that there has been substantial and long-standing isolation of East and West. Further, it is likely that, in addition to just plain "genetic drift," environmental demands and biocultural adaptations differed, yielding present-day differences.

Orientals and Euro-Americans are not the only newborn groups we have examined. We have recorded newborn behavior in Nigeria, Kenya, Sweden, Italy, Bali, India, and Australia, and in each place, it is fair to say, we observed some kind of uniqueness. The Australian aborigines, for example, struggled mightily against the cloth over the nose, resembling the most objecting Caucasian babies; their necks were exceptionally strong, and some could lift their heads up and look around, much like some of the African babies we saw. (Caucasian infants cannot do this until they are about one month old.) Further, aborigine infants were easy to calm, resembling in that respect our easygoing Chinese babies. They thus comprised a unique pattern of traits.

Given these data, I think it is a reasonable conclusion that we should drop two long-cherished myths: (1) No matter what our ethnic background, we are all born alike; (2) culture and biology are separate entities. Clearly, we are biosocial creatures in everything we do and say, and it is time that anthropologists, psychologists, and population geneticists start speaking the same language. In light of what we know, only a truly holistic, multidisciplinary approach makes sense.

For further information:

Caudill, W., and N. Frost. "A Comparison of Maternal Care and Infant Behavior in Japanese-American, American, and Japanese Families." *Influences on Human Development*, edited by Urie Bronfenbrenner and M. A. Mahoney. Dryden Press, 1972.

Chisholm, J. S., and Martin Richards. "Swaddling, Cradleboards and the Development of Children." *Early Human Development*, in press.

Freedman, D. G. "Constitutional and Environmental Interaction in Rearing of Four Breeds of Dogs." *Science*, Vol. 127, 1958, pp. 585–586.

Freedman, D. G. *Human Infancy: An Evolutionary Perspective*. Lawrence Erlbaum Associates, 1974.

Freedman, D. G., and B. Keller. "Inheritance of Behavior in Infants." *Science*, Vol. 140, 1963, pp. 196–198.

Gottesman, I. I. "Developmental Genetics and Ontogenetic Psychology." *Minnesota Symposia on Child Psychology*, Vol. 8, edited by A. D. Pick. University of Minnesota Press, 1974.

Reading 3

Premature Birth: Consequences for the Parent-Infant Relationship

Susan Goldberg

Imagine, if you will, the sound of a young infant crying. For most adults it is a disturbing and compelling sound. If it is made by your own infant or one in your care, you are likely to feel impelled to do something about it. Most likely, when the crying has reached a particular intensity and has lasted for some (usually short) period of time, someone will pick the baby up for a bit of cuddling and walking. Usually, this terminates the crying and will bring the infant to a state of visual alertness. If the baby makes eye contact with the adult while in this alert state, the caregiver is likely to begin head-nodding and talking to the baby with the exaggerated expressions and inflections that are used only for talking to babies. Babies are usually very attentive to this kind of display and will often smile and coo. Most adults find this rapt attention and smiling exceedingly attractive in young infants and will do quite ridiculous things for these seemingly small rewards.

I have used this example to illustrate that normal infant behaviors and the behaviors adults direct toward infants seem to be mutually complementary in a way that leads to repeated social interactions enjoyed by both infants and adults. Consider now the experiences of a baby whose cry is weak and fails to compel adult attention, or the baby (or adult) who is blind and cannot make the eye contacts that normally lead to social play. When the behavior of either the infant or the adult is not within the range of normal competence, the pair is likely to have difficulties establishing rewarding social interactions. Premature birth is one particular situation in which the interactive skills of both parents and infants are hampered.

Recent studies comparing interactions of preterm and full-term parent-infant pairs have found consistently different patterns of behavior in the two groups. Before we turn to these studies, it will be useful to introduce a conceptual framework for understanding parent-infant interaction and a model within which the findings can be interpreted.

A CONCEPTUAL FRAMEWORK

In most mammalian species, the care of an adult is necessary for the survival, growth, and development of the young. One would therefore expect that such species have evolved an adaptive system of parent-infant interaction which guarantees that newborns will be capable of soliciting care from adults and that adults will respond appropriately to infant signals for care. Where immaturity is prolonged and the young require the care of parents even after they are capable of moving about and feeding without assistance, one would also expect the interactive system to be organized in a way that guarantees the occurrence of social (as opposed to caregiving) interactions that can form the basis for a prolonged parent-child relationship. It is not surprising to find that when these conditions are met, the parent-infant interaction system appears to be one of finely tuned reciprocal behaviors that are mutually complementary and that appear to be preadapted to facilitate social interaction. Furthermore, as the example given earlier illustrates, both parents and infants are initiators and responders in bouts of interaction.

This view is quite different from that taken by psychologists in most studies of child development. For most of the relatively short history of developmental psychology it was commonly assumed that the infant was a passive, helpless organism who was acted upon by parents (and others) in a process that resulted in the "socialization" of the child into mature forms of behavior. In popular psychology this emphasis appeared as the belief that parents (especially mothers) were *responsible* for their child's development. They were to take the credit for successes as well as the blame for failures.

In the last fifteen years, the study of infant development has shown that the young infant is by no means passive, inert, or helpless when we consider the environment for which he or she is adapted—that is, an environment which includes a responsive caregiver. Indeed, we have discovered that infants are far more skilled and competent than we originally thought. First, the sensory systems of human infants are well developed at birth, and their initial perceptual capacities are well matched to the kind of stimulation that adults normally present to them. Infants see and discriminate visual patterns from birth, although their visual acuity is not up to adult standards. Young infants are especially attentive to visual movement, to borders of high contrast, and to relatively complex stimuli. When face to face with infants, adults will normally present their faces at the distance where newborns are best able to focus (17–22 cm) and exaggerate their facial expressions and movements. The result is a visual display with constant movement of high contrast borders.

A similar phenomenon is observed in the auditory domain. Young infants are most sensitive to sound frequencies within the human vocal range, especially the higher pitches, and they can discriminate many initial consonants and vocal inflections. When adults talk to infants, they spontaneously raise the pitch of their voices, slow their speech, repeat frequently, and exaggerate articulation and inflection. Small wonder that young infants are fascinated by the games adults play with them!

In addition, researchers have found that when adults are engaged in this type of face-to-face play they pace their behavior according to the infant's pattern of waxing and waning attention. Thus the infant is able to "control" the display by the use of selective attention. At the same time, studies have found that babies are most likely to smile and coo first to events over which they have control. Thus, infants are highly likely to smile and gurgle during face-to-face play with adults, thus providing experiences which lead the adult to feel that he or she is "controlling" an interesting display. We will return to the notion of control and the sense of being effective as an important ingredient in parent-infant relationships.

A second respect in which infants are more skilled and competent than we might think is their ability to initiate and continue both caregiving and social interactions. Although the repertoire of the young infant is very limited, it includes behaviors such as crying, visual attention, and (after the first few weeks) smiling, which have compelling and powerful effects on adult behavior. Almost all parents will tell you that in the first weeks at home with a new baby they spent an inordinate amount of time trying to stop the baby's crying.

Crying is, at first, the most effective behavior in the infant's repertoire for getting adult attention. When social smiling and eye contact begin, they too become extremely effective in maintaining adult attention. In one study, by Moss and Robson (1968), about 80 percent of the parent-infant interactions in the early months were initiated by the infant. Thus, the normally competent infant plays a role in establishing contacts and interactions with adults that provide the conditions necessary for growth and development.

COMPETENCE MOTIVATION: A MODEL

The actual process by which this relationship develops is not clearly understood, but we can outline a plausible model that is consistent with most of the available data. A central concept in this model is that of competence motivation, as defined by White (1959). In a now-classic review of research on learning and motivation in many species, White concluded that behaviors that are selective, directed, and persistent occur with high frequency in the absence of extrinsic rewards. He therefore proposed an intrinsic motive, which he called competence motivation, arising from a need to cope effectively with the environment, to account for behavioral phenomena such as play, exploration, and curiosity. Behavior that enables the organism to control or influence the environment gives rise to feelings of efficacy that strengthen competence motivation. White pointed out that much of the behavior of young infants appears to be motivated in this manner. Why else, for example, would infants persist in learning to walk when they are repeatedly punished by falls and bruises?

At the other extreme, Seligman (1975) has demonstrated that animals, including humans, can quickly learn to be helpless when placed in an unpleasant situation over which they have no control. This learned helplessness prevents effective behavior in subsequent situations where control is possible. It has been suggested that an important part of typical parent-infant interaction in the early months is the prompt and appropriate responses of the parent to the infant's behavior, which enable the infant to feel effective. The retarded development often seen in institutionalized infants may arise from learned helplessness in a situation where, though apparent needs are met, this occurs on schedule rather than in response to the infant's expression of needs and signals for attention. There is a general consensus among researchers in infant development that the

infant's early experiences of being effective support competence motivation, which in turn leads to the exploration, practice of skills, and "discovery" of new behaviors important for normal development.

I have suggested elsewhere (1977) that competence motivation is important to parents as well. Parents bring to their experiences with an infant some history that determines their level of competence motivation. However, their experiences with a particular infant will enhance, maintain, or depress feelings of competence in the parental role. Unlike infants, parents have some goals by which they evaluate their effectiveness. Parents monitor infant behavior, make decisions about caregiving or social interaction, and evaluate their own effectiveness in terms of the infant's subsequent behavior.

When parents are able to make decisions quickly and easily and when subsequent infant behavior is more enjoyable or less noxious than that which prompted them to act, they will consider themselves successful in that episode. When parents cannot make decisions quickly and easily and when subsequent infant behavior is more aversive or less enjoyable than that which led them to intervene, they will evaluate that episode as a failure. Figure 1 illustrates this process, and the following discussion is intended to clarify the model depicted.

The normally competent infant helps adults to be effective parents by being readable, predictable, and responsive. Readability refers to the clarity of the infant's signaling—that is, how easily the adult can observe the infant and conclude that he or she is tired, hungry, eager to play, etc. Although there may be some infants who are easier for everyone to read than others, readability within the parent-infant pair is a joint function of infant behavior and the adult's skill in recognizing behavior patterns.

Predictability refers to the regularity of the infant's behavior—whether sleeping, waking, feeding, and elimination follow a recognizable pattern and whether the infant repeatedly responds to similar situations in a similar fashion. Again, both infant behavior and adult behavior and sensitivity to the infant determine predictability within a given pair. Responsiveness is the infant's ability to react to external stimulation, whether animate or inanimate. To the extent that an infant responds promptly and

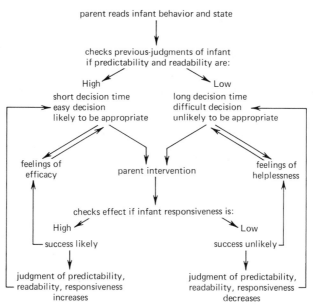

Figure 1   An adult who has experienced a successful interaction with an infant (left) perceives the infant as "readable" and predictable and acquires a feeling of competence in further interactions. The good and sensitive care that results causes the infant to feel more competent in turn at eliciting the appropriate responses, and thus a cycle of successful interaction is established. The reverse of this pattern is illustrated in the right side of the figure.

reliably to adult behavior he or she contributes directly to the adult's feelings of effectiveness as a caregiver.

The left side of Figure 1 shows that when an infant is readable and predictable the adult is able to make caregiving decisions quickly and easily and is highly likely to make decisions that lead to successful or desirable outcomes. When an adult has interacted with an infant in ways that have led to an evaluation of success, the adult is likely to perceive the infant as more readable and predictable than before. Thus, the infant who is readable, predictable, and responsive can capture an initially disinterested adult in cycles of mutually rewarding and effective interaction. Notice also that, in this part of the figure, the adult is able to respond promptly and appropriately to the infant's behavior, providing the infant with what we would describe as good or sensitive care that enhances the infant's feelings of competence. In addition, since these successes make the adult feel efficacious, he or she now has more confidence and is better able to make judgments about infant behavior and caregiving in the future. The right side of the figure illustrates the situation in which the infant is unreadable, unpredictable, and unrespon-

sive as a joint function of poorly organized infant behavior and/or poorly developed adult skills.

PROBLEMS OF PRETERM PAIRS

Under normal conditions, the natural reciprocity of adult and infant behavior guarantees that each member of the pair is provided with frequent opportunities to feel effective. A review of what is known about preterm infants and their parents will indicate that such pairs have a greater probability of falling into the patterns on the right side of the figure than do their full-term counterparts. Most preterm pairs eventually do develop successful relationships. However, the available data also indicate that they must make compensatory adjustments to enable them to overcome initial disadvantages.

Premature infants are those who are born after fewer than 37 weeks of gestation and weigh under 2,500 g. Infants who were born small for their age or with known congenital defects are not included in the samples of the studies I am describing. The most obvious fact of premature birth is that parents are confronted with an infant who is relatively immature and may not have developed the care-soliciting or social behaviors available to the full-term infant.

Several studies, including my own (Goldberg et al., 1978), which have systematically evaluated the behavior of preterm infants (close to term or hospital discharge), have reported that they spent less time alert, were more difficult to keep in alert states, and were less responsive to sights and sounds (a ball, a rattle, a moving face, and a voice) than the full-term comparison group. Furthermore, preterm infants who had experienced respiratory problems following birth rarely cried during the newborn examination, even though some of the procedures (e.g. undressing, testing reflexes) are mildly stressful and provoke crying from full-term infants. This suggests that these preterm infants are not likely to give adults clear distress signals.

The effectiveness of the preterm infant's cry in compelling adult attention has not been studied extensively. However, at the University of Wisconsin (Frodi et al. 1978), mothers and fathers were shown videotapes of full-term and preterm infants in crying and quiescent states. A dubbed sound track made it possible to pair the sound and the picture independently. Physiological recordings taken from the viewing parents indicated that the cry of the premature infant was physiologically more arousing than that of the full-term infant, and particularly so when paired with the picture of the preterm baby. Furthermore, ratings of the cries indicated that parents found that of the premature baby more aversive than that of the full-term infant. Thus, although the preterm infant may cry less often, this can be somewhat compensated for by the more urgent and aversive sound of these cries. If a parent is able to quiet these cries promptly, they clearly serve an adaptive function. If, however, the infant is difficult to pacify or frequently irritable, it is possible that the aversive experience will exceed the parent's level of tolerance or that he or she will experience repeated feelings of helplessness that can be damaging to the interactive relationship.

Thus far, we have assumed that the less competent behavior of the preterm infant is primarily attributable to immaturity. Often prematurity is associated with other medical problems that depress behavioral competence. In addition, the early extrauterine experiences of preterm infants in intensive-care nurseries probably do little to foster interactive

competence and may, in fact, hinder its occurrence. Procedures such as tube feedings, repeated drawing of blood samples, temperature taking, and instrument monitoring often constitute a large proportion of the preterm infant's first encounters with adults. There are few data on the effects of special medical procedures, and since these procedures cannot ethically be withheld on a random schedule, this is a difficult area to study. However, numerous studies have attempted to foster early growth and development of preterm infants by adding specific kinds of experiences.

An example of a study from the first category is one in which 31 preterm infants were gently rocked for 30 minutes, three times each day, from their fifth postnatal day until they reached the age of 36 weeks postconception. They were compared to 31 unrocked preterm babies of similar gestational age, weight, and medical condition. The experimental infants were more responsive to visual and auditory stimulation and showed better motor skills as well.

Other studies have tried to treat preterm infants more like their full-term counterparts. In one study 30 preterm infants weighing 1,300–1,800 grams at birth were randomly assigned to experimental and control groups. The infants in the experimental group were given extra visual stimulation by placing mobiles over their cribs and were handled in the same manner as full-term infants for feeding, changing, and play. The control group received hospital care standard for the preterm nursery, which meant that handling was kept to a minimum. Although initial weights and behavioral assessments had favored the control group, at 4 weeks postnatal age, the experimental group had gained more weight and showed better performance on the behavioral assessment than the controls.

Like these two examples, all of the other studies which provided extra stimulation to preterm infants showed gains in growth and/or development for the babies in the experimental group beyond those of the control group. Thus, although we do not know whether routines of intensive care interfere with early development, we do know that the behavioral competence of preterm infants can be enhanced by appropriate supplemental experiences.

On the parents' side, premature birth means that parenthood is unexpectedly thrust upon individuals who may not yet be fully prepared for it. Beyond the facts of not having finished childbirth preparation classes or having bought the baby's crib, it may be that more fundamental biological and psychological processes are disrupted. A beautiful series of studies by Rosenblatt (1969) has explored the development of maternal behavior in rats. As in humans, both male and female adult rats are capable of responding appropriately to infants. However, the hormonal state of the adult determines how readily the presence of infants elicits such behaviors. Furthermore, hormonal changes during pregnancy serve to bring female rats to a state of peak responsiveness to infants close to the time of delivery. Other animal studies indicate that experiences immediately after delivery are important for the initiation of maternal behavior. In many mammalian species removal of the young during this period may lead to subsequent rejection by the mother.

We do not have comparable hormonal studies of human mothers, but it seems likely that hormonal changes during pregnancy may serve similar functions. There is some evidence that among full-term births, immediate postpartum experiences contribute to subsequent maternal behavior. A series of studies by Klaus and Kennell (1976) and their colleagues provided some mothers with extra contact with their infants soon after birth. In comparison with control groups, these mothers were observed to stay closer to their babies, to touch and cuddle them more, and to express more reluctance to letting others care for their babies after leaving the hospital. Klaus and Kennell have summarized these studies and interpreted them as indicating that there is an optimal or "sensitive" period for initiating maternal behavior in humans. As further evidence they cite studies in which preterm infants are found to be overrepresented among reported cases of child abuse, neglect, and failure to thrive. These disturbing statistics, they suggest, reflect the effects of parent-infant separation during the sensitive period.

Even if one does not accept the idea of the sensitive period as described by Klaus and Kennell (and many developmental psychologists do not), it is clear that parents whose preterm infants must undergo prolonged hospitalization have few opportunities to interact with them. Even in the many hospitals that encourage parents to visit, handle, and care for their babies in intensive care, the experiences of parents with preterm infants are in no way comparable to those of parents with full-term infants.

If you have ever visited a friend under intensive care in the hospital, you will have some idea of the circumstances under which these parents must become acquainted with their infants. Neither parents nor infants in this situation have much opportunity to practice or develop interactive skills or to experience the feelings of competence that normally accompany them. Parents also have little opportunity to learn to read, predict, or recognize salient infant behaviors. In a study conducted at Stanford University, Seashore and her colleagues (1973) asked mothers to choose themselves or one of five other caregivers (e.g. nurse, grandmother) as best able to meet their infants' needs in numerous caregiving and social situations. Mothers who had not been able to handle their first-born preterm infants chose themselves less often than mothers in any other group sampled.

Thus, both infants and parents in preterm pairs are likely to be less skilled social partners than their full-term counterparts, because the development of interactive capacities has been disrupted and because they have had only limited opportunities to get acquainted and to practice. In addition, during the hospital stay, parents of preterm infants already have little self-confidence and lack the feeling of competence. Ordinarily, an interactive pair in which one member has limited competence can continue to function effectively if the partner is able to compensate for the inadequate or missing skills. In the case of parent-infant pairs, because the infant's repertoire and flexibility are limited, the burden of such compensatory adjustments necessarily falls upon the parent.

OBSERVATIONS OF INTERACTIONS

Six studies to date have compared parent-infant interaction in full-term and preterm pairs. They were carried out in different parts of the country with different populations and different research methodologies. Yet there seems to be some consistency in findings that is related to the age of the infant at the time of observation (which also reflects the duration of the parent-infant relationship). Each study involved repeated observation of the same parent-infant pairs, though the number of observations and the length of the studies vary.

Those studies which observed parents and infants in the newborn period typically report that parents of preterm infants are less actively involved with their babies than parents of full-term infants, preterm infants were held farther from the parent's body, touched less, talked to less, and placed in the face-to-face position less often. Subsequent observations of the same pairs usually indicated that the differences between preterm and full-term pairs diminished with time, as parents in the preterm group became more active. Thus, it appears that the initiation of interaction patterns considered "normal" for full-term pairs is delayed in preterm pairs. In my own study (Di Vitto and Goldberg, 1979) I found that for one kind of parental behavior—cuddling the baby—the preterm infants never received as much attention as the full-term infants in spite of increases over time. Over the first four months, parents cuddled preterm infants more at later feeding observations, but they were never cuddled as much as the full-term infants at the very first (hospital) observation. Thus, the development of some kinds of interactions in the preterm group can be both delayed and depressed.

In contrast with these observations of very young infants, studies of older infants reported a very different pattern. Regardless of the observation situation (feeding, social play, or object play), preterm infants were less actively engaged in the task than were full-term infants, and their parents were more active than those of full-term infants. In one study of this type, Field (1977) placed each mother face to face with her baby, who sat in an infant seat, and asked her to "talk to your baby the way you would at home." Infant attention and parent activity were coded. Infants in the preterm group squirmed, fussed, and turned away from their mothers more than those in the full-term group, and preterm mothers were more active than full-term mothers. Instructions that decreased maternal activity ("Try to imitate everything your baby does") increased infant attention in both groups, while those that increased maternal activity ("Try to get your infant to look at you as much as possible") decreased infant attention in both groups.

Field's interpretation of these findings assumed that infants used gaze aversion to maintain their expo-

sure to stimulation within a range that would not overtax their capacities for processing information. Thus, when mothers' activity decreased, infants were able to process the information provided without the need to reduce stimulation. Field also suggested that since the *imitation* condition provided stimulation that was matched to the infant's behavior, it might be more familiar and thus easier for the infant to process. It is possible that the greater initial fussing and gaze aversion reflected information-processing skills that were less developed than those of full-term infants.

Brown and Bakeman (1979) observed feedings in the hospital, one month after discharge, and three months after discharge. Their findings are somewhat different from the overall trend because they were similar at all observations. Behavior segments were assigned to four categories: *mother acts alone, baby acts alone, both act,* and *neither acts.* In comparing preterm and full-term pairs, they reported that preterm infants acted alone less frequently than full-term infants, while mothers of preterm infants acted alone more often than those of full-term infants. Furthermore, in preterm pairs, the *neither acts* state was most likely to be followed by *mother acts alone,* while in the full-term pairs, it was equally likely to be followed by activity by the baby or the mother.

In my own research (Di Vitto and Goldberg, 1979; Brachfeld and Goldberg 1978) there are two sets of data consistent with these findings. First, we found that parent behavior during feedings in the hospital, and at the 4-month home and laboratory visits, was related to infant behavior in the newborn period. Regardless of their condition at birth, infants who had been difficult to rouse as newborns received a high level of functional stimulation from parents (e.g. position changes, jiggling the nipple). Infants who had been unresponsive to auditory stimulation as newborns received high levels of vocal and tactile stimulation during feedings. Thus, the parents of infants who were unresponsive as newborns appeared to work harder during feedings in the first four months than did the parents whose newborns were more responsive.

We also observed the same pairs at 8 months of age in a free-play situation. Four toys were provided and parents were asked to "do what you usually do when [name] is playing." In this situation, both at home and in the laboratory, preterm infants (particularly those who had been very young and small at birth and had respiratory problems) played with toys less and fussed more than the full-term group. Parents in the preterm group stayed closer to their babies, touched them more, demonstrated and offered toys more, and smiled less than those in the full-term group.

Another study with somewhat younger infants also fits this pattern. Beckwith and Cohen (1978) observed one wake–sleep cycle at home one month after discharge. Since babies were born and discharged at different ages, the age of the infants varied: some were relatively young, while others were closer in age to the older groups in other studies. All were born prematurely. However, Beckwith and Cohen found that mothers whose babies had experienced many early complications devoted more time to caregiving than those who had babies with fewer problems.

All these studies concur in indicating that parents with preterm infants or preterm infants with more serious early problems devote more effort to interacting with their babies than do their full-term counterparts. In most of the studies this was coupled with a less responsive or less active baby in the preterm pairs. Thus, it appears that parents adapt to the less responsive preterm baby by investing more effort in the interaction themselves. As Brown and Bakeman put it, the mother of the preterm infant "carries more of the interactive burden" than her full-term counterpart.

From our own laboratory, there is some evidence that other adults have a similar experience with preterm infants. At our regular developmental assessments at 4, 8, and 12 months, staff members rated the preterm group as being less attentive to the tasks, less persistent in solving them, and less interested in manipulating objects than the full-term group. In addition, staff members found it necessary to spend more time with the preterm group to complete the required tasks.

The consistency of these findings suggests that in pairs with a preterm infant, adults use a common strategy of investing extra time and effort to compensate for their less responsive social partner. It is important to note that while this seems to be a widely adopted strategy, it is not necessarily the

most successful one. In Field's study (1977) a decrease in maternal activity evoked infant attention more effectively than an increase. In our own observations of 8-month-old infants, increased parent involvement did not reduce the unhappiness of the sick preterm group, and some play sessions had to be terminated to alleviate infant distress. Hence, while there seem to be some consistent strategies by which parents compensate for the limited skills of their preterm infants, these pairs may continue to experience interactive stress in spite of or even because of these efforts. Continuation of such unrewarding interactions, as Figure 1 indicates, is a threat to continued effective functioning of the interactive system.

The data reviewed above provide little evidence on the duration of interactive differences between full-term and preterm pairs. Among researchers in the field, there seems to be an informal consensus which holds that such differences gradually disappear, probably by the end of the first year. In my own research, a repetition of the play sessions at 12 months revealed no group differences. At 11–15 months, Leiderman and Seashore (1975) report only one difference: mothers of preterm babies smile less frequently than those of full-term babies. However, in Brown and Bakeman's study, group differences were observed as late as preschool age in rated competence in social interactions with adults (teachers) and peers. These data are too meager and scattered to support a firm conclusion on the duration of group differences.

This review has focused only upon the ways in which premature birth may stress the parent-infant interaction system. Preterm infants are generally considered to be at higher risk for subsequent developmental and medical problems than their full-term counterparts. In order to understand the reasons for less than optimal developmental outcomes, it is important to bear in mind that premature births occur with high frequency among population subgroups where family stress is already high (e.g. young, single, black, lower-class mothers). Most of the research designs which would allow us to disentangle the independent contributions of each medical and social variable to long-term development are unethical, impractical, or impossible to carry out with human subjects.

The early approach to studying the consequences of

prematurity was to consider each of these medical and social variables as "causes" and the physical and intellectual development of the child as the "effect." The data reviewed here indicate that we cannot think in such simple terms. Prematurity (or any other event which stresses the infant) stresses the parent-infant interaction system and indeed the entire family. The way in which the family is able to cope with these stresses then has important consequences for the child's development. A major finding of the UCLA study was that for preterm infants, as for full-term infants, a harmoniously functioning parent-infant relationship has beneficial effects on development in other areas, such as language, cognition, motor skills, and general health. Prematurity, like many other developmental phenomena, can best be understood as a complex biosocial event with multiple consequences for the child and the family.

Furthermore, in the absence of sophisticated medical technology, the vast majority of the births we have been discussing would not have produced live offspring. In evolutionary history, though it would have been adaptive for infants' initial social skills to be functional some time before birth was imminent, there was no reason for these preadapted social skills to be functioning at 6 or 7 months gestation. Premature births include only a small proportion of the population, but our ability to make such infants viable at younger and younger gestational ages by means of artificial support systems may be creating new pressures for differential selection. The fact that the majority of preterm pairs do make relatively successful adaptations indicates that the capacity to compensate for early interactive stress is one of the features of the parent-infant interaction system.

REFERENCES

Beckwith, L., and S. E. Cohen. 1978. Preterm birth: Hazardous obstetrical and postnatal events as related to caregiver-infant behavior. *Infant Behav. and Devel.* 1.

Brachfeld, S., and S. Goldberg. Parent-infant interaction: Effects of newborn medical status on free play at 8 and 12 months. Presented at Southeastern Conference on Human Development, Atlanta, GA, April 1978.

Brown, J. V., and R. Bakeman. 1979. Relationships of human mothers with their infants during the first year of life. In *Maternal Influences and Early Behavior,* ed. R. W. Bell and W. P. Smotherman. Spectrum.

DiVitto, B., and S. Goldberg. 1979. The development of early parent-infant interaction as a function of newborn medical status. In *Infants Born at Risk,* ed. T. Field, A. Sostek, S. Goldberg, and H. H. Shuman. Spectrum.

Field, T. M. 1977. Effects of early separation, interactive deficits, and experimental manipulations on mother-infant interaction. *Child Development* 48:763–71.

Frodi, A., M. Lamb, L. Leavitt, W. L. Donovan, C. Wolff, and C. Neff. 1978. Fathers' and mothers' responses to the faces and cries of normal and premature infants. *Devel. Psych.* 14.

Goldberg, S. 1977. Social competence in infancy: A model of parent-infant interaction. *Merrill-Palmer Quarterly* 23:163–77.

Goldberg, S., S. Brachfeld, and B. DiVitto. 1978. Feeding, fussing and play: Parent-infant interaction in the first year as a function of newborn medical status. In *Interactions of High Risk Infants and Children,* ed. T. Field, S. Goldberg, D. Stern and A. Sostek, Academic Press.

Kennell, J. H., and M. H. Klaus. 1976. Caring for parents of a premature or sick infant. In *Maternal-Infant Bonding,* ed. M. H. Klaus and J. H. Kennell. Mosby.

Klaus, M. H., and J. H. Kennell. 1976. *Maternal-Infant Bonding.* Mosby.

Leiderman, P. H., and M. J. Seashore. 1975. Mother-infant separation: Some delayed consequences. In *Parent-Infant Interaction.* CIBA Foundation Symp. 33. Elsevier.

Moss, H. A., and K. S. Robson. The role of protest behavior in the development of parent-infant attachment. Symposium on attachment behavior in humans and animals. Am. Psych. Assoc. Sept. 1968.

Rosenblatt, J. S. 1969. The development of maternal responsiveness in the rat. *Am. J. Orthopsychiatry* 39:36–56.

Seashore, M. J., A. D. Leifer, C. R. Barnett, and P. H. Leiderman. 1973. The effects of denial of early mother-infant interaction on maternal self-confidence. *J. Pers. and Soc. Psych.* 26:369–78.

Seligman, M. R. 1975. *Helplessness: On Development, Depression and Death.* W. H. Freeman.

White, R. 1959. Motivation reconsidered: The concept of competence. *Psych. Review* 66:297–333.

Developmental Consequences of Malnutrition in Early Childhood

Henry N. Ricciuti

The past ten years have witnessed a heightened and continuing concern with malnutrition as a serious public health problem which constitutes a threat to the normal growth and development of many thousands of poor children in various regions of the world, including the United States. Malnutrition tends to occur primarily in poor families confronting the adverse socio-economic and environmental conditions typically associated with poverty, including poor housing and sanitation, exposure to infectious and parasitic disease, inadequate health care, large family size, very limited educational and occupational opportunities, poor feeding and child care practices, etc. Under such circumstances, it is well known that malnutrition may lead to increased early childhood mortality and morbidity, and to substantial impairment of physical growth and brain development, particularly if the nutritional deficits are early, severe, and long lasting without treatment. The possibility that malnutrition may also result in a significant and long lasting impairment of the development of intellectual and social competence, and of adaptive behavior generally, has been a matter of continuing widespread concern during the past 10 years. This issue is obviously not only a matter of substantial scientific importance but one with tremendous social and public policy implications as well.

In the late 60's and early 70's, in the atmosphere of heightened public concern about malnutrition as a public health problem in this country and elsewhere, there was a rather widespread tendency to assume somewhat uncritically that there was a direct causal relationship between early malnutrition and impaired learning and intellectual development, leading in some instances to irreversible mental retardation, (Ricciuti, 1970; Scrimshaw and Gordon, 1968). This assumption was based in large part on human as well as animal studies indicating retarded brain development and brain function resulting from early malnutrition, (Dobbing, 1968; Winick and Rosso, 1969), and on the frequent observation that children having suffered obvious malnutrition tend to show reduced levels of intellectual functioning and school achievement. During the past few years, however, it has become increasingly recognized that the relationship between nutritional deprivation and psychological development in children are quite complicated ones which are methodologically difficult to investigate and are not yet clearly understood.

A substantial body of research has shown quite clearly, for example, that it is extremely difficult, if not impossible, to make a meaningful evaluation of the independent effect of malnutrition *as such* on mental development in children, apart from the influence of various adverse social and environmental conditions typically associated with malnutrition, and capable of having a substantial impact on children's behavior and intellectual development in their own right (Pollitt and Thomson, 1977; Ricciuti, 1977). There has been a tendency therefore, to move away from the assumption of a direct causal relationship between early malnutrition, altered brain development, and impaired intellectual functioning, toward a focussing of greater attention on the following issues:

a more systematic analysis of the ways in which the child's nutritional status and aspects of his social environment and early experience may interact in jointly influencing the course of psychological development, with more precise assessment of nutritional status as well as behavioral outcomes;

b a fuller understanding of the mechanisms through which altered nutritional status may affect behavior and psychological development;

c evaluation of the effectiveness of systematic efforts to prevent or ameliorate the potentially adverse behavioral consequences of early malnutrition.

Since there have been a number of recent extensive reviews of the substantial research literature on malnutrition and behavioral development (Brozek, 1978; Pollitt and Thomson, 1977; Latham, 1974), this paper will not attempt to present another exhaustive review of this literature. Rather, it will endeavor to critically summarize and evaluate the present state of our knowledge in this area, and to delineate in some detail some of the major research issues and priorities which currently represent topics of prime concern to a good many investigators in the field. Attention will be focussed primarily on protein-calorie malnutrition, the most common nutritional problem occurring world-wide in poor populations. Space limitations preclude discussion of such issues as iron deficiency anemia, and the problem of obesity, which is generally considered the most widespread nutritional problem in this country.

We turn first to a brief discussion of the nature of protein-calorie malnutrition and how it is typically assessed, followed by an overview of the major research strategies that have been employed in studies of malnutrition and psychological development.

PROTEIN-CALORIE MALNUTRITION

Definition and Assessment

The major concern of this paper is with malnutrition resulting essentially from an insufficiency of protein and calories in the child's diet, commonly referred to as "protein-calorie malnutrition" (PCM), although more recently alluded to under the generic rubric of "protein and energy deficits". Protein-calorie malnutrition includes the conditions of *nutritional marasmus,* or starvation, usually beginning in the earliest months of life and continuing for an extended period, producing infants whose physical growth and motor development are grossly impaired; and *kwashiorkor,* due primarily to an insufficience of protein, typically occurring as a rather acute illness toward the end of the 1st year or in the 2nd year of life, frequently after the birth of a younger sibling. Many combinations or mixtures of these two conditions are found in practice, and they vary greatly in severity and duration (Scrimshaw, 1963).

The most severe clinical forms of marasmus or kwashiorkor typically occur in combination with various infectious or parasitic disease, and require hospitalization and treatment to ensure the child's survival. Although early and severe malnutrition occurs with considerable frequency in the poorer populations of developing countries (up to 20% in some instances), the most widespread type of malnutrition is that of mild-to-moderate, chronic undernutrition which is most readily noted in some retardation of physical growth and development.

One of the important methodological problems in this area is that it is difficult to secure accurate assessments of nutritional status in children, particularly if one is concerned with measurement throughout a broad range of nutritional variation and not simply with clinically obvious and severe malnutrition. Three types of measures are usually employed: assessment of food intake from detailed dietary information; clinical or physical evaluations, including various anthropometric measures, particularly height, weight, and head circumference; and biochemical evaluations of specific nutrients from blood and urine samples. The interpretation of such measures is considered quite difficult, particularly if one attempts to judge the adequacy of an individual's nutritional status from a single index, and many nutritionists feel that these assessments are most valid when used in combination with one another (Ten State Nutrition Survey, 1972).

A final definitional comment has to do with the importance of distinguishing between hunger and malnutrition. The school child who frequently misses breakfast or lunch may perform poorly because of inattentiveness and distractability associated with hunger. However, these potential influences on school performance and learning, about which we know very little, clearly need to be differentiated from those effects which are the result of long term protein-calorie malnutrition. Many severely malnourished children are characterized by apathy, withdrawal and loss of appetite, rather than by the increased activity and restlessness associated with hunger (Cravioto, DeLicardie, and Birch, 1966).

Major Research Strategies

Most studies of protein-calorie malnutrition have been based on samples of children from poor populations in Latin America, Asia, and Africa. The general strategy has usually involved a comparison of developmental or intelligence test scores, school performance, or other behavioral assessments of children with a known or presumed history of malnutrition, with those of children from the same general population but with a more favorable nutritional history. In the case of early malnutrition serious enough to warrant hospitalization or special treatment, comparative assessments of behavior and development status have sometimes been made during treatment and recovery, as well as a number of years later when the children are of school age. Most studies of school age children have been retrospective, involving a comparison of children with and without a history of hospitalization for severe malnutrition the first two or three years of life.

Studies of the more common mild-to-moderate, chronic malnutrition have usually employed anthropometric indices of growth, such as stature or head circumference, as indices of the pre-school or school-aged child's nutritional history, and correlated these indices with various behavioral outcome measures.

A second research strategy which has been employed more frequently in recent years involves the use of various types of experimental intervention. Children considered at risk of malnutrition are provided with added health care and nutritional supplementation, and an evaluation is made of the behavioral consequences of such intervention, along with the effects on physical growth, nutritional status, and health. More recently, we are beginning to see various forms of environmental stimulation included as an added intervention aimed at promoting behavioral development and physical growth.

A third strategy, less common but potentially extremely valuable, involves the ecologically oriented, detailed longitudinal study of the growth and development of samples of children from birth, in settings where chronic malnutrition is endemic. This approach is best illustrated by Cravioto's recent studies in a rural Mexican village (Cravioto, et al., 1969). The assumption underlying this approach is that the natural variation occurring in such a population will make it possible to study prospectively those conditions which lead to the development of malnutrition in some children and not in others in the same environment.

Studies of Severe Malnutrition

There have been a number of studies indicating that infants examined during and shortly after rehabilitation from severe protein-calorie malnutrition requiring hospitalization in the first several years of life, are substantially retarded in physical growth and motor development, and show appreciably reduced performance on developmental and cognitive tests (Cravioto and Robles, 1965; Chase and Martin, 1970; Brockman and Ricciuti, 1971). The severity of the malnutrition and the associated developmental delay involved here is reflected in the fact, for example, that many of these children might have body weights when hospitalized for treatment at five or six months of age which are no greater or even less than their birthweights, and have made little or

no gain in length; or, they may have body weights at 10 months which are no greater than that of a normal one month old. At the same time, these children may have Developmental Quotients on standard infant tests that are well below 60. Preschool and school-aged children 5 to 11 years of age having experienced severe malnutrition in the first two or three years of life have also frequently been found to perform substantially less well than controls on a variety of intelligence and perceptual/cognitive tests and do less well in school (Cravioto and DeLicardie, 1970; Hertzig, et al., 1972; Champakam, et al., 1968).

It is interesting to note that a number of the investigators reporting these results caution against uncritical interpretation of the findings as evidence of a direct causal relationship between malnutrition and mental sub-normality, since the same socioenvironmental factors which contribute to the development of marasmus or kwashiorkor in some children and not in others in the same environment may well contribute directly to the reduced intellectual performance observed (Chase and Martin, 1970; Champakam, et al., 1968). Moreover, those children who continue to manifest sub-normal levels of intellectual functioning 6 to 10 years after treatment for early, severe malnutrition have typically returned to the same adverse environments which contributed to the severe malnutrition in the first place, and which may be a major determinant of the child's current intellectual functioning.

The importance of variations in the quality of the home environments among very poor families is illustrated in recent work by Richardson (1976) in Jamaica, indicating that children with early, severe malnutrition whose families scored relatively high on several social background factors showed only a minimal reduction in IQ at 6 to 10 years of age relative to comparison cases. On the other hand, children whose families were characterized by more adverse social conditions showed a substantially greater IQ reduction. Thus, the potential effects of even severe early malnutrition on intellectual functioning in the early elementary school years may be considerably attenuated by relatively more favorable social background conditions in the generally very poor families. Somewhat more dramatic evidence of the potential for amelioration of long term effects of severe, early malnutrition is suggested in the recent work of Winick, et al., (1975). Korean orphan girls with a history of malnutrition, as judged by retarded physical growth at 2 to 3 years of age, shortly before adoption by primarily middle class American families, were found to have IQ's and school achievement within the normal range for American children when followed up in grades 1 to 8.

In summary, then, there is reasonably good evidence that severe severe protein-calorie malnutrition in the first several years of life may have substantial adverse effects on children's intellectual development. The effects appear to be more marked the more severe the nutritional deprivation, and the longer it continues without treatment. If nutritional treatment and rehabilitation occur early in the 1st year, the chances of recovery of normal or near normal intellectual functioning appear quite good. There is some evidence, although not entirely consistent, to suggest that severe malnutrition beginning in the second year of life or later, often taking the form of kwashiorkor, appears to produce effects which are not as severe and seem to be more amenable to treatment and remediation. It is still not clear whether malnutrition *as such* is the primary determinant of impaired intellectual functioning, since it is so inextricably intertwined with adverse social and environmental circumstances. Recent studies suggest that the potential long term effects of early, severe malnutrition may be greatly attenuated, or virtually eliminated, by favorable developmentally supportive later environments, or compounded by less favorable environmental conditions. Considerable effort is being made to understand more clearly the mechanisms through which severe malnutrition may exert its influence on behavior and development, as well as to determine which psychological processes are more vulnerable to its potential impact. These topics will be discussed more fully somewhat later in the paper.

Studies of Mild-to-Moderate, Chronic Malnutrition

There have been a good many studies of the intellectual development of children who have presumably experienced the very widespread mild-to-moderate chronic malnutrition which is endemic in many poor populations, as judged primarily on the basis of some physical growth retardation, particularly in height, weight, or head circumference. While these shorter children often tend to show somewhat reduced levels of intellectual functioning, these findings are particularly difficult to interpret because of the problems involved in using simple anthropometric indices like height or head circum-

ference as the principal indices of nutritional status and history. It is well known, for example, that while variations may also reflect a variety of other social characteristics of the environment, or biological characteristics of the individual (including genetic factors), which are themselves capable of influencing the child's intellectual development (Ricciuti, 1977; Pollitt and Ricciuti, 1969).

Several studies of the intellectual competence of tall and short children in Latin America illustrate these interpretive difficulties. In a study of 6 to 11 year old children living in a Guatemalan village, for example, (Cravioto, et al., 1966), tall children tended to make fewer errors than short children in identifying geometric forms on the basis of integrating visual, haptic, and kinaesthetic information. Although the tall and short children came from families with generally equivalent socio-environmental backgrounds, maternal education was markedly higher in the case of the tall children, who may thus have had substantially more intellectual stimulation and opportunities for learning. Similarly, in a Chilean study of 1 to 5 year old poor children considered at risk of mild-to-moderate malnutrition (Monckeberg, et al., 1972), a substantial correlation was found between mothers' IQ and the children's growth in height ($r = .71$). Thus, the lower IQ's found in the shorter children may well be attributable to genetic factors or to reduced levels of intellectual stimulation provided by the less competent mothers.

A number of more recent studies of mild-to-moderate malnutrition have endeavored to evaluate the relative influence of social or environmental factors, and the nutritional variations reflected in physical growth measures, with the use of correlational and multiple regression analyses. In a Guatemala study of 3 to 6 year old village children, for example, Klein, et al., (1972) found that physical growth measures and a composite of social factors showed generally equivalent correlations with tests of language and memory (mostly .20 to .40). On the other hand, in so far as the development of perceptual competence is concerned, their data suggest that nutritional background (height and head circumference) may play a somewhat greater role than social experience (r's were .33 versus .18 for boys, and .33 versus .25 for girls).

Working with considerably younger children in Bogota (6 to 30 months), Christiansen, et al. (1974) found that Griffiths Developmental Quotients were substantially more highly correlated with physical growth (Multiple R for height and weight = .57) than with a composite socio-economic index (Multiple R = .43). Moreover, the predictability of DQ's from height and weight alone was increased by only .05, from . 57 to .62, when the social factors were added. Klein, et al.'s study of 24 month old children (1974) also suggests a somewhat greater influence of nutritional or growth factors rather than social factors on developmental test scores, particularly with regard to motor development.

On the other hand, in Richardson's (1976) previously mentioned study of 6 to 10 year old Jamaica boys who experienced severe malnutrition early in life, a composite family social background index was much more predictive of IQ levels than was the occurrence of the previous history of severe malnutrition. These and other studies indicate that it is very difficult to arrive at any firm, consistent estimates of the magnitude of the independent contributions of nutritional and associated socio-environmental influences to the growth of intellectual competencies. As will be argued more fully somewhat later in this paper, a more fruitful approach would involve a closer examination of the potential interactions between these two major sources of influence, as they jointly shape the course of intellectual development.

In summary, when we consider the chronic, mild-to-moderate malnutrition which is endemic in many economically disadvantaged populations, the research evidence suggesting adverse effects on children's psychological development is substantially weaker and less clear than that dealing with early and severe malnutrition. Generally speaking, the research thus far suggests that mild-to-moderate malnutrition appears to play a relatively minor role in determining children's intellectual development, in comparison with the substantial influence exerted by various social and environmental factors.

Current Research Developments, Needs, and Priorities

Having briefly reviewed some of the major findings of recent research bearing on the relationship between malnutrition and behavioral development in children, we turn next to a somewhat more analytical consideration of contemporary research issues and priorities which appear to this reviewer to represent important directions for continued investigation.

As indicated in the foregoing summary, there is a large body of literature indicating that malnutrition tends to be associated with reduced levels of intellectual functioning in children. In my view, there would be very little to be gained by additional studies which again simply showed that malnourished children perform less well on various intellectual tests than adequately nourished children from the same general population, or even from families with approximately equivalent educational backgrounds. Generally speaking, what is needed at present is a much sharper delineation and analysis of these relationships, with more precise assessments of nutritional status as well as behavioral outcomes. More specifically, as mentioned at the outset, we need to direct our efforts toward a fuller understanding of how malnutrition and other environmental influences interact in combination to influence development, a more complete explanation of the mechanisms or channels of influence through which variations in nutritional status may affect the course of mental development and cognitive functioning, and further studies of the effectiveness of various forms of experimental interventions, including health care, nutritional supplementation, enrichment of the child's social and learning environment, etc. In the long run, these lines of inquiry should not only substantially enhance our understanding of the basic scientific issues involved, but at the same time provide a sounder knowledge base on which to build systematic and effective field programs of prevention and remediation.

In the paragraphs which follow, research issues and needs which seem to this reviewer to be of particularly high priority in each of the three areas just mentioned will be discussed briefly, along with suggested research strategies.

Analyses of Patterns of Interaction between Malnutrition and Socio-Environmental Influences As mentioned in the initial summary, in recent years there has been an increased recognition of the significant role played by various social and environmental conditions typically associated with malnutrition as important determinants of psychological development in children. Various research and analytic strategies have been employed in an effort to evaluate the relationship between nutritional status and intellectual competencies, independent of those socio-environmental influences associated both with malnutrition and behavioral outcomes.

These efforts have sometimes taken the form of comparing the performance of malnourished and better nourished children from the same neighborhoods or general socio-economic levels. Such a strategy, however, does not take into account the likelihood that those poor families whose children are better-nourished may also be living under less adverse socio-economic circumstances than the experimental families, and may be providing a social and learning environment which is more facilitative of their children's intellectual development (Monckeberg, et al., 1972). Other investigators have employed somewhat more refined but still relatively simple indices of variations in family and home environment (type of housing, income, education of parent) and incorporated them in partial correlation or regression analyses aimed at determining how much of the variance in cognitive performance can be accounted for by nutritional status alone, by socio-environmental variations alone, and by the two combined (Klein, et al., 1972; Christiansen, et al., 1974).

From this reviewer's perspective, these kinds of analyses are heuristically useful up to a point, but they are of rather limited value in advancing our understanding of the interactive influences of nutritional and socio-environmental variations on intellectual development. First, the indices of nutritional status and of the family and home environment are typically quite simplistic and hence may be capturing only a small portion of the developmentally relevant variations in each domain. Moreover, obtained estimates of the independent contribution of nutritional versus socio-environmental factors will vary greatly depending on various characteristics of the samples employed (such as age, homogeneity or heterogeneity with respect to environmental and nutritional variation), and also depending on the particular outcome measures utilized (Ricciuti, 1977). Most studies employing this analytic approach typically find that simple indices of nutritional status (ht., wt., h.c.) and of socio-economic background are positively correlated (r's in the .20's to .30's), with correlations of about the same order of magnitude being found between each of these predictors and measures of intellectual competence. Regression analyses tend to show that both social factors and nutritional history make some independent contribution to intellectual competence, with the percentages of variance presumably attributable to each source of influence varying substantially

from study to study (e.g., 29% for social factors versus 5% for severe early malnutrition in the previously mentioned study of 6 to 10 year old Jamaican boys (Richardson, 1976); 18% versus 32% in a study of 6 to 30 month old Colombian children (Christiansen, et al., 1974).

At this point in time, there would appear to be little value in further studies concerned primarily with the question of *how much* of the variation in intellectual competence can be attributed to nutritional status alone or to socio-environmental factors alone. Rather, we need to go beyond such analytic strategies and systematically direct our research at increased understanding of how malnutrition and the child's social environment *interact* in jointly influencing the development of intellectual competencies, employing more refined measures of nutritional status, as well as more precise and detailed analyses of relevant features of the social and physical environment in the home, neighborhood, or community.

The potential value of this line of approach is strongly suggested by several recent studies indicating that within very poor populations where children are known to be generally at risk of early malnutrition, variations in particular features of the child's home and family environment may either increase or reduce substantially the likelihood of severe malnutrition occurring in specific families (DeLicardie and Cravioto, 1974; Richardson, 1974). It is important to note also, that these features of the child's social environment associated with the occurrence of malnutrition include environmental influences which can have a substantial direct effect on the child's mental development (e.g., mother's competence, degree to which child care practices provide nurturance and support for psychological development). For example, in a longitudinal study of several hundred infants born in a poor rural Mexican village (DiLicardie and Cravioto, 1974), those children who experienced severe malnutrition in the first three years of life were found to have lower IQ's than controls at five years of age, and tended to come from homes which, as early as the first year of life, were observed to be lower in the quantity and quality of social, emotional, and cognitive stimulation provided to the child. Moreover, these same features of the early home environment were also related to IQ at five years of age among children without a history of severe malnutrition.

In the present context, it is particularly important to note, as mentioned earlier, that once a child has suffered from early malnutrition, even of the severe type, the risk of subsequent impairment of mental development will also depend very much on the quality of the child's home and family environment. On the basis of both human and animal studies, it has become increasingly apparent that a developmentally facilitative social environment may substantially attenuate or even prevent the potentially unfavorable consequences of early, severe malnutrition (Richardson, 1976; Winick, et al., 1975; Lloyd-Still, et al., 1974; Levitsky, 1978).

The studies just summarized clearly emphasize the importance of our directing more systematic attention toward more precise evaluations of those aspects of the family environment or family functioning which make some families less vulnerable to the occurrence of severe malnutrition than others in the same "at risk" population, and also more capable of "buffering" or attenuating the potentially adverse behavior effects of malnutrition when it does occur. The approach suggested here involves going beyond the well known demographic indicators of increased bio-social stress and risk such as maternal age or health history, family size, parental education, income, exposure to infections or parasitic disease, accessibility of health care, etc. What is needed is a more refined analysis of the coping strengths and strategies used by families, as well as their capacity to provide developmentally facilitative child care or child rearing environments which are supportive of both physical growth and psychological development, in the face of generally adverse socio-environmental circumstances. The identification of these intra-familial strengths or vulnerabilities should certainly enhance significantly our basic understanding of important interactions between nutritional and socio-environmental influences on growth and development. At the same time, from the perspective of prevention and remediation, this added knowledge should provide helpful guidelines or avenues of approach in the development of effective programs of intervention and support for families coping with adversity.

Another example of important inter-relationships between malnutrition and salient aspects of the child's social environment or early experience is reflected in the growing evidence that the infant or young child's altered nutritional status, as reflected in physical appearance and behavior, may affect the manner in which primary caregivers respond to or care for the child, thus potentially altering his early experience in developmentally significant ways (Chavez, et al., 1975; Graves, 1978). Further systematic investigation of these interrelationships should shed additional light on the question of why some children in a given family are severely malnourished while siblings are spared. As our knowledge concerning these developmentally significant patterns of child care and parent-child relationships expands, we should better be able to plan effective preventive or remedial approaches to families where the risk of malnutrition is particularly high.

While the emphasis in the discussion thus far has been upon the interaction of malnutrition and *social* factors in the child's experience and environment, it would similarly be very important to examine more carefully the manner in which malnutrition of various types and degrees of severity might combine with other biological risk factors, such as low birth weight, prematurity, congenital or genetic anomalies, etc., adversely affecting the development of intellectual competencies.

Identification of Mechanisms through Which Altered Nutritional Status May Affect Intellectual Competencies   One of the most important research questions still confronting us in this field is the problem of specifying the mechanisms, or channels of influence, through which malnutrition might exert its impact on the development of various behavioral competencies. In human studies, this problem is being approached in part by efforts to assess a wider array of potential behavioral outcomes of malnutrition in order to determine whether various specific perceptual-cognitive, learning, or motivational processes might be particularly vulnerable to the impact of nutritional deficits (Klein, 1978; Hoorweg, 1976; Pollitt, et al., 1978). The same general approach is being followed in much of the recent animal research, where investigators have also been able to manipulate experimentally the conditions of nutritional deprivation, recovery, and treatment (including added experience) (Levitsky, 1978; Frankova, 1974).

When the concerns about malnutrition as a possible major cause of mental retardation reached a peak in the late 60's and early 70's it was assumed by many that the brain changes produced by malnutrition led directly to an impairment of learning ability and thus to retarded intellectual development, which was often irreversible. On the basis of much human as well as animal research since that time, however, most investigators have tended to discard this view in favor of the hypothesis that malnutrition may exert its major influence on behavioral competencies through dysfunctional changes in attention, responsiveness, motivation, and emotionally, rather than through a more direct impairment of basic ability to learn. In short, the malnourished child's interaction with his environment may be altered in ways that make him less likely to seek out, utilize, and respond to available opportunities for learning and social interaction available in his environment. This state of events would imply quite hopeful prospects for reversibility or remediation, since it may be possible to manipulate the environment so as to make the child's interaction with it more intellectually facilitative (to be discussed more fully later in this review).

This general problem of more precise identification of the mechanisms through which the behavioral effects of malnutrition might be mediated certainly deserves much more systematic attention with human subjects at different age levels, and with different types and severity of nutritional deficits. As indicated earlier, one approach to this problem is to broaden our behavioral assessments so as to include measures specifically intended to determine which psychological processes or competencies are particularly vulnerable to various kinds of malnutrition. Although a good many recent studies have indeed gone beyond general IQ or DQ assessments, particularly with pre-school or school-aged children, it is difficult to find consistent patterns of differential nutritional vulnerability for various perceptual-cognitive functions across studies. Much of this inconsistency is to be expected, since the particular competencies or skills which seem most affected by malnutrition are likely to vary with the age of the children, the severity of the malnutrition, the particular tests used, the degree to which socio-cultural or environmental influences on performance have been controlled, etc.

Nevertheless, perhaps the most common suggestion derivable from much of the research, but particularly from studies of early and severe malnutrition, is that the nutritional deficits seem to alter the child's attentional competencies and responsiveness to the environment. For example, the commonly reported clinical observations of reduced activity or apathy in severe early malnutrition, particularly

of the marasmic type, are supported by recent experimental studies indicating reduced alerting or orienting responses to simple auditory stimuli (Lester, et al., 1975). On the other hand, while these malnourished infants or toddlers seem less responsive to low or moderate levels of stimulation, they appear to be hyper-reactive to higher stimulus levels that are more "intrusive." Non-supplemented young infants, for example, responded more irritably to a moderately stressful stimulus than did supplemented infants, (Vuori, et al., 1978), a finding paralleling reports of heightened "emotionality" and difficulty in extinguishing conditioned responses in malnourished animals. It is interesting to note that this same pattern of reduced attention to moderate stimuli and hyper-reactivity to more intense stimuli is also being found in very recent studies of premature or low-birth weight infants in this country (Rose, et al., 1976). Accompanying this pattern of altered responsiveness in children with early malnutrition are reports of reduced curiosity and exploratory behavior in infants and toddlers (Chavez, et al., 1975; Graves, 1978).

Although the data are much less consistent and clear, there are some suggestions from studies of pre-school and school age children that tasks which require the capacity to mobilize and sustain attention may be particularly affected by malnutrition— e.g., simple tasks of short-term memory, or tasks in which incidental learning is possible. These suggestive findings, which need much more systematic replication, come both from studies of mild-to-moderate malnutrition, (Klein, 1978; Klein, et al., 1979; McKay, et al., 1974), as well as a recent study of teenage children with history of clinical malnutrition in the first two years of life (Hoorweg, 1976). The importance of further systematic research directed at the impact of malnutrition on the child's attentional and motivational competencies is also supported by recent reports of altered work styles, or responses to cognitive demands shown by pre-school children having experienced early clinical malnutrition, (DeLicardie, et al., 1974), as well as less favorable performance on tasks requiring sustained attention by Boston children with iron deficiency (Pollitt, et al., 1978).

Virtually all the research just discussed has involved behavioral assessments of children performing in structured test or experimental situations. There is great need to extend systematically the beginning efforts that have been made recently to examine the potential consequences of malnutrition on various adaptive, intellectual, or learning competencies manifested in various real life settings (Hoorweg, 1976; Nerlove, et al., 1974; Richardson, et al., 1973). Assessments of functional competence based on observations or performance in these natural settings would complement the more common test or laboratory assessments in important ways, not the least of which would be to shed some light on the ecological or functional validity of these more controlled measurements. It is interesting to note that current early intervention research in this country strongly reflects a similar movement away from a heavy dependence on psychological tests or laboratory observations, toward more utilization of evaluations of competence manifested in natural situations.

Effectiveness of Nutritional and Social Interventions in Fostering the Development of Intellectual Competence The systematic utilization of experimental intervention strategies represents one of the most potent research approaches in this field. The hospitalization and treatment of clinically ill children with severe malnutrition obviously represents a basic and widely used form of intervention, which could be more fully exploited for systematic behavioral research purposes than it has been thus far. It is encouraging to note that in the past few years there has been an increasing utilization of nutritional intervention as a research strategy, particularly in connection with efforts to prevent malnutrition in populations where the problem is a chronic and endemic one. Because such studies are carried out within a longitudinal, prospective framework, they provide the opportunity to follow the physical growth and psychological development of children whose nutritional histories have been systematically influenced through the provision of added health care and nutritional supplementation, beginning pre-natally in some instances (Klein, et al., 1979; Brozek, et al., 1977). One of the major advantages of the intervention strategy is that changes or contrasts in children's dietary intake and nutritional status can be monitored prospectively as they occur, along with concurrent social and environmental factors, so that their relationships to contemporary or subsequent developmental outcome measures can be more meaningfully evaluated. This contrasts rather sharply with the situation characterizing many retrospective studies of malnourished chil-

dren, in which information about previous nutritional and developmental histories is often very limited and unclear.

A few recent nutritional intervention studies have begun to incorporate procedures for enrichment or enhancement of the child's social and learning environment as components of the intervention program, along with nutritional supplementation and health care. This intervention has sometimes been provided as an enrichment of experience, or "stimulation" during treatment for severe malnutrition, sometimes as a pre-school program for children typically exposed to chronic undernutrition, and sometimes in the form of a home visiting program to support the mother as a caregiver and promoter of her infant or toddler's development (Brozek, et al., 1977). In my view, this general strategy represents an extremely important approach since it recognizes the fact that the child's health and nutritional status, and his opportunities for learning and social development represent integral components of developmentally supportive child care or child rearing environments.

Let us briefly consider some of these recent intervention studies in somewhat more detail. With regard to severe and early malnutrition, as previously mentioned, it has been apparent for some time that the earlier the treatment and rehabilitation, the less the risk of severe developmental impairment (Pollitt and Thomson, 1977). Also, ensuring that the child is not deprived or adequate social and physical stimulation during treatment and rehabilitation, or providing added experiences during this period, seem to offer some facilitation of the recovery process (McLaren, et al., 1973; Monckeberg and Ruimallo, 1979). The long term benefits of these early treatments and interventions, of course, are very much influenced by the nature of the enduring environments to which the children return after hospitalization. As indicated earlier, the importance of the later developmental environments of children having experienced early and severe malnutrition is emphasized by recent findings indicating that if these environments are favorable and supportive of development there may be a substantial recovery of both physical growth (Winick, et al., 1975; Graham, 1972), as well as intellectual development (Winick, et al., 1975; Lloyd-Still, et al., 1974).

In so far as mild-to-moderate malnutrition is concerned, research thus far suggests that the provision of freely available nutritional supplementation to children and families at risk of mild-to-moderate undernutrition in rural Guatemalan villages has relatively little impact on the enhancement of mental development, particularly when compared with the role played by socio-environmental influences (Klein, 1978; Klein, et al., 1979). In an experimental intervention study with urban poor families in Bogota, during the first 18 months of life children who had received either nutritional supplementation *or* home visiting to promote maternal encouragement of intellectual development showed rather slight advantages in developmental test scores over control children receiving only health care (Mora, et al., 1979). Children who received both treatments showed somewhat more favorable gains in both physical growth and developmental test performance.

While the results just summarized, and a few other behavioral advantages reported for supplemented infants early in the first year of life can be considered somewhat promising, they represent quite modest effects, considering the scope and cost of the interventions involved. On the other hand there may be more subtle but important effects on the families provided with the combined health care, supplementation, and home visiting program, which have not yet been fully assessed.

The recent report from the Cali, Colombia project (McKay, et al., 1978) indicates that some facilitation of cognitive functioning can apparently be produced by a highly structured, cognitively oriented all day pre-school program, which also provides health care and nutritional supplementation. As is the case with many pre-school intervention programs in this country, it is not clear at this point to what extent these apparent benefits will be maintained when the children continue on in the public school system, particularly if no systematic efforts have been made to enhance the continuing environment of the home and family.

In considering the general implications of these recent intervention studies one is inclined to conclude, on the other hand, that the results thus far are mildly promising, at least in the case of the studied which have included social or environmental intervention as well as health care and nutritional supplementation. At the same time, however, these studies also reflect the difficulties of designing and implementing effective early intervention programs which can be shown to produce functionally meaningful enhancement of intellectual competencies. Nevertheless, this reviewer remains convinced that more of our research efforts must be aimed directly at the issue of intervention strategies for optimizing the growth and development of children who live in adverse environments and are at risk of both malnutrition and sub-optimal intellectual development, or have already experienced severe malnutrition. Obviously, in the long run the most effective forms of "intervention" would involve major improvements of the developmentally threatening economic, social, and physical conditions under which large populations of the poor live. Short of these long term political, social and economic changes, however, and working within the framework of resources potentially available in the immediate future, we need to continue to develop and systematically evaluate the effectiveness of various forms of intervention which could eventually be incorporated into realistic, ongoing social programs.

It seems highly possible that the most effective intervention strategies are likely to be those which are simultaneously concerned not only with nutritional and health needs, but also with ensuring necessary socio-environmental supports for optimal psychological development. Our major research goal, then, should be to determine how best to combine these elements in programs which meet the special needs of particular groups of children and families, given our goal of facilitating cognitive development. It seems reasonable to assume, also, that intervention is most likely to be effective, as well as more feasible economically, if it can be focussed so as to reach particularly those children and families considered to be at greatest biological or socio-environmental risk of impaired development.

Summary and Conclusions

It is quite clear that protein-calorie malnutrition represents a significant threat to the normal growth and development of many thousands of children living under the adverse conditions associated with poverty in many regions of the world. While protein-calorie malnutrition may produce substantial retardation of physical growth and brain development, there is relatively little evidence thus far that it has a direct and independent effect in producing intellectual or learning deficits in children, apart from the adverse social and environmental conditions typically associated with malnutrition. Nevertheless, severe and extended malnutrition beginning in the first two years of life may well be implicated as one important determinant of sub-optimal development, particularly if combined with a developmentally unfavorable social and learning environment in the home. Even in such instances, however, it appears that the long term effects of severe malnutrition may be substantially attenuated or minimized by a more favorable, developmentally supportive later environment. Mild or moderate malnutrition appears to play a relatively minor role in determining children's intellectual development, in comparison with the substantial influence exerted by various social and environmental factors.

Much current research is quite properly directed at a fuller understanding of the interactions between malnutrition and specific features of the child's social and physical environment in the home and neighborhood, in order to determine how these two major sources of potential influence may combine to produce either heightened or attenuated risk to normal psychological development. At the same time, considerable research has been focussed on a better understanding of the mechanisms through which malnutrition may exert its influence on behavior, through both human and animal studies. Considerable evidence thus far suggests that malnutrition may alter the child's attentional strategies and competencies, responsiveness to the environment, and emotionality, rather than directly impairing the basic ability to learn.

There has also been a substantial increase in experimental intervention studies concerned with evaluation of the effectiveness of broadly based nutritional supplementation and health care programs in enhancing both physical and mental development. Some of these programs have begun to incorporate efforts to provide added enrichment or enhancement of the child's early social and learning environments as well. While the results of these efforts to enhance children's intellectual development have not been particularly encouraging so far, continued research along these lines is very much needed. Such intervention research should add significantly to our basic understanding of the influence of malnutrition and early experience on behavioral development, while at the same time strengthening the knowledge base required for planning effective social programs aimed at prevention and remediation of sub-optimal development.

REFERENCES

Brockman, L. M. and Ricciuti, H. N. Severe protein-calorie malnutrition and cognitive development in infancy and early childhood. *Dev. Psychol.,* 4:312–319, 1971.

Brozek, J. Nutrition, malnutrition, and behavior. *Ann. Rev. Psychol.,* 1978, 29:157–177.

Brozek, J., Coursin, D. B., and Read, M. S. Longitudinal studies on the effects of malnutrition, nutritional supplementation, and behavioral stimulation. *Bull. Pan. Amer. Health Organ.,* 1977, 11:237–249.

Champakam, S., Srikantia, S. G. and Gopalan, C. Kwashiorkor and mental development. *Am. J. Clin. Nutr.,* 1968, 21:844–852.

Chase, H. P. and Martin, H. P. Undernutrition and child development. *N. Engl. J. Med.,* 1970, 282:933–939.

Chavez, A., Martinez, C., and Yachine, T. Nutrition, behavioral development, and mother-child interaction in young rural children. *Federation Proceedings,* 1975, 34:1574–1582.

Christiansen, N., Vuori, L., Mora, J. O., and Wagner, M. Social environment as it relates to malnutrition and mental development. In Cravioto, et al. (Ed.), *Early Malnut. and Men. Dev.,* Uppsala, Sweden: Almquist and Wiksell, 1974, 186–199.

Cravioto, J., Birch, H. G., DeLicardie, E., Rosales, L. and Vega, L. The Ecology of growth and development in a Mexican pre-industrial community. *Monogr. Soc. Res. Child Dev.,* 1969, 34:1–65.

Cravioto, J. and DeLicardie, E. R. Mental performance in school age children. *Am. J. Dis. Child.,* 1970, 120:404.

Cravioto, J., DeLicardie, E. R. and Birch, H. G. Nutrition, growth and neuro-integrative development: An experimental and ecologic study. *Pediatrics,* 1966, 38:319–372.

Cravioto, J. and Robles, B. Evolution of adaptive and motor behavior during rehabilitation from kwashiorkor. *Am. J. Orthopsychiatry,* 1965, 35:449–464.

DeLicardie, E. R. and Cravioto, J. Behavioral responsiveness of survivors of clinically severe malnutrition to cognitive demands. In Cravioto, et al., eds., *Early Malnutrition and Mental Development.* Uppsala, Sweden: Almquist and Wiksell, 1974, 134–153.

Dobbing, J. Effects of experimental undernutrition on development of the nervous system. In *Malnutrition, Learning and Behavior,* N. S. Scrimshaw and J. E. Gordon, eds., pp. 181–202. Massachusetts Institute of Technology Press, Cambridge, 1968.

Frankova, S. Interaction between early malnutrition and stimulation in animals. In Cravioto, et al., (Ed.), *Early*

Malnut. and Men. Dev., Uppsala, Sweden: Alquist and Wiksell, 1974, 202–209.

Graham, G. Environmental factors affecting the growth of children. *Amer. J. of Clin. Nutr.,* 1972, *25,* 1184–1188.

Graves, P. L. Nutrition and infant behavior: A replication study in the Katmandu Valley, Nepal. *Amer. J. Clin. Nutr.,* 1978, *31*:541–551.

Hertzig, M. E., Birch, H. G., Richardson, S. A. and Tizard, J. Intellectual levels of school children severely malnourished during the first two years of life. *Pediatrics,* 1972, *49*:814–824.

Hoorweg, J. C. *Protein-energy malnutrition and intellectual abilities.* The Hague/Paris: Mouton, 1976.

Klein, R. E. Malnutrition and human behavior: A backward glance at an ongoing longitudinal study. In D. A. Levitsky (Ed.) *Malnutrition, environment, and behavior: New perspectives.* Ithaca, N.Y.: Cornell Univ. Press, 1978, pp. 219–237.

Klein, R. E., Freeman, H. E., Kagan, J., Yarbrough, C. and Habicht, J. P. Is big smart? The relation of growth to cognition. *J. of Health and Soc. Behav.,* 1972, *13,* 219–225.

Klein, R. E., Irwin, M. H., et al. Effects of food supplementation on cognitive development and behavior among rural Guatemalan children. In J. Brozek, ed., *Behavioral Effects of Energy and Protein Deficits.* Bethesda, Md.: DHEW Publications (NIH) 1979, in press.

Klein, R. E., Yarbrough, C., Lasky, R. E., and Habicht, J. P. Correlations of mild to moderate protein-calorie malnutrition among rural Guatemalan infants and preschool children. In Cravioto, et al. (Ed.), *Early Malnut. and Men. Dev.,* Uppsala, Sweden: Almquist & Wiksell, 1974, 168–181.

Latham, M. C. Protein-calorie malnutrition in children and its relation to psychological development and behavior. *Physiological Review,* 1974, *54*(3): 541–565.

Lester, B. M., Klein, R. E., and Martinez, S. J. The use of habituation in the study of the effects of infantile malnutrition. *Developmental Psycho-biology,* 1975, *8,* 541–546.

Levitsky, D. A. (Ed.) Malnutrition, environment, and behavior: New perspectives. Ithaca, N.Y.: Cornell University Press, 1978, in press.

Lloyd-Still, J. D., Hurwitz, I., Wolff, P. H., and Schwachmann, H. Intellectual development after severe malnutrition in infancy. *Pediatrics,* 1974, *54*:306–311.

McKay, H., McKay, A., and Sinisterra, L. Intellectual development of malnourished preschool children in programs of stimulation and nutritional supplementation. In Cravioto, J., et al. *Early malnutrition and mental development.* Uppsala: Almquist and Wiksell, 1974, 226–233.

McKay, H., Sinisterra, L., McKay, H. G., Gomez, H.,

and Lloreda, P. Improving cognitive ability in chronically deprived children, *Science,* 1978, *200*:270–278.

McLaren, D. S., et al. The subsequent mental and physical development of rehabilitated marasmic infants. *Journal of Mental Deficiency Research,* 1973, *17,* 273–281.

Monckeberg, F. and Ruimallo, J. Psychomotor stimulation in recovery of early severe marasmic malnutrition: Experience in recover centers. In J. Brozek (Ed.) *Behavioral effects of energy and protein deficits.* Bethesda, Md.: DHEW Publications (NIH) 1979, in press.

Monckeberg, F., Tisler, S., Toro, S., Gattas, V., and Vegal, L. Malnutrition and mental development. *Amer. J. Clin. Nut.,* 1972, *25,* 766–772.

Mora, J. O., Christiansen, N., Ortiz, N., Vuori, L., and Herrera, M. G. Nutritional supplementation, early environment, and child development during the first 18 months of life. In J. Brozek, ed., *Behavioral Effects of Energy and Protein Deficits.* Bethesda, Md.: DHEW Publications (NIH), 1979, in press.

Nerlove, S. B., Roberts, J. M., Klein, R. E., Yarbrough, C., and Habicht, J. P. Natural indicators of cognitive development: An observational study of rural Guatemalan children. *Ethos,* 1974, *2,* 265–295.

Pollitt, E., Greenfield, D., and Leibel, R. Behavioral effects of iron deficiency among preschool children in Cambridge, Massachusetts. Paper presented at the 62nd Annual Meeting of the Federation of American Societies for Experimental Biology. Atlantic City, New Jersey, April 1978.

Pollitt, E. and Ricciuti, H. Biological and social correlates of stature among children living in the slums of Lima, Peru. *Am. J. Orthopsychiatry,* 1969, *39*:735–747.

Pollitt, E. and Thomson, C. Protein-calorie malnutrition and behavior: A view from psychology. In R. J. Wurtman and J. J. Wurtman (Eds.) *Nutrition and the Brain,* Vol. 2, New York: Raven, 1977, 261–306.

Richardson, S. A. The background histories of school children severely malnourished in infancy. In Schulman, I., ed., *Advances in Pediatrics, 21.* Chicago: Yearbook Medical Publications, 1974, 167–192.

Richardson, S. A. The relation of severe malnutrition in infancy to intelligence of school children with differing life histories. *Pediatric Research,* 1976, *10*:57–61.

Richardson, S. A., Birch, H. G., and Hertzig, M. E. School performance of children who were severely malnourished in infancy. *Am. J. Ment. Defic.,* 1973, *77,* 623–632.

Ricciuti, H. N. Adverse social and biological influences on early development. In H. McGurk, (Ed.) *Ecological factors in human development.* Amsterdam: N. Holland Press, 1977. (Chapt. 12).

Ricciuti, H. N. Malnutrition, learning and intellectual development: Research and remediation. In *Psychology and the Problems of Society.* American Psychological Association, Washington, D.C., 1970.

Rose, S. A., Schmidt, K. and Bridger, W. H. Cardiac and behavioral responsivity to tactile stimulation in premature and full-term infants. *Developmental Psychology,* 1976, *12,* 311–320.

Scrimshaw, N. S. Malnutrition and the health of children. *J. Am. Diet. Assoc.* 1963, *42*:203–208.

Scrimshaw, N. S. and Gordon, J. E., eds. *Malnutrition, Learning and Behavior.* Massachusetts Institute of Technology Press, Cambridge, 1968.

Ten State Nutrition Survey 1968–70. United States Department of Health, Education and Welfare, Health Services and Mental Health Administration. Center for Disease Control, Atlanta, Georgia. Department of Health, Education and Welfare Publication (HSM) 1972, 72–8131.

Vuori, L., de Navarro, L., Christiansen, N., Mora, J. O., and Herrera, M. G. Food supplementation of pregnant women at risk of malnutrition and newborn responsiveness to stimulation. Unpublished manuscript. Boston: Harvard School Pub. Hlth., Dept. of Nutrition, 1978.

Winick, M., Meyer, K., and Harris, R. C. Malnutrition and environmental enrichment by adoption. *Science,* 1975, *190*:1173–1175.

Winick, M. and Rosso, P. Head circumference and cellular growth of the brain in normal and marasmic children. *J. Pediatr.,* 1969, *74*:774–778.

Chapter Two

Infancy and Early Experience

Few areas of research have undergone so radical a change as infancy in recent times. Gone is "the booming, buzzing confusion" that William James described as the world of the infant; nor is the infant viewed any longer as passive, helpless, and at the mercy of his environment. Rather, a new and more positive view of infancy has emerged with infants, characterized as active, competent, and very early ready to make their mark on both their social and physical environment. Owing to rapid and important advances in our methodology for investigating infants, many of the capacities of the infant are just being discovered. As Macfarlane notes in his article in this section, many perceptual and cognitive capacities are available at an earlier age than had previously been assumed. Very young infants are ready to interact with their environment in a meaningful way and through a wide range of senses—vision, hearing, smell, and taste. Nor is infant precocity limited to perceptual capacities; much evidence is accumulating to suggest that infants are prepared for their social roles as well. Infants' early preference for faces and voices over inanimate objects as well as their predisposition to react to human speech sounds are all indicators of the infant's readiness for social interaction.

In spite of the early preparedness of the infant for successful interactions, as Lipsitt argues in his article, "Critical Conditions in Infancy," a great deal of learning takes place in the early weeks and months of life. Lipsitt argues that some of the tragedies that affect young infants, such as "crib death," may be better understood as "abberrations," or failures of learning processes in infancy.

As psychologists have shifted their views of the infant's competence, they have increasingly recognized that the infant plays an important role in determining his or her own course of development. During socialization, the influence process is bi-directional, with both the adult influencing the infant and the infant, in turn, modifying the behavior of his or her caretakers. No one who has been awakened at 3 A.M. by a crying infant would question the impact of infants on their parents. This is one of the themes emphasized by Rutter in his review, "Maternal Deprivation." In this update on the important themes that characterize early infant social development, Rutter also provides a critical discussion of the process of social attachments and the links between early experiences and later parenting behavior.

Finally, both Rutter and Kagan and Klein (1973) remind us that the effects of early infant experiences are not irreversible. The human organism is adaptive and flexible and able to profit from experiences at a variety of age points. For example, early birth traumas and complications can be overcome by a stimulating and responsive child-rearing environment. Similarly, the timing of development in different cultures indicates that slowness in early development does not preclude catch-up advances at later ages. Different cultures, in short, have different timetables for development and demand certain skills at later times than in our American culture. The impressive aspect of the Kagan-Klein report is the reminder that early "deficits" can be overcome; early experience is important, but the early effects are neither inevitable nor irreversible.

What a Baby Knows

Aidan Macfarlane

People used to think that the world of a newborn baby was a confusion of sounds and smells, of shifting light and shadow. Psychologists believed that the infant automatically received all sensations from the environment without exerting any selectivity or discrimination. This is not so. Although we are still in the process of discovering just how competent the newborn baby is, we know that just by being born human the infant fresh from the mother's womb is especially attracted to the features of another human face. This is remarkable because he or she has had no previous experience of the external sight or sound of human beings.

There are many ways of finding out what tiny babies can see, hear, or feel. Undoubtedly the pleasantest is that used by mothers to find out what their babies are thinking—watching them very carefully. One master at baby watching is Peter Wolff of Harvard University, who studied a group of 10 babies in their own homes, observing each for 30 hours a week. He was particularly interested in learning the amount of time infants spend in an attentive state—fully awake, breathing evenly, with eyes wide open, and quiet. Wolff found that the time a baby spends attentively increases from 11 percent in the first week to 21 percent by the fourth. The rest of the time he is either drowsy, asleep, or crying. Wolff also observed that during the first six hours after birth the amount of alert inactivity varied greatly from infant to infant. Some stayed awake for an hour and a half before the first sleep and did not have another alert period of equal length until the end of the first month; others fell asleep within 15 minutes of delivery and did not wake up fully until the second or third day.

I mention this because a newborn baby's reactions to his changing environment largely depend on whether he is drowsy or alert, quiet or crying. The best time to observe a baby's reactions to sights, sounds, and smells is when he is alert but quiet. Unfortunately, as Wolff's study suggests, the time a baby spends like this in the first few days after birth is brief.

Many factors affect a baby's state of alertness. Heinz Prechtl of the State University in Groningen, Holland, gathered from the brain-wave patterns of very small babies that infants under two weeks were never fully awake when flat on their backs; they were much more alert when they were lying at an angle, with their heads higher than their feet, or when they were upright. Alertness may be one reason crying babies often become quiet as soon as they are held up to the shoulder. Once babies are fully alert, the sights and sounds around them take their attention from crying.

A few years ago, many psychologists tested babies when they were flat on their backs, and got negative results. In some cases, they repeated the tests with the babies sitting up, and the babies responded. Today, we frequently use small supportive chairs, inclined at an angle, for babies to sit in. Other factors affecting response include the temperature of the surroundings—too hot and the baby goes off to sleep, too cold and he starts to cry. Touch also matters—if the baby is tightly swaddled, he tends to go to sleep, but he may become distressed if totally naked. Light is an influence—too much and he shuts his eyes with a grimace, too dim and he may go to sleep again. Sound also affects response—many babies go to sleep more quickly when background noise is present.

If the baby is to respond to certain things in the outside world, he needs to encounter certain features that attract his attention, and he has to link them to his previous experiences. If the stimulus is too intense, too bright, too noisy, or has too many novel features, he may defend himself by turning away or crying. If the intensity of the stimulus is too low or too familiar, he may ignore it. These changes in behavior seem to be accompanied by changes in the heart rate. If the baby is attentive to an event he finds interesting, his heartbeat tends to slow down. If a stimulus is too intense or frightening, his heart speeds up, perhaps in preparation for some sort of defense.

Even when a newborn baby is asleep, he will screw up his eyes, frown, and tense his muscles if a bright light suddenly shines on his face. If, however, he is awake and is brought near a window but not into direct sunlight, he will often turn toward the light, indicating that he knows where it is and is attracted by it. There is evidence that a baby responds to light even inside the uterus, and it seems possible that if a bright light were shone on the pregnant mother's belly, the baby might turn toward it. Perhaps some of the baby's movements before birth stem from this attraction to light.

After he is born, a baby is much more discriminating; he looks at some things and not at others. If you move your head slowly from side to side nine inches away from his face, he may follow it for short distances with jerky eye movements. To discover which features of the human face a baby prefers to look at, Robert Fantz of Western Reserve University showed a series of babies three flat objects the size and shape of a head. On the first a stylized face was painted in black on a pink background; the second had the same features as the first, but scrambled; and the third had a solid black patch at one end, equal in area to the features of the first two. The babies tested were from four days to six months old, but regardless of age all of them looked most at the real face, somewhat less at the scrambled face, and least at the object with the black patch.

Most studies on what babies prefer to look at involve showing them two things together and observing their eye movements to see which one they look at more. This method shows that babies are attracted by contrast. They like complex patterns with sharp demarcations, and it is not surprising that they watch the eyes more than other features of the human face. With their whites, darker irises, and black pupils, the eyes present definite contrasts. Obviously it is significant that infants should be attracted to eyes and faces as they are.

It was not realized until recently that very young babies could see at all, because it had not been discovered that they have a fairly rigid distance of focus, approximately nine inches. If you want a baby to look at something, it is best to show it to him at this distance—which is incidentally just about the same distance the mother's face is from her baby's when she is breast-feeding. More recent work shows that this distance may not be completely fixed, for by examining the movements of each eye individually and the distance between the center of the pupils, we can observe that the eyes converge and diverge when babies look at objects 10 to 20 inches away but not when the objects are nearer or farther away. This suggests that babies see objects only within this range.

The baby expects to feel what he can see. Tom Bower of the University of Edinburgh filmed the reactions of a series of babies less than two weeks old while a large object moved at different speeds toward them. Examining the films, he found that as the object approached, the babies pulled back their heads and put their hands between themselves and the object. Apparently they already have a reaction that would defend them against being hit by the object, and they expect it to be solid. The baby's reaction to an object approaching at a certain speed on a "hit path" was specific, but if the object moved away from or to one side of the baby, or if the speed of approach changed, he did not react.

In another experiment, Bower created the optical illusion of an object by using polarized light. If the baby was sitting up in a supportive chair so that his arms and hands were free to move, he appeared to try to grasp the object if it seemed within reach. When he tried to grasp an illusory object only to find that it was not there, he was greatly disturbed. This experiment seems to indicate that at least one aspect of the coordination between eye and hand is present at birth and that the newborn baby expects to be able to touch the objects he sees.

The most common complicated sight a baby sees after birth is his mother's face, not as a still object in one plane, like a photograph, but as a dynamic and continually moving object with varied expressions and different associated contexts such as food and warmth. How soon does a baby come to distinguish his mother's face from others? Genevieve Carpenter of the Behavior Development Research Unit at St. Mary's Hospital in London sat two-week-old babies in supportive chairs and, when they were alert, presented each with either his mother's face or the face of a woman the baby had never seen before in a framed opening in front of him. She observed the babies' general behavior, where they looked, and for how long. At two weeks the babies spent more time looking at their mothers' faces than they did at the strangers' faces. In fact, when they were presented with the other women's faces, they frequently showed strong gaze aversion, looking right away, almost over their shoulders. This kind of withdrawal suggests that the babies found the stimulus too intense or too novel.

It is obvious to most mothers that their babies can hear. If the baby is alert, a loud noise, such as a door slamming, usually makes him tense up or startles him. But during the first few days after birth the middle part of the ear behind the eardrum is full of amniotic fluid that only gradually is absorbed or evaporates. Until it is, sounds reaching the baby's ear are dampened.

Michael Wertheimer of the University of Colorado sounded clicks at either of a newborn's ears and noted that the infant turned his eyes toward the clicks. At four days or even younger, a baby can be taught to turn his head one way for a bell and the other way for a buzzer, by being rewarded when he is right. But we know a baby hears even before he is born. Researchers put a very small microphone on the end of a flexible narrow tube and inserted it into the mother's uterus after her membranes broke— generally a sign that birth will take place within a few hours. The tube was placed close to the baby's ear and recorded the noise actually reaching him. The recordings showed that, before birth, the baby is continuously exposed to the loud rhythmical sounds of the mother's blood flowing through the uterine wall, and to the intermittent sounds of gas rumbling in the mother's intestine. Since it is possible to record an infant's heart rate at this stage, researchers produced a loud noise near the mother's abdominal wall, recorded it from inside the uterus, and noted the effects it had on the baby's heart rate. As might be expected, the baby's heart speeded up.

It seems from this, and from work done with babies right after birth, that patterned, rhythmic sounds produce more response than pure, continuous tones, and that the most effective sound of all is one that includes the fundamental frequencies found in the human voice. There is also evidence from research done by John Hutt at Oxford University that babies respond better to high than to low frequencies. In light of this, it is interesting that both mothers and fathers often pitch their voices higher when talking to their babies than when talking to adults.

It is also true that a newborn baby held upright, with a man talking to him from one side and a woman from the other, often turns more frequently to the woman. If the woman is the mother, it seems as if the baby recognizes her. This may be so, for another study shows that, if a mother consistently calls her baby by name every time she picks him up,

feeds him, or comes near him, by the third day he will frequently turn toward her if she stands out of his line of sight and calls his name. If a woman who is not his mother does the same thing, the baby is much less likely to respond.

A more controlled study of this kind was done by Margaret Mills of the University of Reading in England. She tested babies who were between 20 and 30 days old, and arranged things so that when an infant sucked on a nipple, he heard a recording of either his own mother's or a woman's voice he had not heard before, matched for volume. She found that a baby would suck significantly more to conjure up the sound of his own mother. This is another subtle difference in babies' behavior toward mothers and strangers.

Turning the eyes toward a sound is sophisticated, but five-day-old babies seem to do even better than this. If we disregard his eyes and watch him turn his head instead, we find that he seems able to tell from what angle a sound is coming. Babies will turn their heads more toward a sound coming from an angle of 80 degrees from the midline than they will toward a sound coming from 15 degrees from the midline on the same side.

Also, if you turn your face from side to side in front of the baby's face while talking, his head and eyes follow you—as if he were trying to keep the sound coming from a position between his ears. I have observed babies who under these conditions do not move their eyes at all, but track the face by holding the eyes straight ahead and moving the head only.

Finally, there are the intriguing findings of William Condon of Boston University, who for many years analyzed films of adults talking to one another. He found that people talking seemed to move in synchrony with speech. This "dance" can be detected only by careful film analysis, when even the very smallest movements can be examined. Louis Sander, also of Boston University, later joined Condon in a project of video-taping a series of infants who were between 12 hours and two days old. They showed that even at this incredibly early age the babies seemed to move in precise time to human speech. They did so whether the speech was English or Chinese.

Smell is another way to gather information about people and the world around. Human beings are capable of considerable discrimination among smells, and smells can be evocative. Apparently, smell is a fairly old sense in terms of evolutionary development and is associated with parts of the brain that are themselves ancient in terms of evolution.

That very young babies can smell has been shown in a study conducted at Brown University by Trygg Engen, Lewis Lipsitt, and Herbert Kay. They observed the activity, heart rate, and breathing patterns of 20 two-day-old babies. Each baby was presented with two of four smells: anise oil, asafetida, acetic acid, and phenyl alcohol. When a smell was first presented to the baby, his activity, heart rate, and breathing patterns changed. If the smell continued, the baby gradually learned to take no notice of it (habituation), but when the smell changed, up went the activity and the heart rate, and breathing patterns changed again—the infant recognized the smell as being different from the one he had become used to.

Recent studies I did with newborn babies were designed to test their sense of smell. I had noticed that a baby may turn his face to his mother's breast even before he has looked at it or before his face has been touched by the nipple. This might be because he senses the heat of the breast, and indeed infrared photographs show that the breasts and lips of a lactating woman are the warmest areas of her skin. It might also be that the baby learns very rapidly that when one side of his body is held against his mother he has to turn his head to that side to get fed. But the baby might also be smelling the breast; each time the baby is fed his nose is in such close contact that the food and the smell may become associated.

Initially, I took a four-inch-square gauze breast pad that had been placed inside the mother's bra between feedings, and put it at one side of the baby's head, touching his cheek. At the same time, I put a clean breast pad against his other cheek and for one minute filmed all the movements of the baby's head; at the end of the minute I reversed the pads for another minute. Previous studies had shown that babies tend spontaneously to turn their heads more to the right than to the left, perhaps because mothers tend to hold their babies more often on their own left. Analysis of the films showed that, five days after birth, babies spent more time with their heads turned toward their mothers' pads than toward the clean pads.

To get subtler results I repeated the test using another mother's breast pad instead of a clean one. At two days the babies spent an equal amount of time with both pads, but at six days the babies generally spent more time turned to their own mothers' pads than to the other mothers' pads. At 10 days this effect was even more striking. All the babies were breast-fed and were tested when hungriest, just before a feeding.

This experiment still left open the question of whether it was the breast milk itself, the mother's smell, or a combination of the two that attracted the baby. I did one further experiment, in which the mothers expressed milk from their breasts onto gauze pads and then used those pads as in the previous experiment. This revealed that babies do not turn toward breast milk alone—perhaps the smell of the milk is not strong enough. Here again we witness the ability of the baby to distinguish his own mother from other mothers when he is only six days old.

Perhaps mothers can also recognize their own babies' smells. In a pilot study, we asked a group of mothers to sniff their babies. We blindfolded the mothers and put earphones on them so they could neither see nor hear their babies. When they were given two babies to smell, a significant number managed to identify their own, though I suspect they may have been using other clues.

Taste is a relatively simple sense in human beings, and the fine discriminations that we think we can make by taste we actually make by smell. Two observations indicate that the baby inside the uterus is able to taste. The baby, surrounded by amniotic fluid, swallows it continually and then eliminates it. In certain pregnancies too much fluid accumulates too quickly. Forty years ago a physician developed a novel way of treating this. By sweetening the fluid surrounding the baby with an injection of saccharine, he discovered that he could reduce the amount of fluid, possibly because the baby was encouraged to swallow more.

More recently another doctor found that injecting a substance opaque to x-rays into the amniotic fluid caused a decrease in swallowing; this was clear from the x-ray pictures of the substance being swallowed by the child. The opaque substance he had injected had an extremely unpleasant taste. These observations suggest that a fetus can taste.

Lewis Lipsitt and his colleagues at Brown have been looking at the effect of sweetness on a baby's sucking patterns and on his heart rate. Working with babies two to three days old, they arranged a system by which, each time the baby sucked, he got a tiny fixed amount of fluid containing varying amounts of sugar. They found that the more sugar, the slower the baby sucked and the more his heart rate increased. This is in some ways not what we might expect: Certainly I would have thought that if the baby tasted a sweet substance he would have sucked faster to try to get more. But in this case, where the baby was getting only a very small, fixed amount with each suck, he sucked more slowly. This should mean that less effort was used and the heart should have slowed down, but it did not. One explanation that Lipsitt put forward is that the baby sucks more slowly in order to savor the sweeter fluid, and perhaps the excitement of tasting it increases the heart rate. It is probable, though, that the answer is not this simple.

The findings of David Salisbury of Oxford University are also remarkable. He looked at the effects of different fluids on babies' swallowing, sucking, and breathing patterns. Previous work showed that water, cow's milk, and glucose, when introduced into the back of a calf's throat, interrupted its breathing, while a salt-water solution did not; this suggested that a calf has specialized taste receptors to prevent it from breathing when swallowing. Salisbury studied the effects of feeding different solutions to human babies. He found that, when given salt water, they suppressed breathing very poorly, but when he fed them sterile water, one inhaled it—which suggests that a baby may also have these specialized taste receptors.

Salisbury also examined the swallowing, breathing, and sucking patterns of the infants when fed breast milk or a substitute. Again the patterns were different, indicating that a young baby's taste is sensitive enough to distinguish breast milk from a substitute.

The composition of breast milk alters during the day and during each feeding. At the beginning of a feeding, breast milk is somewhat diluted; it becomes more concentrated toward the end. So the baby gets his fluids at the beginning and his food at the end. Shifting from one breast to another has been likened to having a drink in the middle of a meal.

We still accept the idea that newborn babies are not as susceptible to pain as they are later. This is demonstrated by the practice in the United States of circumcising newborn baby boys without anesthetics or analgesics. If it were necessary to remove an equivalent area of highly sensitive skin from some other part of the body, say the little finger, most people would be horrified if it were done without an anesthetic; yet few demand anesthetics for circumcision.

Little systematic research has been done on a baby's perceptions of pain, since no one wants to hurt babies simply to discover the nature of their reactions. However, watching any baby who has to have a blood test shows us that babies are aware of pain. Blood samples are commonly obtained by pricking a baby's heel with a small stylette and collecting the drops in a container. The normal reaction of the baby to this procedure is immediately to try to withdraw his foot and to wail with anguish. He may also tense all his muscles and turn bright red. His heartbeat and breathing patterns change rapidly as well. But the reaction varies greatly from baby to baby, depending on his temperament and his alertness at the time. And a baby's reactions to pain can be modified: The increases in the heart rate after circumcision can be reduced by having the baby suck at the same time, though the slowed heartbeat is no evidence that the baby feels any less pain.

After a newborn baby has been circumcised, his sleep patterns are disturbed, just as they are after blood has been taken from his heel. In one study the disturbance followed very soon after circumcision; in a second study there was a prolonged period of wakefulness and fussing, which was followed by an increase in quiet sleep. Circumcision has also been implicated in sex differences. Most studies of newborn babies have been done in the United States, where the majority of males are circumcised at birth. It is possible that some reported differences in behavior between male and female babies are results of this surgical procedure instead of any innate differences.

One ability that more than any other demonstrates the sophistication of newborn babies is imitation. In a series of very well controlled studies conducted in England and the United States, Andrew Meltzov demonstrated that at two weeks of age children can stick out their tongues and clench and unclench their hands when they watch someone else do these things. These actions are not immediately obvious to the eye and can be detected only by very close analysis of video tape and film. The baby has to watch another person stick out a tongue, and then he has to realize that his own tongue is equivalent to that person's even though he has never seen his own tongue. Without being able to see what he is doing himself, he must match his movements to the ones he sees. These studies are very recent and are likely to have considerable impact on theories of social development in children.

All this research points in the same direction. It shows that when a baby is born, he already has the capacity to respond selectively and socially to human beings instead of to the things in his new environment. By the age of two weeks, he has learned to recognize the features of individual human beings—especially those of his usual caretaker. At the same time, the baby's appearance and behavior help ensure that his physical and emotional needs are looked after. These systems of mutual attraction and needs did not develop independently, but evolved over millions of years as an interdependent series of factors that ensure the survival of the newborn baby and thus of the human species.

For further information:

Bower, T. G. R. *Development in Infancy.* W. H. Freeman, 1974.

Carpenter, G. "Mother's Face and the Newborn." *New Scientist,* March, 1974.

Crook, J. and Lipsitt, L. P. "Neonatal Nutritive Sucking: Effects of Taste Stimulation upon Sucking Rhythm and Heart Rate." *Child Development,* No. 47, 1976.

Macfarlane, J. A. *The Psychology of Childbirth.* Harvard University Press, 1977.

Macfarlane, J. A. "Olfaction in the Development of Social Preferences in the Human Neonate." *Parent-Infant Interaction.* CIBA Foundation Symposium, No. 33, new series, ASP, 1975.

Richards, M. P. M., J. F. Bernal, and Y. Brackbill. "Early Behavioral Differences: Gender or Circumcision." *Developmental Psychobiology,* No. 9, 1976.

Reading 6

Our Developing Knowledge of Infant Perception and Cognition

Leslie B. Cohen

Over the past two decades, the study of infant development has progressed more rapidly than many other types of research. The field has expanded from a mere handful of investigators in the late 1950s to several hundred today. Each year a higher proportion of articles on infancy are published in major developmental journals. This trend has led to the publication of a new journal devoted exclusively to infant research. Each year more and more papers on infancy are presented at national conventions, culminating in last year's First International Conference on Infancy in Providence, Rhode Island. The conference was attended by over 300 people whose interests centered on many aspects of infant development.

Although there has been a broad-based and dramatic expansion in research on social, language, cognitive, and perceptual development during this period, I would propose that one of the leading areas, if not the leading area, in this advancement has been infant perception. More has been learned about infant perception in the past 15 or 20 years than in all previous years. Many generations have been interested in infant perceptual abilities. As early as 1877, Darwin thrust a candle before his infant son's eyes to test his vision and found him able to fixate. Darwin also noticed that sneezing or producing other unexpected noises elicited a startle response. Other isolated studies of infant perception (e.g., Chase, 1937; Cruickshank, 1941; Ling, 1941; Valentine, 1913–1914) appeared throughout the early 20th century. It was not until Fantz's pioneering work in the late 1950s and early 1960s, however, that research in the area accelerated dramatically. Fantz's early contribution stemmed as much or more from the method he used than from the stimuli he presented or the results he obtained. His work demonstrated that one can simply and reliably measure infant visual fixations. All one must do is

Preparation of this essay was supported in part by Grants HD-03858 and HD-05951 from the National Institute of Child Health and Human Development.

present some visual target, look through a peephole at the infant's eye, and record the amount of time the target is reflected on the infant's cornea (Fantz, 1961). In other words, Fantz devised a simple technique for measuring infant visual perception.

The study of infant perception is intriguing in that infants cannot be asked to express exactly what they are seeing, hearing, or feeling. Yet as Darwin reported so long ago, young infants do react to external stimulation. They must therefore be perceiving something. The question is, Just what are they perceiving? Our natural curiosity about infants, coupled with a viable technique for investigating infant perception, provided the impetus needed for the inauguration of research in this area.

Shortly after the introduction of Fantz's technique, numerous investigators, with a limited amount of inexpensive equipment and little or no prior experience with infants, began to use his procedure to study infant visual perception and cognition. Many used what has become known as the "infant preference" technique (Berlyne, 1958; Fantz, 1958). On each trial, two visual stimuli were presented simultaneously and infants' responses to the stimuli were compared. Actually, all that was usually recorded was the total fixation time to each stimulus. Although some considered this procedure too crude and devised more sophisticated electronic systems for tracking individual eye movements in newborns (Salapatek, 1968), others made ingenious use of this simple procedure ("show them some pictures and see which one they like the most") to examine everything from visual acuity to intermodal coordination. In some of Fantz's earlier work, for example, he showed that infants prefer to look longer at a patterned surface than at a plain one (Fantz, 1963). This simple fact has been used in numerous investigations of the development of infant visual acuity (Fantz, Ordy, & Udelf, 1962; Salapatek, Bechtold, & Bushnell, 1976). One can put vertical black and white stripes on one side and a plain grey stimulus on the other. By decreasing the contrast of the lines or by increasing their spatial frequency, one can determine at what point the infants' preference (and presumably their ability to discriminate between patterned and unpatterned stimuli) disappears. Although actual estimates of infant visual acuity vary somewhat from study to study, we do know that the newborn's acuity is quite poor but that it increases dramatically during the first few months of life (Cohen, DeLoache, &

Strauss, 1979). This knowledge and simple procedure are now beginning to be used on an applied basis in some hospitals to diagnose infants with suspected visual defects (Dobson, Teller, Lee, & Wade, 1978).

In some ways, studies of visual acuity may be considered the limiting case of studies of visual preference. They test whether the infants see something or nothing. Of equal interest are those experiments that present two different perceivable stimuli and test whether or not infants can discriminate between them. Numerous experiments of this sort have shown infant preferences for curved versus straight lines (Frantz & Nevis, 1967; Ruff & Birch, 1974), chromatic versus achromatic stimuli (Fantz, 1963; Oster, Note 1), three-dimensional objects versus two-dimensional representations (Fantz, Fagan, & Miranda, 1975), complex patterns versus simple ones (Brennan, Ames, & Moore, 1966; Fantz, 1965), and schematic faces versus nonfaces (Fantz, 1963; Goren, Note 2). One of the most ingenious recent uses of the technique was devised by Spelke (Note 3) in the study of intermodal perception. Four-month-old infants were simultaneously shown two films: one of a bouncing toy kangaroo and one of a bouncing donkey. The filmed objects each moved at a different rate. From a central speaker, the infants heard the sound appropriate to one of the films. Spelke found that the infants looked significantly longer at the film associated with the sound, thus demonstrating the ability to coordinate auditory and visual information. In a refinement of this procedure in our laboratory, Maynard (1979) showed the identical jumping-kangaroo film on both sides. The only difference between the films was that they were temporally out of phase. Once again, a central speaker produced a sound appropriate to one of the films. Four-month-old males looked significantly longer at the appropriate film, indicating intermodal coordination based solely on the synchrony between auditory and visual information.

As valuable as the visual preference paradigm has proven to be, it does have one inherent drawback. Its effectiveness depends on the infant having greater inborn or automatic preferences for some stimuli. When such a preference occurs, one can use it to infer the infant's ability to discriminate between stimuli, but there are innumerable instances when the infant may be able to discriminate between patterns or objects but does not have any initial preference for one over the other. Once again, we turn to Fantz for the solution of this problem. In addition to infants having a visual preference for certain characteristics of physical stimuli, Fantz reported that infants also have a preference for a novel versus a familiar stimulus (Fantz, 1964). Fantz obtained evidence for novelty preference in the following cleverly designed experiment: On one side of a display screen, he presented the same visual pattern on every trial, and on the other side of the screen, the pattern changed from trial to trial. Over the course of the experiment, the infants gradually looked longer and longer at the side with the novel pattern.

Variations of this novelty preference paradigm have proven to be even more effective tools for assessing infant perceptual discrimination than was the earlier visual preference procedure. The novelty paradigm provides the opportunity to test infants on visual discriminations even when there appears to be no a priori preference for one stimulus. Today, the most commonly used version of the paradigm involves repeatedly presenting a single stimulus until the infant's attention habituates and then testing with the same stimulus versus one or more novel stimuli to determine when recovery of attention occurs. Thus the infant is still responding in terms of a visual preference, but it is an experimentally induced preference for novelty rather than a stimulus preference that the infant brings to the experimental situation.

Within the last 10 years, the habituation or novelty preference paradigm has been employed in countless experiments. From these studies, we know infants can perceive colors, forms, patterns, faces, and even complex events such as subject-object relations (Cohen et al., 1979). The more the paradigm has been used, the more sophisticated the experimental questions have become. There is now evidence that within the first six months of life, infants perceive colors categorically (Bornstein, 1976) and perceive simple forms or angles in terms of the relations among their sides (Schwartz, 1975). Furthermore, infants can perceive simple patterns as gestalts (Vurpillot, Ruel, & Castrec, 1977) and perceive more complex patterns in terms of their components, until about 5 months of age, when they perceive them as compounds (Cohen & Gelber, 1975). A recent example illustrates how the habituation technique may be used. Schwartz (1975) gave 2—4-month-old infants ten 20-second habituation

trials with a single angle whose vertex was oriented to the left. The infants were then tested with the same angle rotated 90° and an acute angle also oriented to the left. Infants looked less at the old angle than at the new one, indicating that they were responding to the relationship between the line segments and not just to the location of independent line segments per se.

In a series of two experiments, my colleagues and I showed that 4-month-old infants perceive simple colored forms in terms of their component parts rather than as a compound. In the first study (Cohen, Gelber, & Lazar, 1971), infants were habituated to a colored form such as a red circle. They were then tested with the red circle, a green circle, a red triangle, and a green triangle. Fixation times recovered somewhat when either color or form was changed but recovered most when both were changed. These results indicated that the infants were perceiving both color and form. In a follow-up study (Cohen & Gelber, 1975), infants were habituated to alternating red circle and green triangles and were then tested with a green circle and a red triangle. Their fixation time remained low in response to these test stimuli, indicating that they had processed the stimuli in terms of their old components rather than as new compounds. A similar study by Fagan (1977) with $5\frac{1}{2}$-month-old infants indicated that at that age, the infants were capable of responding to the compound stimulus as well as to its components.

Summarizing what we now know, the extensive literature on infant visual perception is beginning to yield a consistent picture of how the infant processes visual information during the first few months of life. During the first month or two, infants are capable of processing high-contrast, low-spatial-frequency information. The units of perception are lines, angles, and adjacent high-contrast areas. From 2 until 4 or 5 months of age, simple dimensions such as colors and forms can be processed as units. These units are defined relationally rather than as simple transformations of energy impinging on the retina. Colors are seen categorically; that is, wide ranges of reds, yellows, greens, and blues are perceived as equivalent, whereas there are sharper boundaries between these color categories. Simple forms are perceived as holistic units, that is, in terms of the relation among their parts. It is not until approximately 5 months of age, however, that more complex patterns such as faces or colored forms are perceived as higher order gestalts. This view represents quite a change from the one held a mere two decades ago, when investigators were trying to determine whether the young infant could see at all.

There is no doubt that the habituation or novelty preference paradigm has served us well in our quest for information about how the young infant perceives his or her visual world. But the paradigm has also been valuable in another respect, perhaps more valuable to psychology as a whole than many would have anticipated. In an effort to explain not only what an infant can perceive or discriminate but why the infant habituates or has a novelty preference in the first place, many infant researchers are beginning to ask questions that transcend perception and are more relevant to the early development of memory and cognition. This transition marks the first time that that hardy soul, the infant researcher, has entered the mainstream of developmental psychology and has begun to address the same issues his or her counterparts (working with children or adults) have been investigating. Exploring issues such as recall versus recognition, short-term versus long-term memory, top-down versus bottom-up processing, and the nature of the prototype in concept acquisition has become just as important to the infant researcher as it has long been to colleagues working with older subjects.

The shift to cognition really began to examine seriously the fact that infant habituation implies infant memory. An infant habituates to a stimulus because the stimulus is becoming more familiar. But in order for it to be familiar, it must, in some sense, be remembered. Thus, those experiments which showed that infants preferred a novel color or form to a familiar one also showed that infants remembered the familiar color or form. One could easily do experiments to investigate how long an infant could remember, whether that memory was subject to interference, or whether the same type of information was retained in long-term as in short-term memory.

In order to study long-term memory, all one had to do was to insert a delay between the end of habituation and a subsequent test with novel and familiar stimuli. In one experiment, for example, 5-month-old infants familiarized to a face for two minutes still retained some information about that face after a two-week delay. (Fagan, 1973). In order to investigate interference effects, all one had to do was to insert some irrelevant material before the

test, during the delay interval. Several studies have now shown that infant memory is relatively insensitive to a whole host of interfering stimuli (Cohen, DeLoache, & Pearl, 1977; Fagan, 1977; McCall, Kennedy, & Dodds, 1977).

Although these experiments demonstrated that infant memory is robust and that information can be retained for long periods of time, research is just beginning to examine whether information retained in long-term memory is the same as or different from information retained in short-term memory. In one experiment recently completed in our laboratory (Strauss & Cohen, Note 4), 5-month-old infants were familiarized with a three-dimensional Styrofoam figure. They were then tested immediately, after a 10-minute delay, and after a 24-hour delay, with the same form and one with a different shape, color, size, or orientation. Although the infants exhibited recognition of all four dimensions when tested immediately, they retained only the color and form after 10 minutes and only the form after 24 hours. If one assumes that these dimensions can be arranged hierarchically according to depth of processing or salience of the dimension for knowledge about objects, with form being more salient than color, then this study provides the first evidence that infants retain longest those characteristics that are most salient or important.

One of the more exciting new developments in infant perception is adaptation of the habituation paradigm to investigate concept acquisition in the infant. According to the standard habituation procedure, the infant is repeatedly shown the same stimulus. In a concept study, the infant is shown a variety of different stimuli, all of which belong to the same concept or category, and is then tested with a new member of the category and a nonmember. If the infant has remembered the concept as opposed to the individual stimuli, his or her habituation should generalize more to the new member of category than to the nonmember. These experiments are equivalent to ones with older children in which the subjects are shown several examples from a category and are then asked to select the test items that are members of the same category. Several experiments with infants have now been reported that have used this habituation procedure. Most have used faces as stimuli (Cohen & Strauss, 1979; Cornell, 1974; Fagan, 1974), although there is also evidence of categorization of stuffed animals (Cohen & Caputo, Note 5), photographs of real animals (Cohen & Caputo, Note 5), and shapes regardless of orientation (McGurk, 1972). In one experiment, for example, my co-workers and I habituated 18-, 24-, and 30-week-old infants either to a photograph of a single female face in one orientation, to the same female face in different orientations, or to different female faces in different orientations. All infants were then tested with the original female face, for the first time looking straight ahead, and with a novel female face looking straight ahead. The 30-week-old infants showed not only that they could acquire a concept but that they could acquire different levels of concepts depending on which habituation condition they received. If they had experienced a single face in a single orientation, the infants increased the time they looked at both test stimuli, indicating that they were responding primarily to a change in orientation. If they had been habituated to the same female in different orientations, they spent more time looking at the novel female face only, indicating that they were responding to a specific female face regardless of orientation. Finally, if they had been habituated to different female faces, they did not look long at either test stimulus, indicating a response to female faces in general. In contrast, the two younger groups of infants responded only to the orientation change and not to the more abstract concepts involving faces.

Experiments such as these demonstrate the ability of infants to respond in terms of conceptual categories, but they do not indicate on what basis the categories are formed. Do the infants acquire a concept simply by attending to those specific features in the series of habituation stimuli that remain constant? Or do infants store a more abstract prototype, or best example, of a category even though they may not have experienced that best example as frequently as other poorer examples? This question was examined in what must surely be the most sophisticated study of infant concepts to date (Strauss, 1978). Strauss first familiarized 10-month-old infants with a series of schematic faces in which four facial dimensions—eye separation, nose width, nose length, and face length—varied from trial to trial. During the course of this familiarization, the infants saw 12 extreme examples of each dimension (e.g., six wide noses and six narrow noses) but only two average examples (e.g., two average noses). When tested for the first time with a face containing nothing but extreme values and one

with nothing but average values, the infants generalized more to the average face even though they had seen those average features less frequently. Based on these results, Strauss concluded that when infants acquire a category they are capable of going beyond the specific examples to construct an abstract prototype that is an average of what they have seen before.

It is clear from research such as that presented above that infants at birth can perceive the world around them and from a very early age are organizing their perceptual experience. One goal of future research should be to determine the nature of this organization. To what extent is it hierarchical? To what extent does it change with age or experience? Under what conditions will infants process information at the highest level of their capability, and under what conditions at some lower level? What is the relation between perception and memory or between perception and abstract representation? These are very different questions from the ones traditionally asked by most investigators of infant perception, yet they are crucial from both theoretical and applied viewpoints. They bridge the gap between infancy and later development. They force the investigator of infant development to examine many of the same issues with which his or her colleagues in perception and cognition are struggling in their studies of children and adults. The infant researcher must now be cognizant of a new and diverse experimental literature. As the examination of infant perception and cognition proceeds, the answers found for infants will undoubtedly influence our conceptions of children and adults as well. In short, the field of infant perception is beginning to enter the mainstream of experimental psychology.

From an applied perspective, our expanding knowledge about developmental changes in perception, information processing, and cognition in normal infants is an essential first step toward diagnosis and remediation of specific perceptual or cognitive deficits in high-risk or retarded infants. It is popular these days to assume that infants who have had some perinatal trauma or inadequate environment will be developmentally retarded. Intervention programs for infants are sprouting up all over the country to deal with that assumed retardation. Many of these programs are undoubtedly doing some good, yet because of our current lack of knowledge, most programs are forced to work largely in the dark. Before we can effectively remedy some perceptual or cognitive problem, we must be able to diagnose the specifics of the problem. And before we can make that diagnosis we must learn how the normal infant develops and changes. We already know enough about a few areas, such as the development of visual acuity or color vision, to make early diagnosis possible. Assuming that the current rate of research on infant perception will continue in the next few years, we are likely to achieve that same goal in the more elusive areas of early perceptual organization and cognition. A short time ago, we had to admit that the study of infant development was itself in its own infancy. Today, we can say with some pride that the study of infant development is coming of age.

REFERENCE NOTES

1 Oster, H. S. *Color perception in ten-week-old infants.* Paper presented at the meeting of the Society for Research in Child Development, Denver, April 1975.

2 Goren, C. *Form perception, innate form preferences and visually-mediated head turning in human newborns.* Paper presented at the meeting of the Society for Research in Child Development, Denver, April 1975.

3 Spelke, E. S. *Perceiving bimodally specified events.* Paper presented at the International Conference on Infant Studies, Providence, Rhode Island, March 1978.

4 Strauss, M. S., & Cohen, L. B. *Infant immediate and delayed memory for perceptual dimensions.* Unpublished manuscript, University of Illinois, 1978.

5 Cohen, L. B., & Caputo, N. F. *Instructing infants to respond to perceptual categories.* Paper presented at the meeting of the Midwestern Psychological Association, Chicago, May 1978.

REFERENCES

Berlyne, D. E. The influence of the albedo and complexity of stimuli on visual fixation in the human infant. *British Journal of Psychology,* 1958, *49,* 315–318.

Bornstein, M. H. Infants are trichromats. *Journal of Experimental Child Psychology, 1976, 21,* 425–445.

Brennan, W. M., Ames, E. W., & Moore, R. W. Age differences in infants' attention to patterns of different complexities. *Science,* 1966, *151,* 334–356.

Chase, W. P. Color vision in infants. *Journal of Experimental Psychology,* 1937, *20,* 203–222.

Cohen, L. B., DeLoache, J. S., & Pearl, R. An examination of interference effects in infants' memory for faces. *Child Development,* 1977, *48,* 88–96.

Cohen, L. B., DeLoache, J. S., & Strauss, M. S. Infant perceptual development. In J. D. Osofosky (Ed.),

Handbook of infant development. New York: Wiley, 1979.

Cohen, L. B., Gelber, E. R. Infant visual memory. In L. Cohen & P. Salapatek (Eds.), *Infant perception: From sensation to cognition. Vol. 1. Basic visual processes.* New York: Academic Press, 1975.

Cohen, L. B., Gelber, E. R. & Lazar, M. A. Infant habituation and generalization to differing degrees of stimulus novelty. *Journal of Experimental Child Psychology,* 1971, *11,* 379–389.

Cohen, L. B., & Strauss, M. S. Concept acquisition in the human infant. *Child Development,* 1979, *50,* 419–424.

Cornell, E. H. Infants' discrimination of faces following redundant presentations. *Journal of Experimental Child Psychology,* 1974, *18,* 98–106.

Cruickshank, R. M. The development of visual size constancy in early infancy. *Journal of Genetic Psychology,* 1941, *58,* 327–351.

Dobson, V., Teller, D. Y., Lee, C. P., & Wade, B. A behavioral method for efficient screening of visual acuity in young infants. *Investigative Ophthalmology and Visual Science,* 1978, *17,* 1142–1150.

Fagan, J. F. Infants' delayed recognition memory and forgetting. *Journal of Experimental Child Psychology,* 1973, *16,* 424–450.

Fagan, J. F. Infants' recognition of invariant features of faces. *Child Development,* 1974, *47,* 627–638.

Fagan, J. F. An attention model of infant recognition. *Child Development,* 1977, *48,* 345–359.

Fantz, R. L. Pattern vision in young infants. *Psychological Record,* 1958, *8,* 43–49.

Fantz, R. L. The origin of form perception. *Scientific American,* 1961, *204*(5), 66–72.

Fantz, R. L. Pattern vision in newborn infants. *Science,* 1963, *140,* 296–297.

Fantz, R. L. Visual experience in infants: Decreased attention to familiar patterns relative to novel ones. *Science,* 1964, *146,* 668–670.

Fantz, R. L. Visual perception from birth as shown by pattern selectivity. *Annals of the New York Academy of Science,* 1965, *118,* 793–814.

Fantz, R., Fagan, J., & Miranda, S. Early visual selectivity. In L. Cohen & P. Salapatek (Eds.), *Infant perception: From sensation to cognition. Vol. 1. Basic visual processes.* New York: Academic Press, 1975.

Fantz, R. L., & Nevis, S. Pattern preferences and perceptual-cognitive development in early infancy. *Merrill-Palmer Quarterly,* 1967, *13,* 77–108.

Fantz, R. L., Ordy, J. M., & Udelf, M. S. Maturation of pattern vision in infants during the first six months. *Journal of Comparative and Physiological Psychology,* 1962, *55,* 907–917.

Ling, B. C. Form discrimination as a learning cue in infants. *Comparative Psychology Monographs,* 1941, *17* (2, Whole No. 86).

Maurer, D. Infant visual perception: Methods of study. In

L. Cohen & P. Salapatek (Eds.), *Infant perception: From sensation to cognition. Vol. 1. Basic visual processes.* New York: Academic Press, 1975.

Maynard, J. F. *Infant perception of auditory-visual synchrony.* Unpublished master's thesis, University of Illinois, 1979.

McCall, R. B., Kennedy, C. B., & Dodds, C. The interfering effect of distracting stimuli on the infant's memory. *Child Development,* 1977, *48,* 79–87.

McGurk, H. Infant discrimination of orientation. *Journal of Experimental Child Psychology,* 1972, *14,* 151–164.

Ruff, H. A., & Birch, H. G. Infant visual fixation: The effects of concentricity, curvilinearity, and number of directions. *Journal of Experimental Child Psychology,* 1974, *17,* 460–473.

Salapatek, P. Visual scanning of geometric figures by the human newborn. *Journal of Comparative and Physiological Psychology,* 1968, *66,* 247–258.

Salapatek, P., Bechtold, A. G., & Bushnell, E. W. Infant visual acuity as a function of viewing distance. *Child Development,* 1976, *47,* 860–863.

Schwartz, M. *Visual shape perception in early infancy.* Unpublished doctoral dissertation, Monash University, 1975.

Strauss, M. S. *The abstraction and integration of prototypical information from perceptual categories by ten-month-old infants.* Unpublished doctoral dissertation, University of Illinois, 1978.

Valentine, C. W. The colour perception and colour preferences of an infant during its fourth and eighth months. *British Journal of Psychology,* 1913–1914, *6,* 363–386.

Vurpillot, E., Ruel, J., & Castrec, A. L'organisation perceptive chez le nourrisson: Résponse au tout ou à ses éléments? *Bulletin de Psychologie,* 1977, *327,* 396–405.

Reading 7

Critical Conditions in Infancy: A Psychological Perspective

Lewis P. Lipsitt

The fascination of adults with infants is probably as old as humankind, but the systematic observation and written documentation of infant behavior and development are of recent origin. In 1877, Darwin, inspired by the publication of "an account of the mental development of an infant" by Taine, published a biographical sketch of his own infant son. Darwin waited 37 years to put his account in the literature. He and those following him have used such observations of the earliest human reflexes, sensory–motor coordinations, and emotional expressions to make the evolutionary case for the infant as a bridge between animals and humans.

In 1882 the physiologist Preyer joined the proud parents' parade by publishing careful observations

My work in this area has been supported by grants to the Brown University Child Study Center from the W. T. Grant Foundation and the National Foundation (March of Dimes), and by Grant MCH-000002-01-1 from the U.S. Public Health Service, Bureau of Community Health Services, Office of Maternal and Child Health Service, to the Rhode Island State Department of Health.

I am especially indebted to the following students who have provided background material and have served as sounding boards for some of the ideas: Barbara Burns, Franklin Goodkin, Ann McCullagh, Donna Piazza, Helen Ribbans, and Isabel Smith.

This article is dedicated to Myrtle McGraw, pioneer in the study of brain-behavior relations and their development, on her 80th birthday.

of his son's infancy, pushing still further the comparability of animal and human behavior and furthering the cause that would eventuate in Ernst Haeckel's slogan, popularized by the American psychologist G. Stanley Hall: "Ontogeny recapitulates phylogeny."

It may seem odd to ask what infancy is for, which the evolutionarily oriented developmentalists did as they forged the field of child psychology. Still, it is not unreasonable to ask about the *functions of infancy,* and addressing the normal functions of infancy can provide insight to the origins of developmental aberrations. An evolutionary perspective suggests that infancy serves to provide the new organism with opportunities to test simpler responses before embarking on the hazardous journey into complexities, to learn to cope under reasonably safe conditions of dependency, to experience failure and regain one's position in the flight to maturity, and to test the pleasures of survival and sensation without fear of censure. The "normal" obligations of delaying gratification and of deference to social proscriptions are for later.

Freud was adept in the approach, addressing himself always to the task of creating a theory of normal behavior and development, while seeking to comprehend the origins of the deviant phenomenon, and moving back and forth between the two to enlighten the understanding of both. His theory of the neuroses appealed to an implicit understanding of the normal, and he had a clear conception of neuroses as departure from the norm. The norm, in turn, gave way to intrusions by the abnormal. The interplay between the two reached full flower in Freud's (1904/1960) "Psychopathology of Everyday Life," in which he developed the notion of a continuum of psychological functioning, with occasional slips of the tongue, memory errors, and other abnormal manifestations simply reflecting malfunctions of normal thought processes.

The curiosity is that psychologists have not, for the most part, given credence to the possibility that aberrations of infancy, now so well known as attachment deficits, hospitalism, failure to thrive, and indeed, crib death, might be understood in terms of processes common to the psychology of normal development. Learned behavior is so clearly implicated in so many of life's later developmental crises, for example, accidents, alcoholism, suicide, criminality, and death from controllable obesity or cancer, that one must wonder at the unusual reticence of our field to deal with infantile crises as manifestations of normal developmental and learning processes gone wrong.

THE NORMAL INFANT: A DIGEST

There is a lot to admire in an infant. Out of so little comes so much. About eight pounds at birth, the baby doubles birth weight in 3 months, and triples in 1 year. This decelerative growth function is apparent in many ways. Enormous growth of the body occurs very early, and the brain's growth spurt of the last fetal trimester and the first 3 months postnatally will never be matched again in the child's life. We cannot help being awestruck by the phenomenon.

Our fascination with physical and physiognomic changes in the first year, however, is exceeded by our constant confrontation with the infant's changing behavior. In particular, we are impressed by the mastery process. We are constantly watching babies to note some advance toward our conception of increasing maturity. Was that a smile? Is he about to roll over? After grabbing relentlessly for so long, did she finally reach the coveted (and often forbidden) fruit? The sight of an infant struggling and pulling himself or herself finally to standing for the

first time, or even the second time, gives us great pleasure, and the first step and then walk delights even the most blasé child watcher. When the child finally grunts away at some phoneme that doesn't sound like anything familiar to us, then shapes it into an approximation of our name, and finally blasts forth with a near correct enunciation, our jubilation is unbounded. Nor does our euphoria go unnoticed by the infant, who is positively reinforced by the control, now, over the audience. These are the processes of which learning and advances in development are made (Lipsitt, 1979).

CRISES IN INFANCY: A DEVELOPMENTAL/PROCESS APPROACH

In their studies and developmental conceptualizations, psychologists tend to emphasize the clearly positive features of behavioral change in the first year of life. Among the processes with which we deal most are the beginnings of antigravitational postural controls, such as turning over, pulling to standing, climbing stairs, and holding or transferring objects from hand to hand. In the social sphere, we study the onset of smiling, the beginnings of attachment, the discrimination of family members from others, and the ritualization of eating and other bodily functions. The study of infancy is, for developmental psychologists, mostly the study of positive/appetitive/approach behavioral processes. We do not often deal with the processes underlying events when things do not go right. Information about the dire consequences of the untoward experience and the misadventure has come largely from clinical observers who have been called on to examine afflicted cases, to determine the etiology in specific instances, and to implement remedial measures. We learned of the effects of maternal abandonment and institutionalization from René Spitz, of the grievances of infants in the face of separation from John Bowlby, and of the agonies of the autistic infant from Leo Kanner, Leon Eisenberg, and Michael Rutter. One reason that crib-death and failure-to-thrive syndromes have been so resistant to satisfactory explanation may be that, like the drunk who looks under the lamp post to find his watch that he lost up the dark street, we have left the understanding of morbid conditions of infancy to those who adhere to a disease model. The psychological discipline of infant behavior and development may in fact have the match in its back pocket.

Normal infants are born with all sensory systems functioning. They are capable at birth of engaging in reciprocating relationships with other persons. The first six months is a period of extremely rapid dendritic proliferation and accretion of myelin sheathing of neural tissue. The rate of behavior acquisition, like growth during this period, is phenomenal. The most important aspect of infant development in the first months, however, is the capacity for learning. All of the developmental milestones involve an immense input and appreciation by the baby of sensory stimulation, the registration of that stimulation in memory, and the alteration of behavior style as a function of that experiential input; this is the stuff of which learning is made.

We cannot say any more that learning waits on neurological maturation. This is too simplistic an idea in view of recent studies showing that brain growth itself depends on experiential inputs. Specific neurons are now known to take up specific functions as a consequence of specific identifiable experiences, as has been shown in the pioneering studies of visual development by Hubel and Wiesel, Blakemore, Stryker and Sherk, Hirsch and Spinelli, and others (Lund, 1978). The road between brain development and individual experience is a two-way street. Brain development is as likely to wait on the crucial experience as much as the manifestation of behavior awaits critical neural maturation. The simplistic and stultifying influence of Gesell's (1928) dictum no longer applies: "Acceleration of development . . . is typically an inherent biological characteristic of the individual, most probably hereditary in nature. There is no convincing evidence that fundamental acceleration of development can be readily induced by either pernicious or enlightened methods of stimulation" (pp. 363–364).

Though it remains heresy in some circles to suggest so, the technology has already arrived by which sensory experiential inputs can indeed be shown to produce brain dysfunctions or insufficiencies. It is not so wild a dream, either, that certain developmental anomalies usually though to result from disease or physical injury, overt or covert, might also be the result of subtle and adverse developmental processes involving interplay between brain and behavior.

It is hoped that this brief reminder of the behavioral repertoire of babies and these considerations relating to the nature and functions of infancy are sufficient to make plausible that certain disorders or "accidents" of early human development, like crib death, might be better understood as deviations from, or aberrations of, normative life-development processes.

CRIB DEATH

The sudden infant death syndrome (SIDS) refers to the unexplained death of a child in the first year of life, usually between the ages of 2 and 5 months. *Unexplained* means that there is no clear indication upon autopsy and upon review of the infant's developmental/pediatric history what the cause of death was. The baby simply stops breathing, usually in the night, without apparent cause and without any audible agonal response. Epidemiological statistics indicate that about 2 of every 1,000 births eventuate in crib death, and that some 8,000 crib deaths occur annually in the United States alone. SIDS is responsible for more deaths in the first year of life, after the especially vulnerable 10 days, than any other cause. However, the diagnosis of crib death is essentially a diagnosis of ignorance, in that this term is used when no other perceptible condition or diagnosable ailment can be held responsible. These infants are sometimes reported to have had a mild cold in the days immediately preceding their deaths, but the literature on crib death has consistently reported no major condition of lethal proportions in these children before their demise (Valdes-Dapena, 1978).

Numerous hypotheses about the origin of SIDS have been proposed in the last 10 years. During this time there has been an upsurge of attention to crib death, largely as a result of parental indignation over the lack of knowledge about the phenomenon.

Until fairly recently, the precursors of crib death, let alone the causes, were obscure. In the absence of any satisfactory explanation for SIDS, some attempts have been made to document the conditions that might form the basis of a "risk inventory." Such a listing of signals and signs, especially if utilized in a cumulative and weighted fashion, provides a useful first step in developing a rational model of or cogent hypothesis about the origins of SIDS (Protestos, Carpenter, McWeeny, & Emery, 1973). Moreover, any program of defense against SIDS must ultimately define those conditions likely to be present in infants whose vulnerability demands intervention or extra protection.

Although the mechanisms underlying crib death are by no means understood yet, a better understanding of the phenomenon may come from entertaining the possibility that abberations of the learning process are implicated (Lipsitt, 1976, 1978a, 1978b). Before explicating how such psychological processes may be involved in the origin of SIDS, a brief survey of some known constitutional vulnerabilities of SIDS victims will be useful.

Babies succumbing to SIDS have traditionally been regarded as essentially normal (Valdes-Dapena, 1967, 1978), but there have been several recent studies suggesting that respiratory anomalies of one sort or another are implicated in the final pathway to the infant's death (e.g., Anderson & Rosenblith, 1971; Lipsitt, Sturner, & Burke, 1979; Naeye, Ladis, & Drage, 1976; Steinschneider, 1972; Thoman, Miano, & Freese, Note 1). Steinschneider, for example, believes that apnea, or the spontaneous interruption of respiration, is a significant etiological factor, with the infants particularly prone to apnea during sleep being those most likely to succumb. Thoman et al., on the other hand, suggested that the relevant anomaly is one involving rapid respiration and the absence of normal respiratory pauses. Anderson and Rosenblith, as well as Protestos et al. (1973), also support some kind of respiratory-aberration hypothesis, by documenting that those infants who die of SIDS usually have histories of perinatal/neonatal respiratory distress. Based on data of the National Collaborative Perinatal Project, the studies of Naeye et al. (1976) and Lipsitt et al. (1979) show that respiratory abnormalities were present at birth, months before the infants died.

It appears that infants succumbing to SIDS often endured perinatal stress and had constitutional vulnerabilities that particularly suggested oxygenation deficits. The Lipsitt et al. study found that in comparison with matched control subjects, the 15 crib-death cases from the Providence study of 4,000 infants varied in a number of ways. More blacks than whites succumbed. The Apgar scores of the SIDS group were consistently lower on average than those of the controls; the Apgar scale is a quick assessment of morbidity. Maternal anemia was more frequent in the SIDS group. Several parameters

involving neonatal respiratory anomalies were more frequent in the SIDS than the control infants. Birth weight and body length were smaller in SIDS infants than survivors. Serum bilirubin levels were higher in the SIDS infants. The number of days that the SIDS infants remained in the hospital just after birth was greater than that for the controls. All of these factors suggest that infants who eventually become SIDS cases show early-onset developmental jeopardy even in a study with a rather small incidence of crib death. Various parameters relating to oxygenation of the fetus and newborn infant seem particularly likely to show deficiencies. It might be suggested, therefore, that crib death results from subtle perinatal hazards and constitutional insufficiencies which are compounded by the failure of experience to prepare the infant for later threats to survival. A number of researchers have suggested that respiratory occlusion or the threat of it may lead to abnormal or inadequate responses (Anderson & Rosenblith, 1971; Gunther, 1955, 1961; Shaw, 1968; Swift & Emery, 1973; Wealthall, 1976), and some of these have suggested there is a relationship between inability of the newborn to protect against nasal occlusion, on the one hand, and crib death, on the other.

Though there may be such a relationship between an earlier physical insufficiency and the later lethal outcome, there are a number of reasons to believe that the final pathway to SIDS is complex and that a learning disorder may be implicated. Infants who as newborns are incapable of responding defensively to stimulus hazards could become especially vulnerable at later ages. Babies subjected to poor oxygenation and other physical hazards during the perinatal period probably move less, are less visually alert, such weakly, and generally engage their environment less. They thus experience fewer opportunities for learning than do infants who are not born under such risk conditions. The constellation of pathological signs found in the histories of SIDS cases could dispose them to special danger of acquiring a learning deficiency (Lipsitt, 1976, 1979; Lipsitt et al., 1979).

The inability of the young infant to make appropriate responses in critical situations can conceivably result in debility and ultimately death. That animals and humans will sometimes forego further defense of themselves in apparent despondency when confronted with desperate life stresses has been suggested by Richter (1957) and Seligman (1975), both of whom argue that experiential or learning factors can produce stupor and death.

Let us consider briefly what the mechanisms or processes might be like. Rapid myelinization and dendritic proliferation are characteristics of the period immediately following birth, which may be an especially important one for critical learning events. Very early unconditioned responses, such as the rooting, Babinski, Babkin, and grasping reflexes undergo drastic alterations during the first 2–4 months of life. Vital responses with which the infant is biologically equipped at birth diminish drastically or become considerably altered over time. As McGraw (1943) demonstrated so well, many of these reflexes are supplanted by learned response systems, and the learned patterns of behavior become increasingly functional while their ontogenetic forebears diminish in frequency and vigor. Innate response systems that are strikingly apparent at birth often diminish in frequency and intensity up to 2 or 3 months of age (McGraw, 1943) by which time these response propensities are displaced by "voluntary" or learned responses mediated by higher cortical centers. In consideration of the brain tissue maturation occurring during the first 2 or 3 months of life, it is not unthinkable that this period is quite critical for the development of certain behaviors which, if not adequately learned by the time that the unlearned protective reflexes have diminished, will place the organism in (even lethal) jeopardy.

The enraged response of the normal newborn when struggling against such threats to respiration has been described in detail by Gunther (1955, 1961) and has been included as a test item in the neonate scales of Graham (1956) and Brazelton (1973). It is possible that if the newborn does not have a strong built-in defensive response to respiratory threats, the appropriate voluntary behaviors may not be learned in time to supplant this normal defensive reflex by 2–4 months of age.

Crib-death cases, then, have as a group begun life with some organismic deficits associated with perinatal stresses. Inadequate response to respiratory occlusion (including failure to engage in defensive rage behavior, or in postural and respiratory adjustments when the breathing passages are clogged by mucus) or merely general lethargy of response could lead to oxygen deficiency and utlimately to the infant's death. Until substantial data exist to support other hypotheses that would definitively rule out learning factors in the final pathway to SIDS, a learning-dysfunction hypothesis remains plausible and testable.

FAILURE-TO-THRIVE SYNDROME

That a learning insufficiency may also underlie the still poorly understood failure-to-thrive syndrome in infants has been suggested by Ramey, Hieger, and Klisz (1972). Not based on any known physiological abnormality, the failure-to-thrive syndrome (FTTS) involves failure of a young child; in the absence of organic disturbance, to achieve a physical growth rate within normal limits. The syndrome is estimated to be present in as many as 3% of the general pediatric population, and about 5% of pediatric hospital admissions involve growth failure (Rosen, 1977). Among the identified characteristics of FTTS children less than 4 months of age are unusual watchfulness, lack of cuddliness, little smiling, and few vocalizations, and the documented characteristics of 4–10-month-old FTTS children are lack of appropriate stranger anxiety, few vocalizations (with delay in prespeech complex sound utterances), deficiency in motor skill development, and extreme passivity (Fischoff, Whitten, & Petit, 1971).

A frequent accompaniment of FTTS is some sort of feeding disturbance (Leonard, Rhymes, & Solnit, 1966). FTTS children apparently ingest smaller quantities of food than do normal infants of the same age. Although sometimes, perhaps in as many as 10% of hospital-admitted FTTS children (Bullard, Glaser, Heagarty, & Pivchik, 1967), the FTTS child will show evidence of fractures and contusions, the evidence is not convincing that FTTS is a by-product of battering. Most FTTS cases show onset during early infancy, and the babies are usually hospitalized between 6 and 12 months of age. Retrospective studies of FTTS children strongly suggest a history of adverse perinatal conditions (Shaheen, Alexander, Truskowsky, & Barbero, 1968), but most studies (e.g., Bullard et al., 1967) suggest that, as in SIDS (Carpenter & Emery, 1974), prior indications of gross neurological and physical abnormalities are absent or unremarkable. Indeed, the psychological and emotional difficulties as well as the physical retardation of FTTS children tend to dissipate, and almost all such children resume growing once they are placed in a different environment from that at the time of hospitalization (Koel, 1969; Niven, 1977).

Some of the best documentations of FTTS were those of Spitz (1945). The disorder of "hospitalism," as he termed it, occurred in institutionalized children in the first year of life, and the major manifestations involved emotional disturbance, failure to gain weight, and developmental retardation resulting in poor developmental test performance. A significant etiological factor was gleaned from Spitz's study of infants cared for by their mothers, whom Spitz compared with another group raised in virtual isolation from other infants and from adults. Spitz demonstrated convincingly that even physical illnesses, including infections, are contracted more frequently by infants deprived of environmental stimulation and maternal care. FTTS, according to Spitz, was a direct result of inadequate nurturance. Indeed, he actually documented long-term intellectual deficits in the survivors of the nonnurtured group. Thirty-seven percent of this group had succumbed by 2 years of age, compared with none in the mothered group!

Spitz (1946) said that a condition of "depression" tended to occur in infants separated from their mothers for at least 3 months during the second half of their first year. No child in his study of 123 nursery infants showed such depression who had not experienced maternal separation. The described depression involved decreased interest in environmental stimulation (including that from other humans), retardation of cognitive development, failure to thrive physically, insomnia, and sadness.

Some studies (e.g., Fischoff et al., 1971) suggest that mothers of noninstitutionalized FTTS infants are lacking in ability to relate constructively to their infants and are sometimes regarded as having "character disorders." Certain writers (e.g., Hutton & Oates, 1977), however, have suggested that FTTS children can improve when their mothers are provided with behavioral guidance and encouragement. Some of the most interesting observations of FTTS children and their families (Pollitt & Eichler, 1976; Pollitt, Eichler, & Chan, 1975) have suggested that the mothers of FTTS children differ in the quality of their interactions with their children. FTTS mothers had a tendency to ignore their children or to respond negatively to them, as opposed to control mothers, who evinced a more responsive rapport with them.

Pollitt and his colleagues found that stressful events were prevalent in the personal and family backgrounds of FTTS mothers and that feeding was a time of heightened stress for mothers of FTTS infants. These mothers seemed largely unaware of the needs of their infants (e.g., when they were hungry).

COMMONALITIES

The mechanisms by which FTTS arises are not by any means clear at this time. Because some of the same perinatal and neonatal factors occur in the histories of both crib-death and FTTS infants, similar processes may be involved in both (Lipsitt, 1976, 1977). Both groups, although essentially normal just prior to their crises, tend to have been born under more than the usual conditions of risk and to have manifested some behavioral insufficiencies or aberrations from birth onward. Crib-death infants have been shown to be temperamentally lethargic (Naeye, Messmer, Spect, & Merritt, 1976), and the well-known lack of reciprocating responsivity in the FTTS infant has just been reviewed. Some investigators, moreover, have suggested that emotional deprivation and lack of maternal nurturance can affect neuroendocrine functioning and thus regulation of growth (e.g., Patton & Gardner, 1962). Further reinforcing the supposition that SIDS and FTTS have historical characteristics in common is a study by Sinclair-Smith, Dinsdale, and Emery (1976). Detailed postmortems on 200 SIDS cases revealed that 94% of these infants had growth deficiencies at the time of their deaths and that 50% were in a severe state of growth retardation for a considerable period.

The common characteristic suggested here for both SIDS and FTTS (or at least in many cases of these) is a failure to produce adaptive reciprocating behaviors, perhaps especially under conditions of threat. In order for such a giving-up type of response pattern not to be acquired, it seems reasonable to assume that a modicum of consistent early practice must occur in which reciprocating interactions with others are promoted and reinforced. It is not clear that the specific mechanisms involved here are precisely those proposed by Seligman (1975) for conditioned helplessness or depression, but undoubtedly, infants must acquire an appropriate expectation of reinforcement contingent on their own behavior. Those who achieve the required minimum of practice are perhaps those whose experience in "engaging the environment" has been promoted by an absence or minimum of risk conditions that could jeopardize early (unconditioned) responsivity. These would be the infants who at birth have vigorous responses, for example, to stimulation around the mouth, to the threat of respiratory occlusion, and to other vital environmental events. The lethargy of response of the FTTS baby may have had its earliest representation, as in SIDS cases, in a deficiency of neonatal response patterns or practice. In short, perhaps the premorbid conditions of both classes of infants involve diminished responses due to perinatal stresses, lack of opportunity for the responses present to be fully engaged by the environment, and inadequate learning experiences. These infants may be victims of learning disabilities that we are only beginning to understand.

SUMMARY AND CONCLUSIONS

The heuristic and presently defensible proposition put forth is that the sudden infant death and failure-to-thrive syndromes may have their origins in aberrations of learning processes. As one who has worked in a counseling capacity with parents of crib-death infants, I know that it is very difficult to entertain the prospect that one's child died of a "psychological" cause. One would rather suppose there was a hidden disease, an as yet undiscovered virus, a laryngeal spasm that could not be predicted nor its presence documented postmortem, or a brain tumor that went undetected. Somehow a lethal psychological process leaves us more awestruck than "sudden, unexplained death."

Yet many people do die of psychological causes—in noncaring accidents, through suicide and homicide, by smoking or eating excessively, by resisting treatment, and so on. It is quite possible, in fact, that most people die of psychological or environmentally preventable causes. The prolongation of life in the United States over the past half century, even in the presence of ever-increasing hazards resulting from other environmental events (pollution, technology-associated accidents, etc.), suggests strongly that environmental life supports can be learned and implemented in an advanced society.

Crib death and failure to thrive are two drastic examples of crisis in the first year of human develop-

ment. These tragic conditions serve as enlightening models of infantile, and indeed of parenting, crises, but there are numerous other developmental tragedies that may befall the child under 1 year of age. All the rest of these, like crib death and failure to thrive, need attention of child development researchers and of helping persons who are prepared to minister to human frailties. Infants are not infrequently subjected to physical and psychological abuse, and misadventures of a wide variety do occur, for example, falling from unprotected high places, ingestion of poisonous substances, or failure of the infant's family to achieve safe standards of nutrition or home hygiene.

As it happens, the risk conditions that dispose infants to one hazard are often implicated in the others as well. Lower socioeconomic level, minimal care during pregnancy, crowded or otherwise substandard housing conditions, and low birth weight or prematurity appear as predictive, if not decisive, variables in study after study of developmental risk. An effective research program relating to perinatal risk and developmental crises must place a protective umbrella over those infants most in jeopardy. They are the most needy of intervention of one sort or another, including family counseling or special help in the acquisition of learning skills. Research must begin at or before birth and should pay special attention to the medical, psychological, and socioeconomic conditions of parents at risk for the delivery of a high-risk infant. The definition of risk should be based on actuarial or epidemiological statistics, which are even now quite effective in their identification of the vulnerable ones. We expect no less than this from insurance companies. Should we be satisfied with less than this for our infants?

REFERENCE NOTE

1 Thoman, E., Miano, V. N., & Freese, M. P. The role of respiratory instability in SIDS. In D. J. Willis (Chair), *Sudden infant death syndrome (SIDS)*. Symposium presented at the meeting of the American Psychological Association, Washington, D.C., September 6, 1976.

REFERENCES

Anderson, R. B., & Rosenblith, J. F. Sudden unexpected death syndrome: Early indicators. *Biologia Neonatorum*, 1971, *18*, 395–406.

Brazelton, T. B. *Neonatal behavioral assessment scale.* Philadelphia, Pa.: Lippincott, 1973.

Bullard, D. M. Jr., Glaser, H. H., Heagarty, M. C., & Pivchik, E. C Failure to thrive in the "neglected" child. *American Journal of Orthopsychiatry*, 1967, *37*, 680–690.

Carpenter, R. G., & Emery, J. L. Identification and follow-up of infants at risk of sudden death in infancy. *Nature*, 1974, *250*, 729.

Darwin, C. A biographical sketch of an infant. *Mind*, 1877, *2*, 285–294.

Fischoff, J., Whitten, C. F., & Petit, M. G. A psychiatric study of mothers of infants with growth failure secondary to maternal deprivation. *Journal of Pediatrics*, 1971, *79*, 209–215.

Freud, S. Psychopathology of everyday life. In J. Strachey (Ed.), *The standard edition of the complete psychological works of Sigmund Freud*. London: Hogarth Press, 1960. (First English edition published, 1904.)

Gesell, A. *Infancy and human growth*. New York: Macmillan, 1928.

Graham, F. K. Behavioral differences between normal and traumitized newborns. I. The test procedures. *Psychological Monographs*, 1956, *70*(20, Whole No. 427).

Gunther, M. Instinct and the nursing couple. *Lancet, 1955*, *1*, 575.

Gunther, M. Infant behavior at the breast. In B. M. Foss (Ed.), *Determinants of infant behavior*. New York: Wiley, 1961.

Hutton, M. B., & Oates, R. K. Nonorganic failure to thrive: Long-term follow-up. *Pediatrics*, 1977, *49*, 73–77.

Koel, B. S. Failure to thrive and fatal injury as a continuum. *American Journal of Diseases of Children*, 1969, *118*, 565–567.

Leonard, M. F., Rhymes, J. P., & Solnit, A. J. Failure to thrive in infants: A family problem. *American Journal of Diseases of Children*, 1966, *111*, 600–612.

Lipsitt, L. P. Developmental psychobiology comes of age: A discussion. In L. P. Lipsitt (Ed.), *Developmental psychobiology: The significance of infancy*. Hillsdale, N.J.: Erlbaum, 1976.

Lipsitt, L. P. The study of sensory and learning processes of the newborn. In J. Volpe (Ed.), *Clinics in perinatology* (Vol. 4, No. 1). Philadelphia, Pa.: Saunders, 1977.

Lipsitt, L. P. Assessment of sensory and behavioral functions in infancy. In H. L. Pick, Jr., H. W. Leibowitz, J. E. Singer, A. Steinschneider, & H. W. Stevenson (Eds.), *Psychology: From research to practice*. New York: Plenum, 1978. (a).

Lipsitt, L. P. Perinatal indicators and psychophysiological precursors of crib death. In F. D. Horowitz (Ed.), *Early development hazards: Predictors and precautions*. Boulder, Colo.: Westview Press, 1978. (b).

Lipsitt, L. P. The newborn as informant. In R. B. Kearsley & I. Sigel (Eds.), *Infants at risk: Assessment of cognitive functioning*. Hillsdale, N.J.: Erlbaum, 1979.

Lipsitt, L. P., Sturner, W. Q., & Burke, P. Perinatal indicators and subsequent crib death. *Infant Behavior and Development*, 1979, *2*, 325–328.

Lund, R. D. *Development and plasticity of the brain*. New York: Oxford University Press, 1978.

McGraw, M. B. *The neuromuscular maturation of the human infant*. New York: Hafner, 1943.

Naeye, R., Ladis, B., & Drage, J. S. SIDS: A prospective study. *American Journal of Diseases of Children*, 1976, *130*, 1207–1210.

Naeye, R., Messmer, J., III, Specht, T., & Merritt, F. Sudden infant death syndrome temperament before death. *Journal of Pediatrics*, 1976, *88*, 511–515.

Niven, M. Failure to thrive: The nutritionist's role. *Clinical Proceedings, Children's Hospital National Medical Center*, 1977, *33*, 206–208.

Patton, R. G., & Gardner, L. I. Influence of family environment on growth. *Pediatrics*, 1962, *30*, 957–962.

Pollitt, E., & Eichler, A. Behavioral disturbances among failure-to-thrive children. *American Journal of Diseases of Children*, 1976, *130*, 24–29.

Pollitt, E. Eichler, A. W., & Chan, C. K. Psychosocial development and behavior of mothers of failure to thrive children. *American Journal of Orthopsychiatry*, 1975,*45*, 525–537.

Preyer, W. *Die Seele des Kindes* [Mind of the child] (H. W. Brown, trans.). New York: Appleton, 1888–1889. (Originally published, 1882.)

Protestos, C., Carpenter, R., McWeeny, P., & Emery, J. Obstetric and perinatal histories of children who died unexpectedly (cot death). *Archives of Disease in Childhood*, 1973, *48*, 835–841.

Ramey, C. T., Hieger, L., & Klisz, D. Synchronous reinforcement of vocal responses in failure-to-thrive infants. *Child Development*, 1972, *43*, 1449–1455.

Richter, C. P. On the phenomenon of sudden death in animals and man. *Psychosomatic Medicine*, 1957, *19*, 191–198.

Rosen, G. Reversible growth and developmental retardation in the first year of life. *Clinical Proceedings, Children's Hospital National Medical Center*, 1977, *33*, 193–205.

Seligman, M. E. P. *Helplessness*. San Francisco: Freeman, 1975.

Shaheen, E., Alexander, D., Truskowsky, M., & Barbero, G. Failure to thrive: A retrospective profile. *Clinical Pediatrics*, 1968, *7*, 255–261.

Shaw, E. G. Sudden unexpected death in infancy syndrome. *American Journal of Diseases of Children*, 1968, *116*, 115–119.

Sinclair-Smith, C., Dinsdale, F., & Emery, J. Evidence of duration and type of illness in children found unexpectedly dead. *Archives of Disease in Childhood*, 1976, *51*, 424–429.

Spitz, R. A. Hospitalism. In *The psychoanalytic study of*

the child (Vol. 1). New York: International Universities Press, 1945.

Spitz, R. A. Hospitalism: A follow-up report. In *The psychoanalytic study of the child* (Vol. 2). New York: International Universities Press, 1946.

Steinschneider, A. Prolonged apnea and the sudden infant death syndrome: Clinical and laboratory observations. *Pediatrics*, 1972, *50*, 646–654.

Swift, P. G. F., & Emery, J. L. Clinical observation on response to nasal occlusion in infancy. *Archives of Diseases in Childhood*, 1973, *48*, 947–951.

Valdes-Dapena, M. A. Sudden and unexpected death in infancy. A review of the literature 1954–66. *Pediatrics*, 1967, *39*, 123–138.

Valdes-Dapena, M. A. *Sudden unexpected infant death 1970 through 1975: An evolution in understanding* (Pub. No. (HSA) 78–5255). Bethesda, Md.: U.S. Department of Health, Education, and Welfare, 1978.

Wealthall, S. R. Factors resulting in a failure to interrupt apnea. In J. F. Bosma & J. Showacre (Eds.), *Development of upper respiratory anatomy and function: Implications for sudden infant death syndrome*. Washington, D.C.: U.S. Government Printing Office, 1976.

Reading 8

Cross-cultural Perspectives on Early Development

Jerome Kagan
Robert E. Klein

Most American psychologists believe in the hardiness of habit and the premise that experience etches an indelible mark on the mind not easily erased by time or trauma. The application of that assumption to the first era of development leads to the popular view that psychological growth during the early years is under the strong influence of the variety and patterning of external events and that the psychological structures shaped by those initial encounters have a continuity that stretches at least into early adolescence. The first part of that hypothesis, which owes much of its popularity to Freud, Harlow, and Skinner, has strong empirical support. The continuity part of the assumption, which is more equivocal, is summarized in the American adage, "Well begun is half done."

Many developmental psychologists, certain of the long-lasting effects of early experience, set out to find the form of those initial stabilities and the earliest time they might obtain a preview of the child's future. Although several decades of research have uncovered fragile lines that seem to travel both backward and forward in time, the breadth and

Note: This article was presented by J. Kagan as an invited address to the annual meeting of the American Association for the Advancement of Science, Washington, D.C., December 26, 1972. The research reported in this article was supported by the Association for the Aid of Crippled Children, Carnegie Corporation of New York, Grant HD-4299 and Contract PH 43-65-640 from the National Institute of Child Health and Human Development, and Grant GS-33048, Collaborative Research on Uniform Measures of Social Competence, from the National Science Foundation.

magnitude of intraindividual continuities have not been overwhelming, and each seems to be easily lost or shattered (Kagan & Moss, 1962; Kessen, Haith, & Salapatek, 1970). A recent exhaustive review of research on human infancy led to the conclusion that "only short term stable individual variation has been demonstrated; . . . and demonstrations of continuity in process—genotype continuity—have been rare indeed [Kessen et al., 1970, p. 297]." Since that evaluation violates popular beliefs, the authors noted a few pages later:

> In spite of slight evidence of stability, our inability to make predictions of later personality from observations in the first three years of life is so much against good sense and common observation, to say nothing of the implication of all developmental theories, that the pursuit of predictively effective categories of early behavior will surely continue unabated [p. 309].

The modest empirical support for long-term continuity is occasionally rationalized by arguing that although behaviors similar in manifest form might not be stable over long time periods, the underlying structures might be much firmer (Kagan, 1971). Hence, if the operational manifestations of these hidden forms were discerned, continuity of cognitive, motivational, and affective structures would be affirmed. However, we recently observed some children living in an isolated Indian village on Lake Atitlan in the highlands of northwest Guatemala.

We saw listless, silent, apathetic infants; passive, quiet, timid 3-year-olds; but, active, gay, intellectually competent 11-year-olds. Since there is no reason to believe that living conditions in this village have changed during the last century, it is likely that the alert 11-year-olds were, a decade earlier, listless, vacant-staring infants. That observation has forced us to question the strong form of the continuity assumption in a serious way.

The data to be presented imply absence of a predictive relationship between level of cognitive development at 12—18 months of age and quality of intellectual functioning at 11 years. This conclusion is not seriously different from the repeated demonstrations of no relation between infant intelligence quotient (IQ) or developmental quotient (DQ) scores during the first year of life and Binet or Wechsler IQ scores obtained during later childhood (Kessen et al., 1970; Pease, Wolins, & Stockdale, 1973). The significance of the current data, however, derives from the fact that the infants seemed to be more seriously retarded than those observed in earlier studies, their environments markedly less varied, and the assessment of later cognitive functioning based on culture-fair tests of specific cognitive abilities rather than culturally biased IQ tests.

Moreover, these observations suggest that it is misleading to talk about continuity of any psychological characteristic—be it cognitive, motivational or behavioral—without specifying simultaneously the context of development. Consider the long-term stability of passivity as an example. The vast majority of the infants in the Indian village were homogeneously passive and retained this characteristic until they were five or six years old. A preschool child rarely forced a submissive posture on another. However, by eight years of age, some of the children became dominant over others because the structure of the peer group required that role to be filled. Factors other than early infant passivity were critical in determining that differentiation, and physical size, strength, and competence at valued skills seemed to be more important than the infant's disposition. In modern American society, where there is much greater variation among young children in degree of passivity and dominance, a passive four-year-old will always encounter a large group of dominant peers who enforce a continuing role of submissiveness on him. As a result, there should be firmer stability of behavioral passivity during the early years in an American city than in the Indian village. But the stability of that behavior seems to be more dependent on the presence of dominant members in the immediate vicinity than on some inherent force within the child.

Continuity of a psychological disposition is not solely the product of an inherited or early acquired structure that transcends a variety of contexts. The small group of scientists who champion the view of stability—we have been among them—envision a small box of different-colored gems tucked deep in the brain, with names like intelligent, passive, irritable, or withdrawn engraved on them. These material entities guarantee that, despite behavioral disguises, an inherent set of psychological qualities, independent of the local neighborhood and knowable under the proper conditions, belongs to each individual. This belief in a distinct and unchanging mosaic of core traits—an identity—is fundamental to Western thought and is reflected in the psychological writings of Erik Erikson and the novels of popular Western writers. Only Herman Hesse, who borrowed the philosophy of the East, fails to make a brief for personal identity. *Siddhartha, Magister Ludi,* and *Narcissus and Goldmund* are not trying to discover "who they are" but are seeking serenity, and each appreciates the relevance of setting in that journey.

A secondary theme concerns the interaction of maturation and environment, an issue that has seized academic conversation because of the renewed debate surrounding the inheritance of intelligence. But there is a broader issue to probe. The majority of American psychologists remain fundamentally Lockean in attitude, believing that thought and action owe primary allegiance to experience and that reinforcements and observations of models set the major course of change. Despite Piaget's extraordinary popularity, the majority of American psychologists do not believe that maturation supplies the major impetus for psychological growth during the childhood years. We have forgotten that many years ago Myrtle McGraw (1935) allowed one twin to climb some stairs and prevented his co-twin from practicing that skill. This homely experiment occurred only a few years after Carmichael (1926) anesthetized some *Amblystoma* embryos to prevent them from swimming. The twin not allowed to climb was behind his partner in learning this skill, but he eventually mastered it. Carmichael's embryos swam perfectly when the anesthetic was pumped out of the tank. In both instances, the organisms could not be prevented from displaying species-specific properties.

Our observations in these Indian villages have led us to reorder the hierarchy of complementary influences that biology and environmental forces exert on the development of intellectual functions that are natural to man. Separate maturational factors seem to set the time of emergence of those basic abilities. Experience can slow down or speed up that emergence by several months or several years, but nature will win in the end. The capacity for perceptual analysis, imitation, language, inference, deduction, symbolism, and memory will eventually appear in sturdy form in any natural environment, for each is an inherent competence in the human program. But these competences, which we assume to be universal, are to be distinguished from culturally specific talents that will not appear unless the child is exposed to or taught them directly. Reading, arithmetic, and understanding of specific words and concepts fall into this latter category.

This distinction between universal and culturally specific competences implies a parallel distinction between absolute and relative retardation. Consider physical growth as an illustration of this idea. There is sufficient cross-cultural information on age of onset of walking to warrant the statement that most children should be walking unaided before their second birthday. A three-year-old unable to walk is physically retarded in the absolute sense, for he has failed to attain a natural competence at the normative time. However, there is neither an empirical nor a logical basis for expecting that most children, no matter where they live, will develop the ability to hunt with a spear, ride a horse, or play football. Hence, it is not reasonable to speak of absolute retardation on these skills. In those cultures where these talents are taught, encouraged, or modeled, children will differ in the age at which they attain varied levels of mastery. But we can only classify a child as precocious or retarded relative to another in his community. The data to be reported suggest that absolute retardation in the attainment of specific cognitive competences during infancy has no predictive validity with respect to level of competence on a selected set of natural cognitive skills at age 11. *The data do not imply that a similar level of retardation among American infants has no future implication for relative retardation on culture-specific skills.*

THE GUATEMALAN SETTINGS

The infant observations to be reported here were made in two settings in Guatemala. One set of data came from four subsistence farming Ladino villages in eastern Guatemala. The villages are moderately isolated, Spanish speaking, and contain between 800 and 1,200 inhabitants. The families live in small thatched huts of cane or adobe with dirt floors and no sanitary facilities. Books, pencils, paper, and pictures are typically absent from the experience of children prior to school entrance, and, even in school, the average child has no more than a thin lined notebook and a stub of a pencil.

A second location was a more isolated Indian village of 850 people located on the shores of Lake Atitlan in the northwest mountainous region of the country. Unlike the Spanish-speaking villages, the Indians of San Marcos la Laguna have no easy access to a city and are psychologically more detached. The isolation is due not only to geographical location but also to the fact that few of the women and no more than half of the men speak reasonable Spanish. Few adults and no children can engage the culture of the larger nation, and the Indians of San Marcos regard themselves as an alien and exploited group.

The Infant in San Marcos

During the first 10–12 months, the San Marcos infant spends most of his life in the small, dark interior of his windowless hut. Since women do not work in the field, the mother usually stays close to the home and spends most of her day preparing food, typically tortillas, beans, and coffee, and perhaps doing some weaving. If she travels to a market to buy or sell, she typically leaves her infant with an older child or a relative. The infant is usually close to the mother, either on her lap or enclosed on her back in a colored cloth, sitting on a mat, or sleeping in a hammock. The mother rarely allows the infant to crawl on the dirt floor of the hut and feels that the outside sun, air, and dust are harmful.

The infant is rarely spoken to or played with, and the only available objects for play, besides his own clothing or his mother's body, are oranges, ears of corn, and pieces of wood or clay. These infants are distinguished from American infants of the same age by their extreme motoric passivity, fearfulness, minimal smiling, and above all, extraordinary quietness. A few with pale cheeks and vacant stares had the quality of tiny ghosts and resembled the description of the institutionalized infants that Spitz called marasmic. Many would not orient to a taped source of speech, not smile or babble to vocal overtures, and hesitated over a minute before reaching for an attractive toy.

An American woman who lived in the village made five separate 30-minute observations in the homes of 12 infants 8–16 months of age. If a particular behavioral variable occurred during a five-second period, it was recorded once for that interval. The infants were spoken to or played with 6% of the time, with a maximum of 12%. The comparable averages for American middle-class homes are 25%, with a maximum of 40% (Lewis & Freedle, 1972). It should be noted that the infant's vocalizations, which occurred about 6% of the time, were typically grunts lasting less than a second, rather than the prolonged babbling typical of middle-class American children. The infants cried very little because the slightest irritability led the mother to nurse her child at once. Nursing was the single, universal therapeutic treatment for all infant distress, be it caused by fear, cold, hunger, or cramps. Home observations in the eastern villages are consonant with those gathered in San Marcos and reveal infrequent infant vocalization and little verbal interaction or play with adults or older siblings. The mothers in these settings seem to regard their infants the way an American parent views an expensive cashmere sweater: Keep it nearby and protect it but do not engage it reciprocally.

One reason why these mothers might behave this way is that it is abudantly clear to every parent that all children begin to walk by 18 months, to talk by age 3, and to perform some adult chores by age 10, despite the listless, silent quality of infancy. The mother's lack of active manipulation, stimulation, or interactive play with her infant is not indicative of indifference or rejection, but is a reasonable posture, given her knowledge of child development.

COMPARATIVE STUDY OF INFANT COGNITIVE DEVELOPMENT

Although it was not possible to create a formal laboratory setting for testing infants in San Marcos,

it was possible to do so in the eastern Ladino villages, and we shall summarize data derived from identical procedures administered to rural Guatemalan and American infants. Although the infants in the Ladino villages were more alert than the Indian children of San Marcos, the similarities in living conditions and rearing practices are such that we shall assume that the San Marcos infants would have behaved like the Ladino children or, what is more likely, at a less mature level. In these experiments, the Guatemalan mother and child came to a special laboratory equipped with a chair and a stage that simulated the setting in the Harvard laboratories where episodes were administered to crosssectional groups of infants, 84 American and 80 Guatemalan, at 5½, 7½, 9½, and 11½ months of age, with 10–24 infants from each culture at each age level.

Before describing the procedures and results, it will be helpful to summarize the theoretical assumptions that govern interpretation of the infant's reactions to these episodes. There appear to be two important maturationally controlled processes which emerge between 2 and 12 months that influence the child's reactions to transformations of an habituated event (Kagan, 1971, 1972). During the first six weeks of life, the duration of the child's attention to a visual event is controlled by the amount of physical change or contrast in the event. During the third month, the infant shows prolonged attention to events that are moderate discrepancies from habituated standards. Maintenance of attention is controlled by the relation of the event to the child's schema for the class to which that event belongs. The typical reactions to discrepancy include increased fixation time, increased vocalization, and either cardiac deceleration or decreased variability of heart rate during the stimulus presentation. These conclusions are based on many independent studies and we shall not document them here (Cohen, Gelber, & Lazar, 1972; Kagan, 1971; Lewis, Goldberg, & Campbell, 1970).

However, at approximately eight—nine months, a second process emerges. The infant now begins to activate cognitive structures, called hypotheses, in the service of interpreting discrepant events. A hypothesis is viewed as a representation of a relation between two schemata. Stated in different language, the infant not only notes and processes a discrepancy, he also attempts to transform it to his prior schemata for that class of event and activates hypotheses to serve this advanced cognitive function. It is not a coincidence that postulation of this new competence coincides with the time when the infant displays object permanence and separation anxiety, phenomena that require the child to activate an idea of an absent object or person.

There are two sources of support for this notion. The first is based on age changes in attention to the same set of events. Regardless of whether the stimulus is a set of human masks, a simple black and white design, or a dynamic sequence in which a moving orange rod turns on a bank of three light bulbs upon contact, there is a U-shaped relation between age and duration of attention across the period 3–36 months, with the trough typically occurring between 7 and 12 months of age (Kagan, 1972).

The curvilinear relation between age and attention to human masks has been replicated among American, rural Guatemalan, and Kahlahari desert Bushman children (Kagan, 1971; Konner, 1973; Sellers, Klein, Kagan, & Minton, 1972). If discrepancy were the only factor controlling fixation time, a child's attention should decrease with age, for the stimulus events become less discrepant as he grows older. The increase in attention toward the end of the first years is interpreted as a sign of a new cognitive competence, which we have called the *activation of hypotheses.*

A second source of support for this idea is that the probability of a cardiac acceleration to a particular discrepancy increases toward the end of the first year, whereas cardiac deceleration is the modal reaction during the earlier months (Kagan, 1972). Because studies of adults and young children indicate that cardiac acceleration accompanies mental work, while deceleration accompanies attention to an interesting event (Lacey, 1967; Van Hover, 1971), the appearance of acceleration toward the end of the first year implies that the infants are performing active mental work, or activating hypotheses.

Since increased attention to a particular discrepancy toward the end of the first year is one diagnostic sign of the emergence of this stage of cognitive development, cultural differences in attention to fixed discrepancies during the first year might provide information on the developmental maturity of the infants in each cultural group.

METHOD

Block Episode

Each child was shown a 2-inch wooden orange block for six or eight successive trials (six for the two older ages, and eight for the two younger ages) followed by three or five transformation trials in which a 1½-inch orange block was presented. These transformations were followed by three representations of the original 2-inch block.

Light Episode

The child was shown 8 or 10 repetitions of a sequence in which a hand moved an orange rod in a semicircle until it touched a bank of three light bulbs which were lighted upon contact between the rod and the bulbs. In the five transformation trials that followed, the hand appeared but the rod did not move and the lights lit after a four-second interval. Following the transformations, the original event was presented for three additional trials.

During each of the episodes, two observers coded (a) how long the infant attended to the event, (b) whether the infant vocalized or smiled, and (c) fretting or crying. Intercoder reliability for these variables was over .90.

RESULTS

The Guatemalan infants were significantly less attentive than the Americans on both episodes, and the cultural differences were greater at the two older than at the two younger ages. Figures 1 and 2 illustrate the mean total fixation time to four successive trial blocks for the two episodes. The four trial blocks were the first three standard trials, the last three standards, the first three transformations, and the three return trials.

The American infants of all ages had longer fixation times to the block during every trial block (F ranged from 30.8 to 67.3, $df = \frac{1}{154}$, $p < .001$). The American infants also displayed longer fixations to the light during every trial block (F ranged from 9.8 to 18.4, $df = \frac{1}{141}$, $p < .01$). However, it is important to note that at 11½ months, the American children maintained more sustained attention to the return of the standard than the Guatemalans, who showed a drop in fixation time toward the end

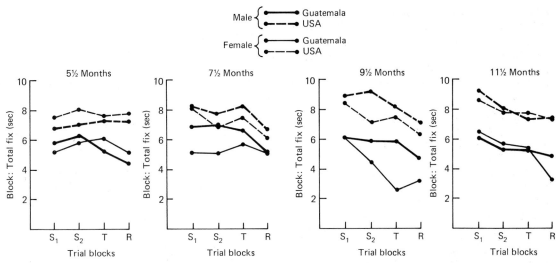

Figure 1 Average total fixation time to the block episode by age and culture.

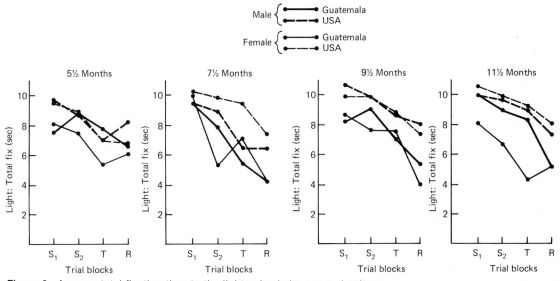

Figure 2 Average total fixation time to the light episode by age and culture.

of the episode. These data suggest that more of the American than of the Guatemalan infants had entered the stage of activation of hypotheses. Since the Ladino infants appeared more mature than the San Marcos children, it is possible that the American one-year-olds were approximately three months advanced over the San Marcos children in the cognitive function.

ADDITIONAL ASSESSMENTS OF DEVELOPMENTAL STATUS

We collected, under less formal conditions in the home, additional information on the developmental status of the San Marcos infant. Not one of the 12 infants between 8 and 16 months reached for an attractive object they watched being hidden, although many would, with considerable hesitation, reach for a visible object placed close to their hands. Furthermore, none of these 12 infants revealed facial surprise following a sequence in which they watched an object being hidden under a cloth but saw no object when that cloth was removed. These observations suggest an absolute retardation of four months in the display of behavioral signs diagnostic of the attainment of object permanence.

A third source of data is based on observations of a stranger anxiety. Each of 16 infants between 8 and 20 months was observed following the first exposure to a strange male (the senior author). The first age at which obvious apprehension and/or crying occurred was 13 months, suggesting a five-month lag between San Marcos and American infants. Finally, the information on nonmorphemic babbling and the onset of meaningful speech supports a diagnosis of absolute retardation. There was no marked increase in frequency of babbling or vocalization between 8 and 16 months among the 12 San Marcos infants observed at home, while comparable observations in American homes revealed a significant increase in babbling and the appearance of morphemic vocalizations for some children. Furthermore, many parents remarked that meaningful speech typically appears first at 2½ years of age, about one year later than the average display of first words in American children.

These data, together with the extremely depressed, withdrawn appearance of the San Marcos infants, suggest retardations of three or more months for various psychological competences that typically emerge during the first two years of life. With the exception of one 16-month-old boy, whose alert appearance resembled that of an American infant, there was little variability among the remaining children. Since over 90% were homogeneously passive, nonalert, and quiet, it is unlikely that the recovery of intellectual functioning to be reported later was a result of the selective mortality of a small group of severely retarded infants.

RESILIENCE OF COGNITIVE DEVELOPMENT

The major theme of this article is the potential for recovery of cognitive functions despite early infant retardation. When the San Marcos child becomes mobile at around 15 months he leaves the dark hut, begins to play with other children, and provides himself with cognitive challenges that demand ac-

commodations. Since all children experience this marked discontinuity in variety of experience and opportunity for exploration between the first and second birthday, it is instructive to compare the cognitive competence of older Guatemalan and American children to determine if differences in level of functioning are still present.

The tests administered were designed to assess cognitive processes that are believed to be part of the natural competence of growing children, rather than the culturally arbitrary segments of knowledge contained in a standard IQ test. We tried to create tests that were culturally fair, recognizing that this goal is, in the extreme, unattainable. Hence, the tests were not standardized instruments with psychometric profiles of test-retest reliabilities and criterion validity studies. This investigation should be viewed as a natural experiment in which the independent variable was degree of retardation in infancy and the dependent variables were performances on selected cognitive instruments during childhood. We assume, along with many psychologists, that perceptual analysis, recall and recognition memory, and inference are among the basic cognitive functions of children (even though they do not exhaust that set), and our tests were designed to evaluate those processes.

Tests of recall and recognition memory, perceptual analysis, and perceptual and conceptual inference were given to children in San Marcos, the Ladino villages, an Indian village close to Guatemala City and more modern than San Marcos, Cambridge, Massachusetts, and to two different groups of children living in Guatemala City. One of the Guatemala City settings, the "guarderia," was a day care center for very poor children. The second group, middle-class children attending nursery school, resembled a middle-class American sample in both family background and opportunity. Not all tests were administered to all children. The discussion is organized according to the cognitive function assessed, rather than the sample studied. The sample sizes ranged from 12 to 40 children at any one age.

Recall Memory for Familiar Objects

The ability to organize experience for commitment to long-term memory and to retrieve that information on demand is a basic cognitive skill. It is generally believed that the form of the organization contains diagnostic information regarding cognitive maturity for, among Western samples, both number of independent units of information and the conceptual clustering of that information increase with age.

A 12-object recall task was administered to two samples of Guatemalan children. One group lived in a Ladino village 17 kilometers from Guatemala City; the second group was composed of San Marcos children. The 80 subjects from the Ladino village were 5 and 7 years old, equally balanced for age and sex. The 55 subjects from San Marcos were between 5 and 12 years of age (26 boys and 29 girls).

The 12 miniature objects to be recalled were common to village life and belonged to three conceptual categories: animals (pig, dog, horse, cow), kitchen utensils (knife, spoon, fork, glass), and clothing (pants, dress, underpants, hat). Each child was first required to name the objects, and if the child was unable to he was given the name. The child was then told that after the objects had been randomly arranged on a board he would have 10 seconds to inspect them, after which they would be covered with a cloth, and he would be required to say all the objects he could remember.

Table 1 contains the average number of objects recalled and the number of pairs of conceptually similar words recalled—an index of clustering—for the first two trials. A pair was defined as the temporally contiguous recall of two or more items of the same category. A child received one point for three contiguous items, and three points for contiguous recall of four items. Hence, the maximum clustering score for a single trial was nine points. As Table 1 reveals, the children showed a level of clustering beyond chance expectation (which is

between 1.5 and 2.0 pairs for recall scores of seven to eight words). Moreover, recall scores increased with age on both trials for children in both villages (F ranged from 11.2 to 27.7, $p < 0.5$), while clustering increased with age in the Ladino village ($F = 26.8$, $p < .001$ for Trial 1; $F = 3.48$, $p < .05$ for Trial 2).

No five- or six-year-old in either village and only 12 of the 40 seven-year-olds in the Ladino village were attending school. School for the others consisted of little more than semiorganized games. Moreover, none of the children in San Marcos had ever left the village, and the five- and six-year olds typically spent most of the day within a 500-yard radius of their homes. Hence, school attendance and contact with books and a written language do not seem to be prerequisites for clustering in young children.

The recall and cluster scores obtained in Guatemala were remarkably comparable to those reported for middle-class American children. Appel, Cooper, McCarrell, Knight, Yussen, and Flavell (1971) presented 12 pictures to Minneapolis children in Grade 1 (approximately age 7) and 15 pictures to children in Grade 5 (approximately age 11) in a single-trial recall task similar to the one described here. The recall scores were 66% for the 7-year-olds and 80% for the 11-year-olds. These values are almost identical to those obtained in both Guatemalan villages. The cluster indices were also comparable. The American 7-year-olds had a cluster ratio of .25; the San Marcos 5- and 6-year-olds had a ratio of .39.[1]

Recognition Memory

The cultural similarity in recall also holds for recognition memory. In a separate study, 5-, 8-, and 11-year-old children from Ladino villages in the East and from Cambridge, Massachusetts, were shown 60 pictures of objects—all of which were familiar to the Americans but some of which were unfamiliar to the Guatemalans. After 0-, 24-, or 48-hours delay, each child was shown 60 pairs of pictures, one of which was old and the other new, and was asked to decide which one he had seen. Although the 5- and 8-year-old Americans performed significantly better than the Guatemalans, there was no statistically

Table 1 Mean Number of Objects and Pairs Recalled

Age	Trial 1		Trial 2	
	Recall	Pairs	Recall	Pairs
Ladino village				
5	5.2	2.1	5.4	2.1
7	6.7	3.3	7.8	3.7
Indian village				
5–6	7.1	3.4	7.8	3.8
7–8	8.6	3.4	8.3	3.6
9–10	10.3	4.9	10.3	4.3
11–12	9.6	3.4	10.1	3.6

[1]The cluster index is the ratio of the number of pairs recalled to the product of the number of categories in the list times one less than the number of words in each category.

Table 2   Mean Percentage of Correct Responses

	Americans			Guatemalans		
		Age				
Delay	**5**	**8**	**11**	**5**	**8**	**11**
0 hours	92.8	96.7	98.3	58.4	74.6	85.2
24 hours	86.7	95.6	96.7	55.8	71.0	87.0
48 hours	87.5	90.3	93.9	61.4	75.8	86.2

Note: Percent signs are omitted.

significant cultural difference for the 11-year-olds, whose scores ranged from 85% to 98% after 0-, 24-, or 48-hour delay (Kagan et al., 1973). (See Table 2.) The remarkably high scores of the American 5-year-olds have also been reported by Scott (1973).

A similar result was found on a recognition memory task for 32 photos of faces, balanced for sex, child versus adult, and Indian versus Caucasian, administered to 35 American and 38 San Marcos children 8–11 years of age. Each child initially inspected 32 chromatic photographs of faces, one at a time, in a self-placed procedure. Each child's recognition memory was tested by showing him 32 pairs of photographs (each pair was of the same sex, age, and ethnicity), one of which was old and the other new. The child had to state which photograph he had seen during the inspection phase. Although the American 8- and 9-year-olds performed slightly better than the Guatemalans (82% versus 70%), there was no significant cultural difference among the 10- and 11-year-olds (91% versus 87%). Moreover, there was no cultural difference at any age for the highest performance attained by a single child.[2] The favored interpretation of the poorer performance of the younger children in both recognition memory studies is that some of them did not completely understand the task and others did not activate the proper problem-solving strategies during the registration and retrieval phases of the task.

It appears that recall and recognition memory are basic cognitive functions that seem to mature in a regular way in a natural environment. The cognitive retardation observed during the first year does not have any serious predictive validity for these two

important aspects of cognitive functioning for children 10–11 years of age.

Perceptual Analysis

The Guatemalan children were also capable of solving difficult Embedded Figures Test items. The test consisted of 12 color drawings of familiar objects in which a triange had been embedded as part of the object. The child had to locate the hidden triangle and place a black paper triangle so that it was congruent with the design of the drawing. The test was administered to rural Indian children from San Marcos, as well as to rural Indians living close to Guatemala City (labeled Indian₁ in Figure 3), the Ladino villages, and two groups from Guatemala City. (See Figure 3.)

The Guatemala City middle-class children had the highest scores and, except for San Marcos, the rural children, the poorest. The surprisingly competent performance of the San Marcos children is due, we believe, to the more friendly conditions of testing. This suggesting is affirmed by an independent study in which a special attempt was made to maximize rapport and comprehension of instructions with a group of rural isolated children before administering a large battery of tests. Although all test performances were not facilitated by this rapport-raising

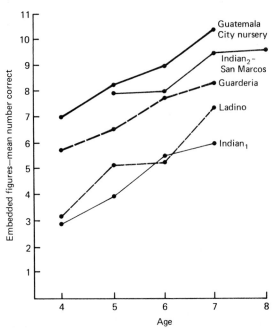

Figure 3   Mean number correct on the Embedded Figures Test.

---

[2]These photographs were also used in an identical procedure with 12 Kipsigis-speaking 10- and 11-year olds from a rural village in eastern Kenya. Despite the absence of any black faces in the set, the percentage of items recognized correctly was 82 for this group of African children.

procedure, performance on the Embedded Figures Test was improved considerably. It is important to note that no five- or six-year-old was completely incapable of solving some of these problems. The village differences in mean score reflect the fact that the rural children had difficulty with three or four of the harder items. This was the first time that many rural children had ever seen a two-dimensional drawing, and most of the five-, six-, and seven-year-olds in San Marcos had had no opportunity to play with books, paper, pictures, or crayons. Nonetheless, these children solved seven or eight of the test items. Investigators who have suggested that prior experience with pictures is necessary for efficient analysis of two-dimensional information may have incorrectly misinterpreted failure to understand the requirements of the problem with a deficiency in cognitive competence. This competence seems to develop in the world of moving leaves, chickens, and water.[3] As with recall and recognition memory, the performance of the San Marcos child was comparable to that of his age peer in a modern urban setting.

Perceptual Inference

The competence of the San Marcos children on the Embedded Figures Test is affirmed by their performance on a test administered only in San Marcos and Cambridge and called Perceptual Inference. The children (60 American and 55 Guatemalan, 5–12 years of age) were shown a schematic drawing of an object and asked to guess what that object might be if the drawing were completed. The child was given a total of four clues for each 13 items, where each clue added more information. The child had to guess an object from an incomplete illustration, to make an inference from minimal information (see Figures 4 and 5).

There was no significant cultural difference for the children 7–12 years of age, although the American 5- and 6-year-olds did perform significantly better than the Indian children. In San Marcos, performance improved from 62% correct on one of the first two clues for the 5- and 6-year-olds to 77% correct for the 9–12-year-olds. The comparable changes for the American children were from 77% to 84%. (See Figure 6.)

Familiarity with the test objects was critical for

[3]This conclusion holds for Embedded Figures Test performance, and not necessarily for the ability to detect three-dimensional perspective in two-dimensional drawings.

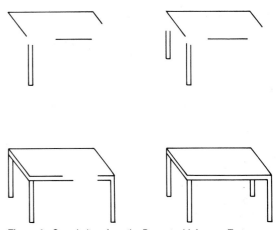

Figure 4 Sample item from the Perceptual Inference Test.

success. All of the San Marcos children had seen hats, fish, and corn, and these items were rarely missed. By contrast, many American children failed these items. No San Marcos child not attending school, and therefore unfamiliar with books, correctly guessed the book item, whereas most of those in school guessed it correctly. As with memory and perceptual analysis, the retardation seen during infancy did not predict comparable retardation in the ability of the 11-year-old to make difficult perceptual inferences.

Conceptual Inference

The San Marcos child also performed well on questions requiring conceptual inference. In this test, the child was told verbally three characteristics of an object and was required to guess the object. Some of the examples included: What has wings, eats chickens, and lives in a tree? What moves trees, cannot be seen, and makes one cold? What is made

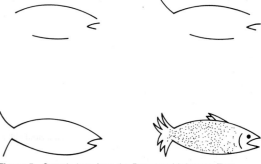

Figure 5 Sample item from the Perceptual Inference Test.

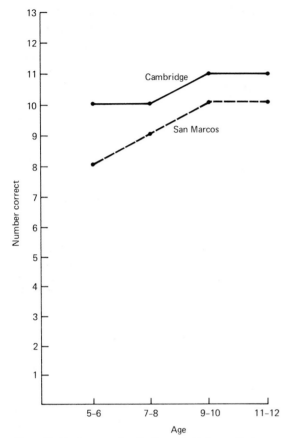

Figure 6 Number correct on the Perceptual Inference Test.

of wood, is used to carry things, and allows one to make journeys? There was improved performance with age; the 5- and 6-year-olds obtained an average of 9 out of 14 correct, and the 11- and 12-year-olds obtained 12 out of 14 correct. The San Marcos child was capable of making moderately difficult inferences from both visual and verbal information.

DISCUSSION

This corpus of data implies that absolute retardation in the time of emergence of universal cognitive competences during infancy is not predictive of comparable deficits for memory, perceptual analysis, and inference during preadolescence. Although the rural Guatemalan infants were retarded with respect to activation of hypotheses, alertness, and onset of stranger anxiety and object permanence, the preadolescents' performance on the tests of

perceptual analysis, perceptual inference, and recall and recognition memory were comparable to American middle-class norms. Infant retardation seems to be partially reversible and cognitive development during the early years and more resilient than had been supposed.

One potential objection to this conclusion is that the tests were too easy for the Guatemalan 11-year-olds and that is why cultural differences were absent. These are two comments that can be addressed to that issue. First, it is not intuitively reasonable to argue that the ability to remember 60 photographs of objects, classify an object from a few sketch lines, or detect the triangle hidden in a two-dimensional drawing is "easy" for children who rarely see photographs, pencils, crayons, or books. Second, we deliberately assessed cognitive functions that we believe all children should master by the time they are preadolescents. The fact that many 11-year-olds approached the ceiling on some tests is support for the basic premise of this article, namely, that infant retardation does not prevent a child from eventually developing basic cognitive competences.

This result is surprising if one believes that each child is born with a certain level of general intellectual competence that is stable from infancy through adulthood. If, on the contrary, one assumes that each stage of development is characterized by a different profile of specific competences and there is no necessary relation between early emergence of the capacities of infancy and level of attainment of the quite different abilities characteristic of childhood, then these results are more reasonable. There is no reason to assume that the caterpillar who metamorphoses a bit earlier than his kin is a better adapted or more efficient butterfly.

Consideration of why the rural Guatemalan children lagged behind the urban children on some tests during the period five through nine years of age comprises a second implication of these data. It will be recalled that on the embedded figures and recognition memory tests the performance of rural children was several years behind both the American and Guatemala City middle-class children. The differences were minimal for the object recall and perceptual inference tests. The approximately three-year lag in performance is paralleled by comparable differences between lower- and middle-class children in urban Western cities. For example, Bosco (1972) found that middle-class first and third graders were able to tolerate smaller interstimulus intervals in a backward masking procedure than lower-class children, but this difference had vanished among sixth-grade children. Similarly, Bakker (1971) compared good and poor readers from urban centers in Holland on a task that required operating simultaneously on two items of information in a temporal integration task. The poor readers performed less well than the good readers at ages six to eight, but were comparable to the good readers during the preadolescent years.

We interpret these results as indicating that the urban lower-class children, like the younger, rural Guatemalans, were not able to mobilize proper problem-solving strategies necessary for task solution, but achieved that level of competence by 11 years of age. Some of these strategies include focused attention, rehearsal of task information and instructions, awareness of and understanding the problem to be solved, maintenance of problem set, and the ability to remember critical information elements in the problem and to operate on that information. It is believed that these functions may emerge a little later in some groups of children than in others, but they are operative in all children by 11–12 years of age. In a recently completed study with Patricia Engle, we found that among rural Guatemalan children, 5 through 11 years of age, the rate of improvement in performance on three memory tasks (memory for numbers, memory for sentences, and auditory blending) was greatest between 9 and 11 years of age, whereas White (1970), using comparable data from American children, found that the greatest rate of improvement was between 5 and 7 years of age—a lag of about three years.

These data have implications for America's educational problems. There is a tendency to regard the poor test performances of economically impoverished, minority group 6-year-olds in the United States as indicative of a permanent and, perhaps, irreversible defect in intellectual ability—as a difference in quality of function rather than slower maturational rate. The Guatemalan data, together with those of Bosco and Bakker, suggest that children differ in the age at which basic cognitive competences emerge and that experiential factors influence the time of emergence. Economically disadvantaged American children and isolated rural Guatemalan children appear to be from one to three years behind middle-class children in demonstrating some of the problem-solving skills characteristic of

Piaget's stage of concrete operations. But these competences eventually appear in sturdy form by age 10 or 11. The common practice of arbitrarily setting 7 years—the usual time of school entrance—as the age when children are to be classified as competent or incompetent confuses differences in maturational rate with permarent, qualitative differences in intellectual ability. This practice is as logical as classifying children as reproductively fertile or sterile depending on whether or not they have reached physiological puberty by their thirteenth birthday.

When educators note correctly that poor children tend to remain permanently behind middle-class children on intellectual and academic performance, they are referring to the relative retardation on the culturally specific skills of reading, mathematics, and language achievement described earlier. That relative retardation is the product of the rank ordering of scores on achievement and IQ tests. The fact that relative retardation on these abilities is stable from age five on does not mean that the relatively retarded children are not growing intellectually (when compared with themselves), often at the same rate as economically advantaged youngsters.

The suggestion that basic cognitive competences, in contrast to culturally specific ones, emerge at different times and that the child retains the capacity for actualization of his competence until a late age is not substantially different from the earlier conclusions of Dennis and Najarian (1957). Although the 49 infants 2–12 months of age living in poorly staffed Lebanese institutions were seriously retarded on the Cattell developmental scale (mean developmental quotient of 68 compared with a quotient of 102 for a comparison group), the 4½—6-year-olds who had resided in the same institution all their lives performed at a level comparable to American norms on a memory test (Knox Cubes) as well as on Porteus mazes and the Goodenough Draw-a-Man Test.

Of more direct relevance is Dennis's (1973) recent follow-up study of 16 children who were adopted out of the same Lebanese institution between 12 and 24 months of age—the period during which the San Marcos infant leaves the unstimulating environment of the dark hut—with an average developmental quotient of 50 on the Cattell Infant Scale. Even though the assessment of later intellectual ability was based on the culturally biased Stanford-Binet IQ test, the average IQ obtained when the children were between 4 and 12 years of age, was 101, and 13 of the 16 children had IQ scores of 90 or above.

Additional support for the inherent resiliency in human development comes from longitudinal information on two sisters who spent most of their infancy in a crib in a small bedroom with no toys.[4] The mother, who felt unable to care for her fourth child, restricted her to the room soon after birth and instructed her eight-year-old daughter to care for the child. One year later, another daughter was born, and she, too, was placed in a crib with the older sister. These two children only left the room to be fed and, according to the caretaker sister who is now a married woman in her twenties, the two infants spent about 23 hours of each day together in a barren crib. When the authorities were notified of this arrangement, the children were removed from the home and taken to a hospital when the younger was 2½ and the older 3½ years old. Medical records reveal that both children were malnourished, severely retarded in weight and height, and seriously retarded psychologically. After a month in the hospital, following considerable recovery, both sisters were placed in the care of a middle-class family who had several young children. The sisters have remained with that family for the last 12 years and regard the husband and wife as their parents. One of us (J. K.) tested the sisters five times when they were between 4 and 9 years of age, and recently interviewed and tested both of them over a two-day period when they were 14½ and 15½ years old.

The younger sister has performed consistently better than the older one over the last 10 years. The IQ scores of the younger girl have risen steadily from a Stanford-Binet IQ of 74 at age 4½ (after two years in the foster home) to a Wechsler Full Scale IQ of 88 at age 14. The older girl's scores have also improved, but less dramatically, from a Stanford-Binet IQ of 59 at age 5 to a Wechsler IQ of 72 at age 15. The author also administered a lengthy battery of tests, some of which were discussed earlier. On the Perceptual Inference Test, the percentage correct was 85 for the younger sister and 61 for the older sister. On the Recognition Memory for Photographs, the percentages were 94 for both. On the Embedded Figures Test, the percentages were 92 and 100, and on the recall memory for objects, the

percentages were 92 and 83 for the younger and older sister, respectively. Moreover, the interpersonal behavior of both girls was in no way different from that of the average rural Ohio adolescent—a group the author came to know well after seven years of work in the area. Although there is some ambiguity surrounding the competence of the older girl, the younger one performs at an average level on a wide range of tests of cognitive functioning, despite 2½ years of serious isolation.

These data, together with the poor predictive relation between scores on infant developmental tests and later assessments of intellectual functioning, strengthen the conclusion that environmentally produced retardation during the first year or two of life appears to be reversible. The importance of the Guatemalan data derives from the fact that the San Marcos 11-year-olds performed so well, considering the homogeneity and isolation of their childhood environment. Additionally, there is a stronger feeling now than there was in 1957 that environmentally produced retardation during the first two years may be irreversible, even though the empirical basis for that belief is no firmer in 1972 than it was in 1957.

More dramatic support for the notion that psychological development is malleable comes from recent experimental studies with animals. Several years ago Harlow's group demonstrated that although monkeys reared in isolation for the first six months displayed abnormal and often bizarre social behaviors, they could, if the experimenter were patient, solve the complex learning problems normally administered to feralborn monkeys. The prolonged isolation did not destroy their cognitive competence (Harlow, Schiltz, & Harlow, 1969). More recently, Suomi and Harlow (1972) have shown that that even the stereotyped and bizarre social behavior shown by six-month-old isolates can be altered by placing them with female monkeys three months younger than themselves over a 26-week therapeutic period. "By the end of the therapy period the behavioral levels were virtually indistinguishable from those of the socially competent therapist monkeys [Suomi & Harlow, 1972, p. 491]."

This resiliency has also been demonstrated for infant mice (Cairns & Nakelski, 1971) who experienced an initial 10 weeks of isolation from other animals. Compared with group-reared mice of the same strain, the isolated subjects were hyperreactive

[4]The authors thank Meinhard Robinow for information on these girls.

to other mice, displaying both extreme withdrawal and extreme aggressiveness. These investigators also attempted rehabilitation of the isolates by placing them with groups of mice for an additional 10 weeks, however, after which their behavior was indistinguishable from animals that had never been isolated.

> By the seventieth day after interchange, the effects of group therapy were complete, and animals that had been isolated for one hundred days following weaning were indistinguishable from animals that had never been isolated [Cairns & Nakelski, 1971, p. 363.].

These dramatic alterations in molar behavior are in accord with replicated reports of recovery of visual function in monkeys and cats deprived of patterned light soon after birth (Baxter, 1966; Chow & Stewart, 1972; Wilson & Riesen, 1966). Kittens deprived of light for one year recovered basic visual functions after only 10 days in the experimenter's home (Baxter, 1966); kittens who had one or both eyes sutured for close to two years were able to learn pattern discriminations with the deprived eye only after moderate training (Chow & Stewart, 1972).

If the extreme behavioral and perceptual sequelae of isolation in monkeys, cats, and mice can be altered by such brief periods of rehabilitative experience, it is not difficult to believe that the San Marcos infant is capable of as dramatic a recovery over a period of nine years. These data do not indicate the impotence of early environments, but rather the potency of the environment in which the organism is functioning. There is no question that early experience seriously affects kittens, monkeys, and children. If the first environment does not permit the full actualization of psychological competences, the child will function below his ability as long as he remains in that context. But if he is transferred to an environment that presents greater variety and requires more accommodations, he seems more capable of exploiting that experience and repairing the damage wrought by the first environment than some theorists have implied.

These conclusions do not imply that intervention or rehabilitation efforts with poor American or minority group preschool children are of no value. Unlike San Marcos, where children are assigned adult responsibilities when they are strong and alert enough to assume them, rather than at a fixed age, American children live in a severely age graded system, in which children are continually rank ordered. Hence, if a poor four-year-old falls behind a middle-class four-year-old on a culturally significant skill, like knowledge of letters or numbers, he may never catch up with the child who was advanced and is likely to be placed in a special educational category. Hence, American parents must be concerned with the early psychological growth of their children. We live in a society in which the relative retardation of a four-year-old seriously influences his future opportunities because we have made relative retardation functionally synonymous with absolute retardation. This is not true in subsistence farming communities like San Marcos.

These data suggest that exploration of the new and the construction of objects or ideas from some prior schematic blueprint must be inherent properties of the mind. The idea that the child carries with him at all times the essential mental competence to understand the new in some terms and to make a personal contribution to each new encounter is only original in our time. Despite the current popularity of Kant and Piaget, the overwhelming prejudice of Western psychologists is that higher order cognitive competences and personality factors are molded completely by the environment. Locke's image of an unmarked tablet on which sensation played its patterned melody has a parallel in Darwin's failure to realize, until late in his life, that the organism made a contribution to his own evolution. Darwin was troubled by the fact that the same climate on different islands in the Galapagos produced different forms of the same species. Since he believed that climatic variation was the dynamic agent in evolution he was baffled. He did not appreciate that the gene was the organism's contributions to his own alteration. Western psychologists have been blocked by the same prejudice that prevented young Darwin from solving his riddle. From Locke to Skinner we have viewed the perfectibility of man as vulnerable to the vicissitudes of the objects and people who block, praise, or push him, and resisted giving the child any compass on his own. The mind, like the nucleus of a cell, has a plan for growth and can transduce a new flower, an odd pain, or a stranger's unexpected smile into a form that is comprehensible. This process is accomplished through wedding cognitive structures to selective attention, activation of hypotheses, assimilation, and accommodation.

The purpose of these processes is to convert an alerting unfamiliar event, incompletely understood, to a recognized variation on an existing familiar structure. This is accomplished through the detection of the dimensions of the event that bear a relation to existing schemata and the subsequent incorporation of the total event into the older structure.

We need not speak of joy in this psychological mastery, for neither walking nor breathing is performed in order to experience happiness. These properties of the motor or autonomic systems occur because each physiological system or organ naturally exercises its primary function. The child explores the unfamiliar and attempts to match his ideas and actions to some previously acquired representations because these are basic properties of the mind. The child has no choice.

The San Marcos child knows much less than the American about planes, computers, cars, and the many hundreds of other phenomena that are familiar to the Western youngster, and he is a little slower in developing some of the basic cognitive competences of our species. But neither appreciation of these events nor the earlier cognitive maturation is necessary for a successful journey to adulthood in San Marcos. The American child knows far less about how to make canoes, rope, tortillas, or how to burn an old milpa in preparation for June planting. Each knows what is necessary, each assimilates the cognitive conflicts that are presented to him, and each seems to have the potential to display more talent than his environment demands of him. There are few dumb children in the world if one classifies them from the perspective of the community of adaptation, but millions of dumb children if one classifies them from the perspective of another society.

REFERENCES

Appel, L. F., Cooper, R. G., McCarrell, N., Knight, J. S., Yussen, S. R., & Flavell, J. H. The developmental acquisition of the distinction between perceiving and memory. Unpublished manuscript, University of Minnesota- Minneapolis, 1971.

Bakker, D. J. *Temporal order in disturbed reading.* Rotterdam: Rotterdam University Press, 1972.

Baxter, B. L. Effect of visual deprivation during postnatal maturation on the electroencephalogram of the cat. *Experimental Neurology,* 1966, 14, 224–237.

Bosco, J. The visual information processing speed of lower

middle class children. *Child Development,* 1972, 43, 1418–1422.

Cairns, R. B., & Nakelski, J. S. On fighting in mice: Ontogenetic and experiental determinants. *Journal of Comparative and Physiological Psychology,* 1971, 74, 354–364.

Carmichael, L. The development of behavior in vertebrates experimentally removed from the influence of external stimulation. *Psychological Review,* 1926, 33, 51–58.

Chow, K. L., & Stewart, D. L. Reversal of structural and functional effects of longterm visual deprivation in cats. *Experimental Neurology,* 1972, 34, 409–433.

Cohen, L. B., Gelber, E. R., & Lazar, M. A. Infant habituation and generalization to differing degrees of novelty. *Journal of Experimental Child Psychology,* 1971, 11, 379–389.

Cole, M., Gay, J., Glick, J. A., & Sharp, D. W. *The cultural context of learning and thinking.* New York: Basic Books, 1971.

Dennis, W. *Children of the Crèche.* New York: Appleton-Century-Crofts, 1973.

Dennis, W., & Najarian, P. Infant development under environmental handicap. *Psychological monographs,* 1957, 71(7, Whole No. 436).

Harlow, H. F., Schiltz, K. A., & Harlow, M. K. The effects of social isolation on the learning performance of rhesus monkeys. In C. R. Carpenter (Ed.), *Proceedings of the Second International Congress of Primatology.* Vol. 1. New York: Karger, 1969.

Kagan, J. *Change and continuity in infancy.* New York: Wiley, 1971.

Kagan, J. Do infants think? *Scientific American,* 1972, 226(3), 74–82.

Kagan, J., Klein, R. E., Haith, M. M., & Morrison, F. J. Memory and meaning in two cultures. *Child Development,* 1973, 44, 221–223.

Kagan, J., & Moss. H. A., *Birth to maturity.* New York: Wiley, 1962.

Kessen, W., Haith, M. M., & Salapatek, B. H. Human infancy: A bibliography and guide. In P. H. Mussen (Ed.), *Carmichael's manual of child psychology.* (3rd ed.) Vol. 1. New York: Wiley, 1970.

Konner, M. J. Development among the Bushmen of Botswana. Unpublished doctoral dissertation, Harvard University, 1973.

Lacey, J. I. Somatic response patterning in stress: Some revisions of activation theory. In M. H. Appley & R. Trumbull (Eds.), *Psychological stress: Issues in research.* New York: Appleton-Century-Crofts, 1967.

Lewis, M., & Freedle, R. *Mother-infant dyad: The cradle of meaning.* (Research bulletin RB72–22) Princeton, N.J.: Educational Testing Service, 1972.

Lewis, M., Goldberg, S., & Campbell, H. A developmental study of learning within the first three years of life: Response decrement to a redundant signal. *Monograph of the Society for Research in Child Development,* 1970, 34(No. 133).

McGraw, M. B. *Growth: A study of Johnny and Jimmy.* New York: Appleton-Century, 1935.

Pease, D., Wolins, L., & Stockdale, D. F. Relationship and prediction of infant tests. *Journal of Genetic Psychology,* 1973, 122, 31–35.

Scott, M. S. The absence of interference effects in pre-school children's picture recognition. *Journal of Genetic Psychology,* 1973, 122, 121–126.

Sellers, M. J., Klein, R. E., Kagan, J., & Minton, C. Developmental determinants of attention: A cross-cultural replication. *Developmental Psychology,* 1972, 6, 185.

Suomi, S. J., & Harlow, H. F. Social rehabilitation of isolate reared monkeys. *Developmental Psychology,* 1972, 6, 487–496.

Van Hover, K. I. S. A developmental study of three components of attention. Unpublished doctoral dissertation, Harvard University, 1971.

White, S. H. Some general outlines of the matrix of developmental changes between 5 and 7 years. *Bulletin of the Orton Society,* 1970, 21, 41–57.

Wilson, P. D., & Riesen, A. H. Visual development in rhesus monkeys neonatally deprived of patterned light. *Journal of Comparative and Physiological Psychology,* 1966, 61, 87–95.

Chapter Three

Emotional Development

The development of emotions in children has puzzled and fascinated investigators since Darwin published his early attempts to understand emotions in his book, *The Expression of Emotions in Man and Animals*. Over a century later, this topic is still receiving a great deal of attention. When and why do babies smile? What causes crying and laughter? Why do infants and children prefer some individuals over others or become "attached" to particular people? Why are we afraid of some things and some people? How can children be helped to overcome their fears? The articles in this section provide some tentative answers to these classic questions about children's emotional development.

In the first paper, Selma Fraiberg describes the ways in which blind babies learn to recognize and eventually to prefer their familiar caregivers over strangers. In contrast to sighted babies, where vision plays an important role in the development of attachment, blind infants rely on their sense of touch for familiarizing themselves with the people in their world. In spite of the fact that the route followed by blind and sighted children is different, both pass the same developmental milestones. Both learn to recognize and eventually to prefer or "become attached" to a few people in their environment. Emotional development can follow a variety of paths to the same goal.

In the second paper, Lewis and Brooks-Gunn provide further evidence of the developmental changes that take place in the infant's reactions to social objects and social situations. In contrast to earlier beliefs that infants routinely show fear of strangers, these investigators show that the type of stranger and the manner in which the strange individual interacts with the infant are important determinants of the infant's reactions to strangers. A playful peer stranger may elicit smiles while an abrupt and imposing adult stranger may elicit fear. The test setting is important as well; a mother who wears a strange mask may elicit laughter at home, while the infant may cry when he sees his masked mother in an unfamiliar laboratory.

Just as people can be either fun or frightening and cause smiles or cries, so can toys elicit either positive or negative reactions in children. In her paper in this section, Gunnar-VonGnechten shows that the ability to control a toy is an important determinant of the child's emotional reaction. If children can control the event, they respond with positive emotions; but if they cannot control it, they are more likely to show a negative emotional response such as fear. The degree of control, then, is one of the important factors that determines our emotional reactions to objects and people in our environment.

In the final paper, Melamed and Siegel show that children can learn to overcome their fears by the use of a film modeling approach. By watching a film of another child who successfully overcomes his fear of surgery, children who are about to undergo surgery show less fear than children who saw an unrelated film. The study demonstrates that emotions such as fear can be modified through learning and suggests that modeling is a powerful way of changing maladaptive emotional reactions.

The Development of Human Attachments in Blind and Sighted Infants

Selma Fraiberg

For the sighted child, the developmental course that leads to stable human partnerships in the course of the first 18 months is charted by us through affective signs and by a sequence of increasingly discriminating behaviors toward the partner which speak for preference and valuation. Without exception, these are signs that are mediated through vision. Differential smiling, discrimination of mother and stranger, and separation and reunion behaviors, unite the affective experience of the mother with sensory pictures, and the picture itself is the synthesizer of all sense experience.

In a world without pictures, how does the infant learn to discriminate his mother from other persons, how does he express preference for and valuation of her? How does the visual deficit affect reciprocity between the baby and his partners and the reading of signs which must underlie every human partnership?

At eighteen months, 9 of our 10 blind babies demonstrated to their parents and to us that the mother had become the most important person in the world and that the world itself was inexhaustibly fascinating. As creepers and toddlers they set out on excursions around the house, returned to touch base with mother, set out again for another trip, pausing sometimes to say "mama" or "hi," waiting for the reassuring voice to come back. They were wary of strangers, took a dim view of the research team, but put up gamely with our presence and our occasional testing nonsense. Without needing invitation or prompting, they gave embraces to mother and father, or lovingly fingered their faces, and almost never favored our observers with such treatment. The absence of the mother for a few minutes or a few hours produced distress and turning away from the ministrations of substitute care-givers. By all signs these blind babies showed us that they had achieved forms of focused human relationships (Yarrow 1967) which compared favorably with those of sighted children of the same age.

Yet the route that led to love and valuation of human partners was in many ways very different from that of the sighted child. I will describe the sequential development of discriminating and preferential behaviors of blind infants toward their human partners and compare these characteristics with those of sighted children during the first two years of life.

DATA SOURCES AND EVALUATION

In examining the course of human attachments in blind babies we recorded and analyzed hundreds of items for each child in a chronological sequence which gave us differential responses to mother, and to other familiar and unfamiliar persons; behaviors showing pleasurable response to and preference for mother; the ability to be comforted by mother; reactions to temporary separation from mother; and tracking and seeking mother (when the baby was mobile). Profiles for each child were constructed, a selection of indicators was made, and a composite profile was developed for 10 babies.

When our data were sorted and evaluated we saw that there were differential responses in certain areas which could be examined in relation to sighted-child criteria and sighted-child norms. There were also a number of indicators of human attachment which appeared in our blind children and which represented the blind baby's exploitation of tactile-auditory modes. These may also be tactile-auditory components of all human attachment that are normally obscured when vision is available to the baby.

INTERVENTION

In examining the development of human attachments in the blind infants who were the subjects of this investigation, it is important to note again that a concurrent education and guidance program was provided for all children in the study. We have reason to believe that our intervention program promoted the attachment of baby and mother, and the presentation of our central findings should be read as the development of human attachments in a group of blind infants who were probably advantaged through an intervention program.

Our guidance in the area of human attachments can be briefly summarized: We gave comfort and support and hope to parents who were without hope and who were still stunned by grief when we first met them. We became the interpreters of the blind baby's experience to his parents. His needs for tactile intimacy and for voice contact were interpreted to his parents and were seen as central to all learning in the early months. We helped our parents to read the alien sign vocabulary of the blind baby, to see the signs of discrimination, preference, and valuation that are often obscured by the absence of mutual gaze. We understood, through our own studies, the developmental deviations and lags in prehension and locomotion which we saw in blind infants, and could share that understanding with the parents along with vital information and guidance which would lead to the child's adaptive solutions. The baby brought his own rewards as we will see in the pages that follow. Our guidance program is described in two papers—Fraiberg, Smith, and Adelson (1969) and Fraiberg (1971a).

The summary that follows is highly selective and may not do justice to the complexities of the problem for the blind baby and his mother in achieving their bonds. Table 1 summarizes the ranges and medians for milestones in human attachment in our group. These milestones will be explicated in the text. Four papers by the author deal with aspects of human attachment in blind infants—Fraiberg (1968), Fraiberg (1971b), Fraiberg (1971e), and Fraiberg (1975).

Smiling

The course of smiling in the blind infant is of exceptional interest and provides an entree through

Table 1   Human Attachment Milestones—C.D.P. Blind Group

Item	Range	Median age
Smiles to familiar voice[a]	1.0– 3.0	
Manual-tactile discrimination familiar-unfamiliar faces	5.0– 8.0	5.0
Stranger avoidance	7.0–15.0	12.5
Person permanence		
Stage 4	10.0–16.0	11.5
Separation protest	11.0–21.0	11.5

Note: Ages rounded to nearest half month. 3 cases corrected for 3 months prematurity.
[a]Parent report credited for this item only. All children had achieved this item at time of entrance to study. All other items credited by our direct observation.

"known territory" to the "unknown territory" of the blind infant's development. In the sighted child, the differentiation of the smile and the increasing selectivity of the smile for the valued partner gives us a sequence of milestones or indicators of human attachment. (Spitz and Wolff 1946; Ambrose 1961; Polak, Emde, and Spitz 1964; Gewirtz 1965; Emde and Koenig 1969.) From the automatic smile at two months to the selective smile which is well established at six months, the prime elicitor of smiling is the visual configuration of the human face. Indeed, the facial gesalt is biologically overdetermined as a stimulus for attention and smiling in the infant.

For the blind infant, the *familiar voice* is the prime elicitor of the smile. As early as the fourth week we have examples of selective (but irregular) smiling to mother's and father's voice. When we, the observers, tried to elicit the smile through our voices in repeated experiments, we failed. The smile to voice is also reported by Wolff (1963) for sighted children of the same age. Emde and Koenig (1969) report, however, that voice is one of a number of unpatterned auditory, tactile and visual stimuli which elicit the smile as an *irregular* response in the period three weeks or two months.

At two and a half months, however, the smile of the sighted child becomes regular and is relatively automatic to the gestalt of the human face. The blind child smiles more frequently to the voice of mother and other familiar persons, but there is no stimulus except gross tactile stimulation (tickling) which *regularly* elicits the smile.

In the period two and a half months to six months the sighted child's smile becomes preferential for mother, with greater frequency for mother than unfamiliar persons. This preferential smile speaks for an affective-cognitive advance in which the baby can discriminate the familiar face from the unfamiliar face. The blind child, whose smile has been "preferential" from the second month on, continues to smile selectively to mother's voice; the smile to voice is still irregular.

In the period six to eleven months the sighted child reserves his smile, alsmost exclusively, for mother and familiar persons (Emde and Koenig 1969). But the blind child's smile is not further differentiated from the earlier stage; it is still an irregular smile to the mother's or familiar persons' voices.

Using sighted-child criteria for smiling as an indicator of attachment behavior, the course of smiling in the blind infant would tell us nothing of the development of human attachments. A preferential smile to voice, which does not undergo a course of further differentiation in the first year, leaves us without vital indicators of progression in human attachment. Yet, even though the blind baby's smile does not inform us of complex discriminations or tell us how he gives unity to the disparate aspects of mother—how he "knows" mother, how he comes to value her—we can demonstrate that there are components of sensorimotor experience which are exploited by the blind baby and his mother and which lead him to a stage in human attachments that becomes recognizable to us immediately as an indicator of a level of human attachments.

Between seven and fifteen months of age, the blind baby, like the sighted baby, repudiates strangers, resists their arms and their ministrations, cries in protest, and is comforted only by mother's voice and embrace. The blind baby has kept his appointment, and meets the sighted baby at a certain time and a certain place on a developmental pathway— but he has gotten there by another route.

The tactile reciprocity between the blind baby and his human partners is, of course, only a component of a tactile-auditory-kinesthetic dialogue. The mother and other partners who hold the baby, rock him, feed him, caress him, and play motor games with him, are at the same time partners who talk, who sing, who create movement for the baby as they walk with him, shift postures, offer him rhythmic experiences. Therefore, in speaking of tactile modes it would be more correct to speak of "predominantly tactile modes."

The hands of the blind baby tell a story which begins in the first months. As the story unfolds in the course of the first year we see the progressive adaptation of the hand as an organ for maintaining contact and, later, for fine discriminations. When we consider that in normal development it is vision that facilitates all adaptive hand behavior, the blind child's exploitation of the hand as a perceptual organ is an extraordinary adaptive feat. In our studies we have compelling evidence that this adaptation, which is unique, of course, for blind children, is given impetus and motive through the primary human attachments and tactile intimacy between the baby and his human partners.

Yet the beginning of the story of the blind baby's hands does not distinguish for our eyes the blind child from the sighted child.

In the early weeks of life, we see a form of tactile-seeking in the blind baby which closely parallels that of the sighted baby. In the mother's arms, both the blind baby and the sighted baby in the second month will engage in a brief pursuit of the mother's hand which has been withdrawn from contact, or in other ways attempt to restore a contact that has been momentarily lost. (Our own protocols for 3 children and Piaget's [1952] protocols for Laurent at 0:1:19 show close correspondence.)

But, for the sighted child, manual tactile experience becomes one of several modes which are available "to maintain contact." By the third month, visual regard and tracking are capable of taking over the functions of "making contact" and "sustaining contact" when the child is at tactile and auditory remove from his mother.

The blind child in the third month and for many months to follow can only maintain contact with his mother when she manifests herself to him through tactile experience and through her voice. When his mother does not manifest herself to him through touch or voice, the blind baby is "not in contact" with her.

Yet the condition of physical proximity to the mother can be exploited fully by the blind child, and what we see is a pantomime of hands which begins in the first month as "chance encounter," then moves toward "tactile seeking," and by five months of age grows progressively more discriminating and intentional. For many months before the ear-hand schemas are coordinated, the blind child's hands send and receive messages in an archaic language: "Are you there? . . . I am here."

Between five and eight months something new emerges in manual-tactile experience. The blind baby's hands begin to explore the face of the mother, father, and other familiar persons:

> Rob, 0:5:18 (on film)
> Now sitting on father's lap, father nuzzling his face and jiggling him on his lap, Robbie's hands are stretched outright. A sequence of Robbie fingering his father's nose and face with great interest follows. Robbie is pinching his father's cheek. Father is talking to him and he strokes father's chin and mouth with his fingers. Now examining with his fingers father's glasses, he grabs hold at one point of the glasses and nearly pulls them off father's nose.

Far less frequently found in our records are examples in which the blind baby explores the observer's face. Our protocols and films give numerous examples from all children in the sample of a sustained, fascinated exploration of facial features of mother, father, siblings, other familiar persons, which gives the sense to the viewer of pleasure in tracing a familiar map and knowing what is to be found. The few examples of manual exploration of the observer's face are qualitatively different; they are brief scannings which appear to give some minimal information. In this behavior the blind child clearly differentiates between the familiar person and the stranger. As an early form of recognition behavior it may be compared fairly with the recognition behaviors which we discern in the sighted child of the same age, in preferential smiling, for example.

The appearance of manual-tactile exploration of faces follows a distribution pattern which is of some interest for comparison. Crediting the first example in the child's protocols of "exploration of the face" we have 5 children at the range five to six months, 2 at seven months, 1 at eight months. (N = 8 for this age period.)

There appears to be some correspondence, then, with forms of discriminatory and recognitory behaviors which appear in the sighted child around the middle of the first year. This was another surprise to us. As the data emerged in first tabulation I found myself disbelieving the evidence, but when I rechecked protocols I was satisfied that the examples were fair. Then I wondered whether our educational program had influenced this distribution pattern and the selective interest in the partner's face. (We had encouraged manual exploration in a number of ways in the early months.) However, when I examined the data for children who had entered the sample between five and eight months (5 children) and those who had been known to us from birth (3 children), the appearance of manual recognitory behavior did not discriminate the 3 "early education" children from the 5 children who had come into the sample with no previous educational advantage. My hypothesis is that the correspondence between visual recognition behavior in the sighted baby and manual-tactile recognition behaviors in the blind baby is a function of brain maturation as well as libidinization of the partner. Both factors must be present, of course, to lead to recognition behavior.

Negative Reactions to the Stranger

On a scale of human attachment, negative reaction to the stranger is regarded as a criterion for the assessment of the positive bonds to the mother and other human partners. (Spitz 1957; Benjamin 1963; Provence and Lipton 1962; Ainsworth 1967; and Yarrow 1967). It speaks for another level of valuation of the mother, in which the positive affect is bound to a partner, in which persons are no longer "interchangeable," and for a new level of cognitive discrimination.

Among sighted children it is the visual discrimination of the stranger's face which elicits avoidance behavior or fear in the child between the ages of seven and fifteen months. (Ranges from Morgan and Ricciutti 1969.) The experimental situations which have been designed to study the developmental characteristics of stranger reaction require, of course, the presentation of the stranger's face and the reactions of the baby to the visual stimulus of the face.

When I now summarize our findings on the stranger reactions of the blind babies in our sample, I do not wish to strain the comparisons between blind and sighted children. The conditions which elicited negative reactions to the stranger for blind children are not identical with those observed and studied in sighted children; a non-visual percept of the stranger is not a true equivalent of a visual percept.

All that can be said with confidence is that in a longitudinal study of 10 babies blind from birth, negative reactions to the stranger were manifest in naturalistic observation and elicited in experimental approaches by the stranger. The first manifestations of stranger avoidance and fear emerged in the period seven to fifteen months for 9 of the 10 children. This correspondence to the period of onset in sighted children invites inquiry.

For both sighted and blind children, discrimination of familiar persons and strangers is manifest some weeks or months before the onset of stranger avoidance or stranger anxiety. We have already seen in our discussion of "smiling" and "tactile language" that the blind baby shows differential responses to familiar persons and strangers in the period under six months of age. I should also add—and this is an important bridge to the material that follows—that the blind baby, like the sighted baby, in the period under six months reacted with squirming and discomfort to subtle postural differences when held in the stranger's arms. Ainsworth (1967) describes similar reactions in sighted children during the same period. But this is not yet fear of the stranger; rather, as Benjamin (1963) suggests, it is the experience of something different, something strange.

As the data emerge from the descriptive protocols and films there is nothing in our records for any child under seven months that can yet be classified as "a negative reaction" to the stranger. Reactions to the observer's voice and to being held in the observer's arms were recorded at each visit.

Between seven and fifteen months, we find that something new begins to emerge in the blind baby's behavior toward the stranger—struggling, straining away, crying—which, for the majority of the babies in our sample, occurs when the observer holds the baby. These fear and avoidance behaviors appear even though the observer, a twice-monthly visitor, is not, strictly speaking, a stranger. At the same time that these reactions are manifest in relation to the observer, we have parallel reports from the mothers, showing that fear of strangers has emerged with other visitors to the house as well.

To the stranger's voice only (no touching or holding) we have only one observation of fear reaction during this period. (See Karen's protocols below.) A typical reaction to "voice only" is something we have called "quieting" in response to the stranger's voice, that is, cessation of activity or vocalizing (without signs of distress) which may last for several minutes, or even longer. I should state at the outset that we have not scored "quieting" as a negative reaction. However, among our blind children it regularly precedes the developmental period in which manifest stranger avoidance or fear occurs. Among sighted children, Ainsworth (1967) and others describe "quieting" or "staring" in the period that precedes fear of the stranger.

In addition to "voice only" we tested the reaction of the baby to being held in the observer's arms at each of the twice-monthly visits. The observer employed a modulated approach to the baby, speaking to him both before picking him up and during the period of his being held. The cumulative record for each child was then analyzed, and examples of the first manifestations of negative reactions to the stranger were sorted and credited, first by me, then jointly in senior staffing where we debated criteria. The credited "first examples" were made through staff consensus.

The problem of setting criteria and making judgments was difficult in the case of blind infants. Many of the criteria used in sighted child studies were inapplicable. "Sobering," for example, scored by some investigators as a negative reaction in sighted children, is inapplicable in the case of blind children. There is actually not enough contrast in the facial expressions of blind babies to produce a valid judgment of "sobering." And, since the blind baby's smiles for the stranger are rare, *not* smiling to the stranger has no value in assessment. "Frowning" is not an expressive sign for all of our blind babies, and we have some evidence that when it appears at all, it occurs among those babies who have minimal light perception. But, as an infrequent or atypical sign in our sample, we cannot use "frowning" as a criterion of negative response. In fact, there is a considerable range of expressive facial behavior, normally modulated through visual experience, which is simply not available to the blind child, and the observer judgments regarding "negative reactions" must be made through other signs.

We are left, then, with a limited number of signs in our blind children that can fairly be called "negative reactions" and "fear responses" to the stranger. Vocal displeasure—whimpering, crying, screaming—remains the same for the blind child as for the sighted one. Avoidance and motor resistance to the approach of unfamiliar persons, followed by active seeking of the mother, will also appear in blind children and can be fairly judged as a negative reaction.

The following examples represent in each case the first instance in our records of the appearance of negative reactions to the stranger.

Toni, 0:7:2
Soon after the observer (S.F.) picks her up, she freezes, then bursts into tears. She scans the face of the observer with her fingers, registers increasing distress on her face, strains away from the observer's body, turns her head and trunk as if seeking to locate her mother by voice. She claws at the examiner's arms. She begins to scream loudly. When she is returned to her mother, she settles, still crying, scans her mother's face with her fingers and is gradually comforted.

Carol, 0:8:22
The observer picks up Carol and holds her. Twice Carol strains away from O's shoulder. When O takes Carol's hand in hers to bring it to O's face, Carol's hand closes in a fist.

Jamie, 0:9:12
E.L. is visiting with the team today. Jamie has never met him before. E.L. picks up the baby and begins to talk to him. As soon as he is picked up, Jamie begins to cry. He is handed to his mother, who diverts him with a game and succeeds in comforting him.

There was 1 subject out of 10 who has not given evidence of stranger avoidance during the first eighteen months. It may be worth reporting on this child to complete the picture.

Robbie

Robbie provided one example of "quieting" to the observer's voice and no examples of negative reactions to strangers at any time in the second year. During the second year he allowed our own observers and other unfamiliar persons to hold him and to play with him. We have examples in our hospital waiting room and other unfamiliar places in which his indiscriminate friendliness to strangers is recorded. He is also the one child in our group whose attachment to his mother was regarded by us as unstable, without signs of active seeking of the mother for pleasure or comfort.

If we can accept, then, those differences in testing reactions which were required when we needed to translate procedures for testing sighted infants into procedures for blind infants, there is fair equivalence in the characteristics of stranger anxiety in our blind baby sample and those reported for sighted children.

Toward the Constitution of Mother as Object

During the period eight to fifteen months, then, we have identified a number of discriminating and preferential behaviors in our blind infants which speak for the affective investment in the mother. We can fairly speak of "focused relationships" (Yarrow 1972), and we can see correspondence between these signs of attachment in blind infants and sighted infants. Moreover, these affective signs speak clearly for cognitive advances which are seen in the forms of tactile and auditory discrimination that are implicit in preferential behaviors.

But now, if we examine our data closely, we will also see divergence from the patterns of sighted children during the period eight to fifteen months. In the pages that follow I will try to show that these are related to the unique problem the blind infant has in the constitution of objects.

The sighted child at 7.7 months (on the Escalona-Corman scale) has achieved stage 4. He demonstrates through his behavior toward the screened toy that he has an elementary belief in permanence, that an object that disappears from his visual field has an existence when not perceived. The baby's elementary deduction leads him to remove the screen and recover the object. In this achievement we also discern that the baby's memory for the object that has left his visual field is sustained for the brief interval of this simple test (Wolff 1960). From the experimental work of Saint-Pierre (1962) and Bell (1970), we also know that there is close temporal correspondence between the attribution of permanence to persons and to things. Person permanence normally inaugurates the stage. The advance in conceptual development in the sighted child moves apace with the libidinal investment of the mother. There is, in fact, a remarkable correspondence between the onset of separation protest in the seven-to-twelve-month period and the emerging concept of mother as object (Ainsworth 1967; Yarrow 1972; Fraiberg 1968; 1969).

Now, if we examine our findings on 10 blind infants we will see points of divergence in the characteristics of human attachments which I believe are related to the extraordinary problems for the blind child in the constitution of the mother as object.

When the blind baby at eight months hears his mother's voice at tactile remove from his person, his smile or his vocalizations or his motor excitement will show selective response to her voice but there is no behavior yet that tells us that his mother's voice is united with the very substantial mother whose touch and embrace are familiar to him. If we watch his hands we see that there is not yet an outward reach to her voice, no motor signs in the fingers that speak for touching or grasping. Yet the same baby in his mother's arms must experience her embrace, her distinctive tactile qualities and her voice as a unified experience. The problem, then, for the blind baby is to reconstitute this unified mother of the embrace in another space, at tactile remove, when only one attribute is presented him—her voice.

The sighted child, as early as five months, has a mother with a picture identity; vision has guaranteed that the mother's voice and touch will be united with the picture. The sighted child does not have to reconstitute his mother from her sensory components; the picture gives unity and coherence to all sensory experience of her.

The blind baby at eight months who does not yet reach out to the mother's voice when she is at tactile remove will also show us that he does not yet reach out for a favorite sound toy when he hears it and when it is within easy range of his hands. We have examples from 9 of our 10 children (age range four to eight months) demonstrating that when a cherished toy is sounded close at hand at midline, the blind baby shows alertness and attention, but makes no attempt to reach. It is as if the musical teddy-bear, gently removed from his hands a moment before, is "not the same teddy-bear" when the baby hears the sound alone. The blind baby cannot yet attribute substantiality or a sound-touch identity to the toy through its sound alone. (See Fraiberg 1968 and Fraiberg, Siegel, and Gibson 1966.)

For 10 children, the range for achievement of "midline reach for and attainment of the toy on sound cue only" was 6:18 to 11:1; median age 8:27.

Proximity-seeking Behaviors: The Emergence of the Concept of Mother as Object

Between the ages of ten months and sixteen months our 10 babies demonstrate for the first time proximity-seeking behaviors toward the mother's voice (with mother at tactile remove). This signifies that the mother has acquired a voice-touch identity, that the baby confers substantiality and an elementary form of permanence (Piaget's stage 4) on his mother when only one of her attributes, voice, is given. Our findings are derived entirely from the descriptive protocols and films. No experimental procedures were employed because we could not know in the design stage of the study how a blind baby would find the solution to the problem of proximity seeking. The baby was to teach us.

The protocols for each child were systematically examined and submitted to these criteria:

1 The mother must be at tactile remove from the baby when she is speaking.
2 The baby must manifest through his behavior a concept of mother as substantial and external to the self.

I credited the following: (a) the baby extends his hands directionally in a reach toward mother upon hearing her voice; (b) if mobile, he creeps directionally toward mother upon hearing her voice; (c) if the word "mama" is now in use as a correct referent, he says "mama."

For (a) I credited 5 children; for (b) 4 children; for (c) 1 child. Crediting the first demonstration in the record, the age range for the attainment of these criteria was from 0:10:5 to 16 months; median age, 11:20.

The concept of mother which is demonstrated in these behaviors has some correspondence with stage 4 for the sighted child; an elementary form of permanence for persons has emerged in which the

mother is constituted as an object when only one of her attributes, voice, is given. The extended hands on voice cue, the directional creep toward mother on voice cue, speak for the expectation of a tactile reunion, which is to say that the auditory and tactile schemas for mother are conceptually unified and the previously experienced unified mother of the embrace can be mentally reconstituted as an object in another space.

In this description the reader may experience the same sense of disbelief that I remember in myself earlier in this investigation. To all of us who have worked extensively with sighted children, the gesture of extended hands toward the mother is familiar from the age of five months (Griffiths 1954). Yet it is not until the last quarter of the first year that this gesture appears among our blind children.

I was well advanced in our study when I understood this. It was very simple. The sighted child's extended hands for mother represent exactly his level of prehension. The sighted child at five months reaches for what he sees, grasps what he reaches, and already, through his advance in prehension, has hundreds of lessons every day which unite the tactile, visual, and auditory experiences of both human and inanimate objects. When the sighted child reaches toward his mother he does not need a concept of mother; he only needs to coordinate eye and hand. The blind child must have an elementary concept of permanence of the mother before he can reach directionally toward his mother, or creep directionally toward her. Tragically, this long delay in achieving the coordination of ear and hand for things and for persons has led many observers and examiners of blind infants to label a child as mentally retarded or unaffectionate, whereas we can now see that this achievement gives eloquent testimony of an advance in conceptual development which demands a high level of inference.

There is, then, an expected correspondence between the blind child's achievement of an elementary concept of permanence for persons and for things. However, our findings on "midline reach for the toy on sound cue only" and "proximity-seeking behaviors for the mother" should be interpreted with caution. The ranges cited for "midline reach for the sound toy" are seven to eleven months. For the person data the ranges are ten to sixteen months. Does this mean that the coordination of ear and hand is achieved earlier for toys than for persons? I think not. The discrepancy in age of onset is more likely attributable to the data sources and the criteria employed for scoring.

Firstly, the toy findings are derived mainly from experimental studies, which means of course that we regularly elicited the highest performance available in the child's repertoire. We did not employ experimental procedures for eliciting the baby's proximity-seeking behaviors in response to mother's voice at tactile remove. These data were derived entirely from naturalistic observation. If the behavior was not manifest spontaneously in the observation session, it did not enter the record.

Secondly, the proximity-seeking behaviors toward mother required a higher level of proficiency in localizing sound and the coordination of tactile-auditory schemas than those required in the toy tests, where we tested reach and attainment of the sound toy at midline. To reach *directionally* toward the mother on voice cue corresponds to a higher level of directional reach identified by Edna Adelson in the prehension studies. To creep toward mother when her voice is heard requires an advance in mobility which was not required, of course, in the toy experiments. To utter the word "mama" in meaningful use when mother's voice is heard is on a still higher level of concept development. In brief, my examination of the emerging concept of permanence for mother credited the first example in the record which spoke for a spontaneous demonstration of a concept of mother and in naturalistic circumstance these demonstrations tapped a repertoire of behaviors which were not available to the child in the toy experiments.

This long, and possibly exhausting, narrative of the blind child's attribution of permanence to persons and to things finally brings us to a milestone of momentous import. When the blind baby demonstrates to us his proximity-seeking behaviors toward mother he tells us that the concept of mother as an object is emerging. His level of concept development has close correspondence with that of the sighted child at stage 4. The sighted child who is fully equipped with a picture memory when he sets out on this journey toward an object world has long ago passed the milestone. Our maps tell us that he passed stage 4 at 7:7 months (Escalona-Corman scale), and was already equipped at that age with a functioning locomotor capability, that he raced on to stage 5 at 9:4 and was advancing steadily toward stage 6 at the close of the first year (mean age 17.2).

The blind child, in a world without picture memory, has pursued this route in a dark labyrinth. At the close of the first year he has achieved stage 4. He has also just invented his own mobility (late, by sighted-child norms), and he ventures forth into the void to begin the mapping of distant space. In customary language we can speak of these late achievements as the "developmental lags" of blind infants. But if we follow the blind infant as he pursues this treacherous route in the labyrinth, we can see these accomplishments as heroic adaptive feats.

Separation and Reunion

For sighted children, there is now a fair consensus among investigators that separation protest or distress emerges in the third quarter of the first year. Stayton, Ainsworth and Main (1971), in a report of their longitudinal studies, place the median age of onset of separation distress in a "mother leave room" situation at 22 weeks or 5.5 months. Other studies (Schaffer and Emerson 1964; Tennes and Lampl 1964; and Spitz 1965) give us a range of six to eight months in average age of onset. However, criteria and observational procedures differed among these studies.

Allowing for these differences among several studies, the age of onset of separation protest or anxiety appears to have some correspondence with the emergence of a concept of permanence for the mother (approximately stage 4). This means, of course, that both an affective investment in the mother and a cognitive advance enter into the experience of separation distress. There must be at least an elementary concept of mother as an object before her absence is perceived as loss.

In briefest summary, we see that between the ages of six and eight months there is a confluence of events in the development of the sighted child in which affective, motor and cognitive advances unite in the service of human attachments. Valuation of and preference for mother, established under six months of age, are now given poignancy by the cognitive awareness of loss, and the baby protests even the momentary disappearance of his mother. An advance in motor development permits him to follow his mother and maintain contact with her. An advance in conceptual development confers upon the mother some measure of permanence as an object, but it is still an uncertain belief which binds her to a place, and it requires frequent confirmation or verification through vision. During the next 12 months the sighted baby's experiments, plus a tremendous advance in representational intelligence, will permit him to account for his mother's displacements in space and finally to constitute his mother as an object (stage 6).

For the blind children in our group, the first manifestations of separation protest and distress appear in the age range 10:22 to 1:9:24; median age, 11:20. There is, then, about a 6-month difference between our blind children and sighted children in the age of onset of separation protest. The age of onset of separation protest shows some correspondence with the onset of proximity-seeking behaviors described in the previous section and suggests links with a stage 4 level of person permanence.

In the following pages I propose to examine the onset of separation protest in relation to (a) the blind child's awareness of "absence and presence"; (b) his concept of mother as an object; (c) tracking on sound; and (d) locomotion as experience in learning the displaceability of objects.

For comparison with sighted children we will find it useful to discriminate among the forms of separation protest and the conditions which elicit them, following Ainsworth (1972).

Ainsworth differentiates between anxiety following prolonged separations ("definitive separations") and "separation protest" in minor everyday situations. In her 1972 essay and elsewhere, she agrees with other authors that separation protest is a criterion of considerable value in the assessment of human attachments, but in her view it should not be employed as the only criterion of attachment. When separation protest is present along with other behaviors ("following" when mother leaves the room, active contact behaviors, affectionate behaviors, approach through locomotion and the use of mother as a secure base to explore, flight to mother as a haven of safety, and clinging) Ainsworth feels that the judgment of "attachment" can be fairly made.

As we examine our blind infant data on separation we will use two classifications: "minor everyday" separation and "prolonged" separations. We found, as Ainsworth reports, a close correspondence between the occurrence of protest and/or anxiety in both types of separation.

Our data on the emergence of separation protest in "minor, everyday situations" are derived entirely from naturalistic circumstance. We recorded descriptively all occurrences in which mother left the room for a few moments and described the baby's reactions. Until the close of the first year we have no examples in which the blind baby registered in any discernible way an awareness of mother "not present," except in circumstances where hunger or an interrupted game with mother were antecedent conditions. To fairly approximate the "neutral conditions" which provided the base for sighted-child observations of "separation protest" (in which neither need states nor interrupted play were factors), I chose only those examples in our records in which the baby's state would not introduce other variables. (For example, the baby is occupied with a toy, or is listening attentively to conversation between mother and others in the room, and mother leaves the room for a few moments.)

Our data on reactions to prolonged separations (mother employed for several hours a day; mother absent for several days) are derived from direct observation *and* parent reports, since such details as the child's reactions when mother is in the hospital, or the child's reactions when mother is working often had to be filled in by the care-giver's reports to the mother.

We might begin with a general frame of reference for the examination of the blind child's experience of separation: How does the blind child experience what we know as "mother not present"?

BLINDNESS AND THE EXPERIENCE OF "PRESENCE" AND "ABSENCE"

In the case of the blind infant even the concept of "momentary separation" must be modified and expanded to include a range of experience that may be called "not in contact" and "maintaining contact." It is more difficult in the case of the blind baby to isolate those conditions that mean mother is "absent" in everyday experience. In the case of the sighted child, mother is absent when she is not seen. Vision also permits the sighted child to give meaning to the "goings" and "comings" of his mother, since he can track her with his eyes to the point at which she leaves his visual field (goes to another room, closes a door, and so on).

For the blind child, even when his mother is present in the room, if she is not in physical proximity and refrains from talking or moving, she has left the child's perceptual field. The silencing of mother's voice, however, is not an equivalent in the blind child's experience to the disappearance of the mother for the sighted child. Vision, by its nature, is continuous; visual tracking confers temporal order to events, and a break or closure of the visual record is read as the sign of "gone." Sound, on the other hand, is discontinuous, and for large periods in a blind child's day, things and people do not manifest themselves to him through sound (or touch). Since there is no predictability in events that are experienced through intermittent sound, the breaking or closure of a sound sequence need not by itself connote "separation" or "loss" or "absence."

For these reasons we chose not to define "separation" for the blind baby at the start of our study, but to examine the experiences of "not in contact" and "maintaining contact" with the mother's voice or her person, with the expectation that at certain as yet unknown points in development during the sensorimotor period, the experience of "loss" would be registered in identifiable ways, and the means of perception of loss would be revealed to us.

In the early weeks of life the sighted child maintains contact with the people and the things of his world by fixating on nearby objects and by tracking movement through vision. As recognition memory becomes available to the baby (and he demonstrates this at under three months in the response smile to the configuration of the human face), he scans his environment and can "rediscover" both human and inanimate objects that are momentarily "absent." Repetition of the game of scanning and recovery probably affords a kind of elementary belief in permanence, that things "lost" can be "found" and are somehow at the disposal of vision (Piaget, stages 1–3). Visual tracking of moving objects, both human and inanimate, affords the sighted child the first practical demonstrations that a person or object (sensory picture) located at point A can appear again or be "rediscovered" at points B and at C, D, E, and so on. And long before the child achieves even an elementary notion of causality, visual tracking prepares him for the discoveries at the end of the first year that an object is not bound to place, that it can be subject to multiple displacements (stage 5) and, finally, between thirteen and eighteen months, to the discovery that the displacements of objects can occur independently of his perception of their movements, which then enables him to take account of invisible displacements and to employ an elementary form of deduction regarding an object's probable route (stage 6). At this stage the sighted child conducts a sustained search for a lost object, which testifies to the emergence of

a belief in permanence; the person or the object "must be someplace."

The human partner leads the way to these discoveries, as psychoanalysts and Piaget have shown. The person-object sequences which lead to object permanence have been experimentally worked out by Saint-Pierre (1962) and Bell (1972) and in these reports we see that *person performance normally precedes toy permanence;* that when the search for the not-present mother takes account of her invisible displacements, discoveries leading to belief in the permanence of inanimate objects follow closely in temporal sequence.

For the blind child during most of the first year there is no equivalent for the sighted child's visual scanning or tracking to locate and maintain contact with the mother if she is momentarily out of the child's perceptual field. And where vision guarantees the perception of movement and the "displaceability" of human and inanimate objects, the blind infant cannot attribute movement to objects, or "comings" and "goings," until his own mobility in the second year gives him the experimental conditions for tracking and recovering persons and toys in multiple displacements.

As we have reported in the preceding section of this chapter, acoustical tracking and localization of sound is not achieved by any child in our sample until the last quarter of the first year. And when he reaches directionally for or creeps toward a person or toy on sound cue only, he demonstrates at the same time an emerging concept of permanence, probably on the level of stage 4. The sound "out there" now connotes a person or a toy, and his reach or his locomotor approach signifies that he confers substantiality, a sound-touch unity to the person or object.

This is, I believe, a virtuoso achievement. From all of our evidence, for most of the first year substantiality is affirmed tactually by the blind child. To endow the sound "out there" with meaning, he can employ only one distance sense, hearing, one that was "intended" in the biological program to evolve in synchrony with vision.

This means, of course, that during the first year the awareness and the experience of "mother not present" for the blind child can emerge only under two types of circumstances: In need states, if the cry or signals of distress do not summon her, if there is a delay in answering the signal or satisfying the need, the blind baby may have an acute sense of "loss" or "not present" and when the mother is constituted as an object, at least on the level of stages 4 and 5 (i.e., if her voice and footsteps connote substantiality to the blind child) "presence" and "absence" become open to objective confirmation. Mother is "present" when she manifests herself through voice or sounds of movement and "absent" when she does not. Under all favorable conditions in which the mother has become the central person, the affectively significant person, awareness of "absence" can also evoke protest, distress and anxiety in ways that are entirely analogous to the experience of separation in sighted children.

For both the blind child and the sighted child, then, the manifestations of separation protest and anxiety are linked to the emergence of object permanence, in which the human partner is endowed with objective attributes. If we can employ my provisional crediting of stage 4 to the level of concept development achieved by our blind children at the close of the first year, the emergence of separation protest and anxiety during the same period has close correspondence with sighted-child data which link the emergence of separation anxiety with stage 4.

Next, we should examine the possible relations between the onset of separation protest and the onset of locomotion in our blind group. Creeping was achieved by 9 of our 10 children in the range of ten and a half to sixteen and a half months; free walking in the range of twelve to twenty months. We also describe the relationship between the onset of self-initiated mobility with the coordination of ear and hand. (No child could creep before he first demonstrated reach and attainment of the sound object.) This links locomotion in the blind child to an elementary form of object permanence.

With the onset of locomotion, the blind baby can begin to conduct a large number of experiments which will inform him of the displaceability of human and inanimate objects and he will now be able to use his newly acquired ability to track movement by sound, along with his newly acquired locomotor skills, in a discovery and rediscovery of his mother dozens of times every day. It is even possible that the discovery, in a sense, of his own "displaceability" through locomotion gives some substance to the concept of "movement" which the blind child cannot perceive in any ways that are analogous to the experience of the sighted—that is, as a sequence of pictures. In all these ways, then,

mobility plays a central role in the blind child's construction of an object world, and specifically, in the problem under examination, in constituting the mother as object.

PROLONGED SEPARATIONS

Our next question brings us to an area of this study which is of very great interest. What happens when the blind child's tracking and locomotor pursuit do not lead to a "rediscovery" of mother? In the early examples from Karen's record of momentary separation, we saw distressed crying, even though she was in her own home, and something close to panic when she lost touch with her mother, tried to find her in the kitchen and could not locate her on sound.

It happened that all of our children, in the first half of the second year, experienced prolonged daily separations from mother (mother working part-time was the most frequent reason), and 5 of the children were separated from their mothers for more than 3 days when either child or mother was hospitalized or a crisis required mother to be away from home. In all these cases, an examination of individual protocols showed that *extreme* forms of distress emerged in minor, everyday situations (mother leaving room) during the period that included prolonged daily separations or prolonged day and night separations. It appeared, then, that the anxiety and panic states seen in these children during the second year were forms of anticipatory anxiety in which "mother not present" signaled the danger of losing mother, which had become actual through the experience of prolonged separations.

In 5 cases, where separation of mother and child lasted for 3 or more days, we saw forms of regression and panic states that I have rarely seen in otherwise healthy children who are sighted. (Clinical examples appear in Fraiberg 1968, 1971a.) Day-and-night screaming, inability to be comforted, and loss of newly acquired achievements in language or mobility appeared during the separation, and persisted even after reunion with the mother. But also, with reunion, we saw forms of clinging to mother which were chilling to witness. The child would press himself against his mother's body in a ventral clasp which united every surface with his mother's body. "He plasters himself against me," one mother said in despair as we witnessed this. We saw primitive forms of clawing at the mother's hands, arms, and face, which the parents, quite naturally, thought was hostile. But it happened, more than once that I, too, held a blind baby who was in a panic state, and I experienced the clawing. To me this was not "hostile." It was an archaic form of anxiety, and I felt that the baby was grasping me, clutching me, digging into me, holding on in a desperate terror. The only analogy which comes to mind is the nightmare experience, in which the dreamer is hanging from a cliff, his hands clutching a ledge, his body pressed against vertical rock—with the void below.

All of the children who experienced these traumatic separations recovered, and we provided much help to the families during these critical periods (Fraiberg 1971b).

In only one case do we have no examples of separation distress or anxiety. This was Robbie. It was Robbie also who never showed stranger avoidance in the first year. As late as three years of age we have no examples of separation distress in his own home. He was, at three, very adequate in language, adaptive hand behavior, and motor skills. There was no question that self-and object-differentiation had been achieved at earlier stages, and that his ego organization was appropriate to his age. But, by all criteria known to us, Robbie could be discrimanated from other children in our group as being a child who was not "securely attached" to his mother.

REFERENCES

Ainsworth, M. D. *Infancy in Uganda: infant care and the growth of love.* Baltimore: Johns Hopkins University Press, 1967.

Ambrose, J. A. The development of smiling response in early infancy. In B. M. Foss (Ed.), *Determinants of infant behavior* (Vol. 1). Ondon: Methuen, 1961, pp. 179–201.

Bell, S. J. The development of the concept of object as related to infant-mother attachment. *Child Development,* 1970, *41,* 291–311.

Benjamin, J. D. Further comments on some developmental aspects of anxiety. In H. S. Gaskill (Ed.), *Counterpoint.* New York: International Universities Press, 1963, 121–153.

Emde, R. N., & Koenig, K. L. Neonatal smiling, frowning, and rapid eye movement states: II, sleep-cycle study. *Journal of American Academy of Child Psychiatry,* 1969, *8,* 637–656.

Escalona, S. K., & Corman, H. H. *Albert Einstein scales of sensorimotor development* (unpublished). From the Child Development Project, Albert Einstein College of Medicine.

Fraiberg, S. Parallel and divergent patterns in blind and sighted infants. *Psychoanalytic Study of the Child, 23,* 1968, 264–300.

Fraiberg, S. Libidinal object constancy and mental representation. *Psychoanalytic Study of the Child,* 1969, *24,* 9–47.

Fraiberg, S. Intervention in infancy: a program for blind infants. *Journal of the American Academy of Child Psychiatry,* 1971a, *10,* 381–405.

Fraiberg, S. Separation crisis in two blind children. *Psychoanalytic Study of the Child,* 1971b, *26,* 355–371.

Fraiberg, S. Smiling and stranger reaction in blind infants. In J. Hellmuth (Ed.), *Exceptional Infant* (Vol. 2). New York: Brunner/Mazel, 1971c, 110–127.

Fraiberg, S. The development of human attachments in infants blind from birth. *Merrill-Palmer Quarterly,* 1975, *21,* 315–334.

Fraiberg, S., Siegel, B., & Gibson, R. The role of sound in the search behavior of a blind infant. *Psychoanalytic Study of the Child,* 1966, *21,* 327–357.

Fraiberg, S., Smith, M., & Adelson, E. An educational program for blind infants. *Journal of Special Education,* 1969, *3,* 121–139.

Gewirtz, J. L. The course of infant smiling in four child-rearing environments in Israel. In B. M. Foss (Ed.), *Determinants of infant behavior* (Vol. 3). New York: Wiley, 1965, pp. 205–248.

Griffiths, R. *The abilities of babies: a study in mental measurement.* London: University of London Press, 1954.

Morgan, G. A., & Ricciuti, H. N. Infants' responses to strangers during the first year. In B. M. Foss (Ed.), *Determinants of Infant Behavior* (Vol. 4). London: Methuen, 1969, pp. 253–272.

Piaget, J. *Origins of intelligence.* New York: International Universities Press, 1952.

Polak, P. R., Emde, R. N., & Spitz, R. A. The smiling response to the human face. I. Methodology quantification and natural history: II. Neural discrimination and the onset of depth perception. *Journal of Nervous and Mental Diseases,* 1964, *139,* 103–109; 407–415.

Provence, S., & Lipton, R. C. *Infants in institutions.* New York: International Universities Press, 1962.

Saint Pierre, J. Etude des differences entre la recherche active de la personne humaine et celle de l'objet inanime. Unpublished master's thesis, University of Montreal, 1962.

Schaffer, H. R., & Emerson, P. E. The development of social attachments in infancy. *Monograph of the Society for Research in Child Development,* 1964, no. 94. Chicago: Child Development Publications.

Spitz, R. A. *No and yes: on the genesis of human communication.* New York: International Universities Press, 1957.

Spitz, R. A. *The first year of life.* New York: International Universities Press, 1965.

Spitz, R. A., & Wolf, K. M. The smiling response: a contribution to the ontogenesis of social relations. *Genetic Psychology Monographs,* 1946, *34,* 57–125.

Stayton, D. J., Ainsworth, M. D., & Main, M. B. The development of separation behavior in the first year of life: protest, following, and greeting. Paper presented in part at the biennial meeting of the Society for Research in Child Development, Minneapolis, April 1971.

Tennes, K. H., & Lampl, E. E. Stranger and separation anxiety. *Journal of Nervous and Mental Diseases,* 1964, *139,* 247–254.

Wolff, P. H. The developmental psychologies of Jean Piaget and psychoanalysis. *Psychological Issues Monograph,* 1960, no. 5, (Vol. 2), I. New York: International Universities Press.

Wolff, P. H. Observations on the early development of smiling. In B. M. Foss (Ed.), *Determinants of infant behavior* (Vol. 2). London: Methuen, 1963, pp. 113–138.

Yarrow, L. J. The development of focused relationships during infancy. In J. Hellmuth (Ed.), *Exceptional infant* (Vol. 1). New York: Brunner/Mazel, 1967, pp. 427–442.

Yarrow, L. J. Attachment and dependency: a development perspective. In J. L. Gewirtz (Ed.), *Attachment and dependency.* Washington, D.C.: Winston and Sons, 1972, pp. 81–137.

Reading 10

Self, Other, and Fear: The Reaction of Infants to People[1]

Michael Lewis
Jeanne Brooks-Gunn

The fears of infants is an important area of inquiry, for it sits squarely on the domains of affect, cognitive and social development. The infant's reactions to other persons may be said to have an affective component: fear of strangers may be an index of attachment. Although attachment usually is defined by a positive approach to the mother, as measured by proximal and distal behaviors (Coates, Anderson & Hartup, 1972; Lewis & Ban, 1971), or by separation from the mother as measured by distress (Ainsworth & Bell, 1970; Goldberg & Lewis, 1969; Schaffer & Emerson, 1964), attachment may also be explored by examining the infant's responses to other persons, either when the mother is or is not present.

Fear of the strange may also be related to cognitive development. Indeed, the theoretical work of Hebb (1946, 1949), as well as of Piaget (1952) and others (Schaffer, 1966), has argued for a relationship between fear and novelty. Moreover, there may be a more indirect relationship, such as increased cognitive capacity leading to greater differentiation, thus producing more strange.

While the strange can include objects and events as well as people, most of the work on fear of the strange has involved people. We will only mention in passing that loud noises, in fact, intensity in general, have the possibility of frightening the infant (see Scarr & Salapatek, 1970). It is not our intention to deal with this dimension of stimulus events. As we have stated before (Lewis, 1971) this stimulus dimension adds little to our understanding of the infant's cognitive development since it acts *upon* the infant, and, as James (1895) has stated, the infant's response is an immediate passive sensory response. Rather, we are interested in stimuli that are defined by the interaction of the organism and the stimulus event (novelty and familiarity are examples of such interaction). We shall restrict our discussion further to include only the infant's social world, leaving out the study of nonsocial stimuli.

Fear of strangers or stranger anxiety has been studied, most of the work growing out of the ethological-attachment literature (Ainsworth & Bell, 1970; Schaffer & Emerson, 1964), Fear of strangers usually appears in the second half of the first year and extends, for some, long into the second year. While the ethological-imprinting position would argue for fear of strangers as a way of binding the infant to his caregivers, we recognize, as do Rheingold and Eckerman (1971), that not all infants exhibit fear of strangers. Some infants may show only signs of wariness or differential smiling towards unfamiliar people.

For all the current research on fear in infancy, there has been relatively little effort directed toward

[1]Paper presented at Eastern Psychological Association meetings, Symposoum on *Infants' Fear of the Strange,* Boston, April 1972. This research was supported in part by a Grant from the Spencer Foundation and by the National Institute of Child Health and Human Development, under Research Grant 1 PO1 HDO1762. Thanks are due to Marcia Weinraub and Gina Rhea who helped to formulate the problem and collect the data.

the social dimensions which elicit fear. Thus far, age of onset, number of infants exhibiting fear, and specific fears of animate objects have received the most attention. We are interested in the infant's fearful response to people, that is, it is the dimension of humanness that we wish to study. While humans and masks have been studied, only one study, that of Morgan and Ricciuti (1969), touches upon the dimensions that interest us. In this study a male and female stranger were used, and the data reveal that the infants were more frightened of the male. No information about the strangers was given. We do not know the sizes and shapes of each, but yet the data suggest differential fear as a function of the nature of the social event. It is to this point that our study is directed. More concretely, our current study comes from an observation of an 8-month-old female. We observed that an approach by an adult stranger produced extreme fear. The infant screamed, cried, and tried desperately to escape. How different when a stranger 3 or 4 years old approached her: smiling, cooing, and reaching behavior was then exhibited. Why should this be—they were equally strange? Would this hold for children who were generally fearful? What does this mean for the cognitive functioning of the infant, let alone its significance for any theory of attachment? As a first step, this casual observation had to be repeated and extended.

In this study we were interested in the infants' responses to five different social events: a strange adult male and female of the same physical size, a strange female child 4 years of age, the infant's mother, and the infant itself. Twenty-four infants, 7–19 months old, were each placed in a pleasant room which was carpeted and had a few pieces of furniture and pictures on the wall. Only infants who were first-born or who had siblings over 5 years of age were included; 20 were first-born. The infant was seated in an infant tenda facing a door about 15 feet away. The mother sat next to the child. Each of the three strangers, one at a time, would first knock on the door. The mother would say, "come in," and each would enter at the far end of the room. The stranger slowly walked toward the infant. Having reached the infant, the stranger would touch the infant's hand. Throughout the episode the stranger smiled but did not vocalize. Movements were deliberately slow to avoid eliciting startle responses. After touching the infant, the stranger slowly turned, walked to the door and left the room. The second and third strangers followed the same proce-

dure. There was approximately a 2-minute wait between visits or until the infant was quiet. After the strangers, the mother went to the door and walked toward the infant in the same manner as the strangers. For the infant-itself condition it was necessary for the infant to see itself. A mirror was used, and to avoid the effect of novelty, the mirror did not approach the infant (mirrors do not walk); rather, the infant approached the mirror. To do this, the mother moved the tenda so that it was directly in front of a mirror placed at the opposite end of the room. She slowly moved the tenda toward the mirror so that the infant was able to see his reflection without observing his mother. When the tenda touched the mirror, the mother moved away. The order was balanced for the three-stranger conditions and between the mother and self conditions.

Three behavioral scales—facial expression, vocalization, and motor activity—were used to rate the infants' reactions to the stranger conditions. The checklist (see Appendix) is similar to the one developed by Morgan and Ricciuti (1969). The infants' responses were measured at four distances. Distance 1, the farthest distance, was when the stranger entered; distance 2 (middle) was when the social event was in the middle of the room; distance 3 (close) was when the event was 3 feet from the infant; and distance 4 (touch) was when the event touched the infant. Observer reliability was measured by the proportion of agreements for two observers who were hidden behind a one-way mirror. The mean percentage of agreement across both the facial and motor scales was .90.

The vocalization scale proved worthless in that there was almost no vocalizing, crying, or fretting. The data to be presented are those for the facial and motor scales, the results of which were almost identical.

The mean data for the five social events are shown in Figures 1 & 2. A score of 3 indicates a neutral response, with 1 being the most negative and 5 being the most positive responses possible. This figure is a combination of the two scales. For the facial expression scale this varied from a broad smile to a puckering crylike expression, while for the motor scale this varied from reaching toward the social event to twisting away from the event and reaching to mother.

The data are rather obvious. Affective social differentiation increases with proximity. Thus, there are no affect differences toward the various social

Facial & Motor Responses

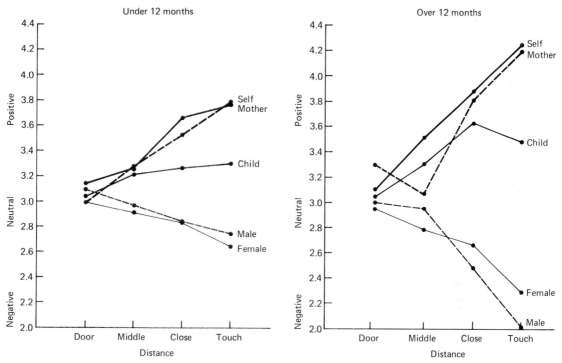

Figure 1 Mean facial and motor responses to the five social events for all infants. A score of 3 indicates a neutral response. Scores less than and more than 3 indicate negative and positive responses respectively.

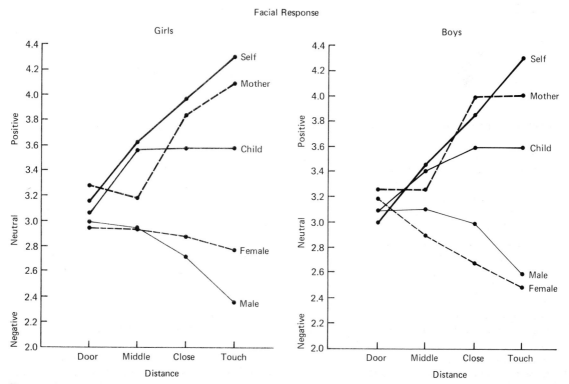

Figure 2 Mean facial responses to the five social events for all infants.

events at the farthest point and affect increases with approach. Social stimuli differ in their effect on the positive and negative affect of the infant. The male and female strangers elicit the most (and only) negative response, while the child stranger elicits a positive response. Moreover, the mother and self elicited the most positive responses. In an analysis of variance with social events and distance as the principal effects, stimulus distance, and stimulus × distance interaction were highly significant ($F = 11.25, p < .001, F = 16.10, p < .001, F = 18.04, p < .001$ respectively).

These findings are consonant with Morgan and Ricciuti's (1969) data and indicate that infants do not exhibit either negative or positive responses until the social event approaches or is in close proximity. This makes good sense since it is a compromise between the need to flee (something strange can hurt) and the need to experience newness in order to alter cognitive structures. The rule might be *stay and attend as long as the event does not get close; if it approaches, withdraw*. Fear and negative affects may be in the service of this escape behavior. Why, though, does the infant not show the positive affect earlier? In order to maintain a parsimonious explanation, we would need to postulate that the intensely positive affects may also interfere with cognitive processes so that they too are only elicited at approach or proximity when social interaction becomes necessary. Of course, a simpler explanation would be related to a time lag notion, wherein the expression of affect, either positive or negative, takes more time. If the social event had waited at the door, would not the same affect have occurred? Morgan and Ricciuti (1969) controlled for this time effect and found it not relevant. On the strength of their results we must reject this hypothesis.

Differentiation of responses to the various social events is also related to age as well as to distance. When the sample is divided by median age, 12 Ss are between 7 and 11.5 months of age and 12 Ss are 12–19 months old. We realize that the small sample size and the arbitrary division of the infants into two age groups limits generalization; however, interesting age differences emerge (see Figure 3). While the patterns for the two age levels are similar, older infants exhibit a greater range of responses than do the younger ones. The older infants are more positive to the self, mother, and child, and are more negative toward the female and male strangers. It is only in amount of negative affect that the two ages

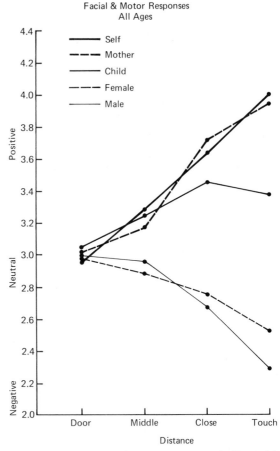

Figure 3 Mean facial and motor responses to the five social events for infants less than and more than 12 months of age.

are significantly different by t-test ($p < .05$ for male plus female strangers) although there is a trend indicating that they also exhibit more positive affect ($p < .10$). It is interesting to note that these age differences are only found when the social event is in close proximity. The greater age and presumably greater cognitive development of the infants more than one year old did not result in prompter affective response. Approach determines the timing, while age affects the intensity of the response.

Age differences in the intensity of fear responses have also been found by others (Morgan & Ricciuti, 1969; Scarr & Salapatek, 1970) and may be influenced by perceptual-cognitive development. However, Scarr and Salapatek (1970) and Schaffer (personal communication) found no relationship either between fear of a female stranger and object permanence (when the age variance was controlled) or between fear of strangers and attention. While these may not be the relevant perceptual cognitive dimensions necessary for eliciting fear, these failures raise the question of what cognitive capacities are relevant to affective responses to social events. While discrimination between familiar and strange is essential, this may be so low a level of cognitive skill that all infants are capable of it and it is not really relevant to the study of the affective responses.

The sex of the infant may be related to the affective response to social events. The negative and positive responses of the boy and girl infants are remarkably similar except for their response to the male stranger. While the infants in general are more frightened of the male stranger, this effect is mostly produced by the girls. It is the girls who seem most frightened by the strange male. This is interesting in light of recent findings in our laboratory (Ban & Lewis, 1971). When one-year-old infants were seen in a playroom with both their mothers and fathers, the girl children appeared to be more reluctant to interact with their fathers than the boys—especially in terms of the distal mode of looking! Although these present results are not significant, they raise the interesting questions of why infants are frightened more of a male stranger and why this is more true of females. No explanation based solely on low levels of paternal interaction as compared to mother's interaction can account for this latter sex difference.

How are we to account for the negative affect directed toward the adult strangers and the positive affect directed toward child stranger and to the mother and self? We would expect fear of the stranger; thus, the negative expression toward the adult strangers comes as no surprise. However, if it is strangeness alone that elicits fear or negative affect, why no fear (in fact, a positive affect) toward the child stranger? This brings into question the whole incongruity hypothesis. Consider the incongruity argument in relation to affect.[2] Briefly, it states that events that are highly incongruent will be those which produce fear, while those that are only partially incongruous will produce little fear. For example, the head of a monkey shown to other monkeys produces extreme fear because of its incongruity (Hebb, 1946). If the judgment of congruity is made with the mother as the referent, then

the strange female is least incongruent, the strange male more so, and the strange female child most. Thus, the child stranger should produce the most fear. In fact, the child stranger produces no fear but positive affect. Incongruity may not be the sole determinant of fear. On the other hand, the mother may not be the only referent for the infant in his observation of social events. Recall that infants also show positive affect to themselves. We will return to this issue of self shortly.

These data also suggest that we reconsider our formulation about the fear of strangers in infants. It now becomes clear that we cannot state that all strange social events that approach infants will elicit the same degree of negative affect. That is, strangeness *per se* is not a sufficient dimension. The social dimensions or space that elicits fear is multidimensional. Strangeness is necessary, but not sufficient. What are the characteristics of the child stranger that *do not* elicit fearful responses? Two appear most likely; the first is size. Clearly, the child stranger is smaller than the adults; also, the child stranger is closer in size to the infant, especially one sitting in a baby tenda. Ethologically it makes sense to postulate that organisms should be more frightened of strange things that are bigger, than of same size or smaller stranger things. Same size or smaller things are less likely or able to hurt. The second dimension is the differential facial configuration between a young child and an adult. Perhaps this is the cue. Observation of the verbal responses of a 12-month-old as she looks through magazines and newspapers containing pictures of adults (these pictures were, of course, miniature) reveals the widely used word "baby" as she points to the figures, suggesting that she was responding to the size of the picture rather than the facial configuration. Whatever the explanation of why the infants were not upset by the child stranger, it is clear that a simple incongruity explanation fails to satisfy the data and that the space of social strangeness is multidimensional, unfamiliar being just one dimension.

The infant's highly positive response to the mother is as we expected; however, the equally positive response to themselves in the mirror is somewhat more interesting. By using the term self we have been making an explicit assumption, one which was quite intentional. There is relatively little information on infants' responses to mirrors, but the anecdotal evidence that does exist all indicates that even at earlier ages there is an intense positive

---

[2]The effect of incongruity on attentive behavior is still being explored. It is important to note that incongruity may produce little attention not because of any cognitive reason but because it produces fear which might result in withdrawal. Gaze aversion is one type of withdrawal.

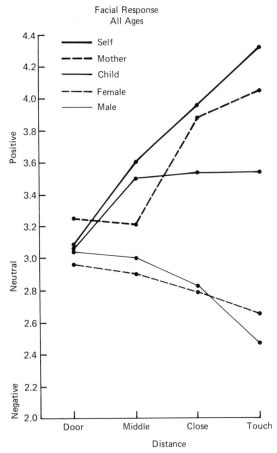

Figure 4 Mean facial responses to the five social events for male and female subjects.

affective response to the mirror. In a recent study of 4-month-olds by Rheingold (1971), further evidence for the positive effect of seeing oneself in the mirror was reported. These infants showed more smiling to a mirror image than to either motion pictures or slides of an infant or to nonsocial stimuli.

Can one talk about the concept of the self at such early ages? Consider two aspects of the self: the first and most common is the categorical self (I am female, or I am intelligent, or I am big or small, or I am capable); the second, and by far the more primitive, is the existential statement "I am." The basic notion of self—probably as differentiated from other (either as object or person, the mother being the most likely other person)—must develop first. There is no reason not to assume that it develops from birth and that even in the early months some notion of self exists. We would argue that this nonevaluative, existential self is developed from the

consistency, regularity, and contingency of the infant's action and outcome in the world. Self is differentiated by reafferent (or information) feedback; for example, each time a certain set of muscles operate (eyes close), it becomes black (cannot see). That is, the immediacy, simultaneity, and regularity of action and outcome produces differentiation and self. The action of touching the hot stove and the immediacy of the pain tells me it's my hand that is on the stove. This self is further reinforced if, when I remove my hand, the pain ceases. The infant's world is full of such relationships and they vary from its own action on objects to its relationship with a caregiver. In these social interactions, the highly directed energy of the caregiver (touch, smile, look, etc.) is contingent and specific to infant action (smile, coo, etc.).

The relationship of self to the mirror is, likewise, related. Looking in the mirror is pleasurable because of the consistency, regularity, and contingency of the viewer's action and the viewed outcome. In no other situation is there such consistent action-outcome pairing. In other words, the mirror experience contains those elements that generally make up the fabric of the infant's growing concept of self. It is not possible for us to know if the infant is aware that the image is himself. Awareness is a difficult concept to study in nonverbal organisms, but it is clear that by the time one-word utterances emerge, such as "self" or "mine," the year-old infant has the concept of self. It is reasonable to assume that the concept existed prior to the utterance. In fact, if we consider the research on the development of object permanence (for example, Charlesworth, 1968), we find that, for the most part, object permanence has been established by 8 months of life, in many cases even earlier. If the infant has the cognition available to preserve memory of objects no longer present, how can we deny them the ability to have self-permanence? Indeed, it is reasonable to talk of object permanence capacity without self-permanence capacity? Given that this first self-other distinction is made very early, the various categorical dimensions of self may also proceed to unfold. The unfolding of the categories, whether sequential, hierarchical, etc., and the dimensions of the various categories are uncertain.

Is our understanding of the phenomenon of fear helped by evoking the concept of self? We would argue, yes. For example, Hebb's (1949, p. 243) study on the fear of monkeys could be explained by this concept. Consider the monkeys were fearful because they saw a monkey without a body and they were aware that they, too, were monkeys. Maybe they too could lose their heads to a mad professor. Would not humans placed in a similar situation show fear for *their* lives or safety?[3] In terms of our data, the notion of self also helps in explaining the data. Perhaps female infants are more frightened than male infants of male adult strangers because, while they are equally strange, the male infant recognizes that the male adult is more like himself. The specific category of self in this case may be gender. The Money, Hampson and Hampson (1957) data on sexual identity suggest that a year-old infant may already possess this category.

That there was a positive response to the child stranger and negative responses to the adult strangers is difficult to explain in any incongruity hypothesis unless we consider that the referent for the social comparison does not always have to be the infant's mother. There could be multiple referents, one of them being the mother, another being the self. Perhaps the positive response to the child stranger is produced because infants find the child like themselves; that is, they use themselves as referent and find the child like them and are therefore not afraid. In this case the categorical dimension of self may have to do with size. I am small vis-à-vis other social events and the child is also small, therefore, like me.[4]

The present data are clear; at least for the social events used, there was significantly different affect elicited as these events approached. The dimensions on which these social events can be ordered are not at all clear. The most likely candidate for the differences between adults and child is size, but since both adults were the same size, the male-female differences cannot be accounted for by this dimension alone. We view this experiment, then, as

a beginning in the study of the dimensions and consequences of social events. Clearly more work is necessary.

In this discussion of fear two major theoretical positions have been evoked, and it would help to clarify the discussion by stating them explicitly. These are the ethological and cognitive approaches. The ethological position rests less (if at all) on a cognitive and more on an imprinting, IRM, instinctual approach. The argument for the present data would be as follows: infant imprinted on parents; all others, strange. Strange at a distance→observe, but do not flee. Strange approach→flee. The only caveat would be that strange has to be bigger than the organism. This model requires the use of no or little cognitive process, and following the ethological approach is rather mechanistic in nature.

The cognitive approach, on the other hand, invokes concepts such as incongruity, novelty and familiarity, and schema. These all rest on the interaction between the organism's past and its present experiences. Moreover, the cognitive approach requires the introduction of such processes as object permanence, at least in terms of remembering the mother. This approach stresses that the child's response to strange is a part of the larger emerging cognitive functions. We would extend this position by considering the concept of self and using it as an additional referent in terms of social interactions and cognitions. While the ethological approach has intrinsic appeal—especially since it evokes a biological simplicity—it is difficult for us to consider infants not responding through the use of elaborate congitive functions which we know are already available to them.

Before concluding this paper, we should like to return to the most interesting of our findings, that of the infant's response to the child. The positive response of the infants to the child stranger is consistent with other primate evidence, all of which suggests that infant-peer interactions may have a special quality. It is well known that infants often follow and learn faster from an older sibling (peer) than from their parents. In fact, peers may serve quite well as adult substitutes in the early attachment relationships (for example, Chamove, 1966; Freud & Dann, 1951). Infants not only show little or no fear toward peers, but, in fact, can engage in a meaningful attachment behavior. We would suggest that these facts have importance for a general theory of interpersonal relationships.

The following speculations are based on these

[3]The Gardners report that in their study of sign language in the chimpanzee, the animal exhibits the concept of self. When shown a mirror Washoe responded with the signs "me Washoe." Thus, it is not unreasonable to attribute the concept of self to other primates.

[4]While there is no direct data to support this, there is a strong suggestion to be found in the data. A correlation matrix was obtained by comparing the children's response consistency across the five social events at the touch distance. As was to be expected, infants who were very fearful of the male stranger were also fearful of the female stranger ($r = .71$, $p < .001$); however, there was no significant relationship between the self and mother ($r = .12$). Thus, while the two strangers were treated alike, the self and mother were not. Moreover, as expected, high negative responses to the adult strangers were associated with more positive responses to both mother and the self; however, they were on the average more than twice as highly associated for the self ($r = -.47$, $p < .05$) than for mother ($r = -.22$).

considerations. Phylogenetically, attachment relationships have changed from infant-peer to infant-adult dyads. Phylogenetically lower organisms attachment behaviors are between peers of the specie. This is especially true if we consider that at the lower end of the scale most information the organism needs for survival is prewired into the system. All that is necessary for the developing species is to practice these skills as they unfold. It would be more logical to practice these skills with someone also somewhat less proficient, for the skills of the adult would be too overwhelming. Moreover, since the adult has little or nothing to teach the infant, there needs to be little attachment to an adult. This would suggest that among birds, for example, the young could be as easily or more easily imprinted on a peer than on an adult member. Whom are the ducklings imprinted on as they swim single file on the pond? The "mother" or the young duckling in front of them? As we proceed along the phylogenetic scale, learning becomes more important for the survival of the organism. As such, peers who are good for practicing present skills are no longer sufficient, and adults who are good in teaching new skills are needed. Thus, attachment on adults rather than peers becomes increasingly important. Single births

and long periods of relative helplessness facilitate the infant-adult relationship; however, the data make clear that if infant-peer relationships can be sustained (as, for example, in laboratory colonies) infant-peer relationships satisfy many of the socioemotional requirements (Harlow & Harlow, 1969; Harlow, Harlow & Suomi, 1971). Its effect on learning, however, should be inhibiting.

The implication for caregiving is vast. We might argue that infant-peer relationships are not substitutes for infant-adult, but rather, are more basic, at least older in a phylogenetic sense. Small families isolated from one another may constitute a rather unique and new experience, not only for the caregivers, but for the infants themselves.

We have come a long way from the observations of the terrified 8-month-old. But we have collected information to indicate that infants of this age are not frightened of young children and often seek and are sustained by their company. In some sense they appear to be attached to all peers, familiar and strange. The social commerce with adults, however, is restricted to those that are familiar, and even then they often prefer their peers. Any theory of interpersonal relationships and fear of social events must come to grips with these facts.

APPENDIX

Scales

	Child				Mother			
	Far	Middle	Close	Touch	Far	Middle	Close	Touch
Facial +2 Smile broad +1 Smile slight 0 Neutral express. −1 Slight frown −2 Puckering, cry								
Motor activity +2 { Reaches to *E* Touches *E* +1 { G.B.M. to *E* Looks at *E* 0 { Inattention Explores room Att. directed away −1 { Neg. express. to *E* Avoids *E* glance Pulls hand away *E* −2 { Attempts to escape *E* Reaches to *M*								

REFERENCES

Ainsworth, M. D. S., & Bell, S. M. Attachment, exploration, and separation: Illustrated by the behavior of one-year-olds in a strange situation. *Child Development,* 1970, *41,* 49–67.

Ban, P., & Lewis, M. Mothers and fathers, girls and boys: Attachment behavior in the one-year-old. Paper presented at Eastern Psychological Association meetings, New York City, April 1971.

Chamove, A. S. The effects of varying infant peer experiences on social behavior in the rhesus monkey. Unpublished M. A. thesis, University of Wisconsin, 1966.

Charlesworth, W. R. Cognition in infancy: Where do we stand in the mid-sixties? *Merrill-Palmer Quarterly,* 1968, *14,* 25–46.

Coates, B., Anderson, E. P., & Hartup, W. W. Interrelations in the attachment behavior of human infants. *Developmental Psychology,* 1972, 6(2), 218–230.

Freud, A., & Dann, S. An experiment in group upbringing. In *The psychoanalytic study of the child, Vol. VI.* New York: International University Press, 1951.

Goldberg, S., & Lewis, M. Play behavior in the year-old infant: Early sex differences. *Child Development,* 1969, *40,* 21–31.

Harlow, H. F., & Harlow, M. K. Effects of various mother-infant relationships on rhesus monkey behaviors. In B. M. Foss (Eds.), *Determinants of inant behavior, Vol. IV.* London: Methuen Press, 1969.

Harlow, H. F., Harlow, M. K., & Suomi, S. J. From thought to therapy: Lessons from a primate laboratory. *American Scientist,* 1971, *59,* 538–549.

Hebb, D. O. On the nature of fear. *Psychological Review,* 1946, *53,* 259–276.

Hebb, D. O. *The organization of behavior.* New York: Wiley, 1949.

James, W. *The principles of psychology.* New York: Dover Publications, 1950 (1895).

Lewis, M. State as an infant-environment interaction: An analysis of mother-infant behavior as a function of sex. Paper presented at the Merrill-Palmer Conference on Research and Teaching of Infant Development, Detroit, February 1971.

Lewis, M., & Ban, S. Stability of attachment behavior: A transformational analysis. Paper presented at Society for Research in Child Development meetings, Symposium on *Attachment: Studies in Stability and Change,* Minneapolis, April 1971.

Money, J., Hampson, J. G., & Hampson, J. L. Imprinting and the establishment of gender role. A.M.A., *Archives of Neurology and Psychology,* 1957, *77,* 333–336.

Morgan, G. A., & Ricciuti, H. N. Infants' responses to strangers during the first year. In B. M. Foss (Ed.), *Determinants of infant behavior,* Vol. IV. London: Methuen Press, 1969.

Piaget, J. *The origins of intelligence in children.* New York: International Universities Press, 1952.

Rheingold, H. L. Some visual determinants of smiling in infants. Unpublished manuscript, University of North Carolina, Chapel Hill, 1971.

Rheingold, H. L., & Eckerman, C. O. Fear of the stranger: A critical examination. Paper presented at Society for Research in Child Development meetings, Minneapolis, April 1971.

Scarr, S., & Salapatek, P. Patterns of fear development during infancy. *Merrill-Palmer Quarterly,* 1970, *16,* 53–90.

Schaffer, H. R. The onset of fear of strangers and the incongruity hypothesis. *Journal of Child Psychology and Psychiatry,* 1966, *7,* 95–106.

Schaffer, H. R., & Emerson, P. E. The development of social attachments in infancy. *Monographs of the Society for Research in Child Development,* 1964, *29* (3, Serial No. 94).

Reading 11

Changing a Frightening Toy into a Pleasant Toy by Allowing the Infant to Control Its Actions

Megan R. Gunnar-VonGnechten

Although the idea that fear in infancy may be a function of the infant's control is not new (Arsenian,

This article is a revised version of a paper presented at the meeting of the Society for Research in Child Development, New Orleans, March 1977. The research was supported by Traineeship Grant MH-12283 from the National Institute for Mental Health. The author wishes to express appreciation to Anne Thompson and Kristie and Kathy Herrera, experimenters and observers in this study. Thanks are also due to Eleanor Maccoby and Daryl Bem for their helpful criticisms of earlier drafts of this article.

1943; Bronson, 1972; Jersild & Holmes, 1935; Rheingold & Eckerman, 1969), its validity has never been clearly demonstrated, nor has it worked its way into the mainstream of theories regarding infant fear. Several studies have indicated that fear reactions increase when limitations are placed on the infant's freedom of movement (Bronson, 1972; Morgan & Ricciuti, 1969). For example, Rheingold and Eckerman (1969) found that 10-month-old infants would explore a strange room without fear if they controlled when they entered and left the room, but would show strong fear reactions if forced to remain alone in the room. However, none of these studies demonstrated that control was the important factor because in each case the infant's freedom of movement was confounded with his/her ability to achieve proximity to his/her mother. This is a serious confound because proximity to the mother itself can reduce fear (Bowlby, 1973).

When control is discussed in regard to fear, it is typically discussed as control over avoiding or terminating the fearful event (Seligman, 1975). Numerous studies conducted with adult and animal subjects have shown that these types of control can reliably reduce fear and stress reactions (Glass & Singer, 1972; Hokanson, DeGood, Forest, & Brittain, 1971; Weiss, 1968). However, there are also some data indicating that control over initiating the occurrence of arousing and potentially frightening events may also affect fear reactions. Steiner, Beer, and Shaffer (1969), using a within-subjects design, gave rats positive brain stimulation for bar pressing. They then gave the same stimulation independent of the rat's actions and found that the rats would actively attempt to escape from the stimulation. Thus, the stimulation was perceived as pleasant when the rat controlled its initiation and aversive when the stimulation was uncontrollable. Furthermore, several studies have shown that positive responses to non-noxious events can be facilitated by allowing the infant to directly control the initiation of the event (Watson & Ramey, 1972; Yarrow, Morgan, Jennings, Gaiter, & Harmon, Note 1).

The following study was conducted to test the hypothesis that a potentially frightening event can be made into a pleasant event merely by giving 1-year-olds direct control over initiating its occurrence. In order to test this hypothesis, two groups of 12-month-old infants were shown a mechanical toy monkey that clapped cymbals together loudly when activated. One group could activate the monkey themselves by hitting a panel. Each hit to the panel caused the monkey to clap the cymbals for 3 sec. A second group served in a yoked, noncontrolling condition, in which the experimenter activated the toy. The monkey was expected to be a frightening toy for the noncontrolling infants and a pleasant toy for the infants who could control its activation.

METHOD

Subjects and Conditions

The subjects were 24 boys and 24 girls, age 12–13 months. Half of the infants of each sex were randomly assigned to a controlling condition, in which they initiated the actions of a mechanical toy monkey by hitting a panel. The other half of the infants were randomly assigned to a yoked, noncontrolling condition, in which they had no control over the toy's activation. The yoking procedure was conducted within sex such that the frequency and pattern of activations generated by a controlling infant determined the pattern of toy activations observed by a noncontrolling infant of the same sex during his/her subsequent test session. From background information obtained at the time of testing, it was determined that all the groups (2 sexes × 2 conditions) were comparable in terms of birth order, length of time walking, number who had colds, and number who were teething.

Procedure

Just prior to participating in the present study all the infants took part in a 10-minute stranger reaction test. The experimenter in the present study served as the stranger. No significant fear of strangers was observed for any of the infants, and there was no indication that group differences in reactions to the toy monkey were related to experiences during this earlier study. Following completion of the stranger episodes, the infants were taken out of the room for 5 minutes while the equipment was set up for the present study. On returning to the room, the mother placed the infant in a low infant seat equipped with a large wooden tray. The tray was bordered in front by a low table. All the infants experienced a brief (2–6 minutes) familiarization period with a pleasant musical merry-go-round toy. This toy was placed in the center of the low table and was just out of the infant's reach.

For the infants in the controlling condition, the familiarization period was used to teach them how to operate the toys by hitting a panel clamped to the upper left-hand corner of the tray. For the first minute with the merry-go-round, the experimenter and the mother demonstrated how the panel worked. Then they both moved back 3 feet from the infant and gave him/her several minutes to demonstrate competence at the task. The criterion for competence was six consecutive directed hits to the panel. Accidental hits with the elbow or arm made while squirming were not counted and were considered to interrupt a chain of directed hits. Once the controlling infant reached criterion, the familiarization period ended. For both sexes the average time to reach criterion was approximately 3.5 minutes, including the first minute of mother and experimenter demonstrations. One infant failed to reach criterion after 6 minutes, and he was dropped from the study.

The infants in the noncontrolling condition experienced a similar sequence of events, with the exception that they did not have the panel and the experimenter turned the merry-go-round on for them approximately every 6 sec. During pretesting we attempted to equate the two groups for the time spent with the merry-go-round. However, we found that doing so often resulted in frustrating or boring the noncontrolling infants, who generally lost interest in the toy fairly quickly. (Recall that the infants could not reach the toy.) Rather than risk producing such emotions prior to showing these infants the monkey, we chose instead to terminate the familiarization period for the noncontrolling infants at the first sign that they were losing interest in looking at the merry-go-round. For both sexes this resulted in an average familiarization period of 2.5 minutes, which was about 1 minute less than that for the controlling infants. Although this minute difference may have affected the results, we are fairly confident it did not because none of the measures of reactions to the monkey was significantly correlated with the amount of time the infants spent with the merry-go-round. In fact, the correlations were all below .22.

Once the familiarization period ended, the merry-go-round was replaced by the cymbal-clapping monkey. For the first 30 sec with the monkey, all the infants remained in the infant seat. Following this they were taken out of the chair by their mothers and stood next to the tray. The mother then moved back away from the infant and the child's reactions were observed for 1 additional minute. The controlling infants were able to activate the monkey both while they were in the chair and while they were out of it. During each controlling infant's tests session, audiotapes were made of their toy activations. Each hit to the panel recorded a click on the tape. The experimenter then listened to these tapes to determine when to activate the toy monkey for the yoked, noncontrolling infants.

Two observers seated behind a one-way mirror recorded the infant's reactions to the monkey using a 6-sec, time-sampling technique. The events noted were fussing and crying, smiling and laughing, looking at the monkey, support looks to the mother (looks that did not include smiles, positive vocalizations, or other indications of pleasure), vocalizations and toy activations. These five events could occur throughout the 1.5-minute test with the monkey, thus for a total of fifteen, 6-sec coding intervals each. Four measures pertained only to the 10 coding intervals, or 1 minute, when the infant was out of the infant seat. These were touching the monkey, touching the mother, being in proximity to the monkey (within 1 foot of the monkey or the panel). The interobserver reliabilities ranged from .80 to .99 using Pearson correlations, with a mean of .94.

If any infant was clearly frightened by the monkey, as indicated by two 6-second coding intervals of full-blown crying, the monkey was removed and the session was terminated early. To account for differences in session length, the frequency of each behavior was calculated as the percentage of coding intervals in which it occurred. The percent scores for each behavior were then analyzed using a 2(sex) $\times$ 2(Conditions) analysis of variance with repeated measures for the conditions factor to take into account the yoking procedure described earlier.

RESULTS

The results showed that the controlling infants did respond more positively to the monkey than did the noncontrolling infants. But, contrary to expectations, only the noncontrolling boys and not the noncontrolling girls were clearly frightened by the toy. Table 1 shows the number of sessions terminated because of strong fear reactions (full-blown

Table 1 Sessions Terminated Because of Full-blown Crying

Group	n	No. terminated	% terminated
Boys			
Noncontrolling	12	9	75
Controlling	12	2	16
Girls			
Noncontrolling	12	2	16
Controlling	12	1	8

crying) in each group. As can be seen, almost all of the sessions had to be terminated for noncontrolling boys, whereas few sessions had to be terminated for the infants in any of the other groups. Furthermore, it was not the case that the infants in the other groups were fussing frequently, but just not crying hard enough for the session to be terminated. This can be seen in Figure 1, which shows the percentage of intervals in which both fussing and crying occurred, with the brackets indicating the .05 confidence intervals around each mean. Negative affect was a function of both control over the toy and the infant's sex, with fussing and crying being significantly greater than zero only for the boys who could not control the toy. For boys, controlling the monkey did change it from a frightening toy to one that was not distressing. For girls the effects of control could not be determined from these data on negative affect because neither group of girls was distressed by the monkey.

For both sexes, however, smiling and laughing at the toy was a function of the infant's control over its actions (see Figure 2). Infants who controlled the monkey's cymbal clapping smiled and laughed more than infants who could not control it. As indicated by the .05 confidence intervals around each mean, smiling was significantly greater than zero only for the infants who could control the toy's actions.

Combining the information on both negative and positive affect, one finds that for boys, controlling the toy changed it from a frightening toy to one that

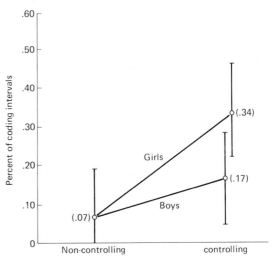

Figure 2 Percentage of intervals in which smiling and laughing occurred. (Brackets indicate .05 confidence intervals around each mean.)

provoked positive affect. For girls, controlling the toy seemed to change it from a toy that provoked neither a significant amount of negative nor positive affect to one that clearly provoked positive emotional responses. We questioned whether the neutral affective reactions of the noncontrolling girls might actually have been an indication of some degree of wariness in the situation. Data on supportive looks toward the mother supported this possibility. For both boys and girls this measure was positively correlated with negative affect, boys $r(23) = +.52, p < .01$; girls $r(23) = +.49, p < .01$. And there was a trend for both sexes of noncontrolling infants to look at their mothers more than controlling infants, $F(1, 22) = 3.52, p < .10$. On the average, noncontrolling infants looked at their mothers during 25% of the coding intervals, as compared to 14% of the intervals for controlling infants.

The measures pertaining only to the time the infants were out of the infant seat presented several problems because these measures could only be obtained for those infants whose sessions were not terminated while they were still in the chair. As might be expected, the greatest loss of cases was for the group of noncontrolling boys. Only 7 of the 12 noncontrolling boys were observed for any length of time while out of the chair, as compared to 11 of the 12 controlling boys and all of the girls in both conditions. Although none of the parametric analyses on the proximity and touching measures yielded any significant differences (perhaps because of the

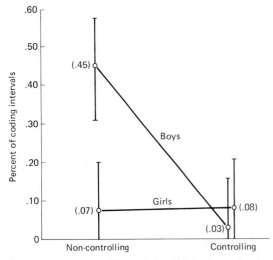

Figure 1 Percentage of intervals in which fussing and crying occurred. (Brackets indicate .05 confidence intervals around each mean.)

reduced sample size and a natural selection for the bolder infants to be observed while out of the chair), nonparametric analyses did yield important differences.

In terms of approaching and touching the monkey, it was noted that although nearly all of the remaining controlling boys did so at least once (9 out of the 11), only 2 of the remaining noncontrolling boys ever approached and touched the toy, $Z = 2.78$, $p < .01$. The number of girls fell somewhere in between, with half of each group touching the toy at least once. In terms of approaching and touching the mother, it was observed that only 27% of the controlling boys ever did so (3 out of 11), as compared to 57% of the noncontrolling boys (4 out of 7). Furthermore, when the reactions of the boys who did not go to their mothers was examined, it was found that two of the three noncontrolling boys had started crying immediately upon being taken out of the chair and had stood crying next to the toy until the session was terminated. This pattern of "freezing" and crying was not observed for any of the controlling boys. The pattern of freezing and crying was observed for one girl in the noncontrolling condition, but in general about half of the girls in each condition approached and touched their mothers during at least one of the coding intervals while they were out of the chair.

Finally, the frequency and pattern of toy activations by the controlling infants was of importance because it both reflected the controlling infants' perceptions of the monkey and, because of the yoking procedure, determined the pattern of activations observed by the noncontrolling infants. These data are shown in Table 2. If the monkey's cymbal clapping had been perceived as aversive by the controlling infants, we might expect that they would not activate the toy more than once or perhaps twice. Although 2 boys and 2 girls showed this

Table 2   Frequency and Pattern of Toy Activations by Controlling Infants

Sex	n	Frequency	Latency to 1st activation	Latency B/W activations[a]
Boys	12	5.25	.92	.90
Girls	12	5.33	1.75	.91

Note. Frequency determined as number of coding intervals (total possible = 15) in which the toy was activated.
[a]This measure was calculated only for the 11 boys and 10 girls who activated the toy more than once.

pattern of activations, on the average both sexes activated the toy during 5 out of the 15 possible coding intervals that it was available, with the .05 t confidence interval ranging from 3 to 7 activations. The pattern of activations also indicated that the cymbal clapping was not aversive to the controlling infants because the latency between activations was quite brief. Furthermore, there were no sex differences in either the frequency or pattern of toy activations generated by the controlling infants, which because of the yoking procedure, meant that there was also no sex difference in toy activations for the noncontrolling infants. Thus, the sex difference in the reactions of the noncontrolling infants cannot be accounted for by any differences in stimulation by the toy.

DISCUSSION

We can conclude that the reactions of 1-year-olds to an arousing event is a function of their control over that event. If they can control it, they respond with positive affect, whereas if they cannot control it, they are fearful, or at least neutral, and perhaps wary. Control, of course, is not the only determinant of their reactions, as indicated by the sex difference observed in the responses of the noncontrolling infants. However, these results clearly indicate that the infant's control, or lack of it, must be taken into account when attempting to predict and explain the infant's fear.

These results also raise several questions, not the least of which is the developmental issue of just when, during the first year, does control become important in regulating fear reactions? Watson and Ramey's (1972) data indicate that as early as 2 months of age, control over initiating actions of a pleasant stimulus event facilitates more positive affective reactions to that event. And, as noted earlier, several studies have indicated that during the latter quarter of the first year, limitations on the infant's freedom of movement in strange situations can facilitate fear reactions. The answer to this developmental question will depend on the mechanisms by which control may operate to reduce fear and facilitate positive affect.

One possibility is that direct control over an event may help the infant assimilate that event and thus reduce its strangeness or discrepancy. During the sensorimotor period, the infant's schemes for events are action schemes, based on how objects or events respond to his/her motor behavior. When the occurrence of a new or strange event clearly depends on the infant's performing of of his/her well-developed action schemes, it may be fairly easy for the infant to assimilate the event to that scheme and thus reduce its discrepancy. Conversely, however, the fear of strangeness may in part reflect the infant's uncertainty or inability to perceive how his/her actions will affect or control the strange object or person, as Kagan, Kearsley, and Zelaro (1975) have recently suggested.

It may also be the case that control operates to reduce fear by increasing the predictability of any given arousing event. In the present study, the infants who could initiate the actions of the monkey were also in a better position to predict when the cymbal clapping would occur than the noncontrolling infants. The possibility that this aspect of control may have played an important role is supported by work with adults and animals, indicating that prediction alone can reduce fear of noxious stimuli (Seligman, 1975).

Control may also reduce fear by allowing the infant to maintain arousal levels within manageable bounds. For example, Waters, Matas, and Sroufe (1975) found that 5–12-month-old infants who were approached by a stranger would often look away from the stranger at the point where the stranger came into close proximity. Using heart rate measures, they found that heart rate increased up to the point at which the infant looked away, at which time there was a significant decrease in arousal. Furthermore, more of the infants who used this controlling action were able to look back at the stranger and engage in positive interactions, whereas more of the infants who did not use this control or avoidance technique increased in arousal and often cried.

As these comments suggest, much more work is needed in order to understand the mechanisms by which control may act to influence the infant's affective reactions. However, the results of the present study clearly indicate that we can no longer discuss the nature of fear in infancy while ignoring the importance of the infant's control over the events he/she encounters.

REFERENCE NOTE

1 Yarrow, L. J., Morgan, G. A., Jennings, K. D., Gaiter, J. L., & Harmon, R. J. *Mastery motivation: A concept in need of measures.* Paper presented at the meeting of the Southeastern Conference on Human Development, Nashville, Tennessee, 1976.

REFERENCES

Arsenian, J. Young children in an insecure situation. *Journal of Abnormal and Social Psychology,* 1943, *38,* 235–249.

Bowlby, J. *Attachment and loss: Separation* (Vol. 2). New York: Basic Books, 1973.

Bronson, G. W. Infant's reactions to unfamiliar persons and novel objects. *Monographs of the Society for Research in Child Development,* 1972, *37*(3, Serial No. 148).

Glass, D. C., & Singer, J. W. *Urban stress: Experiments on noise and social stressors.* New York: Academic Press, 1972.

Hokanson, J. E., DeGood, D. E., Forrest, M. S., & Brittain, T. M. Availability of avoidance behaviors in modulating vascular stress responses. *Journal of Personality and Social Psychology.* 1971, *19,* 60–68.

Jersild, A. T., & Holmes, F. B. Children's fears. *Child Development Monograph,* 1935, *20.*

Kagan, J. Discrepancy, temperament, and infant distress. In M. Lewis & L. Rosenblum (Eds.), *The origins of fear,* New York: Wiley, 1974.

Kagan, J., Kearsley, R. B., & Zelazo, P. R. The emergence of initial apprehension to unfamiliar peers. In M. Lewis & L. Rosenblum (Eds.), *Peer relations and friendships.* New York: Wiley, 1975.

Morgan, G. A., & Ricciuti, H. Infants' responses to strangers during the first year. In B. M. Foss (Ed.), *Determinants of infant behavior* (Vol. 4). New York: Wiley, 1969.

Rheingold, H., & Eckerman, C. The infant's free entry into a new environment. *Journal of Experimental Child Psychology,* 1969, *8,* 271–283.

Seligman, M. *Helplessness: On depression, development and death.* San Francisco: Freeman, 1975.

Steiner, S. S., Beer, B., & Shaffer, M. M. Escape from self-produced rates of brain stimulation. *Science,* 1969, *163,* 90–91.

Waters, E., Matas, L., & Sroufe, A. Infant's reactions to an approaching stranger: Description, validation and functional significance of wariness. *Child Development,* 1975, *46,* 348–356.

Watson, J., & Ramey, C. Reactions to response-contingent stimulation in early infancy. *Merrill-Palmer Quarterly,* 1972, *18,* 219–288.

Weiss, J. M. The effects of coping response on stress. *Journal of Comparative and Physiological Psychology,* 1968, *65,* 251–260.

Reading 12

Reduction of Anxiety in Children Facing Hospitalization and Surgery by Use of Filmed Modeling

Barbara G. Melamed
Lawrence J. Siegel

The literature on hospitalized children suggests that there is a consensus that all children need some kind of psychological preparation for the hospital experience, particularly when accompanied by surgery. The need for such preparation is predicted on the belief that hospitalization and surgery are stressful and anxiety-producing experiences that can lead to transient or long-term psychological disturbances in most children. A number of behavior problems have been observed in children who have been hospitalized for surgery (Chapman, Loeb, & Gibbons, 1956; Gellert, 1958) with estimates for the incidence of these problems ranging from 10% to 35% (Jessner, Blom, & Waldfogel, 1952; Prugh, Staub, Sands, Kirschbaum, & Lenihan, 1953; Schaffer & Callender, 1959). Cassell (1965) reported slight psychological upset in as many as 92% of the hospitalized children studied.

Skipper and Leonard (1968) noted that the hospital experience itself may produce anxiety for the child irrespective of the reason for the hospitalization. In addition to its role in the development of physical and emotional problems, anxiety is of particular interest to the hospital staff because of its influence on the patient's reaction to surgery and its adverse effects on postoperative recovery. Several authors have suggested that preoperative anxiety is a significant factor in impeding recovery from surgery (Dumas, 1963; Giller, 1963; Janis, 1958).

In an attempt to alleviate the stressful effects of hospitalization, several methods of psychological preparation have been utilized. Vernon, Foley, Sipowicz, and Schulman (1965) have suggested that the major purpose of preoperative preparation is to (a) provide information to the child, (b) encourage emotional expression, and (c) establish a trusting relationship with the hospital staff.

The most frequently used method of preparing children for the hospital and surgery is preoperative instruction (Heller, 1967; Mellish, 1969). While a number of different procedures have been used to impart information to the child about the hospital and his operation, they are similar in that they attempt to correct any misinformation that he might have and to help him master the experience by enabling him to anticipate events and procedures and to understand their meaning and purpose.

Puppet therapy (Cassell, 1965) and play therapy (Dimock, 1960; Impallaria, 1955) have also been used as preoperative preparation techniques with children. The child is given the opportunity to act out, draw, or describe the events that he will experience in the hospital. It is believed that such activities permit the child to resolve his fears and concerns with the assistance of a supporting adult.

Several studies have investigated the effectiveness of various methods of preoperative preparation with children (Cassell, 1965; Jackson, Winkley, Faust, & Cermack, 1952; Lende, 1971; Prugh et al., 1953). The results of these studies, however, are equivocal in demonstrating differences between prepared and unprepared subjects on a variety of criterion measures. Most of the measures that purport to measure the child's anxiety are interview questionnaires with the parents or global ratings of the child's response to the treatment procedures. Reliability data on the use of these ratings are not reported. In addition, these investigations suffer from a number of methodological problems that make interpretation of the data difficult. Such factors as previous hospitalizations, age of the child, and prehospitalization personality, which are cited (Vernon et al., 1965) as major determinants of psychological upset, are often uncontrolled.

Recent demonstrations of the therapeutic use of modeling to effectively reduce anxiety-mediated avoidance behavior in children (Bandura, Grusec, & Menlove, 1967; Bandura & Menlove, 1968; Ritter, 1968) suggest that this procedure might also be useful for reducing children's anxiety and fears concerning the hospital and surgery. Vicarious extinction of emotional behavior is typically achieved by exposing the child to a model's approach responses toward a fearful stimulus that does not result in any adverse consequences or that may, in fact, produce positive consequences.

The purpose of this study was to investigate the efficacy of filmed modeling in reducing the emotional reactions of children admitted to the hospital for elective surgery and in facilitating their emotional adjustment during a posthospital period. While several investigations have demonstrated the successful application of therapeutic modeling in alleviating children's fears of dental treatment (Johnson & Machen, 1973; Melamed, Hawes, Heiby, & Glick, 1975; Melamed, Weinstein, Hawes, & Katin-Borland, 1975; White, Akers, Green, & Yates, 1974), there has been only one systematic investigation of this procedure in a hospital setting. Vernon and Bailey (1974) found that children who observed an experimental modeling film exhibited significantly less disruptive and fearful behaviors during induction of anesthesia than a control group that did not observe the modeling film. However, since children in the control group did not observe any film, it is not possible to determine whether the mere act of watching a movie or the content of the movie itself was the critical variable. In addition, the only measure of the film's effectiveness was a "global mood scale" that was used to rate the child's behavior during various phases of the anesthesia-induction procedure.

The current investigation attempts to avoid the methodlological flaws of previous research by controlling for the age, sex, and prior hospitalization history of the subjects. The prehospital personality was assessed through measures of chronic anxiety and behavior maladjustment. The effectiveness of a peer-modeling hospital film in reducing anxiety of the experimental group was compared against a group of children matched in age, sex, and type of surgery who were also exposed to a preadmission film that was not related to the hospitalization. Both groups of children also received preoperative preparation by the hospital staff. Thus the effectiveness of the film was evaluated for its potency above that of procedures already thought to effectively reduce anxiety in these children.

Since anxiety is generally regarded as a multidimensional construct expressing itself in several response classes including physiological, skeletal-muscular, and verbal (cognitive) behavior, a number of dependent measures were used in the present study to assess the children's emotional responses to hospitalization and surgery (Cattell & Scheier, 1961; Lang, 1968). The measures were further selected in order to differentiate between the child's anxiety in specific situations (state anxiety) and his characteristic level of anxiety (trait anxiety) (Cattell & Scheier, 1961; Spielberger, 1966). In addition, these measures were assessed throughout the hospital experience and not just during certain medical procedures. A follow-up assessment of the children was conducted 3–4 weeks after discharge when they returned to the hospital for a postoperative examination by the surgeon.

METHOD

Subjects

The subjects were 60 children between the ages of 4 and 12 years old who were admitted to Rainbow Babies and Children's Hospital, Cleveland, Ohio, for elective surgery. They had no prior history of hospitalization. The subjects were selected from the Division of Pediatric Surgery and were scheduled for either tonsillectomies, hernia, or urinary-genital tract surgery. The length of stay in the hospital for the children ranged from 2 to 3 days.

Thirty matched subjects were assigned to the experimental or control group. Group assignment was conducted in order to counterbalance for age, sex, race, and the type of operation.

Measures of Anxiety

In order to assess the various response classes considered to reflect the multidimensional nature of anxiety, a number of indices of the child's emotional behavior were employed including self-report, behavioral, and physiological measures.

Three measures were used to assess "trait" anxiety, or the long-term effects of the hospital experience. The first measure was the Anxiety scale (Klinedinst, 1971). The 30 items that comprise this scale were rationally derived from the Personality Inventory for Children (Wirt & Broen, 1958). Items on the scale, which the mother rates as true or false about her child, are intended to measure more chronic and stable anxiety.

The Children's Manifest Anxiety Scale (Castaneda, McCandless, & Palermo, 1956) was a second measure of the long-term effects of the hospital experience. The Human Figure Drawing Test (Koppitz, 1968) was the third index of trait anxiety. Koppitz has developed a set of norms for 30 "emotional indicators" that were used to score the subjects' drawings. Average interrater agreement for scoring the drawings, which was computed by

Table 1 Sample Characteristics of the Experimental and Control Groups

Variable	Experi- mental	Control
Age in months		
M	90.4	86.9
SD	26.85	24.97
Sex		
Male	18	19
Female	12	11
Race		
White	23	23
Black	7	7
Type of operation		
Hernia	13	13
Tonsillectomy	4	5
Urinary-genital tract	13	12
No. mothers staying overnight	16	15

dividing the number of agreements of two independent raters by the total number of agreements and disagreements, was 97%.

Situational, or "state," anxiety was assessed by the Palmar Sweat Index, the Hospital Fears Rating Scale, and the Observer Rating Scale of Anxiety.

The Palmar Sweat Index (Johnson & Dabbs, 1967; Thomson & Sutarman, 1953) is a plastic impression method that permits enumeration of active sweat gland activity of the hand. Since the sweat glands of the hand are primarily affected by emotional factors and not other variables such as temperature, the number of active sweat glands provides a measure of transitory physiological arousal. The Palmar Sweat Index was recorded from the index finger of the child's left hand. Rater reliability for two persons independently scoring the same area of the print, as determined by the Pearson product-moment correlation coefficient was .93.

The second measure of situational anxiety was the Hospital Fears Rating Scale. This is a self-report measure comprised of 8 items from the Medical Fears subscale, factor analyzed from the Fear Survey Schedule for Children (Scherer & Nakamura, 1968). Another 8 items with face validity for assessing hospital fears were also included. The Hospital Fears Rating Scale is compromised of these 16 items and 9 nonrelated filler items. Each subject rated his degree of fear for each item on a fear thermometer that ranged from 1 (not afraid at all) to 5 (very afraid). The sum of the ratings on the 16 medical fear items was the subject's score for this measure.

A third measure of situational anxiety was the Observer Rating Scale of Anxiety. This behavioral observation scale was constructed of 29 categories of verbal and skeletal-motor behavior thought to represent behavioral manifestations of anxiety in children. A time sampling procedure was used in which an observer indicated the presence or absence of each response category during three intervals of time in a 9-minute observation period. Examples of items indicative of anxiety include "crying," "trembling hands," "stutters," and "talks about hospital fears, separation from mother, or going home." The frequency of responses observed during the total period of observation was the subject's score on the Observer Rating Scale of Anxiety. Rater reliability was assessed throughout each phase of experimental procedure. Average interrater reliability, which was computed by dividing the number of observer agreements by the total number of categories of behavior that were observed, was 94%.

Procedure

Each subject was asked to report to the hospital 1 hour prior to his scheduled admission time. Upon their arrival, the child and his parents were escorted to a research area of the hospital. The parents and child were separated and taken to adjoining rooms. The parents were questioned to obtain information regarding the child's age and grade, whether he was taking medication, number of previous hospitalizations, whether other siblings had been hospitalized, and whether the mother was planning to remain overnight with the child (the hospital permitted the mother to sleep in the child's room during his stay in the hospital). A consent form was signed by the parents indicating their agreement to have their child participate in a study investigating better methods of preparing children psychologically for hospitalization and surgery.

The mother then completed the Parents' Questionnaire, which asked her to rate 10 statements pertaining to her own anxiety about being a hospital patient, how her child had reacted to past medical procedures, and how she felt her child would respond to the current hospital experience on a 5-point scale. In addition, the mother completed the Behavior Problem Checklist (Peterson, 1961; Peterson, Becker, Shoemaker, Luria, & Hellmer, 1961; Quay & Quay, 1965; Quary & Peterson, Note 1), a 55-item rating scale of behavior problems frequently observed in children. She was instructed to rate the child's behavior during the last 4 weeks. Finally, the mother filled out the Anxiety scale from the Personality Inventory for Children.

The child was taken to a separate room by an experimenter dressed in a white laboratory coat who introduced himself to the child as a doctor. As soon as the child was seated, a second experimenter began observing him with the Observer Rating Scale of Anxiety. The "doctor" placed electrodes on the child's left hand and chest in order to record galvanic skin response and heart rate. The subjects were told that the purpose of the "wires" was to enable the doctor to listen to their heart while they watched a movie. In addition to recording electrophysiological activity, the placement of electrodes provided a sample of behavior with which to measure the subjects' response to an anxiety-evoking situation that closely resembled actual medical procedures encountered by the child in the hospital.

Following the attachment of the electrodes, the doctor left the room to begin the electrophysiological recording. A third experimenter administered the Children's Manifest Anxiety Scale, the Hospital Fears Rating Scale, and the Human Figure Drawing Test. Finally, the Palmar Sweat Index was recorded.

After the measures were completed, the subject was shown the experimental or control film depending on his group assignment. Each film was in the form of an 8-mm cassette that was shown on a Technicolor projector. The experimenter who recorded the behavioral observations left the room prior to the start of the film in order to remain unaware of the treatment condition to which the subject had been assigned. The third experimenter remained in the room with the child during the film.

The experimental film, entitled *Ethan Has an Operation,* depicts a 7-year-old white male who has been hospitalized for a hernia operation. This film, which is 16 minutes in length, consists of 15 scenes showing various events that most children encounter when hospitalized for elective surgery from the time of admission to time of discharge including the child's orientation to the hospital ward and medical personnel such as the surgeon and anesthesiologist; having a blood test and exposure to standard hospital equipment; separation from the mother; and scenes in the operating and recovery rooms. In addition to explanations of the hospital procedures provided by the medical staff, various scenes are narrated by the child, who describes his feelings and concerns that the had at each stage of the hospital experience. Both the child's behavior and verbal remarks exemplify the behavior of a coping model so that while he exhibits some anxiety and appre-

hension, he is able to overcome his initial fears and complete each event in a successful and nonanxious manner. Meichenbaum (1971) has shown that film models who are initially anxious and overcome their anxiety (coping models) result in greater reduction in anxiety than models who exhibit no fear (mastery models).

The subjects in the control group were shown a 12-minute film entitled *Living Things are Everywhere.* The control film was similar in interest value to the experimental film in maintaining the children's attention but was unrelated in content to hospitalization. It presents the experiences of a white preadolescent male who is followed on a nature trip in the country.

Immediately following the experimental or control film, the second experimenter returned to the room to observe the subject with the Observer Rating Scale of Anxiety. The Palmar Sweat Index was recorded, and the Hospital Fears Rating Scale was readministered.

Following the postfilm assessment, the child and his parents were escorted to the hospital lobby. The child was formally admitted to the hospital in the usual manner and taken to the surgical ward.

Later in the afternoon, both the experimental and control subjects were given preoperative instruction by the hospital staff, a standard procedure at the pediatric hospital. This instruction involved a nurse who explained to the child, through pictures and demonstration, what would happen to him the day of surgery, including the things he would observe and experience. The child was also visited by the surgeon and/or anesthesiologist who explained to the child and his parents what his operation would involved, what he would see in the operating room, and the method of anesthesia that would be used. A preoperative teaching communication sheet was completed by the nurse in order to provide a record of the kind of information given to the child to insure that all subjects received similar preoperative instructions.

The subject's level of anxiety was again assessed the evening before he was scheduled for surgery and after preoperative instructions had been completed. Observations of the child with the Observer Rating Scale of Anxiety were made in the child's hospital room while the following took place: first, the child's Palmar Sweat Index was recorded; then Hospital Fears Rating Scale was readministered, a game about hospitalization and surgery called "operation" was played with all subjects. All children were premedicated with Seconal and Atropine. A xylocaine patch was routinely placed on the hand for intravenous induction.

All subjects returned to the hospital for a postoperative physical examination by the surgeon. A follow-up assessment of the child was made at this time. The follow-up session was 20–26 days after the child had been discharged from the hospital. The parents and child were asked to report to the hospital 15 minutes prior to the appointment with the surgeon. After the parents and child were separated, the mother again completed the Anxiety scale from the Personality Inventory for Children and the Behavior Problem Checklist. She was instructed to rate the child's behavior since he left the hospital.

The child was observed with the Observer Rating Scale of Anxiety. Following measurement of the Palmar Sweat Index, the subject was readministered the Children's Manifest Anxiety Scale, the Hospital Fears Rating Scale, and the Human Figure Drawing Test. After all of the measures were completed, the subject was taken to the surgeon's office for his appointment.

Design

A mixed design was employed to evaluate the results of the between-subjects variable and the within-subjects variable. The type of film was the between-subjects variable, with matched groups of children receiving either the hospital-relevant film or an unrelated control film. The within-subjects variable was the time of measurement. Situational measures of anxiety were assessed at four points: prefilm—as the subject was being hooked up to the polygraph; postfilm—immediately after the film viewing was completed; preoperative—the night before surgery (after all preoperative preparation had been concluded a game called operation was played with the child in an attempt to elicit his concern about the impending surgery); postoperative—immediately prior to the surgeon's follow-up examination when the child returned to the hospital 3–4 weeks after discharge. The measures of chronic anxiety and the Behavior Problems Checklist were obtained at the prefilm and postoperative assessments.

The variation in the routine time of preparing the child and the use of premedication immediately prior to surgery made assessment during preoperative medical procedures and the morning of surgery

impractical. Also, since the child was discharged prior to full recovery from anesthesia and pain medication, the effect of immediate recovery from the operation was obtained on a global postoperative recovery questionnaire.

RESULTS

The state measures of anxiety consistently reflected differences between the experimental and control groups. Differences between groups were also found on the prehospitalization to posthospitalization parental ratings of the child's behavior. Measures of trait anxiety did not demonstrate a significant effect of the treatment conditions.

Trait Anxiety Measures

There were no significant differences between prefilm and postoperative assessments between the experimental and control groups on the Children's Manifest Anxiety Scale, the Anxiety Scale of the Personality Inventory for Children, or the Human Figure Drawing Score for anxiety. Because of the wide range of ages, the data were reanalyzed with sex and age taken into account. The children were divided into two age groups defined as younger than 7 years or 7 and older.

The Children's Manifest Anxiety Scale revealed a significant effect of age, $F(1, 52) = 8.39, p < .005$, with the younger children having higher scores on the measure. The significant Sex $\times$ Age $\times$ Time interaction, $F(1, 52) = 4.54, p < .04$, further revealed that young females reported more anxiety on this measure following hospitalization, whereas older females become slightly less anxious. Males reported slightly less anxiety after the hospital experience for both age groups.

On the Anxiety Scale of the Personality Inventory for Children, the main effect of the film condition was significant, $F(1, 52) = 6.21, p < .02$. The mean anxiety rating for the group that viewed the hospital film (5.75) was significantly lower than that of the control group (8.02). The Sex $\times$ Type of Film interaction, $F(1, 52) = 5.08, p < .03$, further revealed that females had significantly lower anxiety scores in the experimental (hospital film) than in the control (unrelated film) group. The difference between conditions was not significant for the males. There was no significant Sex $\times$ Film $\times$ Time of Measurement interaction.

There were no significant differences found with

the Human Figure Drawing Task even when age and sex were evaluated.

Behavior Problems Checklist and Parent Questionnaire

There was a significant Film × Time of Measurement interaction, $F(1, 58) = 5.05, p < .03$. Subsequent t tests revealed that the children in the control group showed a significant increase in the degree of behavior problems from the prehospital to postoperative periods, $t(29) = 2.23, p < .05$. These children showed a mean rating of 10.63 prior to the hospital experience and a mean rating of 12.5 at the postoperative assessment. The experimental subjects did not show any significant increase or decrease in behavior problems across the two assessments. When the data were further evaluated for sex and age, the Film × Time interaction remained significant, $F(1, 52) = 4.4, p < .03$. The significant Age × Sex × Film interaction, $F(1, 52) = 9.13, p < .004$, revealed that the younger females and older males exhibited the most behavior problems in the experimental group, whereas older females had the highest number of behavior problems in the control condition. The Behavior Problem Checklist score (postoperative) correlated significantly with the Anxiety scale of the Personality Inventory for Children ($r = .446, p < .02$). Although there were no group differences, $t(58) = .67, p < .20$, of initial statement of parental anxiety, the Parents' questionnaire, a measure of parental concern, correlated significantly with the Behavior Problem Checklist (postoperative $r = .36, p < .05$).

Situational "State" Anxiety Measures

There were no initial differences between groups for either the Palmar Sweat Index or the Observer Rating Scale for Anxiety. Repeated measures analysis of variance were used to assess the main effect of type of film and the effect of time of measurement and the interactions between these two variables. Since there were group differences on the initial self-report ratings of anxiety on the Hospital Fears Rating Scale, a covariance analysis was employed with this dependent measure. Neuman-Keuls analyses were performed to reveal differences between group means.

Palmar Sweat Index Figure 1 illustrates the significant Film × Time of Measurement interaction, $F(3, 174) = 12.72, p < .0001$. The groups were

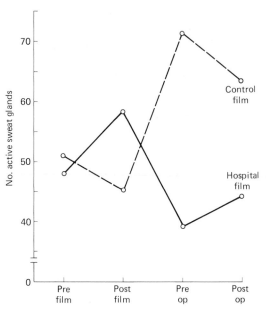

Figure 1 Number of active sweat glands for the experimental and control groups across the four measurement periods.

significantly different the night before surgery (preoperative, $p < .01$) and at the postoperative examination ($p < .05$). The children who viewed the hospital film (experimental group) showed lower levels of sweat gland activity than those who had been exposed to an unrelated control film. Looking at the within-group differences for this same interaction, a Neuman-Keuls analysis revealed that the children who viewed the hospital film showed a significant increase ($p < .05$) in sympathetic arousal (Palmar Sweat Index) from the prefilm to postfilm assessment. However, the experimental group also showed a significant decrease ($p < .01$) in arousal from postfilm to the preoperative assessment. The significant decrease was maintained from the postfilm to the postoperative assessment ($p < .05$).

The control group (unrelated film) on the other hand, showed significant increases in physiological arousal on this measure from prefilm to postoperative assessment ($p < .01$). The means within the control group were also significant (with increased palmar sweating) when the comparisons between prefilm and postoperative assessment ($p < .05$) and postfilm and postoperative assessment ($p < .01$) were examined. When the analysis was made to investigate age and sex variables, the Film × Time interaction remained significant, $F(3, 156) = 14.48$, $p < .00001$, despite a significant Sex × Age interaction, $F(1, 52) = 5.28, p < .02$. Older males exhibited more overall arousal than younger males ($p < .01$), while younger females displayed more arousal than older females ($p < .01$).

Hospital Fears Rating Scale　Figure 2 illustrates the significant Film × Time interaction, $F(2, 115) = 4.74$, $p < .05$, that resulted when a covariance analysis was performed on this scale to statistically control for the initial difference that existed between groups. The control group had a higher fear rating than the experimental group at all assessment times. Statistical significance was achieved at the preoperative ($p < .01$) and postoperative ($p < .01$) measurement across groups. The self-report measure did not yield significant within-group effects across measurement times. There was a significant effect of age, $F(1, 52) = 4.47$, $p < .04$, with the younger children reporting greater fear regardless of film condition. This, however, did not change the significant interaction described above.

Observer Rating Scale of Anxiety　The significant differences in the frequency of observer-rated verbal and nonverbal anxiety responses that resulted between groups across the times of measurement is illustrated by Figure 3, for the Film × Time interaction, $F(3, 174) = 3.33$, $p < .02$. The groups did not differ from each other at prefilm or postfilm assessments. The group that viewed the hospital film exhibited significantly fewer $p < .05$) anxiety-related behaviors than the control group at both the preoperative and postoperative assessments.

In further evaluating the Film × Time interaction by examining the changes within each group on subsequent measurement trials, it was revealed that the experimental subjects showed a significant reduction in this measure of anxiety from both prefilm ($p < .01$) and postfilm ($p < .01$) to the preoperative measurement. There was also a significant reduction on this scale for the comparison of prefilm to postoperative assessment ($p < .05$). It should be noted that although the prefilm to postoperative assessment showed a reduction, there was a significant increase in anxiety-related responses from preoperative to postoperative assessment: ($p < .05$). Both the experimental and control groups showed a significant increase in anxiety-related behavior from preoperative to postoperative assessment ($p < .05$). It is interesting to note, however, that the experimental group evidenced a significant reduction in observed anxiety from the prefilm to postoperative

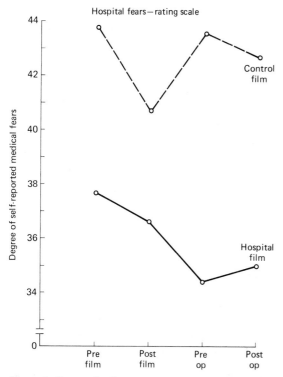

Figure 2　Degree of self-reported medical fears for the experimental and control groups across the four measurement periods.

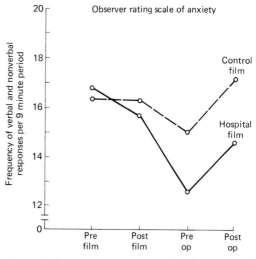

Figure 3　Frequency of observer-rated verbal and nonverbal anxiety responses for the experimental and control groups across the four measurement periods.

assessment period ($p < .05$), whereas there was no significant reduction in anxiety for the control group. There was no significant effect of age or sex on this dependent measure.

DISCUSSION

The efficacy of preoperative preparation using a film of a child undergoing hospitalization for surgery was demonstrated on all measures of transitory, situational anxiety. The experimental subjects who had viewed the hospital peer-modeling film showed lower sweat gland activity, fewer self-reported medical concerns, and fewer anxiety-related behaviors than the control subjects at both the preoperative and postoperative assessments. Since pretreatment assessment revealed that the experimental and control groups were relatively equivalent on the dependent variables, including group characteristics, any differences between groups can be attributed to the treatment conditions that were provided.

The preoperative assessment that took place the night before surgery, and only after all of the children received the typical preoperative counseling and demonstration procedures, reflected the success of the film in reducing anticipatory and situational anxiety beyond that of the staff's efforts. In fact, there was no significant reduction in anxiety for children receiving hospital-initiated preparation. The maintenance of these group differences at the postoperative examination, 3–4 weeks following discharge, further supports the need for more preparation than is ordinarily received once the child is in the hospital.

The 4-week posthospital examination by the surgeon also provided a test of generalization of the film's effectiveness since it presented the child with a similar anticipatory stressful situation that was not specifically depicted in the hospital film. Group differences were maintained on all measures of situational anxiety. Furthermore, experimental subjects showed a significant reduction in anxiety-related behaviors as compared with their initial (prefilm) hospital experience. This would support generalization of the film's effectiveness. There was, however, a significant increment in behaviorally rated anxiety in both groups from the preoperative to postoperative assessments and a trend toward a similar increase, although not significant, in self-reported medical fears and physiological arousal, for the experimental group during the same mea-

surement period. These results may reflect the greater potency of the film under the arousal condition that was present during the initial hospitalization. Another interpretation is that the content of the film, which is specific to procedures during hospitalization, may be a major influence in the reduction of anxiety since the film did not show the child what to expect at the follow-up visit with the surgeon. Finally, the time delay between the viewing of the film and the stress condition (postoperative follow-up) may have attenuated the generalization effects that were obtained.

The specific components that made the film effective will be explored in further parametric investigation. Perhaps the film oriented the child to the hospital procedures, therefore making later preparation more meaningful. Whether the use of a peer coping model enhanced the film's effectiveness must be investigated using appropriate control groups. For instance, one may question whether the film merely familiarized the child with the experiences he would most likely encounter. An experiment comparing peer model, adult model, and demonstration-no-model conditions should be undertaken.

Although the use of the film alone was not possible in the present investigation because of the ethical considerations involved in denying a child preoperative preparation, the research is being replicated in a hospital in which staff-patient ratio does not allow for preoperative preparation. Thus the effectiveness of this film with children who have already been hospitalized needs to be investigated. It would seem that children with one or more hospital experiences may differ sufficiently from the subjects employed in this study since one cannot automatically assume that the film will be equally effective with children having a prior history of hospitalization for surgery.

The increase in arousal level, as measured by the Palmar Sweat Index, for the experimental group from prefilm to postfilm lends some support for the contention of Janis (1958) that a moderate amount of arousal may facilitate response to stress in those facing impending surgery. Therefore, another variable of interest would be the time of presentation of the hospital film. In the present investigation, the children seeing the film immediately prior to admission to the hospital showed an initial increase in arousal. However, their scores on this somatic index as well as the behavioral and self-report measures of situational anxiety decreased from the initial level throughout their hospital and posthospital experiences. Similar results are reported by Florell (1971), who found an increase in transitory anxiety in hospitalized patients immediately following treatment (emotional support and information about the hospital routine) and a decrease in anxiety following surgery, as compared with a control group who exhibited higher transitory anxiety scores after surgery. Schachter and Singer (1962) and Bandur and Rosenthal (1966) provided data that are particularly relevant to the present discussion. They found that moderate levels of physiological and emotional arousal increased imitation of a model's behavior by an observer. Taken together, these results suggest that a particular level of arousal may enhance the modeling effect, and in the case of the present investigation, it may further facilitate attention to the instructions and demonstrations provided by the hospital staff the day before surgery.

One shortcoming of the current investigation was the failure to assess the children's degree of anxiety during actual medical procedures, such as the blood test, the surgeon's examination, etc. However, the time at which these procedures took place was quite variable. In addition, the analysis would not clearly show the effectiveness of the film manipulation since the preoperative teaching by the hospital staff took place throughout the day of admission.

The measures of trait anxiety did not demonstrate a significant effect of the film manipulation. These findings are not surprising in view of the definition of trait anxiety as a stable consistent characteristic of the individual. These results are consistent with Kaplan and Hafner (1959), who found no changes on subjects' scores on the Children's Manifest Anxiety Scale during their hospitalization for surgery. Spielberger, Auerbach, Wadsworth, Dunn, and Taulbee (1973) and Auerbach (1973), using the State-Trait Anxiety Inventory, provided further data indicating the stability of trait measures of anxiety (A-Trait) with hospitalized surgical patients. A-State scores, however, were found to change from presurgery to postsurgery assessments and again during the posthospitalization period.

When the variance due to age and sex was examined in additional analyses of variances, some interesting facts were revealed. Younger children reported higher anxiety on the measure of children's manifest anxiety. Younger females in particular appeared to be more vulnerable to the hospital experience since they reported increased anxiety on this measure at the postoperative examination.

When sex is also significant as a factor contributing to the variance on the Anxiety scale of the Personality Inventory for Children, it was found that lower scores for females on anxiety did occur in the experimental group. Therefore, viewing a male model did not hinder the effectiveness of this film manipulation.

It is interesting that the parents' report of behavior problems occurring 4 weeks following discharge does correspond with how the children reacted to stress during their hospitalization. The children in the control group had an increase in behavior problems during the 3–4 week posthospitalization period before they returned to the hospital for their postoperative examination by the surgeon. They also showed a higher physiological arousal, greater concern about medical fears, and increased anxiety-related behaviors the night prior to surgery and at the follow-up examination. This again supports the contention that in order to avoid posthospital traumatization as observed in psychological disturbances, extensive preoperative preparation is essential.

The use of a multidimensional approach to the measurement of the anxiety proved valuable in understanding the relationships and changes between subjective (self-report), physiological, and behavioral subsystems of human fear response. At least for this sample of children between the ages of 4 and 12, the self-report measure of hospital fears was least sensitive to changes in response at various times during and after hospitalization.

The implications of the research for the measurement and alteration of the stress reaction of normal children to hospitalization and surgery are numerous. The film *Ethan Has an Operation,* which demonstrates a child going through the experiences of being hospitalized for an operation, was more effective in alleviating anxiety than simple verbal, pictorial, or actual demonstration of hospital procedures by the concerned staff. The need for a multidimensional approach to the evaluation of children's responses to stress is supported in view of the differences reflected by trait and state measures of anxiety, as well as between the measures of situational anxiety.

REFERENCE NOTE

1 Quay, H. C., and Peterson, D. R. *Manual for the Behavior Problem Checklist.* Unpublished manuscript, University of Illinois, 1967.

REFERENCES

Auerbach, S. M. Trait-state anxiety and adjustment to surgery. *Journal of Consulting and Clinical Psychology,* 1973, *40,* 264–271.

Bandura, A., Grusec, J. E., & Menlove, F. L. Vicarious extinction of avoidance behaviors. *Journal of Personality and Social Psychology,* 1967, *5,* 16–23.

Bandura, A., & Menlove, F. L. Factors determining vicarious extinction of avoidance behavior through symbolic modeling. *Journal of Personality and Social Psychology,* 1968, *8,* 99–108.

Bandura, A., & Rosenthal, T. L. Vicarious classical conditioning as a function of arousal level. *Journal of Personality and Social Psychology,* 1966, *3,* 54–62.

Cassell, S. Effects of brief puppet therapy upon the emotional responses of children undergoing cardiac catheterization. *Journal of Consulting Psychology,* 1965, *29,* 1–8.

Castaneda, A., McCandless, B. R., & Palermo, D. S. The children's form of the Manifest Anxiety Scale. *Child Development,* 1956, *27,* 317–326.

Cattell, R. B., & Scheier, I. H. *The meaning and measurement of neutroticism and anxiety.* New York: Ronald Press, 1961.

Chapman, A. H., Loeb, D. G., & Gibbons, M. J. Psychiatric aspects of hospitalization of children. *Archives of Pediatrics,* 1956, *73,* 77–88.

Dimock, H. G. *The child in hospital: A study of his emotional and social well-being.* Philadelphia: Davis, 1960.

Dumas, R. G. Psychological preparation for surgery. *American Journal of Nursing,* 1963, *63,* 52–55.

Florell, J. Crisis intervention in orthopedic surgery. (Doctoral dissertation, Northwestern University, 1971). *Dissertation Abstracts International,* 1971, *32,* 3633B. (University Microfilms No. 71–30799, 204).

Gellert, E. Reducing the emotional stress of hospitalization for children. *American Journal of Occupational Therapy,* 1958, *12,* 125–129.

Giller, D. W. Some psychological factors in recovery from surgery. *Hospital Topics,* 1963, *41,* 83–85.

Heller, J. A. *The hospitalized child and his family.* Baltimore: Johns Hopkins Press, 1967.

Impallaria, C. The contribution of social group work: The hospitalized child. *American Journal of Orthopsychiatry,* 1955, *55,* 293–318.

Jackson, K., Winkley, R., Faust, O. A., & Cermack, E. The problem of emotional trauma in the hospital treatment of children. *Journal of the American Medical Association,* 1952, *149,* 1536–1538.

Janis, I. L. *Psychological stress.* New York: Wiley, 1958.

Jessner, L., Blom, G. E., & Waldfogel, S. Emotional implications of tonsillectomy and adenoidectomy in children. In R. S. Eisslen (Ed.), *The psychoanalytic study of the child.* New York: International Universities Press, 1952.

Johnson, R., & Dabbs, J. M. Enumeration of active sweat glands: A simple physiological indicator of psychological changes. *Nursing Research,* 1967, *16,* 273–276.

Johnson, R., & Machen, J. B. Behavior modification techniques and maternal anxiety. *Journal of Dentistry for Children,* 1973, *40,* 272–276.

Kaplan, A. M., & Hagner, A. J. Manifest anxiety in hospitalized children. *Journal of Clinical Psychology, 1959, 15,* 301–302.

Klinedinst, J. K. *Relationship between Minnesota Multiphasic Personality Inventory and Personality Inventory of Children data from mothers of disturbed children.* (Doctoral dissertation, University of Minnesota, 1971). *Dissertation Abstracts International,* 1971, *32,* 4860B. (University Microfilms No. 72–05545, 116).

Koppitz, E. M. *Psychological evaluation of children's human figure drawings.* New York: Grune & Stratton, 1968.

Lang, P. J. Fear reduction and fear behavior: Problems in treating a construct. In J. M. Shlien (Ed.), *Research in psychotherapy* (Vol 3). 1968.

Lende, E. W. *The effect of preparation on children's response to tonsillectomy and adenoidectomy surgery.* (Doctoral dissertation, University of Cincinnati, 1971) *Dissertation Abstracts International,* 1971, *32,* 3642B. (University Microfilms No. 72–01440, 95).

Meichenbaum, D. Examination of model characteristics in reducing avoidance behavior. *Journal of Personality and Social Psychology,* 1971, *17,* 298–307.

Melamed, B. G., Hawes, R. R., Heiby, E., Glick, J. The use of filmed modeling to reduce uncooperative behavior of children during dental treatment. *Journal of Dental Research,* 1975, *54,* 797–801.

Melamed, B. G., Weinstein, D. Hawes, R., & Katin-Borland, M. Reduction of fear-related dental management problems using filmed modeling. *Journal of the American Dental Association,* 1975, *90,* 822–826.

Mellish, R. W. Preparation of a child for hospitalization and surgery. *Pediatric Clinics of North America,* 1969, *16,* 543–553.

Peterson, D. R., Becker, W. C., Shoemaker, D. J., Luria, Z., & Hellmer, L. A. Child behavior problems and parental attitudes. *Child Development,* 1961, *32,* 151–162.

Prugh, D. G., Staub, E., Sands, H. H., Kirschbaum, R. M. & Lenihan, E. A. A study of the emotional reactions of children and families to hospitalization and illness. *American Journal of Orthopsyciatry,* 1953, *23,* 70–106.

Quay, H. C., & Quay, L. C. Behavior problems in early adolescence. *Child Development,* 1965, *36,* 215–220.

Ritter, B. The group desensitization of children's snake phobias using vicarious and contact desensitization procedures. *Behaviour Research and Therapy,* 1968, *6,* 1–6.

Schachter, S., & Singer, J. E. Cognitive, social, and physiological determinants of emotional state. *Psychological Review,* 1962, *69,* 379–399.

Schaffer, H. R., & Callender, W. H. Psychological effects of hospitalization in infancy. *Pediatrics*, 1959, *24*, 528–539.

Scherer, M. W., & Nakamura, C. Y. A fear survey schedule for children (FSS-FC): A factor analytic comparison with manifest anxiety (CMAS). *Behaviour Research and Therapy*, 1968, 173–182.

Skipper, J., & Leonard, R. Children, stress, and hospitalization: A field experiment. *Journal of Health and Social Behavior*, 1968, *9*, 275–287.

Spielberger, C. D. Theory and research on anxiety. In C. D. Spielberger (Ed.), *Anxiety and behavior*. New York: Academic Press, 1966.

Spielberger, C. D., Auerbach, S. M., Wadsworth, A. P., Dunn, T. M., & Taulbee, E. W. Emotional reactions to surgery. *Journal of Consulting and Clinical Psychology*, 1973, *40*, 33–38.

Thomson, M. L., & Sutarman. The identification and enumeration of active sweat glands in man from plastic impressions of the skin. *Transactions of the Royal Society of Tropical Medicine and Hygiene*, 1953, *47*, 412–417.

Vaughan, G. F. Children in hospital. *Lancet*, 1957, *272*, 1117–1120.

Vernon, D. T. A., & Bailey, W. C. The use of motion pictures in the psychological preparation of children for induction of anesthesia. *Anesthesiology*, 1974, *40*, 68–72.

Vernon, D. T. A., Foley, J. M., Sipowicz, R. R., & Schulman, J. L. *The psychological responses of children to hospitalization and illness*. Springfield, Ill.: Charles C Thomas, 1965.

Wirt, R. D., & Broen, W. E. *Booklet for the Personality Inventory for Children*. Minneapolis: Authors, 1958.

White, W., Akers, J., Green, J., & Yates, D. Use of imitation in the treatment of dental phobias in early childhood: A preliminary report. *Journal of Dentistry for Children*, 1974, *26*, 106.

Chapter Four

Language and Communication

Few achievements have captured the imagination of psychologists as much as the child's acquisition of language. A vast effort has been devoted to describing the nature of language development; in other words, how does the nature of children's grammatical constructions shift as the child develops? What are the rule systems that account for the use of sentences, and how does the child's ability to use a system of rules change with development? In his article in this section, Slobin shows the remarkable similarity of children's grammar across a wide variety of different cultures. This is only one of the questions that has concerned students of language, since an analysis of the child's language that was limited to a description of the formal grammatical features of children's sentences was not enough. A second important direction of language research concerns the study of the nonlinguistic context of language. Semantics, or the study of meaning, has emerged as an important and active area of research. Children's language, in short, may be richer, more complex, and more fully understood by a consideration of the context in which the language occurs.

Closely related to this issue is the very difficult task of explaining the language achievements that previous investigators have described. Bruner, in his article in this section, "Learning the Mother Tongue," argues that neither traditional-behaviorist arguments nor Chomskyian-nativist arguments are correct explanations of how children acquire language. Instead he proposes a "fine-tuning theory" that seeks the key to language in the earliest—often nonverbal—exchanges between mother and infant. As a result of the early communication dialogue between adults and infants, the infant gradually learns language.

Not only are there similarities in the development of grammar across a wide range of cultures, there are striking parallels in the pattern or language acquisition of hearing children who acquire a verbal language and deaf children who learn a sign language. (Meadow, this section.) However, Meadow's review of the development of language in deaf children also underlines the difficulty that deaf children encounter in learning language. These investigations indicate that the ability to hear normal speech is an important condition for the adequate development of language. Recent research suggests that deaf children who are exposed to early sign language as well as manual-oral input seem to develop more adequate language skills than deaf children raised in a strictly verbal environment.

In the search for universals, however, we should not forget the obvious differences in the ways in which language is used in different settings and by different groups. Language as a form of communication is highly sensitive to a variety of contextual factors such as the nature of the situation (playground or classroom), the topic, (math problems vs. baseball games) or the audience (teacher vs. your best friends). As Gleason demonstrates in her article in this section, we regularly adjust our language to best suit the situational demands. In fact, a system of language that could not easily be modified to fulfill the functions of a new situation would be of very limited value in communication.

Finally, these performance and stylistic differences that vary across social class and subcultural groups are often viewed as differences in language development. Silverstein and Krate, however, persuasively argue that a deficit model, which suggests that standard English as spoken by middle class whites is superior to black dialects is mistaken. Instead, they propose a difference model, which recognizes that dialects of low-income groups represent parallel language developments. In fact, they note that the structure and syntax of the language of different racial and social class groups is very similar; what differs is style, pronunciation, and vocabulary. Finally, they explore the implications of the discontinuity between the black child's street language and the language of the school culture. As Silverstein and Krate demonstrate, language, thought, and culture interweave and interact in important and complex ways.

It is also clear that our search for the answers to the when, why, and how of language development in children is still far from complete.

Reading 13

Learning the Mother Tongue

Jerome S. Bruner

Learning a native language is an accomplishment within the grasp of any toddler, yet discovering how children do it has eluded generations of philosophers. St. Augustine believed it was simple. Recollecting his own childhood, he said, "When they named any thing, and as they spoke turned towards it, I saw and remembered that they called what they would point out by the name they uttered. . . . And thus by constantly hearing words, as they occurred in various sentences, I collected gradually for what they stood; and having broken in my mouth to these signs, I thereby gave utterance to my will." But a look at children as they actually acquire language shows that St. Augustine was wrong and that other attempts to explain the feat err as badly in the opposite direction. What is more, as we try to understand how children learn their own language, we get an inkling of why it is so difficult for adults to learn a second language.

Thirty years ago, psychologies of learning held sway; language acquisition was explained using principles and methods that had little to do with language. Most started with nonsense syllables or random materials that were as far as researchers could get from the structure of language that permits the generation of rich and limitless statements, speculations, and poetry. Like G. K. Chesterton's drunk, they looked for the lost coin where the light was. And in the light of early learning theories, children appeared to acquire language by associating words with agents and objects and actions, by imitating their elders, and by a mysterious force called reinforcement. It was the old and tired Augustinian story dressed up in the language of behaviorism.

Learning theory led to a readiness, even a recklessness, to be rid of an inadequate account, one that could explain the growth of vocabulary but not how a four-year-old abstracts basic language rules and effortlessly combines old words to make an infinite string of new sentences. The stage was set for linguist Noam Chomsky's theory of LAD, the Language Acquisition Device, and for the Chomskyan revolution.

According to this view, language was not learned;

it was recognized by virtue of an innate recognition routine through which children, when exposed to their local language, could abstract or extract its universal grammatical principles. Whatever the input of that local language, however degenerate, the output of LAD was the grammar of the language, a competence to generate all possible grammatical sentences and none (or very few) that were not. It was an extreme view, so extreme that it did not even consider meaning. In a stroke it freed a generation of psycholinguists from the dogma of association, imitation, and reinforcement and turned their attention to the problem of rule learning. By declaring learning theory dead, it opened the way for a new account. George Miller of The Rockefeller University put it well: We had two theories of language learning—one of them, empiricist associationism, is impossible; the other, nativism, is miraculous. The void between the impossible and the miraculous remained to be filled.

Both explanations begin too late—when children say their first words. Long before children acquire language, they know something about their world. Before they can make verbal distinctions in speech, they have sorted the conceptual universe into useful categories and classes and can make distinctions about actions and agents and objects. As Roger Brown of Harvard University has written, "The concept . . . is there beforehand, waiting for the word to come along that names it." But the mystery of how children penetrate the communication system and learn to represent in language what they already know about the real world has not been solved. Although there is a well-packaged semantic content waiting, what children learn about language is not the same as what they know about the world. Yet the void begins to fill as soon as we recognize that children are not flying blind, that semantically speaking they have some target toward which language-learning efforts are directed: saying something or understanding something about events in a world that is already known.

If a child is in fact communicating, he has some end in mind—requesting something or indicating something or establishing some sort of personal relationship. The function of a communication has to be considered. As philosopher John Austin argued, an utterance cannot be analyzed out of its context of use, and its use must include the intention of the speaker and its interpretation in the light of conventional standards by the person addressed. A speaker may make a request in several ways: by using the conventional question form, by making a declarative statement, or by issuing a command.

Roger Brown observed young Adam from age two until he was four and found that his middle-class mother made requests using a question form: "Why don't you play with your ball now?" Once Adam came to appreciate what I shall call genuine *why* questions (i.e., "Why are you playing with your ball?"), he typically answered these—and these only—with the well-known "Because." There is no instance, either before or after he began to comprehend the genuine causal question, of his ever confusing a sham and a real *why* question.

Not only does conceptual knowledge precede true language, but so too does function. Children know, albeit in limited form, what they are trying to accomplish by communicating before they begin to use language to implement their efforts. Their initial gestures and vocalizations become increasingly stylized and conventional.

It has become plain in the last several years that Chomsky's original bold claim that any sample of language encountered by an infant was enough for the LAD to dig down to the grammatical rules simply is false. Language is not encountered willy-nilly by the child; it is instead encountered in a highly orderly interaction with the mother, who takes a crucial role in arranging the linguistic encounters of the child. What has emerged is a theory of mother-infant interaction in language acquisition—called the fine-tuning theory—that sees language mastery as involving the mother as much as it does the child. According to this theory, if the LAD exists, it hovers somewhere in the air between mother and child.

So today we have a new perspective that begins to grant a place to knowledge of the world, to knowledge of the function of communication, and to the hearer's interpretation of the speaker's intent. The new picture of language learning recognizes that the process depends on highly constrained and one-sided transactions between the child and the adult teacher. Language acquisition requires joint problem solving by mother and infant, and her response to her child's language is close tuned in a way that can be specified.

The child's entry into language is an entry into dialogue, and the dialogue is at first necessarily nonverbal and requires both members of the pair to interpret the communication and its intent. Their relationship is in the form of roles, and each "speech" is determined by a move of either partner. Initial control of the dialogue depends on the mother's interpretation, which is guided by a continually updated understanding of her child's competence.

Consider an infant learning to label objects. Anat Ninio and I observed Richard in his home every two weeks from his eighth month until he was two years old, video-taping his actions so that we could study them later. In this instance he and his mother are "reading" the pictures in a book. Before this kind of learning begins, certain things already have been established. Richard has learned about pointing as a pure indicating act, marking unusual or unexpected objects rather than things wanted immediately. He has also learned to understand that sounds refer in some singular way to objects or events. Richard and his mother, moreover, have long since established well-regulated turn-taking routines, which probably were developing as early as his third or fourth month. And finally, Richard has learned that books are to be looked at, not eaten or torn; that objects depicted are to be responded to in a particular way and with sounds in a pattern of dialogue.

For the mother's part, she (like all mothers we have observed) drastically limits her speech and maintains a steady regularity. In her dialogues with Richard she uses four types of speech in a strikingly fixed order. First, to get his attention, she says "Look." Second, with a distinctly rising inflection, she asks "What's that?" Third, she gives the picture a label, "It's an X." And finally, in response to his actions, she says "That's right."

In each case, a single verbal token accounts for from nearly half to more than 90 percent of the instances. The way Richard's mother uses the four speech constituents is closely linked to what her son says or does. When she varies her response, it is with good reason. If Richard responds, his mother replies, and if he initiates a cycle by pointing and vocalizing, then she responds even more often.

Her fine tuning is fine indeed. For example, if after her query Richard labels the picture, she will virtually always skip the label and jump to the response, "Yes." Like the other mothers we have studied, she is following ordinary polite rules for adult dialogue.

As Roger Brown has described the baby talk of adults, it appears to be an imitative version of how babies talk. Brown says, "Babies already talk like babies, so what is the earthly use of parents doing the same? Surely it is a parent's job to each the adult language." He resolves the dilemma by noting, "What I think adults are chiefly trying to do, when they use [baby talk] with children, is to communicate, to understand and to be understood, to keep two minds focused on the same topic." Although I agree with Brown, I would like to point out that the content and intonation of the talk is baby talk, but the dialogue pattern is adult.

To ensure that two minds are indeed focused on a common topic, the mother develops a technique for showing her baby what feature a label refers to by making 90 percent of her labels refer to whole objects. Since half of the remainder of her speech is made up of proper names that also stand for the whole, she seems to create few difficulties, supposing that the child also responds to whole objects and not to their features.

The mother's (often quite unconscious) approach is exquisitely tuned. When the child responds to her "Look!" by looking, she follows immediately with a query with a gesture or a smile, she supplies a label. But as soon as the child shows the ability to vocalize in a way that might indicate a label, she raises the ante. She withholds the label and repeats the query until the child vocalizes, then she gives the label.

Later, when the child has learned to respond with shorter vocalizations that correspond to words, she no longer accepts an indifferent vocalization. When the child begins producing a recognizable, constant label for an object, she holds out for it. Finally, the child produces appropriate words at the appropriate place in the dialogue. Even then the mother remains tuned to the developing pattern, helping her child recognize labels and make them increasingly accurate. For example, she develops two ways of asking "What's that?" One, with a falling intonation, inquires about those words for which she believes her child already knows the label; the other, with a rising intonation, marks words that are new.

Even in the simple labeling game, mother and child are well into making the distinction between the given and the new. It is of more than passing interest that the old or established labels are the ones around which the mother will shortly be elaborating comments and questions for new information:

Mother (with falling intonation): What's that?
Child: Fishy.
Mother: Yes, and see him swimming?

After the mother assumes her child has acquired a particular label, she generally drops the attention-getting "Look!" when they turn to the routine. In these petty particulars of language, the mother gives useful cues about the structure of their native tongue. She provides cues based not simply on her knowledge of the language but also on her continually changing knowledge of the child's ability to grasp particular distinctions, forms, or rules. The child is sensitized to certain constraints in the structure of their dialogue and does not seem to be directly imitating her. I say this because there is not much difference in the likelihood of a child's repeating a label after hearing it, whether the mother has imitated the child's label, simply said "Yes," or only laughed approvingly. In each case the child repeats the label about half the time, about the same rate as with *no* reply from the mother. Moreover, the child is eight times more likely to produce a label in response to "What's that?" than to the mother's uttering the label.

I do not mean to claim that children cannot or do not use imitation in acquiring language. Language must be partly based on imitation, but though the child may be imitating another, language learning involves solving problems by communicating in a dialogue. The child seems to be trying to get through to the mother just as hard as she is trying to reach her child.

Dialogue occurs in a context. When children first learn to communicate, it is always in highly concrete situations, as when mother or child calls attention to an object, asking for the aid or participation of the other. Formally conceived, the format of communication involves an intention, a set of procedures, and a goal. It presupposes shared knowledge of the world and a shared script by which mother and child can carry out reciprocal activity in that world. Formats obviously have utility for the child. They provide a simple, predictable bit of the world in which and about which to communicate. But they also have an important function for the mother in the mutual task of speech acquisition.

When a mother uses baby talk, her intonation

broadens, her speech slows, and her grammar becomes less complex. In addition, baby talk virtually always starts with the here and now, with the format in which the two are operating. It permits the mother to tune her talk to the child's capabilities. She need not infer the child's general competence for language, but instead judges the child's performance on a specific task at a specific time.

A second major function of speech is requesting something of another person. Carolyn Roy and I have been studying its development during the first two years of life. Requesting requires an indication that you want *something* and *what* it is you want. In the earliest procedures used by children it is difficult to separate the two. First the child vocalizes with a characteristic intonation pattern while reaching eagerly for the desired nearby object—which is most often held by the mother. As in virtually all early exchanges, it is the mother's task to interpret, and she works at it in a surprisingly subtle way. During our analyses of Richard when he was from 10 to 24 months old and Jonathan when he was 11 to 18 months old, we noticed that their mothers frequently seemed to be teasing them or withholding obviously desired objects. Closer inspection indicated that it was not teasing at all. They were trying to establish whether the infants really wanted what they were reaching for, urging them to make their intentions clearer.

When the two children requested nearby objects, the mothers were more likely to ask "Do you really want it?" than "Do you want the X?" The mother's first step is pragmatic, to establish the sincerity of the child's request.

Children make three types of requests, reflecting increasing sophistication in matters that have nothing to do with language. The first kind that emerges is directed at obtaining nearby, visible objects; this later expands to include distant or absent objects where the contextual understanding of words like "you, me," "this, that," and "here, there" is crucial. The second kind of request is directed at obtaining support for an action that is already in progress, and the third kind is used to persuade the mother to share some activity or experience.

When children first begin to request objects, they typically direct their attention and their reach, opening and closing their fists, accompanied by a characteristic intonation pattern. As this request expands, between 10 and 15 months, an observer immediately notes two changes. In reaching for distant objects, a child no longer looks solely at the desired object, but shifts his glance back and forth between the object and his mother. His call pattern also changes. It becomes more prolonged, or its rise and fall is repeated, and it is more insistent. Almost all of Richard's and Jonathan's requests for absent objects were for food, drink, or a book to be read, each having its habitual place. Each request involved the child's gesturing toward the place.

When consistent word forms appeared, they were initially idiosyncratic labels for objects, gradually becoming standard nouns that indicated the desired objects. The children also began initiating and ending their requests with smiles. The development of this pattern is paced by the child's knowledge, which is shared with the mother, of where things are located and of her willingness to fetch them if properly asked. Once the child begins requesting distant and absent objects, the mother has an opportunity to require that the desired object be specified. Sincerity ceases to be at issue, though two other conditions are imposed: control of agency (who is actually to obtain the requested object, with emphasis on the child's increasing independence) and control of "share" (whether the child has had enough).

Requests for joint activity contrast with object requests. I think they can be called precursors to invitation. They amount to the child asking the adult to share in an activity or an experience—to look out of the window into the garden together, to play Ride-a-cockhorse, to read together. They are the most playlike form of request, and in consequence they generate a considerable amount of language of considerable complexity. It is in this format that the issues of agency and share (or turn) emerge and produce important linguistic changes.

Joint activity requires what I call joint role enactment, and it takes three forms: one in which the adult is agent and the child recipient or experiencer (as in early book reading); another in which there is turn taking with the possibility of exchanging roles (as in peekaboo); and a third in which roles run parallel (as in looking around the garden together). Most of what falls into these categories is quite ritualized and predictable. There tend to be rounds and turns, and no specific outcome is required. The activity itself is rewarding. In this setting the child first deals with share and turn by adopting such forms of linguistic marking as *more* and *again*. These appear during joint role enactment and migrate rapidly into formats involving requests for distant objects.

Mothers' questions when children request nearby objects

Type of question	Age in months		
	10-12	13-14	More than 5
About intention ("Do you want it?")	93%	90%	42%
About referent ("Do you want the x?")	7	10	58
Number of questions	27	29	12

Forms of early requests

Request for:	Age in months				
	10-12	13-14	15-16	17-18	20-24
Near and visible object	100%	74%	43%	22%	11%
Distant or invisible object	0	16	24	8	24
Shared activity	0	10	14	23	36
Supportive action	0	0	19	47	29
Minutes of recording	150	120	120	120	150
Number of request/10 minutes	1.5	1.6	1.8	4.3	2.3

Adult responses to children's requests

Type of response	Age in months				
	10-12	13-14	15-16	17-18	20-24
Pronominal question					
Open question (who, what, which)	78%	55%	36%	8%	1%
Closed question (yes, no)	3	10	18	30	22
Comment/Question (yes, no)	6	27	36	25	36
Comment/Question on agency	8	2	0	20	28
"Language lesson"	6	6	9	14	4
Request for reason	0	0	0	3	5
Other	0	0	1	0	4
Number of utterances	36	51	22	116	100

As children's requests change with increasing sophistication (center), their mothers switch from establishing the sincerity of a request to identifying the object wanted (top). The sharp increase in replies having to do with who will get or control an action ("agency") reflects a demand for sharing and a difference in wishes (bottom).

It is also in joint role enactment that the baby's first consistent words appear and, beginning at 18 months, word combinations begin to explode. *More X* (with a noun) appears, and also combinations like *down slide, brrm brrm boo knee, Mummy ride,* and *Mummy read.* Indeed it is in these settings that full-blown ingratiatives appear in appropriate positions, such as prefacing a request with *nice Mummy.*

Characteristically, less than 5 percent of the mother's responses to a child's requests before he is 17 months old have to do with agency (or who is going to do, get, or control something). After 17 months, that figure rises to over 25 percent. At that juncture the mothers we studied began to demand that their children adhere more strictly to turn taking and role respecting. The demand can be made most easily when they are doing something together, for that is where the conditions for sharing are most clearly defined and least likely, since playful, to overstrain the child's capacity to wait for a turn. But the sharp increase in agency as a topic in their dialogue reflects as well the emergence of a difference in their wishes.

The mother may want the child to execute the act requested of her, and the child may have views contrary to his mother's about agency. In some instances this leads to little battles of will. In addition, the child's requests for support more often lead to negotiation between the pair than is the case

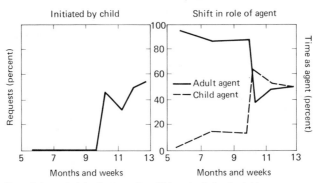

Toward the end of the first year the child gradually begins taking
the lead in give-and-take games. Through such joint activity a child
learns about sharing and taking turns.

when the clarity of the roles in their joint activity makes acceptance and refusal easier. A recurrent trend in development during the child's first year is the shifting of agency in all manner of exchanges from mother to infant. Even at nine to 12 months, Richard gradually began taking the lead in give-and-take games.

The same pattern holds in book reading, where Richard's transition was again quite rapid. Role shifting is very much part of the child's sense of script, and I believe it is typical of the kind of "real world" experience that makes it so astonishingly easy for children to master soon afterwards the deictic shifts, those contextual changes in the meaning of words that are essential to understanding the language. At about this time the child learns that I am *I* when I speak, but *you* when referred to by another, and so too with *you;* and eventually the child comes to understand the associated spatial words, *here* and *there, this* and *that, come* and *go.*

The prelinguistic communicative framework established in their dialogue by mother and child provides the setting for the child's acquisition of this language function. His problem solving in acquiring the deictic function is a *social* task: to find the procedure that will produce results, just as his prelinguistic communicative effort produced results, and the results needed can be interpreted in relation to role interactions.

For a number of years an emphasis on egocentrism in the young child has tended to blunt our awareness of the sensitivity of children to roles, of their capacity to manage role shift and role transforma-

tion. Although there is little doubt that it is more difficult for a young child to take the view of others than it will be for him later, this aspect of development has been greatly exaggerated. In familiar and sufficiently simple situations the child is quite capable of taking another's view. In 1975 Michael Scaife and I discovered that babies in their first year shifted their glance to follow an adult's line of regard, and in 1976 Andrew Meltzoff found in our laboratory that babies only a few weeks old appeared to have a built-in mechanism for mimicking an adult's expression, since they obviously could not see their own faces. More recently, Marilyn Shatz has shown that quite young children are indeed able to "take another's position" when giving instructions, provided the task is simple enough.

According to Katherine Nelson and Janice Gruendel at Yale University, what seems to be egocentrism is often a matter of the child not being able to coordinate his own scripts with those of the questioner, although he is scrupulously following turn taking (which is definitely not egocentric). They found that when "egocentric" four-year-olds do manage to find a joint script, they produce dialogues like the following. Two children are sitting next to each other talking into toy telephones:

Gay: Hi.
Dan: Hi.
Gay: How are you?
Dan: Fine.
Gay: Who am I speaking to?
Dan: Daniel. This is your Daddy. I need to speak to you.
Gay: All right.

Dan: When I come home tonight we're gonna have . . . peanut butter and jelly sandwich . . . uh . . . at dinner time.

Gay: Uhmmm. Where're we going at dinner time?

Dan: Nowhere, but we're just gonna have dinner at 11 o'clock.

Gay: Well, I made a plan of going out tonight.

Dan: Well, that's what we're gonna do.

Gay: We're going out.

Dan: The plan, it's gonna be, that's gonna be, we're going to McDonald's.

Gay: Yeah, we're going to McDonald's. And ah, ah, ah, what they have for dinner tonight is hamburger.

Dan: Hamburger is coming. O.K., well, goodbye.

Gay: Bye.

The child takes into account his or her partner's point of view, phrases his turns properly, and says things that are relevant to the script they are working on jointly. That is surely not egocentrism. But even managing the deictic function of language provides evidence that children realize there are viewpoints other than their own.

The last type of request, the request for supportive action, has a very special property. It is tightly bound to the nature of the action in which the child is involved. To ask others for help in support of their own actions, children need at least two forms of knowledge. One of them represents the course of action and involves a goal and a set of means for getting to it. The second requirement is some grasp of what has been called the arguments of action: who does it, with what instrument, at what place, to whom, on what object, etc. Once children have mastered these, they have a rudimentary understanding of the concepts that will later be encountered in case grammar.

The degree to which a child comes to understand the structure of tasks is the degree to which his requests for support in carrying them out become more differentiated. These requests do not appear with any marked frequency until he is 17 or 18 months old and consist of bringing the "work" or the "action" or the entire task to an adult: A music box needs rewinding, or two objects have to be put together. In time a child is able to do better than that. He may bring a tool to an adult or direct the adult's hand or pat the goal (the chair on which he wants up). He is selecting and highlighting relevant features of the action, though not in a fashion that depends on what the adult is doing. Finally, at about the age of two, with the development of adequate words to refer to particular aspects of the action, the child enters a new phase: He requests action by guiding it successively. The pacemaker of the verbal output is progress in the task itself.

Let me give an instance of this successive guidance system. Richard, it transpires, wishes to persuade his mother to get a toy telephone from the cupboard; she is seated (and very pregnant). Successively, he voices the following requests:

Mummy, Mummy; Mummy come. . . . Up, up. . . . Cupboard. . . . Up cupboard, up cupboard; up cupboard. . . . Get up, get up. . . . Cupboard, cupboard. . . . Cupboard-up; cupboard-up, cupboard-up. . . . Telephone. . . . Mummy. . . . Mummy get out telephone.

His mother objects and asks him what it is he wants after each of the first two requests. She is trying to get him to set forth his request in some "readable" order before she starts to respond—to give a reason in terms of the goal of the action. Richard, meanwhile, achieves something approaching a request in sentence form by organizing his successive utterances in a fashion that seems to be guided by his conception of the needed steps in the action. The initial grammar of the long string of task-related requests is, then, a kind of temporal grammar based on an understanding not only of the actions required, but also of the order in which these actions must be executed. This bit of child language is an interpersonal script based on a young child's knowledge of what is needed to reach the goal in the real world; it is the matrix in which language develops.

In looking closely at two of the four major communicative functions (indicating and requesting), we discovered a great deal of negotiating by the mother about pragmatic aspects of communication: not about truth-falsity and not about well-formedness, but about whether requests were sincere, whose turn it was, whether it should be done independently or not, whether reasons were clear or justified.

There is, of course, more to communication than indicating and requesting. Another major function of speech is affiliation, the forming of a basis for social exchange. This involves matters as diverse as learning to acknowledge presence, to take turns, and to enter what has been called the "cooperative principle" underlying all speech acts.

The final function is the use of communication for generating possible worlds, and it has little to do with asking for help or indicating things in the real world or, indeed, with maintaining social connection. The early utterances of the children we have studied show one clear-cut characteristic: Most of the talking by mother and by child is *not* about hard-nosed reality. It is about games, about imaginary things, about seemingly useless make-believe. What is involved in the generation of possible worlds is quite useful for both conceptual and communicative development—role playing, referring to nonpresent events, combining elements to exploit their variability, etc.

Had we gone on to look at the other two functions, affiliative activity during which mother and child learn the rules for interacting and the sort of play in which possible worlds are created, the case for mother-infant interaction would have been as strong. There is an enormous amount of teaching involved in transmitting the language, though very little of it has to do with language lessons proper. It has to do with making intentions clear, as speaker and as actor, and with overcoming difficulties in getting done in the real world what we want done by the mediation of communicating. And this is why learning a second language is so difficult. The moment we teach language as an explicit set of rules for generating well-formed strings out of context, the enterprise seems to go badly wrong. The rule in natural language learning is that language is learned in order to interact with someone about something the two of you share.

Where does that leave the problem of language acquisition? Well, to my way of thinking it brings it back into the sphere of problem solving—the problem being how to make our intentions known to others, how to communicate what we have in consciousness, what we want done in our behalf, how we wish to relate to others, and what in this or other worlds is possible.

Children still have to learn to use their native lexicons and to do so grammatically. They learn this in use, in order to get things done with words, and not as if they were ferreting out the disembodied rules of grammar. I think we have learned to look at language acquisition not as a solo flight by the child in search of rules, but as a transaction involving an active language learner and an equally active language teacher. That new insight will go a long way toward filling the gap between the impossible and the miraculous.

For further information:

Clark, Herbert, and Eve Clark. *Psychology and Language: An Introduction to Psycholinguistics.* Harcourt Brace Jovanovich, 1977.

De Villiers, Jill G., and Peter A. de Villiers. *Language Acquisition.* Harvard University Press, 1978.

Miller, George A. *Spontaneous Apprentices: Children and Language.* The Seabury Press, 1977.

Snow, Catherine E., and Charles A. Ferguson, eds. *Talking to Children.* Cambridge University Press, 1977.

Reading 14

Children and Language: They Learn the Same Way All around the World

Dan I. Slobin

According to the account of linguistic history set forth in the book of Genesis, all men spoke the same language until they dared to unite to build the Tower of Babel. So that men could not cooperate to build a tower that would reach into heaven, God acted to "confound the language of all the earth" to insure that groups of men "may not understand one another's speech."

What was the original universal language of mankind? This is the question that Psammetichus, ruler of Egypt in the seventh century B. C., asked in

the first controlled psychological experiment in recorded history—an experiment in developmental psycholinguistics reported by Herodotus:

"Psammetichus . . . took at random, from an ordinary family, two newly born infants and gave them to a shepherd to be brought up amongst his flocks, under strict orders that no one should utter a word in their presence. They were to be kept by themselves in a lonely cottage. . . ."

Psammetichus wanted to know whether isolated children would speak Egyptian words spontaneously—thus proving, on the premise that ontogeny recapitulates phylogeny, that Egyptians were the original race of mankind.

In two years, the children spoke their first word: *becos,* which turned out to be the Phrygian word for bread. The Egyptians withdrew their claim that they were the world's most ancient people and admitted the greater antiquity of the Phrygians.

Same We no longer believe, of course, that Phrygian was the original language of all the earth (nor that it was Hebrew, as King James VII of Scotland thought). No one knows which of the thousands of languages is the oldest—perhaps we will never know. But recent work in developmental psycholinguistics indicates that the languages of the earth are not as confounded as we once believed. Children in all nations seem to learn their native languages in much the same way. Despite the diversity of tongues, there are linguistic universals that seem to rest upon the developmental universals of the human mind. Every language is learnable by children of preschool-age, and it is becoming apparent that little children have some definite ideas about how a language is structured and what it can be used for:

Mmm, I want to eat maize.
What?
Where is the maize?
There is no more maize.
Mmm.
[Child seizes an ear of corn]:
What's this?
It's not our maize.
Whose is it?
It belongs to grandmother.
Who harvested it?
They harvested it.
Where did they harvest it?
They harvested it down over there.
Way down over there?
Mmm. [yes]
Let's look for some too.
You look for some.
Fine.
Mmm.
[Child begins to hum]

The dialogue is between a mother and a two-and-a-half-year-old girl. Anthropologist Brian Stross of the University of Texas recorded it in a thatched hut in an isolated Mayan village in Chiapas, Mexico.

Except for the fact that the topic was maize and the language was Tzeltal, the conversation could have taken place anywhere, as any parent will recognize. The child uses short, simple sentences, and her mother answers in kind. The girl expresses her needs and seeks information about such things as location, possession, past action, and so on. She does not ask about time, remote possibilities, contingencies, and the like—such things don't really occur to the two-year-old in any culture, or in any language.

Our research team at the University of California at Berkeley has been studying the way children learn languages in several countries and cultures. We have been aided by similar research at Harvard and at several other American universities, and by the work of foreign colleagues. We have gathered reasonably firm data on the acquisition of 18 languages, and have suggestive findings on 12 others. Although the data are still scanty for many of these languages, a common picture of human-language development is beginning to emerge.

In all cultures the child's first word generally is a noun or proper name, identifying some object, animal, or person he sees every day. At about two years—give or take a few months—a child begins to put two words together to form rudimentary sentences. The two-word stage seems to be universal.

To get his meaning across, a child at the two-word stage relies heavily on gesture, tone and context. Lois Bloom, professor of speech, Teachers College, Columbia University, reported a little American girl who said *Mommy sock* on two distinct occasions: on finding her mother's sock and on being dressed by her mother. Thus the same phrase expressed possession in one context *(Mommy's sock)* and an agent-object relationship in another *(Mommy is putting on the sock).*

But even with a two-word horizon, children can get a wealth of meanings across:

IDENTIFICATION: *See doggie.*
LOCATION: *Book there.*
REPETITION: *More milk.*
NONEXISTENCE: *Allgone thing.*
NEGATION: *Not wolf.*
POSSESSION: *My candy.*
ATTRIBUTION: *Big car.*
AGENT-ACTION: *Mama walk.*
AGENT-OBJECT: *Mama book* (meaning, "Mama read book").
ACTION-LOCATION: *Sit chair.*

ACTION-DIRECT OBJECT: *Hit you.*
ACTION-INDIRECT OBJECT: *Give papa.*
ACTION-INSTRUMENT: *Cut knife.*
QUESTION: *Where ball?*

The striking thing about this list is its universality. The examples are drawn from child talk in English, German, Russian, Finnish, Turkish, Samoan and Luo, but the entire list could probably be made up of examples from two-year old speech in any language.

Word A child easily figures out that the speech he hears around him contains discrete, meaningful elements, and that these elements can be combined. And children make the combinations themselves—many of their meaningful phrases would never be heard in adult speech. For example, Martin Braine studied a child who said things like *allgone outside* when he returned home and shut the door, *more page* when he didn't want a story to end, *other fix* when he wanted something repaired, and so on. These clearly are expressions created by the child, not mimicry of his parents. The matter is especially clear in the Russian language, in which noun endings vary with the role the noun plays in a sentence. As a rule, Russian children first use only the nominative ending in all combinations, even when it is grammatically incorrect. What is important to children is the *word,* not the ending; the *meaning,* not the grammar.

At first, the two-word limit is quite severe. A child may be able to say *daddy throw, throw ball,* and *daddy ball*—indicating that he understands the full proposition, *daddy throw ball*—yet be unable to produce all three words in one stretch. Again, though the data are limited, this seems to be a universal fact about children's sppech.

Tools Later a child develops a rudimentary grammar within the two-word format. These first grammatical devices are the most basic formal tools of human language: intonation, word order, and inflection.

A child uses intonation to distinguish meanings even at the one-word stage, as when he indicates a request by a rising tone, or a demand with a loud, insistent tone. But at the two-word stage another device, a contrastive stress, becomes available. An English-speaking child might say BABY *chair* to indicate possession, and *baby* CHAIR to indicate location or destination.

English sentences typically follow a subject-verb-object sequence, and children learn the rules early. In the example presented earlier, *daddy throw ball,* children use some two-word combinations *(daddy throw, throw ball, daddy ball)* but not others *(ball daddy, ball throw, throw daddy).* Samoan children follow the standard order of possessed-possessor. A child may be sensitive to word order even if his native language does not stress it. Russian children will sometimes adhere strictly to one word order, even when other orders would be equally acceptable.

Some languages provide different word-endings (inflections) to express various meanings, and children who learn these languages are quick to acquire the word-endings that express direct objects, indirect objects and locations. The direct-object inflection is one of the first endings that children pick up in such languages as Russian, Serbo-Croatian, Latvian, Hungarian, Finnish and Turkish. Children learning English, an Indo-European language, usually take a long time to learn locative prepositions such as *on, in, under,* etc. But in Hungary, Finland, or Turkey, where the languages express location with case-endings on the nouns, children learn how to express locative distinctions quite early.

Place Children seem to be attuned to the ends of words. German children learn the inflection system relatively late, probably because it is attached to articles *(der, die, das,* etc.) that appear before the nouns. The Slavic, Hungarian, Finnish and Turkish inflectional systems, based on noun suffixes, seem relatively easy to learn. And it is not just a matter of articles being difficult to learn, because Bulgarian articles which are noun suffixes are learned very early. The relevant factor seems to be the position of the grammatical marker relative to a main content word.

By the time he reaches the end of the two-word stage, the child has much of the basic grammatical machinery he needs to acquire any particular native language: words that can be combined in order and modified by intonation and inflection. These rules occur, in varying degrees, in all languages, so that all languages are about equally easy for children to learn.

Gap When a child first uses three words in one phrase, the third word usually fills in the part that was implicit in his two-word statements. Again, this seems to be a universal pattern of development. It is dramatically explicit when the child expands his own communication as he repeats it: *Want that . . . Andrew want that.*

Just as the two-word structure resulted in idiosyncratic pairings, the three-word stage imposes its own limits. When an English-speaking child wishes to add an adjective to the subject-verb-object form, something must go. He can say *Mama drink coffee* or *Drink hot coffee,* but not *Mama drink hot coffee.* This developmental limitation on sentence span seems to be universal: the child's mental ability to express ideas grows faster than his ability to formulate the ideas in complete sentences. As the child learns to construct longer sentences, he uses more complex grammatical operations. He attaches new elements to old sentences *(Where I can sleep?)* before he learns how to order the elements correctly *(Where can I sleep?).* When the child learns to combine two sentences he first compresses them end-to-end *(the boy fell down that was running)* then finally he embeds one within the other *(the boy that was running fell down).*

Across   These are the basic operations of grammar, and to the extent of our present knowledge, they all are acquired by about age four, regardless of native language or social setting. The underlying principles emerge so regularly and so uniformly across diverse languages that they seem to make up an essential part of the child's basic means of information processing. They seem to be comparable to the principles of object constancy and depth perception. Once the child develops these guidelines he spends most of his years of language acquisition learning the specific details and applications of these principles to his particular native language.

Lapse   Inflection systems are splendid examples of the sort of linguistic detail that children must master. English-speaking children must learn the great irregularities of some of our most frequently used words. Many common verbs have irregular past tenses: *came, fell, broke.* The young child may speak these irregular forms correctly the first time—apparently by memorizing a separate past tense form for each verb—only to lapse into immature talk *(comed, falled, breaked)* once he begins to recognize regularities in the way most verbs are conjugated. These over-regularized forms persist for years, often well into elementary school. Apparently regularity heavily outranks previous practice, reinforcement, and imitation of adult forms in

influence on children. The child seeks regularity and is deaf to exceptions. [See "Learning the Language," by Ursula Bellugi, PT, December 1970.]

The power of apparent regularities has been noted repeatedly in the children's speech of every language we have studied. When a Russian noun appears as the object of a sentence *(he liked the story),* the speaker must add an accusative suffix to the noun—one of several possible accusative suffixes, and the decision depends on the gender and the phonological form of the particular noun (and if the noun is masculine, he must make a further distinction on whether it refers to a human being). When the same noun appears in the possessive form *(the story's ending surprised him)* he must pick from a whole set of possessive suffixes, and so on, through six grammatical cases, for every Russian noun and adjective.

Grasp   The Russian child, of course, does not learn all of this at once, and his gradual, unfolding grasp of the language is instructive. He first learns at the two-word stage that different cases are expressed with different noun-endings. His strategy is to choose one of the accusative inflections and use it in all sentences with direct objects regardless of the peculiarities of individual nouns. He does the same for each of the six grammatical cases. His choice of inflection is always correct within the broad category—that is, the prepositional is always expressed by *some* prepositional inflection, and dative by *some* dative inflection, and so on, just as an English-speaking child always expresses the past tense by a past-tense inflection, and not by some other sort of inflection.

The Russian child does not go from a single suffix for each case to full mastery of the system. Rather, he continues to reorganize his system in successive sweeps of over-regularizations. He may at first use the feminine ending with all accusative nouns, then use the masculine form exclusively for a time, and only much later sort out the appropriate inflections for all genders. These details, after all, have nothing to do with meaning, and it is meaning that children pay most attention to.

Bit   Once a child can distinguish the various semantic notions, he begins to unravel the arbitrary details, bit by bit. The process apparently goes on below the level of consciousness. A Soviet psychologist, D. N. Bogoyavlenskiy, showed five-and six-year-old Russian children a series of nonsense words equipped with Russian suffixes, each word attached to a picture of an object or animal that the words supposedly represented. The children had no difficulty realizing that words ending in augmentative suffixes were related to large objects, and that those ending in diminutives went with small objects. But they could not explain the formal differences aloud. Bogoyavlenskiy would say, "Yes, you were right about the difference between the animals—one is little and the other is big; now pay attention to the words themselves as I say them: *lar-laryonok*. What's the difference between them?" None of the children could give any sort of answer. Yet they easily understood the semantic implications of the suffixes.

Talk   When we began our cross-cultural studies at Berkeley, we wrote a manual for our field researchers so that they could record samples of mother-child interaction in other cultures with the same systematic measures we had used to study language development in middle-class American children. But most of our field workers returned to tell us that, by and large, mothers in other cultures do not speak to children very much—children hear speech mainly from other children. The isolated American middle-class home, in which a mother spends long periods alone with her children, may be a relatively rare social situation in the world. The only similar patterns we observed were in some European countries and in a Mayan village.

This raised an important question: Does it matter—for purposes of grammatical development—whether the main interlocutor for a small child is his mother?

The evidence suggests that it does not. First of all, the rate and course of grammatical development seem to be strikingly similar in all of the cultures we have studied. Further, nowhere does a mother devote great effort to correcting a child's grammar. Most of her corrections are directed at speech etiquette and communication, and, as Roger Brown has noted, reinforcement tends to focus on the truth of a child's utterance rather than on the correctness of his grammar.

Ghetto   In this country, Harvard anthropologist Claudia Mitchell-Kernan has studied language development in black children in an urban ghetto. There, as in foreign countries, children got most of their speech input from older children rather than from their mothers. These children learned English rules as quickly as did the middle-class white children that Roger Brown studied, and in the same order. Further, mother-to-child English is simple—very much like child-to-child English. I expect that our cross-cultural studies will find a similar picture in other countries.

How   A child is set to learn a language—any language—as long as it occurs in a direct and active context. In these conditions, every normal child masters his particular native tongue, and learns basic principles in a universal order common to all children, resulting in our adult Babel of linguistic diversity. And he does all this without being able to say how. The Soviet scholar Kornei Ivanovich Chukovsky emphasized this unconscious aspect of linguistic discovery in his famous book on child language, *From Two to Five:*

"It is frightening to think what an enormous number of grammatical forms are poured over the poor head of the young child. And he, as if it were nothing at all, adjusts to all this chaos, constantly sorting out into rubrics the disorderly elements of the words he hears, without noticing as he does this, his gigantic effort. If an adult had to master so many grammatical rules within so short a time, his head would surely burst. . . . In truth, the young child is the hardest mental toiler on our planet. Fortunately, he does not even suspect this."

Reading 15

Language Development in Deaf Children

Kathryn P. Meadow

It cannot be emphasized too strongly that the basic deprivation of profound congenital deafness is the deprivation of language and not the deprivation of sound. To those who are unfamiliar with deafness and its consequences, this statement may not have full and immediate impact. It reflects the deaf child's inability to communicate in a fully meaningful way about his needs, his thoughts, his feelings, his experiences. It also means that the significant others in his environment cannot communicate their thoughts, demands, questions, reasons. Often the uninitiated social scientist or lay person believes that the worst consequence of deafness is some degree of unintelligible speech, or a need to resort to written notes in order to clarify some difficult point. We take for granted the fact that a 4-year-old hearing member of any culture has a complete working grasp and knowledge of his native language—a knowledge that he has absorbed, processed, and assimilated without formal didactic tutoring. For most deaf children, a limited grasp of oral communication is acquired at the cost of hour upon hour of intensive tutoring, investment of time, and recurring frustration. Methods of teaching language to deaf children have been the subject of bitter controversy for a period of 200 years or more (Bender 1960; Levine 1969a; Schlesinger 1969). The conflict in this area is an important part of the social and cultural context of the deaf child's development because it influences all the developmental issues related to deafness. The observation that the limits of one's language coincide with the limits of one's world has special meaning for language-deprived children and their parents.

There are several previously published reviews of language development in deaf children (Bonvillian, Charrow, & Nelson 1973; Cooper & Rosenstein 1966; Rosenstein 1961). Each of these can be useful for readers who wish to pursue the subject further. Here, research on language development and deafness is presented under four major headings: "First Language Acquisition," "Acquisition of a 'Second Language,'" "Written Language Used by Deaf Children," and "Evaluation of the Linguistic Milieus of Deaf Children."

FIRST LANGUAGE ACQUISITION

In considering the acquisition of language by deaf children, it is helpful to differentiate among three groups of children: (1) those whose deaf parents use the American Sign Language (Ameslan) as their preferred means of everyday communication, at least within the home, and whose socialization therefore takes place through manual communication; (2) those whose (hearing or deaf) parents use a simultaneous combination of signed and spoken English when they communicate with their deaf child; (3) those whose (hearing) parents use spoken English as their only means of communication with their deaf child and who hope and expect that the child's eventual sole communicative mode is oral English.

1. Linguistic Input: American Sign Language

To be considered in this section are those few studies of language acquisition in deaf children whose linguistic socialization takes place through parental use of American Sign Language, or Ameslan. Ameslan is used by approximately three-quarters of deaf American adults (Rainer et al. 1969). It is a language comprised of combinations of symbolic gestures deriving meaning from the shape of the hand, the location of the hand in relation to the body of the signer, and the movement of the hand or hands. Many of the individual signs symbolize concepts rather than individual words. The derivation of some of the signs was iconic; that is, they were apparently based on natural pantomime gestures. Ameslan has long been a stigmatized language. Many have insisted that it was not a language at all. Linguists have only recently begun to study Ameslan seriously and have found that it does have all the characteristics of language, although there are some differences deriving from crossing of modalities (Bellugi & Klima 1972, 1975; McCall 1965; Stokoe 1960; Stokoe, Casterline, & Croneberg 1965). Parents who make use of Ameslan, as "native signers," are with rare exception deaf themselves. This does not mean, however, that *all* deaf parents use Ameslan to communicate with their deaf children. Some deaf parents themselves use only or mostly spoken English as their primary mode of communication. Other deaf parents may use Ameslan with each other but use only spoken English with their deaf child (Stuckless & Birch 1966). A special characteristic of Ameslan as a "native" or "first" language is that the deaf parents of deaf children have in most cases acquired *their* Ameslan from other deaf children in a residential school after the usual and perhaps optimum age of language acquisition. Their own experiences with early language, and with early family interaction, may have been sparse and even painful. Their ideas about parent-child interaction and linguistic socialization may be quite different from those of the hearing parents whose children were the subjects of previous linguistic studies. It is only recently that the language acquisition of young deaf children has received any systematic attention and analysis. There are only three studies available of features of Ameslan acquisition. These were reported by Bellugi (1972), by Hoffmeister and Morres (1973), and by Schlesinger (Schlesinger & Meadow 1972). Schlesinger followed two children of deaf parents. Ann was observed periodically from 8 months to 22 months of age (Schlesinger & Meadow 1972, pp. 54–68). Karen was observed from age 2–6 to age 3–6 (Schlesinger & Meadow 1972, pp. 70–74). Ann's mother was also the child of deaf parents. She used English syntax in her written English and alternated between English and Ameslan syntax in her signed/spoken communications. Ann's father was more likely than her mother to utilize Ameslan syntax in all his communications.

At the age of 10 months, Ann made some first approximation of recognizable signs; at 12 months she signed "pretty" and "wrong"; at 14 months she added "cat" and "sleep" to her vocabulary and combined "bye sleep." When Ann was 17 months old, nine two-sign combinations were recorded. At age 19 months, she had a vocabulary of 117 signs and five manual letters of the alphabet. At age 19½ months, her recorded vocabulary was 142 signs and 14 manual alphabet letters. Thus, Ann had more than 100 signs at the age Lenneberg (1967) estimates that a normal hearing child will have acquired no more than 50 spoken words.

Numerous examples are cited in which Ann used one-word utterances in holophrastic ways just as hearing children use spoken words initially. For example, at age 15 months, she used the sign for smell to mean "I want to go to the bathroom"; "I

am soiled, please change"; and "I want the pretty smelling flower." Schlesinger observed a number of immature variations in Ann's early signs comparable with the baby talk found in the early language of hearing children. The nonstandard variations might be in hand configuration, in placement, or in movement. Thus, context plus the remaining standard features were important in deciphering the meaning of the signed utterance.

Schlesinger emphasizes that the style and feeling of the linguistic input have equal importance with the content. The enjoyment apparent in the language interaction in which Ann and her mother participated were a striking contrast with that observed for many deaf children with their mothers. She suggests that understanding of early meaning, combined with an enjoyment of mother-child communicative events, may represent a necessary feature of normal language development. This theme is elaborated in a later paper on the language development of deaf children (Schlesinger 1972).

The language of the second child in the Schlesinger study, Karen, was analyzed from a body of 200 combinations of two or more signs collected over a period of 8 months. The primary focus of this analysis was a comparison with previously published accounts of children's open and pivot word combinations. Pivot words had been defined as a small group of words used frequently by the young child presumably either first *or* last in two-word combinations. The pivot word would be combined with an unlimited number of open words. Pivot words are more like adult function words (e.g., prepositions), while open words are more like adult content words (e.g., nouns and verbs). Schlesinger's data supported those of several other investigators who were beginning to question the strict definition of the pivot in child language. Karen's pivot signs were found to occur alone as well as in combination with other open signs and in combination with other pivots. Likewise, pivot signs were found sometimes first and sometimes last in two-sign combinations (Schlesinger & Meadow 1972).

Bellugi (1967) was among the first to study the process of child language acquisition among hearing children. More recently she has looked at the (sign) language acquisition of deaf children. A report based on these studies suggests that deaf children learning sign language are systematic, regular, and productive in their language just as were the hearing children studied earlier (Bellugi & Klima 1972).

One child, Pola, provided their initial data on sign language acquisition. Her sign vocabulary apparently covered the full range of concepts expressed by hearing children of a comparable age. Like hearing children, Pola appeared to overgeneralize linguistic rules initially, applying them too broadly at first, but later learning appropriate restrictions on the general linguistic rules. Before she was 3 years old, Pola used spontaneously the signs for name, stay, tomorrow, will, where, who, what, how, dead, know, understand, none, nothing, don't know, and letters of the manual alphabet. Her early sign combinations expressed the full range of semantic relations found in the expressions of hearing children. The increase in the length of her signed expression matched the increase seen in hearing children. Bellugi and Klima conclude (1972) that in spite of the difference in modality the milestones of language development may be the same in the deaf as in the hearing child.

Hoffmeister and Moores (1973) studied the initial language interaction of Alice and her deaf mother at 1-month intervals from the time she was 25 months old until she was 28 months of age. Eight 30-minute videotapes were transcribed and analyzed for the development of the use of the "pointing action" by Alice. The authors concluded that the pointing action was a separate linguistic unit, glossed as "that" or "this." As such it was used in a way very similar to the use of demonstrative pronouns by normal hearing children, but with more apparent precision of meaning. Although normal hearing children use pointing as a gesture, with Alice variations in pointing indicated differential meanings. From their observations of Alice, Hoffmeister and Moores conclude that specific reference, through the pointing action referring to "this" or "that," is an initial stage of sign language acquisition.

The differences between Alice's pointing "sign" and the pointing "gesture" used by hearing children would seem to be difficult to decipher. However, Bellugi and Klima (1975) are working on this very problem with adult signers. That is, they are attempting to develop criteria for differentiating between pantomime and sign. They have observed that certain elements must remain recognizable and constant if a gesture is to be considered to be a specific sign. While Hoffmeister and Moores seem to be observing the same phenomenon in Alice's "this" and "that," the exact differences are nebulous and difficult to pinpoint.

2. Linguistic Input: Bimodal English

A few children who are deaf receive a simultaneous combination of signed plus spoken English as their earliest parental language input. They are the children whose (usually hearing) parents have elected to learn manual communication in some modified version of American Sign Language. Until the very recent past, the use of sign language in any form was seen as an admission of failure on the part of the deaf child, his parents, and his teachers. Since manual communication was believed to interfere with the acquisition of speech and lipreading skills, parents feared to use either nonsytematic gestures or systematic signs. In recent years, the phrase "total communication" has come to be utilized to refer to a communicative mode that combines speech, lipreading, amplification, and the simultaneous use of one of several manual sign systems. Schlesinger (1974) has suggested the term "bimodalism" as a substitute. The manual sign systems are derived from the basic signs of American Sign Language. The variations in the different systems are for the purpose of providing a means for signing a direct and precise gloss of spoken English rather than utilizing the different syntax of American Sign Language. The initial efforts in this direction began in 1962 with the work of Anthony (1966). Bornstein (1973) summarizes four major and competing sign systems currently being developed by groups in different parts of the United States: Signing Exact English, Seeing Essential English, Linguistics of Visual English, and Signed English (Gustason, Pfetzing, & Zawolkow 1972; Kannapell, Hamilton, & Bornstein 1969; O'Rourke 1970). The four systems differ in several ways, but primarily in the extent to which they incorporate traditional signs and in the method for forming the auxiliary verbs, pronouns, articles, and so forth that are not used in American Sign Language. The Rochester Method is another variant of the total communication idea. It utilizes a combination of speech and simultaneous finger spelling (Scouten 1967).

Schlesinger followed the language development of two children. Ruth and Marie, whose hearing parents were utilizing signed and spoken English as well as hearing aids and speech training. Ruth was observed and videotaped from the age of 2–8 to 3–5. Her deafness had been diagnosed at the age of 9 months, and her parents began to learn and to use total communication when she was 15 months old. At 3 years of age. Ruth's vocabulary included a total of 348 words: at 3–4 she had a vocabulary of 604 words, including one or more in each form class. On the basis of three tests of grammatical complexity administered when Ruth was 3, Schlesinger concluded that Ruth was following the same order of grammatical emergence in signed and spoken language that hearing children have previously demonstrated (Schlesinger & Meadow 1972).

Marie was adopted by a hearing family at the age of 6½ months and diagnosed as a deaf child before the age of 12 months. Her parents began to use manual communication with her when she was 3–1; she was followed by Schlesinger from the age of 3–4 to 5–3 (Schlesinger & Meadow 1972, pp. 82–86). Data on Marie's language showed that she was incorporating English syntax, using appropriately such characteristics as plurals and tense that are not part of Ameslan (e.g., "popped" and "broken" at 3–4; glasses, teachers, potatoes, shared, stabbed, working at age 3–5½. Marie's mother played many finger-spelling anagram games with her. At the age of 4–5 Marie demonstrated that she was able to transfer her finger-spelling games to reading material. Marie also gave evidence of the acquisition of negation in the same sequence as has been observed in hearing children in the past. Her lipreading score at age 3–10½ was well above average score for a 5-year-old.

Analysis of early linguistic samples from these children demonstrated the similarities in their acquisition of bimodal language and the acquisition of spoken English by hearing children. Schlesinger's report of data collected somewhat later in the acquisition process illustrates a fascinating difference between these bimodal deaf children and previously observed hearing children. The difference is related to the perceptual salience of various morphemes in visual and auditory modalities. Hearing children typically acquire the "ing" ending for the present progressive before they learn to use the accompanying auxiliary verb (e.g., "girl running" is used for a period before "girl is running"). Apparently hearing children using oral or spoken language pay more attention to the endings of words. This principle did not apply as forcefully for some of the bimodal youngsters studied and may be related to the perceptual salience of various morphemes in the visual or the auditory mode. The perceptual salience appears to be directly related to the amount of residual hearing and to the precision and frequency with which the child's parents use the morphemic

modulations in sign language. Thus the child with the most useable residual hearing acquired the "ing" ending very much as hearing children do, although the auxiliary verb appeared more quickly in the deaf child. Another child subject who is *profoundly* deaf acquired the "ing" and the auxiliary simultaneously. The third youngster, also profoundly deaf but whose linguistic input was less precise for the morphemic modulations, persisted in the use of the auxiliary alone with no trace of the "ing" form for a long period of time. Schlesinger relates these data to Brown's (1973) idea that the relatively late acquisition of the possessive form in hearing children may result from the indistinct and frequently slurred nature of the spoken form.

3. Linguistic Input: Oral English Only

By far the largest number of deaf children (practically all those with hearing parents, or approximately 90% of the total number) have had their initial exposure to language through oral or spoken English. Most parents and educators are committed to the "oral-only" approach to language acquisition for deaf children. There are several methods used. One, called acoupedics, places exclusive reliance on training the deaf child to use his residual hearing. This is also called the unisensory approach because all visual cues, including lipreading, are avoided. Mothers are counseled that they must not accept the idea that their children cannot hear because this implies resignation and will lead eventually to reliance on gestures. Proponents indicate that the program is designed for children who have an average aided hearing loss of less than 60 decibels (Pollack 1964). The Verbotonal approach, developed by Guberina in Yugoslavia, also emphasizes the use of residual hearing (Craig, Craig, & DiJohnson 1972).

Most educators, however, include lipreading within their definition of oral-only approaches to language acquisition. There is a strong commitment to the belief in an exclusively oral environment, which means the conscious elimination of any meaningful gestures from the child's linguistic input during the critical period of language development (DiCarlo 1962). For example, the deaf child would not be allowed to *wave* goodbye because the wave is a meaningful gesture (John Tracy Clinic 1954). The reasoning behind the oral-only approach is that the deaf child who is permitted to use an easier gesture communication system will not work to acquire the harder oral skills of lipreading and speech. Despite the firm convictions attached to what Furth (1966b) has called the myth of least effort, it is only recently that any attempts have been made to test the theory empirically.

Most of the many studies of various aspects of the language development and deficiencies of deaf children have as their subjects children whose early linguistic input was largely unintelligible and therefore meaningless. Much of what is written about language development of the young deaf child is based on nonsystematic observational anecdotal material. There is, it would seem, unanimous concensus that the young deaf child exposed to the difficult spoken English environment is extremely impoverished. DiCarlo comments (1964) that a 5-year-old deaf child probably has fewer than 25 words in his vocabulary unless he has had intensive language instruction. Hodgson (1953) believes that only the unusual 4- or 5-year-old deaf child knows as many as 200 words, whereas the hearing child can be expected to know about 2,000 words at that age. The normal hearing child has been estimated to produce and respond to three words at age 1, 272 words at age 2, 896 words at age 3, and 1,540 words at age 4 (Vetter 1970).

Schlesinger and Meadow (1972) collected language data for 40 deaf and 20 hearing preschoolers. They found that 75% of the deaf children had a language age of 28 months or less when their mean age was 44 months. All of the hearing children scored at the expected age level.

The usual booming buzzing confusion of language is greatly increased for the deaf child. For the orally trained deaf child, reinforcement is not selective. Because his verbalizations are usually grossly distorted and often misunderstood, he often receives inappropriate and contradictory reactions from others. These inconsistent responses to his speech often produce bewilderment and may actually inhibit his future efforts to produce spoken language. He finds it more difficult to generalize, he fails to develop linguistic discrimination, he lacks both primary and secondary reinforcement for his language. It is not surprising that his vocabulary and his language are grossly retarded (DiCarlo 1964). The painfully laborious nature of language acquisition in these circumstances may help to explain not only the impoverished nature of the deaf child's language, but also the absence of any systematic studies of deaf children whose input is spoken English. Fur-

thermore, it has been suggested that discouraging the deaf child's attempts to communicate through the use of natural gestures may well dampen his curiosity about the world around him, thus impeding his capacity for formal cognitive development (Chess et al. 1971).

McNeill (1965) has speculated about the possible effect of the difficulty and delay experienced by deaf children in language acquisition. He suggests that the capacity to acquire language may be transitory, peaking between the ages of 2 and 4, and declining after that. McNeill also points to the greater difficulty experienced in the acquisition of a second language after puberty. These points lead him to observe that early language acquisition for the deaf child is especially crucial.

The production of speech cannot be separated from the reception of speech. Too often, in discussions of deaf children, this is forgotten. There are three aspects to speech development: the learning of motor skills, the mastery of cues for recognition, and the building of linguistic knowledge that is basic to both production and reception (Fry 1966). Available studies of the development of speech and speechreading (or lipreading) skills in deaf children have been conducted, with few exceptions, with oral-only children as subjects. These studies often equate speech development with language development.

Apparently the initial vocalizations of deaf infants have the same tonal quality as those of hearing infants. The one published study touching on early vocalization included only one deaf infant, however (Lenneberg, Rebelsky, & Nichols 1965). The researchers analyzed tape recordings of babies in deaf and in hearing homes. They concluded that crying and cooing depend upon maturational readiness rather than on environmental stimulation. Anecdotal accounts indicate that while deaf babies cry and coo normally at birth, the cooing gradually lessens and is no longer heard after the age of about 6 months. Of seven children whose speech development was followed beginning when they were between the ages of 11 and 32 months, none was judged to have normal vocal quality at the beginning of their training (Lach et al. 1970). After 12 months of training, five of the seven were judged to have normal voices. However, none of the children had produced more than 10 words during the year of training.

The interdependence of all linguistic skills is

illustrated when studies of the speechreading skills of deaf children are evaluated. Speechreading has been found to correlate with both written language and with reading ability, although these correlations have not been entirely consistent from one study to another. O'Neill and Davidson (1956) found no relationship to reading but Craig (1964), Myklebust (1960), and Neyhus (1969) report significant positive correlations. Speechreading has received a great deal of attention from researchers attempting to unravel the mystery of the relative abilities of deaf persons to utilize this method. Of the many factors investigated, amount of residual hearing is the only one which continues to bear an unequivocal positive relationship to the ability to read lips (Donnelly 1969; Farwell 1975). It may well be that the contradictory nature of the results of investigations of other areas may be due to inconsistencies in the selection of research subjects in terms of some of the subtleties of the audiological variables.

Variability of reported correlations between IQ test scores and speechreading ability is great. Most researchers have reported low positive but nonsignificant correlations (Butt & Chreist 1968; Lewis 1972; O'Neill & Davidson 1956; Reid 1947; Simmons 1959). Others have considered the influence of visual synthesis, visual closure, visual memory, concept formation, and rhythm. Most studies report positive correlations between speechreading and chronological age. The fact that the correlations are generally low indicates, however, that speechreading is not a naturally developing compensatory phenomenon. The effects of training on speechreading ability are also unclear. However, training does not appear to have long-term positive effects on speechreading proficiency (Black, O'Reilly, & Peck 1963; Craig 1964; Heider & Heider 1940).

SUMMARY

1 The basic deprivation of deafness is the difficulty it produces for the process of normal language acquisition. This includes the basic inner language abilities as well as the more superficial oral language skills of speech and speechreading.

2 Language acquisition was reviewed for three categories of deaf children whose linguistic milieus and parental inputs differed. The first group includes deaf children of deaf parents who use the American Sign Language, or Ameslan, only in the home. The few existing studies illustrate some of the variations that occur when linguistic socialization takes place in a visual rather than an auditory mode, relying on some features of visual salience. Initial holophrastic usage, progress in combining two or more signs, usage of pivot and open signs, and overgeneralization of first-learned language rules were all similar to observations reported for hearing children.

3 Deaf children of deaf or hearing parents who use some simultaneous combination of signed and spoken English develop bimodal expressive language. Vocabulary growth, grammatical complexity, and syntactical structure all progress in the same way as in hearing children.

4 Deaf children whose parents use oral English only have not received systematic study in terms of the process of their language acquisition. Studies of the language proficiency of these children at various ages make it clear that acquisition is painfully slow. Linguistic retardation continues through adolescence and remains a factor among most deaf adults.

5 Analyses of the written language of deaf children have shown that the vocabulary is limited and sentence structure is simpler and more rigid than for hearing children of the same ages.

6 Analyses of studies that can be utilized for either direct or inferential evidence about the efficacy of various methods of linguistic socialization for deaf children show no reason to support continuing dedication to an oral-only approach. Children exposed to early manual or simultaneous manual-oral input appear to develop more adequate inner language with no reduction in their abilities to use speech and speechreading for communication than do children not so exposed.

REFERENCES

Anthony, C. A. Signing essential English. Unpublished master's thesis, Eastern Michigan University, 1966.

Bellugi, U. The acquisition of negation. Unpublished doctoral dissertation, Harvard University, 1967.

Bellugi, U. Studies in sign language. In T. J. O'Rourke (Ed.), Psycholinguistics and total communication: the state of the art. Washington, D.C.: American Annals of the Deaf, 1972.

Bellugi, U., & Klima, E. S. The roots of language in the sign talk of the deaf. Psychology Today, 1972, 6, 661–64, 76.

Bellugi, U., & Klima, E. S. Aspects of sign language and its structure. Cambridge, Mass.: M.I.T. Press, 1975.

Bender, R. E. The conquest of deafness. Cleveland: Press of Western Reserve University, 1960.

Black, J. W.; O'Reilly, P. P.: & Peck, L. Self-administered training in lipreading. Journal of Speech and Hearing Disorders, 1963, 28, 183–186.

Bonvillian, J. D.; Charrow, V. R.; & Nelson, K. E.

Psycholinguistic and educational implications of deafness. *Human Development*, 1973, *16*, 321–345.

Bornstein, H. A description of some current sign systems designed to represent English. *American Annals of the Deaf*, 1973, *118*, 454–463.

Brown, R. *A first language, the early stages.* Cambridge, Mass.: Harvard University Press, 1973.

Butt, D., & Chreist, F. M. A speechreading test for young children. *Volta Review*, 1968, *70*, 225–235.

Chess, S.; Korn, S. J.: & Fernandez, P. B. *Psychiatric disorders of children with congenital rubella.* New York: Brunner/Mazel, 1971.

Cooper, R. L., & Rosenstein, J. Language acquisition of deaf children. *Volta Review*, 1966, *68*, 58–67.

Craig, W. N. Effects of pre-school training on the development of reading and lipreading skills of deaf children. *American Annals of the Deaf*, 1964, *109*, 280–296.

Craig, W. N.; Craig, H. B.; & DiJohnson, A. Pre-school verbotonal instruction for deaf children. *Volta Review*, 1972, *74*, 236–246.

DiCarlo, L. M. *The deaf.* Englewood Cliffs, N.J.: Prentice-Hall, 1964.

Donnelly, K. An investigation into the determinants of lipreading of deaf adults. *International Audiology*, 1969, *8*, 501–508.

Farwell, R. M. Speechreading, a review of the research. *American Annals of the Deaf.* 1975 (in press).

Fry, D. B. The development of the phonological system in the normal and the deaf child. In F. Smith & G. A. Miller (Eds.), *The genesis of language: a psycholinguistic approach.* Cambridge, Mass.: M.I.T. Press, 1966.

Furth, H. G. *Thinking without language: psychological implications of deafness.* New York: Free Press, 1966. (b)

Gustason, G.; Pfetzing, D.; & Zawolkow, E. *Signing exact English.* Rossmoor, Calif.: Modern Signs Press, 1972.

Heider, F., & Heider, G. M. Studies in the psychology of the deaf, No. 1 Psychological Division, Clarke School for the Deaf. *Psychological Monographs*, 1940, *52*, No. 232.

Hoffmeister, R. J., & Moores, D. F. The acquisition of specific reference in the linguistic system of a deaf child of deaf parents. Research Report No. 53, Research, Development and Demonstration Center in Education of Handicapped Children, University of Minnesota, August 1973.

John Tracy Clinic. Correspondence course for parents of little deaf children. Mimeographed. Los Angeles: John Tracy Clinic, 1954.

Kannapell, B. M., Hamilton, L. B., & Bornstein, H. *Signs for instructional purposes.* Washington, D.C.: Gallaudet College Press, 1969.

Lach, R., Ling, D.; Ling, A. H., & Ship, N. Early speech development in deaf infants. *American Annals of the Deaf*, 1970, *115*, 522–526.

Lenneberg, E. H. *Biological foundations of language.* New York: Wiley, 1967.

Lenneberg, E. H.; Rebelsky, F. G.; & Nichols, I. A. The vocalization of infants born to deaf and to hearing parents. *Human Development*, 1965, *8*, 23–37.

Levine, E. S. Historical review of special education and mental health services. In J. D. Rainer, K. Z. Altshuler, & F. J. Kallmann (Eds.), *Family and mental health problems in a deaf population* (2d ed.) Springfield, Ill.: Thomas, 1969.(a)

Lewis, D. N. Lipreading skills of hearing impaired children in regular schools. *Volta Review, 1972, 74*, 303–311.

McCall, E. A generative grammar of signs. Unpublished master's thesis, University of Iowa, 1965.

McNeill, D. The capacity for language acquisition. In Vocational Rehabilitation Administration, Research on behavioral aspects of deafness, Proceedings of a National Research Conference on behavioral aspects of deafness. New Orleans. May 1965.

Myklebust, H. R. *The psychology of deafness, sensory deprivation, learning and adjustment.* New York: Grune & Stratton, 1960.

Neyhus, A. *Speechreading failure in deaf children.* Washington, D. C.: Office of Education, Department of Health, Education, and Welfare, 1969.

O'Neill, J. J., & Davidson, J. L. Relationship between lipreading and five psychological factors. *Journal of Speech and Hearing Disorders*, 1956, 21, 478–481.

O'Rourke, T. J. *A basic course in manual communication.* Silver Spring, Md.: National Association of the Deaf, 1970.

Pollack, D. Acoupedies: a unisensory approach to auditory training. *Volta Review*, 1964, *66*, 400–409.

Rainer, J. D.; Altshuler, K. Z.; & Kallmann, F. J. (Eds.) *Family and mental health problems in a deaf population* (2d ed.) Springfield, Ill.: Thomas, 1969.

Reid, G. W. A preliminary investigation of the testing of lipreading achievement. *Journal of Speech and Hearing Disorders, 1947, 12*, 77–82.

Rosenstein, J. Perception, cognition, and language in deaf children. *Exceptional Children*, 1961, *27*, 276–284.

Schlesinger, H. S. Beyond the range of sound. *California Medicine*, 1969, *110*, 213–217.

Schlesinger, H. S. Meaning and enjoyment: language acquisition of deaf children. In T. J. O'Rourke (Ed.), *Psycholinguistics and total communication: the state of the art.* Washington, D.C.: American Annals of the Deaf, 1972.

Schlesinger, H. S. The acquisition of sign language. Unpublished manuscript, Department of Psychiatry, University of California, San Francisco, 1974.

Schlesinger, H. S., & Meadow, K. P. *Sound and sign: childhood deafness and mental health.* Berkeley: University of California Press, 1972.

Scouten, E. L. The Rochester method, an oral multisensory approach for instructing prelingual deaf children. *American Annals of the Deaf*, 1967, *112*, 50–55.

Simmons, A. A. Factors related to lipreading. *Journal of Speech and Hearing Research*, 1959, *2*, 340–352.

Stokoe, W. C., Jr. *Sign language structure: an outline of the visual communication systems of the American deaf.* (Studies in linguistics, occasional papers, 8) Buffalo, N.Y.: Department of Anthropology and Linguistics, University of Buffalo, 1960.

Stokoe, W. C., Jr.; Casterline, D. C.; & Croneberg, C. G. *A dictionary of American Sign Language on linguistic principles.* Washington, D.C.: Gallaudet College Press, 1965.

Stuckless, E. R., & Birch, J. W. The influence of early manual communication on the linguistic development of deaf children. *American Annals of the Deaf,* 1966, *III,* 452–460, 499–504.

Vetter, H. J. *Language behavior and psychopathology.* Chicago: Rand-McNally, 1970.

Reading 16

Code Switching in Children's Language[1]

Jean Berko Gleason

Somewhere along the road to language acquisition children must gain control over not only a vast vocabulary and a complicated grammar, but a variety of styles of speaking to different people under different circumstances. The code for addressing a policeman who has just stopped you for speeding is not the same as the code for addressing either little babies or old friends; and anyone studying adult language who restricts himself to one or another of these situations would obviously have only a part of the picture of the complexity and variety that exists in adult language. Paradoxically, until recent times, those of us who have studied child language have restricted ourselves to samples of the child's language to us, the interviewer, or to the child's mother or teacher, and we have assumed that that was it: child language. Whether children, like adults, have control of several codes, and vary their speech in accordance with the situation they are in or the person they are addressing has become an area of increasing interest to a number of researchers in the past few years. In order to investigate code switching in children's language, it is necessary to observe the same child in a number of different speech situations.

This chapter is a preliminary report on a study that Elliot Mishler and I conducted. The findings are observational, rather than quantitative; and it is my hope that experiments with hard data and statistically meaningful results will follow.

In order to investigate the child's emerging control of different styles or codes, we began with the study of the natural conversations that occur in families with several children; this enabled us to study the way that parents alter their style in speaking to children of different ages and sexes, and it put the children in a natural position to a variety of addresses: their parents, ourselves, other children, and babies.

Our basic data were collected from five similarly constituted families who have children attending a private school in Cambridge, Massachusetts. Each of these families has at least three children: a first- or second-grader; a preschool child aged 4 or 5; and an even younger child under the age of 3. All of these families are well-educated and upper middle-class. Most of the data were taped in the families' homes in two 1-hour sessions by Sara Harkness, a doctoral candidate in social anthropology at Harvard, or by myself and Elliot Mishler, head of the Laboratory of Social Psychiatry at the Harvard Medical School. In addition to these tapes we have recorded one other family whose children attend public school in another community. Finally, I made extensive recordings of the 4-year-old son of one of the five families in several different settings: in his own home with his parents; outdoors with his younger and older brothers; at my home talking to me and playing with my 8-year-old daughter, Cindy; and at his nursery school with his friends and teachers. For this one

[1]This research was supported in part by Grant GS-3001 from the National Science Foundation to Elliot Mishler. The paper was written while I was a senior research associate in the Laboratory of Social Psychiatry at the Harvard Medical School. I am grateful to Dr. Mishler for many of the insights reported here.

4-year-old, at least, I have captured a broad variety of speech situations and the stylistic variations that attend them.

ADULT LANGUAGE TO CHILDREN

Since we were observing families, it was inevitable that our sample contain a great deal of language to children from adults, and we examined this adult language for evidence of stylistic variation. Since this adult language is the basic input to the child, some understanding of it is prerequisite to understanding the full significance of the children's productions. It is important to know, for instance, which codes are the children's own, passed on by the peer group, and which codes are passed to the child by adults. Therefore, before discussing the children's language some description of the salient features of the adult codes is in order.

The adults use baby-talk style in talking to the babies. The features of this style have been well reported by others but, briefly, we can say they raised the fundamental frequency of their voices, used simple short sentences with concrete nouns, diminuitives, and terms of endearment, expanded the children's utterances, and in general performed the linguistic operations that constitute baby-talk style. There was a lot of individual variation in the extent to which all of these features might be employed. One mother, for instance, spoke in a normal voice to her husband, a high voice to her 4-year-old, a slightly raised voice to her 8-year-old, and when she talked to her baby she fairly squeaked. Fathers and mothers did not talk in exactly the same way to the babies, and there seemed to be some sex differences, as well, in how the babies were addressed. Some of the boy babies were addressed, especially by their fathers, in a sort of hail-baby-well-met style: While turning them upside down or engaged in similar play, the fathers said things like "Come here, you little nut!" or "Hey fruitcake!" Baby girls were dealt with more gently, both physically and verbally.

Adults used a quite different style to the children who were no longer babies, although there were some common features—the use of endearments, for instance. Both children and babies might be called "sweetie" or have their names played with—one baby was called "funny bunny," for instance, and in a different family a 5-year-old girl was called "Huffy Muffy," so this kind of rhyming play is not uncommon. Otherwise, once the little children's language was comprehensible, expansion and similar devices dropped out while other features assumed salience. Several of these features might be sketched here.

The language addressed to the children we saw who were between the ages of 4 and 8 was basically a language of socialization, and it was a very controlling language in so far as it told the child what to do, what to think, and how to feel.

Although the language was not rich in actual imperatives, the implied imperatives abounded; a mother might say to a child: "Do you want to take your own plate off the table, sweetie?" when the child really had no options in the matter. We saw a lot of dinner-table interaction because we were hoping to get samples of the father's speech as well, and this talk contained many instructions on sitting up, not throwing forks, and generally, how to behave.

The parents typically spelled out explicitly the dangers of situations: a mother might place the food in front of a child while saying, "hot, hot!" One does not give boiling hot food to a little baby, and hostesses do not say, "hot, hot!" as they serve their dinner guests, so this is a special situation. A hostess might, of course, say "Watch out for this dish—it's just out of the oven."

In their conversations with the children of this age, parents typically supplied the entire context. If they asked a question, they included with it the answer. We have, for instance, the following: a father comes to pick up his son at nursery school and says: "Where's your lunchbox? I bet it's inside," or the following conversation between a mother and her 5-year-old son:

Mother: How was school today? Did you go to assembly?

Son: Yes.

Mother: Did the preschoolers go to assembly?

Son: Yes.

Mother: Did you stay for the whole assembly or just part of it?

The child really does not have to do anything but say yes or no—the mother is providing the whole conversation herself, and, undoubtedly, in the process, teaching him to make a conversation and what kind of responses are expected of him.

Another feature of this adult to child language was that the adults frequently exaggerated their responses, almost beyond reason, or reacted in the way they thought the child ought to feel. For instance, the following:

A child in nursery school fills a bucket with a hose. The teacher says: "Hey, wow, that's almost full to the *top!*"

A child shows his mother some old toys that he has just been given by another child. The mother whoops with joy.

A child shows his father a simple model he has made. The father says: "Hey, that's *really* something, isn't it?"

A child tells a neighbor he has been to the circus. The neighbor says: "Boy! That must have been fun."

Since full buckets, old toys, simple models, and even the circus do not really impress adults that much, they must be telling the child how *he* ought to feel.

These are only a few of the special features of the language of socialization.

The transition from this directive socializing language to the colloquial style used by adult familiars is not easily accomplished. Quite to the contrary, parents often persist in addressing their 8-year-olds as if they were 4, much to the dismay of the children. From what we have seen, it is actually because of signals from the child, often very explicit and angry signals, that the adult ceases to address him as if he were very little. Mothers, for instance, typically spell out all the dangers of the situation to young children, as I have said. At some point the child begins to act quite disgusted with what the parents say. When the mother tells him to be careful crossing the street, he says something like, "O.K., O.K., I *know* how to cross the street." This angry negative feedback to her utterances in the language of socialization eventually teaches her to address him in a different style, and perhaps only mention that traffic is very heavy that day. Of course some parents never do seem to understand the angry signals and continue telling their children to wear their rubbers until they are 35.

THE CHILDREN'S LANGUAGE

The children in our sample ranged in age from infancy to 8 years. By and large we were not primarily looking for evidence of baby-talk style. Some things did seem readily evident from observing the very young children and talking to their parents, however. The first is that even the tiniest children make some distinctions. The basic, earliest variation is simply between talking and not talking. Very small children will frequently talk or jabber nonsense to their own parents or siblings, but fall silent in the presence of strangers. When the parent tries to get the baby to say, "Hi," or "Bye-bye," to the interviewer, the baby stares blankly; and the mother says, "I don't know what's wrong. He really can talk. He says bye-bye all the time." The baby remains silent. After the inverviewer leaves, surrounded once more by familiar faces, the baby suddenly springs to life and says a resounding "Bye-bye!" So the first variation is between speech and silence.

Another, more obviously stylistic variation we have seen in the language of the children under 4 as well as those over 4, has been the selective use of whining, by which I mean a repetitive, insistent, singsong demand or complaint, and not crying, which is very difficult for little children to inhibit. The whining basically occurs to parents and parent figures, and a child may abruptly switch to a whine at the sight of his parent, when he has previously been talking to someone else in a quite normal tone. In the nursery school I visited, for instance, one child was talking with his friends when his father arrived. At the sight of his father, he abruptly altered his tone and began to whine, "Pick me up" at him.

In listening to the tapes of the children's speech, we had in mind the generally recognized kinds of language style that linguists talk about. Baby-talk style, peer-group colloquial style, and a more formal style for talking to older people and strangers seemed to be three kinds of codes that all adults have and that we might expect to see emerging in the children as they grow older. We thought that the interviewers or other strange adults would bring out the formal style; that the other children of about the same age—close siblings and the many friends who appeared—would bring out the colloquial style; and that baby-talk style would begin to emerge in the language of these children when they talked to the babies in their families.

We did not originally count on the presence of the language of socialization, but it soon became evident that it was there in many cases where children were talking to somewhat younger children. Part of a conversation between my 8-year-old daughter, Cindy, and the 4-year-old I was studying went as follows. She wanted to give him some of her toys, and she said, "Would you like to have some for you at your house?" When he agreed, she said, "No you just carry them home, and don't run." She then helped him across the street to his house, and when they got there said, "Ricky, you want to show your mother? You want to show your mother that you got these?"

He said, "Yeah. For me." And she replied, "You share them." We have many other instances of older children talking to younger children this way.

We have no real instances of these children using typical adult formal style, probably in part at least because we, as interviewers, were familiar to them and part of their own community. We failed to be formidable strangers, and the parents addressed us in familiar ways as well, so there was very little in the way of formal greetings and farewells, or politeness formulas. Only in one family did we get anything like formal language, and this was the one family outside our Cambridge private school sample that Elliot Mishler and I visited together. In this family, our language and the language of the family proved far more formal. The mother, for example, said to us after we had come in "Have a seat. It's the best one in the house." We had brought some small toys for the children in the family, and the first-grade boy approached Dr. Mishler somewhat later and said, "Thank you for bringing the presents" in a very formal way, with pauses between the words, careful enunciation, and a flat, affectless tone. The other families treated us in a far more colloquial way.

While it was not marked by adult formal features, the children's language to us had its own characteristics. Ricky, the 4-year-old, who said to his father things like "I wanna be up on your shoulder" *fourteen times* in a row, gave me the following explanation of the tooth fairy:

Uh, well, you see, if your teeth come out, the teeth come back and by, uh, a fairy. And, you see, the teeth that came out you have to put under your pillow, and then the fairy comes and takes 'em, you see, and he leaves a little money or a little candy.

This language is far more narrative and far more didactic than anything he directed at either his parents or other children. This is clearly different speech.

The style the children employed in talking to one another was markedly different from their style to adults or to babies, especially in those cases where they were playing together. This peer-group style included a very rich use of expressive words like "yukk" and "blech," and of sound effects. Our tapes are full of bangs, sirens, airplane noises, animal sounds, and explosions. There are some sex differences, since the boys played more violent games and accompanied them with appropriate sounds, but the girls made a lot of noises as well.

The children playing together often launched into chants, rhymes, television commercials, theme songs of favorite shows, and animal acts. They frequently took off from what they were saying into dramatic play involving changing their voices and pretending they were other people or other creatures. This peer-group language was very different from the language directed at adults. Other features of this child-to-child language that might be mentioned are the very frequent use of first names, as in adult-child language, but no endearments, even in those cases where a somewhat older child was speaking to a somewhat younger one as if she were a parent, as I mentioned before. Finally, there was a striking amount of copying behavior in the children's utterances; many instances of one child saying just what another child has said, without any change in emphasis or structure. For instance, the following example from the nursery school:

She: Well, don't you want to see the raspberries?

Malcolm: How 'bout you pick some for me and I'll eat them?

Eric: Yeah, and how 'bout pick some for me and I'll eat them?

The third child adds *yeah, and* to the second child's statement and then repeats it. An adult would not have repeated *and I'll eat them* under the same circumstances, although he might have said, "How 'bout picking some for *me?*" Eric's repetition is quite flat—the intonation contours are the same as Malcolm's, and there is no shift of emphasis. He is really not varying the statement so much as echoing it. Where an adult says just what another adult has said, his intention is usually mockery, but for the children, imitation of this sort is very common, and passes unremarked.

The children's language to the babies in the families was also examined for evidence of baby-talk style. While most of the features of peer group code appeared in the language of the entire 4- to 8-year-old sample, there were age differences in the ability to use baby-talk style. The older children were in control of the basic features of baby-talk style—their sentences to the babies were short and repetitive, and uttered in a kind of singing style. In one family I asked an 8-year-old to ask his 2-year-old brother to take a glass to the kitchen. He said:

"Here, Joey, take this to the kitchen. Take it to the kitchen." (Baby-talk intonation, high voice.)

A little while later, I asked him to ask his 4-year-old brother to take a glass to the kitchen. This time he said:

"Hey, Rick, take this to the kitchen, please." (Normal intonation.) This is clear evidence of code switching in the language of this 8-year-old child.

On the other end of the spectrum, the 4-year-old, Ricky, whom I followed about, did not use baby-talk style to his 2-year-old brother. He typically did not use either a special intonation or repetition. He said to the baby: "Do you know what color your shoes are?" in just the same way he said: "What's the name of the book, Anthony?" to his brother; and "I don't think he know how to climb up" to his father.

Somewhere in between no baby-talk style and full baby-talk style lies slightly inappropriate baby-talk style, which we saw particularly in some 5- and 6-year-old girls. Unlike the 4-year-olds, 5- and 6-year-old children made clear efforts to adjust their language to suit the babies they addressed. We have the following conversation:

2-year-old: Dead bug!
6-year-old: That ant!
2-year-old: That bug!
6-year-old: Hey, Susie, that's ant; that's not bug, that ant!

The 6-year-old is here obviously trying to accommodate the baby sister by talking in what she regards as "her language," but she misses the cues when she says "That's ant." Good baby sentences would be either "That ant," as the child says, or "That a ant," but a copula without an article in "That's ant" doesn't ring true.

Listening to these children begin to use baby-talk style and then use it fluently by the time they are 7 or 8 makes it clear that knowing how to talk to babies is not something you keep with you from having been a baby; you have to learn it again. The young children in the sample who were still completing

their knowledge of regular English syntax were in no position to play with it. They made their sentences the only way they knew how, grinding them out with laborious intensity at times, looking neither to the baby left nor formal right.

The observations we have made thus far are in their preliminary stages, based on only five families, all from the same socioeconomic background and geographical region. The similarities among these families were, however, so great as to make us feel confident that they are generally occurring features, at least in upper middle-class homes. From what we have seen, it seems clear that children are not faced with a vast undifferentiated body of English from which they must make some order as best they can. The parents in these families talked in a very consistent and predictable style to their babies, a style which other researchers have described; and we have found that parents and other adults use a separate style for talking to growing children. This style is different from the informal or colloquial style that teenagers or old friends use to one another, and serves special functions: It is the language of socialization. While baby-talk style is concerned with learning the language, with establishing communication, the language of socialization is filled with social rules. The mother's questions contain answers and in this way show how to make a conversation. The adult emphasizes and exaggerates his own reactions, points up relationships, names feelings, controls and directs the child, and in many ways makes explicit his own world view. The language directed at young children is a teaching language. It tells about the world, and must, because of its special features, be recognized as a separate code.

The original aim of this study was to see if, indeed, children talk in different ways to different people. The answer is yes; infants are selective about whom they talk to at all. Four-year-olds may whine at their mothers, engage in intricate verbal play with their peers, and reserve their narrative, discursive tales for their grown-up friends. By the time they are 8, children have added to the foregoing some of the politeness routines of formal adult speech, baby-talk style, and the ability to talk to younger children in the language of socialization. The details of the emergence of these codes are yet to be elaborated.

Reading 17

Cognitive-Linguistic Development

Barry Silverstein
Ronald Krate

BLACK ENGLISH VERNACULAR: DEFICIT OR DIFFERENCE?

By 1966, low-income urban black children were being described by many psychologists and educators as essentially nonverbal or so deficient in linguistic skills as to be severely inhibited in the development of intellectual abilities and academic achievement. Describing a group of four-year-olds who, they claimed, represented a "fairly unbiased selection from the lower stratum" of an urban black community, Bereiter and Englemann said:

Language for them is unwieldy and not very useful. For some of them, speaking is clearly no fun, and they manage as far as possible to get along without it. Others enjoy social speech and use it a good deal in play and social intercourse, but seldom for purposes of learning or reasoning; their language, as they use it, is not adequate for these purposes.[1]

In addition, Bereiter and Englemann tell us, "preschool disadvantaged children are likely to show distressing tendencies to hit, bite, kick, scream, run wildly about, cling, climb into laps, steal, lie, hide, ignore directions, and defy authority." These behaviors are to be considered simply "inappropriate behaviors for the classroom"; the children's social or emotional needs are of little relevance to understanding them. "Cultural deprivation" is essentially to be understood as "language deprivation." The teacher is instructed to "see the task for what it is: *teaching naïve children how to act in a new situation.*"[2] The four-year-old child has no right to be held in an adult's lap, nor should he be allowed to cling to the teacher. To remedy the children's linguistic deficiencies, the teacher must restrain them from expressing strong emotions or personal concerns and drill them to behave as the controlling adults would have them behave.

In the late 1960s and early 1970s the linguistic-cognitive-deficit explanation of low school achievement among poor black children came under increasing attack. Anthropologically oriented behavioral scientists began to argue that, instead of being deficient or defective in their linguistic-conceptual systems, black children possess linguistic and cognitive systems that are structurally coherent but different from those of white children. Baratz and Baratz, for example, claim:

The current linguistic data . . . do not support the assumption of a linguistic deficit. . . . Many lower-class Negro children speak a well-ordered, highly structured, but different dialect from that of Standard English. These children have developed a language.[3]

From the "cultural-deprivation" viewpoint, black children's linguistic-cognitive abilities are *deficient,* unable to meet the demands of the standard school curriculum without preschool remediation; from the cultural-difference viewpoint, they are *different* and require a different curriculum. The two positions have polarized. Their adherents often fail to take into account the fact that poor black children are *bicultural* and *bidialectical:* They are simultaneously inducted into the urban black community and the more inclusive mainstream, white-dominated society.[4] In socializing their children lower-class black mothers have had to take into account the demands of a widening circle of social systems: the black family, the black community, and the wider society. By the time they reached the upper elementary school grades, most of the children we knew in Central Harlem seemed to comprehend most verbal messages directed to them, whether they were framed in everyday standard English or in black dialect and idiom, although occasionally, because of pronunciation differences, *we* had difficulty understanding a word or two spoken by a child, and sometimes a child would interpret our words in a way we had not intended.

In their own verbal productions the children often used black vernacular vocabulary and syntax, but standard English was not a foreign language to them: The dialect they spoke was a variant of the English language. Just as we reject any image of these children as deficient cognitive machines, so we reject any image of the children as exotic primitives. The children were black and poor, but they were Americans—oppressed Americans, Americans with an African heritage, but Americans living in the contemporary United States.

The linguistic-cognitive-deficit theorists rely heavily on the findings of a long line of studies indicating the middle-class children, from infancy onward, generally appear to be more advanced than working-class or lower-class children in most aspects of language behavior: vocabulary acquisition, sound discrimination, articulation, and sentence structure.[5] There are some exceptions to this trend: Inner-city children, black and white, have been found to respond to verbal stimuli with free word associations at a higher rate than white surburban children (from much higher-income families) at the first-grade level; although they fall behind at the third-grade level, they become equal at the fifth-grade level.[6]

The cultural-deprivation theorists view the poorer linguistic performance of lower-class children as indicative of linguistic-cognitive deficiencies, which they trace to qualitative differences in parent-child interaction associated with social-class level. Middle-class mothers reportedly present their infants, particularly girls, with more face-to-face verbalizations unaccompanied by competing sources of stimulation than working-class mothers. Middle-class girls are reported to be the most advanced group in the rate of linguistic-cognitive development.

With specific regard to lower-class black children, deficit theorists point to research carried out in schools or school-like settings which demonstrates that black children have greater difficulty than middle-class children (black or white) in using words to classify actions or objects.[7] For example, when shown a series of four pictures, each depicting a person engaging in some activity, lower-class black children had considerable difficulty pointing to the one that showed a person "tying," "pouring," "digging," and "picking." The children were not deficient in experience with the referent actions but, rather, had difficulty applying labels to them. This difficulty in making specific connections between words and referents is related causally by deficit

theorists to a relative lack of active verbal interaction between the children and adults in their homes. Deficit theorists see low-income children as less able to use words in thinking, which leads to poor performance on tasks in which words must be used to form categories or express conceptual relationships. Thus, when asked, "Why do these pictures go together?" lower-class black first-graders are more likely to answer: "Because they look the same" or "Because they have legs" than "Because they are all animals." Deficit theorists regard "They are all animals." as a more explicit statement of a concept and, hence, a developmentally more advanced reply; the alternative responses are viewed not as legitimate stylistic ways of ordering perceptions but, rather, as primitive modes of functioning.

The difference theorists argue that many of the researches in support of the conclusion that lower-class black children have linguistic-cognitive deficiencies are based on ethnocentric or racist perceptions. The deficit model is based on the assumption that only standard English as spoken by middle-class whites is acceptable and that any variant, such as the dialects of low-income populations, is a "bad" or "deficient" version. The difference theorists argue that the dialects of low-income whites and blacks as well as their differences from standard English represent parallel development, not deficits.

Cultural-difference theorists claim that no evidence has been found that low-income children have more difficulty acquiring the language of their own community than middle-class children do acquiring theirs.[8] Further, these theorists assert that careful study of the structural differences between the black English vernacular and standard English reveals no grammatical relationship that can be expressed in standard English but not in the black idiom. For example, there is an important distinction between "he workin'" and "he be workin'"—structural forms found in the black English vernacular.[9] "He workin'" means he is working right now; "he be workin'" means he works habitually. In black idiom, the word be is employed as an auxiliary to express the habitual tense, to express action that is of long duration. This is a tense found in West African languages but not in standard English.[10]

Children acquire language not so much through imitation as through problem-solving processes. When two-year-olds are presented with statements to imitate, what the children give back is not a verbatim repetition of what the adult said but the results of their own cognitive processing; the children reduce what was said to their current grammar.[11] Thus, "the pencil is green" is repeated as "pencil green," and "the little boy is eating some pink ice cream" is repeated as "little boy eating pink ice cream."

A similar cognitive-processing system has been revealed in studies of low-income speakers in Harlem. When asked to repeat sentences presented in standard English, Harlem boys aged eleven to fourteen demonstrated that some standard English structures were first *understood,* then *translated* to fit the speaker's own syntactic rules, whereas others were simply *repeated* as presented because they were already in a syntactical form used by the speaker. Thus, "I asked Alvin if he knows how to play basketball" became "I aks Alvin do he know how to play basketball," and "nobody ever" became "nobody never." "Money, who is eleven, can't spit as far as Boo can" was repeated as given, as was "Larry is a stupid fool."[12]

It is important to distinguish between the *production* and the *comprehension* grammars of speakers of black English vernacular. Labov and Cohen have reported variability in the grammatical rules followed by black adults in Harlem depending upon the context in which the speech is produced and the speaker's linguistic experience (e.g., his social-class level and his Northern or Southern background). In general they reported differences in the phonological rules used in careful speech and in casual speech. Middle-class black adults came much closer to the production of standard English in careful speech than did working-class black adults. Thus, in linguistic production, middle-class black adults would appear to be more bicultural than working- or lower-class black adults.

Some lower-middle-class black adults who are economically upwardly mobile have been found to display what Labov has called a "hypercorrect" linguistic pattern.[13] This phenomenon is characterized by an extensive shift from black dialect to standard English forms when changing from casual to careful speech; a sharper tendency than any other group to stigmatize the speech of others; less accurate self-reports of their own speech patterns than others—shifting their perception of their own speech toward the standard norm; the most negative overt feelings about their own speech; and the strongest reactions against their own vernacular. The "hypercorrect" pattern of the lower middle class is found more regularly and in more extreme form among black women than among men. The existence of this pattern suggests that a considerable number of upwardly mobile blacks have accepted the standard white view of black cultural characteristics. They appear to regard their own vernacular as "mistakes" in speech rather than as a second dialect or a different speech system. Such blacks are thus caught in a practical and psychological bind. If, in either-or fashion, they reject standard English, they may restrict their job opportunities in a white-dominated society. If they reject the black idiom, they may experience difficulties in relating to family and friends and, to the extent that they perceive their speech as different from a standard that they believe to be "correct" or "respectable," they may suffer damage to their self-esteem.[14]

The conflict involved in the "hypercorrect pattern" may not develop fully until late adolescence, when the youth begins to comprehend the dimensions of economic discrimination against blacks. As we have noted, low-income black children generally seem able to understand both standard English and their own dialect. However, it is not clear how early lower-class black children will make use of different rules when speaking casually and carefully, as black adults have been observed to do. One study has found some distinctions between the verbal productions of lower-class and middle-class ninth-grade black girls in Chicago depending upon whether they were aiming at "school talk" (standard English) or "everyday talk."[15] A young black field worker met with groups of three girls at a time for discussion. In some groups, the worker asked questions framed in standard English and told the girls to answer in their best "school talk" because their recorded speech would be analyzed by educators. In other groups she framed questions in a style that made use of black English forms and told the girls to use "everyday" talk in replying since their answers would be heard only by the field worker. When the lower-class black girls replied to the field worker using "school talk," their speech became a little more like standard English; however, when they replied in "everyday talk," utilizing the black English vernacular, they gave more elaborate responses. While the middle-class black girls also shifted to more standard English when speaking "school talk," they gave relatively elaborate linguistic responses whether talking "school talk" or "everyday talk." Like the middle-class girls, the lower-class girls were able to change their verbal performance somewhat to meet the performance standards of the mainstream society, but they appeared to feel inhibited in performance situations where mainstream standards would be used to judge their competence. The middle-class girls, on the other hand, gave equally complex performances whether the standard for competence was mainstream or ghetto-specific, suggesting that these girls came closer to being fully bicultural than their lower-class peers.

Although poor quality in verbal performance may seem characteristic of many low-income black children in schools that are white-middle-class-dominated, in other contexts, as we have shown, the children tend to be talkative and highly articulate. The respect accorded to the good talker, the man of words, in the black community and the extent to which verbal performance is utilized as a way to achieve status, particularly in street peer groups, suggests the survival in black America of African oral traditions.[16] Black youth may display a distinct variety of verbal skills in the streets: "Rapping," "shucking," "jiving," "running it down," "copping a plea," "signifying," and "sounding" are all aspects of the black idiom. Each type of talking

> . . . has it own distinguishing features of form, style, and function; each is influenced by, and influences, the speaker, setting, and audience; and each sheds light on the black perspective and the black condition . . . on those orienting values and attitudes that will cause a speaker to speak or perform in his own way within the social context of the black community.[17]

Most ghetto children learn to comprehend and communicate appropriately in these styles of talking.

Smitherman argues that the black idiom cannot be viewed apart from black culture and the black experience in America.[18] She distinguishes two perspectives in looking at black English: linguistic and stylistic. From the linguistic perspective, which emphasizes pronounciation and syntax, Smitherman argues that black English is simply one of many contemporary American dialects; it is likely that the linguistic patterns of black English differ from those of standard English only in surface structure. However, although black people use the vocabulary of the English language, some words are selected out of that lexicon and given a special black semantic slant. Smitherman suggests that the following principles apply:

1 Because of the need of blacks for a code that is unintelligible to whites, the words that are given a special black slant are discarded when they are adopted by whites; e.g., blacks no longer speak of a "hip" brother but of a "together" brother.

2 The concept of denotation *vs.* connotation is not applicable to the black idiom. The black idiom is characterized, instead, by shades of meaning along a connotative spectrum. For example, depending upon the context, "bad" may mean extraordinary, beautiful, good, versatile, or a variety of other terms of positive value. Certain words in the black lexicon may be used to indicate either approbation or denigration, depending upon context; for example, "He's my main nigger" means he is my best friend, whereas "The nigger ain't shit" may indicate a variety of negative characterics, depending upon the context.

3 Approbation and denigration refer to the semantic level; on the grammatical level, the same word may serve two other functions: intensification and completion. Thus, in "Niggers was getting out of there left and right, them niggers was running, and so the niggers said . . .," etc., the word "nigger" may be devoid of real meaning, serving simply to give the sentence a subject and animate the conversation rather than to indicate approbation or denigration. "Cats" or "guys" or "people" would serve as well.

Turning to the stylistic elements of black English, Smitherman enumerates the following elements that differentiate black speakers of English from white speakers:

1 *Call and response.* A speaker's solo voice alternates or is intermingled with responses from the audience. This is basic to the black oral tradition. For example, the congregation responding to the preacher—"Preach, Reverend," "That's right"—or the street audience responding to displays of repartee with laughter, palm-slapping, and such phrases as "get back, nigger," "Git down, baby."

2 *Rhythmic pattern.* This includes cadence, tone, and musical quality. Black speakers often employ a pattern that is lyrical and sonorous and generally emphasizes sound apart from sense through the repetition of certain sounds or words. For example, the preacher's rhythm, "I-I-I-I-I-Oh-I-I-Oh, yeah,

Lord-I-I-heard the voice of Jesus saying . . .," or the rhythmic, fast tempo in delivering toasts such as the signifying monkey.

3 *Spontaneity.* Generally, a speaker's perform- ance is improvisational, including much interaction with the audience, which dictates or directs the flow and outcome of the speech event. The speaker is casual; he employs a lively conversational tone with a quality of immediacy. For example, a preacher declares, "Y'all don' want to hear dat, so I'm gon' leave it lone," and his congregation calls out, "Now, tell it, Reverend, tell it!" and he does.

4 *Concreteness.* A speaker's imagery and ideas center upon contemporary, everyday experiences, and he conveys a sense of identification with the event being described. For example, the toast teller becomes Stag-O-Lee, or the preacher declares, "I first met God in 1925."

5 *Signifying.* To signify, the speaker talks about the entire audience or one of its members, either to trigger a verbal contest or to hammer a point home, without offending the audience. "Pimp, punk, pros- titute, Ph.D.—all the P's—you still in slavery," declared the Reverend Jesse Jackson. Malcolm X delivered this putdown of the nonviolent movement: "In a revolution, you swinging, not singing." The rhythmic alliteration and rhyming in these examples are characteristic of black speakers.

Susan Houston, studying the speech patterns of black and white children in rural Florida, found few important syntactic differences between them.[19] There were real differences, but they were basically in style or pronunciation. In one experiment Hous- ton worked with eighty-six pairs of first-graders from four socio-economic groups: well-to-do whites, well-to-do blacks, poor whites, and poor blacks. She sent one child in each pair out of earshot, then told the other child a story and asked him to retell it exactly to his partner. After the retelling, the partner was asked to repeat the story. All the white children and the middle-class black children tended to reproduce details correctly, according to the norms set by the adult in charge. The poor black children took the given instructions as a baseline upon which to demonstrate spontaneous verbal flair. That is, they reproduced general elements from the story but preferred to supply their own details. Thus, 26 per cent of the stories told by the poor black children contained original material, as against 12 per cent or less for the other groups. Cultural-deprivation theorists would find the poor black children linguistically deficient relative to the other groups; difference theorists would stress their creativity and closer contact with their roots in the black oral tradition.

Another finding of Houston's study is worth noting. The poor black children were the most peer-oriented; they generally interacted far more with other children than did the other groups, and this was true whether they were paired with a white child or another black child. They clearly attended to each other more than to the adult, telling their stories to their partners rather than to the adult for her approval.

To summarize, it appears to us that cultural- difference theory offers a more accurate appraisal of the linguistic-cognitive competence of low-income black children than does cultural-deprivation the- ory. Furthermore, contrary to those cultural- difference theorists who insist that black English must be viewed as a separate language based upon West African linguistic patterns, careful linguistic analysis reveals that it is not based primarily upon West African syntax or grammar, although West African elements are present in the black idiom. From extensive linguistic studies, Labov has con- cluded that, although black English shows internal cohesion,

> . . . it is best seen as a distinct subsystem within the larger grammar of English. Certain parts of the tense and aspect system are clearly separate subsystems in the sense that they are not shared or recognized by other dialects, and we can isolate other such limited areas. But the gears and axles of English grammatical machinery are available to speakers of all dialects, whether or not they use all of them in everyday speech.[20]

Although poor black children may misinterpret some words pronounced by white middle-class speakers because of differences in phonology or usage or unfamiliarity with the vocabulary there is no reason to believe that the children cannot usually comprehend the basic meaning of sentences utilizing standard English grammar and syntax. Here the distinction between competence and performance is essential. Poor black children often do not utilize certain standard English grammatical forms in their verbal productions, but this does not necessarily mean that by late childhood they are not competent to do so. Performance—what one does with one's competence—is affected by a variety of situational determinants. For example, if one is frightened or tired or in a hurry, his linguistic performance is likely to be affected, although his competence, his mastery of the basic grammar of his language, remains unchanged.[21] A college student may feel a bit anxious when speaking to a professor in a speech course and either restrict his utterances or make mistakes in performance that he is not likely to make under other circumstances. Similarly, low-income black children are likely to freeze up or make performance errors, when evaluated by middle-class adults, particularly white adults. However, their poor performance may mask considerable competence. The most significant differences between black English and white English would appear to be in the use made of selected vocabulary and in performance and communication styles.

Cultural-deprivation theorists have a valid point when they observe that middle-class children, black or white, are likely to enjoy richer verbal interaction with adults than their lower-class peers. Low-income black parents have had valid reasons, related to survival in a racist society, to quiet young children and wean them early from dependent interaction. However, these theorists grossly underestimate the linguistic-cognitive competence of low-income black children, for reasons we shall outline below. In addition, they confuse a somewhat slower rate of linguistic-cognitive maturation in lower-class black (or white) children with their own reified theoretical construct—a "cumulative deficit" in basic linguistic-cognitive capacity. They assume that low-income black children will never catch up to middle-class white children, and they employ culturally biased tests, on which low-income blacks perform poorly, to "prove" that blacks continue to be linguistically and cognitively incompetent.

Let us look more closely at the criteria employed by these theorists in judging the linguistic-cognitive competence of low-income black children. Bereiter and Engelmann, for example, report that the children respond to adult questioning, if at all, with gestures, single words, or disconnected words and phrases.[22] Such reports are based upon empirical observation. For example, here is a typical complete interview with a black boy carried out in a New York City school by a friendly white interviewer. The adult places an object on the table in front of the child and says, "Tell me everything you can about this."

12 seconds of silence
Adult: What would you say it looks like?

8 seconds of silence
Child: A spaceship.
Adult: Hmmmmm.
13 seconds of silence
Child: Like a je-et.
12 seconds of silence
Child: Like a plane.
20 seconds of silence
Adult: What color is it?
Child: Orange. (*2 seconds*) An' whi-ite. (*2 seconds*) An' green.
6 seconds of silence
Adult: An' what could you use it for?
8 seconds of silence
Child: A je-et.
6 seconds of silence
Adult: If you had two of them, what would you do with them?
6 seconds of silence
Child: Give one to some-body.
Adult: Hmmm. Who do you think would like to have it?
10 seconds of silence
Child: Cla-rence.
Adult: Mm. Where do you think you could get another one of these?
Child: At the store.
Adult: Oh-ka-ay![23]

Here we have a child in a situation where anything he says may be judged "wrong" and lead to shame or punishment. He plays it safe by saying as little as possible, a survival strategy for dealing with strange adults, particularly whites. The child's defensive behavior is not necessarily a function of ineptness on the part of the adult interviewer, for, as Labov has found, a friendly, competent black male adult interviewer from the community obtained similar results when interviewing eight-year-old Harlem boys in the same manner. However, significant changes in both the volume and the style of speech of the same children occurred when the interviewer brought potato chips, making the interview more like a party; brought along one of the child's friends; reduced the height imbalance by sitting on the floor; and introduced taboo words and topics indicating that the child could say anything without fear of retaliation. These changes were striking, as is clear in this interview with eight-year-old Leon in the presence of eight-year-old Greg:

Adult: Is there anybody who says, "Your momma drink pee?"

Leon: (rapidly and breathlessly) Yee-ah!

Greg: (simultaneously) Yup.

Leon: And your father eat doo-doo for breakfas'!

Adult: Ohhh! *(laughs)*

Leon: And they say your father—your father eat doo-doo for dinner!

Greg: When they sound on me, I say "C.B.M."

Adult: What that mean?

Leon: Congo booger-snatch! *(laugh)*

Greg: (simultaneously) Congo booger-snatcher! *(laughs)*

Greg: And sometimes I'll curse with "B.B."

Adult: What that?

Greg: Oh, that's a "M.B.B." black boy. *(Leon crunching on potato chips)*

Greg: 'Merican black boy.

Adult: Oh.

Greg: Anyway, 'Mericans is same like white people, right?

Leon: And they talk about Allah.

Adult: Oh, yeah?

Greg: Yeah.

Adult: What they say about Allah?

Leon: Allah—Allah is God.

Greg: (simultaneously) Allah—

Adult: And what else?

Leon: I don't know the res'!

Greg: Allah i-Allah is God, Allah is the only God, Allah—

Leon: Allah is the son of God.

Greg: But can he make magic?

Leon: Nope.

Greg: I know who can make magic.

Adult: Who can?

Leon: The God, the real one.

Adult: Who can make magic?

Greg: The son of po'. *(Adult:* Hm?) I'm saying the po'k chop God! He only a po'k chop God! *(Leon chuckles)*[24]

Leon, a boy who barely responded to a traditional interviewer, is now competing actively for the floor. Both boys seem to have no difficulty in using the English language to express themselves. Revealing a strong peer orientation, they talk to each other as much as to the interviewer.

Cultural-deprivation theorists argue that low-income black children's careless articulation and poor auditory discrimination are signs of incompetence. Here an ethnocentric bias often affects judgment: The difficulties poor black children have in pronouncing many words in the manner of middle-class whites often is no more and no less than the problem white middle-class American children would have if asked to speak like Englishmen. All children learn to pronounce words in the manner of those in their immediate community, but cultural-deprivation theorists impose a single standard as an index of precision in articulation. Similarly, the phonology usually presented in auditory-discrimination tests are the sounds of middle-class white English. Thus, many low-income black children may perform poorly not because they have poor auditory discrimination in any absolute sense, but because some of the sounds on the test are not their sounds.[25]

Cultural-deprivation theorists argue also that low-income black children employ shorter sentences and less complex grammar than more privileged children, indicating linguistic-cognitive incompetence. However, sentence length and grammatical complexity typically are assessed by tests like the one described above, in which a strange adult asks questions such as, "Tell me all you can about the object that is on the table." As we have seen, a child who doesn't trust the adult will purposely reply as briefly as possible. Besides, the test itself may seem silly to lower-class children. Why would an adult ask such a question? Can't he see for himself? What does he really want? What trick is he trying to play? Middle-class children are less likely to see the test in this way because they have more experience in being drawn out verbally by their parents. Thus, such tests may tell us more about the manner in which children relate to adults in an evaluative context than about their basic linguistic-cognitive competence.

Further, psychologists and educators seem to have a bias in favor of long sentences and complex grammar. But sentence length and complexity sometimes hide muddled thought, and short, simple sentences may reveal clarity and precision of thought. As a reading of social-science and education journals soon reveals, involved, cumbersome sentences often do not portray reality accurately or make much sense.

Cultural-deprivation theorists and the teachers they have influenced tend to equate class and ethnic differences in grammatical forms with differences in the capacity for logical analysis, to assume that teaching children to mimic the speech patterns of their middle-class teachers is the same as teaching them to think logically, and to favor and reward children who speak the way they do. This preferred treatment may help some children to achieve in school more rapidly than others and this achievement in turn is often seen as evidence that the higher-achieving children were better equipped intellectually from the start.

CLASS AND LINGUISTIC SOCIALIZATION

Middle-class children are likely to approximate their parents' verbalizations somewhat earlier than lower-class children, perhaps because of differences in the linguistic socialization of the two groups. In one study, it was found that low-income black mothers generally relied on more restricted verbal communications in combination with status-oriented discipline in relating to their children than did middle-class black mothers.[26] When the mothers were asked to teach various tasks to their children, the low-income mothers and their children both displayed a greater tendency to act without taking time for reflection or planning. For example, after briefly demonstrating to a child what he was supposed to do, a low-income mother commonly sat silently by, watching the child try to solve a problem until he made an error, whereupon she would punish him immediately. These mothers frequently failed to structure the learning situation so that the children could learn to recognize and correct their errors. They did not stop the children before they made a mistake and ask them to think about the probable outcome of their behavior. Thus, the lower-class child often learned only that his mother wanted him to do something, although she did not specify clearly what it was; no matter what he did, he would probably be punished.

Helen Bee and her associates have also studied social-class differences in the interactions between mothers and young children.[27] Mothers were observed trying to help children carry out specific tasks and while they were in a waiting room well supplied with toys. Mothers were also interviewed concerning their ideas on taking care of children. In general, lower-class mothers appeared to be much more restrictive than middle-class mothers and more inclined to use negative reinforcements. In the helping situation, middle-class mothers tended to allow children to work at their own pace, offering many general suggestions on how to look for a solution to a problem while pointing out what the children were doing that was right. Lower-class mothers, by contrast, tended to behave in ways that did not encourage their children to attend to the basic features of the problem. They tended to tell the children to do specific things, they did not emphasize basic problem-solving strategies, and their "suggestions" were really imperative statements that did not encourage a reply from the child.

The greater verbal interaction between middle-class mothers and their children seems to be "designed" to help the children acquire learning strategies that they can generalize to future problem-solving situations. The middle-class mothers help their children to attend discriminately to various features of the situation and of their own behavior. This selective attending helps children cognitively to take situations and their behaviors apart and to put the pieces together differently in new contexts, thus increasing the range of situations within which the children can respond adaptively. Middle-class mothers tend to ask many more questions of their children when trying to help them. Thus, they help the children to perceive connections between objects and events. The children are also helped to express connections in words and to formulate general rules independent of the particular context within which they are operating. Lower-class mothers, on the other hand, by instructing children in a manner that that does not encourage verbal give-and-take, help their children somewhat to carry out specific tasks, but they do not encourage, and often discourage, a reflective and conceptual orientation to problems.

Studies such as these may be criticized on several grounds. First, the mothers and children were observed in university laboratories, a setting that may be more threatening to lower-class mothers than to their middle-class peers. Thus, the restricted quality of the low-income mothers' performance may have been in part a defense against the possibility of appearing inadequate in the eyes of middle-class observers. Second, the tasks presented by the researchers may have been more familiar to middle-class children, providing a performance advantage. Nevertheless, much of the social-class difference in performance among mothers appears to reflect significant differences in styles of socialization. The behavior of low-income mothers in the laboratory situation is basically consistent with the general socialization orientation of low-income mothers.

Low-income black children have generally not been encouraged to perform linguistically for adult approval or to strive for mastery of skills not immediately necessary for survival. The result is that many such children perform quite poorly in mainstream cultural situations, such as the psychological laboratory or school, in spite of the fact that within their peer group many of them display considerable linguistic-cognitive competence.

The typical middle-class socialization techniques, on the other hand, tend to push children to expand, as rapidly as possible, their capacities for linguistic-cognitive differentiation, categorization, and conceptualization in a widening variety of situations. The parents frequently elaborate on their children's statements, helping them to expand their categorization of experience. They encourage the children to build mental models of experience based on the use of words. By using language to help focus the children's attention on various features of their own behavior and the situations they encounter, middle-class parents provide the children with abundant experience in using the same symbols in a variety of situations. Middle-class children are encouraged to abstract the common meanings of these symbols as used in various situations and to use words as referents for concepts and categories that have generalized meaning, rather than as referents for a narrow range of specific, personalized experiences. Middle-class children are pushed to move beyond the use of language in highly concrete, particularized, situation-specific orientations to the use of language for formal, rule-oriented, conceptually ordered discourse about general aspects of experience. All these skills are socialized by middle-class parents in the expectation that they will be instrumental in the children's future educational and occupational success, helping them to maintain or improve their advantaged position in the social order. These parental behaviors appear to result in accelerated linguistic-cognitive development among middle-class children relative to their lower-class peers, although the magnitude of the differences between them often seems greater than it actually is because of the tendencies of low-income children to perform poorly when tested by adults and because of class and ethnic biases in interpreting low-income children's behavior.

Earlier we discussed the importance of verbal performance in urban black children's peer groups. We also saw that the shift from adult orientation to peer orientation developed at an early age among urban blacks, stimulated by "push" factors that drive children out of the house and by "pull" factors in the lure of the street. Similarly, among black children in a Southern town, the focus of linguistic

socialization has been observed to shift from adults to peers at an early age. Virginia Young, who studied childrearing practices among black residents of a medium-sized town in Georgia, found that about age three there is "an almost complete cessation of the close relationship with the mother and father and a shift in orientation to the children's gang." One of the important features of this change is that

> . . . often speech becomes an indistinct children's patois in contrast to the clear enunciation used by the Knee-baby (younger child) with his parents. Children speak less to adults, and get along adequately with "Yes'm," and "No'm."[28]

We have already noted that low-income black children in the North or the South seemed inclined to direct their verbal performance toward a peer rather than an adult when both peer and adult were available. This relatively early reliance on peers for verbal socialization is likely to delay the child's development of linguistic behavior like his own parents' and to reinforce competence in the language of the streets. While such language is complex, coherent, and creative in vocabulary and style, it is not the language of the schools. Thus, by encouraging linguistic patterns associated with low-income black life-styles and often negating standard English, street peer groups contribute to the child's difficulties in coping with school and his negative attitudes toward school achievement.[29]

NOTES

1 Carl Bereiter and Siegfried Engelmann, *Teaching Disadvantaged Children in the Preschool* (Englewood Cliffs, N.J.: Prentice-Hall, 1966), pp. 39–40.

2 *Ibid.*, p. 41.

3 Stephens S. Baratz and Joan C. Baratz, "Early Childhood Intervention: The Social Science Base of Institutional Racism," *Harvard Educational Review,* 40 (1970): 35.

4 See Vernon J. Dixon and Badi G. Foster, *Beyond Black or White: An Alternate America* (Boston: Little, Brown, 1971); Albert Murray, *The Omni-Americans: New Perspectives on Black Experience and American Culture* (New York: Outerbridge & Dienstfrey, 1970); Charles A. Valentine, "Deficit, Differences, and Bicultural Methods of Afro-American Behavior," *Harvard Educational Review,* 41 (1971): 137–57; and Andrew Billingsley, *Black Families in White America* (Englewood Cliffs, N.J.: Prentice-Hall, 1968).

5 See, for example, Mildred C. Templin, *Certain Lan-*

gauge Skills in Children (Minneapolis: University of Minnesota Press, 1957), and Walter Loban, *The Language of Elementary School Children* (Champaign, Ill.: National Conference of Teachers of English, 1963).

6 See Doris R. Entwisle, "Developmental Sociolinguistics: Inner-City Children," *American Journal of Sociology,* 74 (1968): 37–49, and *idem,* "Semantic Systems of Children," in Frederick Williams, ed., *Language and Poverty* (Chicago: Markham, 1970), pp. 123–39.

7 E.g., see Vera P. John and L. Goldstein, "The Social Context of Language Acquisition," *Merrill-Palmer Quarterly,* 10 (1964): 265–76, and Irving E. Sigal, L. Anderson, and H. Shapiro, "Categorization Behavior of Lower- and Middle-Class Negro Preschool Children: Differences in Dealing with Representations of Familiar Objects," *Journal of Negro Education,* 35 (1966): 218–29.

8 See Paula Menyuk, "Language Theories and Educational Practice," in Williams, ed., *Language and Poverty,* pp. 190–211.

9 W. A. Stuart, "Understanding Black Language," in John F. Szwed, ed., *Black America* (New York: Basic Books, 1970), pp. 121–31.

10 See D. Z. Seymour, "Black English," *Intellectual Digest,* 2 (1972): 78–80, and J. L. Dillard, *Black English* (New York: Random House, 1972), pp. 39–72. The habitual tense is not the same as the present tense, and the difference can be important. For example, "my brother sick" indicates that the sickness is in progress but probably of short duration; "my brother be sick" indicates a long-term condition—a distinction that may be missed by a teacher who is limited to standard English (and who might therefore be labeled "culturally deprived").

11 Dan I. Slobin and C. A. Welsh, "Elicited Imitation as a Research Tool in Developmental Psycholinguistics," unpublished paper, Department of Psychology, University of California, Berkeley, 1967.

12 William Labov and P. Cohen, "Systematic Relations of Standard and Nonstandard Rules in the Grammars of Negro Speakers," *Project Literacy Reports,* No. 8, Cornell University, Ithaca, N.Y., 1967, pp. 66–84.

13 William Labov, "Psychological Conflict in Negro American Language Behavior," *American Journal of Orthopsychiatry,* 41 (1971): 636–37. Essentially the same conflict in speech patterns of upwardly mobile blacks is described in Frantz Fanon, *Black Skin, White Masks* (1952) (New York: Grove Press, 1967), pp. 17–40.

14 See John J. Hartman, "Psychological Conflicts in Negro American Language Behavior: A Case Study," *American Journal of Orthopsychiatry,* 41 (1971): 627–35.

15 B. Wood and J. Curry, " 'Everyday Talk' and 'School

Talk' of the City Black Child," *The Speech Teacher,* 18 (1969): 282–96. See also Menyuk, "Language Theories" (n. 8 *supra*).

16 See Roger D. Abrahams, "Rapping and Capping: Black Talk as Art," in Szwed, ed., *Black America* (n. 9 *supra*(, pp. 132–42, and *idem, Deep Down in the Jungle: Negro Narrative Folklore from the Streets of Philadelphia,* rev. ed. (Chicago: Aldine, 1970).

17 Thomas Kochman, "Rapping in the Ghetto," in Lee Rainwater, ed., *The Black Experience: Soul* (Chicago: Aldine, 1970), p. 51. See also Charles Keil, *Urban Blues* (Chicago: University of Chicago Press, 1966), and Iceberg Slim, *Pimp: The Story of My Life* (Los Angeles: Holloway House, 1967).

18 Geneva Smitherman, "White English in Blackface, or, Who Do I Be?" *The Black Scholar,* 4 (May—June, 1973): 32–39.

19 Susan H. Houston, "Black English," *Psychology Today,* 6 (March, 1973): 45–48.

20 William Labov, *Language in the Inner City: Studies in the Black English Vernacular* (Philadelphia: University of Pennsylvania Press, 1972), p. 64.

21 See Owen P. Thomas, "Competence and Performance in Language," in Roger D. Abrahams and Rudolph D. Troke, eds., *Language and Cultural Diversity in American Education* (Englewood Cliffs, N.J.: Prentice-Hall, 1972), pp. 108–11.

22 Bereiter and Englemann, *Teaching Disadvantaged Children (n. 1 supra),* pp. 34–40.

23 William Labov, "Academic Ignorance and Black Intelligence," *Atlantic Monthly,* June, 1972, p. 60.

24 *Ibid.,* p. 62.

25 See R. Burling, *English in Black and White* (New York: Holt, Rinehart & Winston, 1973), pp. 29–47 and 91–110.

26 Robert D. Hess and Virginia C. Shipman, "Early Experience and the Socialization of Cognitive Modes in Children," *Child Development,* 36 (1965): 869–86. See also *idem,* "Cognitive Elements in Maternal Behavior," in John P. Ill, ed., *Minnesota Symposia on Child Psychology* (Minneapolis: University of Minnesota Press, 1967), 1: 57–81.

27 Helen C. Bee *et al.,* "Social Class Differences in Maternal Teaching Strategies and Speech Patterns," *Developmental Psychology,* 1 (1969): 726–34. See also G. F. Brody, "Socioeconomic Differences in Stated Maternal Child-rearing Practices and in Observed Maternal Behavior," *Journal of Marriage and the Family,* 30 (1968): 656–60.

28 Virginia H. Young, "Family and Childhood in a Southern Georgia Community," *American Anthropologist,* 72 (1970): 282.

29 See William Labov and C. Robbins, "A Note on the Relation of Reading Failure to Peer-Group Status in Urban Ghettos," *Teachers College Record,* 70 (1969): 395–405.

Chapter Five

Cognition and Learning

The articles in this section reflect the marked and continuing increase in research on children's cognitive processes. One of the notable trends in child development over the past 20 years has been the "cognizing" of psychology. This concern with the role of cognitive factors in development is found not only in traditional areas of cognitive study such as in attention, perception, and learning but also in social development. A pervasive theme running through the other sections of this book is how the cognitive processes or capabilities of children moderate or mediate their responses to such things as attachment, discipline, loss of a parent, the behavior of teachers and peers, and a broad array of other social factors.

Although much of the original impetus to the cognitive development movement was attributable to the theory and research of Jean Piaget (described in the first paper by David Elkind), the papers in this section reflect the more contemporary cognitive processing approach to investigating issues in cognitive development.

Rochel Gelman's paper emphasizes the competence of infants and young children. In the past, infants and preschool children were frequently viewed as less capable than they really were because inadequate techniques were used to assess their cognitive functioning. Cognitive development in these years was often described in terms of what infants and young children could not do rather than what they could do. The increased knowledge we have about early developmental capabilities in perception, information processing, and cognition in infants and young children may serve as the foundations for developing preschool intervention and educational experiences.

The paper by Siegel and Schadler attempts to assess the development of young children's internal representation of large-scale space, in this case their kindergarten classroom. It may be because of recent interest on the impact of environment and ecology on behavior that psychologists are becoming interested in how children perceive, and remember aspects of the larger environment.

In his paper on metacognition and cognitive monitoring, John Flavell presents another new area of concern to developmental psychologists. What do children know about knowing and how do they monitor their own cognitive activities such as attention, perception, memory, and comprehension?

The last paper by Ross Parke deals with cognitive factors in socialization. In the process of socialization, some behaviors often need to be suppressed or inhibited. Parke's article outlines some of the factors that alter the impact of punishment as a control technique. In this area as well as in other areas of child development, the child's cognitive capacities are receiving recognition; specifically, reasoning techniques are found to become increasingly effective inhibitory tactics as the child develops. Moreover, in light of the ethical problems involved in the use of punishment, for both parents and researchers, this reorientation to cognitive forms of control is a welcome change. Finally, these studies remind us of a recurring theme: the child plays an active role in determining the type or intensity of disciplinary techniques that adults will select. The child plays an active role in the learning process.

Reading 18

Giant in the Nursery—Jean Piaget

David Elkind

In February, 1967, Jean Piaget, the Swiss psychologist, arrived at Clark University in Worcester, Mass., to deliver the Heinz Werner Memorial Lectures. The lectures were to be given in the evening, and before the first one a small dinner party was arranged in honor of Piaget and was attended by colleagues, former students and friends. I was invited because of my long advocacy of Piaget's work and because I spent a year (1964–1965) at his Institute for Educational Science in Geneva. Piaget had changed very little since I had last seen him, but he did appear tired and mildly apprehensive.

Although Piaget has lectured all over the world, this particular occasion had special significance. Almost 60 years before, in 1909, another famous European, Sigmund Freud, also lectured at Clark University. Piaget was certainly aware of the historical parallel. He was, moreover, going to speak to a huge American audience in French and, despite the offices of his remarkable translator, Eleanor Duckworth, he must have had some reservations about how it would go.

Piaget's apprehension was apparent during the dinner. For one who is usually a lively and charming dinner companion, he was surprisingly quiet and unresponsive. About half way through the meal there was a small disturbance. The room in which the dinner was held was at a garden level and two boys suddenly appeared at the windows and began tapping at them. The inclination of most of us, I think, was to shoo them away. Before we had a chance to do that, however, Piaget had turned to face the children. He smiled up at the lads, hunched his shoulders and gave them a slight wave with his hand. They hunched their shoulders and smiled in return, gave a slight wave and disappeared. After a moment, Piaget turned back to the table and began telling stories and entering into animated conversation.

Although I am sure his lecture would have been a success in any case and that the standing ovation he received would have occurred without the little incident, I nonetheless like to think that the encounter with the boys did much to restore his vigor and good humor.

It is Piaget's genius for empathy with children, together with true intellectual genius, that has made him the outstanding child psychologist in the world today and one destined to stand beside Freud with respect to his contributions to psychology, education and related disciplines. Just as Freud's discoveries of unconscious motivation, infantile sexuality and the stages of psychosexual growth changed our ways of thinking about human personality, so Piaget's discoveries of children's implicit philosophies, the construction of reality by the infant and the stages of mental development have altered our ways of thinking about human intelligence.

The man behind these discoveries is an arresting figure. He is tall and somewhat portly, and his stooped walk, bulky suits and crown of long white hair give him the appearance of a thrice-magnified Einstein. (When he was at the Institute for Advanced Study at Princeton in 1953, a friend of his wife rushed to a window one day and exclaimed, "Look, Einstein!" Madame Piaget looked and replied, "No, just my Piaget.") Piaget's personal trademarks are his meerschaum pipes (now burned deep amber), his navy blue beret and his bicycle.

Meeting Piaget is a memorable experience. Although Piaget has an abundance of Old-World charm and graciousness, he seems to emanate an aura of intellectual presence not unlike the aura of personality presence conveyed by a great actor. While as a psychologist I am unable to explain how this sense of presence is communicated, I am nevertheless convinced that everyone who meets Piaget experiences it. While talking to me, for example, he was able to divine in my remarks and questions a significance and depth of which I was entirely unaware and certainly hadn't intended. Evidently one characteristic of genius is to search for relevance in the apparently commonplace and frivolous.

Piaget's is a superbly disciplined life. He arises early each morning, sometimes as early as 4 A.M., and writes four or more publishable pages on square sheets of white paper in an even, small hand. Later in the morning he may teach classes and attend meetings. His afternoons include long walks during which he thinks about the problems he is currently confronting. He says, "I always like to think on a problem before reading about it." In the evenings, he reads and retires early. Even on his international trips, Piaget keeps to this schedule.

Each summer, as soon as classes are over, Piaget gathers up the research findings that have been collected by his assistants during the year and departs for the Alps, where he takes up solitary residence in a room in an abandoned farmhouse. The whereabouts of this retreat is as closely guarded as the names of depositors in numbered Swiss bank accounts; only Piaget's family, his long-time colleague Bärbel Inhelder and a trusted secretary know where he is. During the summer Piaget takes walks, meditates, writes *and* writes. Then, when the leaves begin to turn, he descends from the mountains with the several books and articles he has written on his "vacation."

Although Piaget, now in his 72d year, has been carrying his works down from the mountains for almost 50 summers (he has published more than 30 books and hundreds of articles), it is only within the past decade that his writings have come to be fully appreciated in America. This was due, in part, to the fact that until fairly recently only a few of his books had been translated into English. In addition, American psychology and education were simply not ready for Piaget until the fifties. Now the ideas that Piaget has been advocating for more than 30 years are regarded as exceedingly innovative and even as avant-garde.

His work falls into three more or less distinct periods within each of which he covered an enormous amount of psychological territory and developed a multitude of insights. (Like more creative men, Piaget is hard put to it to say when a particular idea came to him. If he ever came suddenly upon an idea which sent him shouting through the halls, he has never admitted to it.)

During the first period (roughly 1922–1929), Piaget explored the extent and depth of children's spontaneous ideas about the physical world and about their own mental processes. He happened upon this line of inquiry while working in Alfred Binet's laboratory school in Paris where he arrived,

still seeking a direction for his talents, a year after receiving his doctorate in biological science at the University of Lausanne. It was in the course of some routine intelligence testing that Piaget became interested in what lay behind children's correct, and particularly the incorrect, answers. To clarify the origins of these answers he began to interview the children in the open-ended manner he had learned when serving a brief internship at Bleler's psychiatric clinic in Zurich. This semiclinical interview procedure, aimed at revealing the processes by which a child arrives at a particular reply to a test question, has become a trademark of Piagetian research investigation.

What Piaget found with this method of inquiry was that children not only reasoned differently from adults but also that they had quite different worldviews, literally different philosophies. This led Piaget to attend to those childish remarks and questions which most adults find amusing or nonsensical. Just as Freud used seemingly accidental slips of the tongue and pen as evidence for unconscious motivations, so Piaget has employed the "cute" sayings of children to demonstrate the existence of ideas quite foreign to the adult mind.

Piaget had read in the recollections of a deaf mute (recorded by William James) that as a child he had regarded the sun and moon as gods and believed they followed him about. Piaget sought to verify his recollection by interviewing children on the subject, and he found that many youngsters do believe that the sun and moon follow them when they are out for a walk. Similar remarks Piaget either overheard or was told about led to a large number of investigations which revealed, among many similar findings, that young children believe that anything which moves is alive, that the names of objects reside in the objects themselves and that dreams come in through the window at night.

Such beliefs, Piaget pointed out in an early article entitled "Children's Philosophies," are not unrelated to but rather derive from an implicit animism and artificialism with many parallels to primitive and Greek philosophies. In the child's view, objects like stones and clouds are imbued with motives, intentions and feelings, while mental events such as dreams and thoughts are endowed with corporality and force.

Children also believe that everything has a purpose and that everything in the world is made by and for man. (My 5-year-old son asked me why we have snow and answered his own question by saying, "It is for children to play in.")

The child's animism and artificialism help to explain his famous and often unanswerable "why" questions. It is because children believe that everything has a purpose that they ask, "Why is grass green?" and "Why do the stars shine?" The parent who attempts to answer such questions with a physical explanation has missed the point.

In addition to disclosing the existence of children's philosophies during this first period, Piaget also found the clue to the egocentrism of childhood. In observing young children at play at the *Maison des Petits,* the modified Montessori school associated with the Institute of Educational Science in Geneva, Piaget noted a peculiar lack of social orientation which was also present in their conversation and in their approaches to certain intellectual tasks. A child would make up a new word ("stocks" for socks and stockings) and just assume that everyone knew what he was talking about as if this were the conventional name for the objects he had in mind. Likewise, Piaget noted that when two nursery school children were at play they often spoke *at* rather than *to* one another and were frequently chattering on about two quite different and unrelated topics. Piaget observed, moreover, that when he stood a child of 5 years opposite him, the child who could tell his own right and left nevertheless insisted that Piaget's right and left hands were directly opposite his own.

In Piaget's view, all of these behaviors can be explained by the young child's inability to put himself in another person's position and to take that person's point of view. Unlike the egocentric adult, who can take another person's point of view but does not, the egocentric child does not take another person's viewpoint because he cannot. This conception of childish egocentrism has produced a fundamental alteration in our evaluation of the preschool child's behavior. We now appreciate that it is intellectual immaturity and not moral perversity which makes, for example, a young child continue to pester his mother after she has told him she has a headache and wishes to be left alone. The preschool child is simply unable to put himself in his mother's position and see things from her point of view.

The second period of Piaget's investigations began

when, in 1929, he sought to trace the origins of the child's spontaneous mental growth to the behavior of infants; in this case, his own three children, Jaqueline, Lucienne and Laurent. Piaget kept very detailed records of their behavior and of their performance on a series of ingenious tasks which he invented and presented to them. The books resulting from these investigations, "The Origins of Intelligence in Children," "Play, Dreams and Imitation in Children" and "The Construction of Reality in the Child" are now generally regarded as classics in the field and have been one of the major forces behind the scurry of research activity in the area of infant behavior now current both in America and abroad. The publication of these books in the middle and late nineteen-thirties marked the end of the second phase of Piaget's work.

Some of the most telling observations Piaget made during this period had to do with what he called the *conservation of the object* (using the word conservation to convey the idea of permanence). To the older child and to the adult, the existence of objects and persons who are not immediately present is taken as self-evident. The child at school knows that while he is working at his desk his mother is simultaneously at home and his father is at work. This is not the case for the infant playing in his crib, for whom out of sight is literally out of mind. Piaget observed that when an infant 4 or 5 months old is playing with a toy which subsequently rolls out of sight (behind another toy) but is still within reach, the infant ceases to look for it. The infant behaves as if the toy had not only disappeared but as if it had gone entirely out of existence.

This helps to explain the pleasure infants take in the game of peek-a-boo. If the infant believed that the object existed when it was not seen, he would not be surprised and delighted at its re-emergence and there would be no point of the game. It is only during the second year of life, when children begin to represent objects mentally, that they seek after toys that have disappeared from view. Only then do they attribute an independent existence to objects which are not present to their senses.

The third and major phase of Piaget's endeavors began about 1940 and continues until the present day. During this period Piaget has studied the development in children and adolescents of those mental abilities which gradually enable the child to construct a world-view which is in conformance with reality as seen by adults. He has, at the same time, been concerned with how children acquire the adult versions of various concepts such as number, quantity and speed. Piaget and his colleagues have amassed, in the last 28 years, an astounding amount of information about the thinking of children and adolescents which is only now beginning to be used by psychologists and educators.

Two discoveries made during this last period are of particular importance both because they were so unexpected and because of their relevance for education. It is perhaps fair to say that education tends to focus upon the static aspects of reality rather than upon its dynamic transformations. The child is taught how and what things are but not the conditions under which they change or remain the same. And yet the child is constantly confronted with change and alteration. His view of the world alters as he grows in height and perceptual acuity. And the world changes. Seasons come and go, trees gain and lose their foliage, snow falls and melts. People change, too. They may change over brief time periods in mood and over long periods in weight and hair coloration or fullness. The child receives a static education while living amidst a world in transition.

Piaget's investigations since 1940 have focused upon how the child copes with change, how he comes to distinguish between the permanent and the transient and between appearance and reality. An incident that probably played a part in initiating this line of investigation occurred during Piaget's short-lived flirtation with the automobile. (When his children were young, Piaget learned to drive and bought a car, but he gave it up for his beloved bicycle after a couple of years.) He took his son for a drive and Laurent asked the name of the mountain they were passing. The mountain was the Saleve, the crocodile-shaped mass that dominates the city of Geneva. Laurent was in fact familiar with the mountain and its name because he could see it from his garden, although from a different perspective. Laurent's question brought home to Piaget the fact that a child has difficulty in dealing with the results of transformations whether they are brought about by an alteration in the object itself or by the child's movement with respect to the object.

The methods Piaget used to study how the child comes to deal with transformations are ingenuously simple and can be used by any interested parent or teacher. These methods all have to do with testing the child's abilities to discover that a quantity remains the same across a change in its appearance. In other words, that the quantity is conserved.

To give just one illustration from among hundreds, a child is shown two identical drinking glasses filled equally full with orangeade and he is asked to say whether there is the "same to drink" in the two glasses. After the child says that this is the case, the orangeade from one glass is poured into another which is taller and thinner so that the orangeade now reaches a higher level. Then the child is asked to say whether there is the same amount to drink in the two differently shaped glasses. Before the age of 6 or 7, most children say that the tall, narrow glass has more orangeade. The young child cannot deal with the transformation and bases his judgement on the static features of the orangeade, namely the levels.

How does the older child arrive at the notion that the amounts of orangeade in the two differently shaped glasses is the same? The answer, according to Piaget, is that he discovers the equality with the aid of reason. If the child judges only on the basis of appearances he cannot solve the problem. When he compares the two glasses with respect to width he must conclude that the wide glass has more while if he compares them with respect to the level of the orangeade he must conclude that the tall glass has more. There is then no way, on the basis of appearance, that he can solve the problem. If, on the other hand, the child reasons that there was the same in the two glasses before and that nothing was added or taken away during the pouring, he concludes that both glasses still have the same drink although this does not appear to be true.

On the basis of this and many similar findings, Piaget argues that much of our knowledge about reality comes to us not from without like the wail of a siren but rather from within by the force of our own logic.

It is hard to overemphasize the importance of this fact, because it is so often forgotten, particularly in education. For those who are not philosophically inclined, it appears that our knowledge of things comes about rather directly as if our mind simply copied the forms, colors and textures of things. From this point of view the mind acts as a sort of mirror which is limited to reflecting the reality which is presented to it. As Piaget's research has demonstrated, however, the mind operates not as a passive mirror but rather as an active artist.

The portrait painter does not merely copy what he sees, he interprets his subject. Before even commencing the portrait, the artist learns a great deal about the individual subject and does not limit himself to studying the face alone. Into the portrait goes not only what the artist sees but also what he knows about his subject. A good portrait is larger than life because it carries much more information than could ever be conveyed by a mirror image.

In forming his spontaneous conception of the world, therefore, the child does more than reflect what is presented to his senses. His image of reality is in fact a portrait or reconstruction of the world and not a simple copy of it. It is only by reasoning about the information which the child receives from the external world that he is able to overcome the transient nature of sense experience and arrive at that awareness of permanence within apparent change that is the mark of adult thought. The importance of reason in the child's spontaneous construction of his world is thus one of the major discoveries of Piaget's third period.

The second major discovery of this time has to do with the nature of the elementary school child's reasoning ability. Long before there was anything like a discipline of child psychology, the age of 6 to 7 was recognized, as *the age of reason*. It was also assumed, however, that once the child attained the age of reason, there were no longer any substantial differences between his reasoning abilities and those of adolescents and adults. What Piaget discovered is that this is in fact not the case. While the elementary school child is indeed able to reason, his reasoning ability is limited in a very important respect—he can reason about things but not about verbal propositions.

If a child of 8 or 9 is shown a series of three blocks, ABC, which differ in size, then he can tell by looking at them, and without comparing them directly, that if A is greater than B and B greater than C, then A is greater than C. When the same child is given this problem, "Helen is taller than Mary and Mary is taller than Jane, who is the tallest of the three?" the result is quite different. He cannot solve it despite the fact that it repeats in words the problem with the blocks. Adolescents and adults, however, encounter no difficulty with this problem because they can reason about verbal propositions as well as about things.

This discovery that children think differently from adults even after attaining the age of reason has educational implications which are only now beginning to be applied. Robert Karplus, the physicist who heads the Science Curriculum Improvement Study at Berkeley has pointed out that most teachers use verbal propositions in teaching elementary school children. At least some of their instruction is thus destined to go over the heads of their pupils. Karplus and his co-workers are now attempting to train teachers to instruct children at a verbal level which is appropriate to their level of mental ability.

An example of the effects of the failure to take into account the difference between the reasoning abilities of children and adults comes from the New Math experiment. In building materials for the New Math, it was hoped that the construction of a new language would facilitate instruction of set concepts. This new language has been less than successful and the originators of the New Math are currently attempting to devise a physical model to convey the New Math concepts. It is likely that the new language created to teach the set concepts failed because it was geared to the logic of adults rather than to the reasoning of children. Attention to the research on children's thinking carried out during Piaget's third period might have helped to avoid some of the difficulties of the "New Math" program.

"In the course of these many years of research into children's thinking, Piaget has elaborated a general theory of intellectual development which, in its scope and comprehensiveness, rivals Freud's theory of personality development. Piaget proposes that intelligence—adaptive thinking and action—develops in a sequence of stages that is related to age. Each stage sees the elaboration of new mental abilities which set the limits and determine the character of what can be learned during that period. (Piaget finds incomprehensible Harvard psychologist Jerome Bruner's famous hypothesis to the effect that "any subject can be taught effectively in some intellectually honest form to any child at any stage of development.") Although Piaget believes that the order in which the stages appear holds true for all children, he also believes that the ages at which the stages evolve will depend upon the native endowment of the child and upon the quality of the physical and social environment in which he is reared. In a very real sense, then, Piaget's is both a nature *and* a nurture theory.

The first stage in the development of intelligence

(usually 0–2 years) Piaget calls the sensory-motor period and it is concerned with the evolution of those abilities necessary to construct and reconstruct objects. To illustrate, Piaget observed that when he held a cigarette case in front of his daughter Jaqueline (who was 8 months old at the time) and then dropped it, she did not follow the trajectory of the case but continued looking at his hand. Even at 8 months (Lucienne and Laurent succeeded in following the object at about 5 months but had been exposed to more experiments than Jaqueline) she was not able to reconstruct the path of the object which she had seen dropped in front of her.

Toward the end of this period, however, Jaqueline was even able to reconstruct the position of objects which had undergone hidden displacement. When she was 19 months old, Piaget placed a coin in his hand and then placed his hand under a coverlet where he dropped the coin before removing his hand. Jaqueline first looked in his hand and then immediately lifted the coverlet and found the coin. This reconstruction was accomplished with the aid of an elementary form of reasoning. The coin was in the hand, the hand was under the coverlet, the coin was not in the hand so the coin is under the coverlet. Such reasoning, it must be said, is accomplished without the aid of language and by means of mental images.

The second stage (usually 2–7 years), which Piaget calls the preoperational stage, bears witness to the elaboration of the symbolic function, those abilities which have to do with representing things. The presence of these new abilities is shown by the gradual acquisition of language, the first indications of dreams and night terrors, the advent of symbolic play (two sticks at right angles are an airplane) and the first attempts at drawing and graphic representation.

At the beginning of this stage the child tends to identify words and symbols with the objects they are intended to represent. He is upset if someone tramps on a stone which he has designated as a turtle. And he believes that names are as much a part of objects as their color and form. (The child at this point is like the old gentleman who when asked why noodles are called noodles, replied that "they are white like noodles, soft like noodles and taste like noodles so we call them noodles.")

By the end of this period the child can clearly distinguish between words and symbols and what they represent. He now recognizes that names are arbitrary designations. The child's discovery of the arbitrariness of names is often manifested in the "name calling" so prevalent during the early school years.

At the next stage (usually 7–11 years) the child acquires what Piaget calls concrete operations, internalized actions that permit the child to do "in his head" what before he would have had to accomplish through real actions. Concrete operations enable the child to think about things. To illustrate, on one study Piaget presented 5-, 6- and 7-year-old children with six sticks in a row and asked them to take the same number of sticks from a pile on the table. The young children solved the problem by placing their sticks beneath the sample and matching the sticks one by one. The older children merely picked up the six sticks and held them in their hands. The older children had counted the sticks mentally and hence felt no need to actually match them with the sticks in the row. It should be said that even the youngest children were able to count to six, so that this was not a factor in their performance.

Concrete operations also enable children to deal with the relations among classes of things. In another study Piaget presented 5-, 6- and 7-year-old children with a box containing 20 white and seven brown wooden beads. Each child was first asked if there were more white or more brown beads and all were able to say that there were more white than brown beads. Then Piaget asked, "Are there more white or more wooden beads?" The young children could not fathom the question and replied that "there are more white than brown beads." For such children classes are not regarded as abstractions but are thought of as concrete places. (I once asked a pre-operational child if he could be a Protestant and an American at the same time, to which he replied, "No," and then as an afterthought, "only if you move.")

When a child thought of a bead in the white "place" he could not think of it as being in the wooden "place" since objects cannot be in two places at once. He could only compare the white with the brown "places." The older children, who had attained concrete operations, encountered no difficulty with the task and readily replied that "there are more wooden than white beads because all of the beads are wooden and only some are white." By the end of the concrete operational period, children are remarkably adept at doing thought problems and at combining and dividing class concepts.

During the last stage (usually 12–15 years) there gradually emerge what Piaget calls formal operations and which, in effect, permit adolescents to think about their thoughts, to construct ideals and to reason realistically about the future. Formal operations also enable young people to reason about contrary-to-fact propositions. If, for example, a child is asked to assume that coal is white he is likely to reply, "But coal is black," whereas the adolescent can accept the contrary-to-fact assumption and reason from it.

Formal operational thought also makes possible the understanding of metaphor. It is for this reason that political and other satirical cartoons are not understood until adolescence. The child's inability to understand metaphor helps to explain why books such as "Alice in Wonderland" and "Gulliver's Travels" are enjoyed at different levels during childhood than in adolescence and adulthood, when their social significance can be understood.

No new mental systems emerge after the formal operations, which are the common coin of adult thought. After adolescence, mental growth takes the form—it is hoped—of a gradual increase in wisdom.

This capsule summary of Piaget's theory of intellectual development would not be complete without some words about Piaget's position with respect to language and thought. Piaget regards thought and language as different but closely related systems. Language, to a much greater extent than thought, is determined by particular forms of environmental stimulation. Inner-city Negro children, who tend to be retarded in language development, are much less retarded with respect to the ages at which they attain concrete operations. Indeed, not only inner-city children but children in bush Africa, Hong Kong and Appalachia all attain concrete operations at about the same age as middle-class children in Geneva and Boston.

Likewise, attempts to teach children concrete operations have been almost uniformly unsuccessful. This does not mean that these operations are independent of the environment but only that their development takes time and can be nourished by a much wider variety of environmental nutriments than is true for the growth of language, which is dependent upon much more specific forms of stimulation.

Language is, then, deceptive with respect to thought. Teachers of middle-class children are often misled, by the verbal facility of these youngsters, into believing that they understand more than they actually comprehend. (My 5-year-old asked me what my true identity was and as I tried to recover my composure he explained that Clark Kent was Superman's true identity.) At the other end, the teachers of inner-city children are often fooled by the language handicaps of these children into thinking that they have much lower mental ability than they actually possess. It is appropriate, therefore, that preschool programs for the disadvantaged should focus upon training these children in language and perception rather than upon trying to teach them concrete operations.

The impact which the foregoing Piagetian discoveries and conceptions is having upon education and child psychology has come as something of a shock to a good many educators and psychological research in America, which relies heavily upon statistics, electronics and computers. Piaget's studies of children's thinking seem hardly a step beyond the prescientific baby biographies kept by such men as Charles Darwin and Bronson Alcott. Indeed, in many of Piaget's research papers he supports his conclusions simply with illustrative examples of how children at different age levels respond to his tasks.

Many of Piaget's critics have focused upon his apparently casual methodology and have argued that while Piaget has arrived at some original ideas about children's thinking, his research lacks scientific rigor. It is likely that few, if any, of Piaget's research reports would have been accepted for publication in American psychological journals.

Other critics have taken somewhat the opposite tack. Jerome Bruner, who has done so much to bring Piaget to the attention of American social scientists, acknowledges the fruitfulness of Piaget's methods, modifications of which he has employed in his own investigations. But he argues against Piaget's theoretical interpretations. Bruner believes that Piaget has "missed the heart" of the problem of change and permanence or conservation in children's thinking. In the case of the orangeade poured into a different-sized container, Bruner argues that it is not reason, or mental operations, but some "internalized verbal formula that shields him [the child] from the overpowering appearance of the visual displays." Bruner seems to believe that the syntactical rules of language rather than logic can account for the child's discovery that a quantity remains unchanged despite alterations in its appearance.

Piaget is willing to answer his critics but only when he feels that the criticism is responsible and informed. With respect to his methods, their casualness is only apparent. Before they set out collecting data, his students are given a year of training in the art of interviewing children. They learn to ask questions without suggesting the answers and to test, by counter-suggestion, the strength of the child's conviction. Many of Piaget's studies have now been repeated with more rigorous procedures by other investigators all over the world and the results have been remarkably consistent with Piaget's findings. Attempts are currently under way to build a new intelligence scale on the basis of the Piaget tests, many of which are already in widespread use as evaluative procedures in education.

When it comes to criticisms of his theoretical views, Piaget is remarkably open and does not claim to be infallible. He frequently invites scholars who are in genuine disagreement with him to come to Geneva for a year so that the differences can be discussed and studied in depth. He has no desire to form a cult and says, in fact, "To the extent that there are Piagetians, to that extent have I failed." Piaget's lack of dogmatism is illustrated in his response to Bruner:

"Bruner does say that I 'missed the heart' of the conservation problem, a problem I have been working on for the last 30 years. He is right, of course, but that does not mean that he himself has understood it in a much shorter time . . . Adults, just like children, need time to reach the right ideas . . . This is the great mystery of development, which is irreducible to an accumulation of isolated learning acquisitions. Even psychology cannot be learned or constructed in a short time." (Despite his disclaimer, Piaget has offered a comprehensive theory of how the child arrives at conservation and this theory has received much research support.)

Piaget would probably agree with those who are critical about premature applications of his work to education. He finds particularly disturbing the efforts by some American educators to accelerate children intellectually. When he was giving his other 1967 lectures, in New York, he remarked:

"If we accept the fact that there are stages of development, another question arises which I call 'the American question,' and I am asked it every time I come here. If there are stages that children reach at given norms of ages can we accelerate the stages? Do we have to go through each one of these stages, or can't we speed it up a bit? Well, surely, the answer is yes . . . but how far can we speed them up? . . . I have a hypothesis which I am so far incapable of proving: probably the organization of operations has an optimal time . . . For example, we know that it takes 9 to 12 months before babies develop the notion that an object is still there even when a screen is placed in front of it. Now kittens go through the same sub-stages but they do it in three months—so they're six months ahead of the babies. Is this an advantage or isn't it?

"We can certainly see our answer in one sense. The kitten is not going to go much further. The child has taken longer, but he is capable of going further so it seems to me that the nine months were not for nothing . . . It is probably possible to accelerate, but maximal acceleration is not desirable. There seems to be an optimal time. What this optimal time is will surely depend upon each individual and on the subject matter. We still need a great deal of research to know what the optimal time would be."

Piaget's stance against using his findings as a justification for accelerating children intellectually recalls a remark made by Freud when he was asked whatever became of those bright, aggressive shoeshine boys one encounters in city streets. Freud's reply was, "They become cobblers." In Piaget's terms they get to a certain point earlier but they don't go as far. And the New York educator Eliot Shapiro has pointed out that one of the Negro child's problems is that he is forced to grow up and take responsibility too soon and doesn't have time to be a child.

Despite some premature and erroneous applications of his thinking to education, Piaget has had an over-all effect much more positive than negative. His findings about children's understanding of scientific and mathematical concepts are being used as guidelines for new curricula in these subjects. And his tests are being more and more widely used to evaluate educational outcomes. Perhaps the most significant and widespread positive effect that Piaget has had upon education is in the changed attitudes on the part of teachers who have been exposed to his thinking. After becoming acquainted with Piaget's work, teachers can never again see children in quite the same way as they had before. Once teachers begin to look at children from the Piagetian perspective they can also appreciate his views with regard to the aims of education.

"The principal goal of education," he once said, "is to create men who are capable of doing new things, not simply of repeating what other generations have done—men who are creative, inventive and discoverers. The second goal of education is to form minds which can be critical, can verify, and not accept everything they are offered. The great danger today is of slogans, collective opinions, ready-made trends of thought. We have to be able to resist individually, to criticize, to distinguish between what is proven and what is not. So we need pupils who are active, who learn early to find out by themselves, partly by their own spontaneous activity and partly through materials we set up for them; who learn early to tell what is verifiable and what is simply the first idea to come to them."

At the beginning of his eighth decade, Jean Piaget is busy as ever. A new book of his on memory will be published soon and another on the mental functions in the preschool child is in preparation. The International Center for Genetic Epistemology, which Piaget founded in 1955 with a grant from the Rockefeller Foundation, continues to draw scholars from around the world who wish to explore with Piaget the origin of scientific concepts. As Professor of Experimental Psychology at the University of Geneva, Piaget also continues to teach courses and conduct seminars.

And his students still continue to collect the data which at the end of the school year Piaget will take with him up to the mountains. The methods employed by his students today are not markedly different from those which were used by their predecessors decades ago. While there are occasional statistics, there are still no electronics or computers. In an age of moon shots and automation, the remarkable discoveries of Jean Piaget are evidence that in the realm of scientific achievement, technological sophistication is still no substitute for creative genius.

Reading 19

Preschool Thought

Rochel Gelman

I find it noteworthy that this special issue has provided for a separate essay on preschool thought. Until very recently, almost all researchers of cognitive development have made a habit of contrasting the preschooler with the older child. Preschoolers have been characterized as lacking the classification abilities, communication skills, number concepts, order concepts, memorial skills, and a framework for reasoning about causal relationships between events that older children are granted. Indeed, had one written an essay on preschool thought five years ago, the conclusion might have been that preschoolers are remarkably ignorant. In this essay I review some of the evidence that has begun to pile up

against the view that preschoolers are cognitively inept. I then consider why we failed to see what it is that preschoolers can do and possible misinterpretations of the recent findings.

It is commonplace to read about the egocentrism of preschool children. The idea is that the young child either is unable to take the perspective of another child or adult or, worse yet, believes his or her own perspective is the same as that of others. Such general statements derive support from a variety of studies. When asked to describe an abstract shape for another child, a preschooler will sometimes use private labels, for example, "mommy's hat" (Glucksberg, Krauss, & Weisberg, 1966). The child's talk in the presence of others often goes on without any attempt to coordinate this talk with that of other speakers; the child seems not

Preparation of this essay was supported in part by National Science Foundation Grant BNS 03327 and National Institute of Child Health and Human Development Grant HD 10965.

to care who else is speaking, what they say, or whether he or she is being listened to. "He feels no desire to influence his listener nor to tell him anything; not unlike a certain type of drawing room conversation where everyone talks about himself and no one listens" (Piaget, 1955, p. 32). When asked to choose a picture that represents the view of a mountain seen by someone opposite the child, the child selects the representation that matches what the child sees (Piaget & Inhelder, 1956)!

In 1973, Marilyn Shatz and I reported on our studies of the speech used by 4-year-olds when they talked to 2-year-olds, peers, or adults. We found that our subjects generally used short and simple utterances when they described the workings of a toy to their 2-year-old listeners. In contrast, these same 4-year-old children used longer and more complex utterances when describing the same toy to their peers or adults (Shatz & Gelman, 1973). Was it possible that these children, who were presumed to be egocentric speakers by the research community at large, were adjusting their speech in accordance with their perception or conception of their listeners' different abilities and needs? As it turns out, yes. We (Gelman & Shatz, 1977) found that 4-year-olds' speech to a 2-year-old serves different functions and contains somewhat different messages than does their speech to adults. Speech to 2-year-olds serves to show and tell to focus, direct, and monitor attention; speech to adults includes talk about the child's own thoughts and seeks information, support, or clarification from adults. Adult-directed speech also contains hedges about statements of fact, indicating that the child recognizes that he or she may be wrong and that the adult could challenge his or her statements. The children in our experiments were clearly taking the different needs and capacities of their listeners into account when talking to them. They hardly seem egocentric!

What about the claim that preschoolers think their visual perspective is the same as that of another person? Here again the presumed is contradicted. In an elegant series of experiments with 1–3-year-old children, Lempers, Flavell, and Flavell (1977) demonstrated over and over again that it is simply wrong to deny preschoolers an ability to distinguish their perspective from that of others. In the "show-toy task," 1½–3-year-old children showed toys to adults so that the front side was visible to the adult. This means they turned away from themselves the front of the toy and thereby deprived themselves of their original perspective. When asked to show pictures, almost all the 2- and 3-year-olds turned the front side to the adult and thereby ended up seeing the blank back of the picture. Still younger children showed the picture horizontally rather than egocentrically, that is, they did not simply hold the picture upright and thus show the back to their adult cohort in the task.

More recently, Flavell, Shipstead, and Croft (Note 1) dispelled the rumor that preschoolers believe that the closing of their own eyes deprives others of visual information about them. In fact, there is so much evidence now coming in about the perspective-taking abilities of preschoolers (for reviews, see Gelman, 1978; Shatz, 1978) that I find it hard to understand how I or anyone else ever held the belief that preschoolers are egocentric.

In retrospect one might argue that the perspective-taking abilities of preschoolers make sense. Young children do interact with others and they do talk. If they did not have any perspective-taking abilities, how could they ever communicate (cf. Fodor, 1972)? The argument might continue that we may have been wrong on the perspective-taking front, but surely we were correct in our characterization of other cognitive abilities. After all, number concepts seem much removed from the daily interactions of a preschooler. Besides, they constitute abstract ideas—the kind of ideas that everyone knows are very late in cognitive development. All of this may well be true; nevertheless, preschoolers know a great deal about the nature of number. I and my collaborators have shown that children as young as $2\frac{1}{2}$ years honor the principles of counting and are able to use a counting algorithm to reason numerically, for example, to determine that an unexpected change in the numerical value of a set occurred because of surreptitiously performed addition or subtraction. (See Gelman & Gallistel, 1978, for a review of the arithmetic reasoning abilities of preschoolers.)

Successful counting involves the coordinated application of five principles (Gelman & Gallistel, 1978). These are as follows: (1) The one–one principle—each item in an array must be tagged with one and only one unique tag. (2) The stable-order principle—the tags assigned must be drawn from a stably ordered list. (3) The cardinal principle—the last tag used for a particular count serves to designate the cardinal number represented by the array. (4) The abstraction principle—any set of items may be collected together for a count. It does not matter whether they are identical, three-dimensional, imagined, or real, for in principle, any discrete set of materials can be represented as the contents of a set. (5) The order-irrelevance principle—the order in which a given object is tagged as one, two, three, and so on, is irrelevant as long as it is tagged but once and as long as the stable-order and cardinal principles are honored. Number words are arbitrary tags. The evidence clearly supports the conclusion that preschoolers honor these principles. They may not apply them perfectly, the set sizes to which they are applied may be limited, and their count lists may differ from the conventional list, but nevertheless the principles are used. Thus, a 2½-year-old may say "two, six" when counting a two-item array and "two, six, ten" when counting a three-item array (the one-one principle). The same child will use his or her own list over and over again (the stable-order principle) and, when asked how many items are present, will repeat the last tag in the list. In the present example, the child said "ten" when asked about the number represented by a three-item array (the cardinal principle).

The fact that young children invent their own lists suggests that the counting principles are guiding the search for appropriate tags. Such "errors" in counting are like the errors made by young language learners (e.g., "I runned"). In the latter case, such errors are taken to mean that the child's use of language is rule governed and that these rules come from the child; we are not likely to hear speakers of English using such words as *runned, footses, mouses, unthirsty,* and *two-six-ten.* We use similar logic to account for the presence of idiosyncratic count lists.

Further facts about the nature of counting in young children support the idea that some basic principles guide their acquisition of skill at counting. Children spontaneously self-correct their count errors, and perhaps more important, they are inclined to count without any request to do so. If we accept the idea that the counting principles are available to the child, the fact that young children count spontaneously without external motivation fits well. What's more, the self-generated practice trials make it possible for a child to develop skill at counting.

Still other cognitive domains exist for which it has been possible to reveal considerable capacity on the part of the young child. There are conditions under which preschoolers classify according to taxonomic categories (Rosch, Mervis, Gray, Johnson, & Boyes-Braem, 1976), classify animate and inanimate objects separately (Keil, 1977; Carey, Note 2), and use hierarchical classifications (Keil, 1977; Mansfield, 1977; Markman & Siebert, 1976). They can be taught to use a rule of transitive inference (Trabasso, 1975). They can be shown to be sensitive to temporal order (Brown, 1976). They believe, as do adults, that causes precede their effects (Bullock & Gelman, 1979; Kun, 1978). They use rules to solve problems (Siegler, 1978), and so on. In short, they have considerable cognitive abilities. Why, then, has it taken us so long to see them? I think there are two related reasons.

First, we simply did not look. Indeed, we seemed to choose to ignore facts that were staring us in the face. Consider the case of counting prowess in the young child. It is now clear that preschoolers can and do count. But many of us, myself included, who researched number concepts in children started out with the view that preschoolers were restricted to the use of a perceptual mechanism for number abstraction. The idea was that their representation of number was governed by the same pattern-recognition abilities that are used to distinguish one object from another. Just as they distinguish "cowness" and "treeness," they presumably distinguished "twoness" and "threeness." I don't remember how many times I saw preschoolers counting in my various experiments before I finally recognized they were indeed able to count, no matter what our theories led us to believe. I do remember one 3-year-old telling me that he much preferred one task over another, that being the one in which it was possible to count! And it took us a while to recognize the ubiquitous tendency for 4-year-olds to talk down to 2-year-olds.

The failure to recognize facts that contradict existing theories is not unique to those who study cognitive development. Time and time again we read in the history of science of similar cases. It seems as if we have a general tendency to resist new facts if their recognition means giving up a theory without being able to come up with another that will account for the new as well as the old facts. I believe that we now know enough about the nature of the development of number concepts to be able to deal with the apparent contradictions between the new and old research findings. The young child seems unable to reason about number without reference to representations of specific numerosities, representations obtained by counting. With development, the child's reasoning moves from a dependence on specific representations to an algebraic stage in which specific representations of numerosity are no longer required. In the conservation task, the child has to make inferences about equivalence and nonequivalence on the basis of one-to-one correspondence. It matters not what the particular numbers of items in the two displays are. If they can be placed in one-to-one correspondence, then they are equal by definition. If we are correct, then the abilities we have uncovered can be seen as the beginning understanding of number. In this light their existence need not be seen as contradictory findings. Indeed, once one begins to talk about precursors of later cognitive abilities it is no longer unreasonable to start the search for those concepts and capacities the preschooler must have if he or she is to acquire complex cognitive abilities. We should expect to find domains in which they are quite competent—if only we look.

Recent work on the learning and memorial abilities of young children endorses my belief that there are many cases in which it will suffice to decide to look for competence in order for us to take note of it. As Carey (1978) pointed out, young children perform an incredible task by learning the lexicon of their native language. She estimated that 6-year-old children have mastered to some degree about 14,000 words. To do this, the children need to learn about nine new words a day from the time they start speaking until the time they reach their sixth birthday. This is truly a remarkable accomplishment. So what if the preschooler fails on a task that requires him or her to sort consistently by taxonomic category? The same child has to have some classification abilities in order to learn the lexicon so rapidly. To be sure, the child probably does not learn the full meaning of every new word the first time that word is heard. But as Carey showed, "One or a very few experiences with a new word can suffice for the child to enter it into his or her mental lexicon and to represent some of its syntactic and semantic features." Given this and the continued exposure to that word, it is then possible for a child to learn more about it and to reorganize his or her lexicon and the conceptual framework involved therein.

Nelson (1978) made it clear that young children readily learn the scripts that describe the class of events they encounter. Others (e.g., Mandler, in press) have shown young children to have excellent memories for stories—a fact that really should not surprise us, given the young child's interest in hearing stories.

Although some abilities are so pervasive that simply deciding to attend to them will make them evident, this is not true for a wide variety of cognitive skills, for example, reading and metacognitive skills. This brings me to the second reason for our failure, until recently, to acknowledge the cognitive capacities of preschoolers.

Many of the young child's cognitive abilities are well concealed and require the modification of old tasks or the development of new tasks for their revelation. I return to the question of early number concepts. Young children systematically fail Piaget's number conservation task. With this task, they behave as if they believe that the number of objects in a row changes when items are pushed together or spread apart. They thus begin by agreeing that two rows placed in one-to-one correspondence represent equal amounts; when they see one row lengthened, however, they deny the continued equivalence.

In an effort to control for a variety of variables that might have interfered with the child's possible belief in the invariance of the numerical value of a set despite the application of a lengthening transformation, my colleagues and I developed what we call "the magic task" (Gelman, 1972). The task involves two phases. The first establishes an expectancy for the continued presence of two sets of two given values, say, 3 and 2, despite the repeated covering and uncovering of those sets. To avoid reference to number or the use of ambiguous terms such as *more* or *less,* one of these displays is designated "the winner," and the other "the loser." These are covered and children have to find the winner and tell us why they have or have not done so once they uncover a display. As luck would have it, preschoolers decide on their own that numerical value is the determinant for winning and losing status. They thus establish an expectancy for two particular numerical values. Then, unbeknownst to the child, the second phase of the experiment begins when the experimenter surreptitiously alters one of the expected displays. Across different conditions and experiments, the changes involve addition, subtraction, displacement, change in color of the original objects, and even a change in identity of the original objects. Children who encounter a change in number produced by subtraction or addition say that the expected number has been violated, typically identify the number of elements present and the number that should be present, and make explicit reference to the transformation that must have been performed—even if they did not see it. In contrast, children who encounter the effects of irrelevant transformations say the number of elements is as expected despite the change in length of a display, or in the color, or in the identity of an element in that display.

According to the results of the magic task, preschoolers know full well that lengthening or shortening an array does not alter the numerical value of a display. Still, these same children fail the conservation task. But note how different these tasks are. In the conservation task the child has to judge equivalence on the basis of one-to-one correspondence, correctly interpret questions that are ambiguous, watch the transformation being performed, and then ignore the effect of that transformation. In the magic task the child need not make judgments of equivalence based on one-to-one correspondence, he or she need not (indeed cannot) see the transformation being performed, and there are no ambiguous terms to misinterpret. In other words, the magic task is a very stripped down version of the conservation task. Likewise, many other tasks that show preschoolers in a positive light have downgraded the complexity of the tasks that they fail, altered the instructions, changed the stimuli used, embedded the question of interest in games preschoolers play, provided extensive pretraining before testing on the target task—In short, in many cases it has been necessary to develop tasks and experimental settings to suit the preschool child (Gelman, 1978). This is easier said than done. Consider the magic game which *was* designed to meet our best guesses as to how to elicit the number-invariance rules honored by the young child.

Bullock and Gelman (1977) modified the magic task in order to determine whether preschoolers could compare two number pairs. In particular, the question was whether they would recognize that the number pair 1 and 2 was like 3 and 4 insofar as 1 and 3 were both "less" and 2 and 4 were both "more." Children between the ages of 2½ and 4 were first shown one-item and two-item displays, and they established expectancies for a set of one and a set of two items. Half the children were told that the one-item array was the winner; half were told that the two-item array was the winner. From the

experimenter's point of view this was also a more-less comparison task. To determine whether the 2½–4-year-old children in the experiment knew this, we surreptitiously replaced the original displays with three-item and four-item displays and asked which of these was the winner. Many of the older children were confused by this question and said that neither was the winner—an observation which in point of fact was correct. When asked to make the best possible choice, the children then went on to choose the display that honored the relation they were reinforced for during the expectancy training. Apparently the children did not immediately realize that it was all right to make a judgment of similarity, given the fact that neither of the new displays was identical to either of the original displays. Our variation in question format served to tell them that the transfer task called for a similarity judgment. My point here is that we started out with a task that was designed for young children and still we found that the task presented problems.

This example of the subtle ways in which a task can confound the assessment of those early cognitive abilities that are generally buried is not an isolated one. I have discussed others elsewhere (Gelman, 1978), and for me they are very sobering. They make it clear that in many cases, it takes more than a decision to look for early cognitive abilities. It is often exceedingly difficult to know how to design tasks so that they will be suitable for use with young children. I believe this derives in part from the fact that many of the preschoolers' cognitive abilities are fragile and as such are only evident under restricted conditions—at least compared with the conditions under which older children can apply their knowledge. This brings me to my next point.

Some might take the recent demonstrations of early cognitive abilities to mean that preschoolers are miniature adults as far as their cognitions are concerned. This is not what I want people to conclude, and should they so conclude it would not be in the best interests of either those who study cognitive development or the child. The fact remains that despite the recent demonstration of some complex cognitive abilities, young children fail a wide range of tasks that seem so simple for older children. I believe that many of the best insights into the nature of development will come from understanding exactly what conditions interfere with the use and accessibility of those capacities the young child does possess. These insights may also be of the greatest educational relevance. However, these insights can only come after we have uncovered the basic capacities that make cognitive growth a possibility.

What I do want people to realize is that we have been much too inclined to reach conclusions about what preschoolers cannot do, compared with what their older cohorts can do on a variety of tasks. We must cease to approach young children with only those tasks that are designed for older children. The time has come for us to turn our attention to what young children can do as well as to what they cannot do. Without a good description of what young children do know, it's going to be exceedingly difficult, if not impossible, to chart their course as they travel the path of cognitive development. What's worse, we run the serious risk of making unwarranted statements about the nature of preschool curricula. I have had people tell me that there is no point in teaching young children about numbers, since preschoolers cannot conserve numbers. This, I submit, is a non sequitur. The conservation task is but one index of numerical knowledge, and it is beginning to look like it is an index of a rather sophisticated knowledge.

My message is quite straightforward. We should study preschoolers in their own right and give up treating them as foils against which to describe the accomplishments of middle childhood. We have made some progress in recent years, but there is still plenty of room for those who are willing to take on the mind of the young child.

REFERENCE NOTES

1 Flavell, J. H., Shipstead, S. G., & Croft, K. *What young children think you see when their eyes are closed.* Unpublished manuscript, Stanford University, 1978.

2 Carey, S. *The child's concept of* animal. Paper presented at the meeting of the Psychonomic Society, San Antonio, Texas, November 1978.

REFERENCES

Brown, A. L. The construction of temporal succession by preoperational children. In A. D. Pick (Ed.), *Minnesota symposium on child psychology* (Vol. 10). Minneapolis: University of Minnesota Press, 1976.

Bullock, M., & Gelman, R. Numerical reasoning in young children: The ordering principle. *Child Development,* 1977, *48,* 427–434.

Bullock, M., & Gelman, R. Preschool children's assump-

tions about cause and effect: Temporal ordering. *Child Development,* 1979, *50,* 89–96.

Carey, S. The child as word learner. In M. Halle, J. Bresnan, & G. A. Miller (Eds.), *Linguistic theory and psychological reality.* Cambridge, Mass.: Massachusetts Institute of Technology Press, 1978.

Fodor, J. A. Some reflections on L. S. Vygotsky's *Thought and language. Cognition,* 1972, *1,* 83–95.

Gelman, R. Logical capacity of very young children: Number invariance rules. *Child Development,* 1972, *43,* 75–90.

Gelman, R. Cognitive development. In L. W. Porter & M. R. Rosenzweig (Eds.), *Annual review of psychology* (Vol. 29). Palo Alto, Calif.: Annual Reviews, 1978.

Gelman, R., & Gallistel, C. R. *The child's understanding of number.* Cambridge, Mass.: Harvard University Press, 1978.

Gelman, R., & Shatz, M. Appropriate speech adjustments: The operation of conversational constraints on talk to two-year-olds. In M. Lewis & L. A. Rosenblum (Eds.), *Interaction, conversation, and the development of language.* New York: Wiley, 1977.

Glucksberg, S., Krauss, R. M., & Weisberg, R. Referential communication in nursery school children: Method and some preliminary findings. *Journal of Experimental Child Psychology,* 1966, *3,* 333–342.

Keil, F. *The role of ontological categories in a theory of semantic and conceptual development.* Unpublished doctoral dissertation, University of Pennsylvania, 1977.

Kun, A. Evidence for preschoolers' understanding of causal direction in extended causal sequences. *Child Development,* 1978, *49,* 218–222.

Lempers, J. D., Flavell, E. R., & Flavell, J. H. The development in very young children of tacit knowledge concerning visual perception. *Genetic Psychology Monographs,* 1977, *95,* 3–53.

Mandler, J. M. Categorical and schematic organization. In C. R. Puff (Ed.), *Memory, organization, and structure.* New York: Academic Press, in press.

Mansfield, A. F. Semantic organization in the young child: Evidence for the development of semantic feature systems. *Journal of Experimental Child Psychology,* 1977, *23,* 57–77.

Markman, E. M., & Siebert, J. Classes and collections: Internal organization and resulting holistic properties. *Cognitive Psychology,* 1976, *8,* 561–577.

Nelson, K. How young children represent knowledge of their world in and out of language: A preliminary report. In R. Siegler (Ed.), *Children's thinking: What develops?* Hillsdale, N.J.: Erlbaum, 1978.

Piaget, J. *The language and thought of the child.* London: Routledge & Kegan Paul, 1955.

Piaget, J., & Inhelder, B. *The child's conception of space.* London: Routledge & Kegan Paul, 1956.

Rosch, E., Mervis, C. B., Gray, W. D., Johnson, D. M.,

& Boyes-Braem, P. Basic objects in natural categories. *Cognitive Psychology,* 1976, *8,* 382–439.

Shatz, M. The relationship between cognitive processes and the development of communication skills. In C. B. Keasey (Ed.), *Nebraska symposium on motivation* (Vol. 26). Lincoln: University of Nebraska Press, 1978.

Shatz, M., & Gelman, R. The development of communication skills: Modifications in the speech of young children as a function of listener. *Monographs of the Society for Research in Child Development,* 1973, *38*(2, Serial No. 152).

Siegler, R. S. The origins of scientific reasoning. In R. S. Siegler (Ed.), *Children's thinking: What develops?* Hillsdale, N. J.: Erlbaum, 1978.

Trabasso, T. R. Representation, memory and reasoning: How do we make transitive inferences. In A. D. Pick (Ed.), *Minnesota symposium on child psychology* (Vol. 9). Minneapolis: University of Minnesota Press, 1975.

Reading 20

Metacognition and Cognitive Monitoring: A New Area of Cognitive–Developmental Inquiry

John H. Flavell

Preschool and elementary school children were asked to study a set of items until they were sure they could recall them perfectly (Flavell, Friedrichs, & Hoyt, 1970). The older subjects studied for a while, said they were ready, and usually were, that is, they showed perfect recall. The younger children studied for a while, said they were ready, and usually were not. In another study, elementary school children were asked to help the experimenter evaluate the communicative adequacy of verbal instructions, indicating any omissions and obscurities (Markman, 1977). Although the instructions were riddled with blatant emissions and obscurities, the younger subjects were surprisingly poor at detecting them. They incorrectly thought they had understood and could follow the instructions, much as their counterparts in the study by Flavell et al. (1970) incorrectly thought they had memorized and could recall the items.

Results such as these have suggested that young children are quite limited in their knowledge and cognition about cognitive phenomena, or in their *metacognition,* and do relatively little monitoring of their own memory, comprehension, and other cognitive enterprises (see, e.g., Brown, 1978; Flavell, 1978; Flavell & Wellman, 1977; Kreutzer, Leonard, & Flavell, 1975; Flavell, Note 1, Note 2, Note 3; Markman, Note 4). Investigators have recently concluded that metacognition plays an important

The preparation of this essay was supported by National Institute of Child Health and Human Development Grant NDMH 10429.

role in oral communication of information, oral persuasion, oral comprehension, reading comprehension, writing, language acquisition, attention, memory, problem solving, social cognition, and various types of self-control and self-instruction; there are also clear indications that ideas about metacognition are beginning to make contact with similar ideas in the areas of social learning theory, cognitive behavior modification, personality development, and education (Flavell, Note 1, Note 2, Note 3). Thus, the nature and development of metacognition and of cognitive monitoring/regulation is currently emerging as an interesting and promising new area of investigation. What might there be for a child or adolescent to learn in this area? That is, what adultlike knowledge and behavior might constitute the developmental target here, toward which the child gradually progresses? The following model is my attempt to answer this question. For further details about the model see my papers on the subject (Flavell, Note 2, Note 3).

A MODEL OF COGNITIVE MONITORING

I believe that the monitoring of a wide variety of cognitive enterprises occurs through the actions of and interactions among four classes of phenomena: (a) *metacognitive knowledge,* (b) *metacognitive experiences,* (c) *goals* (or *tasks*), and (d) *actions* (or *strategies*). Metacognitive knowledge is that segment of your (a child's, an adult's) stored world knowledge that has to do with people as cognitive creatures and with their diverse cognitive tasks, goals, actions, and experiences. An example would be a child's acquired belief that unlike many of her friends, she is better at arithmetic than at spelling. Metacognitive experiences are any conscious cognitive or affective experiences that accompany and pertain to any intellectual enterprise. An example would be the sudden feeling that you do not understand something another person just said. I assume that metacognitive knowledge and metacognitive experiences differ from other kinds only in their content and function, not in their form or quality. Goals (or tasks) refer to the objectives of a cognitive enterprise. Actions (or strategies) refer to the cognitions or other behaviors employed to achieve them. Below, I pay particular attention to the nature and functions of metacognitive knowledge and metacognitive experiences, with goals and actions discussed in the course of describing these first two.

Metacognitive Knowledge

Metacognitive knowledge consists primarily of knowledge or beliefs about what factors or variables act and interact in what ways to affect the course and outcome of cognitive enterprises. There are three major categories of these factors or variables— *person, task,* and *strategy.*

The person category encompasses everything that you could come to believe about the nature of yourself and other people as cognitive processors. It can be further subcategorized into beliefs about intraindividual differences, interindividual differences, and universals of cognition. Examples of the first and second subcategories would be, respectively, your belief (a) that you can learn most things better by listening than by reading, and (b) that one of your friends is more socially sensitive than another. The following are possible examples of beliefs about universal properties of cognition that the children might gradually acquire. They could learn that there are various degrees and kinds of understanding (attending, remembering, communicating, problem solving, etc.). You may not understand some person or thing you hear, see, or read about if you do not attend closely—and also, sometimes, even if you do attend closely. Moreover, you can fail to understand something or someone in two different ways: (a) by not achieving any coherent representation at all, or (b) by understanding incorrectly, that is, misunderstanding. The growing

individual will also learn that it can sometimes be difficult to determine how well you know or remember a social or nonsocial object of cognition, for example, whether you know it well enough to reach some social or nonsocial goal involving that object. There is the further insight that how well you understand something now may not be an accurate predictor of how well you will understand it later. For instance, you may forget later what you can easily bring to mind now, and you may remember later what you cannot bring to mind now. I think such tacit beliefs may play important roles in the cognitive enterprises of older children and adults the world over and that the acquisition of these beliefs would be interesting to study.

One subcategory of the task category concerns the information available to you during a cognitive enterprise. It could be abundant or meager, familiar or unfamiliar, redundant or densely packed, well or poorly organized, delivered in this manner or at that pace, interesting or dull, trustworthy or untrustworthy, and so on. The metacognitive knowledge in this subcategory is an understanding of what such variations imply for how the cognitive enterprise should best be managed and how successful you are likely to be in achieving its goal. To take a social–cognitive example, the child needs to learn that the quantity and quality of available information can sometimes be insufficient to warrant confident judgments about what another person is really like. Another subcategory includes metacognitive knowledge about task demands or goals. The child will come to know that some cognitive enterprises are more demanding and difficult than others, even given the same available information. For example, it is easier to recall the gist of a story than its exact wording.

As for the strategy category, there is a great deal of knowledge that could be acquired concerning what strategies are likely to be effective in achieving what subgoals and goals in what sorts of cognitive undertakings. The child may come to believe, for example, that one good way to learn and retain many bodies of information is to pay particular attention to the main points and try to repeat them to yourself in your own words. As is shown below, it is possible to acquire metacognitive strategies as well as cognitive ones.

Finally, most metacognitive knowledge actually concerns interactions or combinations among two or three of these three types of variables. To illustrate a combination involving all three, you might believe that you (unlike your brother) should use Strategy A (rather than Strategy B) in Task X (as contrasted with Task Y).

Several things follow from the assumption, made above, that metacognitive knowledge is not fundamentally different from other knowledge stored in long-term memory. Thus, a segment of it may be activated as the result of a deliberate, conscious memory search, for example, for an effective strategy. On the other hand, and no doubt more commonly, the segment may be activated unintentionally and automatically by retrieval cues in the task situation. However activated, it may and probably often does influence the course of the cognitive enterprise without itself entering consciousness. Alternatively, it may become or give rise to a conscious experience (called a metacognitive experience in the present model of cognitive monitoring). Finally, and again like any other body of knowledge children acquire, it can be inaccurate, can fail to be activated when needed, can fail to have much or any influence when activated, and can fail to have a beneficial or adaptive effect when influential. I believe that metacognitive knowledge can have a number of concrete and important effects on the cognitive enterprises of children and adults. It can lead you to select, evaluate, revise, and abandon cognitive tasks, goals, and strategies in light of their relationships with one another and with your own abilities and interests with respect to that enterprise. Similarly, it can lead to any of a wide variety of metacognitive experiences concerning self, tasks, goals, and strategies, and can also help you interpret the meaning and behavioral implications of these metacognitive experiences.

Metacognitive Experiences

Metacognitive experiences can be brief or lengthy in duration, simple or complex in content. To illustrate, you may experience a momentary sense of puzzlement that you subsequently ignore, or you may wonder for some time whether you really understand what another person is up to. These experiences can also occur at any time before, after, or during a cognitive enterprise. For instance, you may feel that you are liable to fail in some upcoming enterprise, or that you did very well indeed in some previous one. Many metacognitive experiences have to do with where you are in an enterprise and what sort of progress you are making or are likely to make: You believe/feel that you have almost memo-

rized those instructions, are not adequately communicating how you feel to your friend, are suddenly stymied in your attempt to understand something you are reading, have just begun to solve what you sense will be an easy problem, and so forth.

My present guess is that metacognitive experiences are especially likely to occur in situations that stimulate a lot of careful, highly conscious thinking: in a job or school task that expressly demands that kind of thinking; in novel roles or situations, where every major step you take requires planning beforehand and evaluation afterwards; where decisions and actions are at once weighty and risky; where high affective arousal or other inhibitors of reflective thinking are absent (cf. Langer, 1978). Such situations provide many opportunities for thoughts and feelings about your own thinking to arise and, in many cases, call for the kind of quality control that metacognitive experiences can help supply.

Some metacognitive experiences are best described as items of metacognitive knowledge that have entered consciousness. As one example, while wrestling with some stubborn problem, you suddenly recall another problem very like it that you solved thus and so. Some metacognitive experiences clearly cannot be described that way, however. For instance, the feeling that you are still far from your goal is not in itself a segment of metacognitive knowledge, although what you make of that feeling and what you do about it would undoubtedly be informed and guided by your metacognitive knowledge. Thus, metacognitive knowledge and metacognitive experiences form partially overlapping sets: Some experiences have such knowledge as their content and some do not; some knowledge may become conscious and comprise such experiences and some may never do so.

Metacognitive experiences can have very important effects on cognitive goals or tasks, metacognitive knowledge, and cognitive actions or strategies. First, they can lead you to establish new goals and to revise or abandon old ones. Experiences of puzzlement or failure can have any of these effects, for example.

Second, metacognitive experiences can affect your metacognitive knowledge base by adding to it, deleting from it, or revising it. You can observe relationships among goals, means, metacognitive experiences, and task outcomes and—Piagetian fashion—assimilate these observations to your existing metacognitive knowledge and accommodate the knowledge to the observations. Although metacognitive knowledge can undoubtedly undergo at least some modification without metacognitive experiences, I suspect that these experiences play a major role in its development during childhood and adolescence.

Finally, metacognitive experiences can activate strategies aimed at either of two types of goals—cognitive or metacognitive. As an example of the former, you sense (metacognitive experience) that you do not yet know a certain chapter in your text well enough to pass tomorrow's exam, so you read it through once more (cognitive strategy, aimed at the straightforward cognitive goal of simply improving your knowledge). As an example of the latter, you wonder (metacognitive experience) if you understand the chapter well enough to pass tomorrow's exam, so you try to find out by asking yourself questions about it and noting how well you are able to answer them (metacognitive strategy, aimed at the metacognitive goal of assessing your knowledge, and thereby, of generating another metacognitive experience). Cognitive strategies are invoked to *make* cognitive progress, metacognitive strategies to *monitor* it. However, it is possible in some cases for the same strategy to be invoked for either purpose and also, regardless of why it was invoked, for it to achieve both goals. For instance, you could have asked yourself questions about the chapter with the deliberate aim of improving your knowledge rather than monitoring it, and even if your aim had been to monitor rather than to improve it, an improvement in your knowledge as well as an assessment of its quality would likely result. I am arguing, then, that your store of metacognitive knowledge is apt to contain knowledge of metacognitive strategies as well as of cognitive ones. Skimming a set of directions to get a rough idea of how hard they are going to be to follow or remember is a metacognitive strategy. Another is to paraphrase aloud what someone has just told you to see if she will agree that that is, in fact, just what she meant. A third is to add a column of figures a second time to ensure that your total is accurate.

Recall that according to this model, the monitoring of cognitive enterprises proceeds through the actions of and interactions among metacognitive knowledge, metacognitive experiences, goals/tasks, and actions/strategies. A hypothetical but true-to-life example of this dynamic interplay at work might be a useful way of concluding this summary of the model. Let us begin at the point where some self-imposed or externally imposed task and goal are established. Your existing metacognitive knowledge concerning this class of goals leads to the conscious metacognitive experience that this goal will be difficult to achieve. That metacognitive experience, combined with additional metacognitive knowledge, causes you to select and use the cognitive strategy of asking questions of knowledgeable other people. Their answers to your questions trigger additional metacognitive experiences about how the endeavor is faring. These experiences, again informed and guided by pertinent metacognitive knowledge, instigate the metacognitive strategies of surveying all that you have learned to see if it fits together into a coherent whole, if it seems plausible and consistent with your prior knowledge and expectations, and if it provides an avenue to the goal. This survey turns up difficulties on one or more of these points, with the consequent activation by metacognitive knowledge and experiences of the same or different cognitive and/or metacognitive strategies, and so the interplay continues until the enterprise comes to an end.

DEVELOPMENTAL AND EDUCATIONAL IMPLICATIONS

This model suggests the existence of a number of possible developments that researchers might find it worthwhile to investigate (Flavell, Note 3). In the case of universals (person category of metacognitive knowledge), for instance, children might at first distinguish only between understanding and not understanding things; they might know only that inputs sometimes lead them to feel puzzled, confused, unable to act, uncertain about what is intended or meant, and that they sometimes lead to the absence of these feelings, to a clear representation of something, to a definite sense of what they should do next. The distinction, within the latter state, between accurate or real understanding and inaccurate or illusory understanding may only be acquired after this initial, more basic differentiation has been made. The acquisition of the second distinction may then pave the way for still more sophisticated metacognitive knowledge in this area; possible examples include the recognition that accuracy of understanding can sometimes be hard to attain and to assess, and knowledge of some of the person variables that can decrease accuracy, such as personal biases, intense affect, and mental or physical illness. Additional developmental hypotheses can be derived from other parts of the model. Here as elsewhere (see Gelman, 1979, this issue), it will naturally be very important to try to discover the early competencies that serve as building blocks for subsequent acquisitions rather than merely cataloging the young child's metacognitive lacks and inadequacies. We also need to try to explain development in this area as well as to describe it, but there is little to say about explanatory factors at present (Flavell, Note 1).

For those with educational interests who would rather assist development than describe and explain it, I think there is a very great deal that is worth assisting in this area. It is certainly true that some basic preliminary questions need answers. For example, how much good does cognitive monitoring actually do us in various types of cognitive enterprises? Also, might it not even do more harm than good, especially if used in excess or nonselectively? Think of the feckless obsessive, paralyzed by incessant critical evaluation of his own judgments and decisions.

Such questions suggest legitimate caveats about educational interventions in this area. Lack of hard evidence notwithstanding, however, I am absolutely convinced that there is, overall, far too little rather than enough or too much cognitive monitoring in this world. This is true for adults as well as for children, but it is especially true for children. For example, I find it hard to believe that children who do more cognitive monitoring would not learn better both in and out of school than children who do less. I also think that increasing the quantity and quality of children's metacognitive knowledge and monitoring skills through systematic training may be feasible as well as desirable (Flavell, Note 2). To illustrate what may be feasible here, Brown, Campione, and Barclay (Note 5) trained educable retarded children (mental age = 8 years) in self-testing strategies for assessing and checking their readiness to recall errorlessly by rote a list of unrelated words—the same type of cognitive monitoring task that was described in the first sentence of this article. One year later, the subjects spontaneously used these metacognitive strategies when confronted with the same task and, even more impressively, appeared to apply modifications of these strategies effectively to the quite different memory task of recalling the gist of prose passages. Brown, Campione, and others

(e.g., Baker, Note 6) at the University of Illinois Center for Research in Reading are currently doing research ultimately aimed at finding out how children may be effectively taught to monitor their comprehension, especially while reading. Psychologists in other laboratories have also begun to do research on similar problems (e.g., Meichenbaum & Asarnow, 1979; Forrest & Barron, Note 7).

I can also at least imagine trying to teach children and adolescents to monitor their cognition in communication and other social settings (cf. Flavell, Note 2). In many real-life situations, the monitoring problem is not to determine how well you understand what a message means but to determine how much you ought to believe it or do what it says to do. I am thinking of the persuasive appeals the young receive from all quarters to smoke, drink, take drugs, commit aggressive or criminal acts, have casual sex without contraceptives, have or not have the casual babies that often result, quit school, and become unthinking followers of this year's flaky cults, sects, and movements. (Feel free to revise this list in accordance with your own values and prejudices.) Perhaps it is stretching the meanings of metacognition and cognitive monitoring too far to include the critical appraisal of message source, quality of appeal, and probable consequences needed to cope with these inputs sensibly, but I do not think so. It is at least conceivable that the ideas currently brewing in this area could someday be parlayed into a method of teaching children (and adults) to make wise and thoughtful life decisions as well as to comprehend and learn better in formal educational settings.

REFERENCE NOTES

1 Flavell, J. H. Metacognition. In E. Langer (Chair), *Current perspectives on awareness and cognitive processes.* Symposium presented at the meeting of the American Psychological Association, Toronto, August 1978.

2 Flavell, J. H. *Cognitive monitoring.* Paper presented at the Conference on Children's Oral Communication Skills, University of Wisconsin, October 1978.

3 Flavell, J. H. *Monitoring social-cognitive enterprises: Something else that may develop in the area of social cognition.* Paper prepared for the Social Science Research Council Committee on Social and Affective Development During Childhood, January 1979.

4 Markman, E. M. *Comprehension monitoring.* Paper presented at the Conference on Children's Oral Com-

munication Skills, University of Wisconsin, October 1978.

5 Brown, A. L., Campione, J. C., & Barclay, C. R. *Training self-checking routines for estimating test readiness: Generalization from list learning to prose recall.* Unpublished manuscript, University of Illinois, 1978.

6 Baker, L. *Do I understand or do I not understand: That is the question.* Unpublished manuscript, University of Illinois, 1978.

7 Forrest, D. L., & Barron, R. W. *Metacognitive aspects of the development of reading skills.* Paper presented at the meeting of the Society for Research in Child Development, New Orleans, March 1977.

REFERENCES

Brown, A. L. Knowing when, where, and how to remember: A problem of metacognition. In R. Glaser (Ed.), *Advances in instructional psychology.* New York: Halsted Press, 1978.

Flavell, J. H. Metacognitive development. In J. M. Scandura & C. J. Brainerd (Eds.), *Structural/process theories of complex human behavior.* Alphen a. d. Rijn, The Netherlands: Siithoff & Noordhoff, 1978.

Flavell, J. H., Friedrichs, A. G., & Hoyt, J. D. Developmental changes in memorization processes. *Cognitive Psychology,* 1970, *1,* 324–340.

Flavell, J. H., & Wellman, H. M. Metamemory. In R. V. Kail & J. W. Hagen (Eds.), *Perspectives on the development of memory and cognition.* Hillsdale, N.J.: Erlbaum, 1977.

Gelman, R. Preschool thought. *American Psychologist,* 1979, 34, 900–905.

Kreutzer, M. A., Leonard, C., & Flavell, J. H. An interview study of children's knowledge about memory. *Monographs of the Society for Research in Child Development,* 1975, *40*(1, Serial No. 159).

Langer, E. J. Rethinking the role of thought in social interaction. In J. H. Harvey, W. J. Ickes, & R. F. Kidd (Eds.), *New directions in attribution research* (Vol. 2). Hillsdale, N.J.: Erlbaum, 1978.

Markman, E. M. Realizing that you don't understand: A preliminary investigation. *Child Development,* 1977, *48,* 986–992.

Meichenbaum, D., & Asarnow, J. Cognitive-behavior modification and metacognitive development: Implications for the classroom. In P. Kendall & S. Hollon (Eds.), *Cognitive-behavioral interventions: Theory, research and procedures.* New York: Academic Press, 1979.

Reading 21

The Development of Young Children's Spatial Representations of Their Classrooms

Alexander W. Siegel
Margaret Schadler

Concomitant with recent interest in the social and psychological consequences of the environment and ecology on the lives of individuals (Proshansky 1976; Wohlwill 1970) there has been considerable interest on the part of architects, geographers, and urban planners in how adults and children perceive, represent, and remember arrangements of objects in the

This research was supported by the University of Pittsburgh's Learning Research and Development Center, which is funded in part by the National Institute of Education, and by grant HD-09694 from the National Institute of Child Health and Human Development to the senior author. We would like to thank Marvin Morris for his assistance in testing subjects and for his invaluable skill in photography. We would also like to thank Harold D. Fishbein, Robert V. Kail, Jr., and Harold W. Stevenson for their helpful criticisms on earlier versions of this manuscript. Requests for reprints should be sent to Alexander W. Siegel, Department of Psychology, University of Pittsburgh, Pittsburgh, Pennsylvania 15260.

large-scale environment (cf. Appleyard 1970; Downs & Stea 1973; Lynch 1960). For the most part, however, psychologists have paid little attention to this topic.

With few exceptions (e.g., Acredolo, Pick, & Olsen 1975) experimental research on the development of children's knowledge of macrospace has been limited to the study of knowledge in novel, artificial, and/or simple environments (e.g., Maier 1936). Little attention has been paid to the investigation of children's knowledge of actual and familiar large-scale spaces, yet it is within these domains that children develop, acquire, and use their spatial knowledge. The child's classroom is prototypic of such domains, especially the preschool or kindergarten classroom (which typically is more complex and varied than a classroom whose central feature is multiple rows of desks). Even though age-related differences in children's knowledge of large spaces within which they move has been examined in recent studies (e.g., Acredolo et al. 1975), no attempt has been made to examine the development of children's knowledge over relatively long spans of time. Surely, one would expect that kindergartners somehow have a more accurate spatial representation of their classroom in June than they do in September. The present study is an initial attempt to determine what young children know and remember about the arrangements of objects in their own classroom at the beginning and end of a school year.

The experimental task involved the construction by the child of a model of his or her classroom. Three groups of children were tested, two in the spring of 1973 and one in the following fall. One group tested in the spring was given four accurately placed landmarks prior to model construction. Acredolo et al. (1975) and Siegel and White (1975) have argued that familiarity and differentiated landmarks are important variables influencing the development of accurate representations of large-scale space in both children and adults. Thus it was expected that accuracy of the children's models should be least when children have little familiarity with the classroom and are given no cues to guide their performance; it should be better when the children are familiar with their classroom even though not given cues; and accuracy of construction should be greatest when the children are both familiar with their classroom and are provided cues to guide their performance.

METHOD

Design

The design was a 2 (sex) × 3 (condition: 1–2 months' experience, no cue; 8 months' experience, no cue; 8 months' experience, cue) factorial design with five children per cell.

Subjects

Fifteen boys and 15 girls from the same kindergarten classroom in the Pittsburgh public school participated in the experiment. Ten boys and 10 girls (mean CA = 5–8, range = 5–4 to 6–3) were tested in the spring of 1973, while five boys and five girls (mean CA = 5–2, range = 4–8 to 5–6) were tested in the subsequent fall. Children tested in the fall thus

had been in their classroom for 1–2 months, while children tested in the spring had about 8 months of experience.

Materials

The materials were scale models (1 inch = 2 feet) of the kindergarten classroom and its contents. A 12 × 20-inch Masonite frame with 5-inch-high walls was used to represent the classroom; 4 × 2¾-inch rectangular holes were cut in each end of the unpainted frame, their position corresponding to the location of the two doors in the actual classroom. Forty scale models (1 inch = 2 feet) of the furniture and other major items in the classroom (e.g., piano, tables, TV, chalkboards, cabinets, etc.) were cut from balsa wood, and the primary identifying features were inked or colored on them. Children easily recognized the items.

Procedure

Individual children were brought into the testing room and seated in front of a table opposite the experimenter. The child was shown the model on the table and told that it represented his classroom. (All children viewed the model from the same perspective.) The doors leading to the hall and street were pointed out, and children were required to identify each of these doors before proceeding. In the cued condition, the experimenter named and then accurately placed four items in the model: the teacher's desk (on the hall door wall), the piano (on the adjacent wall), and two of the movable walls of the "playhouse" (on the street-door wall). This part of the procedure was omitted for children in the uncued conditions.

The child was then asked to tell the experimenter some of the furniture that belonged in his or her classroom. When the child named an item he was given the model of that item and told to put it in the model where it belonged—"just like it goes in your classroom." When the subject stopped naming items spontaneously, the experimenter randomly selected one of the remaining items hidden behind a screen, named it, showed it to the child, and asked if it belonged in the child's classroom. If the child said it belonged, he was asked to place it; if the child said that the item did not belong, it was put aside. The procedure continued until all 40 items (36 in the cued condition) had been identified and either placed in the model or rejected. (Virtually all items were correctly recognized and placed somewhere in the model by all children.) The child was not bound to his initial placement of any item and was free to relocate any items at any time. No feedback as to accuracy of identification or placement was given at any time; however, the child was given frequent encouragement to ensure attention and task engagement. A female and a male experimenter each tested approximately an equal number of boys and girls in each condition.

Each test session was audiotaped. In addition, an observer recorded each item the child named and its location in the child's model on a small grid map not visible to the child. The child's final production was photographed from above. All measurements and scoring were performed on the basis of these 8 × 10-inch black-and-white photographs. The audiotapes and observer's records were used to confirm the identification of the items in the photographs.

Scoring

A schematic diagram of the layout of items in a classroom is presented in Figure 1. Children's performance was scored in three different ways, each reflecting accuracy of placement at different levels of spatial specificity—from the Cartesian coordinates of single items to interrelations of single items to interrelations of clusters of items (independent of Cartesian coordinates).

Absolute Accuracy   This measure was designed to reflect the accuracy with which the child placed a given item in the model with respect to that item's position in the classroom. One point was given for each item that was placed within 2 inches of where it actually belonged in the model (i.e., within 4 feet of where it belonged in the actual 24 × 40 foot classroom). Since children in the uncued conditions could place a possible 40 items, while those in the cued conditions could place only 36 (the experimenter having already placed four), these scores were converted to proportion correct.

Local Relational Accuracy   This measure was designed to reflect the accuracy with which the child placed a given item in the model with respect to items adjacent to it in the classroom. Of the 40 items used, 32 belonged to five "clusters," each containing four to nine items. These clusters were determined intuitively on the basis of the perceptual grouping within the classroom and on the basis of the teacher's judgment. The clusters had three common characteristics: *(a)* items within a cluster were in close physical proximity and were relatively isolated

from other clusters; *(b)* each cluster had a central or key item that was used by children to identify the location of other items in the cluster; *(c)* the key item in a cluster was the functional center for children's activities (i.e., teacher's desk, piano, TV, playhouse, chalkboard). One point was given for each relation correctly reproduced. For example, the chalkboard cluster consisted of two chalkboards and two crayon tables. The following five relations, if properly reproduced, earned one point each: *(a)* crayon tables adjacent; *(b)* both crayon tables between chalkboards; *(c)* inner edges of chalkboards between 1 and 3 inches apart; *(d)* all objects on or along a wall; *(3)* no other objects intruding in the cluster. Thus, if the child had these five relations correct he got 5 points regardless of whether the cluster was on the correct wall or not. The number of relations scored for each of the clusters varied from four to six; total possible score was 25. Each child's score was converted to proportion correct. This measure and the following one were used because a child could have (but no child did) constructed a mirror-image model of the classroom, thus obtaining a score of 0 on the first measure. In actuality, he might have constructed a model in which the interitem relations were highly accurate.

Global Relational Accuracy   This measure was designed to reflect the accuracy with which the child placed clusters in relation to each other. For each pair of clusters two relations were measured (and given one point each if correct): *(a)* each cluster was roughly to the left, to the right, or opposite of every other cluster; *(b)* each cluster was roughly on the same, perpendicular, or opposite wall relative to every other cluster. For example, the piano cluster should be to the left of and on the same wall as the TV cluster. The maximum possible number of points for this measure was 16. Each child's score was converted to proportion correct.

RESULTS

All children spontaneously recalled and/or correctly recognized at least 39 of the 40 items (35 of 36 in the cued condition). Thus, subsequent differences found on the three measures cannot be attributed to differences in item recognition. Since preliminary analyses indicated that the scores of children tested by the two experimenters did not differ, the scores were combined in all subsequent analyses. A 2 (sex) × 3 (conditions) analysis of variance was performed

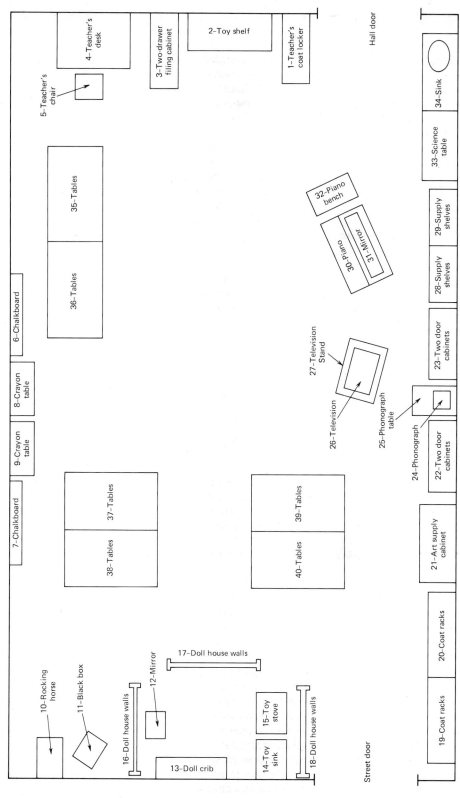

Figure 1 Schematic diagram of the classroom layout. The clusters are as follows: items 1-5, 6-9, 10-18, 22-27, 28-32.

on each of the three dependent measures. (Since analyses performed on both raw and arc-sine-transformed proportions yielded essentially identical results, only the analyses on raw proportions are reported here.) All three analyses yielded significant main effects for sex and condition and nonsignificant sex × condition interactions.

The mean absolute accuracy of boys was significantly greater than that of girls, $F(1,24) = 7.51, p < .05$: Boys placed .40 of the items within 2 inches of their correct position in the model, whereas girls placed only .27 of the items accurately. The effect of condition was highly significant, $F(2,24) = 9.88, p < .001$: When not given cues, children with 8 months of experience had higher absolute placement scores (.40) than did children with only 1–2 months of experience (.16). For children with 8 months of classroom experience, those given cues were not significantly more accurate (.53) than those not given cues (.40).

Since age and experience in the classroom are highly confounded, it could be argued that the performance difference between children tested in the fall (1–2 months' experience) and children tested in the spring (8 months' experience) was due to maturation, independent of experience. To assess this possibility, the scores of the youngest and the oldest children in the fall and spring no-cue groups were compared. If the effects obtained were due to age, as opposed to experience, then younger and older children in the fall group should differ, but younger children in the spring group should not do better than the older children in the fall group. Although the subsample sizes were small, this maturational explanation was ruled out. The five youngest (mean CA = 61 months) and the five oldest children (mean CA = 65 months) tested in the fall did not differ (.19 vs. .13); the five youngest (mean CA = 66 months) and the five oldest children (mean CA = 70 months) tested in the spring did not differ (.38 vs. .42). However, the five youngest children in the spring group were significantly more accurate than the five oldest children in the fall group, $t(8) = 1.87, p < .05$ (one-tailed).

The mean local relational accuracy of boys (.69) was, again, significantly greater than that of girls (.47), $F(1,24) = 8.82, p < .01$. Mean local relational accuracy (i.e., proportion of relations among spatially proximal items correctly reproduced) was also affected by condition, $F(2,24) = 4.53, p < .05$. The pattern of condition differences was different from

that found for the absolute accuracy measure. Children in the spring uncued condition (.56) did not have significantly higher local relational accuracy than children in the fall uncued condition (.45). However, the performance of spring children given cues (.73) was significantly greater than that of either group of children given no cues.

Boys correctly reproduced nearly twice as many relations (.90) between clusters of items as did girls (.48), $F(1,24) = 24.05, p < .001$. Once again, global relational accuracy was also affected by condition, $F(2,24) = 5.61, p < .01$, in a way similar to that found with the measure of local relational accuracy. In the uncued conditions, children who had 8 months of experience (.58) were no more accurate on this measure than children who had only 1–2 months of experience (.61). Insofar as children in the cued condition (spring) were given four "key" cluster items, it is not surprising that their "between-cluster" (or global relational) accuracy was very high (.89) and significantly greater than that for both groups of children in the uncued conditions. (Six of the 10 children in this condition, five boys and one girl, had scores of 1.00, reflecting perfect performance.)

For the entire sample, scores on all three measures were highly intercorrelated, r's$(28) \geq .68, p < .001$. Although the intercorrelations were all significant those for the girls were somewhat higher, r's$(13) \geq .78, p < .001$, than those for boys, r's$(13) \geq .53, p < .05$. The global relational accuracy scores for children in the cued condition were high, and the correlations between this and the other measures might have been spurious (due to the restricted range). Thus, separate correlations were computed for the 20 children in the uncued conditions. Once again, all three correlations were highly significant, r's$(18) \geq .64, p < .01$.

DISCUSSION

In general, the results support the notion that both increases in familiarity and the provision of significant landmarks (differentiated cues) enhance young children's spatial representations of their classrooms. At least for the kindergarten children tested, these effects were found to be independent of maturational factors alone. The pattern of results indicated that increased experience in the classroom significantly facilitated the absolute accuracy of the children's spatial representation (i.e., the extent to which the positions of individual items were accurately reproduced) but had relatively little effect on the extent to which clusters of items and their interrelations were accurately reproduced. Insofar as all children had at least some (i.e., 1–2 months) experience in the classroom, it would be of interest to look at the differential effects of less experience (e.g., a week or so) on the spatial representations (inferred from their models) of these young children.

Providing "landmarks" for the children had only a slight facilitatory effect on the accuracy with which children placed individual items but had a marked effect on the local relational and global relational accuracy scores. This is not surprising: Giving the children properly placed central or key items in three of the five clusters provided them with both mnemonic and perceptual cues around which to organize the spatial representation.

Sex differences in a variety of tasks have been documented (Maccoby & Jacklin 1974), and consistent differences favoring males have been found in a number of spatial tasks (Harris 1977; Smith 1964). However, these sex differences have seldom been found much before 9 or 10 years of age, with maximal differences not usually found until adolescence (Harris 1977). For example, sex differences in preschool and elementary school children have not been found in tasks involving coordination of perspectives (e.g., Fishbein, Lewis, & Keiffer 1972) or in tasks involving memory for locations in large (Acredolo et al. 1975) or small environments (Fehr & Fishbein 1976). Thus, the striking performance differences between boys and girls of kindergarten age was somewhat surprising. When we watched the children in action in the classroom, no obvious differences in their patterns of interaction with the environment were noted; both boys and girls seemed to know their way around, and certainly none of the children had trouble locomoting in the space of the classroom or locating objects in the room.

The interpretation of the obtained sex difference is thus not clear. The difference might be due to the girls' relative inability (or inefficiency) to encode and remember positional information in a large spatial environment. Alternatively, the difference could be attributed to girls' relative inability to deal with small-scale models and the spatial transformations they require (e.g., minification, translating the child's-eye view of the classroom to an aerial

perspective, understanding that the model "stands for" the classroom). Recently collected data from our laboratory seem to shed some light on the issues. Herman (Note 1) walked kindergarten, second-grade, and fifth-grade children through a large model town (16 × 20 feet) and subsequently asked them to reproduce the locations of eight buildings in the town. No sex differences in performance were found at any grade level, indicating that the sex differences obtained in the present study are most probably not due to children's ability to encode and remember positional information in a large space. Kail and Siegel (1977) presented third-grade, sixth-grade, and college students sets of five or seven letters in a 4 × 4 matrix and asked them to remember either the names of the letters or their positions within the matrix. At all grade levels females' recall of positional information was markedly inferior to that of males. This substantiates the finding of the present study of a relative inability of females to encode and/or remember positional information in a small-scale space. Insofar as the children's knowledge of positional information was tested in a relatively small space in the present experiment, this could have contributed to the obtained sex difference. Additionally, Fehr and Fishbein (1976) and Fishbein et al. (1972) used relatively simple small-scale layouts with only three or four objects and found no sex differences. It is possible that in simple situations minimal stress is placed on the spatial system; under conditions of minimal stress, sex differences are not obtained. In the present study the layout was complex and had a very large number of objects (40). This situation can be conceptualized as placing much greater stress on the spatial system; under stress, the relatively less powerful spatial representational system of the girls became "overloaded," producing poorer performance. Clearly, further research in which cognitive "load" or stress is manipulated systematically is necessary to answer this question.

The three measures of accuracy used seemed to us to reflect children's ability to reproduce locational information at three different levels of spatial specificity: the item, the cluster, and global relations between clusters. The high and significant intercorrelations among the three measures could be interpreted as evidence that all three measures are tapping the same underlying spatial function. However, it is also possible that the high intercorrelations are partially an artifact of methodological interdependence (e.g., reversing the positions of the piano and the TV results in two absolute errors as well as one global relational error).

Finally, the global relational, local relational, and absolute measures might appear to reflect the different kinds of spatial knowledge suggested by Piaget and Inhelder (1965): Euclidean, topological, and projective. However, we would argue that the three measures can be best conceptualized along a continuum of increasing differentiation of spatial knowledge (Werner 1948). The explication and development of these kinds of levels of spatial knowledge deserve further study.

REFERENCE NOTE

1 Herman, J. F. The development of spatial representations of large environments: an exploratory study. Unpublished master's thesis, University of Pittsburgh, 1976.

REFERENCES

Acredolo, L. P.; Pick, H. L.; & Olsen, M. G. Environmental differentiation and familiarity as determinants of children's memory for spatial location. *Developmental Psychology*, 1975, *11*, 495–501.

Appleyard, D. Styles and methods of structuring a city. *Environment and Behavior*, 1970, *2*, 100–118.

Downs, R. M., & Stea, D. (Eds.). *Image and environment.* Chicago: Aldine, 1973.

Fehr, L. A., & Fishbein, H. D. The effects of an explicit landmark on spatial judgments. In P. Suedfeld & J. Russell (Eds.), *The behavioral basis of design.* Vol. 1. Stroudsburg, Pa., Dowden, Hutchinson & Ross, 1976.

Fishbein, H. D.; Lewis, S.; & Keiffer, K. Children's understanding of spatial relations: coordination of perspectives. *Developmental Psychology*, 1972, *7*, 21–33.

Harris, L. J. Sex differences in spatial ability: possible environmental, genetic, and neurological factors. In M. Kinsbourne (Ed.), *Hemispheric asymmetries of function.* Cambridge: Cambridge University Press, 1977.

Kail, R. V., & Siegel, A. W. Sex differences in retention of verbal and spatial characteristics of stimuli. *Journal of Experimental Child Psychology*, 1977.

Lynch, K. *The image of the city.* Cambridge, Mass.: M.I.T. Press, 1960.

Maccoby, E. E., & Jacklin, C. W. *The psychology of sex differences.* Stanford, Calif.: Stanford University Press, 1974.

Maier, N. R. F. Reasoning in children. *Journal of Comparative Psychology*, 1936, *21*, 357–366.

Piaget, J., & Inhelder, B. *The child's conception of space.* New York: Norton, 1967.

Proshansky, H. M. Environmental psychology and the real world. *American Psychologist*, 1976, *31*, 303–310.

Siegel, A. W., & White, S. H. The development of spatial representations of large-scale environments. In H. W. Reese (Ed.), *Advances in child development and behavior.* Vol. *10*. New York Academic Press, 1975.

Smith, I. M. *Spatial ability.* San Diego, Calif.: Knapp, 1964.

Werner, H. *Comparative psychology of mental development.* New York: International Universities Press, 1948.

Wohlwill, J. F. The emerging discipline of environmental psychology. *American Psychologist*, 1970, *25*, 303–312.

Reading 22

Some Effects of Punishment on Children's Behavior—Revisited[1]

Ross D. Parke

A casual review of magazines, advice to parent columns, or (until recently) the psychological journals quickly reveals that there is considerable controversy concerning the usefulness of punishment as a technique for controlling the behavior of young children. For many years, the study of the impact of punishment on human behavior was restricted to

armchair speculation and theorizing. In part, this paucity of information was due to the belief that punishment produced only a temporary suppression of behavior and that many undesirable side-effects were associated with its use. Moreover, ethical and practical considerations prohibited the employment of intense punishment in research with human subjects—especially children—thus contributing to this information gap.

Through both studies of child rearing and labora-

[1]The preparation of this paper and some of the studies that are reported here were supported in part by Research Grant GS 1847, National Science Foundation.

tory investigations, however, some of the effects of punishment on children's social behavior are being determined. It is the main aim of this paper to review these findings and assess the current status of our knowledge concerning the effects of punishment.

TIMING OF PUNISHMENT

A number of years ago at Harvard's Laboratory of Human Development, Black, Solomon and Whiting (1960) undertook a study of the effectiveness of punishment for producing "resistance to temptation" in a group of young puppies. Two training conditions were used. In one case, the dogs were swatted with a rolled-up newspaper just *before* they touched a bowl of forbidden horsemeat. The remaining pups were punished only *after* eating a small amount of the taboo food. On subsequent tests—even though deprived of food—the animals punished as they approached the food showed greater avoidance of the prohibited meat than did animals punished after committing the taboo act. This study is the prototype of a number of studies recently carried out with children, and it illustrates the importance of the *timing* of the punishment for producing effective control over children's behavior.

In recent studies of the effects of timing of punishment on children's behavior, the rolled-up newspaper has been replaced by a verbal rebuke or a loud noise, and an attractive toy stands in place of the horsemeat. For example, Walters, Parke and Cane (1965) presented subjects with pairs of toys—one attractive and one unattractive—on a series of nine trials. The six- to eight-year-old boys were punished by a verbal rebuke, "No, that's for the other boy," when they chose the attractive toy. As in the dog study, one group of children was punished as they approached the attractive toy, but before they actually touched it. For the remaining boys, punishment was delivered only after they had picked up the critical toy and held it for two seconds. Following the punishment training session, the subjects were seated before a display of three rows of toys similar to those used in the training period and were reminded not to touch the toys. The resistance-to-deviation test consisted of a 15-minute period during which the boy was left alone with an unattractive German-English dictionary and, of course, the prohibited toys. The extent to which the subject touched the toys in the absence of the external agent was recorded by an observer located

behind a one-way screen. The children's data paralleled the puppy results: the early punished children touched the taboo toys less than did the boys punished late in the response sequence. This timing of punishment effect has been replicated by a number of investigators (Aronfreed & Reber, 1965; Parke & Walters, 1967; Cheyne & Walters, 1969).

Extensions of this experimental model indicate that this finding is merely one aspect of a general relation: *the longer the delay between the initiation of the act and the onset of punishment, the less effective the punishment for producing response inhibition.* This proposition is based on a study in which the effects of four delay of punishment positions were examined (Aronfreed, 1965). Using a design similar to Walters, Parke and Cane (1965), Aronfreed punished one group of children as they reached for the attractive toy. Under a second condition, the subject was permitted to pick up the attractive toy and was punished at the apex of the lifting movement. Under a third condition, six seconds elapsed after the child picked up the toy before punishment was delivered. In the final group, six seconds after the child picked up the toy he was asked to describe the toy and only then was punishment administered. The time elapsing between the experimenter's departure until the child made the first deviation steadily decreased as the time between the initiation of the act and the delivery of punishment increased.

Punishment may be less effective in facilitating learning as well as less effective in facilitating resistance to temptation if the punishment is delayed. Using a learning task in which errors were punished by the presentation of a loud noise combined with the loss of a token, Walters (1964) found that punishment delivered immediately after the error speeded learning more than did punishment which was delayed 10 seconds or 30 seconds.

Since it is often difficult to detect and punish a response in the approach phase of a transgression sequence, the practical implications of these studies may be questioned. However, Aronfreed (1968) has noted one feature of naturalistic socialization that may dilute the importance of punishing the act in the execution phase. "Parents frequently punish a child when he is about to repeat an act which they dislike" (p. 180). In this case, punishment may be delivered in the early stages of the next execution of the act, even though it is delayed in relation to the previously completed commission of the same deviant behavior.

In addition, the importance of timing of punishment may be contingent on a variety of other features of punishment administration, such as the intensity of the punishment, the nature of the agent-child relationship, and the kind of verbal rationale accompanying the punishment. The effects of these variables will be examined in the following sections.

INTENSITY OF PUNISHMENT

It is generally assumed that as the intensity of punishment increases the amount of inhibition will similarly increase. It is difficult to study severity of punishment in the laboratory due to the obvious ethical limitations upon using potentially harmful stimuli in experimentation with children. Until recently most of the evidence concerning the relative effectiveness of different intensities of punishment derived either from animal studies or from child-rearing interview studies.

The animal studies (e.g., Church, 1963), in which electric shock is most often used as the punishing stimulus, have supported the conclusion that more complete suppression of the punished response results as the intensity of the punishment increases. On the other hand, the child-rearing data relation to the effects of intensity on children's behavior have not yielded clear cut conclusions. It is difficult, however, to assess the operation of specific punishment variables using rating scales of parent behavior because most of these scales confound several aspects of punishment, such as frequency, intensity, and consistency (Walters & Parke, 1967). Differences between scale points may, therefore, be due to the impact of any of these variables, either alone or in combination.

Recent laboratory studies have avoided some of these short-comings and have yielded less equivocal conclusions concerning the effects of punishment intensity on children's behavior. Using the resistance-to-deviation approach already described, Parke and Walters (1967) punished one group of boys with a soft tone (65 decibels) when they chose an attractive but prohibited toy. A second group heard a loud tone (96 decibels) when they chose the attractive toy. In the subsequent temptation test, children who were exposed to the loud punisher were less likely to touch the prohibited toys in the experimenter's absence than were boys exposed to a less intense version of the tone. This finding has been confirmed using a noxious buzzer as the

punishing stimulus (Cheyne & Walters, 1969; Parke, 1969).

This research has also yielded some suggestive evidence concerning the impact of intensity variations on other aspects of punishment such as timing (Parke, 1969). Under conditions of high intensity punishment, the degree of inhibition produced by early and late punishment was similar. Under low intensity conditions, however, the early punished subjects showed significantly greater inhibition than did subjects punished late in the response sequence. Thus, timing of punishment may be less important under conditions of high intensity punishment. However, the generality of this conclusion is limited by the narrow range of delay of punishment intervals that have been investigated. Perhaps when punishment is delayed over a number of hours, for example, this relationship would not hold. Further research is clearly required.

Other research has indicated, however, that high intensity punishment may not always lead to better inhibition or be more effective in controlling children's behavior than low intensity punishment. A study by Aronfreed and Leff (1963), who investigated the effects of intensity of punishment on response inhibition in a temptation situation, illustrates this possibility. Six- and seven-year-old boys were given a series of choice trials involving two toys roughly comparable in attractiveness, but which differed along certain stimulus dimensions that the child could use to distinguish between punished and nonpunished choices. For two groups, a simple discrimination between red and yellow toys was required; the other groups of subjects were exposed to a complex discrimination between toys which represented passive containers and toys with active internal mechanisms. The punishment consisted of verbal disapproval (no), deprivation of candy, and a noise. The intensity and quality of the noise were varied in order to control the noxiousness of the punishment. Following training, each child was left alone with a pair of toys of which the more attractive one was similar in some respects to the toys that had been associated with punishment during the training procedure. Provided that the discrimination task was relatively simple, response inhibition was more frequently observed among children who received high intensity punishment. When the discrimination task was difficult, however, "transgression" was more frequent among children under the high intensity punishment than among children who received the milder punishment. Thus, the complex discrimination task combined with high intensity punishment probably created a level of anxiety too high for adaptive learning to occur. When subtle discriminations are involved, or when the child is uncertain as to the appropriate response, high intensity punishment may create emotional levels that clearly interfere with learning and therefore retard inhibition of undesirable behaviors.

NATURE OF THE RELATIONSHIP BETWEEN THE AGENT AND RECIPIENT OF PUNISHMENT

The nature of the relationship between the socializing agent and the child is a significant determinant of the effectiveness of punishment. It is generally assumed that punishment will be a more effective means of controlling behavior when this relationship is close and affectional than when it is relatively impersonal. This argument assumes that any disciplinary act may involve in varying degrees at least two operations—the presentation of a negative reinforcer and the withdrawal or withholding of a positive one (Bandura & Walters, 1963). Physical punishment may, in fact, achieve its effect partly because it symbolizes the withdrawal of approval or affection. Hence, punishment should be a more potent controlling technique when used by a nurturant parent or teacher.

Sears, Maccoby and Levin (1957) provided some evidence in favor of this proposition. Mothers who were rated as warm and affectionate and who made relatively frequent use of physical punishment were more likely to report that they found spanking to be an effective means of discipline. In contrast, cold, hostile mothers who made frequent use of physical punishment were more likely to report that spanking was ineffective. Moreover, according to the mothers' reports, spanking was more effective when it was administered by the warmer of the two parents.

A study by Parke and Walters (1967) confirmed these child-rearing findings in a controlled laboratory situation. In this investigation, the nature of the experimenter-child relationship was varied in two interaction sessions prior to the administration of punishment. One group of boys experienced a 10-minute period of positive interaction with a female experimenter on two successive days. Attractive constructional materials were provided for the children and, as they played with them, the female experimenter provided encouragement and help and warmly expressed approval of their efforts. A second group of boys played with relatively unattractive materials in two 10-minute sessions while the experimenter sat in the room without interacting with the children. Following these interaction sessions, the children underwent punishment training involving verbal rebuke and a noxious noise for choosing incorrect toys. In the subsequent test for response inhibition, children who had experienced positive interaction with the agent of punishment showed significantly greater resistance to deviation than boys who had only impersonal contact.

It is difficult to determine whether this effect is due to an increase in the perceived noxiousness of the noise when delivered by a previously friendly agent or whether the result derives from the withdrawal of affection implied in the punitive operation. Probably it was a combination of these two sources of anxiety which contributes to our findings. A study by Parke (1967), while not directly concerned with the relative importance of these two components, shows that nurturance-withdrawal alone, unaccompanied by noxious stimulation, can effectively increase resistance to deviation in young children. Two experimental treatments were employed. In one condition—the continuous nurturance group—the subjects, six- to eight-year-old boys and girls, experienced 10 minutes of friendly and nurturant interaction with either a male or female experimenter. Subjects in the nurturance-withdrawal group experienced five minutes of nurturant interaction, followed by five minutes of nurturance-withdrawal during which the experimenter turned away from the child, appeared busy, and refused to respond to any bid for attention. Following these manipulations, all subjects were placed in a resistance-to-deviation situation, involving a display of attractive, but forbidden, toys. In the instructions to the subject, it was made clear that if the subject conformed to the prohibition, the experimenter would play with him upon returning. In this way the link between resistance-to-deviation and nurturance was established. As in previous experiments, a hidden observer recorded the child's deviant activity during the 15-minute period that the adult was absent from the room. The results provided support for the hypothesis, with subjects in the nurturance-withdrawal group deviating significantly less often than subjects in the continuous-nurturance condition. However, it was also found that nurturance-withdrawal influenced girls to a greater degree than boys, and that the effect was most marked with girls experiencing withdrawal of a female agent's nurturance.

These data are consistent with previous studies of nurturance-withdrawal, which have indicated that withdrawal of affection may motivate the previously nurtured child to engage in behavior that is likely to reinstate the affectional relationship (e.g., Hartup, 1958; Rosenblith, 1959, 1961). . . .

REASONING AND PUNISHMENT

In all of the studies discussed, punishment was presented in a relatively barren cognitive context. Very often, however, parents and teachers provide the child with a rationale for the punishment they administer. Is punishment more effective when accompanied by a set of reasons for nondeviation? Field studies of child rearing suggest that the answer is positive. For example, Sears, Maccoby and Levin (1957), in their interview investigation of child-rearing practices, found that mothers who combine physical punishment with extensive use of reasoning reported that punishment was more effective than mothers who tended to use punishment alone. Field investigations, however, have yielded little information concerning the relative effectiveness of different aspects of reasoning. In the child-training literature, reasoning may include not only descriptions of untoward consequences that the child's behavior may have for others, but also the provision of examples of incompatible socially acceptable behaviors, explicit instructions on how to behave in specific situations, and explanations of motives for placing restraints on the child's behavior. Moreover, these child-training studies do not indicate the manner in which the provision of reasons in combination with punishment can alter the operation of specific punishment parameters such as those already discussed—timing, intensity, and the nature of the agent-child relationship.

It is necessary to turn again to experimental studies for answers to these questions. First, laboratory investigations have confirmed the field results in that punishment is more effective when accompanied by a rationale. Parke (1969), for example, found that when children, in addition to being punished, were told that a toy was "fragile and may break," greater inhibition occurred than when children were punished without an accompanying rationale. In a later experiment, Parke and Murray

(1971) found that a rationale alone is more effective than punishment alone. However, comparison of the results of the two studies indicates that the combination of punishment and a rationale is the most thoroughly effective procedure.

To understand the impact of reasoning on the timing of punishment effect, let us examine a pioneering set of studies by Aronfreed (1965). In the earlier timing experiments, cognitive structure was minimized and no verbal rationale was given for the constraints placed on the child's behavior. In contrast, children in a second group of experiments were provided, in the initial instructions, with a brief explanation for not handling some of the toys. In one variation, for example, the cognitive structuring focused on the child's intentions. When punished, the child was told: "No, you should not have *wanted* to pick up that thing." The important finding here was that the addition of reasoning to a *late*-timed punishment markedly increased its effectiveness. In fact, when a verbal rationale accompanied the punishment the usual timing of punishment effect was absent; early- and late-timed punishments were equally effective inhibitors of the child's behavior. Other investigators have reported a similar relation between reasoning operations and timing of punishment (Cheyne & Walters, 1969; Parke, 1969). In these latter studies, the reasoning procedures presented in conjunction with punishment did not stress intentions, but focused on the consequences of violation of the experimenter's prohibition.

The delay periods used in all of these studies were relatively short. In everyday life, detection of a deviant act is often delayed many hours or the punishment may be postponed, for example, until the father returns home. An experiment reported by Walters and Andres (1967) addressed itself directly to this issue. Their aim was to determine the conditions under which a punishment delivered four hours after the commission of a deviant act could be made an effective inhibitor. By verbally describing the earlier deviation at the time that the punishment was administered, the effectiveness of the punishment was considerably increased in comparison to a punishment that was delivered without an accompanying restatement. An equally effective procedure involved exposing the children to a videotape recording of themselves committing the deviant act just prior to the long-delayed punishment. A partially analogous situation, not studied by these investigators, involves parental demonstration of the deviant behavior just before delivering the punishing blow. In any case, symbolic reinstatement of the deviant act, according to these data, seems to be a potent way of increasing the effectiveness of delayed punishment.

A question remains. Do reasoning manipulations alter the operation of any other parameters besides the timing of the punishment? Parke (1969) examined the modifying impact of reasoning on the intensity and nurturance variables. When no rationale was provided, the expected intensity of punishment effect was present: high intensity punishment produced significantly greater inhibition than low intensity punishment. However, when a rationale accompanied the punishment, the difference between high and low intensity of punishment was not present.

As noted earlier, children who experience nurturant interaction with the punishing agent prior to punishment training deviate less often than subjects in the low nurturance. However, this effect was present in the Parke (1969) study only when no rationale accompanied the noxious buzzer. When the children were provided with a rationale for not touching certain toys, the children who had experienced the friendly interaction and the children who had only impersonal contact with the agent were equally inhibited during the resistance-to-deviation test period. Taken together, these experiments constitute impressive evidence of the important role played by cognitive variables in modifying the operation of punishment.

A common yardstick employed to gauge the success of a disciplinary procedure is the permanence of the inhibition produced. It is somewhat surprising, therefore, that little attention has been paid to the stability of inhibition over time as a consequence of various punishment training operations. One approach to this issue involves calculating changes in deviant activity occurring during the resistance-to-deviation test session in experimental studies. Does the amount of deviant behavior increase at different rates, for example, in response to different training procedures? As a first step in answering this question, Parke (1969) divided the 15-minute resistance-to-deviation test session into three five-minute periods. As Figure 1 indicates, the low cognitive structure subjects (no rationale) increased their degree of illicit toy touching over the three time periods while the degree of deviation over the three intervals did not significantly change

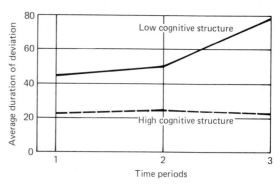

Figure 1 Stability of duration of deviation over three five-minute periods for high-cognitive and low-cognitive structure conditions.

for the high cognitive structure (rationale provided) subjects. Cheyne and Walters (1969) have reported a similar finding. These data clearly indicate that the stability of inhibition over time was affected by the reasoning or cognitive structuring procedures. The most interesting implication of this finding is that inhibition—or internalization—may *require* the use of cognitively-oriented training procedures. Punishment techniques that rely solely on anxiety induction, such as the noxious noises employed in many of the experiments discussed or the more extreme forms of physical punishment sometimes used by parents, may be effective mainly in securing only short-term inhibition.

However, children often forget a rationale or may not remember that a prohibition is still in force after a lengthy time lapse. A brief reminder or re-instatement of the original punisher or rationale may be necessary to insure continued inhibition. To investigate the impact of such re-instatement on the stability of inhibition was the aim of an experiment by Parke and Murray (1971). In this study, following the typical punishment training procedure, the seven- to nine-year-old boys were tested immediately for resistance-to-deviation and then re-tested in the same situation one week later. Half of the children were "reminded" of the earlier training by the experimenter. For example, in the case of the boys who were punished by a buzzer during the training session, the experimenter sounded the buzzer a single time and reminded the children that it signalled that they should not touch the toys ("You shouldn't touch the toys"). For children who received rationales unaccompanied by any punishment, the experimenter merely re-stated the rationale ("Remember, those toys belong to another boy" or "They are fragile and may break") before leaving the children alone with the toys. For the remaining children, no reminder or re-instatement of the earlier training was provided. As Figure 2 indicates, re-instatement of the original training clearly increased the permanence of the response inhibition.

However, the effectiveness of different types of reasoning procedures for producing inhibition varies with the developmental level of the child. Cheyne (1972) for example, found that third grade children increased their resistance to deviation in response to a prohibitory rationale stressing the norm of ownership, while first graders responded equally to both a rationale and a simple verbal prohibition. However, as Parke and Murray (1971) have demonstrated, the type of rationale is important for achieving optimal inhibition with children of different ages. It is necessary to match the type and complexity of the rationale with the level of the child's cognitive development. Only if children can readily comprehend the bases of the rationale will it be an effective inhibitor. To test this proposition, Parke and Murray exposed 4-year- and 7-year-old children to two types of rationales that varied in degree of abstractness. The first—an object-oriented appeal—was relatively concrete and focused on the physical consequences of handling the toy ("the toy is fragile and might break"). This emphasis on the physical consequences of an action is similar to the types of justificatory rationales that young children use in their moral judgments (Kohlberg, 1964). The second rationale was a property rule which stressed the ethical norm of ownership. This person-oriented rationale was more abstract and assumed that children understand the rights of other individuals. In Kohlberg's moral

judgment system this understanding represents a more sophisticated level of moral development. It was predicted that the property rationale would be most effective with the older children and that the concrete rationale would be more effective with the younger children. The results were consistent with this prediction. The concrete rationale was significantly more effective than was the property rationale in producing response inhibition in the younger children. At the older age level the effectiveness of the two rationales was approximately equal, the property rule being slightly more effective.

Rationales do not vary only in terms of their object *vs.* person-oriented qualities. As a number of writers (Aronfreed, 1968; Hoffman, 1970; LaVoie, 1974) have stressed, rationales vary in terms of their focus on either (A) the consequences or outcomes of the rule violation or (B) the motivation or intention underlying the deviation. Since children utilize consequences as the basis for judging rule infractions at an earlier age than they utilize the actors' intentions, it is likely that appeals which focus on the consequences of misbehavior would be more effective for producing response inhibition than appeals which focus on the child's intentions. In fact, LaVoie (1974) recently evaluated this proposition; seven-, nine-, and eleven-year-old children heard either a consequence focused rationale ("That toy might get broken or worn out from you playing with it") or an intention focused rationale (It is wrong for you to *want* to play with that toy or think about playing with that toy"). As expected the consequence rationale was equally effective at all ages, but the intention-focused rationale increased in effectiveness across age. For younger children, focusing on the consequences of the act yields more effective control than focusing on intentions.

Other types of rationales have been investigated as well. For example, Sawin and Parke (1980) examined the relative effectiveness of different types of emotional appeals on response inhibition in children at different ages. Children at two age levels (3-4 and 6-7 years of age) were exposed to either a fear-based rationale or an empathy-based rationale. The fear rationale focused on expressions of adult anger directed toward the child (i.e. "I will be angry if you touch the toys") while the empathy rationale focused on the negative affect that rule violation would generate in the adult ("I will be sad if you touch the toys"). The effectiveness of these two types of rationales in producing resistance to devia-

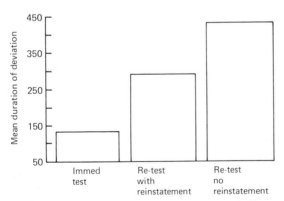

Figure 2 Stability of inhibition over one week with and without reinstatement.

tion in the toy touching situation varied with the age of the child. The provision of the fear invoking (angry) rationale increased the effectiveness of the prohibition for children at both age levels. However, the empathy-invoking consequences were less effective for the young children than the older children. These findings suggest that empathetic appeals are relatively ineffective with young children.

Another factor to be considered is the length of the explanation; since young children have shorter attention spans than older children, lengthy explanations may simply not be very effective with young children. Hetherington (1975), in fact, found that parents who used brief explanations gained better control over their children than parents who used long and involved explanations.

Together the findings emphasize the importance of considering developmental factors in studies of different types of control tactics. Finally, by using cognitively based control tactics, age changes in behavioral aspects of moral development are clearly demonstrated. The task of charting in more detail age changes in relation to specific types of prohibitory rationales would appear to be worthwhile.

CONSISTENCY OF PUNISHMENT

In naturalistic contexts, punishment is often intermittently and erratically employed. Consequently, achieving an understanding of the effects of inconsistent punishment is a potentially important task. Data from field studies of delinquency have yielded a few clues concerning the consequences of inconsistency of discipline. Glueck and Glueck (1950) found that parents of delinquent boys were more "erratic" in their disciplinary practices than were parents of nondelinquent boys. Similarly, the McCords (e.g., McCord, McCord, & Howard, 1961) have found that erratic disciplinary procedures were correlated with high degrees of criminality. Inconsistent patterns involving a combination of love, laxity, and punitiveness, or a mixture of punitiveness and laxity alone were particularly likely to be found in the background of their delinquent sample. However, the definition of inconsistency has shifted from study to study in delinquency research, making evaluation and meaningful conclusions difficult (Walters & Parke, 1967).

To clarify the effects of inconsistent punishment on children's aggressive behavior, Parke and Deur

(Parke & Deur, 1970; Deur & Parke, 1970) conducted a series of laboratory studies. Aggression was selected as the response measure in order to relate the findings to previous studies of inconsistent discipline and aggressive delinquency. An automated Bobo doll was used to measure aggression. The child punched the large, padded stomach of the clown-shaped doll and the frequency of hitting was automatically recorded. In principle, the apparatus is similar to the inflated punch toys commonly found in children's homes. To familiarize themselves with the doll, the boys participating in the first study (Parke & Deur, 1970) punched freely for two minutes. Then the children were rewarded with marbles each time they punched the Bobo doll for a total of 10 trials. Following this baseline session, the subjects experienced one of three different outcomes for punching: termination of reward (no outcome), receipt of marbles on half the trials and a noxious buzzer following the other half, or consistent punishment by the buzzer. Half the children were also told that the buzzer indicated that they were playing the game "badly," while the remaining boys were informed that the buzzer was a "bad noise." All the boys had been informed that they could terminate the punching game whenever they wished. The main index of persistence was the number of hitting responses that the child delivered before voluntarily ending the game. The results were clear: subjects in the no outcome group made the greatest number of punches, while the continuously punished children delivered the fewest punches; the inconsistently punished children were in the intermediate position. The results were not affected by the labeling of the buzzer; whether the buzzer meant "playing the game badly" or a "bad noise" made no difference. This laboratory demonstration confirms the common child-rearing dictum that intermittent punishment is less effective than continuous punishment.

Parents and other disciplinary agents often use consistent punishment only after inconsistent punishment has failed to change the child's behavior. To investigate the effectiveness of consistent punishment *after* the child has been treated in an inconsistent fashion was the aim of the next study (Deur & Parke, 1970). Following the baseline period, subjects underwent one of three different training conditions. One group of boys was rewarded for 18 trials, while a second group of children received marbles on nine trials and no outcome on the remaining trials. A final group of boys was rewarded on half of the trials but heard a noxious buzzer on the other nine trials. The children were informed that the buzzer indicated that they were playing the game "badly."

To determine the effects of these training schedules on resistance to extinction (where both rewards and punishers were discontinued) and on resistance to continuous punishment (where every punch was punished) was the purpose of the next phase of the study. Therefore, half of the children in each of the three groups were neither rewarded nor punished for hitting the Bobo doll and the remaining subjects heard the noxious buzzer each time they punched. The number of hitting responses that the child made before voluntarily quitting was, again, the principal measure.

The results are shown in Figure 3. The punished subjects made fewer hitting responses than did subjects in the extinction condition, which suggests that the punishment was effective in inhibiting the aggressive behavior. The training schedules produced particularly interesting results. The inconsistently punished subjects showed the greatest resistance to extinction. Moreover, these previously punished children tended to persist longer in the face of consistent punishment than the boys in the other training groups. The effects were most marked in comparison to the consistently rewarded subjects. The implication is clear: the socializing agent using inconsistent punishment builds up resistance to

future attempts to either extinguish deviant behavior or suppress it by consistently administered punishment.

The particular form of inconsistency employed in this study represents only one of the variety of forms of inconsistency which occurs in naturalistic socialization. Consistency, as used in the present research, refers to the extent to which a single agent treats violations in the same manner each time such violations occur.

What are the effects of inter-agent inconsistent punishment? Sawin and Parke (1979) recently investigated this issue. Employing the Bobo doll paradigm, 8-year-old boys were exposed to two female socializing agents who reacted in one of the following ways to the boys punching behavior: (1) the two agents were both rewarding, (2) the two agents were both punishing, or (3) one agent was rewarding, while the other agent was punishing. The results revealed that the boys persisted longer in punching when the agents were inconsistent than when the two agents were consistently punitive. Nor are the effects of inter-agent inconsistency restricted to aggression. In an earlier study, Stouwie (1972) demonstrated that inconsistent instructions between two agents in a resistance to deviation situation lessened the amount of subject control. Unfortunately, little is known concerning the impact of inter-agent inconsistency on the persistence of the behavior under extinction or consistent punishment. Nor do we know about the generalizability of these effects. Do inconsistent parents make it more difficult for teachers to gain control over children's behavior?

THE CHILD'S ROLE IN SPARING THE ROD

Research and theories of childhood socialization have traditionally been based on an undirectional model of effects; it was assumed that the rewarding and punishing activities of socializing agents serve to shape the behavior patterns of children. In fact, the research that we have discussed so far in this chapter reflects this orientation. The child, it implies, is acted upon by adults; the child is a passive recipient of adult-controlled input. However, this model is inadequate and a bi-directional model is necessary, in which the child is explicitly recognized as an active participant and modifier of adult behavior. As Bell (1968) has so persuasively argued, children shape adults just as adults shape children. Moreover, this

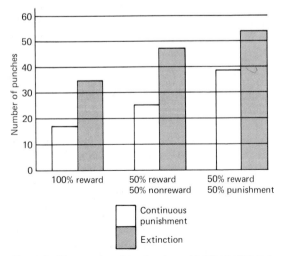

Figure 3 Mean number of punches in post-training period as a function of consistency of reward and punishment.

general principle has recently been shown to operate in important ways in disciplinary contexts (Parke, 1974). Specifically, the child can modify the degree and amount of adult punitiveness by their reactions after violation of a rule or by their behavior following the administration of discipline by an adult. The following studies by Sawin and Parke (1975) will illustrate the role of the child in modifying adult disciplinary tactics.

In their study, adult females were given the opportunity to administer rewards and punishments to a 7-year-old boy. They were first shown a video-tape of two boys sitting at desks in a school-like context. They were asked to assist in assessing "how adults and children can interact by means of a remote closed circuit television monitoring and control system that might be used in understaffed day care facilities to supplement regular person to person contacts." The adult was asked to evaluate the boys' behavior by delivering or removing points that could be later traded in for varying amounts of free play time. In fact, the children's behavior on the video-tapes was pre-recorded and the adult's feedback to the child was surreptitiously recorded by the experimenter. To evaluate the impact of children's behavior on adult disciplinary actions, adults saw one of four video-taped sequences, which were similar except for one section of the tape. All tapes showed one boy pushing a second child's workbook off his desk. Prior to the adult's opportunity to discipline or reward the child, the deviant child gave one of four reactions: (1) reparation—offered to pick up the book, (2) plead—pleaded for leniency, (3) ignore—turned his back to the adult, (4) defiance—acted in a defiant fashion by saying "It was a dumb book anyway." Although all of the children were punished, the amount of punishment varied. The adults who saw the reparative child, who offered to correct his misbehavior, delivered the least amount of punishment while the adults who saw the child ignore the adult or behave in a defiant fashion delivered the harshest punishment. The way that a child reacts after misbehaving but before the adult administers punishment can significantly modify the severity of the adult's disciplinary behavior.

In a related study, the impact of the child's reaction *after* being disciplined on the adults' later disciplinary actions was examined. As in the earlier study, an adult monitored children on a video-tape. Again one of the children misbehaved but this time the adult was allowed to finish punishing the child

before viewing the child's reaction to being punished. One of four reactions followed: (1) reparation, (2) plead, (3) ignore, or (4) defiance. Immediately following the target child's reaction to being punished the adult was signalled to respond again; this was the crucial test trial since it followed immediately on the child's reaction to the prior discipline. As Figure 4 illustrates, the subsequent discipline was significantly affected by the child's reaction to the earlier adult discipline. In fact, the adults who witnessed the child make reparation were *not* even punitive, but were mildly rewarding. As in the earlier study, the defiance and ignore reactions elicited the most severe punitive reactions from the adults. The study clearly demonstrates that children's reactions to discipline serve as determinants of how severely they will be dealt with on future occasions. Children can play a role in sparing the rod!

UNDESIRABLE CONSEQUENCES OF PUNISHMENT

The foregoing paragraphs indicate that punishment is effective in producing response suppression. Nevertheless, punishment may have undesirable side-effects which limit its usefulness as a socializing technique. In the first place, the teacher or parent who employs physical punishment to inhibit undesirable behaviors may also serve as an aggressive model. Bandura (1967) has summarized this viewpoint as follows: "When a parent punishes his child physically for having aggressed toward peers, for example, the intended outcome of this training is that the child should refrain from hitting others. The child, however, is also learning from parental dem-

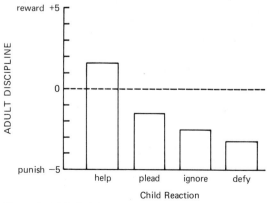

Figure 4 Adult discipline in response to children's reactions to prior punishment.

onstration how to aggress physically. And the imitative learning may provide the direction for the child's behavior when he is similarly frustrated in subsequent social interactions" (1967, p. 43).

Evidence supporting this position is, at best, indirect. There is a sizable body of data indicating a relation between the frequent use of physical punishment by parents and aggressive behavior in their children (Becker, 1964). However, the increases in aggression could possibly be due to the *direct* encouragement that punitive parents often provide for behaving aggressively outside the home situation. Alternatively, highly aggressive children may require strong, physically punitive techniques to control them. Thus, even if it is assumed that the punitive parent acts as an aggressive model there is no evidence demonstrating that children imitate the aggressive behaviors the disciplinarian displays while punishing the child. It is recognized that exposure to aggressive models increases aggressive behavior in young children (Bandura, 1967). It is of questionable legitimacy, however, to generalize from Bobo doll studies to children imitating a physically punitive adult who is often carrying out a justified spanking in line with his role as parent or teacher.

Fortunately, a direct test of the modeling hypothesis has recently been reported. (Gelfand, Hartmann, Lamb, Smith, Mahan, and Paul, 1974) These investigators exposed 6-to-8-year-old children to rewarding, punishing or unresponsive adults in a marble drop game. When each child was later given the opportunity to train another child to play the game, he employed techniques strikingly similar to those he had previously experienced himself. Of particular importance was the finding that children who themselves had been punished by the adult used punitive techniques in interactions with another child.

Another negative side effect is the avoidance of the punishing agent. This is illustrated in a recent study by Redd, Morris, and Martin (1975) in which five-year-old children interacted with three different adults who employed various strategies. One adult behaved in a positive manner and smiled and made positive comments ("Good," "Nice boy," "Tremendous") while the child performed a color-sorting task. A second adult dispensed mild verbal reprimands whenever the child deviated from the sorting task (for example, "Stop throwing the tokens around," "Don't play with the chair"). A third adult

was present but didn't comment on the child's behavior. While the results indicated that the punitive adult was most effective in keeping the child working on the task, the children tended to prefer the positive and neutral agents more than the punitive adult. When asked to indicate which adult they wished to work with a little longer, the children always chose the positive adult. Similarly, the children always avoided the punitive adult as their partner on other tasks or as a playmate. The implication is clear: punishment may be an effective modification technique, but the use of punishment by adults may lead the child to avoid that socializing agent and therefore undermine the adult's effectiveness as a future influence on the child's behavior.

Conditions such as the classroom often prevent the child from physically escaping the presence of the agent. Continued use of punishment in an inescapable context, however, may lead to passivity and withdrawal (Seligman, Maier & Solomon, 1969) or adaptation to the punishing stimuli themselves. In any case, whether escape is possible or not, the quality of the agent-child relationship may deteriorate if punishment is used with high frequency; punishment administered by such an agent will, therefore, be less effective in inhibiting the child.

The undesirable effects of punishment mentioned here probably occur mainly in situations where the disciplinary agents are indiscriminately punitive. In child-training contexts where the agent rewards and encourages a large proportion of the child's behavior, even though selectively and occasionally punishing certain kinds of behavior, these side-effects are less likely to be found (Walters & Parke, 1967).

REINFORCEMENT OF INCOMPATIBLE RESPONSES: AN ALTERNATIVE TO PUNISHMENT

In light of these undesirable consequences, it may be worthwhile to consider other ways in which deviant behavior can be controlled. Reinforcement of incompatible responses is one such technique. Brown and Elliot (1965) asked several nursery school teachers to ignore aggressive acts and only encourage behaviors that were inconsistent with aggression, such as cooperation and helpfulness. Encouraging these alternative behaviors resulted in a marked decrease in classroom aggression. More recently, Parke, Ewall and Slaby (1972) have found that encouraging college subjects for speaking helpful words also led to a decrease in subsequent aggression. In an extension of this work, Slaby (1970) found a similar effect for eight- to 12-year-old children. The lesson is clear: speaking in a manner that is incompatible with aggression may actually inhibit hostile actions. Words, as well as deeds, can alter our physical behaviors. The advantage of the incompatible response technique for controlling behavior is that the unwanted side-effects associated with punishment can be avoided.

CONCLUSION

This review leaves little doubt that punishment can be an effective means of controlling children's behavior. The operation of punishment, however, is a complex process and its effects are quite varied and highly dependent on such parameters as timing, intensity, consistency, the affectional and/or status relationship between the agent and recipient of punishment, and the kind of cognitive structuring accompanying the punishing stimulus.

The decision to employ punishment in child-rearing, however, cannot be evaluated simply in terms of its effectiveness as a suppressor of undesirable behavior. The decision to use a particular disciplinary tactic is inevitably intertwined with the wider socio-political and moral issue of children's rights. A number of writers are beginning to question whether or not children's rights to humane treatment are not being violated by adult use of physically punitive control tactics (Parke, 1976). As the research reviewed here indicates, children *can* both understand and effectively utilize cognitively based rationales to govern their behavior; in short, continued reliance on physical punishment as a control tactic is probably unjustified. By focusing on the task of promoting acceptable and pro-social behaviors, our need to rely on punishment to socialize our children will diminish.

REFERENCES

Aronfreed, J. Punishment learning and internalization: Some parameters of reinforcement and cognition. Paper read at biennial meeting of Society for Research in Child Development, Minneapolis, 1965.

——, *Conduct and Conscience.* New York: Academic Press, 1968.

Aronfreed, J. & Leff, R. The effects of intensity of punishment and complexity of discrimination upon the learning of an internalized inhibition. Unpubl, mss., Univ. of Pennsylvania, 1963.

Aronfreed, J. & Reber, A. Internalized behavioral suppression and the timing of social punishment, *J. pers. soc. Psychol.,* 1965, 1, 3–16.

Bandura, A. The role of modeling processes in personality development. In W. W. Hartup & Nancy L. Smothergill (Eds.), *The Young Child: Reviews of Research.* Washington: National Association for the Education of Young Children, 1967, pp. 42–58.

Bandura, A. & Walters, R. H. *Social Learning and Personality Development.* New York: Holt, Rinehart & Winston, 1963.

Becker, W. C. Consequences of different kinds of parental discipline. In M. L. Hoffman & L. W. Hoffman (Eds.), *Review of Child Development Research,* Vol. 1. New York: Russell Sage Foundation, 1964. Pp. 169–208.

Bell, R. Q. A reinterpretation of the direction of effects of socialization. *Psychological Review,* 1968, 75, 81–95.

Black, A. H., Solomon, R. L. & Whiting, J. W. M. Resistance to temptation in dogs. Cited by Mowrer, O. H. *Learning Theory and the Symbolic Processes.* New York: John Wiley, 1960.

Brown, P. & Elliot, R. Control of aggression in a nursery school class. *J. exp. child Psychol.,* 1965, 2, 103–107.

Cheyne, A. Punishment and reasoning in the development of self-control. In R. D. Parke (Ed.), *Recent Trends in Social Learning Theory.* New York: Academic Press, 1972.

Cheyne, J. A. & Walters, R. H. Intensity of punishment, timing of punishment, and cognitive structure as determinants of response inhibition. *J. exp. child Psychol.,* 1969, 7, 231–244.

Church, R. M. The varied effects of punishment on behavior. *Psychol. Rev.,* 1963, 70, 369–402.

Cowan, P. A. & Walters, R. H. Studies of reinforcement of aggression: I Effects of scheduling. *Child Develpm.,* 1963, 34, 543–551.

Deur, J. L. & Parke, R. D. The effects of inconsistent punishment on aggression in children. *Develpm. Psychol.,* 1970, 2, 403–411.

Gelfand, D. F., Hartmann, D. P., Lanb, A. K., Smith, C. L., Mahan, M. A., and Paul, S. C. The effects of adult models and described alternatives on children's choice of behavior management techniques. *Child Develpm.,* 1974, 45, 585–593.

Glueck, S. & Glueck, E. *Unraveling Juvenile Delinquency.* Cambridge: Harvard Univ. Press, 1950.

Hetherington, E. M. Children of Divorce. Paper presented at Biennial meeting of Society for Research in Child Development, Denver, 1975.

Hoffman, M. L. Moral development. In P. Mussen (Ed.), *Manual of Child Psychology,* New York: Wiley, 1970.

Hartup, W. W. Nurturance and nurturance-withdrawal in relation to the dependency behavior of preschool children. *Child Develpm.,* 1958, 29, 191–201.

Kohlberg, L. Development of moral character and moral ideology. In M. L. Hoffman and Lois W. Hoffman

(Eds.), *Review of Child Development Research,* Vol. 1. New York: Russell Sage Foundation, 1964, Pp. 383–431.

LaVoie, J. C. Cognitive determinants of resistance to deviation in seven, nine and eleven year old children of low and high maturity of moral judgment. *Developm. Psychol.,* 1974, 10, 393–403. (b).

McCord, W., McCord, J. & Howard, A. Familial correlates of aggression in non-delinquent male children. *J. abnorm. soc Psychol.,* 1961, 62, 79–93.

Parke, R. D. Nurturance, nurturance-withdrawal and resistance to deviation. *Child Develpm.,* 1967, 38, 1101–1110.

―――. The role of punishment in the socialization process. In R. A. Hoppe, G. A. Milton, & E. C. Simmel (eds.), *Early Experiences and the Processes of Socialization.* New York: Academic Press, 1970. Pp. 81–108.

―――. Effectiveness of punishment as an interaction of intensity, timing, agent nurturance and cognitive structuring. *Child Develpm.,* 1969, 40, 213–236.

Parke, R. D. Rules, roles and resistance to deviation in children: Explorations in punishment, discipline and self control. In A. Pick (ed.), *Minnesota symposia on child psychology,* Vol. 8. Minneapolis: University of Minnesota Press, 1974.

Parke, R. D. Socialization into child abuse: A social interactional perspective. In J. L. Tapp and F. J. Levine (Eds.), *Law, justice and the individual in society: Psychological and legal issues.* New York: Holt, Rinehart and Winston, 1976.

Parke, R. D. & Deur, J. The inhibitory effects of inconsistent and consistent punishment on children's aggression. Unpubl. mss., Univ. of Wisconsin, 1970.

Parke, R. D., Ewall, W. & Slaby, R. G. Hostile and helpful verbalizations as regulators of nonverbal aggression. *J. pers. soc. Psychol.,* 1972, 23, 243–248.

Parke, R. D. & Murray, S. Re-instatement: A technique for increasing stability of inhibition in children. Unpubl. mss., Univ of Wisconsin, 1971.

Parke, R. D. & Walters, R. H. Some factors determining the efficacy of punishment for inducing response inhibition. *Monogr. Soc. Res. Child Develpm.,* 1967, 32 (Serial No. 109).

Redd, W. H., Morris, E. K., and Martin, J. A. Effects of positive and negative adult-child interactions on children's social preferences. *J. exp. child Psychol.,* 1975, 19, 153–164.

Rosenblith, J. F. Learning by imitation in kindergarten children. *Child Develpm.,* 1959, 30, 69–80.

―――. Imitative color choices in kindergarten children. *Child Develpm.,* 1961, 32, 211–223.

Sawin, D. B. and Parke, R. D. The child's role in sparing the rod. Paper presented at the American Psychological Association, Chicago, September, 1975.

Sawin, D. B. and Parke, R. D. The effect of inter-agent inconsistent discipline on aggression in young boys. *J. exp. child Psychol.,* 1979.

Sawin, D. B. and Parke, R. D. The impact of fear and empathy-based rationales on children's inhibition. *Merrill-Palmer Quarterly,* 1980.

Sears, R. R., Maccoby, E. E. & Levin, H. *Patterns of Child Rearing.* Evanston, Ill.: Row, Peterson, 1957.

Seligman, M. E. P., Maier, S. F. & Solomon, R. L. Unpredictable and uncontrollable aversive events. In F. R. Brush (Ed.), *Aversive Conditioning and Learning.* New York: Academic Press, 1969.

Slaby, R. G. Aggressive and helpful verbalizations as regulators of behavioral aggression and altruism in children. Unpubl. doctoral dissertation, Univ. of Wisconsin, 1970.

Stouwie, R. J. An experimental study of adult dominance and warmth, conflicting verbal instructions, and children's moral behavior. *Child Developm.,* 1972, 43, 959–972.

Walters, R. H. Delay-of-reinforcement effects in children's learning. *Psychonom. Sci.,* 1964, 1, 307–308.

Walters, R. H. & Andres, D. Punishment procedures and self-control. Paper read at Annual Meeting of the American Psychological Association, Washington, D. C., Sept., 1967.

Walters, R. H. & Parke, R. D. The influence of punishment and related disciplinary techniques on the social behavior of children: Theory and empirical findings. In B. A. Maher (Ed.), *Progress in Experimental Personality Research,* Vol. 4. New York: Academic Press, 1967. Pp. 179–228.

Walters, R. H., Parke, R. D. & Cane, V. A. Timing of punishment and the observation of consequences to others as determinants of response inhibition. *J. exp. child Psychol.,* 1965, 2, 10–30.

Chapter Six

Individual Differences in Intelligence

Few topics have stimulated more controversy and research than that of the effects of transactions between biological and environmental factors on intellectual development. In most cases, studies in this area have involved the use of standardized intelligence tests and the obtained intelligence quotient, or IQ, as a measure of intelligence. Sometimes educational level, professional achievements, Piagetian tasks, and less frequently social problem-solving are also used to estimate cognitive level.

Many of the problems in interpretation of these studies rest in disparate views of what IQ scores represent, others are based on confusion about the concept of heritability. The layman tends to regard IQ as a measure of the innate capacity to learn that remains relatively stable throughout life. As the student will learn in reading the papers in this section this is not true. The IQ is a measure of performance on an intelligence test relative to the performance of a group of individuals on whom the test has been standardized. As the IQ goes above 100 it means the individual is performing better than the average person of his or her age in the standardization group; as it drops below 100 the individual is performing less well than the average person in the standardization group. The problem-solving performance measured on an intelligence test is most closely related to performance and achievement in academic settings and less closely to competence in social situations, practical problems in everyday life, and earning power.

The student should note first that IQ is a measure of performance, not innate capacity. This performance will be a result of the interaction among many variables: innate intellectual capacity, life experiences, the environment in which the individual is raised, condition at the time of testing, the particular items on the test, and the conditions under which the test is administered. Second the student should keep in mind that IQ is always a relative performance score. The group with whom we compare the performance of the individual should be one with a similar background and shared life experiences. Finally there are considerable fluctuations in IQ for the same individual over the life span. This is in part attributable to the fact that very different types of items which may be testing different cognitive competences are used with children of different ages. In the prelinguistic child under two years of age, items relying heavily on sensory or motor skills are used. With the onset of language, intelligence tests become more heavily weighted with items involving verbal skills. It has been argued that these early sensorimotor measures involve a different kind of cognitive competence than do verbal or abstract reasoning items. Some support for this position is found in the extremely low relationship between IQ scores obtained in the first two years of life and those from later ages. In addition the pattern and rate of intellectual development varies for different individuals. Just as children may show plateaus and spurts in physical growth at different ages, wide individual variations in patterns of cognitive development occur.

Closely related to misconceptions about the IQ is confusion about the meaning of heritability. In its simplest form, heritability is a statistical concept which reflects the percentage of variability that is associated with differences in the genetic composition of individuals in a group (McCall, 1975). Scarr-Salapatek in her article on unknowns in the IQ equation emphasizes that the heritability of IQ will vary in different populations. The percentage of variability in IQ associated with inherited factors and with experiential factors will vary for groups raised in different environments. Scarr-Salapatek uses this argument to rebut the positions of Jensen, Eysenck, and Herrnstein that the lower IQs obtained by blacks and lower-class whites relative to middle-class whites are largely based on genetic differences in intellectual abilities. If the heritability coefficient for IQ is lower for a group raised in one environment than those raised in another setting, it may mean that the environment may be suppressing or restricting the expressions of intellectual ability. Jensen's figure of 80 percent heritability of IQ, which is frequently cited, is largely based on twin and adoption studies of middle-class white populations. Scarr-Salapatek finds much lower proportions of heritability of IQ in black and lower-class white populations, which she attributes to the social and economic disadvantages suffered by these groups, particularly by the deleterious effects of the racial caste system imposed upon blacks.

Scarr-Salapatek and her colleague Richard Weinberg have extended her investigations on race and IQ in the interracial adoption study which is presented in the last paper in this section. In this paper they examine the effects of cross-fostering on the IQs of black children and find that the social and cognitive environment of middle-class white adoptive homes was associated with increases in IQ in black adopted children. They propose that *if* high IQs are considered desirable some restructuring of the social system within black homes is necessary to facilitate the development of intellectual skills measured by intelligence tests.

The two papers by Zajonc and by Maccoby, Doering, Jacklin, and Kraemer should be read as a pair since they suggest alternative interpretations of the frequently reported birth-order effects in cognitive performance. Zajonc suggests that differences in experiential and social factors can explain the superior performance on IQ tests of first-born children and later-born children from families in which there are widely spaced births. Maccoby and her colleagues suggest that these findings could also be associated with hormone depletions found in later-born, closely spaced children. It may well be that both social and biological factors must be considered in any adequate explanation of the relation between birth order and intelligence.

REFERENCES

McCall, R. B. *Heritability*. Homewood: Richard Irwin, 1975.

Reading 23

Unknowns in the IQ Equation

Sandra Scarr-Salapatek

IQ scores have been repeatedly estimated to have a large heritable component in United States and Northern European white populations *(1)*. Individual differences in IQ, many authors have concluded, arise far more from genetic than from environmental differences among people in these populations, at the present time, and under present environmental conditions. It has also been known for many years that white lower-class and black groups have lower IQ's, on the average, than white middle-class groups. Most behavioral scientists comfortably "explained" these group differences by appealing to obvious environmental differences between the groups in standards of living, educational opportunities, and the like. But recently an explosive controversy has developed over the heritability of between-group differences in IQ, the question at issue being: If individual differences within the white population as a whole can be attributed largely to heredity, is it not plausible that the average differences between social-class groups and between racial groups also reflect significant genetic differences? Can the former data be used to explain the latter?

To propose genetically based racial and social-class differences is anathema to most behavioral scientists, who fear any scientific confirmation of the pernicious racial and ethnic prejudices that abound in our society. But now that the issue has been openly raised, and has been projected into the public context of social and educational policies, a hard scientific look must be taken at what is known and at what inferences can be drawn from that knowledge.

The public controversy began when A. R. Jensen, in a long paper in the *Harvard Educational Review,* persuasively juxtaposed data on the heritability of IQ and the observed differences between groups.

Jensen suggested that current large-scale educational attempts to raise the IQ's of lower-class children, white and black, were failing because of the high heritability of IQ. In a series of papers and rebuttals to criticism, in the same journal and elsewhere *(2),* Jensen put forth the hypothesis that social-class and racial differences in mean IQ were due largely to differences in the gene distributions of these populations. At least, he said, the genetic-differences hypothesis was no less likely, and probably more likely, than a simple environmental hypothesis to explain the mean difference of 15 IQ points between blacks and whites *(3)* and the even larger average IQ differences between professionals and manual laborers within the white population.

Jensen's articles have been directed primarily at an academic audience. Herrnstein's article in the *Atlantic* and Eysenck's book (first published in England) have brought the argument to the attention of the wider lay audience. Both Herrnstein and Eysenck agree with Jensen's genetic-differences hypothesis as it pertains to individual differences and to social-class groups, but Eysenck centers his attention on the genetic explanation of racial-group differences, which Herrnstein only touches on. Needless to say, many other scientists will take issue with them.

EYSENCK'S RACIAL THESIS

Eysenck has written a popular account of the race, social-class, and IQ controversy in a generally inflammatory book. The provocative title and the disturbing cover picture of a forlorn black boy are clearly designed to tempt the lay reader into a pseudo-battle between Truth and Ignorance. In this case Truth is genetic-environmental interactionism *(4)* and Ignorance is naive environmentalism. For the careful reader, the battle fades out inconclusively as Eysenck admits that scientific evidence to date does not permit a clear choice of the genetic-differences interpretation of black inferiority on intelligence tests. A quick reading of the book, however, is sure to leave the reader believing that scientific evidence today strongly supports the con-

Scarr-Salapatek's paper is a review of three publications:

(1) "Environment, heridity, and intelligence," a collection of articles comprising a statement by Arthur R. Jensen and rebuttals by leading psychologists. *Harvard Educational Review* Spring 1969 (subsequently published by the *Review* as a special reprint).

(2) H. J. Eysenck, *The IQ Argument,* New York: Library Press, 1971.

(3) Richard Herrnstein, "I.Q." *Atlantic* 288 No. 3 (1971):44–64.

clusion that U.S. blacks are genetically inferior to whites in IQ.

The basic theses of the book are as follows:

1 IQ is a highly heritable characteristic in the U.S. white population and probably equally heritable in the U.S. black population.
2 On the average, blacks score considerably lower than whites on IQ tests.
3 U.S. blacks are probably a non-random, lower-IQ, sample of native African populations.
4 The average IQ difference between blacks and whites probably represents important genetic differences between the races.
5 Drastic environmental changes will have to be made to improve the poor phenotypes that U.S. blacks now achieve.

The evidence and nonevidence that Eysenck cites to support his genetic hypothesis of racial differences make a curious assortment. Audrey Shuey's review *(5)* of hundreds of studies showing mean phenotypic differences between black and white IQ's leads Eysenck to conclude:

All the evidence to date suggests the strong and indeed overwhelming importance of genetic factors in producing the great variety of intellectual differences which we observe in our culture, and much of the difference observed between certain racial groups. This evidence cannot be argued away by niggling and very minor criticisms of details which do not really throw doubts on the major points made in this book [p. 126].

To "explain" the genetic origins of these mean IQ differences he offers these suppositions:

White slavers wanted dull beasts of burden, ready to work themselves to death in the plantations, and under those conditions intelligence would have been counter-selective. Thus there is every reason to expect that the particular sub-sample of the Negro race which is constituted of American Negroes is not an unselected sample of Negroes, but has been selected throughout history according to criteria which would put the highly intelligent at a disadvantage. The inevitable outcome of such selection would of course be a gene pool lacking some of the genes making for higher intelligence [p. 42].

Other ethnic minorities in the U.S. are also, in his view, genetically inferior, again because of the selective migration of lower IQ genotypes:

It is known [sic] that many other groups came to the

U.S.A. due to pressures which made them very poor samples of the original populations. Italians, Spaniards, and Portuguese, as well as Greeks, are examples where the less able, less intelligent were forced through circumstances to emigrate, and where their American progeny showed significantly lower IQ's than would have been shown by a random sample of the original population [p. 43].

Although Eysenck is careful to say that these are not established facts (because no IQ tests were given to the immigrants or nonimmigrants in question?), the tone of his writing leaves no doubt about his judgment. There is something in this book to insult almost everyone except WASP's and Jews.

Despite his conviction that U.S. blacks are genetically inferior in IQ to whites, Eysenck is optimistic about the potential effects of radical environmental changes on the present array of Negro IQ phenotypes. He points to the very large IQ gains produced by intensive one-to-one tutoring of black urban children with low-IQ mothers, contrasting large environmental changes and large IQ gains in intensive programs of this sort with insignificant environmental improvements and small IQ changes obtained by Head Start and related programs. He correctly observes that, whatever the heritability of IQ (or, it should be added, of any characteristic), large phenotypic changes may be produced by creating appropriate, radically different environments never before encountered by those genotypes. On this basis, Eysenck calls for further research to determine the requisites of such environments.

Since Eysenck comes to this relatively benign position regarding potential improvement in IQ's, why, one may ask, is he at such pains to "prove" the genetic inferiority of blacks? Surprisingly, he expects that new environments, such as that provided by intensive educational tutoring, will not affect the black-white IQ differential, because black children and white will probably profit equally from such treatment. Since many middle-class white children already have learning environments similar to that provided by tutors for the urban black children, we must suppose that Eysenck expects great IQ gains from relatively small changes in white, middle-class environments.

This book is an uncritical popularization of Jensen's ideas without the nuances and qualifiers that make much of Jensen's writing credible or at least responsible. Both authors rely on Shuey's review

(5), but Eysenck's way of doing it is to devote some 25 pages to quotes and paraphrases of her chapter summaries. For readers to whom the original Jensen article is accessible, Eysenck's book is a poor substitute; although he defends Jensen and Shuey, he does neither a service.

It is a maddeningly inconsistent book filled with contradictory caution and incaution; with hypotheses stated both as hypotheses and as conclusions; with both accurate and inaccurate statements on matters of fact. For example, Eysenck thinks evoked potentials* offer a better measure of "innate" intelligence than IQ tests. But on what basis? Recently F. B. Davis *(6)* has failed to find any relationship whatsoever between evoked potentials and either IQ scores or scholastic achievement, to which intelligence is supposed to be related. Another example is Eysenck's curious use of data to support a peculiar line of reasoning about the evolutionary inferiority of blacks: First, he reports that African and U.S. Negro babies have been shown to have precocious sensorimotor development by white norms (the difference, by several accounts, appears only in gross motor skills and even there is slight). Second, he notes that by three years of age U.S. white exceed U.S. black children in mean IQ scores. Finally he cites a (very slight) negative correlation, found in an early study, between sensorimotor intelligence in the first year of life and later IQ. From exaggerated statements of these various data, he concludes:

> These findings are important because of a very general view in biology according to which the more prolonged the infancy the greater in general are the cognitive or intellectual abilities of the species. This law appears to work even within a given species [p. 79].

Eysenck would apparently have us believe that Africans and their relatives in the U.S. are less highly evolved than Caucasians, whose longer infancy is related to later higher intelligence. I am aware of no evidence whatsoever to support a within-species relationship between longer infancy and higher adult capacities.

The book is carelessly put together, with no index; few references, and those not keyed to the text; and long, inadequately cited quotes that carry over several pages without clear beginnings and ends.

*A measure of the electrical activity in the brain.

Furthermore, considering the gravity of Eysenck's theses, the book has an occasional jocularity of tone that is offensive. A careful book on the genetic hypothesis, written for a lay audience, would have merited publication. This one, however, has been publicly disowned as irresponsible by the entire editorial staff of its London publisher, New Society. But never mind, the American publisher has used that and other condemnations to balance the accolades and make its advertisement *(7)* of the book more titillating.

HERRNSTEIN'S SOCIAL THESIS

Thanks to Jensen's provocative article, many academic psychologists who thought IQ tests belonged in the closet with the Rorschach inkblots have now explored the psychometric literature and found it to be a trove of scientific treasure. One of these is Richard Herrnstein, who from a Kinnerian background has become an admirer of intelligence tests—a considerable leap from shaping the behavior of pigeons and rats. In contrast to Eysenck's book, Herrnstein's popular account in the *Atlantic* of IQ testing and its values is generally responsible, if overly enthusiastic in parts.

Herrnstein unabashedly espouses IQ testing as "psychology's most telling accomplishment to date," despite the current controversy over the fairness of testing poor and minority-group children with IQ items devised by middle-class whites. His historical review of IQ test development, including tests of general intelligence and multiple abilities, is interesting and accurate. His account of the validity and usefulness of the tests centers on the fairly accurate prediction that can be made from IQ scores to academic and occupational achievement and income level. He clarifies the pattern of relationship between IQ and these criterion variables: High IQ is a necessary but not sufficient condition for high achievement, while low IQ virtually assures failure at high academic and occupational levels. About the usefulness of the tests, he concludes:

> An IQ test can be given in an hour or two to a child, and from this infinitesimally small sample of his output, deeply important predictions follow—about schoolwork, occupation, income, satisfaction with life, and even life expectancy. The predictions are not perfect, for other factors always enter in, but no other single factor matters as much in as many spheres of life [p. 53].

One must assume that Herrnstein's enthusiasm for intelligence tests rests on population statistics, not on predictions for a particular child, because many children studied longitudinally have been shown to change IQ scores by 20 points or more from childhood to adulthood. It is likely that extremes of giftedness and retardation can be sorted out relatively early by IQ tests, but what about the 95 percent of the population in between? Their IQ scores may vary from dull to bright normal for many years. Important variations in IQ can occur up to late adolescence (8). On a population basis Herrnstein is correct; the best early predictors of later achievement are ability measures taken from age five on. Predictions are based on correlations, however, which are not sensitive to absolute changes in value, only to rank orders. This is an important point to be discussed later.

After reviewing the evidence for average IQ differences by social class and race, Herrnstein poses the nature-nurture problem of "which is primary" in determining phenotypic differences in IQ. For racial groups, he explains, the origins of mean IQ differences are indeterminate at the present time because we have no information from heritability studies in the black population or from other, unspecified lines of research which could favor primarily genetic or primarily environmental hypotheses. He is thoroughly convinced, however, that individual differences and social-class differences in IQ are highly heritable at the present time, and are destined, by environmental improvements, to become even more so:

> If we make the relevant environment much more uniform (by making it as good as we can for everyone), then an even larger proportion of the variation in IQ will be attributable to the genes. The average person would be smarter, but intelligence would run in families even more obviously and with less regression toward the mean than we see today [p. 58].

For Herrnstein, society is, and will be even more strongly, a meritocracy based largely on inherited differences in IQ. He presents a "syllogism" (p. 58) to make his message clear:

1 If differences in mental abilities are inherited, and
2 If success requires those abilities, and
3 If earnings and prestige depend on success,
4 Then social standing (which reflects earnings

and prestige) will be based to some extent on inherited differences among people.

Five "corollaries" for the future predict that the heritability of IQ will rise; that social mobility will become more strongly related to inherited IQ differences; that most bright people will be gathered in the top of the social structure, with the IQ dregs at the bottom; that many at the bottom will not have the intelligence needed for new jobs; and that the meritocracy will be built not just on inherited intelligence but on all inherited traits affecting success, which will presumably become correlated characters. Thus from the successful realization of our most precious, egalitarian, political and social goals there will arise a much more rigidly stratified society, a "virtual caste system" based on inborn ability.

To ameliorate this effect, society may have to move toward the socialist dictum, "From each according to his abilities, to each according to his needs," but Herrnstein sees complete equality of earnings and prestige as impossible because high-grade intelligence is scarce and must be recruited into those critical jobs that require it, by the promise of high earnings and high prestige. Although garbage collecting is critical to the health of the society, almost anyone can do it; to waste high-IQ persons on such jobs is to misallocate scarce resources at society's peril.

Herrnstein points to an ironic contrast between the effects of caste and class systems. Castes, which established artificial hereditary limits on social mobility, guarantee the inequality of opportunity that preserves IQ heterogeneity at all levels of the system. Many bright people are arbitrarily kept down and many unintelligent people are artificially maintained at the top. When arbitrary bounds on mobility are removed, as in our class system, most of the bright rise to the top and most of the dull fall to the bottom of the social system, and IQ differences between top and bottom become increasingly hereditary. The greater the environmental equality, the greater the hereditary differences between levels in the social structure. The thesis of egalitarianism surely leads to its antithesis in a way that Karl Marx never anticipated.

Herrnstein proposes that our best strategy, in the face of increasing biological stratification, is publicly to recognize genetic human differences but to reallocate wealth to a considerable extent. The IQ have-nots need not be poor. Herrnstein does not delve into the psychological consequences of being publicly marked as genetically inferior.

Does the evidence support Herrnstein's view of hereditary social classes, now or in some future Utopia? Given his assumptions about the high heritability of IQ, the importance of IQ to social mobility, and the increasing environmental equality of rearing and opportunity, hereditary social classes are to some extent inevitable. But one can question the limits of genetic homogeneity in social-class groups and the evidence for his syllogism at present.

Is IQ as highly heritable throughout the social structure as Herrnstein assumes? Probably not. In a recent study of IQ heritability in various racial and social-class groups (9), I found much lower proportions of genetic variance that would account for aptitude differences among lower-class than among middle-class children, in both black and white groups. Social disadvantage in prenatal and postnatal development can substantially lower phenotypic IQ and reduce the genotype-phenotype correlation. Thus, average phenotypic IQ differences between the social classes may be considerably larger than the genotypic differences.

Are social classes largely based on hereditary IQ differences now? Probably not as much as Herrnstein believes. Since opportunities for social mobility act at the phenotypic level, there still may be considerable genetic diversity for IQ at the bottom of the social structure. In earlier days arbitrary social barriers maintained genetic variability throughout the social structure. At present, individuals with high phenotypic IQ's are often upwardly mobile; but inherited wealth acts to maintain genetic diversity at the top, and nongenetic biological and social barriers to phenotypic development act to maintain a considerable genetic diversity of intelligence in the lower classes.

As P. E. Vernon has pointed out (10), we are inclined to forget that the majority of gifted children in recent generations have come from working-class, not middle-class, families. A larger percentage of middle-class children are gifted, but the working and lower classes produce gifted children in larger numbers. How many more disadvantaged children would have been bright if they had had middle-class gestation and rearing conditions?

I am inclined to think that intergenerational class mobility will always be with us, for three reasons. First, since normal IQ is a polygenic characteristic,

various recombinations of parental genotypes will always produce more variable genotypes in the offspring than in the parents of all social-class groups, especially the extremes. Even if both parents, instead of primarily the male, achieved social-class status based on their IQ's, recombinations of their genes would always produce a range of offspring, who would be upwardly or downwardly mobile relative to their families of origin.

Second, since, as Herrnstein acknowledges, factors other than IQ—motivational, personality, and undetermined—also contribute to success or the lack of it, high IQ's will always be found among lower-class adults, in combination with schizophrenia, alcoholism, drug addiction, psychopathy, and other limiting factors. When recombined in offspring, high IQ can readily segregate with facilitating motivational and personality characteristics, thereby leading to upward mobility for many offspring. Similarly, middle-class parents will always produce some offspring with debilitating personal characteristics which lead to downward mobility.

Third, for all children to develop phenotypes that represent their best genotypic outcome (in current environments) would require enormous changes in the present social system. To improve and equalize all rearing environments would involve such massive intervention as to make Herrnstein's view of the future more problematic than he seems to believe.

RACE AS CASTE

Races are castes between which there is very little mobility. Unlike the social-class system, where mobility based on IQ is sanctioned, the racial caste system, like the hereditary aristocracy of medieval Europe and the caste system of India, preserves within each group its full range of genetic diversity of intelligence. The Indian caste system was, according to Dobzhansky (11), a colossal genetic failure—or success, according to egalitarian values. After the abolition of castes at independence, Brahmins and untouchables were found to be equally educable despite—or because of—their many generations of segregated reproduction.

While we may tentatively conclude that there are some genetic IQ differences between social-class groups, we can make only wild speculations about racial groups. Average phenotypic IQ differences between races are not evidence for genetic differences (any more than they are evidence for environmental differences). Even if the heritabilities of IQ are extremely high in all races, there is still no warrant for equating within-group and between-group heritabilities (12). There are examples in agricultural experiments of within-group differences that are highly heritable but between-group differences that are entirely environmental. Draw two random samples of seeds from the same genetically heterogeneous population. Plant one sample in uniformly good conditions, the other in uniformly poor conditions. The average height difference between the populations of plants will be entirely environmental, although the individual differences in height within each sample will be entirely genetic. With known genotypes for seeds and known environments, genetic and environmental variances between groups can be studied. But racial groups are not random samples from the same population, nor are members reared in uniform conditions within each race. Racial groups are of unknown genetic equivalence for polygenic characteristics like IQ, and the differences in environments within and between the races may have as yet unquantified effects.

There is little to be gained from approaching the nature-nurture problem of race differences in IQ directly (13). Direct comparisons of estimated within-group heritabilities and the calculation of between-group heritabilities require assumptions that few investigators are willing to make, such as that all environmental differences are quantifiable, that differences in the environments of blacks and whites can be assumed to affect IQ in the same way in the two groups, and that differences in environments between groups can be "statistically controlled." A direct assault on race differences in IQ is vulnerable to many criticisms.

Indirect approaches may be less vulnerable. These include predictions of parent-child regression effects and admixture studies. Regression effects can be predicted to differ for blacks and whites if the two races indeed have genetically different population means. If the population mean for blacks is 15 IQ points lower than that of whites, then the offspring of high-IQ black parents should show greater regression (toward a lower population mean) than the offspring of whites of equally high IQ. Similarly, the offspring of low-IQ black parents should show less regression than those of white parents of equally low IQ. This hypothesis assumes that assortative mating for IQ is equal in the two races, which could be

empirically determined but has not been studied as yet. Interpretable results from a parent-child regression study would also depend upon careful attention to intergenerational environmental changes, which could be greater in one race than the other.

Studies based on correlations between degree of white admixture and IQ scores *within* the black group would avoid many of the pitfalls of between-group comparisons. If serological genotypes can be used to identify persons with more and less white admixture, and if estimates of admixture based on blood groups are relatively independent of visible characteristics like skin color, then any positive correlation between degree of admixture and IQ would suggest genetic racial differences in IQ. Since blood groups have not been used directly as the basis of racial discrimination, positive findings would be relatively immune from environmentalist criticisms. The trick is to estimate individual admixture reliably. Several loci which have fairly different distributions of alleles in contemporary African and white populations have been proposed (14). No one has yet attempted a study of this sort.

h^2 [HERITABILITY] AND PHENOTYPE

Suppose that the heritabilities of IQ differences within all racial and social-class groups were .80, as Jensen estimates, and suppose that the children in all groups were reared under an equal range of conditions. Now suppose that racial and social-class differences in mean IQ still remained. We would probably infer some degree of genetic difference between the groups. So what? The question now turns from a strictly scientific one to one of science and social policy.

As Eysenck, Jensen, and others have noted, eugenic and euthenic strategies are both possible interventions to reduce the number of low-IQ individuals in all populations. Eugenic policies could be advanced to encourage or require reproductive abstinence by people who fall below a certain level of intelligence. The Reeds (15) have determined that one-fifth of the mental retardation among whites of the next generation could be prevented if no mentally retarded persons of this generation reproduced. There is no question that a eugenic program applied at the phenotypic level of parents' IQ would substantially reduce the number of low-IQ children in the future white population. I am aware of no studies in the black population to support a similar program, but some proportion of future retardation could surely be eliminated. It would be extremely important, however, to sort out genetic and environmental sources of low IQ both in racial and in social-class groups before advancing a eugenic program. The request or demand that some persons refrain from any reproduction should be a last resort, based on sure knowledge that their retardation is caused primarily by genetic factors and is not easily remedied by environmental intervention. Studies of the IQ levels of adopted children with mentally retarded natural parents would be most instructive, since some of the retardation observed among children of retarded parents may stem from the rearing environments provided by the parents.

In a pioneering study of adopted children and their adoptive and natural parents, Skodak (16) reported greater *correlations* of children's IQ's with their natural than with their adoptive parents' IQ's. This statement has been often misunderstood to mean that the children's *levels* of intelligence more closely resembled their natural parents', which is completely false. Although the rank order of the children's IQ's resembled that of their mothers' IQ's, the children's IQ's were higher, being distributed, like those of the adoptive parents, around a mean above 100, whereas their natural mothers' IQ's averaged only 85. The children, in fact, averaged 21 IQ points higher than their natural mothers. If the (unstudied) natural fathers' IQ's averaged around the population mean of 100, the mean of the children's would be expected to be 94, or 12 points lower than the mean obtained. The unexpected boost in IQ was presumably due to the better social environments provided by the adoptive families. Does this mean that phenotypic IQ can be substantially changed?

Even under existing conditions of child rearing, phenotypes of children reared by low-IQ parents could be markedly changed by giving them the same rearing environment as the top IQ group provide for their children. According to DeFries (17), if children whose parents average 20 IQ points below the population mean were reared in environments such as usually are provided only by parents in the top .01 percent of the population, these same children would average 5 points *above* the population mean instead of 15 points below, as they do when reared by their own families.

Euthenic policies depend upon the demonstration

that different rearing conditions can change phenotypic IQ sufficiently to enable most people in a social class or racial group to function in future society. I think there is great promise in this line of research and practice, although its efficacy will depend ultimately on the cost and feasibility of implementing radical intervention programs. Regardless of the present heritability of IQ in any population, phenotypes can be changed by the introduction of new and different environments. (One merit of Eysenck's book is the attention he gives to this point.) Furthermore, it is impossible to predict phenotypic outcomes under very different conditions. For example, in the Milwaukee Project (18), in which the subjects are ghetto children whose mothers' IQ's are less than 70, intervention began soon after the children were born. Over a four-year period Heber has intensively tutored the children for several hours every day and has produced an enormous IQ difference between the experimental group (mean IQ 127) and a control group (mean IQ 90). If the tutored children continue to advance in environments which are radically different from their homes with retarded mothers, we shall have some measure of the present phenotypic range of reaction (19) of children whose average IQ's might have been in the 80 to 90 range. These data support Crow's comment on h^2 in his contribution to the *Harvard Educational Review* discussion (p. 158):

> It does not directly tell us how much improvement in IQ to expect from a given change in the environment. In particular, it offers no guidance as to the consequences of a new kind of environmental influence. For example, conventional heritability measures for height show a value of nearly 1. Yet, because of unidentified environmental influences, the mean height in the United States and in Japan has risen by a spectacular amount. Another kind of illustration is provided by the discovery of a cure for a hereditary disease. In such cases, any information on prior heritability may become irrelevant. Furthermore, heritability predictions are less dependable at the tails of the distribution.

To illustrate the phenotypic changes that can be produced by radically different environments for children with clear genetic anomalies, Rynders (20) has provided daily intensive tutoring for Down's syndrome [i.e., so-called Mongoloid] infants. At the age of two, these children have average IQ's of 85 while control-group children, who are enrolled in a variety of other programs, average 68. Untreated children have even lower average IQ scores.

The efficacy of intervention programs for children whose expected IQ's are too low to permit full participation in society depends on their long-term effects on intelligence. Early childhood programs may be necessary but insufficient to produce functioning adults. There are critical research questions yet to be answered about euthenic programs, including what kinds, how much, how long, how soon, and toward what goals?

DOES h^2 MATTER?

There is growing disillusionment with the concept of heritability, as it is understood and misunderstood. Some who understand it very well would like to eliminate h^2 from human studies for at least two reasons. First, the usefulness of h^2 estimates in animal and plant genetics pertains to decisions about the efficacy of selective breeding to produce more desirable phenotypes. Selective breeding does not apply to the human case, at least so far. Second, if important phenotypic changes can be produced by radically different environments, then, it is asked, who cares about the heritability of IQ? Morton *(21)* has expressed these sentiments well:

> Considerable popular interest attaches to such questions as "is one class or ethnic group innately superior to another on a particular test?" The reasons are entirely emotional, since such a difference, if established, would serve as no better guide to provision of educational or other facilities than an unpretentious assessment of phenotypic differences.

I disagree. The simple assessment of phenotypic performance does not suggest any particular intervention strategy. Heritability estimates can have merit as indicators of the effects to be expected from various types of intervention programs. If, for example, IQ tests, which predict well to achievements in the larger society, show low heritabilities in a population, then it is probable that simply providing better environments which now exist will improve average performance in that population. If h^2 is high but environments sampled in that population are largely unfavorable, then (again) simple environmental improvement will probably change the mean phenotypic level. If h^2 is high and the environments sampled are largely favorable, then novel environmental manipulations are probably required to change phenotypes, and eugenic programs may be advocated.

The most common misunderstanding of the con-

cept "heritability" relates to the myth of fixed intelligence: if h^2 is high, this reasoning goes, then intelligence is genetically fixed and unchangeable at the phenotypic level. This misconception ignores the fact that h^2 is a population statistic, bound to a given set of environmental conditions at a given point in time. Neither intelligence nor h^2 estimates are fixed.

It is absurd to deny that the frequencies of genes for behavior may vary between populations. For individual differences within populations, and for social-class differences, a genetic hypothesis is almost a necessity to explain some of the variance in IQ, especially among adults in contemporary white populations living in average or better environments. But what Jensen, Shuey, and Eysenck (and others) propose is that genetic racial differences are necessary to account for the current phenotypic differences in mean IQ between populations. That may be so, but it would be extremely difficult, given current methodological limitations, to gather evidence that would dislodge an environmental hypothesis to account for the same data. And to assert, despite the absence of evidence, and in the present social climate, that a particular race is genetically disfavored in intelligence is to scream "FIRE! . . . I think" in a crowded theater. Given that so little is known, further scientific study seems far more justifiable than public speculations.

REFERENCES

1 For a review of studies, see L. Erlenmeyer-Kimling and L. F. Jarvik, *Science* 142, 1477 (1963). Heritability is the ratio of genetic variance to total phenotypic variance. For human studies, heritability is used in its broad sense of total genetic variance/total phenotypic variance.

2 The *Harvard Educational Review* compilation includes Jensen's paper, "How much can we boost IQ and scholastic achievement?," comments on it by J. S. Kagan, J. McV. Hunt, J. F. Crow, C. Bereiter, D. Elkind, L. J. Cronbach, and W. F. Brazziel, and a rejoinder by Jensen. See also A. R. Jensen, in J. Hellmuth, *Disadvantaged Child,* vol. 3 (Special Child Publ., Seattle, Wash., 1970).

3 P. L. Nichols, thesis, University of Minnesota (1970). Nichols reports that in two large samples of black and white children, seven-year WISC IQ scores showed the same means and distributions for the two racial groups, once social-class variables were equated. These results are unlike those of several other studies, which found that matching socio-economic status did not create equal means in the two racial groups [A. Shuey *(5):* A. B. Wilson, *Racial Isolation in the Public Schools,* vol. 2

(Government Printing Office, Washington, D.C., 1967)]. In Nichols's samples, prenatal and postnatal medical care was equally available to blacks and whites, which may have contributed to the relatively high IQ scores of the blacks in these samples.

4 By interaction. Eysenck means simply $P = G + E$, or "heredity and environment acting together to produce the observed phenotype" (p. 111). He does not mean what most geneticists and behavior geneticists mean by interaction; that is, the *differential* phenotypic effects produced by various combinations of genotypes and environments, as in the interaction term of analysis-of-variance statistics. Few thinking people are not inter-actionists in Eysenck's sense of the term, because that's the only way to get the organism and the environment into the same equation to account for variance in any phenotypic trait. How much of the phenotypic variance is accounted for by each of the terms in the equation is the real issue.

5 A. Shuey, *The Testing of Negro Intelligence* (Social Science Press, New York, 1966), pp. 499–519.

6 F. B. Davis, *The Measurement of Mental Capacity through Evoked-Potential Recordings* (Educational Records Bureau, Greenwich, Conn., 1971). "As it turned out, no evidence was found that the latency periods obtained . . . displayed serviceable utility for predicting school performance or level of mental ability among pupils in preschool through grade 8" (p. x).

7 *New York Times,* 8 Oct. 1971, p. 41.

8 J. Kagan and H. A. Moss, *Birth to Maturity* (Wiley, New York, 1962).

9 S. Scarr-Salapatek, *Science,* 1971, *174,* 1285–1292.

10 P. E. Vernon, *Intelligence and Cultural Environment* (Methuen, London, 1969).

11 T. Dobzhansky, *Mankind Evolving* (Yale Univ. Press, New Haven, 1962), pp. 234–238.

12 J. Thoday, *J. Biosocial Science 1,* suppl. 3, 4 (1969).

13 L. L. Cavalli-Sforza and W. F. Bodmer, *The Genetics of Human Populations* (Freeman, San Francisco, 1971), pp. 753–804. They propose that the study of racial differences is useless and not scientifically supportable at the present time.

14 E. W. and S. H. Reed, *Science* 165, 762 (1969); *Am. J. Hum. Genet.* 21, 1 (1969); C. MacLean and P. L. Workman, paper at a meeting of the American Society of Human Genetics (1970, Indianapolis).

15 E. W. Reed and S. C. Reed, *Mental Retardation: A Family Study* (Saunders, Philadelphia, 1965); *Social Biol.* 18, suppl. 42 (1971).

16 M. Skodak and H. M. Skeels, *J. Genet. Psychol.* 75, 85 (1949).

17 J. C. DeFries, paper for the C.O.B.R.E. Research Workshop on Genetic Endowment and Environment in the Determination of Behavior (3–8 Oct. 1971, Rye, N.Y.).

18 R. Heber, *Rehabilitation of Families at Risk for Mental Retardation* (Regional Rehabilitation Center, Univ. of Wisconsin, 1969), S. P. Strickland, *Am. Ed.* 7, 3 (1971).

19 I. I. Gottesman, in *Social Class, Race, and Psychological Development,* M. Deutsch, I. Katz, and A. R. Jensen, Eds. (Holt, Rinehart, and Winston, New York, 1968), pp. 11–51.

20 J. Rynders, personal communication, November 1971.

21 N. E. Morton, paper for the C.O.B.R.E. Research Workshop on Genetic Endowment and Environment in the Determination of Behavior (3–8 Oct. 1971, Rye, N.Y.).

Reading 24

The War over Race and IQ:
When Black Children Grow Up in White Homes

Sandra Scarr-Salapatek
Richard A. Weinberg

Black children in this country, as a group, score lower on IQ tests than white children do. The difference between the two groups is about 15 points, a gap that generally corresponds to the white children's greater success in school.

The IQ difference is agreed upon by all parties in the continuing debate about race and intelligence. But there has been no resolution to the burning question of why it exists, and the efforts to explain it have generated anguish, bitterness and opprobrium among educators, makers of social policy, and laymen.

Three camps are now continuing the argument. One believes that the IQ is fixed genetically, and that efforts to change a child's score by changing his environment or giving him compensatory education must fail [see "The Differences Are Real," *pt,* December 1973]. This genetic view also maintains that IQ tests are valid because they reliably predict the academic success of all children, black and white, equally well. The second group, largely liberal and activist, retorts that black children show an IQ deficit because they live and grow in environments that are physically and intellectually impoverished. Change the environment, their argument runs, and the IQ will follow. The environmentalists consider IQ tests to be biased in favor of white middle-class children, and thus invalid measures of intelligence for minorities.

The third group, who might be called the pacifists, argues that no resolution of the debate is possible until black children are raised in exactly the same surroundings as whites. If equally rich environments close the IQ gap, then the genetic argument falls apart.

We have now completed a study on transracial adoption that provides a first look at what happens to the IQs of black children who live in white homes. Adoption changes a child's entire lifestyle around the clock, in contrast to compensatory-education programs or special classes that are wedged into the school curriculum and, at best, affect some part of the child's life between 9:00 and 3:00. If black children raised in white worlds do better on IQ tests than blacks raised in black environments, all groups in the controversy would have their answer.

White Parents, Black Children In the mid-'60s thousands of white families adopted children of other racial and national origins, partly because few white infants were available for adoption, and partly because many of these families were personally committed to racial equality. We did not deal with the value judgment of whether transracial adoption is good or bad for the children and families involved; we simply seized the opportunity to see whether radical environmental change closes the IQ gap.

Over the past two years we have studied 101 white families who adopted black children. We reached them through the Minnesota Open Door Society, a group of such families, and the Adoption Unit of the Minnesota State Department of Public Welfare. In the Minneapolis area, where the black population is only 1.9 percent, black-white relationships are not as tense and troubled as they are in other states and cities. For this reason, parents can adopt children of different races easily, and the surrounding community exacts no social price, from parents or adopted children, for doing so.

A team of interviewers visited each family twice and gave every member over the age of four an IQ test: the Stanford-Binet for four- to eight-year-olds,

the Wechsler Intelligence Scale for Children (WISC) for eight- to 16-year-olds, and the Wechsler Adult Intelligence Scale (WAIS) for children over 16 and their parents. The tests were all scored by an experienced psychometrician who was unaware of the children's race or adoptive status. We also interviewed the parents about the family's lifestyle, the circumstances of the adoption, and their experiences in raising children of different races.

The fathers in our transracial families tend to be professionals—ministers, engineers and lawyers. Nearly half of the mothers are employed at least part-time as secretaries, nurses, or teachers. Most of the parents are college graduates, but they are not especially wealthy. Many live in areas with a few black neighbors but most rarely see blacks in their daily lives. The households themselves often resembled miniversions of the United Nations, for a number of families adopted children of several races or nationalities in addition to having their own. The average number of children in a family was four, with a range from one to 14.

Of the 321 children in the study, 145 were natural and 176 adopted; 130 of the adoptees were black and 46 either white, Asian, or American Indian. Among the black children, 22 percent had two black parents, 52 percent had one black and one white parent, and 26 percent had one black parent and a parent of unknown or Asian ancestry.

Adoption and IQ The typical adopted child in these families—of any race—scored above the national average on standard IQ tests. But the child's age at adoption and his or her experiences before moving to the new family were strongly related to later IQ. The earlier a child was placed, the fewer disruptions in his life, and the better his care in the first few years, the higher his later IQ score was likely to be. The white adopted children, who found families earlier than any other group, scored 111 on the average; the black adopted children got IQ scores averaging 106; and the Asian and Indian children, who were adopted later than any other group, and more of whom had lived longer in impersonal institutions, scored at the national average, 100.

If the black adopted children had been reared by their natural parents, we would expect their IQ scores to average about 90. We infer these scores from the level of education and the occupations of their biological parents. The black adopted children, however, scored well above the national averages of both blacks and whites, especially if they were adopted early in life. In fact, the *lowest* score of an early-adopted black child, 86, was close to the average for all black children in the nation.

When we compare black and white adoptees, it seems that the white children still have an IQ advantage, 111 to 106. However, the black children had lived with their adoptive families for fewer years than the white children and were younger when we tested them. Adoption at an early age increased the scores of black children to an average of 110. There was a trend for early adoption to increase the IQ scores of white children too, but we have only nine cases in that category.

True to their higher IQ scores, the black adopted children also did better at school, a real-life criterion of intellectual achievement. They scored above the average for Minnesota schoolchildren and above the national average as well on aptitude and achievement tests. In reading and math they scored in the 55th percentile; in comparison, the average ranking for all black children in the Minneapolis-St. Paul area is the 15th percentile.

The adoptive families are clearly doing something that develops intellectual skills in all of their children, adopted or not. These parents were a particularly bright group—with an average IQ of 121 for the fathers and 118 for the mothers—that is reflected in their high levels of education. Their natural children, who have lived in such enriched environments since their birth, scored above the adopted children and slightly below the parents.

The Influences of Birth vs. Breeding When it comes to explaining just why individual children differ in IQ, however, we still don't have a perfect way to separate genetic and environmental influenc-

es. Consider Daniel and Sara, two black children who were adopted before they were six months old. Daniel's adoptive father is a professor of biology and his mother is a high-school English teacher; both have high IQs. They had two children before adopting Daniel. The boy's black natural parents were college students. At the age of eight, Daniel tested out with an IQ of 123.

Sara's adoptive father is a minister, and her mother a housewife; their IQs are average. They have four other children, two of whom were also adopted. Sara's black mother was a nurse's aide who had a 10th-grade education, and her father a construction worker who quit high school in the 11th grade. At the age of eight, Sara's IQ was 98.

Daniel and Sara had a different biological heritage and rearing environment. Which contributed more?

Children are not dealt randomly into adoptive homes like poker hands. Adoption agencies usually try to match the backgrounds of the natural and adoptive parents. As a result, children like Daniel, whose natural parents were well-educated, tend to get placed with adoptive parents who also are bright and have professional careers. So adopted children show an intellectual ability related to that of their natural parents, even though they were not raised by them.

To answer the genetic argument that blacks have lower IQ scores than whites because of their African ancestry, we compared the IQ scores of children who had had one black parent with those who had had two. The 19 children of two black parents got an average score of 97, while the 68 with only one black parent scored 109.

One might leap to the old genetic-deficiency explanation, but the confounding problem is that the two groups had very different placement histories and their mothers differed in amount of education. The children who had two black parents were significantly older when they were adopted, had been in their new homes a shorter time when we tested them, and had had more placements before being adopted. Further, their black natural mothers had less education than the white natural mothers and probably underwent more risks during pregnancy. Prenatal problems can affect a child's intellectual ability.

Intelligence, then—at least as measured by IQ tests—is a result both of environment and genetics, but overall, our study impressed us with the strength of environmental factors. Children whose natural parents had relatively little education and presum-

	IQ scores		
	Number	Average	Range
All adopted children			
Black	130	106	68-144
White	25	111	62-143
Other	21	100	66-129
Early adopted children			
Black	99	110	86-136
White	9	117	99-138
Other		only three cases	
Natural children	144	117	81-150

Comparison of Adopted Children Having either One or Two Black Natural Parents:

	Children with two black parents (29)	Children with one black and one white parent (68)*
IQ	97	109
Age at adoption (in months)	32	9
Length of time in new family (in months)	42	61
Natural mother's education (in years)	10.9	12.4
Adoptive father's IQ	119.5	121.4
Adoptive mother's IQ	116.4	119.2

*Note in all but two of these cases, the pattern was a white woman and a black man.

ably below-average IQs can do extremely well if they grow up in enriched surroundings. If a different environment can cause the IQ scores of black children to shift from a norm of 90 or 95 to 110, then the views advanced by the genetic determinists cannot account for the current IQ gap between blacks and whites. Our work does not rule out genetic contributions to intelligence, but it does demonstrate that a massive environmental change can increase black IQ scores to an above-average level. Social factors, such as age at placement and the adoptive family's characteristics play a strong role in accounting for this increase.

Cooling Out the Controversy The touchy and troubling question is, now what? Schools, as presently run, do not have the far-reaching, intensive impact of the family in the formation and enhancement of a child's intelligence. But no one would be so arrogant or foolhardy to endorse transracial adoption as social policy, shipping black children into white homes with the same furious effort now devoted to bussing them into white schools. On the contrary, many black-action groups are now putting pressure on adoption agencies to make sure that transracial adoption does not occur.

Now we need to find out what goes on in these adoptive families that enhances IQ. From personality tests and observations of the parents we worked with, we know they are generally warm, comfortable, free of anxiety, and relaxed with children. They run democratic households in which adults and kids participate in many activities together. These factors, along with the intellectual stimulation that the children are exposed to, are doubtless involved in their children's higher IQs. We need to look for other intangibles in the things parents give their children and do with them that increase intelligence.

And after we've found all the intangibles, we may want to ask whether IQ should be an overriding middle-class value at all. Intelligence tests do measure how well a child will get on in a white middle-class schoolroom, but tell us nothing about a person's empathy, sociability and altruism, a few blessed virtues that tend to get brushed off the psychologist's test battery.

But for the moment, at least, we have evidence that the black-white IQ gap is neither inevitable nor unchangeable. Smug whites have no cause to rest on biological laurels. The question no longer is why blacks do more poorly on IQ tests than whites. The question is what we are prepared to do about it.

Reading 25

Family Configuration and Intelligence

R. B. Zajonc

In 1962 the average Scholastic Aptitude Test score of high school seniors was 490. In 1975 it barely surpassed 450. This decline has been steady over the last 12 years, and it appears to be continuing. Some

This article is based on the author's contribution to an earlier paper, "Intellectual Environment and Intelligence," by R. B. Zajonc and Gregory B. Markus, which was awarded the AAAS Socio-Psychological Prize for 1975.

educational authorities blame it on television, on the erosion of interest in language skills, or on a widespread craving for freedom of expression that is at odds with disciplined learning, but there is no evidence to support any of these opinions. Nor is there any evidence that the decline in SAT averages is due to the rising numbers of poor and minority students who have taken the tests. In fact, the proportion of such students remained stable in the last several years while SAT scores continued to decrease (1).

In all likelihood a number of diverse conditions converged to precipitate the decline. In this paper, however, the focus is entirely on one set of such factors, those associated with changing family patterns. I shall try to show generally that variations in aggregate intelligence scores are closely associated with variations in patterns of family configuration, and that these aggregate family factors are deeply implicated in the declining SAT scores as a special case of a general phenomenon that manifests itself also in a variety of national, ethnic, regional, racial, and sex differences in intellectual test performance. For the purpose of this argument, I will first summarize a recent theoretical analysis that specifies the conditions under which family configuration may foster or impede intellectual growth. I will then examine some relevant empirical findings, and finally return to the special case of the SAT's.

Table 1 is based on a study by Breland (2) in which the averages of nearly 800,000 candidates on the National Merit Scholarship Qualification Test (NMSQT) were examined as a function of family size and birth order. Five features of these results are of particular significance: (i) NMSQT scores generally decline with increasing family size; (ii) within each family size they decline with birth order; (iii) the rate of decline decreases with successive birth orders; (iv) there is a discontinuity for the only child, who scores below a level that would be expected had intelligence declined monotonically with increasing family size; (v) twins have comparatively low scores.

Such effects of birth order and family size on intellectual test performance have been recently explicated in a theory called the confluence model

(3). In this model, Markus and I try to capture the effects of the immediate intellectual environment on intellectual growth, and to specify how individual differences emerge in the social context of the family. The basic idea of the confluence model is that within the family the intellectual growth of every member is dependent on that of all the other members, and that the rate of this growth depends on the family configuration. Different family configurations constitute different intellectual environments. "Intellectual environment" can be thought of in this context as being some function of the average of the absolute intellectual levels of its members. Note that we are not considering IQ, which is a quantity relative to age, but rather an absolute quantity such as mental age. If the intellectual environment is conceived as an average of all the members' absolute "contributions," then it changes continually as the children develop, and it manifests the most dramatic changes when there is an addition to or departure from the family. Of course, abrupt changes in the environment need not have immediate effects.

The confluence model defines intellectual growth of the individual as a function of his age and represents changes in the rate of this growth by a parameter α_τ which is a function of the intellectual environment in the family at time τ. The following examples illustrate, in a simplified form, the dependence of intellectual growth on the changing family configuration. For the purpose of these examples consider the absolute intellectual levels of the parents to be 30 arbitrary units each, and of the newborn child to be zero. Thus, the intellectual environment at the birth of the first child has an average value of 20. Suppose the second child is born when the intellectual level of the firstborn reaches 4. The second born then enters into an environment of $(30 + 30 + 4 + 0)/4 = 16$. (Note that since the intellectual environment is an average of the absolute intellectual levels of all family members, the individual is included as a part of his own environment.) If a third child is born when the intellectual level of the firstborn has reached, say, 7 and that of the secondborn is at 3, the family intellectual environment will then be reduced to 14.

These examples illustrate a number of significant consequences that the confluence model predicts. It might appear from these examples that intellectual environment should decline with birth order. That is not so. In itself birth order is not an important variable. The model predicts that its effects are

Table 1   Mean Scores on the National Merit Scholarship Qualification Test, 1965, by Place in Family Configuration. [Data from (2)]

Family size	Birth order				
	1	2	3	4	5
1	103.76				
2	106.21	104.44			
3	106.14	103.89	102.71		
4	105.59	103.05	101.30	100.18	
5	104.39	101.71	99.37	97.69	96.87
Twins	98.04				

mediated entirely by the age spacing between siblings. Observe that if the second child is not born until the first reaches an intellectual level of 24, for example, then the newborn enters an environment of $(30 + 30 + 24 + 0)/4 = 21$, which is more favorable than the one of 20 entered by the first-born. Hence, with large enough age gaps between siblings (allowing sufficient time for the earlier born to mature), the negative effects of birth order can be nullified and even reversed.

In principle, the negative effects of family size can also be overcome by age spacing between children. If each child were to be born only after its predecessors reached maturity (to take an extreme example), each successive sibling would enter a progressively more favorable environment, and the average intellectual levels would increase with family size. Of course, older children tend to leave home eventually. Furthermore, biological constraints set limits on the covariation of family size and spacing. Demographic data show that birth intervals invariably decline as family size increases.

The examples above deal only with environment at birth. The confluence model considers the intellectual growth process over time and evaluates all changes in the rates of family members' growth that are caused by the resulting changes in intellectual environment (4).

The growth parameter α_τ, represents an important aspect of this analysis, for it reflects all significant changes in the individual's intellectual environment. But it also reflects the confluent nature of intellectual development within the family context. The intellectual development of all family members is affected by the common familial intellectual milieu. Therefore α_τ is the same for all members at the point in family history τ, a feature of the model which underscores the mutuality of intellectual influences among family members. It may be noted that the later these influences occur in the individual's life, the smaller is their effect (5).

Representing intellectual environment as some function of the average absolute intellectual levels within the family is obviously a simplification of what is an enormously complex process. Clearly, intellectual growth will not be greatly enhanced by a highly favorable environment if there is no interaction between the child and the people around him. The influence of the parents' and siblings' intellectual levels on the child's growth is necessarily mediated by diverse processes of social interaction that vary from family to family. Ideally the parameter α_τ should represent not only the intellectual levels of the family members but also the amount of time each family member spends with the child. The nature of social interaction in the home also influences intellectual growth; a game of tag may not be as conducive to the development of intelligence as a game of chess. This sort of articulation of the parameter α_τ is impracticable at present, not only because of the formal complexity that it would entail but also because we do not yet know how various forms of social interaction contribute to intellectual growth. It will be shown, however, that even though the confluence model ignores much of the richness of the social processes that mediate intellectual growth, it leads to a variety of empirically supported inferences about differences in intellectual test performance among individuals and groups.

FAMILY SIZE

In addition to Breland's study of NMSQT candidates, there are three other studies in which the intellectual test performance of large populations was examined for its relationship to the sort of family variables that, according to the confluence model, influence intellectual development. The earliest of these was carried out in Scotland on 70,000 school children (6). The more recent ones come from France (7) and the Netherlands (8) and report data for 100,000 and 400,000 individuals respectively. They are summarized in Fig. 1. To make them roughly comparable, all the averages have been converted into standard deviation units $[X' = (X - X)/\sigma$, where X's are cell means and X's and σ's are the means and the standard deviations of the samples]. There are a number of interesting similarities and differences among the four samples which can be understood if we analyze them in terms of the confluence model.

All four sets of data, even though they are derived from different tests of intellectual performance, different age groups, different cohorts, and different countries, indicate that intellectual level generally declines with family size. Even in the NMSQT sample, which consists of promising students, there is decline with family size. As a result of the selective factor, however, the effect is attenuated in that sample. In others the effect is quite substantial. In the French and Scottish samples the difference between the IQ's of children from the smallest and

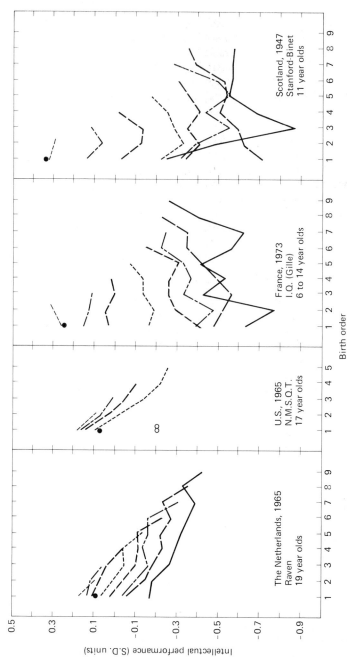

Figure 1 Intellectual performance of four large populations, plotted as function of birth order and family size. Separate curves in each graph represent different family sizes, which can be read from the last birth order on each curve. Solid circles represent only children. The double open circle in the U.S. data represents twins. The years show when data were collected. The means of the Dutch, American, French, and Scottish data set are 2.82, 102.5, 99.2, and 36.74 respectively. The corresponding standard deviations are 1.43, 21.25, 14.53, and 16.10.

the largest families is about one standard deviation (15 points).

It is well known that family size differs across socioeconomic strata and so does intellectual test performance. The possibility that socioeconomic factors mediated these results must be considered. Three socioeconomic levels (SES) were differentiated in the Dutch sample, six in the French. Both sets of data (Fig. 2) reveal that intellectual performance declines with increasing family size independently of SES. In the French sample the partial correlation between family size and IQ was −.45. In fact, it appears that SES contributes to the family size effects only a little, for the correlation rises to only −.47 when SES is allowed to vary freely. Needless to

say, socioeconomic status does affect intelligence scores, a fact that is clear from Fig. 2. The partial correlation between them is .66.

BIRTH ORDER AND SPACING OF SIBLINGS

It is strikingly apparent in Fig. 1 that in the Dutch and American samples intellectual test performance declines with birth order whereas in the French and Scottish there is no such decline *(9)*. According to the confluence model, the effects of birth order are totally mediated by the age gaps between successive children, hence these differences in the effects of birth order must be associated with differences in age gaps.

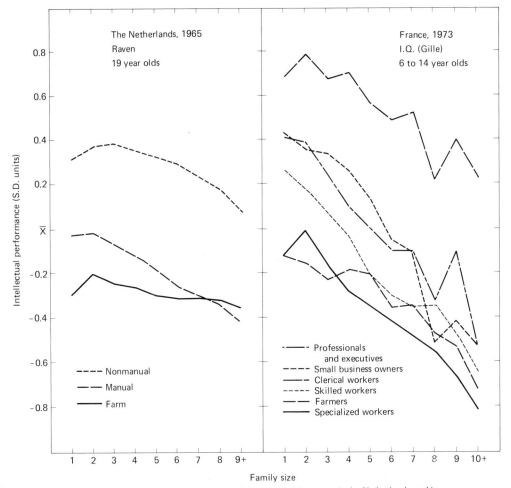

Figure 2 Relation of family size and socioeconomic status to intellectual performance in the Netherlands and in France.

While there is no specific and direct empirical information about age gaps in the four samples, information about national averages in these countries taken from census data can be used. Unfortunately, data on birth intervals are not collected uniformly. (In Scotland no such data were tabulated at all in 1936, when the children in the Scottish sample were born.) Hence, comparisons with regard to birth intervals must rely on indirect indices.

One reliable correlate of birth intervals is, of course, birthrate. When birthrate is high or rising, intervals between successive births are normally quite short; during a period of low or declining birthrate they are longer. For the Dutch subjects (who were born in 1944 to 1946) the corresponding birthrate was rising, from 24.0 in 1944 to 30.2 in 1946. The birthrate in the United States in the year 1948, when most of the NMSQT respondents were born, was 24.2 and also rising. For the French cohorts, however, the birthrate averaged over the years of their births was 18.2 and declining, and the Scottish birthrate in 1936 was 17.9 and declining as well *(10)*. Hence the differences in intellectual performance associated with birth order (Fig. 1) are entirely consistent with the pattern of differences in birthrates in the four countries. Where birth order is

least detrimental to intellectual performance, namely in Scotland, is also where birthrate is lowest.

National averages for intervals between successive births in completed families, that is, families known to have had their last children, have been collected only recently, and they are available for the cohorts from which the French sample was drawn *(11)*. The intervals for completed families of two to six children are reproduced in Fig. 3. They are generally quite long. For some of the points in Fig. 3 comparable data are available from U.S. births of about 1959 *(12)* and from Dutch births of about 1944, both estimated from data on births since marriage tabulated by birth order *(13)*. The American and Dutch intervals are considerably shorter than the French. For example, the intervals between the first and second births in American and Dutch two-child families were 45.7 and 44.6 months respectively; the French interval was over 60 months. The intervals between the second and third births in American and Dutch three-child families were 45.8 and 47.0 months, again more than one year shorter than in the French. Hence the pattern of differences in birth order effects (Fig. 1) is paralleled by a pattern of differences in birth intervals in the four countries such as the confluence model leads us to

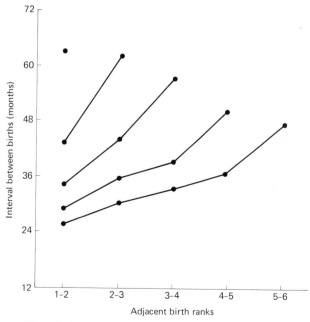

Figure 3 Intervals between successive children in completed French families of two to six children, according to a 1962 survey (11).

expect. For the Dutch and American cohorts, in which there is a general decline in intellectual performance with birth order, birth intervals seem generally to be short. For the French and Scottish samples, which do not show such a decline, they are substantially longer.

An interesting trend is observed in Fig. 3: each successive child appears to be separated from the preceding sibling by an increasingly longer gap. Last children, therefore, come after the longest gap. This trend may explain why there is a quadratic component in the birth order curves shown in Fig. 1, and why there seems to be in some cases an upswing in intelligence for later-born children (14).

One other important factor no doubt contributed to the pattern of results in the French and Scottish birth order data. These scores come from children 6 to 14 years of age and 11 years of age respectively. Obviously, children of those ages who are among the eldest in large families cannot be very widely separated in age from their siblings. The youngest in large families, however, can come from sibships with large or small gaps, hence there is no reason to suppose that the gaps of the later-born children differed from the national averages, which we noted were relatively high. If the short age gaps of earlier-born children depress their intellectual performance, their advantage in order of birth could be nullified. Longer gaps between later-born children in these samples may compensate for the depressing effects of late birth order. Together, these factors would produce a pattern of birth order effects such as was found in the French and Scottish samples. These considerations suggest that the differences in birth order effects among the four national samples in Fig. 1 are associated with differences in age gaps.

There is some other more direct information which indicates that children with large age gaps between them and their younger siblings attain higher intellectual levels than children close in age to younger siblings. In a family of two children, for example, the larger the age separation the longer the older child can remain in an environment undiluted by the presence of an intellectually immature sibling. Long birth intervals give older children the benefits of being in a small family for a longer period of time and during an early phase of growth, which is sensitive to environmental effects. It is also to the advantage of the younger child to postpone its birth, because the later it arrives the more mature will be the environment which it enters at birth and

in which it will develop. Higher IQ's for pairs of widely spaced children than for closely spaced pairs were indeed found by Tabah and Sutter (15). More recently, an extensive study of perinatal effects (16) found that children born after long intervals score four points higher on the Stanford-Binet scale than children born after shorter intervals, a difference that was independent of the socioeconomic status of parents.

EVIDENCE FROM TWINS

Twins score consistently and substantially lower on intelligence tests and other tests of intellectual performance than do nontwins. For example, in the National Merit Scholarship sample (2) twins achieved an average score of 98.0, singly born children an average of 102.57. Tabah and Sutter (15) report an average IQ of 89.2 for twins and 101.2 for singly born children among French 6- to 12-year-olds. Other studies agree with these findings (17, 18). Record, McKeown, and Edwards (19) found an average verbal reasoning score of 95.7 for twins and 91.6 for triplets, which are deficits of .30 and .58 S.D. unit. Admittedly, biological factors may be involved here, but deficits for twins and larger multiple births would also be expected according to the confluence model. Twins have of course the shortest possible gaps between successive siblings. Thus, a family with two singly born children and a family with twins represent quite different intellectual environments. For twins who are the first offspring the intellectual environment at birth is $(30 + 30 + 0 + 0)/4 = 15$. In a two-child family the environment of the first-born is 20, and it must be higher than 15 at the birth of the second child because $(30 + 30 + x + 0)/4 > 15$, since $x > 0$. Hence, with other factors constant, the intellectual environment for twins must necessarily be lower than for either of two singly born siblings.

Perhaps the most important evidence of environmental effects on the intellectual growth of twins comes from another aspect of the Record-McKeown-Edwards study (19). It follows from the confluence model that the intellectual performance of twins who were separated early in life should be higher than of twins reared together. Record et al. report that twins whose co-twins were stillborn or died within four weeks achieve nearly the same average intelligence as nontwins. Table 2 reproduces these data together with the average birth weights of

Table 2 Mean Verbal Reasoning Scores and Mean Birth Weights of Twins, by Fate of Their Co-twins. [Data from (19)]

Sex	Twins whose co-twins					
	Were stillborn, or died in first four weeks			Survived		
	N	Verbal reasoning score	Birth weight (kg)	N	Verbal reasoning score	Birth weight (kg)
Males	85	98.2	2.34	967	93.9	2.58
Females	63	99.3	2.22	948	96.5	2.45
Both sexes	148	98.7	2.29	1924	95.2	2.52

the subjects. The fact that the birth weights of twins who both survive are higher than of those of whom one dies early suggests that physiological factors, for example oxygen deficiency, that are postulated as explaining the relatively low intelligence of multiple-birth children may have been exaggerated (20).

PARENTAL ABSENCE

It follows directly from the confluence model that a one-parent home constitutes an inferior intellectual environment and should result in intellectual deficits, and that early loss of a parent should produce greater deficits than a loss occurring at a later age. In most studies of this effect the absent parent is the father, and their results agree with these inferences (16, 21, 22). For example, fatherless students scored in the 55th percentile on the American College Entrance Examination test, while a comparable group from intact homes scored in the 65th percentile (23). A recent extensive study of desegregation (24) found children from intact homes scoring 100.64 (S.D. 15.05) on a combined mathematical and verbal achievement test, and children from single-parent homes 95.37 (S.D. 13.95)—a difference of one-third of a standard deviation. Other studies show similar effects (25–29). Differences in intelligence and in intellectual performance found between children from fatherless homes and from intact homes are greater the longer the father's absence and the younger the child when loss of the parent occurred (25–27). Interestingly, the most severe deficits are often in the quantitative skills (22, 26). It appears also that, in comparison with other causes of loss of parent, death may have an especial-

ly depressing effect on intellectual performance (30). Although being deprived of a parent is generally accompanied by stress in the home from other sources, such as marital conflict or bereavement, intellectual deficits occur even when the father's absence is temporary and free from these stressful correlates. Children of men in the service (26), for example, and children whose fathers are frequently absent or not readily available because of their occupation, show substantial intellectual and academic lags (25). Restoration of adult presence has beneficial effects. Remarriage of the remaining parent, especially if it occurs early in the child's life, results in improved intellectual performance (30).

Many of the cited studies did not control for socioeconomic factors such as sharp drops in income due to fathers' absence. But deficits in the intellectual test performance of fatherless children are also found when comparisons are made within a single socioeconomic stratum (16). For example, Carlsmith's subjects (26) were all Harvard undergraduates whose fathers had been in military service; absence of these fathers would not have caused appreciable drop in income. Santrock (30) found similar deficits in samples of white lower-class children.

ONLY AND LAST CHILDREN

In all four sets of data in Fig. 1 the only child shows a distinct discontinuity with the family size effect; that is, only children score below a level that would be expected if intelligence increased monotonically with decreasing family size. The discontinuity is fairly pronounced. In three out of the four samples, the only children have lower averages than children from families of two, and in the American and the Dutch data lower than from families of three.

A possible explanation may be that only children have fewer opportunities to be teachers. Children with siblings, especially the older children, show their brothers and sisters how to hold a bat or skip rope, help them tie their shoes, explain to them the meanings of new words and rules of new games, warn them about what may get them into trouble, divulge what they may get away with, spot errors and ineptitude and offer critique. One who has to explain something will see from the other's reactions whether the explanation was well understood, and be prompted to improve the explanation, with the consequence that his or her own understanding of the matter is improved. An active participation in an intellective process is decidedly more instructive than a passive participation (31). Only children do not usually have the chance to serve as such intellectual resources.

Viewing the only child from this perspective makes him or her seem like a lastborn child rather than an anomalous firstborn, which has been the usual characterization (32). The last child also is usually a nonteacher, since he is unlikely to have skills or information that his older siblings might require. It is interesting that the last child, in at least one of the sets of data in Fig. 1, like the only child creates a discontinuity in the observed patterns. The discontinuity of the last child, however, is with respect to the effects of birth order. In the Dutch sample the last child declines more than other children, and this decline occurs in all family sizes. In the Dutch data the discontinuity for the last child is equivalent in magnitude to the discontinuity for the only child (33). Altus (34) reports Scholastic Aptitude Test data from the University of California at Santa Barbara that also fit the foregoing pattern. In two-child families the decline from the first to the second (that is, last) was 20.1 (over one-sixth of a standard deviation). In three-child families the decline from the first to the second child was only 2.1 SAT points, but from the second to the last child was 21.9 points.

The nonteacher deficit can be counteracted in the case of last children. The last child who is born many years after the birth of the next to the last enters an environment of intellectually more mature children—a condition that may overcome the nonteacher handicap. Recall that in France, where lastborns tended to show an upswing rather than a decline (Fig. 1), intervals for last children were especially long (Fig. 3). Intervals for last children are also longer than for earlier ones in the United States (12). Moreover, the teacher role is not entirely closed off to last children, for there must be some occasions when they, too, can serve as resources. For only children the nonteacher handicap cannot be offset or diminished in these ways. The only children should, therefore, produce a consistent discontinuity in the overall family size effect, whereas the discontinuity of the last children in the effect of birth order should be less consistent because of its vulnerability to the effects of spacing. Where the gaps are known to be especially long, as in France, the inordinate drop for the last child disappears (Fig. 1).

If we consider the effects of gaps together with the nonteacher deficit, then the first child represents an interesting case. As was suggested above, a large gap will allow the firstborn to remain in an "undiluted" environment for a longer period of time and hence benefit his or her intellectual development. But during all this time the child must continue to suffer the nonteacher handicap, which may obliterate the favorable effects of an undiluted environment. The trade-off value between the two opposing factors is not known at present. However, since last children have nothing to lose from the postponement of their arrival, they should show greater beneficial effects of large gaps than should first children. Breland (2) reports just such findings for the NMSQT sample. In two-child families, firstborns with large gaps scored .18 S.D. unit and those with short gaps .17 S.D. unit above the mean of the entire sample. In these families, however, secondborn children with long age separations scored .12 unit above the mean and those with short gaps only .05 S.D. unit. In three-child families the pattern was similar.

In general, it would be expected, according to the confluence model, that the larger the interval between adjacent siblings the more likely that the birth-order effect would be reversed, so that the younger child might surpass the older in intellectual attainment. Breland's data are based on observations of individuals who come from different families. Other studies on the effects of age gaps also utilize subjects whose siblings' intelligence scores are not known. There are very few such studies and they show conflicting results (35). Most informative would be within-family differences in IQ and their relation to differences in age gaps. One report (36) that meets this criterion contains intelligence scores of a small number of entire families. The percentages of pairs of adjacent siblings in which the elder surpassed the younger in IQ were computed in each of four categories of age gaps. These were 59.2, 54.9, 51.6, and 51.1 percent for gaps of 12, 24, 36, and 48 or more months respectively.

NATIONAL, REGIONAL, ETHNIC, AND RACIAL DIFFERENCES

There are by now a large number of studies reporting differences in intellectual test performance among different national, regional, and ethnic groups. Some investigators have attempted to find genetic explanations but most of these differences have, in fact, gone unexplained. It is clear that these differences share at least one factor: variations in family configuration. Setting aside the important question of whether the various tests used are appropriate measures of intellectual ability in different populations, we may consider whether the national, regional, ethnic, and racial differences in test performance can perhaps be better understood on the basis of differences in family configuration of populations. For example, in 1960 the American white family contained on the average 2.27 children, the American black family 3.05. White and black families also differ in the length of intervals between children. In the white population the average intervals between the first and second child, the second and third, and the third and fourth were 26.7, 31.8, and 30.6 months respectively. The corresponding figures for the black population were 23.1, 23.0, and 22.3. The IQ's of children born to older mothers are consistently higher (35). It is interesting, therefore, that the white mother is on the average nearly three years older when she bears her first child than is the black mother. Yet another important aspect of family configuration is the presence of adults in the home; we noted above that the absence of a parent has a depressing effect on intellectual development. Among white Americans, in 1960, 1968, 1970, and 1974 there were respectively 6.1, 7.7, 7.8, and 10.4 percent of households with only the mother present. The comparable figures for black households are 19.8, 27.6, 29.3, and 37.8 (37). It would be surprising if these differences in family configuration between whites and blacks were not seriously implicated in the differences sometimes found between these groups in intellectual test performance.

The evidence examined thus far has involved comparisons of intellectual test performance of the individuals' own family patterns. Studies that compare test performance of national or ethnic groups do not as a rule contain family pattern data of their own respondents. However, since they are sampled from populations whose characteristic patterns of family configuration are often known or can be estimated, the association between family factors and intellectual test performance can be examined indirectly. For example, the average IQ's of 5504 children of various ethnic backgrounds in the United States (38) have a correlation with family size in the respective ethnic groups that varies between −.49 and −.69, depending on what demographic index is used to estimate family size (39). A recent international study obtained measures of reading comprehension for three age groups of school children in a number of countries (40). In Fig. 4 reading comprehension scores of one of the age groups (ten-year-olds) is plotted against birthrates in these countries. The intellectual performance scores were obtained in 1971–72; the birthrates are those of 1961–62. The relationship of these scores with the corresponding birthrates is quite strong, and it is nearly as strong in the other age groups.

The French survey referred to earlier (7) reports clear differences in IQ among children from different regions of the country. These are paralleled by differences in family configuration. Table 3 shows both the average IQ in each region and another aggregate index of family configuration—average order of births—which combines two important factors of intellectual environment, family size and birth rank. In many countries birth records include information about the mother's previous pregnancies and that information is summarized in demographic yearbooks. Average order of births can be readily calculated from these reports (41). High values of average order of births for a given year indicate that children born that year have on the average more older siblings and come from larger families. The association between this index and average IQ is clearly evident.

There are, of course, other important differences among groups, regions, and countries besides those in birth rates, order of births, and family size. Differences in economic resources, educational opportunities, linguistic habits, and literacy rates, for example, would contribute to these differences in intellectual performance scores. It is not being argued here that variation in family pattern is the only factor implicated in the intellectual differences.

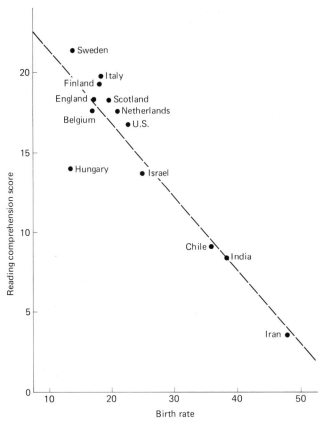

Figure 4 Reading comprehension scores and birth rates (per 1000 population) in 13 countries (40).

SEX DIFFERENCES

The sort of confounding with socioeconomic or genetic factors which obscure the source of the association between family pattern and regional or ethnic differences in intelligence is totally absent with respect to sex differences. In the United States, the Scholastic Aptitude Test scores of males have tended to be somewhat higher on the average than those of females. In the speculation about factors that might account for sex differences in SAT's the possible contribution of family configuration has been thus far overlooked. There are two consistent differences between the position of males and females in the family configuration. First, the intervals following male births are somewhat longer than those following female births *(42)*, probably because of parental preference for male offspring. Second, females are more likely to come late in the sibship

than are males *(43)*. This difference in the average order of births of the two sexes is quite small, but in the United States, for example, it has occurred without exception for at least the last 28 years. A preference regarding the sex of offspring cannot explain this second difference. There are more fetal deaths among males than among females. Also, fetal deaths are more likely to occur in later pregnancies *(44)*. These two factors could combine to produce the consistent sex differences in aggregate birth order.

If sex differences in SAT's are associated with differences in the kinds of family environments that surround males and females, then the magnitudes of sex differences in SAT's should be systematically related to the magnitudes of sex differences in the order of births. In Fig. 5 this association (with both differences expressed in ratios) is shown for years in

Table 3 **Average Order of Live Births in France in 1962 and Average Intelligence of French Children Tested in 1973, by Region (41).**

Region	Mean order of births	Mean IQ	X−X̄
Picardie-Champagne	3.09	96.5	−.19
Nord	3.08	97.7	−.10
Normandie	3.01	98.7	−.03
Poitou-Centre	2.90	98.1	−.08
Bourgogne-Lorraine	2.86	99.8	.05
Bretagne-Loire	2.82	96.5	−.19
Limousin-Auvergne	2.70	97.5	−.12
Alsace-Strasbourg	2.68	98.6	−.04
Sud-Ouest	2.52	99.1	−.01
Sud-Est	2.42	101.1	.13
Region Parisienne	2.27	102.9	.25

which SAT data were published by sex. Except in 1957, the relation between the two ratios is quite strong. In the large NMSQT sample *(2)* the pattern is similar: males achieved an average score of 103.45 and females 101.28, a ratio of 1.021. The ratio of birth orders in that sample, female/male, was 1.013. Since the female high school students who take SAT's (or the NMSQT) come from the same populations as the male, economic, regional, or linguistic differences could not have contributed to this relationship.

TRENDS IN FAMILY CONFIGURATION

Return now to the marked decline in SAT scores. As with the sex differences, short temporal trends in these scores cannot be attributed to socioeconomic factors, let alone to genetic effects. The proportion of poor and minority students remained fairly stable in the period of declining scores *(1)*. Moreover, if the decline in scores were due to increases in the numbers of poor and minority students taking the tests, the main change in the distribution of the scores would be an increase in the proportion of low scorers, without any changes in the absolute numbers of high scorers. That has not been the case. In 1972, for example, there were 53.794 high school seniors with verbal SAT scores of over 650 (two S.D.'s above the mean). In 1973, when the mean

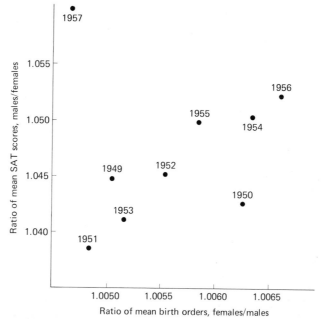

Figure 5 Differences in mean SAT scores of males and females (expressed in ratios) and their relation to sex differences in average orders of live births (also expressed as ratios).

verbal score dropped by 8 points, only 39,779 seniors had such scores *(1)*.

High school seniors for whom average SAT scores are known were born between 1940 and 1957, and the scores can be compared with the corresponding average birth orders of children born in those years (Fig. 6). Except in the World War II years, the association is close indeed *(45)*. During the war years there was considerable fluctuation in birthrate and thus in average orders of births. Also, the proportion taking SAT's was smaller among those cohorts than it is today. But even for the wartime cohorts SAT scores reflect birth order fluctuations to some extent. After 1946 the two trends are virtually parallel. For some recent years the number of high school students with SAT scores above 500 is known. When we compare the percentage of such

students with the percentage of firstborns in the respective cohorts (Fig. 7) the correspondence is also quite striking.

As may also be seen in Fig. 6, in 1962 the average birth order begins to rise markedly. Of the 1947 births 42 percent were first children. In 1962 only 27 percent were first children, but the proportion has been steadily increasing, and last year's births include as large a proportion of firstborns as did the 1947 births. Children born in 1963 will be taking the SAT's in 1980. If average orders of births are reliable predictors of SAT scores, in 1980 ± 2 the alarming downward trend should be reversed. This prospect can be partially verified on younger children, for scores on school tests of children born around 1963 should begin showing increments now. Temporal changes in test scores of Iowa children

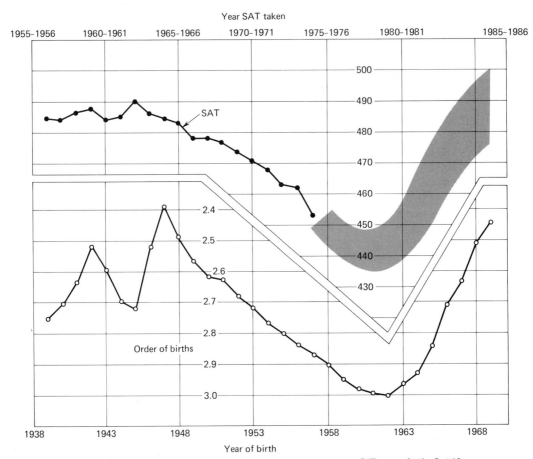

Figure 6 Average order of live births in the United States, 1939 to 1969, and average SAT scores for the first 18 cohorts. Future SAT averages are predicted to lie within the shaded area.

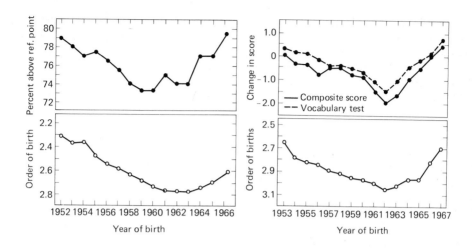

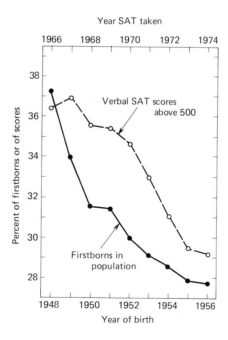

Figure 7 (left). Percentage of SAT scores above 500, 1966 to 1974, and percentage of firstborns in the corresponding cohorts. **Figure 8** (center). Average order of live births in Iowa, 1953 to 1967, and changes in Iowa Basic Skills scores of these cohorts (grades 3 to 8). In the Iowa Basic Skills Testing Program 1965 was designated as the base year, and all scores are reported as deviations from the 1965 average score (46). **Figure 9** (right). Average order of live births in New York State, 1952 to 1966, and percent of third-, sixth-, and ninth-grade pupils who surpassed 1966 reference point in reading skill (47).

born between 1953 and 1967, together with aggregate orders of births in that state, are shown in Fig. 8 *(46)*. There is indeed a rise in scholastic performance which begins exactly with the children born in 1962, when birth orders begin to rise. Similar trends are observed among third-, sixth-, and ninth-graders in New York State (Fig. 9). That state established a testing program in 1966, at which time a "reference point" was chosen for each of the three grades. The percentages of pupils who surpassed that reference point in reading skills (Fig. 9) parallel the changing average order of live births of the cohorts *(47)*. Beginning with children born in 1963 there is a definite rise in test scores which is coincidental with the sharp reversal in birth trends. Several other states have also reported rising test scores recently in lower elementary grades.

SUMMARY AND CONCLUSION

A variety of findings reveal the impact of family configuration on intelligence: (i) Intellectual performance increases with decreasing family size. (ii) Children born early in the sibship perform better on intelligence tests than later children when intervals between successive births are relatively short. (iii) Long inter-sibling spacing appears to cancel the negative effects of birth order and in extreme cases to reverse them. (iv) In general, long intervals enhance intellectual growth. (v) The adverse effects of short intervals are reflected in the typically low IQ's of children of multiple births. (vi) In the special case of only children, the benefits of a small family are apparently counteracted by the lack of opportunities to serve as teachers to younger children. (vii) Last children suffer that handicap too. (viii) Absence of a parent is associated with lower intellectual performance by the children. (ix) Temporal changes in family patterns such as birthrates, average orders of births, intervals between children, and family size are reflected in temporal changes in aggregate measures of intellectual performance. (x) Differences in family patterns between different countries, between different regions of the same country, and between ethnic or racial groups are also associated with differences in aggregate intellectual performance. (xi) Males and females differ in average birth order, and this difference is reflected in aggregate intellectual performance scores.

The pattern of these diverse data is consistent with the analysis of intellectual development based on the confluence model. Of course, not all variation in intelligence is accounted for by variation in family configuration. For example, in the United States the large decline in SAT scores (over ⅓ S.D. in 12 years) cannot be a function of changes in family configuration alone because it is considerably larger than we would expect on the basis of a simple extrapolation from the four national samples in Fig. 1. Nor is all of the sex difference in SAT scores accounted for by the sex difference in orders of births. It should not be overlooked, however, that the average birth orders in these data are based on entire cohorts, whereas SAT's were taken by only 25 percent of the children in these cohorts.

Nor is it claimed that the confluence model generates a unique interpretation of all these facts. For each of them one could probably supply another reasonable explanation. The intellectual deficit of twins could have a biological basis, for example, and the higher intelligence of twins who lost their co-twins may involve unknown genetic factors. The drop in SAT's may be due to a general decline in intellectual interests, and the lower intelligence scores of children living in one-parent homes may be due to a history of conflict or stress. Future research will shed light on these questions. At the moment, however, the confluence model has the advantage of parsimony. And because it makes rather specific predictions, it can be readily verified.

Lest premature implications be drawn from this paper for family planning, education, population growth, or composition of day care centers, another word of caution is called for. IQ isn't everything. Large families may contribute to growth in attributes other than intelligence: social competence, moral responsibility, or ego strength, for example. These or similar family effects are still to be verified, however.

What contribution can the confluence model make to the controversy between the hereditarian and the environmentalist view of intelligence? Clearly, on the basis of the empirical evidence now available, we cannot evaluate the relative importance of the two factors, and the controversy will not be resolved until we know precisely how these factors influence intellectual development. Hereditarians lack information about genetic loci that might transmit intelligence, and environmentalists have not been able to identify the critical features of the environment that generate intellectual effects *(48)*. And the two groups suffer equally from ambiguities about what abilities intelligence tests are assumed to measure in different populations *(49)*. Generally, the environmental case has relied more on attacking the inadequacies of the genetic position than on positive evidence that would establish the role of environmental factors in intellectual development. Moreover, the hereditarian view has had the advantage of a formal model—the polygenic model of parent-offspring resemblance *(50)*—while up to now there has been no parallel formalization of environmental effects.

Some specific derivations with implications for the analysis of genetic effects on intelligence follow directly from the confluence model. Such analysis utilizes estimates of heritability, some of which involve comparisons between correlations of the intelligence of twins and correlations of the intelligence of nontwin siblings. According to the confluence model, such comparisons must suffer from a confounding with birth intervals. The age gap for twins is, of course, constant at zero, whereas age gaps between other siblings vary. If variations in birth intervals affect the early and the later children differentially (as seems to be the case), heritability indices based on sibling correlations without regard to birth intervals are inaccurate. Similarly, parent-offspring correlations, which are also parts of heritability estimates, are inaccurate if they do not control for birth order, birth intervals, and family size. If there is in fact a close relation between IQ of parents and children, and if family factors influence the intercept of the corresponding regression line, then combining over birth order and family size simply adds variance around all the points of the regression line and thus attenuates the over-all coefficient. Third, the interpretation of the close intellectual similarity of separated twins may have underestimated the contribution of environmental factors. According to the confluence model, placing twins in two separate environments makes these environments more similar. If two families of the same size adopt twins (or two other individuals who do not differ in mental age), the average intellectual levels of these families will be necessarily more similar after adoption than previously. These effects may be quite small. Nevertheless, in inferences about genetic effects drawn from adoption studies the influence that the foster child may have on the foster family environment should be considered.

While aggregate data support the confluence model in a variety of ways, its full usefulness can only be determined when its predictions are tested against a substantial sample of family configurations, examined repeatedly over a period of several years. From such data the relation of the environmental variables that it specifies to the total IQ variance in the sample can be measured. Since it is sometimes asserted that as much as 86 percent of this variance is genetically determined, it would be of some interest to establish just how much can be assigned to environmental factors when the analysis begins with them. Judging from the consistency and magnitude of some of the effects reviewed here, it would be surprising if the variables specified by the confluence model did not account for more than the small fraction allowed by heritability analysis to environmental factors and to error. When we have calculated the variance in IQ that is associated with the environmental variables of family size, birth rank, birth intervals, parental absence, and presence of other adults in the home, and with the portion of the parent-offspring covariation that has no genetic bases, the interplay of genetic and environmental forces in intellectual performance will be better understood.

REFERENCES AND NOTES

1. S. A. McCandless, paper presented at the western regional meeting of the College Entrance Examination Board, San Francisco, 1975.
2. H. M. Breland, *Child Dev.* **45,** 1011 (1974).
3. R. B. Zajonc and G. B. Markus, *Psychol. Rev.* **82,** 74 (1975).
4. Absolute intellectual level M*t* attained by a given child at age *t* is assumed to develop as a sigmoid function of age. The only child grows according to the function $f(t) = \alpha_1 [1 - \exp(-k^2t^2)]$, where α_1, the intellectual environment in the family at birth of the child, is a function of the average of the intellectual levels of all family members including the newborn child, and k is an arbitrary constant that varies with the type of intellectual ability examined or with the scale used for its measurement. The first child of a larger family also grows according to the function $f(t)$ until a sibling is born, at which time the firstborn will shift from $f(t)$ to some other function. $g(t) = \alpha_2[- \exp(-k^2t^2)]$, where α_2 is the new intellectual environment that coincides with the birth of the second child. If there is another child still later, the intellectual growth of the firstborn would change to yet another function, $h(t) = \alpha_3[1 - \exp(-k^2t^2)]$, and so on. If the second child is born when the first is t_1 years old, we can estimate the firstborn's absolute intellectual level M at t_2 from the

sum of the two functions $f(t)$ and $g(t)$, where the first is evaluated from age t_0 to age t_1 and the second from t_1 to t_2.

$$M_{12} = f(t)\Big|_{t_0}^{t_1} + g(t)\Big|_{t_1}^{t_2} = \alpha_1[1 - \exp(-k^2t^2)] +$$

$$\alpha_2[1 - \exp(-k_2t_2^2)] - \alpha_2[1 - \exp(-k^2t_1^2)]$$

5 In social and developmental psychology, environmental effects have been generally treated as independent of the individual. Such an approach simplifies analysis, but it is decidedly a misrepresentation of reality. Perhaps when the individual-environment interaction is examined at a fixed point in time an independence of this sort may be assumed. However, when developmental processes and changes over time are involved, specific features of the individual-environment interdependence must be incorporated in the analysis, for if at one time individual A influences the state of individual B, and if later B's state affects the state of A, then A's initial state affects A via changes in B.

Moreover, treating the environment and the individual as independent units not only violates intuitive notions of social reality, it also leads to inaccurate theoretical implications. If the confluence model did not include the individual in calculating his or her own intellectual environment, later-born children would always be predicted to have environments superior to those of earlier-borns. For example, at the birth of the second child the environment of the firstborn would be $(30 + 30 + 0)/3 = 20$ and of the secondborn $(30 + 30 + x)/3 > 20$, because $x > 0$. This advantage of the secondborn would continue throughout the growth process, and a negative birth order effect would invariably be predicted, a theoretical result that is in clear conflict with data in Table 1 and with other results which will be reviewed below.

6 *The Trend of Scottish Intelligence* (Univ. of London Press, London, 1949): the data used in this article were computed from pp. 101–117.

7 *Enquête Nationale sur le Niveau Intellectuel des Enfants d'Age Scolaire* (Institut National d'Etudes Démographiques, Paris, 1973): the data used in this article are from pp. 25–115.

8 Dutch data in this article were recomputed from L. Belmont and F. A. Marolla. *Science* **182**, 1096 (1973).

9 It was conflicting results of this type which prompted some scholars to doubt whether birth order deserves "the heavy investment needed to carry out any more definitive studies" [C. Schooler, *Psychol. Bull.* **78**, 161 (1972)].

10 *Demographic Yearbook* (United Nations Publications, New York, 1954), pp. 252–261: *ibid.* (1965). pp. 276–299. Birthrates are births per 1000 population.

11 J. C. Deville, *Enquête de 1962* (Institut National de la Statistique et des Etudes Economiques, Paris, 1962). The tables were supplied by L. Henry, Institut National d'Etudes Démographiques. Very similar results are reported for 1954 by J. Magaud and L. Henry, *Population* **23**, 879 (1968).

12 Bureau of the Census, *Current Population Reports*, Series P-20, No. 108 (Government Printing Office, Washington, D.C., 1961), pp. 46–48.

13 *Mouvement de la Population* (Institut National de la Statistique et des Etudes Economiques, Paris, 1967), p. 260; *ibid.* (1969), pp. 159, 212, 266. The Dutch data were supplied by H. G. Moors and were calculated by G. B. Markus.

14 The quadratic trend is amplified by averaging sigmoid function assumed here to represent intellectual growth.

15 L. Tabah and J. Sutter, *Ann. Hum. Genet.* **19**, 120 (1954).

16 S. H. Broman *et al.*, *Preschool IQ: Prenatal and Early Developmental Correlates* (Erlbaum, Hillsdale, N.J., 1975).

17 H. L. Koch, *Twins and Twin Relations* (Univ. of Chicago Press, Chicago, 1966).

18 R. B. McCall, M. I. Appelbaum, P. S. Hogarty, *Monogr. Soc. Res. Child Dev.* **38**, 1 (1973); S. N. Mehrotra and T. Maxwell, *Popul. Stud.* **3**, 295 (1949); L. L. Thurstone and R. L. Jenkins, *J. Educ. Psychol.* **20**, 641 (1929).

19 R. G. Record, T. McKeown, J. H. Edwards, *Ann. Hum. Genet. Soc.* **34**, 11 (1970).

20 Prematurity of birth, which is common in twins, was found by Koch *(17)* to be unrelated to twin intelligence. Premature twins were not lower on any of the intellectual performance measures than full-term twins.

21 H. B. Biller, *Parental Deprivation* (Lexington Books, Toronto, 1974).

22 D. B. Lynn, *The Father: His Role in Child Development* (Brooks-Cole, Monterey, Calif., 1974).

23 B. Sutton-Smith, B. G. Rosenberg, F. Landy, *Child Dev.* **39**, 1213 (1968).

24 H. B. Gerard and N. Miller, *School Desegregation* (Plenum, New York, 1975).

25 R. W. Blanchard and H. B. Biller, *Dev. Psychol.* **4**, 301 (1971).

26 L. Carlsmith, *Harv. Educ. Rev.* **34**, 3 (1964).

27 F. Landy, B. G. Rosenberg, B. Sutton-Smith. *Child Dev.* **40**, 941 (1969).

28 E. E. Lessing, S. W. Zagorin, W. Nelson, *J. Genet. Psychol.* **117**, 181 (1970).

29 Note that the early intellectual environment of twins $[(30 + 30 + 0 + 0)/4 = 15]$ is equivalent to that of the single child in a one-parent home $[(30 + 0)/2 = 15]$. It is interesting, therefore, and supportive of the confluence model, that the deficits in test scores of twins and of children from one-parent homes are similar in magnitude.

30 J. W. Santrock, *Child Dev.* **43**, 455 (1972).

31 E. Burnstein, *Psychol. Monogr.* **76**, No. 35 (1962): F. I. M. Craik and R. S. Lockhart, *J. Verb. Learn. Verb. Behav.* **11**, 671 (1972); R. B. Zajonc, *J. Abnorm. Soc. Psychol.* **67**, 96 (1960).

32 J. Sadger, *Fortschr. Med.* **29**, 601 (1911): S. Schachter, *Am. Sociol. Rev.* **28**, 757 (1963).

33 See (*3*, p. 81). The handicap of the lastborn is represented by a separate parameter λ in the confluence model (*3*, p. 86).

34 W. D. Altus, *J. Consult. Psychol.* **29**, 202 (1965).

35 V. G. Cicirelli, *Child Dev.* **38**, 481 (1967): B. G. Rosenberg and B. Sutton-Smith, *Dev. Psychol.* **1**, 661 (1969). A factor that complicates the effects of birth intervals is mother's age at birth of child. Intelligence scores show an increase with maternal age (*16*) that is independent of the effects of birth order [R. G. Record, T. McKeown, J. H. Edwards, *Ann. Hum. Genet.* **33**, 61 (1969)]. The relation between the effects of mother's age and birth interval, however, remains to be determined.

36 M. C. Outhit, *Arch. Psychol.* **149**, 1 (1933).

37 R. Farley and A. Hermalin, *Am. Sociol. Rev.* **36**, 1 (1971). Data for 1970 and 1974 are from an unpublished study by the same authors.

38 N. D. M. Hirsch, *Genet. Psychol. Monogr.* **1**, 231 (1926).

39 Family sizes were computed from *16th Census of the United States* (Government Printing Office, Washington, D.C., 1940), pp. 127–128, 135–136.

40 Data on reading comprehension are from R. L. Thorndike, *Reading Comprehension Education in Fifteen Countries* (Wiley, New York, 1973), birth rates from *Demographic Yearbook*. (United Nations Publications, New York, 1962 to 1964). The data were plotted against birth rates rather than against average orders of births because the latter figures were not available for three of the countries.

41 Order of live births was computed from *Mouvement de la Population* (Institut National de la Statisque et des Etudes Economiques, Paris, 1969, pp. 535–536. Average order of live births is $\Sigma(B_i i)/\Sigma B_i$ where B_i is the number of live births of the order *i*. Eighth and later births were combined letting $(i \geq 8) = 10$.

42 M. P. Schutzenberger, *Sem. Hôp. Paris* **26**, 4458 (1950); G. Wyshak, *J. Biosoc. Sci.* **1**, 337 (1969).

43 M. S. Teitelbaum, *J. Biosoc. Sci.* **2**, Suppl., 61 (1970).

44 J. N. Norris and J. A. Heady, *Lancet* **268** (1955).

45 Birthrates show very similar relationships with SAT trends. For example, the correlation of SAT scores with crude birthrate (births per 1000 population) over the last 18 years is −.61 and with fertility (births per 1000 women of childbearing age) −.71. Minnesota collects scholastic aptitude tests from high school juniors. Over the last 13 years the association between those scores and birth orders in the state was equally high. The scores are in E. O. Swanson. *Student Counseling Bureau Reviews,* vol. 25 (Student Counseling Bureau, University of Minnesota, Minneapolis, 1973), pp. 69–72. The average orders of live births in Minnesota come from *Vital Statistics of the United States,* 1943 to 1955 (Bureau of the Census, Washington, D.C., 1945, 1946; Government Printing Office, Washington, D.C., 1947 to 1957).

46 These figures were computed from data supplied by W. E. Coffman, Director, Iowa Testing Programs. The figures supplied for 1973 and 1974 had been interpolated from 1972 and 1975. Orders of live births for Iowa were computed from *Vital Statistics of the United States. 1953 to 1964 (Government Printing Office, Washington, D.C., 1955 to 1966).*

47 These figures were averaged from data supplied by V. A. Taber, Director, Division of Educational Testing. State University of New York. Albany.

48 L. Erlenmeyer-Kimling and I. F. Jarvik, *Science* **142**, 1477 (1963); J. Hirsch, *Educ. Theory* **25**, 3 (1975); C. Jencks *et al., Inequality: A Reassessment of the Effects of Family and Schooling in America* (Basic Books, New York, 1972); A. R. Jensen, *Harv. Educ. Rev.* **39**, 1 (1969): D. Layzer, *Science* **183**, 1259 (1974): I. A. Rondal, *Psychol. Belg.* **14**, 149 (1974): S. Scarr-Salapatek, *Science* **174**, 1285 (1971), P. Urbach, *Brit. J. Phil. Sci.* **25**, 99 (1974).

49 T. A. Cleary, I. G. Humphreys, S. A. Kendrick, A. Wesman, *Am. Psychol.* **30**, 15 (1975): L. J. Cronbach, *ibid.,* p. 1; D. Wechsler, *ibid.,* p. 135.

50 C. Burt, *Brit. J. Psychol.* **57**, 137 (1966).

51 This research was supported by grant 1-R01 HD08986-01 from the National Institute of Child Health and Human Development. This paper was completed while I held a fellowship at the Center for Advanced Study in the Behavioral Sciences. I am grateful to Patricia B. Gurin, Gregory B. Markus, Richard E. Nisbett, Howard Schuman, Beth Shinn, and especially Hazel J. Markus for their helpful comments and critique. I also thank Benno G. Fricke, Harold B. Gerard, Albert A. Hermalin, Louis Henry, Sam McCandless, Hein G. Moors, and E. W. Swanson for allowing me to have data they collected and for directing me to important sources of other data, and to Louis Gottfried, David Reames, and David Ravid for their assistance in tabulating some of the results reported here.

Reading 26

Concentrations of Sex Hormones in Umbilical-Cord Blood: Their Relation to Sex and Birth Order of Infants

Eleanor E. Maccoby
Charles H. Doering
Carol Nagy Jacklin
Helena Kraemer

There is considerable interest in the role that prenatal and perinatal hormonal factors may play in the postnatal behavioral differentiation of male and female children. Possible influences of biochemical factors in differentiation associated with ordinal position have not been considered. Any differences that have been found in the development of first-born as compared with later-born children have almost always been ascribed to environmental factors, such as parental experience and the presence of siblings in the home. However, some research has found behavioral differences between firstborns and later borns very shortly after birth (e.g., Waldrop & Bell 1966), before family environmental forces have been brought to bear. Such early birth-order differences might be assumed to reflect such parity-related factors as maternal age (and correlated difficulties of pregnancy) or length of labor. However, the possibility exists that some aspects of differential development between first and later borns might be associated with variation in hormonal concentrations at or prior to birth. The present paper reports data on five sex hormones present in the cord blood of three groups of human infants. The behavioral development of these infants is being studied longitudinally through the first 6 years of childhood, and relationships between cord-blood hormones and subsequent behavioral development will be reported elsewhere. The primary objective of the present report is to determine whether, and how, cord-blood hormones are related to the infant's sex and birth order.

The five hormones measured in the present study

are two androgens—testosterone and androstenedione, two estrogens—estrone and estradiol, and progesterone. Out of a large number of reports of hormone concentrations in human umbilical-cord blood only a few report data by sex or birth order. For testosterone, Forest and co-workers have reported higher concentrations in cord blood of males than females (Forest, Cathiard, Bourgeois, & Genoud 1974; Forest, Sizonenko, Cathiard, & Bertrand 1974). With a relatively small number of subjects, Mizuno and colleagues found higher concentrations of androstenedione in the cord blood of males (Mizuno, Lobotsky, Lloyd, Kobayashi, & Murasawa 1968) while Forest and Cathiard (1978) report no sex difference in this hormone. Laatikainen found higher concentration of progesterone in boys (Laatikainen & Peltonen 1974). Forest and Cathiard, on the other hand (1978) report that levels of 17-α-hydroxyprogesterone (a derivative of progesterone) are higher in the cord blood of female infants. No sex differences have been reported for estrogens, but an effect of birth order on estrogen concentrations has been described (Shutt, Smith, & Shearman 1974; Smith, Shutt, & Shearman 1975).

Hormone concentrations have also been studied in the feto-placental unit of subhuman primates. Resko (1974) reports significantly higher levels of testosterone in cord blood of male rhesus monkeys through the last two-thirds of gestation. Conversely, higher levels of estradiol and of progesterone were found in the cord blood of late gestational female fetuses (Resko 1975; Resko, Ploem, & Stadelman 1975). Higher progesterone levels in fetal circulation of female rhesus monkeys were also reported by Hagemenas and Kittinger (1972). The opposite, however, was reported by McDonald and colleagues for rhesus and another species of macaques (McDonald, Yoshinaga, & Greep 1973). It is evident that the existing data on sex and ordinal position differences in concentrations of cord-blood hormones are incomplete and sometimes contradictory.

Data on three new samples of human newborns

The research reported herein was supported by grants from the Ford and Spencer Foundations and from the National Institutes of Health, grant no. ND-09814-03. While the work was in progress, the senior author served as a Fellow at the Boys Town Center, Stanford University. The authors wish to express their indebtedness to Jeff Shindelman for supervising laboratory work on the hormone assays, to Drs. David Hamburg and Keith Brodic for consultation during the planning phases of the project and for their indispensable cooperation in making laboratory facilities available in the Stanford Medical School, and to Sue Dimiceli for the examination of outlying cases that led to the childbirth spacing hypothesis.

are presented here with the objective of amplifying and clarifying existing information.

Method

Subjects   Three groups of infants are included in the study: cohort 1, with 40 males and 35 females, cohort 2, with 32 males and 42 females, and cohort 3, with 53 males and 54 females, for a total of 256 infants.

The infants in cohort 1 were born at a university hospital during July and August 1973. This hospital serves primarily the families of relatively high-income professional and business people, with a smaller admixture of welfare mothers. The infants in cohorts 2 and 3 were born at a nearby general hospital serving a broader socioeconomic group. They were born from January to March 1974 (cohort 2) and August through November 1974 (cohort 3). An infant was included in the study only if no complications occurred during delivery and if its 5-min Apgar score was at least 7. Caesarian births were excluded.

Procedure   At the time of each infant's birth, at least 12 ml of blood were taken from the umbilical cord as soon as it was severed. The blood was predominantly venous, with relatively smaller amounts from the cord artery. The blood was allowed to clot in a refrigerator and the serum was frozen at $-25°$. On the day following the infant's birth, the mother was asked for permission to include the infant in the longitudinal study. For the infants so enrolled (a large majority of those eligible) the frozen serum samples were subsequently analyzed for five hormones. Androstenedione (4-androstene-3, 17-dione), testosterone (17β-hydroxy-4-androsten-3-one), estrone (3-hyroxy-1,3,5(10)-estratrien-17-one), and estradiol (1,3,5(10)-estratriene-3, 17β-diol) were estimated by radioimmunoassay methods established in our laboratory. Progesterone (4-pregnene-3,20-dione) was assayed by a competitive protein binding method. Since not all infants whose cord blood was analyzed remained in the study, the analyses in the remainder of the present paper of sex and birth-order effects involves 234 subjects.

Results

Table 1 shows the mean values for each of the five hormones by sex and birth order. Male infants were

Table 1   Mean Concentrations of Five Cord-Blood Hormones, by Sex and Birth Order (Cohorts combined)

	Male infants		Female infants		F values		
	First-borns	Later borns	First-borns	Later borns	Sex	Birth order	Sex by birth-order interaction
Testosterone:							
Mean (ng/ml)	.297	.266	.212	.213	74.5***	3.62	4.00*
SD	.083	.059	.040	.045	...	...	...
N	60	55	51	65	...	...	...
Androstenedione:							
Mean (ng/ml)	.945	.983	.891	.936	1.60	1.06	.04
SD	.316	.355	.297	.244	...	...	...
N	58	54	52	64	...	...	...
Estrone:							
Mean (ng/ml)	24.74	22.25	25.72	22.51	.017	3.83	.06
SD	9.94	19.34	13.21	10.90	...	...	...
N	61	55	53	65	...	...	...
Estradiol:							
Mean (ng/ml)	8.89	6.87	7.53	6.29	2.57	7.44**	.42
SD	5.59	4.58	3.89	3.87	...	...	...
N	61	55	53	65	...	...	...
Progesterone:							
Mean (μ/ml)	.918	.790	.889	.706	2.16	16.40***	.51
SD	.332	.299	.318	.220	...	...	...
N	61	55	53	65	...	...	...

*$p < .05$.
**$p < .01$.
*** $p < .001$.

born with significantly higher levels of testosterone than female infants. In both sexes firstborns have significantly higher concentrations of estradiol and progesterone than later borns; there is a tendency for them to have more estrone as well ($p < .06$). First-born males have higher levels of testosterone than later-born males, but there is no birth-order difference among females for this hormone.

What accounts for the relationship between cord-blood hormones and birth order? Inspection of the distributions revealed several outlying cases—cases of later-born children who were aberrant in that they had unusually high progesterone concentrations. When these cases were examined in detail, it was found that an unusually long time had elapsed since the birth of their next-older sibling. Following this lead, the hormone values for later-born children in all three cohorts were analyzed in relation to the spacing in age between each child and its next-older sibling. For some of the families in the original analysis of sex by birth order, information concerning the spacing of children could not be obtained (due to families moving away from the area). Hence, only 218 subjects were analyzed.

Figure 1 shows that for later-born male infants testosterone levels are decreased for children born less than 4 years after the preceding sibling. After 4 years or more has elapsed, testosterone levels are approximately equivalent to the levels found in first-born children. Testosterone levels in females remain lower than for males at all points along the spacing continuum, and they are no lower for closely spaced children than they are for first-borns.

For infants of both sexes, progesterone concentrations are lower for closely spaced later borns than they are for firstborns (see fig. 2). For male infants, progesterone values increase as the spacing between siblings increases, so that after a lapse of 4 or more years since the birth of the previous child progesterone values are near to (or even higher than) those of first-borns. Girls do not clearly show this recovery effect.

For boys, values of androstenedione, estrone, and estradiol are lower for closely spaced later borns, with a recovery to or above the firstborn levels as spacing becomes wider. For girls, there is a similar lowering of concentrations for closely spaced later borns, but only a suggestion of recovery with increased spacing. The effects of spacing on the hormone levels of later-born children are clearly greater for male infants. It should be noted, howev-

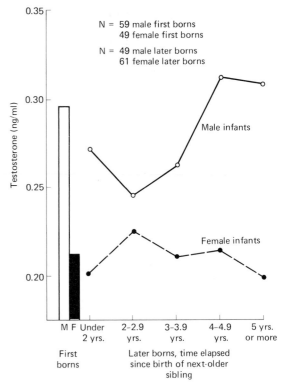

Figure 1 Cord-blood testosterone in relation to spacing of childbirths.

er, that at least in the case of the estrogens and progesterone the interaction is carried primarily by the small group of infants born after a lapse of 5 years or more. The seven boys in this group have extraordinarily high concentrations, with large standard deviations, while the 10 girls have unusually low concentrations. Apart from this group of 10 girls, there is some indication of a recovery curve among female as well as male infants in progesterone and the two estrogens.

The possible implications for subsequent development of males' higher concentrations of testosterone have been widely discussed elsewhere (see Gorski 1977 and Reinisch 1974 for reviews). For our present purposes only a few issues need be mentioned. The first concerns the relation of the hormonal situation prevailing at birth to the long series of biochemical events occurring during gestation. From the time that the fetal testes first become active in the male (at about 6 weeks gestational age), males have higher serum concentrations of testosterone than females, although the females do have small

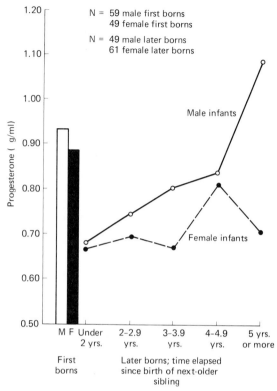

Figure 2 Cord-blood progesterone in relation to spacing of childbirths.

amounts of testosterone derived primarily from androstenedione. The sex difference in concentrations of testosterone is much greater at about 12–16 weeks gestational age than at the time of birth (Faiman, Reyes, & Winter 1974). The critical period during which testosterone directs the male fetus toward development of male rather than female genitalia occurs fairly early in gestation, at the time of greatest activity of the testes (Gandy 1977). Since these events occur so long a time prior to birth, is there any reason to believe that the levels of hormones present in cord blood would have any relevance to subsequent development? A first point is that there are great individual differences, both within and between sexes, in the concentrations of cord-blood testosterone. It may be that these variations reflect the individual differences that were present at earlier points in development, even though the absolute levels were previously higher. At present, nothing is known about whether correlations of this kind exist.

It is important to note that even though the critical period for genital differentiation may occur early in gestation we do not have good information concerning the critical period (if any) for other aspects of physical and behavioral dimorphism between the sexes. There may be several critical periods, some coming much closer to the time of birth. Experiments with lower mammals, in which testosterone has been injected at birth or shortly thereafter, have shown later effects on sexual behavior and other sex-dimorphic behavior (Reinsich 1974). Furthermore, it is known that a relatively high proportion of the testosterone in cord blood is unbound (and hence available to enter target tissues) relative to the state of affairs that prevails a few months after birth. And the nervous system is still in a state of plasticity fostering the uptake of hormonal agents by the relevant target tissues. Thus there is reason to believe that hormones present at or near the time of birth may have effects on subsequent development whether or not they index the levels present at earlier periods of gestation.

The relationships between hormone levels and birth order are largely unexpected. Smith et al. (1975) did find substantially lower estrogen levels in cord blood in multiparous births than in primiparous ones. They were unable to offer an explanation for this observation, especially since there was no significant difference in the duration of labor between multiparous and primiparous parents (Shutt et al. 1974; Smith et al. 1975). We have also found significantly lower concentrations of estradiol in later borns of both sexes, and borderline parity differences in estrone, but the differences are of much smaller magnitude than those reported by Smith et al. (1975). The substantially lower levels of progesterone in later borns were not anticipated in previous work, nor were the birth-order differences in testosterone in male infants. We have found that the birth-order effects in progesterone and testosterone are *not* due to several other factors that covary with birth order: length of labor, mother's age, and the birth weight of the infant. Among later borns (most clearly among later-born males), hormone levels are found to be related to the spacing of childbirths, with closely spaced infants showing lowered levels and widely spaced infants returning to the level of firstborns, or even above.

During gestation, large amounts of progesterone are produced by the placenta. This progesterone is further converted to other sex hormones in the feto-placental unit (Beling 1977; Gandy 1977) with, of course, an additional contribution of testosterone from the testes in the case of male infants. Our findings are consistent with the view that time is required, following childbirth, for the recovery of certain maternal physiological processes involved in gestation, and that the placenta may not be as active in producing progesterone and other hormones derived from it when pregnancies are closely spaced. It is not clear why this "depletion" effect should be greater—and perhaps, recovery from it faster—if the mother is carrying a male fetus.

What are the possible implications of lowered levels of progesterone for the development of closely spaced later borns? The most directly relevant research is that by Dalton (1968), who studied certain aspects of postnatal development of a group of children whose mothers had received at least 500 mg of progesterone during pregnancy as treatment for preeclamptic toxemia. These children were compared with a control group composed of the next child born to a mother in the same hospital ward as the progesterone-treated mother. Dalton reported that the children whose mothers had received the progesterone treatment during gestation were developmentally advanced in standing and walking at the age of 1 year. When these same children were followed up at the age of 9 and 10 years, the progesterone children scored higher on a variety of achievement tests. A follow up of a subgroup in adolescence provided partial confirmation of these findings (Zussman, Note 1), with the advantage of the progesterone-treated group being greatest on tests of quantitative ability. In the most recent follow up (Dalton 1976), a higher proportion of the progesterone-treated group than the control groups is reported to have successfully completed A-level examinations and entered university. A recent reanalysis of Dalton's data has questioned the validity of some of the original conclusions concerning achievement scores (Lynch & Mychalkiw 1978).

A follow-up study of children treated prenatally with medroxyprogesterone (MPA) has not found an effect upon the children's intellectual performance when they are compared with a matched control group (Meyer-Bahlburgh & Ehrhardt 1977). And Reinisch and Karow (1977), studying the effects of prenatal administration of synthetic progestins on the later development of a group of children (compared with their untreated siblings), also report no effects upon intellectual performance. In these studies, the substances administered during preg-

nancy were not identical with that used by Dalton. Therefore their findings may not be regarded as failures to replicate, since their effects upon the CNS (if any) may be quite different. Clearly, however, there is need to replicate Dalton's work on new samples of mothers and infants. Meanwhile, the possibility that variations in concentrations of prenatal progesterone affect postnatal intellectual development must be taken as hypothesis only. If the Dalton claim is supported by further research, then it is possible that our present findings on the relationship between progesterone and the spacing of childbirths has some bearing upon the work of Zajonc and Markus (1975). These investigators show that tested intelligence is greater for firstborns than later borns. Their model also assumes that intelligence will be greater for later borns who are not closely spaced. Their hypothesis is a social one: that intellectual development is facilitated the more a child's interaction partners have a higher mental age than the child's own. The hypothesis may be true, but the present findings suggest that there may be hormonal factors related to spacing which would have similar effects and that these would need to be controlled before the Zajonc and Markus hypothesis can be validly examined.

There may also be implications of lowered hormonal levels for closely spaced later borns with respect to other aspects of development than the intellectual ones. Yalom, Green, and Fisk (1973) have studied the sons of a group of diabetic women to whom exogenous estrogens and progesterone were administered during pregnancy to facilitate carrying the fetus to term. At age 6, these boys were somewhat less interested in sports and somewhat less aggressive than sons of diabetic mothers who did not receive hormonal treatment. At age 16, similar tendencies were identified. In the Zussman follow up of the Dalton sample, adolescent boys who had had prenatal progesterone treatment were somewhat less involved than normal controls in dating and other heterosexual activities. Progesterone-treated girls in this study less often reported that they had been "tomboys" during their primary school years. Reinisch and Karow (1977) report effects of prenatal progestins on personality test scores, and some recent unpublished work by Ehrhardt and Meyer-Bahlberg finds a relationship between prenatal MPA and lowered tomboyism in girls. None of these studies reports relationships strong enough to account for a great deal of variance. Nonetheless they do suggest that the relationships between childbirth-spacing and the cord-blood hormones of infants may have some implications for their future development in the social as well as the intellectual spheres.

REFERENCE NOTE

Zussman, J. U.; Zussman, P. P.; & Dalton, K. Effects of prenatal progesterone on adolescent cognitive and social development. Paper presented at the meeting of the International Academy of Sex Research, Bloomington, Illinois, August 1977.

REFERENCES

Beling, C. Estrogens. In F. Fuchs & A. Klopper (Eds.), *Endocrinology of pregnancy*. 2d ed. New York: Harper & Row, 1977.

Carr, B. R.; Mikhail, G.; & Flickinger, G. L. Column chromatography of steroids on Sephadex LH-20. *Journal of Clinical Endocrinology and Metabolism*, 1971, **33**, 358–360.

Carstensen, H.; Amer, B.; Amer, I.; & Wide, L. The postoperative decrease of plasma testosterone in man after major surgery, in relation to plasma FSH and LH. *Journal of Steroid Biochemistry*, 1973, **4**, 45–50.

Dalton, K. Ante-natal progesterone and intelligence. *British Journal of Psychiatry*, 1968, **114**, 1377–1382.

Dalton, K. Prenatal progesterone and educational attainment. *British Journal of Psychiatry*, 1976, **129**, 438–442.

Doerr, P., & Pirke, K. M. Cortisol-induced suppression of plasma testosterone in normal adult males. *Journal of Clinical Endocrinology and Metabolism*, 1976, **43**, 622–628.

Edqvist, L. E., & Johannson, E. D. B. Radioimmunoassay of oestrone and oestradiol in human and bovine peripheral plasma. *Acta Endocrinologica*, 1972, **71**, 716–730.

Folman, C.; Reyes, F. I.; & Winter, J. S. D. Serum gonadotropin patterns during the perinatal period in man and chimpanzee. In M. G. Forest and J. Bertrand (Eds.), *Endocrinologie sexuelle de la période périnatale*. (Les Colloques de l'Institut National de la Santé et de la Recherche Médicale. Vol. **32**.) Paris: Inserm, 1974.

Forest, M. G., & Cathiard, A. M. Ontogenic study of plasma 17-α Hydroxyprogesterone in the human, I: Postnatal period: evidence for a transient ovarian activity in infancy. *Pediatric Research*, 1978, **12**, 5–11.

Forest, M. G.; Cathiard, A. M.; Bourgeois, J.; & Genoud, J. Androgènes plasmatiques chez le nourrisson normal et prémature, relation avec la maturation de l'axe hypothalamo-hypophysogonadique. Vol. **32**. Paris: Inserm, 1974.

Forest, M. G.; Sizonenko, P. C.; Cathiard, A. M.; &

Bertrand, J. Hypophysogonadal function in humans during the first year of life. *Journal of Clinical Investigation*, 1975, **53**, 819–828.

Gandy, H. M. Androgens. In F. Fuchs & A. Klopper (Eds.), *Endocrinology of Pregnancy* (2d ed.). New York: Harper & Row, 1977.

Gorski, R. A. Gonadal hormones and the perinatal development of neuroendocrine function. In F. Fuchs and A. Klopper (Eds.), *Endocrinology of pregnancy* (2d ed.). New York: Harper & Row, 1977.

Hagemenas, F. C., & Kittinger, G. W. The influence of fetal sex on plasma progesterone levels. *Endocrinology*, 1972, **91**, 253–256.

Kreuz, L. E.; Rose, R. M.; & Jennings, J. R. Suppression of plasma testosterone levels and psychological stress. *Archives of General Psychiatry*, 1972, **26**, 479–482.

Laatikainen, T., & Peltonen, J. Levels of estriol, estriol sulfate, progesterone, and neutral steroid mono- and disulfates in umbilical cord arterial and venous plasma. Vol. **32**. Paris: Inserm, 1974.

Lynch, A., & Mychalkiw, W. Prenatal progesterone, II: Its role in the treatment of pre-eclamptic toxaemia and its effects on the offspring's intelligence: a reappraisal. *Early Human Development*, 1978, **2**(4), 323–339.

McDonald, G. J., Yoshinaga, K., & Greep, R. O. Progesterone values in monkeys near term. *American Journal of Physical Anthropology*, 1973, **38**, 201–206.

Matsumoto, K.; Takeyasu, K.; Mitzutani, S.; Hamanaka, Y.; & Uozumi, T. Plasma testosterone levels following surgical stress in male patients. *Acta Endocrinologica*, 1970, **65**, 11–16.

Meyer-Bahlburg, H., & Ehrhardt, A. A. Effects of prenatal hormone treatments on mental abilities. In R. Gemme & C. C. Wheeler (Eds.), *Progress in sexology*. New York: Plenum, 1977.

Mizuno, M.; Lobotsky, J.; Lloyd, C. W.; Kobayashi, T.; & Murasawa, Y. Plasma androstenedione and testosterone during pregnancy and in the newborn. *Journal of Clinical Endocrinology and Metabolism*, 1968, **28**, 1133–1142.

Murphy, B. E. P. Some studies of the protein-binding of steroids and their application to the routine micro and ultramicro measurement of various steriods in body fluids by competitive protein-binding radioassay. *Journal of Clinical Endrocrinology and Metabolism*, 1967, **28**, 973–990.

Reinisch, J. M. Fetal hormones, the brain, and human sex differences: a heuristic, integrative review of the recent literature. *Archives of Sexual Behavior*, 1974, **3**, 51–87.

Reinisch, J. M., & Karow, W. G. Prenatal exposure to synthetic progestins and estrogens: effects on human development. *Archives of Sexual Behavior*, 1977, **6**, 257–288.

Resko, J. A. Sex steroids in the circulation of the fetal and neonatal rhesus monkey: a comparison between male and female fetuses. Vol **32.** Paris: Inserm, 1974.

Resko, J. A. Fetal hormones and their effect on the differentiation of the central nervous system in primates. *Federation Proceedings,* 1975, **34,** 1650–1655.

Resko, J. A.; Ploem, J. G.; & Stadelman, H. L. Estrogens in fetal and maternal plasma of the rhesus monkey. *Endocrinology,* 1975, **97,** 425–430.

Rodbard, D. Statistical quality control and routine data processing for radioimmunoassays and immuno radiometric assays. *Clinical Chemistry,* 1974, **20,** 1255–1270.

Shutt, D. A.; Smith, I. D.; & Shearman, R. P. Fetal plasma steroids in relation to parturition, III: The effect of parity and method of delivery upon umbilical plasma oestrone and oestradiol levels. *Journal of Obstetrics and Gynaecology of the British Commonwealth,* 1974, **81,** 968–970.

Smith, I. D.; Shutt, D. A.; & Shearman, R. P. Foetal plasma steroid concentrations related to gestational age and method of delivery. *Journal of Steroid Biochemistry,* 1975, **6,** 657–662.

Waldrop, M., & Bell, R. Q. Effects of family size and density of newborn characteristics. *American Journal of Orthopsychiatry,* 1966, **36,** 544–550.

Yalom, I. D.; Green, R.; & Fisk, N. Prenatal exposure to female hormones: effect on psychosexual development in boys. *Archives of General Psychiatry,* 1973, **28,** 554–561.

Zajonc, R. B., & Markus, G. B. Birth order and intellectual development. *Psychological Review,* 1975, **82,** 74–88.

Chapter Seven

The Family

The family has traditionally been viewed as the primary and most powerful agent of socilaization of children. Parents are the initial and most enduring social contacts the child encounters. These early contacts with parents are likely to be critical in shaping children's self-concepts, their expectations in interpersonal relations, and their competence in social situations. In addition the actions, attitudes, and values of the parents which are communicated to the child will serve as a cognitive framework around which the child will organize his or her subsequent perceptions of social standards and appropriate social behavior.

In the United States the nuclear family, consisting of a mother and father and one or more children, has been regarded as the most desirable child-rearing unit. Although shifts in family roles and structure are occurring, the majority of American children and adults still view parental roles in a stereotypical fashion with the father being seen as the powerful, coping decision maker, disciplinarian, and provider, and the mother as the sensitive, nurturant caretaker. In addition, until the past decade the child has been regarded as a passive object of socialization. The use of terms like "child rearing" and "child training" reflects the dominant American behavioristic orientation in which parents are seen to shape the development of children in a unilateral fashion.

Recent changes in theorizing and conceptualizations about family processes and their role in socialization have been some of the most dramatic to occur in the history of child psychology. The family is viewed as an interactive system with the behavior of each family member modifying those of other members in the system. Children are shaping and socializing their parents and siblings as the parents are socializing them.

This mutual shaping of behavior is particularly clearly presented in the paper by Hetherington, Cox, and Cox on family interaction following divorce. Obviously a unidirectional model of family functioning is incomplete and inaccurate whether it is one of the child shaping the parents or the parents shaping the child. The family can be understood only as a multidirectional interactive system.

A second way in which theorizing and research on the family system has changed is in the increasing emphasis on the role of the father. Until recently psychological research on the family was focused on such topics as mother-child relations, mother love, disrupted or deviant mothering, or maternal deprivation. Somehow fathers remained shadowy figures in the background who were seldom mentioned and rarely studied. In reading the papers in this section the student will become aware that this is no longer true. Psychologists are talking about parenting and fathering rather than just mothering. This can be regarded as another reflection of the emphasis on the family as an interactive system. Parke and Sawin in their paper expose some of the fallacies in our beliefs about fathers based on their careful analyses of parent-infant interaction. Hetherington, too, in her study is concerned with the impact of divorce on the entire family system.

Finally, our theorizing and research on the functioning of the American family is changing. Many of these changes are associated with intentional or unintentional shifts in sex roles, particularly in maternal and paternal roles in the family. How has the rising divorce rate and increase in unwed mothers, and maternal employment, or the breakdown in the intended family and other family support systems contributed to the welfare or lack of well-being of our children? What will be the impact of the women's liberation movement, or of greater accessibility of day care and other child-care innovations, on the family?

The family system is changing and alternate life-styles emerging so rapidly that viewing the nuclear family as the only acceptable social unit in which to facilitate the development of competence in children seems naïve. In a country in which one out of every six children is growing up in a single-parent home, it is necessary to study these families and alternative life-styles to discover what aspects of their functioning interfere with or enhance the well-being of children. In situations where social or political experiments in restructuring the family and child-rearing unit have occurred, such as those reported in David Lynn's article, what are the effects on family members?

Neither the nuclear family nor the alternatives to it provide an ideal milieu for the fulfillment of its members. Social institutions cannot remain stable. They must change and evolve in the search for satisfaction of the needs of their members. Alternative life-styles and alterations in family structure can be regarded as a positive step in the quest for an improved society. However, transitions often have unfortunate concomitants. Society needs to provide a variety of support systems to parents and children in their exploration of new social contexts in which to grow and develop.

Day care has been viewed as an important support system, especially for families in which both parents work and for single parent households. Belsky and Steinberg review the effects of day care on children.

Finally, although the family has been viewed as the most important early agent of socialization, the child is engaged in many other social systems such as the peer system, the school, and the neighborhood. Little is known about relationships among these systems. George and Main study the social interactions of young abused children and find that the effects of child abuse extend beyond the boundaries of the home into relations with caretakers and peers in day care centers. As we move on to look at some of the extrafamilial agents of socialization such as peers and the school and mass media in the following sections it is important to remember that none of these systems functions in isolation; each is part of the broad interacting social network of the child.

Reading 27

Father-Infant Interaction in the Newborn Period: A Re-evaluation of Some Current Myths

Ross D. Parke
Douglas B. Sawin

In spite of the theoretical interest and research activity in the area of mother-infant interaction, the role of the father in infancy remains relatively unexplored. Although the father is often recognized in theoretical discussions as playing an important role in the child's development, it is generally assumed that his role begins to take on importance only in late infancy and early childhood. This theoretical assumption is combined with the fact that fathers are also assigned a secondary position by both the culture as well as by psychology theorists. There are a number of strands of evidence that have maintained this view.

    1 Cultural
    2 Historical
    3 Animal evidence
    4 Hormonal evidence

CULTURAL

In Western, industrialized society there has been a clear set of roles prescribed for males and females, with child care being assigned almost exclusively to the mother. In fact, as Josselyn (1956) has noted, it is even considered inappropriate in our culture for fathers to be nurturant toward their infants. Nor is the attitude restricted to our own culture: an examination of other cultures suggests a similar demarcation of roles with the mother nearly always being the primary caretaker. In part, this was due to the assumption that the feeding context was critical for adequate development of social responsiveness.

HISTORICAL

In addition to cross-cultural comparisons, historical roles have been examined with the same result. Over a wide span of history and across a large variety of economies, the father has played a minor role in the care of infants and children.

Paper presented as part of a symposium, "Fathers and Infants," at the American Psychological Association, Chicago, September 1, 1975.

ANIMAL COMPARISONS

In addition to cultural and historical sources, evidence from the organization and behavior of animals has been examined, in part, to determine the extent to which these role allocations are prevalent among animals. Typically cited are studies of non-human primates either in captivity or in the wild. For example, DeVore (1963) found that the cynocephalus baboons take little interest in infants and play a protective role for the troupe as a whole. Few instances of either play or caretaking were observed.

Lab studies often present a similar picture. In a study from Harlow's lab, a 20–40 day old infant was introduced to male-female pairs of preadolescent monkeys. Again, the males played a lesser role: females were 4 times as likely to express nurturant behavior to an infant while the male was 10 times as hostile.

HORMONAL BASES OF "CARETAKING BEHAVIOR"

Although there is little information at the human level, there is considerable evidence that "caretaking behavior" is to some extent under hormonal control. Studies with rats (Rosenblatt & Moltz) have demonstrated that virgin females treated with female hormones show maternal behavior more rapidly. In short, the hormones associated with pregnancy and parturition "prime" the female to engage in caretaking activities.

On the basis of this kind of evidence a series of "myths" about fathers and their role in relation to the young infant has emerged. Let me list a few of the "father myths."

MYTHS

    1 Fathers are uninterested in and uninvolved with newborn infants.
    2 Fathers are less nurturant toward infants than mothers.

3 Fathers prefer non-caretaking roles and leave the caretaking up to mother.

4 Fathers are less competent than mothers to care for newborn infants.

To examine the validity of the propositions, let us take two approaches. First, let us point out the exceptions and qualifications surrounding the cultural, historical, animal and hormonal arguments. Secondly, and more importantly, let me briefly review some of the recent research evidence from our laboratory concerning the father's role in the newborn period.

First, there are cultures in which males and females play a more equal role in the care of young children. For example, among the Trobrianders of Melanesia the father has considerable share in the care of young children—feeding them, carrying them, and caretaking them.

Second, the historical argument is usually misused, because it implies an inevitability that role relations are biased by prior arrangements. Moreover, the argument ignores secular trends that reflect shifts in technological and economic spheres which are supporting the possibilities of new roles for males and females. As students of socialization it is important to consistently monitor shifts in the larger social and economic structure may, in turn, affect the definition and allocation of sex roles. In our preoccupation with the research for general laws, too often we have ignored the tenuousness of our findings in light of shifts in social economic and possibly medical practices.

To cite a single example, consider the impact of bottle feeding;by a single stroke, fathers were able to overcome a biological difference which limited their participation in caretaking of young infants.

In a similar vein, research evidence can often affect historical trends. For example, Harlow—a notorious advocate of traditional sex typed roles—is, in part, responsible for the recent interest in fathers by his demonstrations that "contact comfort" was probably more important than the feeding situation for social development. Even without the invention of bottle feeding, fathers were suddenly put in a position where they were just as capable as mothers of providing the important ingredients for proper early development. Harlow, to date, has not commented on his apparently inadvertent contribution to the women's liberation movement.

Closely related to this issue is the old distinction within psychology that needs to be brought to bear on the present context, namely the competence/performance distinction. Too often the fact of low father involvement throughout history in the caretaking of children has been extended to the conclusion that the low involvement indicated low competence. However, the fact that historical, social and economic arrangements meant that fathers were allocated to other roles *need not necessarily imply that they are incapable of assuming a caretaking function.*

In fact, recent animal evidence has demonstrated that males can assume a parental role via-à-vis infants. As Mitchell, Redican & Gomber (1974) point out: "While adult male rhesus monkeys rarely display parental behavior in the wild, they are certainly capable of doing so when given the opportunity in the laboratory" (pg. 8).

Nor can the hormonal evidence remain unqualified. As Maccoby & Jacklin (1974) recently concluded, "the hormones associated with pregnancy, childbirth and lactation are not necessary for the appearance of parental behavior. With sufficient exposure to newborns, virgin females and males will show parental behavior—although the behavior is not so readily aroused as it is in a female that has been hormonally primed" (p. 219). In short, hormones help, but are necessary for the arousal of maintenenace of parental responsivity.

In light of this evidence, it will come as little surprise that most of the "myths" are just that. Let us take each myth in turn.

Myth 1 Fathers are uninterested and uninvolved with newborn infants. *Evidence:* To evaluate this proposition, an observational study was conducted involving the mother-father-infant triad. Observations took place in the mother's hospital room between 6 and 48 hours after delivery. The sample was white, middle-class and well educated. All fathers but one were present at labor and delivery. About half of the couples attended Lamaze classes. All were first born. The procedure was as follows: the child was brought to the mother's room and the parents were asked, "Whom shall I give the baby to?" This permitted an evaluation of who held the baby first and for how long. The family was observed for 10 minutes and a time sampling observational procedure was used. The 10-minute period was divided into 40 15-second intervals and for each interval, the observer recorded the occurrence of the following infant or parent behaviors. For the infant: cry, vocalize, move, mouth movements with or without object, look at mother, father, around. For the parents: looks, smiles, vocalizes, hold, kiss, touch, imitate, explore, feed, hand over to other parent.

First, the results indicated that fathers were just as involved as mothers and the mothers and fathers did not differ on the majority of measures. In fact, fathers tended to hold the infant more than mothers and rock the infant in their arms more than mothers. Fathers, in short, in a context where it is *unnecessary* to participate are just as involved as the mother in interaction with their infants.

However, there is a variety of questions that could be raised about this study. First, the context is unique since the mother and father were together and possibly the high degree of father-infant interaction observed in the initial study was due to the supporting presence of the mother. Therefore, in the next study, the father was observed alone with the newborn as well as with the mother.

Moreover, the sample of fathers in the original study were unqiue in other ways that may have contributed to their high degree of interaction with their infant. Over half of the fathers had attended Lamaze childbirth classes and with one exception, all fathers were present during the delivery of the child. Both of these factors are likely to have increased the fathers' later involvement with their infants.

Finally, these fathers were well educated and middle class, and their high degree of involvement may be unique to middle-class groups; parental involvement may be less in lower-class samples due to a more rigid definition of parental roles among lower-class parents. To overcome the sample limitations of the original study, a group of lower-class fathers who neither participated in childbirth classes nor were present during delivery were observed. This study permitted a much more stringent test of father-infant involvement and permitted wider generalization of the previous findings. Little support is available for Myth 1.

But possibly fathers are less nurturant than mothers—Myth 2. A close look at the types of activities that mothers and fathers engaged in provides little support for this argument. Fathers were just as nurturant as mothers. In a first study, they touched, looked, vocalized, and kissed their newborn offspring just as often as did mothers. In a second study, an even more striking picture

emerged—with the father exhibiting more nurturant behavior in the triadic context than the mother and an equal amount when alone with the baby.

There was a single nurturant behavior—smiling—in which the mother surpassed the father—in both studies.

The triadic context, however, did affect the rate of smiling: both mothers and fathers smiled more at the baby when a spouse was present than absent.

Two myths down, two to go. Myth 3 states that fathers play a less active role in caretaking activities than mothers. In both studies, the parents were free to feed the baby, but were not requested to do so. In the first study, mothers did feed more than fathers—but with 13 of 19 families breast feeding, this is no great surprise. A more legitimate comparison comes from our second study in which all babies were bottle fed. While fathers were more likely to feed than mother when both parents were present, fathers fed significantly *less* than mothers when they were along with the baby.

Additional evidence comes from a more recent study, which provides a more detailed examination of early parent-infant interaction in a specific context—feeding. Instead of a time-sampling procedure, behaviors were recorded in sequence along a continuous time line. For this purpose, a Datamyte keyboard was used, which is a 10-key device permitting behaviors which have been assigned numerical values to be punched into the system. The keys are tone-related and record the auditory pattern on a cassette tape; in turn, this produces a printout of numerical values (*i.e.,* behaviors) in their order of occurrence and their time of occurrence.

This permits the following types of data: (1) frequency of occurrence of each parent and infant behavior; (2) duration of each parent and infant behavior; (3) the average duration of each parent and infant behavior; (4) a set of rules have been developed which define contingent sequences of interaction between the infant and his caretaker. Two sets of sequences are derived from the interaction data: (a) infant-elicited parent behavior, whereby the probability of occurrence of various parental behaviors are determined in response to an infant-signal (*e.g.,* crying, moving, sucking, etc.); (b) parent-elicited infant behavior whereby the probability of occurrence of various infant behavior is determined in response to a parental stimulus input (touch, rock, vocalize, etc.).

Again, mothers spend more time engaged in caretaking activities, such as burping, wiping the baby's face, checking and changing diapers and grooming activities than fathers.

In summary, Myth 3 is not completely invalid: mothers do spend more time engaged in feeding and related caretaking activities than fathers in the newborn period.

The correlated Myth 4, however, needs to be explored as well. This myth states that fathers are less competent than mothers to care for newborn infants. How do we measure "competence?" A variety of approaches is possible, but one approach is to measure the parent's sensitivity to infant cues in the feeding context. Success in caretaking, to a large degree, is dependent on the parent's ability to correctly "read" or interpret the infant's behavior so that their own behavior can be regulated in order to achieve some interaction goal. To illustrate, in the feeding context, the aim of the parent is to facilitate the food intake of the infant; the infant, in turn, by a variety of behaviors, such as sucking, burping, coughing, provides the caretaker with feedback concerning the effectiveness and ineffectiveness of their current behavior in maintaining the food intake process. In this context, one approach to the competence issues involves an examination of the degree to which the caretaker modifies his/her behavior in response to a set of infant cues.

Let me briefly describe how this was measured. We asked what changes in probability of a particular parental behavior occurred in the 10-second interval following an infant behavior. In other words, if an infant emits behavior, what happens in the next 10-second interval in terms of the parent's behavior

A brief methodological note is in order. Since behaviors occur with different frequencies throughout an interaction session it is necessary to determine the unconditional or baseline probabilities of the occurrence of the target parent behavior. To do this, the probability that a parent behavior occurred in each of the sixty 10-second intervals of the interaction session was calculated. If there are no sequential dependencies of any behavior with the infant trigger variable, we would expect the behaviors to follow the infant trigger in proportion to their unconditional occurrence in the total data set.

To illustrate how this system works, consider the following example. A powerful infant signal in the feeding context is an auditory distress signal, such as a cough, spit up, or sneeze. The main reaction of parents to this signal is, quite sensibly, to stop feeding and the parent does this with a conditional probability .33. However the unconditional probability of this parent behavior—stop feed—occurring is quite low (.05). Similarly, parents vocalize with an unconditional probability of .27, but vocalize with a probability of .45 when the infant sneezes, spits up, or coughs. In addition, the parent unconditional probability of looking closely is .12, which doubles to .25 whenever the infant spits or coughs. Touching, on the other hand, is inhibited slightly by this type of infant signal. Mothers and fathers differ but only slightly: mothers have a probability of stopping their feeding activity of (.27) while fathers cease feeding with a high probability (.35). Similarly, mothers look more closely (.28) than do fathers (.21) in this feeding context. Finally, touching is dramatically reduced for fathers, (.03) from a baseline probability of .12 while mothers increase their touching slightly to .14.

There are sex of parent × sex of infant interactions as well. Mothers are more likely to stop feeding a boy (.40) than a girl (.23) when the infant spits up or coughs. Second, mothers touch a boy (.23) to a much greater extent than girls (.02) in response to this type of signal. Similarly, she is more likely to vocalize to a girl (.48 for conditional probability vs. baseline probability of .23) than a boy (.40 for conditional vs. .27 for baseline). The importance of this approach becomes clear by comparing these results with the previously noted patterns yielded by both the frequency and duration of lesser involvement of the father in the feeding context—either in terms of time spent in this task or in terms of the extent to which paternal behavior was significantly related to feeding related infant cues. However, these conditional probability results suggest a corrective to this earlier pattern. Although he may spend less time overall, *he is as sensitive as the mother to infant cues in the feeding context.* Moreover, the amount of milk consumed by the infants with their mothers and fathers was very similar (1.3 oz. vs. 1.2 of mothers and fathers respectively). By further adjusting, for the difference in amount of time engaged in feeding the mothers and fathers amount is nearly identical. In short, fathers and mothers are not only similar in their sensitivity, but also strikingly similar in the amount of milk that they succeed in feeding the baby.

In terms of our fourth myth, then, our data indicate that fathers are competent in caretaking as indexed by our sensitivity and feeding induces.

Overall, our data indicate that:

a fathers are interested in newborns and if provided with the opportunity, do become involved;

b are just as nurturant in their interactions with newborns as mothers;

c apparently do engage in less caretaking, but;

d are capable and competent to execute at least some caretaking activities.

Before leaving our data, however, let me point out that there are qualitative differences between mothers and fathers that emerge from an examination of the sex and ordinal position of the infant. Moreover, some of the differences are clearly consistent with cultural stereotypes concerning parent preferences and especially father preferences. Let me cite one example to illustrate the necessity for qualification of these general patterns. In one of our studies (Parke & O'Leary, 1975), we found that fathers touched first born boys more than either later born boys or girls of either ordinal position. Fathers vocalized more to first born boys than first born girls, while they vocalized equally to later born infants irrespective of their sex. A similar finding has emerged from our sequential analyses of the impact of infant vocalizations on parent behavior. Fathers are particularly likely to react to this infant cue by vocalizing—but especially in the case of the male infant. Clearly there may be some bases to the claim that fathers really do prefer boys—especially first born boys. These data are consistent with Pedersen's (1975) recent finding that variations in father behavior were related to the behavior of male three-month-old infants—but there was no relationship for fathering and female infants. Caution must be exercised in generalizing from these data since all observations were made in the newborn period. Moreover, there is little doubt that father's role and involvements shifts with age of the infant. However, in view of the assumption that involvement typically comes later in the infant's development, our data take on increased corrective significance. Observational data on the father-infant interaction in the home is currently being collected in order to determine whether or not the amount and/or patterns of father-infant interaction during the newborn period are of predictive value for later behavior.

However, the newborn period need not be viewed as simply a starting point for observation, but as a potentially important intervention point as well. For fathers, in spite of their interest and competence, clearly need support—just as mothers need support. Moreover, it is assumed that paternal behavior can be modified, both quantitatively and qualitatively by early intervention. As Klaus, Leiderman, and others have shown, mothers who are given extended contact with their infants over the first three post-delivery days were more stimulating later at one month and even one year. In light of this demonstration, it is probably important to provide this opportunity for fathers as well, if their nurturant and caretaking capacities are to be fully actualized in post-hospital contexts.

In fact, there is recent evidence from Sweden (Lind, 1974) that fathers who were provided the opportunity to learn and practice basic caretaking skills during the post-partum hospital period were more involved with their infants at six months.

The next task is to provide cultural supports for these potential activities—by modifying hospital visiting arrangements, providing paternity leaves, making available training classes so that fathers will have the opportunity to both learn and practice caretaking skills which in turn will not only make it more likely that he will share these responsibilities, but that he will execute these tasks effectively and view these behaviors as role consistent.

The slaying of myths should be viewed as only a first step; the important task of specifying the changes in father-infant interaction and involvement and indicating how these shifts will affect both the mother and the infant remains to be undertaken. In conclusion, it seems that Margaret Mead's famous dictum that "fathers are a biological necessity, but a social accident" is no longer valid.

REFERENCES

Biller, H. B. *Father, child and sex role.* Lexington, Mass.: D. C. Heath, 1971.

Chamove, A., Harlow, H. F., and Mitchell, G. D. Sex differences in the infant-directed behavior of preadolescent rhesus monkeys. *Child Development,* 1967, *38,* 329–335.

DeVore, I. Mother-infant relations in free ranging baboons. In H. L. Rheingold (Ed.), *Maternal behavior in mammals.* New York: Wiley, 1963.

Harlow, H. F. The nature of love. *American Psychologist,* 1958, *13,* 673–685.

Josselyn, I. M. Cultural forces, motherliness, and fatherliness. *American Journal of Orthopsychiatry,* 1956, *26,* 264–271.

Lind, R. Observations after delivery of communications between mother-infant-father. Paper presented at the International Congress of Pediatrics. Buenos Aires, October, 1974.

Lynn, D. B. *The father: His role in child development.* Monterey: Brooks Cole, 1974.

Maccoby, E. E., & Jacklin, C. N. *The psychology of sex differences.* Stanford: Stanford University Press, 1974.

Mitchell, G. D. Paternalistic behavior in primates. *Psychological Bulletin,* 1969, *71,* 399–417.

Mitchell, G. D., Redican, W. K., & Gomber, J. Males can raise babies. *Psychology Today,* 1974, *7,* 63–67.

Moltz, H., Lubin, M., Leon, M., & Numan, M. Hormonal induction of maternal behavior in the overiectomized rat. *Physiology and Behavior,* 1970, *5,* 1373–1377.

Parke, R. D., & O'Leary, S. E. Father-mother-infant interaction in the newborn period: Some findings, some observations and some unresolved issues. In K. Riegel

& J. Meacham (Eds.), *The developing individual in a changing world, Vol. II, Social and environmental issues.* The Hague: Mouton, 1975.

Parke, R. D., O'Leary, S. E., & West, S. Mother-father-newborn interaction: Effects of maternal medication, labor and sex of infant. *Proceedings of the American Psychological Association,* 1972, 85–86.

Parke, R. D., & Sawin, D. B. Infant characteristics and behavior as elicitors of maternal and paternal responsibility in the newborn period. Paper presented at the Biannual meeting of the Society for Research in Child Development, Denver, April, 1975.

Pedersen, F. A. Mother, father and infant as an interactive system. Paper presented at the Annual Convention of the American Psychological Association, Chicago, September, 1975.

Rosenblatt, J. S. The development of maternal responsiveness in the rat. *American Journal of Orthopsychiatry,* 1969, *39,* 36–56.

Stephens, H. N. *The family in cross-cultural perspective.* New York: Holt, Rinehart, & Winston, 1963.

Reading 28

The Aftermath of Divorce

E. Mavis Hetherington
Martha Cox
Roger Cox

The incidence of divorce has increased dramatically over the past decade. If the divorce rate stabilized at its 1974 level, it is estimated that over 40% of new marriages will ultimately end in divorce. In addition, although the birth rate in the United States is declining, the number of divorces involving children is rising. While the rate of remarriages has also risen, it has not kept pace with the divorce rate, especially in families where children are involved. Thus, during the past ten years there has been an increase in the proportion of divorced persons, particularly divorced parents, relative to partners in intact marriages (Bronfenbrenner, 1975).

In divorces in which children are involved, except under unusual circumstances, the mother usually gains custody of the child. Although the proportion of children living with their divorced fathers is increasing, in the latest yearly Population Survey by the Census Bureau only 8.4% of children of divorced parents were reported to reside with their father (Current Population Report Series P-20,

1975). Thus the most frequently found family condition in the immediate post-divorce situation is one in which a child is living in a home with a single mother, and is having intermittent or no contact with the father. It may be because of these circumstances that, in studying divorce, social scientists have focused on the impact of divorce on mothers and children rather than on the entire family system including the father. Even in studies with these restricted perspectives, the approach has been largely descriptive. The characteristics of divorced mothers and their children are described and compared to those of mothers and children in intact homes (Biller 1974; Herzog & Sudia 1973; Hetherington & Deur 1971; Lynn 1974). Attempts to study changes in family interaction and functioning following divorce are rare.

Divorce can be viewed as a critical event which affects the entire family system, and the functioning and interactions of the members within that system. In order to get a true picture of the impact of divorce, its effects on the divorced parents and on the children must be examined.

The findings to be reported are part of a two-year longitudinal study of the impact of divorce on family functioning and the development of children. The first goal of the larger study was to examine responses to the family crisis of divorce and patterns of reorganization of the family over the two-year period following divorce. It was assumed that the family system would go through a period of disorganization immediately after the divorce, followed by recovery, reorganization, and eventual attainment of a new pattern of equilibrium. The second goal was to examine the characteristics of family members that contributed to variations in family processes. The third goal was to examine the effects of variations in family interaction and structure on the development of children.

In this paper we will focus on change and stresses experienced by family members and factors related to alterations in parent-child interaction in the two years following divorce.

METHOD

Subjects

The original sample was composed of 72 white, middle-class children (36 boys, 36 girls) and of their divorced parents from homes in which custody had been granted to the mother, and the same number of children and parents from intact homes. The mean ages of the divorced mothers and fathers, and of mothers and fathers from intact families, were 27.2, 29.6, 27.4 and 30.1, respectively. All parents were high school graduates and the large majority of the parents had some college education or advanced training beyond high school. Divorced parents were identified and contacted through court records and lawyers. Only families with a child attending nursery school, who served as the target child, were included in the study. The intact families were a sample selected on the basis of having a child of the same sex, age, and birth order in the same nursery school as a child from a divorced family. In addition, an attempt was made to match parents on age, education, and length of marriage. Only first- and second-born children were used in the study. The final sample consisted of 24 families in each of the groups, a total of 96 families on which complete data was available. Sample attrition was largely due to

remarriage in the divorced families (19 men, 10 women), separation or divorce in the intact sample (five families), relocation of a family or parent, lack of cooperation by schools which made important measures on the child unavailable, and eight families who no longer wished to participate in the study. Since one of the interests in the investigation was to determine how mothers and children functioned in father-absent homes and how their functioning might be related to deviant or nondeviant behavior in children, families with stepparents were excluded from this study but remained in a stepparent study. In the analyses to be presented, six families were randomly dropped from groups to maintain equal sizes in groups.

When a reduction in sample size occurs from 144 families to 96 families, bias in the sample immediately becomes a concern. On demographic characteristics such as age, religion, education, income, occupation, family size, and maternal employment there were no differences between subjects who dropped out or were excluded from the sample and those who remained. When a family was no longer included in the study, a comparative analysis was done of their interaction patterns and those of the continuing families. Some differences in these groups will be subsequently noted. In general, there were few differences in parent-child interactions in families who did or did not remain in the study. However, there were some differences in the characteristics of parents who remarried and how they viewed themselves and their lives.

Procedure

The study used a multimethod, multimeasure approach to the investigation of family interaction. The measures used in the study included interviews with structured diary records of the parents, observations of the parents and child interacting in the laboratory and home, behavior checklists of child behavior, parent rating of the child's behavior, and a battery of personality scales on the parents. In addition, observations of the child were conducted in nursery schools, peer nomination and teacher ratings of the child's behavior, and measures of the child's sex-role typing, cognitive performance and social development also were obtained. The parents and children were administered these measures at two months, one year, and two years following divorce.

Parent interviews and personality tests, diary

records, observations of the parent and child in an interaction situation in the laboratory, a checklist of the child's behavior kept by the parents, and parent-rating scales of the child's current behavior will be the procedures presented in detail, although related findings on other measures will occasionally be referred to.

Parent Interview Parents were interviewed separately on a structured parent interview schedule designed to assess discipline practices and the parent-child relationship; support systems outside the family household system; social, emotional and heterosexual relationships; quality of the relationship with the spouse; economic stress; family disorganization; satisfaction and happiness; and attitudes towards themselves. The interviews were tape-recorded. Each of the categories listed in Table 1 were rated on scales by two judges. In some cases the category involved the rating of only a single 5- or 7-point scale. In others it represented a composite score of several ratings on a group of subscales. Interjudge reliabilities ranged from .69 to .95 with a mean of .82. The interviews were derived and modified from those of Baumrind (1967, 1971), Sears, Rau and Alpert (1965), Martin and Hetherington (1971), and others.

Parent-Personality Inventories The parent personality measures include the Personal Adjustment Scale of the Adjective Checklist (Gough & Heilbrun, 1965), the Socialization Scale of the California

Personality Inventory (Gough, 1969), Rotter's I-E Scale (Rotter, 1966) and the Speilberger's State-Trait Anxiety Scale (Speilberger, Gorsuch & Lushene, 1970).

Structured Diary Record Each parent was asked to complete a structured diary record for three days (one weekday, Saturday, and Sunday). Fathers were asked to include at least one day when they were with their children. The diary record form was divided into half-hour units and contained a check list of activities, situations, people, and five 7-point bipolar mood-ratings scales. The dimension on the mood-rating scales included: (1) anxious-relaxed; (2) hostile, angry-friendly, loving; (3) unhappy, depressed-happy; (4) helpless-competent, in control; and (5) unloved, rejected-loved. Each 30-minute unit was subdivided into three 10 minute units. If very different events had occurred in a 30-minute period, the subject was encouraged to record these separately and sequentially. For example, if a father had a fight with his boss and a phone call from his girl friend in the same half hour, these were recorded sequentially in separate columns. The parent was instructed to check off what he was doing, where he was, who he was with, and how he was feeling on the mood scales in each 30-minute unit from the time he rose in the morning until he went to sleep at night. The record sheet also left space for any additional comments the parent might care to make. Although the parents were encouraged to record at the end of each 30-minute period,

---

Table 1

Control of child	Problems in running household
Maturity demands of child	Relationship with spouse
Communication with child	Emotional support in personal matters
Nurturance of child	Immediate support system
Permissiveness-restrictiveness with child	Social life and activities
Negative sanctions with child	Contact with adults
Positive sanctions with child	Intimate relations
Reinforcement of child for sex-typed behaviors	Sexuality
Paternal availability	Number of dates
Maternal availabillity	Happiness and satisfaction
Paternal face-to-face interaction with child	Competence as a parent
Maternal face-to-face interaction with child	Competence as a male/female
Quality of spouse's relationship with the child	Self-esteem
Agreement in treatment of the child	Satisfaction with employment
Emotional support in child rearing from spouse	Conflict preceding divorce
Economic stress	Tension in divorce
Family disorganization	

the situation in which they found themselves sometimes made this impossible. When retrospective recording was done, it was noted, and the time at which the entry was made was also recorded. In the first session, a series of standardized scales dealing with affect, stress, and guilt has been included in the battery of parent measures; however, since the diary mood-rating scales were found to be better predictors of behavior than these more time-consuming tests, the standardized scales were subsequently dropped from the study.

Parent-Child Laboratory Interaction   Each parent was observed separately interacting with the child in the laboratory in a half-hour free-play situation and in a half-hour structured situation involving puzzles, block building, bead stringing, and sorting tasks. The interaction sessions with each parent were scheduled on different days, separated by a period of about a month. Half of the children interacted with the mother first and half with the father first. All sessions were videotaped in order to permit the use of multiple coding of behavior. Behavior was coded in the categories in Table 2. The coding procedure was similar to that used by Patterson and his colleagues (Patterson et al. 1969) where the observation period was divided into 30-second intervals, and an average of approximately five behavior sequences of interactions between the subject and other family members was coded in

the 30-second interval. However, in order to improve reliability, a tone sounded every six seconds during the recording interval. Two raters rated all sessions; interjudge agreement or individual responses averaged .83%.

Checklist of Child Behavior   Although at least 3 hours of observations of the parent and child interacting in the home situation were collected at each of the three time points, this was not a sufficient time period to obtain an adequate sample of the children's behavior in which we were interested and which occurred relatively infrequently. Parents were given a behavior checklist and a recording form divided into half-hour units, and were asked to record whether a given child's behavior had occurred in a particular half-hour period. Three hours of recording were available for fathers, but 24 hours were available for mothers. These behaviors included both acts regarded as noxious by parents, such as yelling, crying, whining, destructiveness, noncompliance, etc., and those regarded as desirable, such as helping, sharing, cooperative activities, compliance, sustained play or independent activities.

Parent-Rating Scales of Child Behavior   A parent-rating scale of child behavior was constructed and standardized on a group of 100 mothers and fathers. Items used in previous observation questionnaires and rating scales or which seemed relevant to the interests of this study were included in an initial pool of 96 items. The parents were asked to rate their children on these items using a 5-point scale ranging from 1 (never occurs, occurs less often than in most children) to 5 (frequently occurs, occurs more often than in most children). Items which correlated with each other, which seemed conceptually related, or which had been found to load on the same factor in previous studies, were clustered in seven scales containing a total of 49 items. Only items which correlated with the total score in the scales were retained. Items were phrased to describe very specific behavior since many of these same items were also used on the Checklist of Child Behaviors previously described. The seven scales were aggression, inhibition, distractibility, task orientation, prosocial behavior, habit disturbance, and self-control. Divorced parents were asked to rate each item on the basis of the child's current behavior.

Table 2   Interaction Coding

Parent behavior	Child behavior
Command (positive)	Opposition
Command (negative)	Aversive opposition
Question (positive)	Compliance
Question (negative)	Dependency
Nonverbal intrusion	Negative demands (whining,
Ignore	complaining, angry tone)
Affiliate (interact)	Aggression (tantrum, destruc-
Positive sanctions	tiveness)
Negative sanctions	Requests
Reasoning and explanation	Affiliate
Encourages	Self-manipulation
Dependency	Sustained play
Indulgence	Ignore
Opposition	Cry
Compliance	
Encourages independence	

Data Analysis

Repeated measure manovas involving test session (two months, one year, two years), sex of child, sex of parent, and family composition (divorced versus intact) were performed for each measure on the interview and laboratory interaction task, and on the mood ratings, and on the amount of time spent in various activities reported in the structured diary records, and on the checklist and rating scales. A repeated measure manova excluding the sex of child variable was performed for the parents' personality measures. Correlational analyses of all variables within and across sub-groups also were performed. In addition, multiple regression and cross-lagged panel correlations were calculated for selected parent and child variables in an attempt to identify functional and causal relationships contributing to changes in the behavior of family members across time.

RESULTS

The results of the study will not be presented separately for each procedure used. Instead, the combined findings of the different procedures will be used to discuss alterations in life style, stresses and coping by family members, family relations, and how these factors change in the two years following divorce.

Change, Stress and Coping in Divorce

How does the life of a single parent differ from that of married parents? In changing to a new single life-style, what kind of stresses and satisfactions are experienced by members of a divorced couple? How might these be related to parent-child relations? The main areas in which change and stress were experienced were, first, those related to practical problems of living such as economic and occupational problems and problems in running a household; second, those associated with emotional distress and changes in self concept and identity; and third, interpersonal problems in maintaining a social life, in the development of intimate relationships and in interactions with the ex-spouse and child.

Practical Problems The main practical problems of living encountered by divorced parents were those related to household maintenance, economic and occupational difficulties. Many divorced men, particularly those from marriages in which conven-

tional sex roles had been maintained and in which the wife had not been employed, initially experienced considerable difficulty in maintaining a household routine, and reported distress associated with what one termed "a chaotic lifestyle."

One of the sets of interview scales was family disorganization, which dealt with the degree of structure in prescribed household roles, problems in coping with routine household tasks, and the regulating and scheduling of events. On this scale and in the structured diaries the households of the divorced mothers and fathers were more disorganized than those of intact families, although this disorganization was most marked in the first year following divorce and had significantly decreased by the second year. Members of separated households were more likely to get pick-up meals at irregular times. Divorced mothers and their children were less likely to eat dinner together. Bedtimes were more erratic; the children were read to less before bedtime, and they were more likely to arrive at school late. Divorced men were less likely to eat at home than were married men. They slept less, had more erratic sleep patterns, and had difficulty with shopping, cooking, laundry, and cleaning. Some relief from stress associated with housework occurred with six of the fathers when female friends or an employed cleaning woman participated in household tasks.

Eleven of the 48 divorced fathers reported little difficulty in household maintenance, and said they enjoyed having full responsibility for ordering their lives. Most of these men had participated actively in household tasks and child care during their marriages, and following divorce were more likely to assist their ex-wives in maintenance of her home than were fathers who previously had difficulty in coping with such tasks.

Greater economic stress in divorced couples as opposed to married couples was apparent in our sample. Although the average income of the divorced families was equal to that of the intact families, the economic problems associated with maintaining two households led to more financial concerns and limitations in the purchasing practices of divorced couples. Divorced fathers were more likely than married fathers to increase their work load in an attempt to raise their income. This created some duress in the first year following divorce when many fathers reported feeling immobilized by emotional problems and unable to work effectively. In addition, financial conflicts were one of the main sources of disagreement between divorced couples.

It had been suggested by Herzog and Sudia (1973) that many of the deleterious effects of a father's absence on children could be eliminated if economic stability was provided for mothers with no husband in the home. However, in our study the number of significant correlations was not above chance between income or reported feelings or economic stress, and parents' reported or observed interactions with their children or with behavior of the child in nursery school. This was true whether we use the total income for divorced husbands and wives, or the separate income for each of the households of the divorced spouses in the analyses. It may be that in our middle-class sample with an average combined maternal and paternal income of about $22,000, the range is not great enough to detect the effects of economic stress. In a lower-class sample, the greater extremes of economic duress might be associated with variations in parent-child interaction or the development of the child.

Changes in Self-Concepts and Emotional Adjustment of Parents Interview findings, diary mood ratings, and parents' personality tests show many differences between the self-concepts and emotional adjustments of parents in divorced and intact families. Many of these differences diminish over the two-year period following divorce, with a marked drop occurring between one year and two years following divorce. In the first year following divorce, divorced mothers and fathers feel more anxious, depressed, angry, rejected, and incompetent. The effects are more sustained for divorced mothers, particularly for divorced mothers of boys who at the end of two years are still feeling less competent, more anxious, more angry, and more externally controlled as measured by the I-E Scale than are married mothers or divorced mothers of girls. The diary record indicates that these negative feelings are most likely to occur in episodes involving interactions with their sons. This finding should be noted since the position is later going to be advanced that the mother-son relationship is particularly problematic in divorced families.

Divorced parents also score lower on the socialization scale of the California Personality Inventory and Personality Scale of the Adjective Checklist throughout the three sets of measures. Does this

mean that divorced people are less well-adjusted than married couples, or that an adverse response to the stresses associated with a conflictual marriage and divorce endure over the two-year post-divorce period? This can't be answered from our data. The five couples in the larger, intact sample who subsequently divorced scored lower on these scales than the nondivorcing couples and as more external on the I-E Scale only in the period immediately preceeding the divorce, which suggests that these scales may be affected by the conflict associated with an unsatisfying marriage and divorce.

Perhaps because he leaves the home and suffers the trauma of separation from his children, the divorced father seems to undergo greater initial changes in self-concept than does the mother, although the effects are longer-lasting in the mother. The continued presence of children and a familiar home setting gave mothers a sense of continuity which fathers lacked. Mothers complained most often of feeling physically unattractive, having lost the identity and status associated with being a married woman, and a general feeling of helplessness. Fathers complained of not knowing who they were, being rootless, and having no structure or home in their lives. The separation induced great feelings of loss, previously unrecognized dependency needs, guilt, anxiety, and depression. Changes in self-concept and identity problems were greatest in parents who were older or who had been married longest. Although two months following divorce about one-third of the fathers and one-quarter of the mothers reported an ebullient sense of freedom, which alternated with apprehension and depression, by one year the elation had been largely replaced by depression, anxiety, or apathy. These negative feelings markedly decreased by two years.

A pervasive concern of the fathers was the sense of loss of their children. For most this declined with time, but for many it remained a continued concern. Eight fathers who had initially been highly involved, attached, and affectionate parents reported that they could not endure the pain of seeing their children only intermittently, and by two years after divorce had coped with this stress by seeing their children infrequently although they continued to experience a great sense of loss and depression. However, it should not be thought that all divorced fathers felt less satisfied with their fathering roles following divorce. Ten of the fathers reported that their relationships with their children had improved, and that they were enjoying their interchanges more. Most of these fathers came from marriages in which there had been a high degree of husband-wife conflict.

One of the most marked changes in divorced parents in the first year following divorce was a decline in feelings of competence. They felt they had failed as parents and spouses, and they expressed doubts about their ability to adjust well in any future marriages. They reported that they functioned less well in social situations, and were less competent in heterosexual relationships. Nine of the divorced fathers reported an increased rate of sexual dysfunction. In addition to these feelings specifically related to marriage, 36 of the divorced fathers reported that they felt they were coping less well at work.

The flurry of social activity and self-improvement which occurred during the first year following divorce, particularly in divorced fathers, seemed to be an attempt to resolve some of the identity and loss of self-esteem problems experienced by the divorced parents.

One year after the divorce the father was in a frenzy of activity. Although at this time contacts with old friends had declined, dating and casual social encounters at bars, clubs, cocktail parties, and other social gatherings had increased. In this period many of the divorced men and women were also involved in programs of self-improvement. Twenty-eight of the divorced fathers, in contrast to 13 of the unseparated fathers, and 20 of the divorced mothers, in contrast to 14 married mothers, were engaged in activities such as night-school courses in photography, languages, potting, jewelry making, modern dance, and creative writing, structured physical-fitness programs, tennis, golf, or sailing lessons. However, by two years following divorce, both social life in divorced fathers and self-improvement programs for both divorced parents had declined. It should be noted that although these activities kept the parents busy and were associated with more positive emotional ratings, the most important factor in changing the self-concept two years after divorce was the establishment of a satisfying, intimate, heterosexual relationship. Only one father became involved in a homesexual relationship. He happened to have low ratings of self-esteem and happiness. It is obvious that on the basis of this finding, no conclusion can be drawn about the relative satisfaction of homosexual or heterosexual relationships.

Interpersonal Problems, Social Life, and Intimate Relationships An area in which stresses are experienced by most divorced couples are in social life and in establishing meaningful, intimate, interpersonal relationships. Almost all of the divorced adults in this study complained that socializing in our culture is organized around couples and that being a single adult, particularly a single woman with children, limits recreational opportunities. Both the interview findings and the diary records kept by parents indicated that social life was more restricted in the divorced couples in the two years following divorce and that this effect initially was most marked for women. Divorced parents reported that two months following divorce married friends were supportive, and diary records indicated that considerable time was spent with them. However, these contacts rapidly declined. The dissociation from married friends was greater for women than for men, who were more often included in social activities and sometimes participated in joint family outings on visitation days. Shared interests and concerns led to more frequent contact with other divorced, separated, or single persons. Divorced mothers reported having significantly less contact with adults than did married parents, and often commented on their sense of being locked into a child's world. Several described themselves as prisoners and used terms like being "walled in" or "trapped." This was less true of working than nonworking mothers. Many nonworking mothers complained that most of their social contacts had been made through professional associates of the husband, and that with divorce these associations terminated. In contrast, the employed mothers had contact with their co-workers and these relations often extended into after-hour social events. Although the employed women complained that it was difficult to get household chores done and of their concern about getting adequate care for their children, most felt the gratifications associated with employment outweighed the problems. Social life for our total sample of divorced women increased over the two year period; however, it always remained lower than that of married women.

Divorced men had a restricted social life two months after divorce, followed by a surge of activity at one year, and a decline in activity to the wife's level by two years. In contrast to divorced women who felt trapped, divorced men complained of feeling shut out, rootless, and at loose ends, and of a need to engage in social activities even if they often were not pleasurable. Divorced men and women who had not remarried in the two years following divorce repeatedly spoke of their intense feelings of loneliness.

Heterosexual relations play a particularly important role in the happiness and attitudes toward the self of both married and divorced adults. Happiness, self-esteem, and feelings of competence in heterosexual behavior increased steadily over the two year period for divorced males and females, but they were not as high even in the second year as those for married couples. It should be noted, however, that the subjects who later remarried and were shifted from this study of divorce and father absence to a stepparent study scored as high on happiness, although lower on self-esteem and feelings of competence, as did parents in intact families. Frequency of sexual intercourse was lower for divorced parents than married couples at two months, higher at one year for males, and about the same at two years. Divorced males particularly seemed to show a peak of sexual activity and a pattern of dating a variety of women in the first year following divorce. However, the stereotyped image of the happy, swinging single life was not altogether accurate. One of our sets of interview ratings attempted to measure intimacy in relationships. Intimacy referred to love in the sense of valuing the welfare of the other as much as one's own, of a deep concern and willingness to make sacrifices for the other, and a strong attachment and desire to be near the other person. It should be understood that this use of the term intimacy is not synonomous with sexual intimacy although, of course, the two frequently occur together. Intimacy in relationships showed strong positive correlations with happiness, self-esteem, and feelings of competence in heterosexual relations for both divorced and married men and women. Table 3 shows that in the divorced sample, but not in the married sample, if subjects were divided into those above and below the median in terms of intimacy in relationships, happiness correlated negatively with frequency of intercourse in the low-intimacy group and positively in the high-intimacy group. The same pattern held for self-esteem. This was true for both divorced males and females. The only nonsignificant correlation was for low-intimacy males immediately following divorce. Many males but few females were pleased at the increased opportunity for sexual experiences with a variety of partners immediately

Table 3 Correlations between Frequency of Sexual Intercourse and Happiness in High and Low Intimacy Divorced Groups

	High intimacy		Low intimacy	
	Male (N=24)	Female (N=24)	Male (N=24)	Female (N=24)
Two months	+.40*	+.43*	−.09 (n.s.)	−.42*
One year	+.40**	+.47**	−.41*	−.46*
Two years	+.54**	+.52**	−.48**	−.57**

* p<.05
** p<.01

following divorce. However, by the end of the first year both divorced men and women were expressing a want for intimacy and a lack of satisfaction in casual sexual encounters. Women expressed particularly intense feelings about frequent casual sexual encounters, often talking of feelings of desperation, overwhelming depression, and low self-esteem following such exchanges. A pervasive want for intimacy which was not satisfied by casual encounters characterized most of our divorced parents, and the formation of an intimate relationship seemed to be a powerful factor in the development of happiness and satisfaction.

Relationships between Divorced Partners At two months following divorce, relations with the ex-spouse and children remained the most salient and preoccupying concern for divorced parents. Most (66%) of the exchanges between divorced couples in this period involved conflicts. The most common areas of conflict were those dealing with finances and support, visitation and child rearing, and intimate relations with others. In spite of the fact that the relationship between all but four of our divorced couples was characterized by acrimony, anger, feelings of desertion, resentment and memories of painful conflicts, this was tempered by considerable ambivalence. Attachments persisted, and in some cases increased, following the escape from daily confrontations. Six of the 48 couples had sexual intercourse in the two months following divorce. Thirty-four of the mothers and 29 of the fathers reported that in the case of a crisis the ex-spouse would be the first person they would call. Eight of the fathers continued to help the mother with home maintenance and four babysat when she went out on dates. With time both conflict and attachment decreased, although anger and resentment were sustained longer in mothers than fathers. The establishment of new intimate relations and remarriage were particularly powerful factors in attenuating the intensity of the divorced couples' relationship.

At one year after divorce, which seemed to be the most stressful period for both parents, 29 of the fathers and 35 of the mothers reported that they thought the divorce might have been a mistake, and that they should have tried harder to resolve their conflicts; the alternative life-styles available to them were not satisfying. By the end of the second year, only 12 of the mothers and 9 of the fathers felt this way.

In our larger sample which included parents who remarried, remarriage of the spouse was accompanied by a reactivation of feelings of depression, helplessness, anger, and anxiety, particularly in mothers. Many reported that their feelings of panic and loss were similar to those experienced at the time of the original separation and divorce. Anger by the mother was almost an invariable concomitant of remarriage by the ex-husband even if the mother was the first to remarry. Sometimes this took the form of reopening conflicts about finances or visitation, sometimes it was directed at the children and their split loyalties, and often it focused on resentment and feelings of competition with the new wife. Five of the 10 men whose ex-wives remarried reported approval of the new husband, in contrast to only 4 of the 19 women whose husbands remarried. The new wives seemed to exacerbate these feelings by entering a particularly hostile competitive relationship with the ex-wife in which criticism of the children and the wives' child rearing often were used as the combatative focus.

Parent-Child Relations Thus far we have been focusing mainly on changes in the divorced partners in the two years following divorce, and have seen that they encounter and cope with many stresses. We will now look at differences in family functioning and in parent-child interactions as measured both in the interview and in direct observations in the laboratory situation.

The interaction patterns between divorced parents and children differed significantly from those of intact families on many variables studied in the interview, and on many of the parallel measures in the structured interaction situation. On these meas-

ures the differences were greatest during the first year, whereas a process of re-equilibration seemed to be taking place by the end of the second year, particularly in mother-child relationships. However, even at the end of the second year, on many dimensions parent-child relations in divorced and intact families still differed. It is noteworthy that although there are still many stresses in the parent-child interactions of divorced parents at the end of two years, almost one-quarter of the fathers and one-half of the mothers report that their relationships with their children have improved over the time during the marriage when parental conflict and tensions had detrimental effects.

Some of the findings for fathers must be interpreted in view of the fact that divorced fathers become increasingly less available to their children and ex-spouse over the course of the two-year period. Although at two months divorced fathers were having almost as much face-to-face interaction with their children as were fathers in intact homes who are often highly unavailable to their children (Blanchard & Biller 1971), this interaction declines rapidly. At two months about one-quarter of the divorced parents even reported that fathers, in their eagerness to maximize visitation rights and maintain contact with their children, were having more face-to-face contact with their children than they had before the divorce. This contact was motivated by a variety of factors in the divorced fathers. Sometimes it was based on a deep attachment to the child or continuing attachment to the wife; sometimes it was based on feelings of duty or attempts to assuage guilt; often it was an attempt to maintain a sense of continuity in their lives; unfortunately, it was frequently at least partly motivated by a desire to annoy, compete with, or retaliate against the spouse. By two years after divorce, 19 of the divorced fathers were seeing their children once a week or more, 14 fathers saw them every two weeks, 7 every three weeks, and 8 once a month or less.

The results of the diary record, of the interview findings, and of laboratory observations relating to parent-child interaction will be presented in a simplified fashion and wherever possible, presented together. The patterns of parent-child interaction showed considerable congruence across these measures.

Divorced parents make fewer maturity demands of their children, communicate less well with their children, tend to be less affectionate with their children, and show marked inconsistency in discipline and lack of control over their children in comparison to married parents. Poor parenting is most apparent when divorced parents, particularly the divorced mothers, are interacting with their sons. Divorced parents communicate less, are less consistent, and use more negative sanctions with their sons than their daughters. Additionally, in the laboratory situation divorced mothers exhibited fewer positive behaviors such as positive sanctions and affiliation, and more negative behaviors such as negative commands, negative sanctions, and opposition to requests of the child, with sons than with daughters. Sons of divorced parents seem to be having a hard time of it, and this may in part explain why, as we shall see shortly, the adverse effects of divorce are more severe and enduring for boys than for girls.

Fortunately, people, even parents, learn to adapt to problem situations, and by two years after divorce the parenting practices of divorced mothers have improved. Poor parenting seems most marked, particularly for divorced mothers, one year after divorce, which seems to be a peak of stress in parent-child relations. Two years following the divorce, mothers are demanding more autonomous mature behavior of their children, communicate better, and use more explanation and reasoning. They are more nurturant and consistent, and are better able to control their children than they were before. A similar pattern occurs for divorced fathers in maturity demands, communication and consistency, but they become less nurturant and more detached from their children with time. In the laboratory and home observations, divorced fathers were ignoring their children more and showing less affection.

The interviews and observations showed that the lack of control divorced parents have over their children was associated with very different patterns of relating to the child for mothers and fathers. The divorced mother tries to control her child by being more restrictive and giving more commands which the child ignores or resists. The divorced father wants his contacts with his child to be as happy as possible. He begins by initially being extremely permissive and indulgent with his children and becoming increasingly restrictive over the two year period, although he is never as restrictive as fathers in intact homes. The divorced mother uses more

negative sanctions than the divorced father does, or than parents in intact families do. However, by the second year her use of negative sanctions is declining as the divorced father's is increasing. In a parallel fashion, the divorced mother's use of positive sanctions increases after the first year as the divorced father's decreases. The "every day is Christmas" behavior of the divorced father declines with time. The divorced mother decreases her futile attempts at authoritarian control and becomes more effective in dealing with her child over the two-year period.

The lack of control that divorced parents have over their children, particularly one year following divorce, was apparent in both home and laboratory observations. The observed frequency of a child's compliance with parents' regulations, commands, or requests could be regarded as a measure either of parental control or resistant child behavior. A clearer understanding of functional relationships in parent-child interaction may be obtained by examining the effectiveness of various types of parental responses in leading to compliance by the child, and the parents' responses to the child following compliance or noncompliance. It can be seen in Table 4 that boys are less compliant than girls and that fathers are more effective than mothers in obtaining compliance from children. This may be at least partly based on the fact that mothers give over twice as many commands as do fathers, and that divorced mothers give significantly more commands than do divorced fathers, or mothers and fathers in intact families. The curvilinear effect with the least effectiveness of any type of parental behavior at one year and a marked increase in control of the child by two years is again apparent, although the divorced mothers and fathers never gain as much control as their married counterparts. Since developmental psychologists have traditionally regarded reasoning and explanation as the font of good discipline from which all virtues flow, the results relating to type of parental demands were unexpected. Negative commands are less effective than positive commands, and, somewhat surprisingly, in the two months and one year groups, reasoning and explanation are less effective than either positive or negative commands. By the last test session, the effectiveness of reasoning and explanation have significantly increased over reasoning in the previous sessions. Two things are noteworthy about the pattern of change in reasoning. First, it should be remembered that the average

Table 4

	Intact				Divorced			
	Girl		Boy		Girl		Boy	
	Father	Mother	Father	Mother	Father	Mother	Father	Mother

Percentage of compliance to parental commands (positive)

	Father	Mother	Father	Mother	Father	Mother	Father	Mother
Two months	60.2	54.6	51.3	42.6	51.3	40.6	39.9	29.3
One year	63.4	56.7	54.9	44.8	43.9	31.8	32.6	21.5
Two years	64.5	59.3	57.7	45.3	52.1	44.2	43.7	37.1

Percentage of compliance to parental commands (negative)

	Intact				Divorced			
	Girl		Boy		Girl		Boy	
	Father	Mother	Father	Mother	Father	Mother	Father	Mother
Two months	55.7	49.3	47.5	36.4	47.0	34.8	35.6	23.4
One year	59.2	51.5	50.3	38.8	39.1	27.2	28.3	17.2
Two years	60.5	54.6	53.6	39.0	49.9	39.7	39.7	31.8

Percentage of compliance to parental reasoning and explanation

	Intact				Divorced			
	Girl		Boy		Girl		Boy	
	Father	Mother	Father	Mother	Father	Mother	Father	Mother
Two months	49.1	43.3	41.0	31.1	41.3	29.2	29.6	18.4
One year	55.4	48.0	46.2	34.5	26.3	23.1	24.5	14.1
Two years	62.3	58.1	58.1	47.6	50.3	42.5	41.4	36.9

age of the subjects is two years older at the final session. The mean age at the two-month session was 3.92 years, at the one year's session was 4.79, and at the final session was 5.81 years. It may be that, as children become more cognitively and linguistically mature, reasoning and explanation is more effective because the child can understand it and has a longer attention span. It may also be that internalization and role taking are increasing, and that explanations which involve appeals to the rights or feelings of others become more effective. Some support for the position that younger children may not fully comprehend or attend to explanations is found in a point biserial correlational post hoc analysis between the number of words in explanations and compliance or noncompliance of children. On going back over videotapes to see what was happening in cases where there was high use of reasoning and explanation and low compliance, it was observed that the parents often were using long-winded, often conceptually complicated explanations and that the child seemed to rapidly become inattentive, distractible, and bored. Thereupon, the child either continued or resumed his or her previous activity or ignored and made no response to the parent. The averaged point biserial correlation and noncompliance and number of words across group as $-.58$ for two months, $-.44$ for one year, and $-.13$ for two years. "Short and sweet" would seem to be an effective maxim in instructing young children. The same type of analyses was performed on the home observations which had been recorded with audio but not videotape, and the same pattern of results was obtained. Long explanations were associated with noncompliance to parents in younger children. The second thing to be noted about these findings is that the superiority of reasoning over negative parental commands in obtaining compliance is true for boys, with the exception of sons interacting with their divorced fathers, but is not found for girls. Why should reasoning be relatively more effective in gaining compliance in boys? Barclay Martin (1974) in his recent review of research on parent-child interactions suggests that coercive parental responses are more likely to be related to oversocialization and inhibition in girls but to aggression in boys. It may be that the greater aggressiveness frequently observed in preschool boys and greater assertiveness in the culturally prescribed male role necessitates the use of reasoning and explanation to develop the cognitive mediators necessary for self-control in boys. Some support for this is found in a greater number, significantly larger, and more consistent correlations for boys than for girls between the communication scale on the parent interview and also frequency of observed parental reasoning and explanation, with parent's ratings of their children's prosocial behavior, self-control, and aggression. A similar pattern of correlations was obtained between these parental measures and the frequency of negative and positive behavior on the behavior checklist. In contrast, high use of negative commands was positively related to aggression in boys but not in girls. In summary: although reasoning and explanation are not clearly superior to other commands in gaining short-term compliance, in the long term development of self-control, inhibition of aggression, and prosocial behavior in boys, they are more effective.

After reviewing the interview and observational findings, one might be prone to state that disruptions in children's behavior following divorce are attributable to emotional disturbance in the divorced parents and poor parenting, especially by mothers of boys. However, before we point a condemning finger and say fie upon these parents, especially upon the divorced mothers who face the day-to-day problems of child rearing, let us look at their children. The findings on the behavior checklist, recording the occurrence of positive and negative behaviors in the home in 30-minute units, show not only that children of divorced parents exhibit more negative behavior than do children of intact families, but also that these behaviors are most marked in boys and have largely disappeared in girls

by two years after divorce. They are also significantly declining in the boys. Children exhibit more negative behavior in the presence of their mothers than their fathers; this is especially true with sons of divorced parents.

These checklist results were corroborated by the home and laboratory observations and by parent ratings of their children's behavior. Divorced mothers may give their children a hard time, but mothers, especially divorced mothers, get rough treatment from their children. As previously remarked, children are more likely to exhibit oppositional behavior to mothers and comply to fathers. They also make negative complaining demands of the mother more frequently. Boys are more oppositional and aggressive; girls are more whining, complaining, and compliant. Divorced children show an increase in dependency over time, and exhibit less sustained play than children of intact families. The divorced mother is harassed by her children, particularly her sons. In comparison with fathers and mothers of intact families, her children in the first year don't obey, affiliate, or attend to her. They nag and whine, make more dependency demands, and are more likely to ignore her. The aggression of boys with divorced mothers peaks at one year, then drops significantly, but is still higher than that of boys in intact families at two years. Some divorced mothers described their relationship with their child one year after divorce as "declared war," a "struggle for survival," "the old Chinese water torture," or "like getting bitten to death by ducks." As was found in the divorced parents' behavior, one year following divorce seemed to be the period of maximum negative behaviors for children and great improvement occurred by two years, although the negative behaviors were more sustained in boys than in girls. The second year appears to be a period of marked recovery and constructive adaptation for divorced mothers and children.

Who is doing what to whom? It has been proposed, most recently by Gerald Patterson in a paper entitled "Mothers: The Unacknowledged Victims" (1976), that the maternal role is not a very rewarding or satisfying one. Patterson demonstrates that the maternal role, particularly with mothers of problem children, demands high rates of responding at very low levels of positive reinforcement for the mothers. He assumes that mothers and their aggressive children get involved in a vicious circle of coercion. The lack of management skills of the mothers accelerates the child's aversive behavior for which she is the main instigator and target. This is reciprocated by increased coercion in the mother's parenting behavior, and feelings of helplessness, depression, anger, and self-doubt. In his study Patterson shows that decreases in the noxious behaviors of aggressive children through treatment procedures aimed at improving parenting skills are associated with decreases of maternal scores on a number of clinical scales on the MMPI, with a decrease in anxiety on the Taylor manifest anxiety scale, and with improvement on several other measures of maternal adjustment. Patterson's model may be particularly applicable to divorced mothers and children in our study. High synchronous correlations between reported and observed poor parenting in divorced mothers, and reported and observed negative behavior in children, occurred at each time period. The greater use of poor maternal parenting practices and higher frequency of undesirable behaviors in children from divorced families, even in the first sessions with mothers and sons, suggests that the coercive cycle was already underway when we first encountered our families two months after divorce. Stresses and conflicts preceding or accompanying the divorce may have initiated the cycle. High rates and durations of negative exchanges between divorced mothers and their sons were apparent throughout the study. Sequence analyses of the home and laboratory observations showed that divorced mothers of boys are not only more likely than other parents to trigger noxious behavior, but also that they are less able to control or terminate this behavior once it occurs.

We attempted to use cross-lagged panel correlations between selected parent and child measures at times 1 and 2 and times 2 and 3 to identify causal effects in these interactions. There were many significant synchronous correlations between parent and child behavior. Poor parenting practices and coercive behavior in parents correlate with undesirable and coercive behaviors in children, particularly in divorced mothers and sons. This suggests that the coercive cycle is already under way. Causal direction for poor-parenting practices and noxious child behavior could not be identified consistently by the panel correlations. However, the observational measures and child checklist measures, but not the interview and rating measures, indicate that poor parenting by divorced mothers at two months causes problem behaviors in children at one year. These

effects are similar but not significant between one year and two years.

A striking finding is that self-esteem, feelings of parental competence as measured by the interview, state anxiety as measured by the Speilburger State-Trait Anxiety Scale, and the divorced mother's mood ratings of competence, depression, and anxiety on the Structured Diary Record not only show significant synchronous correlation with ratings of children's aggression and checklist frequency of noxious behaviors, but also yield significant cross-lagged panel correlations that suggest that the child's behavior, particularly that of the son, is causing the emotional responses of the mother. The findings are similar but less consistent for mothers in intact families. Mothers from both divorced and intact families show more state and trait anxiety, feelings of external control and incompetence, and depression than do fathers. This suggests that the feminine maternal role is not as gratifying as the paternal role, regardless whether the family is intact or divorced. The more marked findings in divorced women seem in accord with Patterson's view that mothers of problem children are trapped in a coercive cycle that leads to debilitating attitudes towards themselves, adverse emotional responses, and feelings of helplessness.

In Patterson's study and others comparing parents of problem and nonproblem children, fathers were found to be much less affected by a problem child than were mothers. Fathers, particularly divorced fathers, spend less time with their children than do mothers, thereby escaping some of the stresses imposed by a coercive child and obtaining more gratification in activities outside the family. In addition, fathers seem less likely to get involved in such a coercive vicious cycle because children exhibit less deviant behavior in the presence of their fathers; furthermore, fathers are more able to control deviant behavior in their children once it occurs, as is shown in fathers' ratings of their child's behavior, frequencies of behavior on the checklist, and in observations in the laboratory and home.

The cross-lagged panel correlations showed a larger proportion of effects going in the direction of fathers causing children's behavior than in children causing fathers' behavior relative to the number found in mother-child interactions. Children's behavior showed few effects on the state anxiety, mood ratings, or self-esteem of fathers, especially divorced fathers. In addition, in intact families, negative child behaviors at one and two years following divorce seemed to be partially caused by poor control, low nurturance and high use of negative sanctions by fathers in the earlier time periods.

The 48 divorced fathers involved in this study were probably more concerned about their children and interacted more with them than most divorced fathers do. The fact that they were available for study and willing to participate may reflect a more sustained and greater degree of paternal involvement than is customarily found. However, in spite of this possible bias, the impact of divorced fathers on children declined with time, and was significantly less than that of fathers in intact families. At two months following divorce, the number of significant correlations between paternal characteristics and behavior, and child characteristics is about the same as those in intact families. However, two years after the divorce, divorced fathers clearly are influencing their children less and divorced mothers more. Divorced mothers are becoming increasingly salient relative to the divorced father in the social, cognitive and personality development of their children. This decrease is less marked for divorced fathers who maintain a high rate of contact with their children.

It would seem that in the period during and following divorce, parents are going through many role changes and encountering many problems and would benefit from support in coping with these problems.

Effectiveness in dealing with the child is related to support in child rearing from the spouse and agreement with the spouse in disciplining the child in both divorced and intact families. When support and agreement occurred between divorced couples, the disruption in family functioning appeared to be less extreme, and the restablizing of family functioning occurred earlier, by the end of the first year.

When there was agreement in child rearing, a positive attitude toward the spouse, low conflict between the divorced parents, and when the father was emotionally mature as measured by the Socialization Scale of the California Personality Inventory (Gough 1969) and the Personal Adjustment scale of the Adjective Checklist (Gough & Heilbrun 1965), frequent contact of the father and child was associated with positive mother-child interactions and with more positive adjustment of the child. When there was disagreement and inconsistency in attitudes toward the child, and conflict and ill will between

the divorced parents, or when the father was poorly adjusted, frequent visitation was associated with poor mother-child functioning and disruptions in the children's behavior. Emotional maturity in the mother was also found to be related to her adequacy in coping with stresses in her new single life and relations with her children.

Other support systems such as that of grandparents, siblings, close friends, especially other divorced friends or male friends with whom there was an intimate relationship, or a competent housekeeper, also were related to the mother's effectiveness in interacting with the child in divorced but not in intact families. However, none of these support systems were as salient as a continued, positive, mutually supportive relationship of the divorced couple and continued involvement of the father with the child. For the father, women with whom he was intimately involved, married friends, and relatives offered the next greatest support in his relationship with his child.

In our forty-eight divorced couples only six mothers and four fathers sought professional counselling or therapy. The main factor which seemed to motivate parents to enter therapy was having other friends who had been in therapy and who encouraged the divorced parent to try it. However, in our larger sample of seventy-two divorced couples we were able to identify eleven mothers and six fathers who entered therapy, on whom we had records for one year following entry into therapy. The only subgroup in which both the divorced mother and the child demonstrated improved adjustment was in five mothers who were involved in programs focused on the improvement of parenting skills and in which 24-hour telephone contact with the parent trainer was available. This is obviously not a large enough group on which to draw firm conclusions about the efficacy of therapy as a support system, but it does suggest that focusing on effective parenting may alleviate some of the problems encountered by the divorced mother and child.

DISCUSSION AND SUMMARY

In summary, in this study divorced mothers and fathers encountered marked stresses in the area of practical problems of living, of self-concept and emotional distress, and in interpersonal relations following divorce. Low self-esteem, loneliness, depression, and feelings of helplessness were characteristic of the divorced couple. Although the establishment of new intimate relations helped mitigate these effects, divorced parents were still less satisfied with their lives two years after the divorce than were parents in intact families.

In many divorced families, disruptions occurred in parent-child relations. Divorced parents infantalized and communicated less well with their children than did parents in intact families. In addition, they tended to be more inconsistent, less affectionate, and have less control over their children's behavior. The children in divorced families were more dependent, disobedient, aggressive, whining, demanding, and lacking in affection. These effects were most marked in mother-son interactions. A peak of stress in parent-child interactions appeared one year after divorce and marked improvement, particularly in mother-child relations, occurred thereafter. Both personal and emotional adjustment and parent-child relations deteriorated in the year following divorce. This seemed to be a period where members of divorced families were testing a variety of coping mechanisms in dealing with changes and stresses in their new life situation. Many of these mechanisms were unsuccessful in reducing stress. However, by the second year following divorce a process of restabilization and adjustment was apparent.

In our current culture the myth of romantic love and marriage is being replaced by the romance of divorce. The literature on divorce is replete with titles such as *Creative Divorce, Divorce: Chance of a New Lifetime,* and *Divorce: The Gateway to Self-Realization.* Many couples, on initiating divorces, are prepared for a reduction in stress and conflict, the joys of greater interpersonal freedoms, and the delights of self-discovery and self-actualization associated with liberation. Few are prepared for the traumas and stresses they will encounter in attaining these goals following divorce, even if the goals are ultimately reached.

Since this was a longitudinal study it presented an opportunity to examine how family members responded and coped with the crisis of divorce. Some of the audience may object to the term crisis used to describe the divorce experience. However, in the families we studied there were none in which at least one family member did not report distress or exhibit disrupted behavior, particularly during the first year following divorce. We did not encounter a victimless divorce. Most of the members of divorced families in our study were able ultimately to cope with many of their problems, but the course of adjustment was often unexpectedly painful.

Since this study only lasted two years it is impossible to state whether the restabilizing process in the divorced family had reached an asymptote and was largely completed at two years, or whether this readjustment would continue over a longer period of time until it would ultimately more closely resemble that in intact families.

It should be remembered that the results reported in a study such as this represent averages, and that there are wide variations in coping and parenting within intact and divorced families. There are many inadequate parents and children with problems in intact families. Our study and previous research shows that a conflict-ridden intact family is more deleterious to family members than a stable home situation in which parents are divorced. Divorce is often a positive solution to destructive family functioning and the best statistical prognostications suggest that the rate of divorce is likely to increase. Since this is the case, it is important that parents and children be realistically prepared for problems associated with divorce which they may encounter. More research and applied programs oriented toward the identification and application of constructive parenting and coping following divorce should be initiated. Divorce is one of the most serious crises in contemporary American life. It is a major social responsibility to develop support systems for the divorced family in coping with changes associated with divorce and in finding means of modifying or eliminating the deleterious sequelae of divorce.

REFERENCES

Baumrind, D. Child care practices anteceding three patterns of preschool behavior. *Genetic Psychology Monograph,* 1967, *75,* 43–88.

Baumrind, D. Current patterns of parental authority. *Developmental Psychology Monograph,* 1971, *4* (4, Pt. 2).

Biller, H. B. *Paternal deprivation.* Lexington, Mass.: Lexington Books, D. C. Heath & Co., 1974.

Blanchard, R. W., & Biller, H. B. Father availability and academic performance among third grade boys. *Development Psychology,* 1971, *4,* 301–305.

Bronfenbrenner, U. *The Changing American Family.* Paper presented at the Society for Research in Child Development meetings. Denver, April 1975.

Gough, H. G., & Heilbrun, A. B. Jr. *The Adjective Checklist.* Palo Alto, Calif.: Consulting Psychologists Press, Inc. 1965.

Gough, H. G. *Manual for California Personality Inventory.* Palo Alto, Calif.: Consulting Psychologists Press, Inc. 1969.

Herzog, E., & Sudia, C. E. Children in fatherless families. In B. M. Caldwell & H. Riccuiti (Eds.) *Review of Child Development Research,* p. 141–232. Chicago: University of Chicago Press, 1973.

Hetherington, E. M., & Deur, J. The effects of father absence on child development. *Young Children,* 1971, *26,* 233–248.

Kenney, D. A. A quasi-experimental approach to assessing treatment effects in the nonequivalent control group design. *Psychological Bulletin,* 1975, *82*(3), 345–362.

Lynn, D. B. *The father: His role in child development.* Belmont, Calif.: Wadsworth Publishing Company, Inc. 1974.

Martin, B. Parent-child relations. In F. D. Horowitz (Ed.) *Review of Child Development Research.* Chicago, Ill.: University of Chicago Press. 1975.

Martin, B., & Hetherington, E. M. *Family interaction in withdrawn, aggressive and normal children.* Unpublished manuscript. 1971.

Patterson, G. R., Ray, R. S., Shaw, D. A., & Cobb, J. A. *A manual for coding of family interaction,* 1969 revision. NAPS Document #01234.

Patterson, G. *Mothers: The unacknowledged victims.* Paper presented at the Western Regional Meetings for the Society for Research in Child Development. Oakland, California. April 1976.

Rotter, J. B. Generalized expectancies for internal versus external control of reinforcement. *Psychological Monographs,* 1966, *80,* (1, Whole No. 609).

Sears, R. R., Rau, L., & Alpert, R. *Identification and child rearing.* Stanford, Calif.: Stanford Press. 1965.

Speilberger, C. D., Gorsuch, R. L., & Lushene, R. *State-Trait Anxiety Inventory.* Palo Alto, Calif.: Consulting Psychologist Press, Inc. 1970.

Reading 29

Social Interactions of Young Abused Children: Approach, Avoidance, and Aggression

Carol George
Mary Main

There is increasing emphasis on intervention and prediction in the study of child abuse. Perhaps for this reason, most studies of child abuse emphasize the detection, care, and protection of abused children, or situations and personality characteristics of both parent and child which increase the child's vulnerability toward abuse (see Maden & Wrench [1977] and Parke & Collmer [1975], for major reviews of the literature).

To date there has been little concern with the actual

This article is based on a master's thesis submitted by Carol George to Mary Main. The research was supported by Biomedical Research Support grant 1-444036-3204 to Main, who received further support from the Zenturm für interdisziplinare Forschung, Bielefeld, Germany, as this study was being completed. We are grateful to the families who gave permission for these observations. We also thank Diane Sumner, Loretta Townsend, David George, and the many Berkeley students who helped to collect and analyze these data. We also thank Ross Parke, Lewis Petrinovitch, Arnold Sameroff, Everett Waters, and John Watson for helpful reviews of earlier editions of this manuscript.

behavior of the abused child, and few studies have offered more than incidental reports. Most have consisted of incidental characterizations of children seen in child-protection units or in conjunction with child-protection services. It is only very recently that careful descriptions of the behavior of abused and/or neglected children have become available (see Gaensbauer & Sands, in press; Martin & Beezley 1977; Gaensbauer, Mrazek, & Harmon, Note 1). Control groups have not been used.

The present study is the first controlled investigation of the social interactions of physically abused infants between 1 and 3 years of age. The impetus for the present study lies in studies of normal mother-infant interaction rather than in previous studies of abuse. Working with several samples of normal 1-year-old infants and mothers, Main 1977; 1981; Note 2) has sought to describe and explain the avoidance of the attachment figure which appears in some infants in stress situations and the effects of rejection by the attachment figure.

Main defines "rejection" in terms of two separate variables, each involving observable aspects of maternal behavior shown in videotaped play sessions: movements of avoidance/rejection of physical contact with the infant, and angry behavior noted in voice, posture, and facial expression. In some cases the origins of these patterns of maternal behavior may reside in difficulties presented by the infant as early as the newborn period; in others, in temporary or enduring characteristics of the mother which appear irrespective of early infant behavior.

Whatever the origins of this kind of maternal behavior, Main suggests that an attached infant must experience a strong and theoretically irresolvable conflict when it is stressed by maternal rebuff and yet not permitted physical access to its mother as attachment figure. This conflict, if continuing, may influence much of infant social behavior. Main has found the mother's rejection of contact and her angry behavior correlated with a syndrome of several kinds of infant behavior. First, normal infants who are rejected in this manner tend to avoid the mother rather than approach her or otherwise show attachment behaviors following brief separations. Maternal rejection is also related (1) to the infant's failure to approach other friendly adults at the moment that they attempt to establish social interaction; (2) to active visual and physical avoidance of these persons under these same conditions; and (3) to hitting and threatening to hit the mother, active disobedience to the mother, and to other forms of angry behavior. In strongly rejected infants, approach-avoidance movements are sometimes noted. The rejection observed within these normal samples is, of course, limited.

The set of correlates of rejection described above suggested a simple analogy. Since abuse is an extreme form of threatening or rejecting parental behavior, many abused children might experience extreme rejection of physical contact and threats of abuse as well as the relatively rare incidents of abuse itself. This conjunction between abuse and rejection is not inevitable; some abused infants have been abused only once and otherwise enjoy a relationship of mutual affection. Nonetheless, many abused

children might be expected to fall at an extreme with respect to the syndrome described above.

As part of the preparation for the present study, George (Note 3) conducted a microanalysis of the filmed behavior of one infant in a normal sample who was severely punished by the mother but not actually physically abused. She found that this infant's behavior did fall at the extreme of the described pattern. The infant not only avoided her mother, but she was also highly avoidant when an unfamiliar adult attempted to establish a social relationship with her. Moreover, she "approached" the adult in a peculiar manner, that is, by turning about and backstepping. This latter behavior had not been observed in most rejected infants.

The present study was undertaken to determine whether abused children would resemble relatively rejected children in normal samples. Abused toddlers were observed during social interactions with caregivers and with peers in special daycare centers: Their behavior was compared with that of matched controls from families experiencing stress. We expected that the abused infants would show relatively more aggression, more avoidance, and more approach-avoidance conflict.

METHOD

Participants Twenty children (10 physically abused children and 10 matched controls) participated in this study. Each group was composed of four females and six males, ranging in age from 1 to 3 years. The participants were contacted through four metropolitan daycare centers. Two of these had been established as child-protection centers exclusively for battered children. The two control centers specialized in serving "families under stress" in the neighboring community. The object of the 1-year search for subjects was to obtain, as far as possible, a sample differing only in histories of physical abuse. Sexual abuse and neglect cases were excluded.

This was the first daycare experience for the entire sample. The control children had experienced a few more months of care than the abused children, but the groups did not differ significantly in current hours per week in care.

The two groups of children were matched as completely as possible to the following demographic characteristics: sex, age, race, marital status of parents, mother's education and occupation, father's education and occupation (not always known), and finally the adult(s) with whom the child was living at the time of the study.

Centers The abused children were obtained from daycare centers in which they had been placed by city protective services. Within the group severity of abuse ranged from severe punishment to skull fractures, broken collar bones, and severe burns, but the marks of abuse were visible on only a few children. Our agreement with both centers and families to ensure the anonymity of participants prohibits more detailed descriptions of the circumstances.

Both the control centers served only "families under stress" in need of care for their children. Participation was on a voluntary basis. Stress was defined at these centers as social or emotional factors which made it necessary for the family or individual parent to seek care for the child. In some cases psychological treatment was needed for the parents, but in no case was the child pervasively neglected or abused.

Center A_1 (abuse) and center C_1 (control) were very similar in space provided and also in size (20 children) and child-caregiver ratio (in both centers, 3:1). Both care for infants up to 3 years. In both centers caregivers were responsible for the entire group of children. Seven abused children and six controls were drawn from these centers.

The physical structures of centers A_2 and C_2 were less well matched. Center A_2 cared for a smaller group of children (approximately 15) ranging in age from 1 to 7 years. In contrast, center C_2 was very large, extending care to approximately 30 children who ranged in age from 8 months to 4 years but were separated into small groups according to age. The caregiver-to-child ratio at Center A_2 was 3:1, and at center C_2 it was 4:1 for children over one year of age. Three abused and four control children were drawn from these two centers.

Procedure Written permission to observe each toddler was obtained from parents or legal guardians.

Five trained student observers made a continuous narrative account of the behavior of the children from the floor of the daycare centers. Each observer followed one infant for 30 min. The observers were instructed to be unobtrusive and to ignore gently any initiations by the child for each interaction. Four half-hour observations of each child were collected over a period of 3 months for each center.[1] No more than 1 week separated each observation for a particular child.

The instructions to the trained student observers were identical to those they had received from Main in previous observations and studies: to record social behavior as closely as possible, including even small movements such as backstepping. Since observation instructions were unchanged, four of the five observers were successfully kept blind to the specific hypotheses of this study. It was impossible for observers, however, to be kept blind regarding the identity of abuse and control centers. Centers were located in different areas of the community, caregivers conversed in the presence of observers, and finally, the physical condition of some of the children identified them as abused.

Description of Measures Social interaction as reported in the narrative records was coded into four mutually exclusive categories: approach, avoidance, approach-avoidance, and aggression. For each of these categories, the "target" person (whether child or caregiver) was noted.

Approach behavior was split into two main categories: head-turning and locomotor approach. "Head-turning only" referred to turning the head or upper body toward the target person. If locomotion was also used, the event was categorized instead as a "locomotor approach." Locomotor approach was further described in terms of the child's orientation to the target person as the child approached. Approaches made by moving directly forward toward the person, effectively in his or her full vision

---

[1]Only three half-hour observations were available for three of the children (two abused and one control) and the data for these have been prorated.

and while facing him/her, were described as direct approaches. Following a person who was moving away was also counted as a direct approach. Indirect approaches included approaches to the person's side, which occurred frequently; and approaches to the person's back (excepting the above) or to the person's "front" made by backstepping or scooting backwards so that the child could not see the person he was "approaching." These extreme forms of indirect approach are considered here as a single special category: approaches to the rear and/or backstepping. It is included as such because it had been seen in the severely punished infant studied by George (Note 3).

Any of these approach behaviors could occur either as spontaneous approach or in response to commands or to friendly overtures of others (see below).

Avoidance behaviors were also broken down into two main categories: head-turning only (including looking away, turning the head away, and turning the upper body away) and locomotor avoidance (walking away, creeping away, etc.). If locomotor avoidance occurred in addition to visual (head turning) avoidance, the event was categorized as locomotor avoidance only. Avoidance was categorized as such only when it occurred with definite reference to the appearance or behavior of a particular target person.

Approach-avoidance was a separate category of behavior. This was used when a child showed approach and avoidance behaviors either simultaneously ("she crawls toward the caregiver but with head averted") or in rapid sequence ("she creeps toward him but suddenly veers away"). The combinations of locomotor approach with gaze aversion and visual orientation with moving away were singled out as a subcategory of approach-avoidance entitled "head moves opposed to body."

The incidence in each of the above categories for each child was totaled over the 2 hours of observation, with special attention, in the case of approaches, to spontaneous approach.

Approach, avoidance, and approach-avoidance data were then examined for all instances of what were called "friendly approaches" (or overtures) made either by caregivers or other children. Examples of friendly approach are: efforts to assist the child in an activity or to make a friendly check on his/her mood or status, the initiation of friendly physical contact, and offering of toys or nourishment. We then determined the proportion of friendly approaches to which the child responded by showing approach, avoidance, or approach-avoidance behavior.

Two separate systems were used for the analysis of aggressive behavior. First, we simply counted the incidence of physical assault (hitting, kicking, pinching, spitting, slapping, or aggressively grabbing the body of another person) and the incidences of threats of assault of the same kind (where these were expressed physically). Second, we followed a schema provided by Margaret Manning (Manning, Heron, & Marshall, 1978) which divided occurrences of aggressive behavior (verbal as well as nonverbal) into the following three categories:

"Specific hostility" is defined as reactive aggression, a reaction to a specific preceding event, most commonly the loss of property. Examples of specific hostility in our sample include: grabbing keys away from a child who has just stolen them, yelling back at a child who has just taken a toy away, and pushing a child back after being pushed.
"Harassment" is, in contrast, defined as malicious behavior, behavior having the apparent intent of obtaining a distress reaction from the victim. Conceivably, harassment could be preceded by an offense on the part of the victim, such as removal of a toy or a verbal correction. Harassment, however, predominantly occurred spontaneously, unpredictably, and without apparent cause. Examples of harassment in our sample included: threatening another child with a shovel as the child entered the play area, slapping a nearby child after being corrected by a caregiver, kicking a child who is on the crossbars of the jungle gym, and spitting on a caregiver.

"Teasing" is defined as any behavior which interferes with an activity by holding onto to taking away a toy, taunting, etc. Teasing was often playful in nature, in contrast to the other forms of hostile behavior. Examples of teasing in our sample included: smiling which actively ignoring the command of a caregiver, and laughing while tentatively trying to take away another child's truck.

Interobserver Agreement Six reliability records were obtained; these involved each of the four main observers.[2]

Observer reliability was estimated using strict criteria. Observers were scored as being in disagreement if either observer missed the occurrence of a behavior. To be scored as being in agreement regarding a particular instance of approach, avoidance, or approach-avoidance, however, the two observers had to agree on every one of the following categories: the behavior, the mode (head turning or locomotor), the target, and the preceding event (e.g., whether or not the behavior was preceded by a friendly approach from the target). Observer agreement for approach, avoidance, and approach-avoidance categories ranged from 86% to 91%, with a mean of 89%. To be scored as being in agreement regarding aggressive behavior, the observers had to agree on the category of aggressive behavior and the target of the behavior. Observer agreement for aggressive behavior ranged from 89% to 92% with a mean of 90%.

For the purposes of coding, 10 half-hour narrative records were randomized. Two coders blind to the child's group placement coded the approach, avoidance, and approach-avoidance data. Two other coders blind to group placement coded the aggressive behavior. Intercoder agreement was estimated using the criteria described above. Coder agreement on the approach, avoidance, and approach-avoidance systems was 86%. Coder agreement on the aggressive behaviors was 88%.

RESULTS

Each of the three major categories of social behavior listed above was correlated (across groups, Pearson product-moment coefficient) with age, the number of months in daycare, and the number of hours per week in care. The only significant correlation was between approach behavior and age ($p <$ .05).

Caregivers approached the abused children an aver-

[2]So few reliability observations were undertaken because each of the four day-care centers was geared to the care of children under stress, and none welcomed having two observers simultaneously. Interobserver reliabilities for data collected outside of these care centers were even higher than those reported here.

age of 29.13 times over the 2 hours of observation, the control children an average of 32.55 times. Other children approached abused children an average of 20.08 times, the control children 21.19 times. The t tests for matched subjects showed that these differences were not significant.

Approach The abused infants approached caregivers only about half as often as the control children did ($t = 6.82$, $p <$ .0005), but for the most part they did not differ from the controls in approach to other infants.

It is interesting, however, that there were no significant differences in *spontaneous* approach. It is exactly when the caregiver made a friendly overture that the abused children, in contrast to the control children, failed to approach. When they did approach in response to a friendly overture from the caregiver, the abused children were far more likely than the controls to approach indirectly, that is, to the side, the rear, or by turning about and backstepping ($p <$ .01). Six of the abused infants but only two of the control infants responded by approaching to the rear or turning about and backstepping.

Avoidance The abused children avoided other children almost four times as often as the control children. When other children made friendly overtures, the abused children responded on the average by physically moving away 11% of the time, the control children only 2.6% of the time.

The abused children also avoided caregivers about three times as often as the controls avoided them. Furthermore, they responded to friendly approaches by turning or moving away 11% of the time, whereas the control children did so only 3% of the time.

Approach-avoidance Ten of the abused children but none of the control children responded to friendly overtures from other children with approach-avoidance behavior. Six of the abused children but none of the controls responded to other children with the odd form of approach-avoidance behavior in which the head moves in opposition to the body. Seven of the abused children but only one of the control children engaged in approach-avoidance behavior with caregivers.

Aggressive Behaviors   The abused infants physically assaulted other infants twice as often as the controls did. Five of the abused infants but none of the control infants assaulted or threatened to assault caregivers.

When all of Manning's categories of verbal and nonverbal aggressive behaviors were considered together, the abused infants were found to aggress against caregivers over four times as often as the control infants.

No group differences were found in teasing or in specific hostility: a majority of the abused children, however, "harassed" their caregivers.

DISCUSSION

In many articles which have appeared prior to this one, battered children have been described as unusually aggressive or angry (e.g., Curtis 1963; Galdston 1965; Green 1978; Johnson & Morse 1968; Martin 1972; Ten Broeck 1974). In previous reports, however, distinctions have not been drawn between types of aggression and among targets of aggressive behavior. These distinctions were made and were found helpful in the present study. Although for every measure of aggressive incidence, the abused children exceeded the control children, the strongest group differences occurred in behavior with caregivers. The abused children were the only children in the sample to assault or threaten to assault their caregivers, and seven of the abused children but only two of the control children "harassed" their caregivers.

This means that infants who have had some cause to regard caregiving figures as dangerous are more likely than other infants to assault and harass them. This may seem surprising, but there is a parallel from normal samples. Main (in press; Note 2) finds that both the mother's apparent aversion to physical contact with her infant and her angry behavior toward the infant are related to infant assault and threat of assault on the mother. Indeed, the mother's aversion to contact in the first three months of life is related to assault and threat of assault 9 months later.

Several explanations for this behavior can be suggested; they are compatible rather than mutually exclusive. The abused infants may be expressing a generalized anger toward caregiving figures, and/or they may be seeking interaction or attention, and/or in some way they may be imitating their own treatment at the hands of caregivers. Harassment is the one form of aggression whose aim seems to be "the discomfiture of the victim" (Manning, Heron, & Marshall, in press), and the harassment of caregivers may warrant special attention. Manning and her colleagues at Edinburgh found that preschool children who "specialized" in harassment in the nursery setting had mothers who enforced rules "strictly, often severely." In a follow-up study at the ages of 7 and 8, these children were found difficult and even disturbed in their school behavior.

The differences between the abused children and the control children in aggressive behavior were significant, but merely significant, differences. There were, in contrast, highly significant differences in approach and avoidance behavior. Other investigators have also noted avoidance, approach-avoidance, or affective withdrawal in abused children (Gaensbauer & Sands, in press; Martin & Beezley 1977; Gaensbauer, Mrazek, & Harmon Note 1).

That abused infants are avoidant or withdrawn is perhaps not surprising; apprehension in such infants is to be expected. In our own sample, however, the division of approaches into "spontaneous" approaches and approaches in response to friendly overtures yielded somewhat puzzling findings.

Between-group differences in approach behavior in our sample appeared for the most part with caregivers. Even if the abused infants are more generally apprehensive, it would seem most reasonable that they should show the greatest apprehension in situations in which the caregiver has failed to signal his own affiliative intentions. Thus in the absence of the "safety" signal of a friendly overture, it would seem intuitively reasonable to expect that abused children would approach less frequently, less directly, and with more avoidant movement than nonabused children would; whereas, when the signal is given the abused child might reasonably be expected to more closely approximate the control in its behavior.

In fact, of course, the reverse was obtained. There

were no significant differences in spontaneous loco-motor approaches to caregivers and none in orientation so long as the approach was spontaneous. It was precisely when their caregivers made friendly overtures that the abused children failed to approach them. Affiliative gestures from caregivers inhibited approach or resulted in spatial distortions in approach behavior. Affiliative gestures from caregivers or from peers resulted in avoidance or in combined approach-avoidance movements.

The simplest interpretation of the avoidant movements of the abused child is that the child is fearful and expressing this fearfulness in abbreviated movements of flight. A second, less simple interpretation may also be offered. This is that the infant's avoidance functions to permit the maintenance of control over its own prospective reactions to the attention of the partner-reactions which might be composed of fear, but also of anger, or distress, or all of these emotions/tendencies together.

This interpretation of the occurrence of avoidant movements in seemingly positive social circumstances was first put forth by the ethologist Michael Chance (1962). According to Chance, for many animals sight of even a well-intentioned prospective social partner interacting in close proximity is threatening: Hence sight of the prospective social partner under these conditions almost inevitably arouses tendencies toward flight, aggression, or both. Movements of avoidance in such situations do not merely "express" fear; by momentarily directing visual attention away from the attending partner they function to reduce the arousal of *any* disorganizing, negative emotions/tendencies. Control over such tendencies is desired because expression has negative effects on the behavior of the partner and is therefore dangerous to the maintenance of a socially positive proximity, and because full expression is disorganizing even for the performing animal. Shifts in attention away from the partner permit the maintenance of proximity and the maintenance of voluntary control.

This theory certainly suggests that an infant might be more apprehensive in situations in which attention of any kind was directed to it and correctly predicts increased avoidance in response to friendly overtures. What the theory adds is the suggestion that avoidance may function to reduce the likelihood

of flight, that avoidance may function to reduce the likelihood of expressions of anger or distress instead of or as well as those of flight, and that the infant is maintaining voluntary control in this fashion, rather than merely engaging in involuntary expressions of fearfulness.

This interpretation can neither be supported nor disconfirmed in an observational study in which film could not be employed for data collection. Nonetheless, in our opinion, it fits well with the data. (1) For abused infants, interaction and mutual attention with caregivers has sometimes led to disappointing, unpleasant, or even dangerous consequences. (2) At the same time, these consequences are likely to have aroused distress, fear, and anger. (3) Mutual attention is therefore especially threatening to maintenance of control for these infants. (4) So long as the infant is approaching solely on its own, it is relatively safe from this. (5) If the prospective partner does direct attention to the infant, the infant can maintain control through avoidance. (6) If the partner does direct attention to the infant and the infant approaches, the infant can still control the degree of arousal by approaching in such a way that the likelihood of reciprocal attention is limited, that is, by approaching to the side, to the rear, or by approaching with head averted, or by turning about and backstepping. All this suggests, of course, that the abused toddler may have special difficulty looking at the caregiver as the caregiver looks at it. This is further supported by still another strong difference in our data, one which was completely unexpected: Only two of the abused infants ever *simply* turned to look at caregivers making friendly overtures, while every one of the control infants did so.

CONCLUSIONS

1 *The social behavior of this sample of abused children does resemble that of relatively rejected children found within normal samples.* The results reported in this study affirmed our expectation that abused toddlers would display the syndrome of behavior which Main (1977; in press; Note 3) has described as appearing in rejected infants in normal samples: Compared with their matched controls, we found abused children aggressive, inhibited in approach, and avoidant in response to friendly overtures.

Maternally rejected infants in normal samples additionally tend to avoid the mother following separations in a strange environment (Ainsworth, Bell, & Stayton 1971; Main, Note 2). In a study of normal infants placed in daycare, Blanchard and Main (in press) found avoidance of the parent (whether observed on reunion in the laboratory or in the daycare setting) negatively related to social-emotional adjustment in the daycare environment. In this study, we were not able to observe toddlers with the abusing parent. Gaensbauer, Mrazek, and Harmon (Note 1) have, however, begun to conduct separation studies with parents of abused and/or neglected infants. According to their report, an unnumbered but apparently substantial percentage of these infants pay no attention to the mother or explicitly avoid interactions with her following brief separations in a strange environment. Taken together, these several studies suggest that avoidance of the attachment figure is a highly significant behavior pattern.

From these first studies it is not possible to tell what proportion of abused children will exhibit this avoidant-aggressive syndrome. Abused toddlers do not present a unitary picture, and interaction patterns differ among dyads (Martin & Beezley 1977; Gaensbauer, Mrazek, & Harmon, Note 1). However, the particular pattern described here is a coherent one. It leads to several further conclusions.

2 *Abused children differ from their matched controls. Since they are not only more aggressive, but also respond negatively to friendly overtures, they may readily be termed more "difficult."* There is evidence that many children who will later be abused begin life as difficult newborns (Martin, Note 4); low birth weight, prematurity, birth complications, and neonatal illness are associates of abuse, and each of these factors may make the caregiving task more difficult (Lynch 1975; Sameroff & Chandler 1975). This given, it is not surprising that not every child within a family is abused; usually only one child is singled out, sometimes one whom the parents describe as especially "difficult" (Friedrich & Boriskin 1976; Justice & Duncan 1975; Lynch 1975; Morse, Sahler, & Friedman 1970; Smith & Hanson 1974).

Our study was not addressed to the question of how these particular children came to be selected for parental abuse. It does affirm, however, that even this early in childhood the infant who has been abused can be "difficult."

3 *In broad aspects of their social behavior, abused infants bear some resemblance to their parents.* Although many efforts to provide an identifying profile for abusing parents have been undertaken, no single coherent profile emerges: Seemingly only two general conclusions can be drawn (see Parke & Collmer 1975). These are, first, that abusing parents suffer a general difficulty with the control of aggression, one which extends beyond the episodes of abuse of a particular child (Kempe, Silverman, Steele, Droegenmueller, & Silver 1962; Martin & Beezley 1977; Spinetta & Rigler 1972; Steele & Pollock 1968; Young 1964). Second, that abusing families tend to be both personally and socially isolated from the rest of the community and extended family resources (Elmer 1967; Garbarino & Crouter 1978; Merrill 1962; Smith & Hanson 1975; Young 1964; Martin, Note 4). This could be explained in part by their rejection by the community, but much of their isolation seems self-imposed.

In early childhood their children are already showing excessive aggression and rudimentary self-isolating mechanisms. These behaviors make the children of abusing parents "difficult." At the same time they may separate them from those who can offer help in the face of stress.

4 *If future studies of abused toddlers should confirm and elaborate on the present study, interventions in the abused-abusing cycle should begin directly with the infant.* According to Parke & Collmer (1975), the child-rearing histories of abusing parents reveal "a consistent picture of aggressive, physically punitive childhood experiences." Many investigators have further reported that parents who abuse their children were abused as children themselves (Curtis 1963; Justice & Duncan 1975; Kempe et al. 1962; Silver 1969; Spinetta & Rigler 1972; Steele & Pollock 1968). Note that this does not imply that the majority of abused children become abusing parents, but only that abusing parents have themselves been abused. Nonetheless, these studies establish evidence for intergenerational continuity.

Despite this evidence, family intervention in child abuse has to date meant primarily help for the abusing parents, aimed at the prevention of further abuse. If, however, succeeding samples of abused infants show distortions in social behavior similar to those we have reported, intervention in the future should probably deal directly with the infant as well as the parent. One clear possibility for intervention is the establishment of specially staffed daycare centers, perhaps centers in which abused infants are placed with nonabused.

The absolute seriousness ·of distortions in social behavior cannot be determined in a study such as this one, which merely establishes the existence of differences between groups. These distortions are not random, however; they form an expected and coherent pattern. The discovery of this pattern represents an important if early step toward understanding the development of children who have undergone abuse.

REFERENCE NOTES

1 Gaensbauer, T. J.; Mrazek, D.; & Harmon, R. J. Affective behavior patterns in abused and/or neglected infants. Unpublished manuscript, 1978.
2 Main, M. Avoidance of the attachment figure in infancy. Unpublished manuscript, 1978.
3 George, C. Microanalysis of the social behavior of a severely punished toddler. Unpublished manuscript, 1975.
4 Martin, H. P. The abusive environment and the child's adaptation. Paper presented at the meeting of the American Psychological Association, San Francisco, August 1977.

REFERENCES

Ainsworth, M. D. S., Bell, S. M. V., & Stayton, D. Individual differences in strange situation behavior of one-year-olds. In H. R. Schaffer (Ed.), *The origins of human social relations.* London: Academic Press, 1971.

Blanchard, M., & Main, M. Avoidance of the attachment figure and social-emotional adjustment in daycare infants. *Developmental Psychology,* in press.

Chance, M. R. S. An interpretation of some agonistic postures: the role of "cut-off" acts and postures. *Symposia of the Zoological Society of London,* 1962, **8,** 71–89.

Curtis, G. Violence breeds violence—perhaps? *American Journal of Psychiatry,* 1963, **120,** 386–387.

Elmer, E. *Children in jeopardy: a study of abused minors and their families.* Pittsburgh: University of Pittsburgh Press, 1967.

Friedrich, W. N., & Boriskin, J. A. The role of the child in abuse: a review of the literature. *American Journal of Orthopsychiatry,* 1976, **46,** 580–590.

Gaensbauer, T. J., & Sands, K. Distorted affective communications in abused/neglected infants and their potential impact on caretakers. *Journal of the American Academy of Child Psychiatry,* in press.

Galdston, R. Observations on children who have been physically abused and their parents. *American Journal of Psychiatry,* 1965, **122,** 440–443.

Garbarino, J., & Crouter, A. Defining the community context for parent-child relations: the correlates of child maltreatment. *Child Development,* 1978, **49,** 604–616.

Green, A. H. Psychopathology of abused children. *Journal of the American Academy of Child Psychiatry,* 1978, **17,** 92–103.

Johnson, B., & Morse, H. A. Injured children and their parents. *Children,* 1968, **15,** 147–152.

Justice, B., & Duncan, D. F. Physical abuse of children. *Public Health Reviews,* 1975, **4,** 183–200.

Kempe, C. H., Silverman, F. N., Steele, B. B., Droegenmueller, W., & Silver, H. K. The battered-child syndrome. *Journal of of the American Medical Association,* 1962, **181,** 17–24.

Lynch, M. A. Ill-health and child abuse. *Lancet,* August 16, 1975.

Maden, M. F., & Wrench, D. F. Significant findings in child abuse research. *Victimology,* 1977, **2,** 196–244.

Main, M. Analysis of a peculiar form of reunion behavior seen in some daycare children: its history and sequelae in children who are home-reared. In R. Webb (Ed.), *Social development in childhood: daycare programs and reasearch.* Baltimore: Johns Hopkins University Press, 1977.

Main, M. Avoidance in the service of proximity. In K. Immelmann, G. Barlow, M. Main, & L. Petrinovitch (Eds.), *Behavioral development: the Bielefeld interdisciplinary project.* New York: Cambridge University Press, 1981.

Manning, M., Heron, J., & Marshall, T. Styles of hostility and social interactions at nursery, at school and at home: an extended study of children. In L. Hersov & M. Berger (Eds.), *Aggression and conduct disorder in childhood and adolescence.* New York: Pergamon Press, 1978.

Martin, H. P. The child and his development. In C. Kempe & R. Helfer (Eds.), *Helping the battered child and his family.* Chicago: University of Chicago Press, 1972.

Martin, H. P., & Beezley, P. Behavioral observations of abused children. *Developmental Medicine and Child Neurology,* 1977, **19,** 373–387.

Merrill, E. J. Physical abuse of children: an agency study. In V. de Francis (Ed.), *Protecting the battered child.* Denver: American Humane Association, 1962.

Morse, W., Sahler, O. J., & Friedman, S. B. A three-year follow-up of abused and neglected children. *American Journal of Diseases of Children,* 1970, **120,** 439–446.

Parke, R. D., & Collmer, C. W. Child abuse: an interdisciplinary analysis. In E. M. Hetherington (Ed.), *Review of child development research.* Vol. **5.** Chicago: University of Chicago Press, 1975.

Sameroff, A. J., & Chandler, M. J. Perinatal risk and the continuum of caretaking casualty. In F. D. Horowitz, E. M. Hetherington, S. Scarr-Salapatek, & G. Siegel (Eds.), *Review of child development research,* Vol. **4.** Chicago: University of Chicago Press, 1975.

Siegel, S. *Nonparametric statistics.* New York: McGraw-Hill, 1956.

Silver, L. B. Does violence breed violence? Contributions from a study of the child abuse syndrome. *American Journal of Psychiatry,* 1969, **3,** 126.

Smith, S. M., & Hanson, R. Battered children: a medical and psychological study. *British Medical Journal,* 1974, **3,** 666–670.

Smith, S. M., & Hanson, R. Interpersonal relationships and childbearing practices in 214 parents of battered children. *British Journal of Psychiatry,* 1975, **127,** 513–525.

Spinetta, J. J., & Rigler, D. The child-abusing parent: a psychological review. *Psychological Bulletin,* 1972, **77,** 296–304.

Steele, B. F., & Pollock, D. A psychiatric study of parents who abuse infants and small children. In R. E. Helfer & C. H. Kempe (Eds.), *The battered child.* Chicago: University of Chicago Press, 1968.

Ten Broeck, E. The extended family center: a home away from home for abused children and their parents. *Children Today,* 1974, **3,** 2–6.

Young, L. *Wednesday's children: a study of child neglect and abuse.* New York: McGraw-Hill, 1964.

Reading 30

What Does Research Teach Us about Day Care?
A Follow-Up Report

Jay Belsky
Laurence D. Steinberg

In its 1978 report to Congress, evaluating the appropriateness of Federal Interagency Day Care Requirements, the Department of Health, Education, and Welfare reported that approximately 2.5 million infants and toddlers as well as 3.7 million preschoolers were enrolled in day care on a full- or part-time basis.[1] If recent trends provide any indication of what to expect in the near future, it is clear that the demand for day care in the United States will continue to grow over the next few years. Given this state of affairs, it is legitimate to ask, from the vantage points of social policy, science and concerned parents: What are the consequences of this form of child care?

Writing in the January-February 1972 issue of *Children Today,* Bettye Caldwell and Edith Grotberg provided some preliminary answers to this question.[2] This article is intended to update their analyses by discussing the present status of our knowledge concerning the effects of day care. Our summary of research findings is based on a review of day care we recently completed for the Department of Health, Education, and Welfare.[3] It considers the impact of day care upon the three aspects—intellectual, emotional and social—of children's development.

INTELLECTUAL DEVELOPMENT

On the basis of the research available in 1972, Caldwell concluded that the cognitive and intellectu-al development of children under three are "not harmed by experiences in a day care environment . . . and, in fact, many young children benefit significantly from such exposure." Since Dr. Caldwell's report appeared additional research has been undertaken and the results tend to support her conclusions. In fact, in our recent review of more than 40 investigations, we concluded "that the day care experience has neither salutary nor adverse effects on the intellectual development (as assessed by standardized tests) of most children. For economically disadvantaged children, however, day care may have an enduring positive effect, for it appears that such day care experience may attenuate declines in test scores typically associated with high-risk populations after 18 months of age."[4]

Several recently completed longitudinal studies of infant day care provide the clearest documentation of the validity of this conclusion. For example, Jerome Kagan's Boston-based investigation of Chinese-American and Caucasian children from working class families revealed few differences between matched young children in day care and those reared at home when an extensive battery of cognitive assessments (tapping memory, concept formation, vocabulary and language comprehension) were administered periodically when the children were between the ages of six and 29 months.[5]

The work of Craig Ramey and his colleagues in North Carolina.[6] and of Mark Golden and his associates in New York City,[7] provide evidence that early exposure to day care may have positive consequences for children from economically disadvantaged households. What is most intriguing about these results is the fact that while the children studied in North Carolina attended an extremely high-quality, cognitively-enriched, university-sponsored day care program, those participating in the New York City research were enrolled in publicly and privately funded, community-sponsored centers much more likely to be representative of model day care in this country than the focal centers in Boston and North Carolina.

Clearly these results must be encouraging to those hopeful that day care in the first few years of life can function as an effective early intervention to prevent the cognitive declines so repeatedly discerned among children from economically disadvantaged homes.[8] Despite this optimism, however, caution must be exercised in interpreting these findings since there is still no evidence that these positive benefits persist into and through the school-age years. Furthermore, it must be recognized that the research findings in the New York City project apply only to day care centers, not family day care homes. Finally, notice must be taken of the fact that the positive effect described refers only to the attenuation of the declines commonly observed among the populations studied; the evidence simply does not suggest that the IQ scores of high risk children enrolled in day care increase as a function of the day care experience.

From a more general standpoint, the results summarized above are qualified by one very significant consideration. In almost all the studies that we evaluated, investigators examining the effects of day care upon cognitive functioning relied upon standardized tests of intellectual performance. As a result, it remains unclear whether the data derived from these measures (IQ scores) are readily generalizable to real-life settings. For only when evaluations geared toward assessing children's motivation and ability to function purposefully, effectively and successfully in the course of their daily interchanges are made, will it be possible to conclude that these positive effects associated with day care are significant in terms of the children's later functioning in school and society.

EMOTIONAL DEVELOPMENT

Although the results of research on day care and cognitive development are encouraging, especially in light of earlier fears that care outside the home in the first years of life would irreparably harm a child, the issue of paramount importance to many is whether day care affects the emotional bond between mother and child. Historically, this bond has been a prime focus of concern for those interested in the more general issue of the influence of early experiences on later development. Since psychoanalytic theory and prior research on institutionalized children suggested that any arrangement that deprives a child of continuous access to his or her mother would impair the development of a strong maternal attachment, and so adversely affect the child's emotional security, it is no wonder that a great deal of attention has been devoted to learning whether child care outside the home disrupts the child's emotional bond to his or her mother.[9]

Although the early evidence summarized by Caldwell on this issue could be considered, in her words, "very reassuring," a report that appeared in 1974 suggested that her conclusion—that no differences in children's attachments to their mothers were shown by children in day care as opposed to those reared at home—may have been premature. In fact, Mary Curtis Blehar's investigation of a sample of day care and home-reared children in Baltimore indicated that day care may have fostered anxious and ambivalent, as opposed to secure, attachments to mothers.[10]

More recently, a number of investigations have been conducted which challenge Blehar's findings. Again and again researchers have discerned no differences in the mother-child bond between children in day care and home-reared children. Quoting again from our earlier review: "The total body of evidence reviewed regarding the effect of day care on the child's attachment to his mother offers little support for the claim that day care disrupts the child's ties to his mother. . . . With the exception of Blehar's report, *not a single study provided evidence documenting the existence of substantial, systematic differences* between day care and home-reared children . . ." In fact, not only do day care children appear as equally attached to their mothers as their home-reared counterparts but they even do not seem to prefer their caregivers to their parents. More specifically, several studies clearly indicate that young children are more likely to stay in the proximity of, or interact with, their mothers as opposed to their familiar caregivers when confronted with situations of stress and boredom or which demand assistance in problem solving.[11]

The absence of evidence for the deleterious effects of day care in existing research does not mean, however, that no such effects may occur. Once again the results reviewed must be qualified, this time not only in terms of the investigatory procedures employed by day care researchers to assess emotional development but also in terms of the populations studied. The majority of children whose relationships with mothers have been investigated have come from day care programs that simply cannot be considered representative of those available to most parents: high quality centers run by universities for research purposes. Thus we must be extremely cautious in applying the results summarized above to the kinds of day care most prevalent in this country—family day care, church-based day care and community center day care.[12] Until more investigations of children from such programs are carried out, the only conclusion that is empirically justifiable is that day care need not disrupt the child's emotional bond with his or her mother. Given the fears of many concerning the potential for developmental disturbance in children as a result of receiving day care, such a limited conclusion should not be considered inconsequential.

The investigatory strategy employed by researchers to assess emotional development, or more accurately the mother-child relationship, must also be scrutinized. If the term "relationship" implies an enduring, generalized pattern of reciprocal feelings and acts which cut across time and settings, there is reason to wonder whether a one-time procedure (that evaluates the child's approach-avoidance responses following repeated separations from mother, in the presence of a strange adult, in an unfamiliar university laboratory) can adequately diagnose the quality of the mother-child bond, as day care researchers seem to believe it can. Recent evidence from basic research suggests that individual differences between children discerned in such a "strange situation," as it is so aptly called, are stable between 12 and 18 months, and can predict children's motivation and competence in a problem-solving situation at the age of two.[13] Nevertheless, we suggest that to meaningfully assess the mother- and father-child relationship, serious attention must also be paid to what goes on in the real world, that is, in day care children's homes.

At present, we really know very little about the nature of daily parent-child interaction patterns in families with children in day care. It seems reasonable to ask, then, whether and to what degree day care impacts on the mother-child and also on the father-child relationship. Until such evaluations are made, we must remain cautious in generalizing any findings concerning the effects of day care on emotional development.

SOCIAL DEVELOPMENT

In the realm of social development, defined as relations with persons other than the child's parents, the available research on the effects of day care may be least encouraging. When compared with age-mates reared at home, day care children tend to interact more with peers, in both positive *and* negative ways. That is, they are more likely to cooperate with as well as aggress against their agemates. Some evidence suggests, moreover, that children enrolled in day care for extended periods of time show increased apprehension towards adults and decreased cooperation with them, as well as a lessened involvement in educational activities once they enter school.

In evaluating the significance of our findings, we feel it is essential to emphasize the important point that such social consequences of day care are more likely to be functions of particular socialization values—individualism vs. the group and competition vs. cooperation—than of day care in general. This conclusion is based on two points: evidence from other countries (Russia, China and Israel) indicating that group care there results in outcomes very different from those summarized above[14] and our belief that the social development of children in day care programs in this country most often reflects the characteristically stressed American values of aggressiveness, impulsivity and egocentrism.[15] Indeed, as we go on to suggest in our more lengthy review of day care research, "Like all social or educational efforts, day care programs are likely to reflect, and in some measures achieve, the values held explicitly or implicitly by their sponsor, and, through them, the community at large."[16]

It is no wonder then that another set of investigators, Macrae and Herbert-Jackson, proposed that with respect to social development the effects of day care may be program specific.[17] If cross-cultural evidence can be used to document the fact that varied value systems can differentially affect the social products of group rearing, then there is little doubt as to the validity of this analysis. More important, there should, consequently, also be little doubt that the results summarized above, which will certainly be discouraging to some, in no way represent the inevitable by-products of the day care experience.

CONCLUSION

Since the reviews by Caldwell and Grotberg appeared, a great deal of additional research has been conducted in the field of day care. As we and others have noted, much still remains to be done, and not only concerning the effects of day care on intellectual and emotional development, as previously suggested. With the recent completion of the National Day Care Study, conducted for the Administration for Children, Youth and Families by Abt Associates, inroads are being made to expand the focus of traditional day care research.[18] Moreover, the foresightful planners of this large-scale investigation were able to assure that data of critical importance to public policy decision making were gathered. Most significant in this regard are the study findings concerning group size, staff-child ratio and the training of caregiving personnel in center-based day care.

With respect to group size, the information gathered on 1,800 preschool children, 1,200 parents and 300 staff members from 150 centers in Atlanta, Detroit and Seattle revealed that children in smaller groups, consisting, for example, of about 16 to 18 children, learned more and acted more positively than did their counterparts enrolled in larger groups. In fact, as group size got smaller, the study found, children had a better experience in day care. Interestingly, staff-child ratio was not observed to have as important an impact on the quality of care provided as did group size—except in the case of infant and toddler care. The study also found that specialized training of staff members, or education of staff personnel in fields related to the development of young children, was significantly related to the quality of care provided.

In sum, smaller groups, especially those supervised by trained personnel, tended to be characterized by activity and harmony. Children in such groups showed less hostility and conflict, less aimless wandering, less apathy and more involvement. There was also more warmth and positive interaction between caregivers and children. That such

results have direct bearing on the administration of day care programs and federal regulation of them is self-evident. Indeed, it is clear that data of the sort gathered in the National Day Care Study are the kind that can assure that program designs maximize the benefits that children may receive from day care.

The findings of the National Day Care Study are of critical importance to parents, policy makers and program planners. The study has broadened the scope of day care research which, until recently, was focused primarily upon the effects of day care on the children receiving such care. Nevertheless, it must be recognized that there still exist many "unknowns in the day care equation."[19] For example, we have little idea at present how variations in day care environments other than staff training and group size (such as segregation by age groups and presence of male caregivers) systematically affect development. Most important in this regard are the potentially differential effects of being reared in centers as opposed to family day care homes, or even in one's own home by babysitters. Dr. Moncrieff Cochran of Cornell University has recently documented, in a study of day care in Sweden, that children's experiences in centers and in homes differ markedly.[20] For example, in centers children experienced fewer restrictions and played with toys more, but they also explored non-toy objects, such as plants and lamps, less frequently. In this country, Dr. Judith Rubenstein of Tufts University has discerned similar differences between rearing environments.[21] Clearly these investigations document the well-known fact that day care programs differ. Is it not reasonable to question, then, whether such systematic variation between center and family day care programs have differential consequences for children?

In all likelihood, the effects of day care, whether center- or family-based, are mediated by children's experiences at home. If day care encourages parents to "abdicate" their childrearing responsibilities to the day care programs in which their children are enrolled, it is difficult to see how day care could support healthy psychological development. After all, day care-reared children will spend far more time over the course of their lives at home with their parents than in the day care programs which they must eventually leave.

If, on the other hand, day care supports parents in their childrearing efforts, as most day care proponents believe, then day care is likely to have beneficial consequences, not only for the child, but for the entire family as well. In fact, it is likely that supportive day care would enhance the quality of the time mothers and fathers spend with their children and, possibly, even the quality of the relationship that exists between spouses. At the community level, it is also worth noting, day care may stimulate the development of adult friendships and natural helping networks, factors which we known are important in supporting families in their childrearing roles. Unfortunately, these wider effects of day care have yet to receive the systematic attention they deserve.

Another important issue that needs to be addressed in future work is the interface of day care and the home. What are the effects, for example, of being reared in two different rearing contexts, in which socialization demands systematically vary?

As a first step toward answering this question, Douglas Powell of the Merrill-Palmer Institute has conducted interviews with over 200 parents and almost 100 caregivers from 12 Detroit area day care centers.[22] While caregiver-parent communication was observed to be frequent, especially during transition points in the day (drop-off and pick-up times), the data gathered revealed minimal attempts to coordinate children's socialization processes in the home and in the center. From these findings Powell was led to conclude that "the social world of day care children . . . is one of fragmentation and discontinuity." Although this descriptive study of parent-caregiver communication provides no evidence as to whether such experience negatively affects the child, it most certainly highlights the need to explore how the day care/home interface impacts on the child's functioning, both at home and in day care.

Clearly a tremendous amount of study needs to be done on the growing situation of day care before we can truly evaluate its overall effects. Given such research, the future should provide information pertinent to the issues raised here, as well as to many others. In another seven years, if not before, it should be time for another follow-up report on "What Does Research Teach Us About Day Care?"

FOOTNOTES

1 *The Appropriateness of the Federal Interagency Day Care Requirements (FIDCR): Report of Findings and Recommendations,* Washington, D.C., Office of Assistant Secretary for Planning and Evaluation, U.S. Department of Health, Education, and Welfare, 1978.

2 B. Caldwell, "What Does Research Teach Us About Day Care: For Children Under Three" and E. Grotberg, "What Does Research Teach Us About Day Care: For Children Over Three," *Children Today,* Jan.-Feb. 1972.

3 U. Bronfenbrenner, J. Belsky and L. Steinberg, "Day Care in Context: An Ecological Perspective on Research and Public Policy," paper prepared for the Office of the Assistant Secretary for Planning and Evaluation, Department of Health, Education, and Welfare, 1976 (revised 1977) and J. Belsky and L. Steinberg, "The Effects of Day Care: A Critical Review," *Child Development,* December 1978.

4 Belsky and Steinberg, op. cit.

5 J. Kagan, R. Kearsley and P. Zelazo, *Infancy: Its Place in Development,* Harvard University Press, 1978.

6 C. Ramey and B. Smith, "Assessing the Intellectual Consequences of Early Intervention with High-Risk Infants," *American Journal of Mental Deficiency,* January 1977, and C. Ramey and F. Campbell, "The Prevention of Developmental Retardation in High-Risk Children," in P. Mittler (Ed.), *Research to Practice in Mental Retardation: Vol. 1, Care and Intervention,* Baltimore, Md., University Park Press, 1977.

7 M. Golden, et al., *The New York City Infant Day Care Study,* New York, Medical and Health Research Association of New York City, Inc., 1978.

8 For summary of evidence documenting such declines, see M. Golden and B. Birns, "Social Class and Infant Intelligence," in M. Lewis (Ed.), *Origins of Intelligence,* New York, Plenum Press, 1976.

9 J. Bowlby, *Maternal Care and Child Health,* Geneva, World Health Organization, 1951; W. Goldfarb, "The Effects of Early Institutional Care on Adolescent Personality," *Journal of Experimental Education,* December 1943; and R. Spitz, "Hospitalism: An Inquiry into the Genesis of Psychiatric Conditions in Early Childhood," Vol. 1, *Psychoanalytic Study of the Child,* 1945.

10 M. Blehar, "Anxious Attachment and Defensive Reactions Associated with Day Care," *Child Development,* September 1974.

11 H. Ricciuti, "Fear and Development of Social Attachments in the First Year of Life," in M. Lewis and L. Rosenblum (Eds.), *The Origins of Human Behavior: Fear,* New York, Wiley, 1974; D. Farran and C. Ramey, "Infant Day Care and Attachment Behavior Towards Mothers and Teachers," *Child Development,* September 1977; and Kagan et al., op. cit.

12 In fact, recent research by Steinberg suggests that different types of day care may have different patterns of effects on children and their families: see L. Steinberg and C. Green, "Three Types of Day Care: Choices, Concerns and Consequences," unpublished manuscript, available from L. Steinberg, University of California at Irvine.

13 L. Matas, R. Arend and L. Sroufe, "Continuity and Adaptation in the Second Year: The Relationship Between Quality of Attachment and Later Competence," *Child Development,* September 1978 and E. Waters, "The Reliability and Stability of Individual Differences in Infant-Mother Attachment," *Child Development,* June 1978.

14 See, for example, U. Bronfenbrenner, *Two Worlds of Childhood: U.S. and U.S.S.R.,* New York, Russell Sage Foundation, 1970 and U. Bronfenbrenner, "Reaction to Social Pressure From Adults Versus Peers Among Soviet Day School and Boarding School Pupils in the Perspective of an American Sample," *Journal of Personality and Social Psychology,* July 1970.

15 J. Schwarz, R. Strickland and C. Krolick, "Infant Day Care: Behavioral Effects at Preschool Age," *Developmental Psychology,* July 1974.

16 J. Belsky and L. Steinberg, op. cit.

17 J. Macrae and E. Herbert-Jackson, "Are Behavioral Effects of Infant Day Care Program Specific?" *Developmental Psychology,* May 1975.

18 See Executive Summary of Vol. 1 of the final study report, *Children at the Center: Summary Findings and Policy Implications of the National Day Care Study,* Cambridge, Mass., Abt Associates, March 1979. (Single copies are available free from the Day Care Division, ACYF, P.O. Box 1182, Washington, D.C. 20013.)

19 For a more extensive analysis of such unknowns see J. Belsky, "An Ecological Analysis of Unknowns in the Day Care Equation," invited address, Conference on Day Care and the Family, Auburn University, September 1977.

20 M. Cochran, "A Comparison of Group Day and Family Child-rearing Patterns in Sweden," *Child Development,* September 1978.

21 J. Rubenstein and C. Howes, "Caregiving and Infant Behavior in Day Care and In Homes," *Developmental Psychology,* January 1979.

22 D. Powell, "Interpersonal Relationship Between Parents and Caregivers In Day Care Centers," *American Journal of Orthopsychiatry,* October 1978.

Reading 31

Cultural Experiments in Restructuring the Family

David B. Lynn

From each according to his ability.
To each according to his need.

A *kibbutz* principle

Many of the families in the cultures reviewed in Chapter Three are dominated by authoritarian fathers, if not traditionally patriarchal. Now we will examine some systematic efforts to eradicate patriarchy. The People's Republic of China, the U.S.S.R., and Sweden have methodically attacked patriarchy on a nationwide scale. Efforts have also been made to eliminate patriarchy among groups within the broader culture; for example, in the *kibbutz* of Israel and in communes in North America. We will discuss the father role in the Soviet Union, Sweden, the *kibbutz,* and the communes of North America.

THE SOVIET EXPERIMENT

The prerevolutionary legal code of Russia gave the husband unlimited power in his family, but follow-ing the Revolution the government and much of the urban population denounced patriarchal patterns as backward and unenlightened "remnants" of an outmoded, decadent way of life.

The chief target was the patriarchal institution of the Church and its tradition of ascribing inferior status to women. This tradition was especially strong among the peasants, who clung to the old patriarchal mores. The attitude of the Communist officials versus that of the peasants can be seen in the Party's attack on jealousy as an extension of the concept of private property. Because emancipated women could not longer be regarded as property, it became one of the worst crimes to kill a woman for jealousy. Equality of power and authority between husband and wife within the family not only was encouraged but became law. No legal distinctions remain between the sexes regarding domestic rights and duties. Husband and wife enjoy full freedom of choice concerning their individual occupation and place of residence. Each spouse is required to support the other if he or she is in need and unable to work, and husband and wife are jointly responsible for the support and upbringing of the children.

Equality of the sexes went beyond legal parity. The state's plan was that after private ownership of property was abolished, after women were engaged in production on an equal footing with men, and after the state assumed most of the functions of the family, then couples could bear children without having to assume the obligations usually involved in family life. The separation of the housewife from the kitchen was to be a more significant event than the separation of the church and state. Communal kitchens, dining halls, laundries, and children's homes and preschool centers would be established. Even the possibility of separate residences for husband and wife was proposed to assure genuine emancipation of women.

These and other measures were designed to abolish traditional parent-child ties as well. Motivation for these measures stemmed partly from the fact that parents were apt to be more resistant to the new regime than children and should therefore have less influence over their children. In addition, the measures were designed to abolish the advantages in wealth, education, and position that some parents were able to afford for their children, and instead to offer equal opportunity to all children.

The Soviets have been only partly successful with their reforms. Although the role of women in the society has improved in many respects, men still predominate in governing and managerial positions. The much-heralded predominance of women in clinical medicine in Russia is easily misinterpreted as symbolizing equality of the sexes. The fact is that clinical medicine (as opposed to medical research and teaching) is considered one of the nurturing professions, like grade-school teaching and nursing, and therefore especially suited to women. Clinical medicine is not given the prestige it receives in our society.

Most schoolteachers are women, although some men do teach especially in the secondary schools; but the greater proportion of female teachers is even more pronounced than in North America. Activities in the home are still sex-typed. The primary responsibility of the husband is to provide material security for the family, while the wife's is to care for young children, prepare food, wash clothes, and so on. Most Soviet women are both wife and mother on the one hand and full-time worker on the other, a dual role that is a strain on them and their families.

Soviet men, Communists as well as others, are amused when told that American men don't mind helping women wash dishes, sweep floors, and change diapers. To them these are strictly women's tasks, and the equality of the sexes proclaimed by the revolution does not extend to sharing household chores.

Men seem more willing to work under women in public life than to relinquish dominance in the home, and this fact is a bitter pill for women. One woman wrote to the newspaper that her husband, an important activist, had forbidden her to engage in political activity. She complained that in those very meetings that he forbids her to attend, and which she attends secretly, he makes thunderous speeches about the active role that women should play in the revolution. What he needs, she wrote, is a cook and a mistress. Although women carry their burden cheerfully, on the whole, they deeply resent the fact that life seems easier for their husbands. Even so, cooperation and good comradeship seem to prevail in Soviet marraiges; indeed, everything in the couple's background and training has equipped them for cooperative living.

Although preschool centers and collective dining facilities are not as prevalent as early proponents had envisioned, over 10 percent of all Soviet children from 3 months to 2 years of age are currently enrolled in public nurseries, and about 20 percent of the children between 3 and 6 years of age attend preschool institutions. About 5 percent of all school-age children (7 years old and over) are enrolled in boarding schools or extended-day schools. In the extended-day school, pupils arrive early in the morning and leave at about six o'clock in the evening. Priority for admission to these facilities is given to children from families in which one parent is absent or away for long periods, or in which the parents work on different shifts. So although most women have not been relieved of the obligations involved in family life, as was the original plan, considerable headway has been made in providing some families with public nurseries, boarding schools, and extended-day schools.

Although most children live with their parents, primary responsibility for rearing children does not center in the family. Soviet parents are not without authority, but their authority is only the reflected power of the state. The duty of the father toward his children is a particular form of his duty toward society: to do a good job of raising its citizens. The state, in fact, expects parents to give their children love as part of that correct upbringing. Schools, camps, children's institutions, and youth programs provide the child with formalized character training aimed at the development of Communist collectivist morality (duty, honor, conscience, patience, perseverance, proper attitude toward work and public property, and so on), responsible attitudes toward learning, good conduct, esthetic appreciation, and physical culture and sports.

Most of the child's activities, including those in the home, are taught him in the children's collective of which he is a member. Each classroom is a unit of the Communist youth organization appropriate to that grade level. The child is instructed to engage in certain activities at home: for example, in the first grade he is taught to greet parents upon arising, to thank them after meals, and to take care of his own things (including sewing on buttons). In the fifth grade, he is instructed to assist in the home garden and to help care for the elderly members of the family. These activities are rehearsed through role playing and systematically reported on in school. The schools may ask parents to submit reports on the child's behavior at home; they also recommend appropriate punishment. As the children mature, collectively and individually, they become increasingly responsible for their own behavior. First-grade children are appointed as monitors to record achievements and conduct. Older children learn public self-criticism. Occasionally an older child is disciplined by the collective through a trial conducted by his peers.

From our perspective, the Soviet state intrudes upon the domain of the family. In fact, though, the values of the state and those of the parents seem generally to coincide, so that the home and the collective reinforce each other. The child experiences continuity between home and society, and both are strong sources of security, support, and satisfaction. In both, deviance is interpreted as betrayal and elicits withdrawal of acceptance, which produces guilt (Bronfenbrenner, 1970).

Soviet parents lavish both affection and demands on their children. Babies are held more often than are American babies. Breast feeding is virtually universal, and babies are frequently held even when they are not being fed. Young Russian children receive considerably more hugging, kissing, and cuddling than American children. On the other hand, they are given little opportunity for freedom

and initiative. There is concern to protect them from discomfort, illness, injury, and drafts. Children in the park are expected to stay in the immediate vicinity of their accompanying adult.

The American psychologist Urie Bronfenbrenner, who did research in Russia, reports (1970) that when his children, aged 9 and 4, would run about the park well within his view, kindly citizens of all ages would bring them back by hand, often with a reproachful word about his lack of parental concern. It is common when sitting in a crowded public conveyance to have a child placed on one's lap by strangers.

Older children of both sexes also show a lively interest in young children and are much more comfortable handling them than our society. Urie Bronfenbrenner reports that once when his 4-year-old son was walking briskly ahead of him, a group of teen-age boys coming from the opposite direction scooped him up, hugged him, kissed him resoundingly, and passed him from one to the other. Then they began a merry children's dance, caressing him with words and gestures.

What differentiates Russian parents from their American counterparts is the emotional loading of the parent-child relationship, both in its positive and negative aspects. On the one hand, the parents are more demonstrative toward the child. On the other hand, any departure from proper behavior evokes a prompt withdrawal of affection, expressed to the child by gesture, word, intonation, or eloquent silence. The child is made to feel that he has ungratefully betrayed an affectional bond with his parent.

Despite the affection, patience, and nurturance of the Soviet father toward his child, the mother still has primacy in child rearing. It is still common practice in Russia to give a man work assignments in a locality away from his family, with no apparent concern either for the consequences of separating father from child or for leaving the mother with the entire responsibility for child rearing during his absence. The popular literature on bringing up children is addressed to the mother and portrays her as the principal decision maker where the child is concerned.

Since the child is accustomed from birth to the nurturance of strangers, it is not surprising that he easily transfers his dependence from his mother to the collective as the primary source of security and incontestable authority. The evidence suggests that the combined force of the values held in common by parents and the collective does produce a child who conforms to adult standards of good conduct. A study (Bronfenbrenner, 1970) of 12-year-olds in different countries, including the U.S.S.R., tested children's readiness to engage in morally disapproved behavior, such as cheating on a test or denying responsibility for property damage. Hypothetical situations involving such behavior were presented under three different conditions: (1) no one would know their answers; (2) only parents and teachers would be informed of their answers; and (3) only classmates would be informed of their answers. Under all three conditions, Soviet children proved much less willing to engage in antisocial behavior than their age-mates in the United States, England, and East Germany. When told that their classmates would know of their actions, American children were even more inclined to take part in misconduct than if no one knew. Soviet youngsters showed just the opposite tendency; in fact, their classmates were about as effective as their parents in inhibiting misbehavior.

In another study (Bronfenbrenner, 1970), which compared Swiss and Soviet boarding-school children, the child was asked to tell what he would do if he learned that a classmate or friend had engaged in some form of misconduct. The Soviet child was much more likely than the Swiss to talk to the misbehaving comrade or to invoke the help of other children in dealing with the problem, and much *less* likely to tell an adult or simply to do nothing at all about it. Taken together, the results of these studies strongly indicate that the collective upbringing, reinforced in the home, does achieve some of its intended effects, at least at the school-age level. Not only does the child's peer group in the U.S.S.R. support behavior consistent with the values of the adult society, but it also succeeds in inducing its members to take personal initiative and responsibility for maintaining such behavior in others (Bronfenbrenner, 1970; Geiger, 1968; Mace & Mace, 1963).

THE SWEDISH EXPERIMENT

Sweden has swept away almost all traces of statutory patriarchy. Its laws make few distinctions between men and women in rights and obligations, and the few remaining distinctions are under review. But it is not satisfied with statutory sex-role egalitarianism alone; the government is also trying to alter the very structure of its institutions and the attitude of all its people to make its legal ideal a living reality.

The Swedish ideology specifies that the conditions in the society should be such that men and women have the same obligations to society and the same opportunities to participate in all cultural roles; this equality includes the opportunity for a man to stay home and mind the house and children while his wife works, if the couple so chooses. The government knows that equal opportunities are not afforded people through legislation alone, but that prejudices and preconceptions about masculine and feminine roles must be eradicated, and that facilitating institutions (such as day-care centers) must be created and the supporting economic structure established before true equality can be achieved.

Perhaps it is a sign of the future that a rugged Nordic male mannequin in a window of a large Stockholm department store was shown ironing, and that Swedish boys as well as girls are now taught to cook, sew, and care for children. In this regard, Prime Minister Olaf Palme of Sweden said, "If any responsible Swedish politician should say today that men and women should have separate life roles, he would be regarded as being from the Stone Age" (Choate, 1971). Men should no longer be mainly breadwinners and women mainly caretakers of the children; men should be educated for child care and given the same parental rights and duties as those enjoyed by women, and women should bear their share of responsibility for child support. The expression "male emancipation" has been coined to denote the right of a husband to remain at home while his children are small. There is a demand for legislation whereby the father would receive a leave of absence with pay to stay home with newborn babies, bringing the rights of men in line with those of Swedish women, who are already entitled to such a leave with pay.

In a society in which each human being can develop his own intellectual and emotional possibilities to the maximum without being hampered by preconceptions about sex roles, men should have the right to experience their children to the full. This right is thought to benefit not only the man but the child. Swedish leaders are impressed by recent research associating boys' delinquency and other disturbances with father absence and with the general lack of adult male models in the growing boy's environment. They use this research to bolster their arguments for paid leaves for fathers of newborns, shorter working hours for men with children, and for hiring males in child-care institutions.

The goal of sex-role equality is an ideal not realized even in Sweden except in a very patchy way. For example, little direct effort has been made to change the concept of what a father is, although some changes have been instituted that may later revise the definition of fatherhood. Granting men shorter working hours and leaves to be with young children would seem more practical if there were more women in the labor force. To this end, Sweden has launched a special program designed to increase the proportion of working women. Although over half of Swedish mothers with children under 17 already work full or part time, those women have frequently done so at a considerable sacrifice. Although Sweden has accomplished more toward developing low-cost day-care facilities than most other nations, there is still a lack of adequate inexpensive day care for children. To cope with this shortage, the government recently announced that it would give priority to constructing more day-care centers. It has also modified the tax laws to make it financially more attractive for women to work.

Even if many more women did join the labor force, however, a new definition of the father role in Sweden would still perhaps have to wait a more equitable occupational distribution of the sexes. Women are still found predominantly in the lowest-paid jobs; only an extremely low proportion hold managerial and high-level technical positions. This inequity is likely to continue for some time because women are not preparing for careers as thoroughly as men are. For example, not nearly as many women as men graduate from the universities; not as many girls as boys take vocational training; and women who do choose vocational training take shorter courses.

Parity between the sexes comes slowly; in Sweden, as in the rest of the world, working women still bear the brunt of the housework on top of their work outside the home. Despite definite steps toward equality in sex roles, the Swedes have a long way to go. We will simply have to wait and see how the role of the father will be defined if true equality of the sexes is in fact achieved (Anér, 1966; Linnér,

1969; *The Status of Women in Sweden,* 1968; Thorsell, 1969).

THE *KIBBUTZ* EXPERIMENT

Most family patterns throughout the world, rooted in abiding traditions, are taken for granted by the people living them; the cultural family pattern is considered to be simply "the way folks live." In societies in which the traditional family organization is breaking down, there is more awareness of the possibility of structuring family life in more than one way. Such awareness seems particularly acute in societies in which realigning family roles is a clear-cut national goal, such as in the U.S.S.R. and Sweden.

Experiments in restructuring family life occur not only on a national scale, however, but also among groups within the nation, such as the *kibbutz* collectives of Israel or the communal families within our own country. Communes are by no means new; the dream of a communal rather than a competitive order traces to Plato's *Republic,* which proposed collectivization of property under the authority of the ruling aristocracy. Religious sects, such as the Anabaptists, Separatists, and Moravians, formed communes shortly after the Reformation, seeking to live "as the early Christians did." Let's examine the role of the father first in the *kibbutz* and then in recent North American experiments in communcal living.

A *kibbutz* is an agricultural collective in Israel whose main features include communal living, collective ownership of all property, and the communal rearing of children. Its guiding principle is "from each according to his ability, and to each according to his needs." Although there is a basic *kibbutz* structure, there are important differences among individual *kibbutzim* (plural of *kibbutz*); keep in mind that what is described here may not be true in every particular in all *kibbutzim* (Bettelheim, 1969). There are, in fact, about 83,000 people living in over 200 *kibbutzim* in Israel.

A *kibbutz* couple lives in a single bedroom-living room; meals are eaten in a communal dining room. Their children live separately from them and are reared in a communal children's dormitory. The children's own parents do not provide directly for their physical care. The children sleep and eat in special "children's houses," obtain their clothes from a communal store, and when ill are taken care of by the "nurses." Although the *kibbutz* as a whole is vested with the parental power to control and care for the child and plan his future, a strong parent-child relationship does exist and is characteristically more significant than one might expect.

Although their nurses and teachers are responsible for the education and socialization of *kibbutz* children, parents do spend time with their children. An infant's mother often comes to play with him and to nurse him. *Kibbutz* parents are free to visit their children any time during the day. If a father passes his child's dwelling on his way to work or on an errand, he may stop to visit for a few minutes. In general, whether a parent visits frequently or only to fetch the child in the evening depends on whether his work is located in or near the living area of the *kibbutz* or out in the fields. Since mothers are more likely to work nearby, they are apt to visit more often than fathers do. As the child grows older, he may go to his parents' room whenever he chooses during the day, although he must return to the children's house at night. Because of his schooling and his parents' work, he is usually with his parents for only an hour or two before the evening meal, but he may also spend all day Sunday with them.

The time children spend with parents within the *kibbutz* compares favorably with findings on some American families. A study of conventional families in Michigan (Thorpe, 1957) found that those families spent only about an hour a day together, most of that time during meals. In that study, farm families spent even less time together than did urban families (Thorpe, 1957).

Neither *kibbutz* parent is the primary disciplinarian; since the nurses bear that responsibility, the child-parent interaction is free of that source of tension. The child's attachment, which in non-*kibbutz* families usually focuses on parents, is, within the *kibbutz,* shared by his nurses and peers. The child grows up from the very beginning among a group of peers who are viewed virtually as siblings and with whom he is constantly encouraged to cooperate and share. Age-mates are viewed so strongly as siblings that fellow members of the same *kibbutz* typically do not marry each other, although there are no rules either discouraging or prohibiting their doing so.

The roles the father actually plays within the *kibbutz* are particularly interesting when one bears in mind both the authority characteristic of the traditional Judaic patriarch and the goals of the *kibbutzim.* The theme of emancipation from bondage to the authoritarian father pervades the literature of the *kibbutz* founders. They aimed to achieve equality in status of men and women and thus the destruction of the father's formal authority. The goal was that women, relieved of their domestic burdens by means of the various institutions of collective living, could take their place as men's equals in all activities. The communal dining room would free a woman from the burden of cooking; the communal nurseries, from the responsibilities of raising children; and the couple's small room, from excessive cleaning.

Equality of men and women has not, however, been fully realized. The original settlers did indeed divide labor equally. Women, like men, worked the fields and drove tractors; men, like women, worked in the kitchen and did laundry. Although some women were capable of performing extremely strenuous physical tasks, many of them simply could not do the arduous jobs of which the men were capable, such as tractor driving or harvesting. Moreover, a pregnant woman could not work too long, even in the vegetable garden, and a nursing mother had to work near the nursery. When these women temporarily left the "productive" branches of the economy and entered the "service" branches, their places were filled by men. Thus some women ended up without the variety of cooking *and* sewing *and* baking *and* cleaning characteristic of traditional households, but instead either cooked *or* sewed *or* took care of the children *eight hours a day.* This new housekeeping is more boring and less rewarding than the traditional type. The end result in the *kibbutz* is that men predominate in the agricultural branches of the economy and women in the service branches. Women are the teachers in the early grades, although men are found teaching at the high-school level. With such clear-cut distinctions prevailing in sex roles, it is not surprising to find that little girls play at being nurses while boys play at being truck drivers (a high-prestige job in the *kibbutz*).

Although males tend to hold the jobs with higher prestige, the father is not the specific breadwinner for his particular child, since the *kibbutz* as a whole provides for the children. A bachelor contributes just as much to a child's economic well-being as his father does. Elimination of economic dependence on the father nullifies, at least in theory, one source of paternal authority. Major decisions that shape the child's destiny are made not by his parents but by the collective, and minor daily decisions are made by his nurses. Instead, the father, along with the mother, plays a crucial role in the psychological development of the child by providing love, emotional security, and an adult model that no one else can provide.

That the *kibbutz* child is also attached to nurses and peers does not imply that he is less attached to his parents than a child in our own society. At least one observer considers the attachment of young *kibbutz* children to be stronger (Spiro, 1954). Fathers generally display an interest in their infants from the first, holding them, bouncing them, discussing their particular characteristics with their wives and other mothers, and boasting of their new accomplishments. If a mother is away from the *kibbutz,* the father may come to the nursery to give his baby a bottle or to the toddler's house to feed him. His interest increases as the child matures. An observer's impression is that the father interacts with the child in approximately the same ways as the mother. One study of *kibbutz* children (Spiro, 1966) revealed few differences between mothers and fathers in the way children characterized their socialization roles.

Because he is male, the father may have advantages over the mother in his relationship with the child. First, he gains by holding the more prestigious job; second, he gains by *not* being a woman, as the nurses are. The younger child is with the nurses all day, and his father is virtually the only man he sees. Moreover, the nurses inevitably must sometimes punish, since they are the primary disciplinarians. The child's ambivalent feelings toward nurses may be transferred to the mother, another woman. The father, in contrast, is an exclusively permissive and nurturant figure—perhaps the nurturant figure *par excellence.* One observer (Spiro, 1966) noted that when the younger children cry for their parents during the day, they cry for their fathers more frequently than for their mothers, and when a nurse discusses the important persons in a particular child's life, the father emerges as the dominant figure. In interviews, most of the children spontaneously expressed a preference for their fathers, although they were not even asked to state a preference. The observer (Spiro, 1966) noted that this preference was expressed by males and females alike, and that it seemed most intense in two females

who showed signs of deep emotional involvement with their fathers. One said that she could ask him anything because he knew everything and always made the right decisions. She left the dining room in anger when a visitor replied to her boasts that he had never heard of her father.

Despite the observation that *kibbutz* children do not perceive many differences between the socialization practices of their mothers and their fathers, there is some evidence that the children of several *kibbutzim* did feel that the parent of the same sex related to them in a very different way from the parent of the opposite sex. In this investigation, eighth-grade *kibbutz* children were asked who made decisions at home, who demanded more of them, and to whom they turned for advice. Boys generally answered "father," and girls answered "mother." On the other hand, girls generally thought that their fathers were kinder to them than their mothers, but boys thought that the mothers were more considerate and took their side in arguments (Kugelmass & Breznitz, 1966).

It is interesting that when the same questions were asked of an urban Israeli high school. where the children were *not* from *kibbutzim,* the children did not perceive nearly so many differences in the same sex and the opposite-sex parent related to them. This study revealed that fathers tended to make decisions at home for both boys and girls, and that girls thought that their mothers, not their fathers, were kinder to them, and agreed with the boys that their mothers were also more considerate and took their side in arguments (Breznitz & Kugelmass, 1965). This investigation concluded that, despite strong efforts to eradicate sex roles within the family, boys and girls within the *kibbutzim* had different preceptions of their relationship with their father.

Kibbutz children tend to choose their parents' occupation, but they do not necessarily choose that of the parent of the same sex. Despite the differentiation of occupations along sex lines described above, one study (Spiro, 1966) showed that half of the adult males had chosen the same branch of agriculture as their *mothers,* and half had chosen the branch of their fathers. It may be that it is difficult for boys to identify with the father as a way of learning the adult male role. With his child, the father "lets down" and acts as an affectionate, nurturant playmate, a role similar to the mother's. Since the young boy is in the charge of women during the day, he does not experience the father as the responsible person he actually is. Although in most conventional families the boy does not experience the father at work either, he *does* experience his father's discharge of responsibilities within the home, an experience that may give the boy some cues to his adult masculine role.

One investigation, which compared the fantasies of 9- and 11-year-old *kibbutz* and non-*kibbutz* boys, suggests that boys in conventional families are more likely to model themselves after the father, whereas *kibbutz* boys may be as likely to pattern themselves after the mother or their siblings. The boys were given the Blacky Pictures Test, which showed cartoonlike pictures representing various scenes in the life of a dog called Blacky, his mama, his papa, and a sibling named Tippy. The boys ascribed imaginary thoughts to the characters in each cartoon. Fewer of the *kibbutz* boys said that Blacky would prefer to be like his father; more said that he would rather be like his mother or like Tippy (Rabin, 1958).

YOUTH EXPERIMENTS IN COMMUNAL LIVING

Turning to communes in North America, let us keep in mind that today's communal movement is a reawakening of the search for Utopia that started in America as early as 1680, when religious sects first retreated to the wilderness to live as a community. The transcendental movement of the nineteenth century produced a variety of communal groups, including the Fourierists, Shakers, Zoarites, Perfectionalists, and Spiritualists. While experiments in communal living have always been part of the American landscape, only a few dozen—such as the Shakers, the Amana community, and the Hutterites—survived for more than a few years.

Within the past few years, a significant new element has appeared in America's communal movement as thousands of young people, most from middle-class homes, have rejected the life style of the prevailing culture in favor of communal living. Hundreds of "hippie" communes have appeared in the United States, particularly in California and Oregon. A belief in mysticism and nonviolence, derived, at least in part, from the use of psychedelic drugs, especially LSD, mescaline, and marijuana, seems to be common to most. A drug as powerful as LSD sometimes shatters the conventional view of the social order and allows concepts of possible new life styles to emerge; its ingestion is also commonly

accompanied by mystical or spiritual experiences (Smith & Sternfeld, 1970).

Present-day communes may be found in either urban or rural areas. They vary widely in structure: at one end of the continuum is the anarchistic commune seeking intimacy and involvement, characterized by little structure, no overt concern with permanence, a vague philosophical foundation, open membership, and a weak financial base; at the other end is the highly organized commune, with an integrative and explicit philosophical system, stringent entrance requirements, fixed daily routines, and a solid financial footing, usually through economic ties with the rest of society. Communes without an adequate financial base dominate. Even most agricultural communes are not self-sufficient, and, even when some of their members work in the community, their most common sources of support are welfare, unemployment compensation, food stamps, and money from home.

Communes also vary in sexual patterns. Some encourage sexual experimentation, attempting group marriages or encouraging random and unrestricted sexual promiscuity; but the available evidence suggests that such are the minority. Although sexual mores are usually very liberal, communes also range from an emphasis on the solidarity of the traditional nuclear unit within the larger communal family to the practice of regarding the child as "belonging" to the commune as a whole, each adult member sharing responsibility for the child's welfare and upbringing.

Child rearing in many contemporary American communes, reminiscent of attitudes and practices in the *kibbutz,* is self-consciously founded on a rejection by its members of their own restrictive upbringing. Although their rebellion may well be against an authoritarian style characteristic of many fathers in our society, there is some evidence that in many cases it may, in fact, be against their mothers, not their fathers. Some young people who have adopted a hippie life style seem to be reacting against a restrictive mother who contrasts sharply with a father who encouraged independence, curiosity, and open exploration. This evidence was gathered in a study (Kendall & Pittell, 1969) of young people who had come to the Haight-Ashbury Research Project in San Francisco to participate in an intensive psychological and sociological investigation of the drug-based hippie culture. The research did not attempt to find out how many of the subjects lived in urban communes at that time or sought communal living later. It is known that many Haight-Ashbury residents did later seek refuge in rural communes.

In this study, one group, labeled "contented," often freely described themselves as "hippies" and expressed a philosophical commitment to that life style. Members of this group reported that their fathers talked things over and reasoned with them, joked with them, and encouraged them to be curious, to question, and to make decisions on their own. They generally characterized their relationship with their fathers as warm and understanding. Their mothers, on the other hand, had been authoritarian with them, worried about bad and sad things that could happen to them, and punished them by taking away privileges. The mothers, unlike the fathers, were not warm and understanding and did not encourage independence.

Another group of subjects, labeled "dysphoric," seldom described themselves as "hippies" although they lived in the Haight-Ashbury community and participated in the drug culture. Most of them had experienced adverse drug reactions; all of them found the hippie culture unsatisfactory. This group had had a generally negative relationship with a rejecting and rigid father who did not allow them to question his decisions and often felt angry with them. Their mothers, in contrast, were said to be warm and supportive and to encourage independence.

Since the hippie culture characteristically values aesthetic experience, cooperation, nonviolence, tenderness, and warmth—values typically cherished more by mothers than by fathers in our society—it may be that the "contented" group in this study was seeking and finding a substitute for a mother who lacked these matristic values herself. At the same time, this group felt supported by their fathers' attitudes. The "dysphoric" group, in contract, might be actively rebelling against the strictness of their fathers. In rearing their own children, each group might rebel against the values of one of their parents: the "contented" group against the values of their mothers and the "dysphoric" group against the values of their fathers. In either case, both groups would be apt to value child-rearing practices of tolerance, permissiveness, little guidance and protection, much warmth and affection, and open and egalitarian communication. These were indeed found to be the child-rearing values of West Coast urban hippie adults. The single exception to highly permissive child-rearing attitudes was suppression of the child's aggression. The men held child-rearing values much more characteristic of mothers than of fathers in our society (Blois, 1971).

An investigation of families preparing for communal living found that the fathers promoted nonconformity in their preschool children and were not authoritarian with them. Like the mothers, they encouraged independence and individuality, tried to enrich the children's environment, and were very accepting of the children (Baumrind, 1971b).

The research discussed above did not differentiate between those who were living in communes and those who were not. Now let us discuss what little is known about fathers in communes. Bennett Berger and his colleagues (1971) studied child rearing in rural communes in northern California. Each commune included at least five adults and two children who had been sharing resources and facilities in a common household or domestic establishment for at least six months. Most of the communes regarded themselves as extended families, consciously using the term. In one case they actually adopted a common surname. A typical way of settling disputes among children was to appeal to kinship, even when the children were unrelated: "Mary is your sister, don't hit her." This approach is reminiscent of the way *kibbutz* children relate to peers as though they were siblings. Within the larger communal family were found a variety of nuclear units: legally married spouses and children, unmarried couples with and without children, couples in which the male partner is not the father of the child, and even one case in which the female partner was not the mother of the man's child.

In most of the communes observed in this study, sexual fidelity was approved as a general pattern; at the same time, the concept of the partner as sexual property was rejected. Although the researchers observed couples who remained together despite occasional sexual relations with others, they also observed that deep tensions sometimes resulted from infidelity. Apparently the ideology that condemns viewing another person as sexual property is often incapable of overriding the deeply entrenched motive demanding exclusive rights of the other. A vivid example of the strength of the desire for exclusive ownership of the partner was reported by Sara Davidson (1970) at the Wheeler Ranch. A group marriage between two teen-age girls, a 40-year-old man, and two married couples ended abruptly when one of the husbands saw his wife with another man in the group, pulled a knife, and dragged his wife off, yelling, "She belongs to me."

The entire commune, including the children, is frequently present at the birth of a baby. The father of the child is encouraged to assist directly in delivery, on the assumption that actual participation in the birth process encourages a profound attachment to his child. This belief is consistent with findings from animal research that early contact between adult male and infant seems to enhance paternal behavior (see Chapter 2, Question 1). In one instance, not only was childbirth ritually celebrated, but a photographic record was made of the entire process and the father composed an invocational poem in praise of life.

Even when the biological father is absent, there is usually a man present who is considered a father to the child and regarded as stable even if he and the mother have been together only a short time and have not yet settled on the degree of commitment they have to each other. Children may refer to having had many "fathers" in their young lives.

The distinction is by no means clear between the rights of parents and the rights of another commune member. One observer saw an argument between the mother of a 4-year-old girl and an adult male commune member (neither the father of the child nor the mother's "old man"). He was holding the child on his lap and feeding her at the dinner table. The man reproached the mother for interfering with him and the child while they were doing their "dinner thing" together, implying that in this instance the mother had no special rights over her child.

The dominant child rearing ideology is to let the child "do his thing," to allow maximum expression of his individuality and creativity. If forced to choose between training the next generation toward the communal life and training it to be free, most communes would choose the latter. Generally, only mild pressures toward conformity are exercised; in one instance, a father refused to take by force an adult's pipe from his 16-month-old son, who insisted upon smoking it and would not give it up, even as he was coughing on the smoke.

It remains to be seen whether children raised in these communes will follow in their parents' footsteps or whether, as has been typical in utopian communities in the history of this country, they will reject the communal values of their parents and become "uptight" businessmen and suburban housewives.

SUMMARY

This chapter has explored several experiments in uprooting traditional family roles. The Soviet Union and Sweden have not fully achieved their goal of equality between the sexes. Both, however, have gone far in eradicating the authoritarian father figure. In the Soviet Union, the parents and the collective reinforce each other in inducing the desired values and conduct in children (Bronfenbrenner, 1970; Geiger, 1968; Mace & Mace, 1963). But in both the Soviet Union and Sweden, the mother still dominates in child rearing. In the Israeli *kibbutz,* although parental power rests with the collective, the father may become the child's favorite source of nurturance and affection. In the youth communes of America, even in cases in which the biological father is absent, there is usually some man present who is considered a father to the child. Commune fathers and mothers encourage maximum freedom and exercise minimum guidance and control.

These first four chapters have raised questions that are beyond the powers of this writer to resolve. Does human fathering have some animal base, or at least primate base? To what extent do the varieties of human fathering, brought about by cultural differences, represent a primary distinction between man and other animals? The focus of Chapters Three and Four has been on the influence of economic and cultural-historical conditions on fatherhood. Viewed from another perspective, do styles of fathering influence the economic conditions of a culture, and ultimately, its history?

REFERENCES

Anér, K. *Swedish women today.* Stockholm, Sweden: The Swedish Institute, 1966.

Baumrind, D. Harmonious parents and their preschool children. *Developmental Psychology,* 1971, 4, 99–102.

Berger, B., Hackett, B., Cavan, S., Zickler, G., Miller, M., Noble, M., Theiman, S., Farrell, R., and Rosenbluth, B. Child-rearing practices of the communal family. In A. S. Skolnick and J. H. Skolnick (Eds.), *Family in transition.* Boston: Little, Brown, 1971. Pp. 509–523.

Bettelheim, B. *Children of the dream.* New York: Macmillan, 1969.

Blois, M. S. Child-rearing attitudes of hippie adults. *Dissertation Abstracts,* 1971, *31* (7-A), 3329–3330.

Bronfenbrenner, U. *Two worlds of childhood: U.S. and U.S.S.R.* New York: Russell Sage Foundation, 1970.

Choate, R. Swedes iron out differences. *San Francisco Chronicle,* March 29, 1971.

Davidson, S. Open land: Getting back to the communal garden. *Harper's,* June, 1970, 91–102.

Geiger, K. *The family in Soviet Russia.* Cambridge, Massachusetts: Harvard University Press, 1968.

Kendall, R. F., and Pihell, S. M. Life history antecedents of subjective contentment and dysporia in a hippie culture. Paper presented at the meeting of the Society for Research in Child Development, March, 1969.

Kugelmass, S., and Breznitz, S. Perception of parents by kibbutz adolescents. *Human Relations,* 1966, 19, 117–122.

Linnér, B. *Society and sex in Sweden.* Stockholm, Sweden: The Swedish Institute, 1969.

Mace, D., and Mace, V. *The Soviet family.* Garden City, New York: Doubleday, 1963.

Rabin, A. I. Some psychosexual differences between kibbutz and non-kibbutz Israeli boys. *Journal of Projective Techniques,* 1958, 22, 328–332.

Smith, D. E., and Sternfield, J. The hippie communal movement: Effects on child birth and development. *American Journal of Orthopsychiatry,* 1970, 40, 527–530.

Spiro, M. E. *Children of the kibbutz: A study in child training and personality.* New York: Schocken Books, 1966.

Spiro, M. E. Is the Family universal? *American Anthropologist,* 1954, 56, 840–846.

The status of women in Sweden: Report to the United Nations 1968. Stockholm, Sweden: The Swedish Institute, 1968.

Thorpe, A. C. Patterns of family interaction in farm and town homes. Michigan Agricultural Experiment Station, Technical Bulletin No. 260, 1957.

Thorsell, S. *For children's minds—Not just to mind the children.* Stockholm, Sweden: The Swedish Institute, 1969.

Chapter Eight

Peers

Although the family is the earliest agent of socialization, as the child grows older his or her values are influenced by other social agents and institutions. Schools, churches, law enforcement agencies, and many other social institutions are established with the inculcation and maintenance of socially desired values and behaviors as one of their main missions. Peers, although less formally oriented toward shaping social attitudes and behavior, also remain one of the most influential forces in socialization.

Peer interactions are encouraged early by parents, and the influence of peers increases rapidly in the preschool years. Children's views of themselves, of social standards, and of other people are modified by their experience with peers.

What factors are associated with friendship formation and acceptance by peers? In the paper by Asher, Oden, and Gottman the relation of personal and situational characteristics and social skills in successful or unsuccessful interactions with peers is explored. One of the consistent findings is that physically unattractive children are unpopular with their peers and are viewed as having more undesirable social characteristics than are their attractive peers. Is this in the eye of the beholder or is it a behavioral reality? Langlois and Downs study the behavior of preschool children and find that with increasing age, unattractive children show more noxious, aggressive behavior than do attractive children.

What can be done when children are unsuccessful in interactions with peers? Asher, Oden, and Gottman discuss shaping, modeling, and coaching techniques which are effective in teaching social skills to young children. The paper by Furman, Rahe, and

Hartup presents a program of rehabilitation of socially-withdrawn preschool children through interactions with mixed-age or same-age peers.

Most interactions of young peers take place during the course of play. A particular type of play, pretend play, increases dramatically from the age of two to six. Greta Fein discusses the relation of pretend play to the cognitive and socioemotional development of the child. Peer interactions and play serve an important role in developing social and intellectual competencies in children.

Reading 32

Children's Friendships in School Settings

Steven R. Asher
Sherri L. Oden
John M. Gottman

INTRODUCTION

As children grow older their social interaction typically increases and their friendships become more stable (Horrocks & Buker, 1951; Parten, 1932; Shure, 1963). Still, there are many children who go through the preschool and elementary school years without friends or with few friends. One study found that 6% of third to sixth graders had no classroom friends and an additional 12% had only one friend (Gronlund, 1959).

The consequences of low acceptance by peers has been extensively documented. Children who are socially isolated are more likely to drop out of school (Ullmann, 1957), be later identified as juvenile delinquents (Roff, Sells, & Golden, 1972), and have mental health problems in later life (Cowen, Pederson, Babijian, Izzo, & Trost, 1973). The consequences of low peer acceptance may be more severe than the consequences of low achievement. In one study (Cowen *et al.*, 1973), extensive data were gathered on third-grade children. Measures included absenteeism, grade point average, IQ scores, achievement test performance, teacher ratings, and peer ratings. Eleven years later the research team examined a community mental health register to learn which of these children were being seen by a mental health professional. Of all the measures taken in third grade the one that best predicted which children would later have emotional problems was peer ratings. Children who were less liked by their peers were more likely to be receiving treatment for mental health problems eleven years later.

This paper reviews research on children's friendships in nursery school and elementary school settings. Since school dominates many of the hours of a child's day, it is obviously an important setting in which to study social as well as academic events. Most of the research on children's friendships reflects this fact. While there is some research on friendships in camps, neighborhood settings, etc., the size of this literature is dwarfed in comparison to what is known about social relationships in school.

In reviewing this research, we have tried to select studies that have implications for educational practice. Most of the studies are rather well designed and well executed. We have not hesitated, however, to include less rigorous research if its conception or findings might stimulate further research or suggest ideas for educational practice.

The first part of the paper is concerned with the influence of enduring personal characteristics on peer relations. In this section we consider some of the stereotypes that affect children's friendships and offer a few suggestions about ways to overcome these biasing factors. Next, we review research on the influence of the school environment on friendships. Classroom and school situation variables affect social interactions and the extent to which children will make friends with one another. In the third section we examine research on the kinds of social skills that are important to achieving peer acceptance. Many children lack friends because they do not have the necessary social skills. Finally, the paper concludes with a discussion of the ways in which children who lack social skills can be taught how to make friends. A number of teaching methods can be quite effective in increasing the social interaction and peer acceptance of formerly isolated children. It *is* possible to have classrooms in which far fewer children are socially isolated!

PERSONAL CHARACTERISTICS AND FRIENDSHIP

Among the determinants of peer acceptance are personal characteristics that are rather enduring. One's name, physical appearance, race, and sex are not easily changed. Yet all of these variables influence friendship selection and peer acceptance.

Names

In every generation, a few first names which were previously uncommon become popular. This is particularly true for girls' names. A recent survey of New York City hospitals (Beadle, 1973) indicated that seven of the ten most popular names given to boys in 1972 were among the ten most popular names given to boys in 1948. However, none of the girls' names appeared on both lists.

But does it make a difference what names children are given? Apparently so. Names like John, Sherri, and Steven are among those common appellations that would seem to minimize social discomfort. On the other hand, names like Frances, Hugo, and Hilda seem to carry with them social risks.

McDavid and Harari (1966) asked a group of 10- to 12-year-old children in a community center to indicate their friends while another group of children, unfamiliar with children in the first group, rated the desirability of the children's names. The correlation between desirability of names and the popularity of children with these names was significant. Children with more desirable names were better liked. In a follow-up study Harari and McDavid (1973) found that teachers were also affected by children's names. Teachers graded student essays lower when those essays were randomly paired with rare, unpopular, and unattractive names.

What accounts for the relationship between names and peer acceptance? One possibility is that the simple unfamiliarity or strangeness of certain names leads people to dislike or avoid their bearers. Perhaps children initially behave differently toward a Herbert than a Bill and in so doing set up a cycle of less positive interaction. An alternative explanation is that parents who lack social skills are more likely to give their children odd names and fail to teach effective social skills. In this case, peers would be reacting more to the child's behavior than to the child's name.

If the unfamiliarity explanation is correct, then teachers could help an oddly-named child to be included by making the child's name more of an "everyday household word." Repeated classroom use may help. Associating the name with a famous person in history, science, music, etc., may also be effective. But if the issue is not the child's name, per se, but the associated lack of social skills, then the child should be helped to learn social skills. Thus, for each child the teacher should assess whether the child's name is the real cause of his social difficulty.

One last word: It is important not to overestimate the importance of names. It is only one of many variables that influence social acceptance. United States Presidents in the twentieth century have

included a Theodore, Woodrow, Warren, Calvin, Herbert, Franklin, Dwight, and Lyndon. The last five elected Vice-Presidents have included an Alben, Hubert, and Spiro. It may be that many Americans will vote for a man they would not want as a friend; a more plausible interpretation is that names are not everything.

Physical Attractiveness

In American society there seems to be considerable agreement about who is or is not physically attractive. In one study (Cross & Cross, 1971), seven-, twelve-, and seventeen-year-olds, as well as adults, were shown twelve sets of photographs. Each set contained six faces of a particular race, sex, and age group. Respondents were asked to select from each set the most beautiful face and then were asked to rate the twelve faces that had been selected. Results showed no significant difference in the evaluations of beauty made by different age groups. Even the youngest tested shared the conception of beauty held by older people.

Not only is there consensus about physical attractiveness, but there is a strong tendency for children's friendship selection to be influenced by appearance. Young and Cooper (1944) studied factors that influence popularity among elementary school children. They correlated over 30 variables with social acceptance. The most significant was attractiveness of the child's facial appearance. The better looking children were better liked. An interesting aspect of the results was that when the ratings of attractiveness were made by children the relationship between attractiveness and popularity was stronger than when adults made the ratings. In both cases the raters did not know the children they rated and could not have been influenced by any previous associations with the children.

What accounts for the relationship between physical attractiveness and social acceptance? As with names, the cause of greater attraction is unclear. Perhaps better looking children are responded to more positively and thereby develop more effective social skills. Dion and Berscheid (1974) found that nursery school children attributed more negative social behavior to their less attractive peers.

Adults also tend to respond to physical appearance in judging children. Dion (1972) gave college students a photo of a second grade child along with a description of a behavioral episode. The photo showed either an attractive or less attractive child. The behavioral episode consisted of some unacceptable kind of behavior. After the subjects read the episodes, they were asked, among other questions, to predict how likely the child would be to do the same thing again. The physically attractive child was judged to be less likely to repeat the unacceptable behavior. Furthermore, on a series of six personality ratings the attractive child was judged to be more honest and pleasant than the less attractive child. These findings are striking since the behavior being judged was identical; only physical appearance varied.

One group of children who tend to be considered low in physical attractiveness are the physically disabled. In one study (Richardson, Goodman, Hastorf, & Dornbusch, 1961) ten- and eleven-year-old children from many different social classes, regions, and ethnic backgrounds were found to rank figures of disabled children lower in desirability. Furthermore, the same rank ordering occurred in every sample. From most to least liked they were: the normal child, a child with crutches and brace, a child in a wheelchair, a child with a left hand missing, a child with a facial disfigurement, and finally, an obese child.

Many explanations have been offered to account for people's rejection of the disabled. One view is that the disabled are victimized by an excessive societal value on beauty (Wright, 1960). Undoubtedly, this at least partially explains children's feelings toward the less attractive, in general, and the disabled, in particular. Another interpretation (Wright, 1960) is that the disabled are less liked because they are presumed to be different. N. W. Asher (1975) has found that people attribute different attitudes and personality characteristics to disabled and able-bodied individuals. In another study (N. W. Asher, 1973) she found that the extent to which college students perceived a disabled person as similar did indeed influence their feelings toward the person.

It is plausible that the same trend would be found with children since children are more attracted to those who are attitudinally similar to themselves (Byrne & Griffit, 1966). If children could discover for themselves areas of similarity with a disabled person, friendships might be possible. The emphasis should be on guided discovery. In the studies mentioned, the subject was not told that he or she

was similar to the person being rated. The subject discovered the similarity when reading the person's attitude profile. Adults often tell children: "He is really just like you" but it is likely that this message is believed most when children discover similarities for themselves. This line of reasoning suggests that teachers should provide situations in which children can discover their similarities of attitude, personalities, values, etc.

The variable of similarity-dissimilarity can, of course, cut both ways. If, in interactions with disabled persons, able-bodied children discover more differences than similarities, increased rejection rather than acceptance could result. Rejection might occur, for example, in an environment which stressed physical prowess above all other skills or where the disabled child was overprotected, given unnecessary preferential treatment, or prevented from developing skills and interests of value to children.

Race

Racial awareness comes quite early in life. Children three years of age and older are clearly aware of racial labels and can appropriately identify their own racial membership (Clark & Clark, 1947; Durrett & Davy, 1970; Hraba & Grant, 1970).

Children also use race as a criterion for selecting friends. Criswell (1939) asked New York City children in three schools to write down the names of classmates they would like to sit next to. Results indicated that children were significantly more likely to choose friends from among their own race. What is interesting, however, is that children did make a considerable number of cross-race selections. Forty percent of their choices would have been cross-race selections if they had been making choices without regard to race. When we averaged Criswell's results across all schools, the results indicated that approximately 25% of the selections were cross-race. Thus, although there was a tendency to prefer children of one's own race many cross-race friendships did exist.

Some recent evidence shows a similar pattern of results. S. R. Asher (1973) asked fourth- and fifth-grade children in a middle-sized Midwestern city to write down the names of their five best friends. About 40% of the school population was black. Each month from October to April approximately 55 children, randomly selected, were asked to name their five best friends. The results showed that children made fewer cross-race selections than would be expected by chance. Still, approximately 18% of white children's selections and 44% of black children's selections were cross-race.

In another study Shaw (1973) asked fourth-, fifth-, and sixth-grade children in February and in June whom they most preferred to be with. Approximately 80% of the children were white and 20% black. Both blacks and whites over-selected members of their own race. Nonetheless, both whites and blacks chose members of the other race. Overall, about 33% of black children's selections were white and 6% of white children's selections were black.

The studies reviewed thus far show less racial bias among children than one might expect given the history of poor race relations in the United States. One possibility is that children might show more racial bias if they were asked not only to name a few friends, but to describe their feelings about each classmate. A child might feel quite positively about a few members of another race while feeling negatively about the majority of opposite-race children. A recent study by Singleton (1974) is relevant to this issue. Third-grade classrooms were surveyed in eleven different schools in a single moderate-size city. These children had experienced desegregated education throughout their public school careers and school system personnel were interested in the children's race relations.

Children were asked to rate each of their classmates on two scales: how much they like to work with other children in their class and how much they like to play with other children. The scales were constructed so that "1" indicated "I don't like to" and "5" indicated "I like to a lot." The results were that both blacks and whites rated members of their own race higher than members of the other race. This result was statistically significant. As in the Criswell, Asher, and Shaw studies, however, there was considerable cross-race acceptance. For example, on the play item, blacks gave blacks an average rating of 3.58 and whites an average rating of 3.17. Whites gave whites an average rating of 2.96 and blacks a rating of 2.86. Thus, children's cross-race ratings were in reality not very different from their same-race ratings.

Although the interracial picture in the preschool and elementary school years is surprisingly positive, the pattern in high school is less hopeful. In one study of high school students (Silverman & Shaw, 1973) social interaction was observed at a popular meeting place in the school. The school's population was 70% white and 30% black. Of all the interactions observed, those between white and black students averaged below 3%. It may be that the "threat" of interracial dating draws students at this age apart. If so, we need to provide children with models of positive interracial relationships so that their teen-age years are not characterized by nearly complete racial separation.

What conditions promote positive or negative relations between children of different races? S. R. Asher (1973) and Shaw (1973), both of whom collected data across the school year, found little systematic change in children's acceptance of members of another race from the beginning to the end of the school year. It is clear from this that contact per se does not guarantee unbiased friendship selections. It is undoubtedly the nature of the interracial experience that influences the extent to which children make friends across ethnic and racial lines.

One critical issue is the extent to which contact leads children of different races to perceive themselves as similar versus dissimilar. There is evidence that white children more positively evaluate black children when they discover them to hold similar attitudes (Insko & Robinson, 1967). To the extent that children share the same social class, values, life-style, level of educational attainment, etc., it is likely that more interracial acceptance will occur. One way that a classroom teacher may be able to increase cross-race friendships is by attending to similarities of interests between black and white children. In one study (S. R. Asher, 1975), fifth-grade children were asked to rate the interest value of a series of 25 pictures. The correlation between black male and white male ratings was strongly significant. The correlation between white females and black females, although lower, was also significant. So within each sex there appeared to be considerable similarity of interest between black and white children. For example, both white males and black males rated basketball and race cars highly. Commonly held interests may provide a basis for bringing together children of different races.

Another factor that contributes to interracial acceptance is parent attitude. Analysis of integration case reports suggests that the school atmosphere is far more positive when parents are supportive rather than opposed to the integration process.

Authorities, whether Supreme Court justices, the President, or parents, serve to legitimize certain points of view. There was, for example, a marked increase in pro-integration sentiment after the 1954 Supreme Court decision. If children perceive their parents as supportive of integration they are probably far more likely to make an effort to reach out to children of another race.

Sex

Although racial factors influence friendship choice, the sex of the child is a more important factor. American social scientists, heavily committed to the elimination of racial bias, have sometimes underestimated the extent to which sociometric data contains evidence of the existence of two separate cultures: boys' and girls'. The degree to which children chose same-sex friends can be seen in three of the studies discussed in the previous section.

Criswell (1939) summarized her data with the comment that "cleavage between the sexes was greater than racial cleavage," and that "a given group of boys or girls nearly always preferred classmates of the same sex but different race to those of the same race but different sex [p. 18]." S. R. Asher (1973) found a strong preference in children for friends of the same sex. Approximately 95% of children's friendship choices were same-sex choices and there was little variation from month to month. Singleton (1974) also discovered strong and statistically significant acceptance of same-sex and rejection of opposite-sex children. On her 1-5 play scale, boys rated boys 3.95 and rated girls 2.08. Girls rated girls 3.78 and boys 2.26. Comparison of these results with those presented for race in the previous section indicate the extent to which sex is an important factor in friendship selection.

A study by Challman (1932) indicates the early age at which children exclude members of the opposite sex. He observed 33 nursery school children, recording the names of children who were in the same group. Results of over 200 hours of observation indicated predominantly same-sex grouping even among children between the ages of 27 to 45 months. Only one boy and one girl showed strong preferences for opposite-sex friendships. More recently, Omark and Edelman (1973) observed playground interaction and found that kindergarten, first-, and second-grade children interacted predominantly with members of the same sex.

One very interesting finding is that when cross-sex friendships are formed they tend to be quite unstable. Gronlund (1955) gave two sociometric surveys four months apart. Only 20% of the cross-sex friendship choices made on the first survey were also made on the second survey. In contrast, children's same-sex choices were about three times as stable.

One concomitant of restricted interaction between boys and girls is a sharp differentiation of interests. Even young children show strong sex-typing of interests. Shure (1963), for example, found that four-year-old nursery school boys spent more time in the block area while girls spent time in the art, book, and doll areas. The same study that showed a high degree of cross-race similarity of interests (S. R. Asher, 1975) found that the correlation of boys' and girls' interest ratings was low. Among white children the top five interests of boys and girls were completely different. Among black children only one of the top five interests was common to boys and girls. Finally, there is evidence that children's interests are highly related to traditional sex-role conceptions. Markell and Asher (1974) had judges rate the "masculinity" and "femininity" of 25 pictures. When these ratings were correlated with children's interest in the same pictures, the results showed that boys were more interested in "masculine" pictures and girls were more interested in "feminine" pictures.

It seems likely, then, that in the long run the occurrence of many cross-sex friendships depends upon diminishing sex-role rigidity. If boys and girls were reared to have a wider range of interests and to enjoy a wider range of activities there would probably be many more boy-and-girl friendships. An interesting question is whether educational programs such as "Free to be You and Me" or "Sesame Street" will produce change in children's sex-role concepts and friendship patterns.

In the short run, one way to bring boys and girls together may be to provide common or superordinate goals (Sherif, 1958). In a study by DeVries and Edwards (1974), seventh-grade math classes were organized so that children worked individually in two classes and were rewarded for individual achievement while in two other classes boys and girls were teamed together and children were rewarded according to their team's performance. After the four-week experiment was over, children were asked a number of questions; one of these requested them to list their friends. In the two "no team" classes, the number of children's choices that crossed sex lines was 21 and 17%. In the "team" classes, however, the number of cross-sex choices was 33 and 27%. The findings of this experiment suggest that using superordinate goals may help overcome the social distance between boys and girls.

SITUATIONAL CHARACTERISTICS AND FRIENDSHIP

One way to increase friendships among children is to structure the educational environment so that friendships are likely to develop and endure. Many children may lack friends or have few friends because the environment does not promote friendship. A variety of situational factors which influence friendship will be discussed.

Population Mobility

Although contact alone is not sufficient to create peer acceptance, children who have prolonged contact with the same peers should at least have greater opportunity to form friendships. Following this line of reasoning, researchers have investigated the effect of residential mobility of individual children and school populations in relation to peer acceptance. In a study of individual mobility (Young & Cooper, 1944), the five least and five most accepted children in each of eleven elementary school classrooms were compared on the length of time in the current school and the number of schools previously attended. The most accepted and least accepted children did not differ on either of these measures. More recently, Roistacher (1974) found that the degree of an individual child's mobility had no relationship to the number of peers in school who knew him. Neither study, then, found evidence that the more mobile child is at a social disadvantage. It should be noted, however, that neither study controlled for within-school differences in socioeconomic status or social skill repertoire. If the more mobile children within schools were socioeconomically more advantaged they may have had skills which offset potential disadvantages of mobility. There is evidence, for example, that middle class children are more effective communicators than lower class children (Gottman, Gonso, & Rasmussen, 1975; Heider, 1971).

While individual mobility may not be an important factor, the mobility of an entire school population may well be important. In one study (Roistacher, 1974), four inner city and four suburban schools were compared. The inner city schools had an annual pupil turnover rate of over 35%; in contrast, the turnover rate in the suburban schools averaged below 10%. Eighth-grade boys in each school were asked to indicate those students they knew well. In schools with high turnover fewer children were known by others. Furthermore, these results were obtained even when other differences between the schools, such as income and racial composition, were statistically controlled.

It would seem, then, that children who attend "high turnover" schools have a social disadvantage when it comes to making friends. In this type of environment, it is necessary for the school staff and community to take special steps to bring children in contact with one another. Other environments with high population turnover (e.g., universities, military bases) provide a variety of social activities for integrating new members and building cohesiveness. Perhaps schools could adopt some of their techniques. Having children eat or play with children from different classrooms might help. especially if the teacher made sure that children learned each other's names. It might also help if children could learn about each other's background, where they lived before, their interests, etc. In a high-mobility environment, children, like adults, need to identify characteristics in others that will help them to rapidly build relationships.

Opportunities for Participation

Situations vary in the extent to which they allow people to participate fully in social interaction. For example, if there is a large variety of social roles to be filled and a limited number of potential "actors," more people will get involved. This is the type of situation that exists in smaller schools. Whatever the size of the school, there are a certain number of roles that must be filled (e.g., band member, club member, student council member, etc.). Thus, students who attend small schools should have greater opportunities for participation. Indeed, Gump and Friesen (1964) and Wicker (1969) have found that students in small high schools participated in a wider range of activities and held more positions of responsibility than students in large schools.

Size of classroom also appears to be an important influence on social participation. Dawe (1934) observed teacher-led discussions in kindergartens ranging in size from 14 to 46 children. As one might expect, the average number of comments contributed by each child decreased as size increased. The average child in the 14-person class spoke nearly seven times while children in classes about 30 spoke fewer than two times each. There is, after all, a finite amount of "air time" which must be shared among classroom members.

The higher participation characteristic of small school settings should lead students to be better known by their peers. Interestingly, Roistacher (1974) found that junior high school students in smaller schools knew more fellow students, in absolute numbers, than did students in larger schools. These data should give pause to those who urge consolidation of smaller school districts into large ones. It may be that there are social disadvantages that offset the potential economic or academic advantages to be gained from consolidation.

If participation and responsibility are important determinants of peer acceptance, then increasing participation and responsibility should promote peer acceptance. A study by McClelland and Ratliff (1947) found this to be the case. They worked in a junior high school where a particularly large number of children seemed to have no friends. They decided to intervene in one class of 35 students. On a pretest measure, 12 students received no sociometric choices on any of four sociometric questions. (With whom would you like to go to a show? With whom would you like to study? Whom would you like to have as a guest in your home? With whom would you rather share a secret?)

One part of their intervention consisted of providing isolated children with special classroom roles (e.g., chairman of the hospitality committee who had responsibility for sending cards to sick classroom members). The class was also divided into small groups based on seating rows. Each group had a captain and various activities such as parties and charity drives were conducted by the groups so that individual member participation was increased. Sociometric choices made after this intervention indicated that only two children were still ignored on all four questions. These results, although based on only a single classroom, are promising. Creating new roles which give children a chance to participate may be a powerful way to overcome isolation.

The importance of participating in a visible and valued classroom role is also demonstrated in a study by Chennault (1967). Two isolated children from 16 special education classes were grouped with the two most popular children from the same classes. Each group's task was to produce a skit for their classroom. They met for 15 minutes twice a week for 5 weeks, and then presented their skit to the class. Sociometric ratings taken after this activity indicated that the participating isolated children were more accepted than a control group of isolated children who had not been involved with the skit.

A follow-up study (Rucker & Vincenzo, 1970) shows that maintenance of this type of change is dependent on continued participation. Isolated children from special education classes met with the most popular members of their class for 45 minutes. The group met twice weekly for two weeks to produce a classroom carnival. The group planned events, decorated the room, awarded prizes, etc. A sociometric measure given three days after the carnival indicated that the participating isolated children were far more accepted than the control group of isolated children. However, a follow-up measure taken one month after the carnival showed that these children were no longer more accepted than the control group. Once their participation ceased, the level of peer acceptance they experienced also declined. The same pattern of initial gain followed by long-run decline has also been found by Lilly (1971). These results suggest that isolated children may be unable to maintain relationships which have been situationally nurtured.

Rewarding Social Interaction

One critical situational component is whether children are rewarded or reinforced by the teacher or by peers for engaging in friendship-making behavior. When the environment rewards certain behavior, the likelihood is greater that the behavior will occur again. If rewards are withheld, the behavior is less likely to occur. Children, like adults, are reinforced by approval of their conduct.

The power of reinforcement was demonstrated in a study by Blau and Rafferty (1970). They paired children together to play a game in which a light went on when the children cooperated. One group of children played the game without receiving any reward from the experimenter. In other groups, each time children cooperated they received a ticket redeemable for prizes. After playing, the same children rated how much they liked each other. These ratings indicated that the children rewarded for cooperation regarded each other more highly than children who were not rewarded.

An important point is that reinforcement has to be maintained to some degree if the desired behavior is to continue. One study (Hauserman, Walen, & Behling, 1973) examined the effect of reinforcing black and white first-grade children for sitting with each other in the lunchroom. The study was carried out in a school lunchroom where children usually sat in racially separate groups. The teachers introduced a game in which children drew papers out of a hat. Each paper had the name of one black and one white child and children were told to sit with their "new friend." At the end of the lunch session, children who had carried out this instruction received tickets, redeemable for candy. In the next phase of the experiment, the name drawing was discontinued. Instead, children simply were encouraged to sit with "new friends" and were reinforced if they sat with an interracial group. In the final phase, reinforcement procedures were terminated.

Results of the study indicated an increase of interracial interaction in the lunchroom during the experimental phase. More important, this effect also generalized to a free play session held in the classroom after lunch. Here, too, children engaged in more cross-race interaction. However, once reinforcement procedures were ended, children once again sat with members of their own race. These results demonstrate the power that environmental reward has on children's social interactions.

Success and Failure

Another important situational variable is the extent to which the school helps the child to succeed academically. The cognitive and social areas of development are interrelated. Children who have difficulty with cognitive tasks are also likely to have greater problems in social relationships. This is demonstrated by the finding that low achieving children tend to have fewer friends in school (Gronlund, 1959).

Why might academic progress be related to peer acceptance? One possibility is that success leads children to "feel good" and be more concerned for other children. Isen, Horn, and Rosenhan (1973) performed an experiment in which they arranged for some children to succeed at a game while others failed. After playing the game, children were asked by an adult experimenter to contribute money to buy toys for poor children. When contributions were made without the experimenter watching, the children who had succeeded at the game were more generous than those who had failed. When the contributions were made publicly, the two groups gave similar amounts.

While success leads children to feel good, school failure probably leads many children to be aggressive and unkindly disposed toward their peers. And from avaiable evidence, the aggressive child (Hartup, Glazer, & Charlesworth, 1967), particularly the inappropriately aggressive child (Lesser, 1959), is disliked and rejected.

Such results suggest that environments which provide children with opportunities for feeling successful would simultaneously be promoting positive peer relations. This means first of all that the curriculum should provide children with a chance to succeed. Second, evaluation of student progress should emphasize the child's own rate of progress (Hill, 1972). In environments where children are compared with one another ("grading on a curve"), a certain percentage of children experience failure regardless of their level of performance and rate of progress.

Activities

Observation of classrooms indicates that the type of available activities influences the kinds of social interaction which may occur. A study by Charlesworth and Hartup (1967) was concerned with activities in which children interacted positively with each other. They observed four nursery school classrooms and counted the frequency of four categories of positive social response: giving positive attention and approval, giving affection and personal acceptance, submission (passive acceptance, imitation, allowing another child to play), and token giving (spontaneously giving physical objects such as toys or food). Sixty-five percent of the positive responses given by children occurred in what the authors termed dramatic play activities (housekeeping area, blocks, trucks, puppet play, etc.). In contrast, table activities (puzzles, manipulative table toys, art activities, stories, flannel board, etc.) were less likely to elicit positive social behaviors. Finally, when children were wandering about the room without engaging in any activity, they were also less likely to interact positively with others.

Another relevant variable is the number of activity resources available. Since limited resources can lead to conflict and aggression, one way to minimize disturbance and keep children "on task" would be to provide lots of available resources. Indeed, evidence exists (Doke & Risley, 1972) that providing children with activity options, increasing the amount of materials, and dismissing children individually (rather than en masse) from one activity to another results in greater participation by children with the materials. Each of these techniques has the effect of increasing the ratio of available materials per child.

But is a high degree of participation with materials totally desirable? A second look suggests that the picture is more complicated. When the children worked with no activity options and were dismissed en masse, it appeared that ". . . children spent more time talking to each other" (Doke & Risley, 1972, p. 416). Since talking can lead to social learning, some nonparticipation with materials may be valuable. Having fewer material resources may be functional in another sense; the conflict and frustration that result provide children with opportunities to learn how to share and cooperate.

SOCIAL SKILLS AND FRIENDSHIP

Many children may lack friends not because the situation is particularly interfering or constraining but because they do not have certain important social skills. Help for these children requires that they be taught necessary social behaviors. In this section we will consider some of the behaviors associated with being liked and having friends.

Responding Positively

One important set of behaviors involves a child's ability to interact positively with others. As children grow older, they are likely to engage in more positive social responses with one another (Charlesworth & Hartup, 1967). The extent to which children behave constructively toward peers seems to be pretty consistent within a single context. Kohn (1966) observed kindergarten children throughout the school year. He found that the degree of positive interaction shown by children in the fall semester correlated with the degree of positive interaction in the spring. One reason for the stability of positive interaction is that children who give a lot of positive responses also tend to receive a lot. For example, Kohn (1966) found a high correlation between the percentage of positive acts made by a child and the percentage of positive acts which others made toward him or her. Charlesworth and Hartup (1967), in their study of nursery school children, found that the number of children to whom a child

responded positively was correlated significantly with the number of children who responded positively to him.

From these data we can hypothesize that children who engage in a high degree of positive interaction would also be chosen as friends on a sociometric measure. Studies in which children are asked to name their friends support this hypothesis. For example, Hartup et al. (1967) observed social interaction in a nursery school and correlated the type of interaction each child displayed with the number of acceptances and rejections received on a sociometric test. Social behavior was categorized as positive or negative. The first category included giving attention and approval, giving affection and personal acceptance, submitting to another's wishes, and giving things to another. Negative behaviors included noncompliance, interference, derogation, and attack. Peer acceptance and rejection were measured by asking children to identify three children they "especially like" and three they "don't like very much." Results of this study indicated that in both classrooms the number of positive responses a child made toward peers was positively correlated with peer acceptance. Furthermore, children who gave the most negative responses to peers were the most rejected. It seems, then, that children, who lack friends tend not to positively reinforce interpersonal contact.

In teaching a child to be more socially effective with peers, it is necessary to develop those behaviors that will be perceived by a child's peers as positive. These behaviors may vary across settings. Gottman, Gonso, and Rasmussen (1975) correlated social interaction patterns with peer acceptance in third- and fourth-grade classrooms. One-half of the classrooms were in a middle class school and one-half were in a working class school. As in the Hartup et al. (1967) study, the frequency of positive and negative social interactions was recorded. However, the observation categories were extended to include verbal and nonverbal behavior. The results indicated that the children who were liked in the middle class school were those who engaged in positive verbal interaction. In the working class school, the most liked children were those who engaged in positive nonverbal interaction. Middle class children who engaged in positive nonverbal behavior actually tended to be more disliked. These data imply that it is important for children to learn what types of behavior are reinforcing to other children. A child must learn to "psych out" the environment to figure out what kinds of behavior will lead to acceptance or rejection.

Communicating Accurately

Another skill that appears to be important is the ability to communicate accurately with another person. In one study (Rubin, 1972) children played a communication game in which a speaker described unusually shaped patterns to a listener. Data were also collected on children's three friendship play choices. The correlation between having friends and doing well on the patterns communication task was strongly significant in kindergarten and second grades. The correlations were nonsignificant in fourth and sixth grades. A more recent study (Gottman, Gonso, & Rasmussen, 1975) also found a relationship between having friends and communicating effectively.

Why might poorer communicators be less liked? One reason, perhaps, is that it is not very reinforcing or personally validating to be with someone who cannot express his ideas clearly and who may not be an especially good listener either. Another reason is that effective collaboration, whether it be in play or at work, depends on two people having a common idea of what they are about. The child who communicates poorly may also be playing or working at cross-purposes with peers.

Whatever the reason, it is important to identify possible reasons for poor communication performance. Some children may communicate poorly because they have less adequate vocabularies. Kingsley (1971) found that kindergarten children who did poorly on a communication task had more limited vocabulary. Second, some children may not recognize that effective communication often involves making fine distinctions. Asher and Parke (1975) found that young children can communicate as effectively as older children if fine distinctions are not required but do poorly when fine distinctions are required. Third, some children may not be considering the listener's perspective when communicating with another person. In one study (Flavell, Botkin, Fry, Wright, & Jarvis, 1968), elementary school children taught a game to a listener who was either sighted or blind. The children gave rather useful information to the sighted person but far less useful information when the listener was blind. For example, they would say "Put this piece here"; or "Take the red one and put it next to the blue one." This type of behavior suggests that the children were not thinking about the listener's point of view.

Research is needed on whether teaching children to be more accurate communicators increases their acceptance by other children. There is evidence that communication skills can be improved through practice or teaching (Chandler, Greenspan, & Barenboim, 1974). One study (Gottman, Gonso, & Schuler, in press) included sociometric measures and found that isolated children who were taught to be better communicators were more accepted by their classmates. No firm conclusion can be drawn since communication skill training was only one of a number of interventions with the children. Still, the results suggest that future exploration is warranted. If an isolated child is also a poor communicator, it could help to teach communication skills.

Being Expert

One way for a child to gain peer acceptance is to be very good at something valued by other children. For example, being a competent athlete is likely to be a social asset. McCraw and Tolbert (1953) compared the sociometric status of junior high school boys with their athletic ability. They measured sociometric status by asking boys to indicate the three children they like best in their class, grade level, and school. From these ratings a total status score was derived for each individual. Athletic ability was measured by an index composed of performance on the 50-yard dash, the standing broad jump, and the softball distance throw. At each grade level and in each class, the correlation between athletic ability and being liked was significant.

One group of children who are relatively lacking in expertise are the retarded. A study by Goodman, Gottlieb, and Harrison (1972) found that elementary school children expressed less liking for a sample of educably mentally retarded children from their school than for a sample of nonretarded children. Furthermore, there was evidence that increased contact through integrated classrooms led to increased *rejection* of the retarded. The retarded children in integrated classrooms were more rejected as potential friends. A follow-up study by Gottlieb and Budoff (1973) also found rejection of the retarded as friends and provided additional evidence that increased contact between retarded and nonretarded may lead to increased rejection. In a school with no interior walls, retarded children were more rejected than in a school with walls and segregated classrooms. As long as people judge others by their abilities, increased contact with those who are relatively less expert may lead to less rather than more acceptance.

How might the retarded be more successfully integrated with the nonretarded? The hypothesis that expertness is a critical determinant of peer acceptance suggests that activities should be emphasized in which the retarded have a chance to perform at or near the same level as nonretarded children. There are many areas in which EMR children are nearly indistinguishable from "normal" children. For example, they are likely to be more competent on the playground than in the classroom. Gottlieb (1971) found that children in Norway express more positive attitudes about playing with retarded children than working with them. It is likely that the same is true for American children.

If expertness is an important determinant of being liked, not just for the retarded, but for all children, then it should be possible to improve the status of an isolated child by making an existing talent more visible to the class. For example, while working in a third-grade class, two of the authors had an isolated child plan, with two other children, a puppet show which was presented to the class. Follow-up data indicated that the child gained a friend. If a child lacks skills valued by the group, it should be possible to increase his acceptance by teaching him a valued skill, For example, in a classroom where children emphasize athletics, teaching an isolated child to play a better game of basketball should increase his acceptance into the group. Although we know of no formal research that has evaluated the effectiveness of either of these strategies, many teachers report positive results from their own experience. It remains for researchers to evaluate what may be an effective practice.

Initiating a Relationship

It is conceivable that some children are positively responsive, effective communicators, and expert in certain areas but still lack friends. One possibility is that they may not know how to go about making a friend. In one study (Gottman, Gonso & Rasmussen, 1975), third- and fourth-grade children were asked individually to pretend that the experimenter was a new child in school and that he or she wanted to make friends. The children's responses were scored according to whether they offered a greeting,

asked the "new child" for information (e.g., "Where do you live?"), attempted to include (e.g., "Wanna come over to my house sometime?"), or gave information (e.g., "My favorite sport is basketball."). In addition to participating in this role play, the children were asked to name their best friends. Children who were chosen as a friend by six or more peers were found to be much more skillful on the "new friend" role-play than children who received five choices or less.

TEACHING SOCIAL SKILLS

If children have few friends because they lack effective social behaviors, then teaching social skills can be helpful. In this section we will review research on teaching friendship-making behavior to isolated children. Our focus is on teaching startegies that have practical value for the nursery school or elementary school classroom.

Shaping

Shaping uses positive reinforcement to change behavior gradually. The first step is to wait until the child's behavior somewhat approximates the behavior to be learned and then give the child a reinforcer. As the child's behavior further approaches the desired behavior, he or she is again reinforced. This shaping process continues until the new behavior is learned. One of the first studies to demonstrate the effects of shaping on an isolated child's behavior was done by Allen, Hart, Buell, Harris, and Wolf (1964). Their subject was Ann, a four-year-old nursery school child, who, after six weeks of school, was isolated from other children and engaged in a variety of behaviors to gain the teachers' attention. The study began with a five-day baseline period in which Ann's behavior was observed but no attempts were made to change her behavior. During this baseline period, Ann was observed to interact approximately 10% of the time with peers and approximately 40% of the time with teachers.

In the next phase of the study, the teacher reinforced Ann by giving her attention as she interacted with other children. At first, she was reinforced for standing close to another child or playing beside another child. Later, she was reinforced only for direct interaction. The researchers discovered that direct comments to Ann such as "Ann, you are making dinner for the whole family" had the effect of leading Ann away from the children into interaction with the teacher. Reinforcing statements that focused on Ann as a member of a group (e.g., "You three girls have a cozy house! Here are some more cups, Ann, for your tea party.") were quite successful; interaction with adults fell below 20% and interaction with children increased to about 60%.

Then the procedure was reversed. Ann was reinforced for being alone or interacting with teachers and ignored when she interacted with peers. Her behavior returned to the baseline level. This reversal to her previously isolated situation indicates the power of the teacher's attention. Ann's behavior was strongly influenced by what she was reinforced for doing. As a final test, the teachers once again reinforced Ann only for interacting with children. As before, her time spent interacting with children increased and her time with adults decreased.

What happens to isolated children weeks after reinforcement procedures are terminated? A study by O'Connor (1972) is relevant. Eight isolated children were reinforced for making social contact. The amount of time they spent in social interaction dramatically increased. However, when reinforcement was terminated their behavior reverted back to the baseline level. The failure to produce longer lasting effects is somewhat surprising. One might think that isolated children would find it reinforcing to be with other children and that the experience of being included by others would adequately sustain the new behavior. Perhaps the isolated children were socially unskilled and other children found them unpleasant to be with.

One approach to the problem of maintaining change is to gradually decrease or fade out the reinforcement rather than abruptly terminate it. A case study (Coats, 1967, reported in Baer & Wolf, 1970) with a four-year-old child found that when the teacher gradually decreased the frequency of reinforcing the child's social behavior the behavior lasted. Perhaps the gradual decrease in reinforcement gave the isolated child more time to learn and practice social skills. In this case, over a period of time his peers would begin to reinforce the child for social interaction. They would take over, as it were, the reinforcing function.

The studies considered here have been primarily concerned with increasing a child's tendency to approach other children. How do you teach an isolated child what to do once he approaches his peers? One method would be to shape appropriate

behavior by reinforcing closer and closer approximations of the desired behavior. This approach might be inefficient for teaching complex social skills; one could wait a long time for even an approximation of the appropriate behavior to occur. The next two teaching strategies to be discussed are more direct and possibly more efficient. Modeling and coaching can provide children with rules or general strategies of social interaction. These rules can guide the child's behavior so that he is reinforcing to be with.

Modeling

One way to learn something is to watch someone do it. In every culture a tremendous amount of information is transmitted from one generation to the next. Much of this information is acquired through observation. Children watch their parents shave, hunt, get up early for work, cook, make a bed, ride a bike, read, etc. By watching they learn. There has been a growing interest in using observational methods to change the behavior of children. Just as watching an aggressive model can lead children to be more aggressive (Bandura, Ross, & Ross, 1961), models may serve more positive functions. For example, children have been found to imitate models who reflect thoughtfully on a problem (Ridberg, Parke, & Hetherington, 1971), contribute to charity (Rosenhan & White, 1967), and express moral judgments characteristic of older children (Turiel, 1966).

If children learn by observing others, then an isolated child's social involvement could be increased by showing him a model of a socially effective person. O'Connor (1969) identified socially isolated children in nine nursery school classes by using a combination of teacher nominations and direct behavioral observation. Half of the isolated children saw a social interaction modeling film; the other half, the control group, saw a film about dolphins. The modeling film, 23 minutes long, consisted of 11 episodes in which a child entered a group of other children. The situations were graduated from low threat (sharing a book or toy with two other children) to high threat (joining a group of children who were gleefully tossing play equipment around the room). The model was always well received by the children (e.g., offered a toy, talked to, smiled at, etc.). A narrator described the action as it occurred in order to call children's attention to the relevant behaviors. For example, in one sequence the narrator says "Now another child comes up close to watch. She wants to play, too. She waits for them to see her. Now she gets a chair and she sits down with them so they will play with her. She starts to do what they are doing so they will want to play with her. . . ."

After seeing the film, each child returned to the classroom where postfilm observations were immediately made. Results showed that the social interaction of children in the modeling group greatly increased. In fact, they were interacting somewhat more frequently than a sample of nonisolated children. The control group that watched the dolphin film did not change at all. These are impressive results, particularly in the light of the brief nature of the "therapy."

But does it last? A second study by O'Connor (1972) is relevant. Again, isolated children were selected from nursery school classrooms. One group of children saw the modeling film. As in the previous study, the behavior of the children following the film was as interactive as that of the nonisolated children. In addition, follow-up observations were made weeks after the film. The children who saw the modeling film continued to interact with their peers. Another study using the modeling film observed children one month after exposure to the film model and also found that social interaction continued at a high level (Evers & Schwarz, 1973).

One intriguing issue left unresolved by this research is why isolated children learn from O'Connor's film models but have not learned from the real-life peer models who are in their classes. Nearly every class has highly popular children who are also socially quite skillful. One possible explanation is that the film narrator draws the children's attention to appropriate social details that they otherwise miss. Perhaps in the flow of events in the real world the isolated child fails to attend to significant elements of the popular child's behavior.

This analysis suggests that making the peer model's presence explicit could have positive results. A study of disruptive behavior by Csapo (1972) is suggestive. She paired six emotionally disturbed children with six peers who were exemplars of classroom decorum. The disturbed children sat next to their classmate model and were told to watch the model and do what he was doing so that he could learn how to get along better in class. Observations indicated that all six disruptive children improved their behavior dramatically. Follow-up data were

collected for ten days after the intervention was concluded and the six children continued their socially appropriate behavior.

Coaching

The development of language is a significant advance in a child's educational potential. Once children comprehend language, they can acquire new social behavior through direct instruction. Teachers and peers can become coaches who verbally transmit rules of social behavior. As we are using it here, coaching has a number of components. First, the child is provided with a rule or standard of behavior. In simple terms he is told what he should do. Second, the child has opportunities to rehearse or practice the behavior. Finally, there are opportunities for feedback in which the child's performance is discussed and suggestions for improvements made. The studies we will review here use at least two of these three components.

Studies of assertiveness training with college students can be used to illustrate coaching. McFall and Twentyman (1973) were interested in teaching assertive behaviors to unassertive people. As part of the training, the trainee was confronted with a series of simulated, or role-play, situations which typically pose difficulty for unassertive people (e.g., saying "no" to an illegitimate request). In each situation the trainee was given verbal instructions on how best to handle the situation. Coaching was found to be effective in improving assertive behavior in the training situation and in a real-life situation. Of particular interest was the finding that trainees who had a chance to rehearse or practice the new behavior improved more than those whose training did not include opportunities for practice.

Coaching can also be effective with young children. Using verbal reasoning techniques appears to be one of the best ways to insure that children internalize rules of social behavior. For example, studies of child-rearing methods suggest that verbal reasoning leads to more prosocial behavior by the child than physical punishment (e.g., Hoffman & Saltzstein, 1967). More recently, Parke (1970) has found that punishment, when it is administered, is more effective if accompanied by a verbal rationale. Parke suggested that rationales might include various kinds of information such as descriptions of consequences of behavior, examples of acceptable behavior, and explicit instructions on what to do in specific situations.

These types of rationales were provided in a study by Chittenden (1942). A critical situation for young children is one in which there are limited play resources (e.g., two children and one toy). Chittenden chose this situation and sought to teach children to take turns with materials, divide or share the materials where possible, or play cooperatively with the materials. She selected 19 nursery school children whose play with others included a high proportion of dominating behavior and a low proportion of cooperation. Ten of these children received training in how to play cooperatively with others; the other nine children served as the control group.

Chittenden's training situation was ingenious. Each child was introduced to two dolls named "Sandy" and "Mandy." In a series of situations, the dolls confronted the problem of how to play with a single toy. Sometimes they were unsuccessful and their interaction ended in a fight. At other times they were successful and they took turns, shared, or played cooperatively. Eleven training sessions were held. In the first session Sandy and Mandy were introduced; and in the next ten sessions the dolls faced a series of limited resource situations. Chittenden provides scripts for each of the sessions that could be used to repeat her training. Briefly, the first sessions served to teach the children to discriminate unhappy outcomes such as fighting, anger, etc., from happy outcomes such as sharing, having a good time, etc. In later sessions, the dolls sometimes played successfully, thereby modeling appropriate behavior. At other times they fought and the experimenter-teacher and child discussed possible ways of resolving conflicts the dolls faced. In still later sessions the child was asked to show the dolls what they could do to play more successfully. For example, after Sandy and Mandy fought over who was to use some toy cars the experimenter-teacher asked "What would you do? Show them what to do." These situations provided tests of the child's understanding.

More than a week after training, the children were observed in a real-life play situation. The results showed that the trained children had significantly decreased in their amount of dominating behavior. They also increased in cooperative behavior but the increase was not statistically significant. The control group children showed little change in their behavior from pre- to posttest.

A more recent coaching study by Zahavi (1973) has also obtained impressive results. She selected eight nursery school children who had been the most aggressive during six hours of observation over a two-week period. The head teacher, who was highly regarded by the children, met individually with four of the eight children for approximately fifteen minutes. The meeting consisted of three phases. First, the teacher explained to each child that hitting others causes harm; second, that the other children would not like the child if he hit them and that hitting does not solve the problem; and third, the child was asked to think of alternative behaviors to hitting such as sharing or taking turns. At each phase, the teacher asked the child questions so that he would participate in formulating these concepts. Six hours of follow-up observation conducted during the two weeks after training indicated that two of the four children greatly decreased their amount of aggressive activity. Furthermore, the decrease in aggression was accompanied by an increase in positive behaviors. The four control group children did not change. Next, these four children were coached by the teacher. Observations made one week later indicated that three of these four children dramatically changed their behavior. These results are quite impressive in the light of the short coaching session held by the teacher. They provide testimony to the way a teacher can verbally guide the behavior of even very young children.

Neither of these studies measured sociometric progress so there is no way of knowing whether children gained friends as a result of their change in behavior. Two recent coaching studies have included measures of friendship. In one (Gottman, Gonso, & Schuler, 1976), "low-friend" children from a single third-grade classroom were selected. Two of the children received training and two were control subjects. The training consisted of modeling and coaching in which the child saw a video tape of a girl entering a group of peers. The video tape was discussed and the "low-friend" child role-played situations in which she was a new child in class and wanted to make friends. After this role play the child was taught to be a more effective communicator. The emphasis of the training was on thinking of the listener's perspective when talking to another person.

Results of this study indicated that the two coached children were rated more highly by peers while the two control children received ratings quite similar to their earlier ones. Observation in class suggested that none of the children increased their frequency of interaction. However, the two coached children changed in the kind of children they interacted with. One girl sought out more popular children and the other interacted more with other "low-friend" children. Apparently the training affected children's selection strategies.

In another coaching and friendship study (Oden & Asher, 1975) three "low-friend" children in eleven different third- and fourth-grade classrooms were identified based on sociometric measures. One of the three was coached. This child, in five separate sessions, played a game with a classmate. Each session the child played with a different classmate. Before playing, the child was advised on how to have the most fun. The coach suggested such things as participating fully, cooperating, communicating, and showing interest in the other person. The child was asked to think of examples for each of these categories. After playing the game the coach asked the child "how it went" and the child discussed his experience in terms of issues such as participation, cooperation, communication, and showing interest. One of the other three "low-friend" children in each classroom participated in the same number of play sessions but received no coaching. The remaining "low-friend" child from the classroom came out of the room with a classmate, received no coaching, and played a game alone.

The experiment lasted for four weeks. About five days later the children were once again asked to indicate how much they liked to play with and work with the other children in the class and to name their friends. The results were encouraging. On the "play with" measure the coached children received a significantly higher rating; the rating of the children who were paired but did not receive coaching actually went down slightly; and the rating of children who played alone did not change. On the "work with" rating and the naming of friends measure the results were generally in the same direction but not significant.

In summary, it appears from a number of studies that coaching can improve children's social skills and lead to increased peer acceptance. Given the capacity of children to learn from verbal instruction and the opportunity to practice, a teacher would be wise to include coaching as a method for helping socially isolated children.

SUMMARY

We have considered some of the characteristics that are associated with having friends. It is important to keep in mind that children who lack friends may do so for different reasons. Social relationships are affected by the child's personal characteristics, varied aspects of the situation, and the child's social skills. With careful observation and informal "experimenting," it should be possible to infer the reasons for a particular child's social difficulty.

If a child's personal characteristics seem to be distracting from his or her friendship-making capability, emphasis could be placed on the child's similarity to other children such as having a common interest or goal. If the situation seems to be constraining peer relationships, there are a number of classroom features that could be changed. Introducing opportunities for children to participate in activities, rewarding social interaction, facilitating success experiences, and providing socially conducive activities can make a difference. Research to date suggests that it is important to maintain changes in the situation if friendships are to continue. If children lack friends due to limited social skills, a variety of teaching methods can be used. Shaping, modeling, and coaching have been found to improve the social interaction of isolated children. The results are particularly encouraging given the short-term nature of the "treatment" employed in most training research.

In terms of teaching social skills there are two areas, in particular, that we need to know more about. First, do the effects of social skill training last? To date, there have been no long-term follow-up studies. Results gathered about one month after training are encouraging, but there is a need for more longitudinal information. A formerly isolated child may need the psychological equivalent of "booster shots."

Second, we need to know which changes in social behavior lead to increased peer acceptance. For example, in shaping and modeling studies, the proportion of time children spend interacting with peers increases. Typically, however, no sociometric data are gathered, so it is impossible to say whether increased friendships result. For example, it is hard to know how the other children are perceiving the new behavior. It is possible that a formerly isolated child's classmates are thinking: "What a kid! He used to be by himself all the time; now he's always hanging around." The attention of the teacher and researcher should, therefore, be directed toward changes in both behavior *and* sociometric status.

Although we need to know more about how friendships develop and how they can be facilitated, we do know enough right now to improve the social relationships of children. The best strategy may be to use multiple methods of teaching social skills. The combined effects of shaping, modeling, and coaching would probably be more effective than any single technique alone. Finally, it would probably be best to consider situational variables when teaching social skills. Children need a suitable environment in which to practice newly developing abilities.

REFERENCES

Allen, K. E., Hart, B., Buell, J. S., Harris, F. R., & Wolf, M. M. Effects of social reinforcement of isolate behavior of a nursery school child. *Child Development,* 1964, *35,* 511–518.

Asher, N. W. Manipulating attraction toward the disabled: An application of the similarity-attraction model. *Rehabilitation Psychology,* 1973, *20,* 156–164.

Asher, N. W. Social stereotyping of the physically handicapped. Submitted for publication, 1975.

Asher, S. R. The influence of race and sex on children's sociometric choices across the school year. Unpublished manuscript, University of Illinois, 1973.

Asher, S. R. The effect of interest on reading comprehension of black children and white children. Unpublished manuscript, University of Illinois, 1975.

Asher, S. R., & Parke, R. D. Influence of sampling and comparison processes on the development of communication effectiveness. *Journal of Educational Psychology,* 1975, *67,* 64–75.

Baer, D. M., & Wolf, M. M. Recent examples of behavior modification in preschool settings. In C. Neuringer & J. L. Michael (Eds.), *Behavior modification in clinical psychology.* New York: Appleton-Century-Crofts, 1970.

Bandura, A., Ross, D., & Ross, S. A. Transmission of aggression through imitation of aggressive models. *Journal of Abnormal and Social Psychology,* 1961, *63,* 575–582.

Beadle, M. The game of the name. *N.Y. Times Magazine,* October 21, 1973, pp. 38–39, 120–126, 128–130.

Blau, B., & Rafferty, J. Changes in friendship status as a function of reinforcement. *Child Development,* 1970, *41,* 113–121.

Byrne, D., & Griffit, W. A developmental investigation of the law of attraction. *Journal of Personality and Social Psychology,* 1966, *4,* 699–702.

Challman, R. C. Factors influencing friendships among preschool children. *Child Development,* 1932, *3,* 146–158.

Chandler, M. J., Greenspan, S., & Barenboim, C. Assessment and training of role-taking and referential communication skills in institutionalized emotionally disturbed children. *Developmental Psychology,* 1974, *10,* 546–553.

Charlesworth, R., & Hartup, W. W. Positive social reinforcement in the nursery school peer group. *Child Development,* 1967, *38,* 993–1003.

Chennault, M. Improving the social acceptance of unpopular educable mentally retarded pupils in special classes. *American Journal of Mental Deficiency,* 1967, *72,* 455–458.

Chittenden, G. F. An experimental study in measuring and modifying assertive behavior in young children. *Monographs of the Society for Research in Child Development,* 1942, *7,* No. 1 (Serial No. 31).

Clark, K. B., & Clark, M. K. Racial identification and racial preference in Negro children. In T. Newcomb & E. Hartley (Eds.), *Readings in social psychology.* New York: Holt, 1947.

Cowen, E. L., Pederson, A., Babijian, H., Izzo, L. D., & Trost, M. A. Long-term follow-up of early detected vulnerable children. *Jounral of Consulting and Clinical Psychology,* 1973, *41,* 438–446.

Criswell, J. H. A sociometric study of race cleavage in the classroom. *Archives of Psychology,* 1939, No. 235, 1–82.

Cross, J. F., & Cross, J. Age, sex, race, and the perception of facial beauty. *Developmental Psychology,* 1971, *5,* 433–439.

Csapo, M. Peer models reverse the "one bad apple spoils the barrel" theory. *Teaching Exceptional Children,* 1972, *5,* 20–24.

Dawe, H. C. The influence of size of kindergarten upon performance. *Child Development,* 1934, *5,* 295–303.

DeVries, D. L. & Edwards, K. J. Student teams and learning games: Their effects on cross-race and cross-sex interaction. *Journal of Educational Psychology,* 1974, *66,* 741–749.

Dion, K. K. Physical attractiveness and evaluation of children's transgressions. *Journal of Personality and Social Psychology,* 1972, *24,* 207–213.

Dion, K. K., & Berscheid, E. Physical attractiveness and peer acceptance among children. *Sociometry,* 1974, *37,* 1–12.

Doke, L. A., & Risley, T. R. The organization of day-care environments: Required vs. optional activities. *Journal of Applied Behavior Analysis,* 1972, *5,* 405–420.

Durrett, M. E., & Davy, A. J. Racial awareness in young Mexican-American, Negro, and Anglo children. *Young Children,* 1970, *26,* 16–24.

Evers, W. L., & Schwarz, J. C. Modifying social withdrawal in pre-schoolers: The effects of filmed modeling and teacher praise. *Journal of Abnormal Child Psychology,* 1973, *1,* 248–256.

Flavell, J. H., Botkin, P. T., Fry, C. L., Wright, J. W., & Jarvis, P. E. *The development of role-taking and communication skills in children.* New York: Wiley, 1968.

Goodman, H., Gottlieb, J., & Harrison, R. H. Social acceptance of EMRs integrated into a nongraded elementary school. *American Journal of Mental Deficiency,* 1972, *76,* 412–417.

Gottlieb, J. Attitudes of Norwegian children toward the retarded in relation to sex and situational context. *American Journal of Mental Deficiency,* 1971, *75,* 635–639.

Gottlieb, J., & Budoff, M. Social acceptability of retarded children in nongraded schools differing in architecture. *American Journal of Mental Deficiency,* 1973, *78,* 15–19.

Gottman, J., Gonso, J., & Rasmussen, B. Social interaction, social competence and friendship in children. *Child Development,* 1975, *46,* 709–718.

Gottman, J., Gonso, J., & Schuler, P. Teaching social skills to isolated children. *Journal of Abnormal Child Psychology,* 1976, *4,* 179–197.

Gronlund, N. E. The relative stability of classroom social status with unweighted and weighted sociometric choices. *Journal of Educational Psychology,* 1955, *46,* 345–354.

Gronlund, N. E. *Sociometry in the classroom.* New York: Harper, 1959.

Gump, P. V., & Friesen, W. V. Participation in nonclass settings. In R. G. Barker & P. V. Gump (Eds.), *Big school, small school: High school size and student behavior.* Stanford, Calif.: Stanford University Press, 1964.

Harari, H., & McDavid, J. W. Name stereotyping and teachers' expectations. *Journal of Educational Psychology,* 1973, *65,* 222–225.

Hartup, W. W., Glazer, J. A., & Charlesworth, R. Peer reinforcement and sociometric status. *Child Development,* 1967, *38,* 1017–1024.

Hauserman, N., Walen, S. R., & Behling, M. Reinforced racial integration in the first grade: A study in generalization. *Journal of Applied Behavior Analysis,* 1973, *6,* 193–200.

Heider, E. R. Style and accuracy of verbal communication within and between social classes. *Journal of Personality and Social Psychology,* 1971, *18,* 33–47.

Hill, K. T. Anxiety in the evaluative context. In W. W. Hartup (Ed.), *The young child: Reviews of research,* Vol. 2. Washington, D.C.: National Association for the Education of Young Children, 1972.

Hoffman, M. L., & Saltzstein, H. D. Parent discipline and the child's moral development. *Journal of Personality and Social Psychology,* 1967, *5,* 45–57.

Horrocks, J. E., & Buker, M. E. A study of the friendship fluctuations of preadolescents. *The Journal of Genetic Psychology,* 1951, *78,* 131–144.

Hraba, J., & Grant, G. Black is beautiful: A reexamination of racial preference and identification. *Journal of Personality and Social Psychology,* 1970, *16,* 398–402.

Insko, C. A., & Robinson, J. E. Belief similarity versus race as determininants of reactions to Negroes by southern white adolescents: A further test of Rokeach's theory. *Journal of Personality and Social Psychology,* 1967, *7,* 216–221.

Isen, A. M., Horn, N., & Rosenhan, D. L. Effects of success and failure on children's generosity. *Journal of Personality and Social Psychology,* 1973, *27,* 239–247.

Kingsley, P. Relationship between egocentrism and children's communication. Paper presented at the biennial meeting of the Society for Research in Child Development, Minneapolis, 1971.

Kohn, M. The child as a determinant of his peers' approach to him. *The Journal of Genetic Psychology,* 1966, *109,* 91–100.

Lesser, G. S. The relationships between various forms of aggression and popularity among lower-class children. *Journal of Educational Psychology* 1959, *50,* 20–25.

Lilly, M. S. Improving social acceptance of low sociometric status, low achieving students. *Exceptional Children,* 1971, *37,* 341–347.

Markell, R. A., & Asher, S. R. The relationship of children's interests to perceived masculinity and femininity. Paper presented at the annual meeting of the American Educational Research Association, Chicago, 1974.

McClelland, F. M., & Ratliff, J. A. The use of sociometry as an aid in promoting social adjustment in a ninth grade home-room. *Sociometry,* 1947, *19,* 147–153.

McCraw, L. W., & Tolbert, J. W. Sociometric status and athletic ability of junior high school boys. *The Research Quarterly,* 1953, *24,* 72–80.

McDavid, J. W., & Harari, H. Stereotyping of names and popularity in grade-school children. *Child Development,* 1966, *37,* 453–459.

McFall, R. M., & Twentyman, C. T. Four experiments in the relative contributions of rehearsal, modeling, and coaching to assertiveness training. *Journal of Abnormal Psychology,* 1973, *81,* 199–218.

O'Connor, R. D. Modification of social withdrawal through symbolic modeling. *Journal of Applied Behavior Analysis,* 1969, *2,* 15–22.

O'Connor, R. D. Relative efficacy of modeling, shaping, and the combined procedures for modification of social withdrawal. *Journal of Abnormal Psychology,* 1972, *79,* 327–334.

Oden, S. L., & Asher, S. R. Coaching children in social skills for friendship making. Paper presented at the biennial meeting of the Society for Research in Child Development. Denver, 1975.

Omark, D. R., & Edelman, M. S. A developmental study of group formation in children. Paper presented at the annual meeting of the American Educational Research Association, New Orleans, 1973.

Parke, R. D. The role of punishment in the socialization process. In R. A. Hoppe, G. A. Milton, & E. C. Simmel (Eds.), *Early experiences and the processes of socialization.* New York: Academic Press, 1970.

Parten, M. B. Social participation among preschool children. *Journal of Abnormal and Social Psychology,* 1932, *27,* 243–269.

Richardson, S. A., Goodman, N., Hastorf, A. H., & Dornbusch, S. A. Cultural uniformity in reaction to physical disabilities. *American Sociological Review,* 1961, *26,* 241–247.

Ridberg, E. H., Parke, R. D., & Hetherington, E. M. Modification of impulsive and reflective cognitive styles through observation of film-mediated models. *Developmental Psychology,* 1971, *5,* 369–377.

Roff, M., Sells, S. B., & Golden, M. M. *Social adjustment and personality development in children.* Minneapolis: University of Minnesota Press, 1972.

Roistacher, R. C. A microeconomic model of sociometric choice. *Sociometry,* 1974, *37,* 219–238.

Rosenhan, D., & White, G. W. Observation and rehearsal as determinants of prosocial behavior. *Journal of Personality and Social Psychology,* 1967, *5,* 424–431.

Rubin, K. H. Relationship between egocentric communication and popularity among peers. *Developmental Psychology,* 1972, *7,* 364.

Rucker, C. N., & Vincenzo, F. M. Maintaining social acceptance gains made by mentally retarded children. *Exceptional Children,* 1970, *36,* 679–680.

Shaw, M. E. Changes in sociometric choices following forced integration of an elementary school. *Journal of Social Issues,* 1973, *29,* 143–157.

Sherif, M. Superordinate goals in the resolution of intergroup conflicts. *American Journal of Sociology,* 1958, *63,* 349–356.

Shure, M. B. Psychological ecology of a nursery school. *Child Development,* 1963, *34,* 979–992.

Silverman, I., & Shaw, M. E. Effects of sudden mass desegregation on interracial interaction and attitudes in one southern city. *Journal of Social Issues,* 1973, *29,* 133–142.

Singleton, L. *The effects of sex and race on children's sociometric choices for play and work.* Urbana, Illinois: University of Illinois, 1974. (Eric Document Reproduction Service No. ED 100520.)

Turiel, E. An experimental test of the sequentiality of the developmental stages in the child's moral judgements. *Journal of Personality and Social Psychology,* 1966, *3,* 611–618.

Ullmann, C. A. Teachers, peers and tests as predictors of adjustment. *Journal of Educational Psychology,* 1957, *48,* 257–267.

Wicker, A. Cognitive complexity, school size, and participation in school behavior settings: A test of the frequency of interaction hypothesis. *Journal of Educational Psychology,* 1969, *60,* 200–203.

Wright, B. A. *Physical disability—A psychological approach.* New York: Harper & Row, 1960.

Young, L. L., & Cooper, D. H. Some factors associated with popularity. *Journal of Educational Psychology,* 1944, *35,* 513–535.

Zahavi, S. Aggression-control. Unpublished master's thesis, University of Illinois, 1973.

Reading 33

Peer Relations as a Function of Physical Attractiveness: The Eye of the Beholder or Behavioral Reality?

Judith H. Langlois
A. Chris Downs

A child's physical appearance provides highly visible cues which indicate age, sex, race, and physical attractiveness. However, there has been little systematic study of the role these characteristics play as elicitors or modifiers of children's *behavior* in social interactions. The lack of research on the influence of appearance on behavior is particularly surprising

This research was supported in part by a grant from the Spencer Foundation to Judith H. Langlois. Portions of this paper were presented at the biennial meeting of the Society for Research in Child Development, New Orleans, March 1977. The authors thank the director, teachers, and children of the Little Red School House, Austin, Texas, for their participation and cooperation; Robert Young and John Loehlin for statistical advice; and Douglas Sawin, Walter Stephan, and Cookie Stephan for helpful comments and suggestions on the manuscript.

considering the implicit and explicit cultural values associated with beauty and ugliness (Berscheid & Walster 1973). For example, through fairy tales we all know that Cinderella is beautiful, good, and kind, while her stepsisters are ugly, wicked, selfish, and cruel; and that the ugly duckling who is rejected by his "peers" finds happiness only when he grows up to become a beautiful swan. Indeed, there is now considerable evidence that both adults and children make *inferences* about the behavior of others on the basis of physical appearance; desirable traits are attributed to attractive individuals, while undesirable traits are attributed to unattractive persons (Dion 1973; Dion, Berscheid, & Walster 1972).

In one such study, the physical attractiveness of a child who committed a transgression was found to influence adult evaluations of the child: unattractive children were perceived as dishonest, unpleasant, and as chronically anti-social compared with attractive children (Dion 1972). Clifford and Walster (1973) and Lerner and Lerner (1977) found that attractive children were rated by teachers as having greater academic ability, better social relations and adjustment, and as more likely to become successful in life than unattractive children.

Not only do adults evaluate children differentially based on physical attractiveness, but children evaluate each other differentially. Preschoolers and young elementary school children have the same behavioral stereotypes associated with appearance as do adults and prefer unfamiliar attractive peers as potential friends, while they dislike unfamiliar unattractive children (Dion 1973). Indeed, in triethnic investigations of elementary school children, Kleck, Richardson, and Ronald (1974) and Langlois and Stephan (1977) have found results suggesting that physical attractiveness may be more powerful than race in determining peer preferences and positive and negative behavioral expectations.

Taken together, these findings strongly suggest that physical attractiveness plays an important role in the development and expression of peer preferences and peer interactions. However, the processes which mediate the relationship between *perceptions* of behavior of attractive and unattractive children and the *actual behavior* emitted by these children remain largely unexplored. For example, do adults and children react differentially to attractive and unattractive children because these children in fact behave differently? That is, are unattractive children aggressive and anti-social while attractive children are friendly and behave prosocially? Or, are there no real behavioral differences between attractive and unattractive children but, rather, are they merely perceived by others to behave in this manner? Perhaps both children and adults have assimilated cultural stereotypes based on physical attractiveness which distort the perception of the behavior of others to fit these stereotypes. Finally, these two processes may interact. That is, because of cultural stereotypes we may expect attractive children to behave in one way and unattractive children in another. These expectations may then activate a self-fulfilling prophecy in which attractive children learn to behave in prosocial ways while unattractive children learn to behave in unacceptable, anti-social ways.

In the present study, we wished to determine whether or not behavioral differences exist between children judged attractive or unattractive. If no behavioral differences are found between attractive and unattractive children, it might be suggested that children are only perceived to behave differently. Age differences, however, would suggest that stereotypic expectations of behavior based on physical attractiveness and a self-fulfilling prophecy may interact such that no behavioral differences are found at younger ages but such differences become evident in older children. Finally, demonstrating substantial differences in behavior in both younger and older attractive and unattractive children might indicate that children learn these cultural stereotypes at younger ages than expected, or even perhaps that there is some biological relationship between appearance and behavior.

Children who were classmates and well acquainted were the focus of the investigation. Such an approach was taken in light of recent arguments for studying children in their natural ecological environments (Bronfenbrenner 1977; Lewis, Young, Brooks, & Michalson 1975). In addition, previous work with both preschool (Styczynski & Langlois 1977) and elementary school children (Styczynski & Langlois, Note 1) suggested that it may not be appropriate to generalize conclusions about the impact of physical attractiveness to acquainted children from research on unacquainted children. While the children in these studies rated unknown age-mates in a manner consistent with the "beauty is good" stereotype (Berscheid & Walster 1973; Dion 1972, 1973; Dion et al. 1972), this was not always the case for acquainted children. Rather, these preschool and elementary school children preferred unattractive male classmates over attractive male classmates.

METHOD

Subjects

A full-face black-and-white photograph was taken of 110 white children, all from a large, middle-class nursery school in Austin, Texas. All photographs were cropped at chin level to eliminate clothing cues. Children with eyeglasses or facial deformities were not included in the original stimulus set. Photographs of children within each age and sex were ranked, from a random display, from most to least attractive by 20 adult females who were unacquainted with the subjects. Judges were told to rank each photo on the basis of overall facial attractiveness. Interjudge agreement on ranking was significant. From these rankings, 64 children were selected: the 16 most attractive girls, the 16 most attractive boys, the 16 most unattractive girls, and the 16 most unattractive boys as judged by the adult raters. Half of the subjects were 3-year-olds with a mean age of 3 years, 4 months while the other half were 5-year-olds with a mean age of 5 years, 1 month. These ages were selected for the sample on the basis of previous work (Dion 1973, 1977; Dion & Berscheid 1974; Styczynski & Langlois 1977).

Apparatus

A portable child-study device, consisting of two wooden panels placed in the corner of a room, was erected in an unused room in the nursery school. The structure formed a play area of 3.05×3.05m. Five toys (blocks, riding truck, dolls, ball, puzzles) were available in the play area.

Design

Same age and sex dyads were formed on the basis of physical attractiveness. For each age and sex, four types of dyads were formed in a factorial design: dyads consisting of two attractive children (AA dyads), dyads of unattractive children (UU dyads), and two types of mixed dyads consisting of one attractive and one unattractive child (AU or UA dyads). The first child was designated as the subject the second as the peer. Within each age, sex, and physical-attractiveness category, all children were paired randomly with the stipulation that pairs must be classmates. All dyads were observed twice, yielding eight observations for each dyad type within each sex and age.

Procedure

Children were allowed to play in the playroom on several occasions prior to data collection in order for the children to adapt to the playroom situation. During data collection, one observer recorded the behavior of one member of the dyad while a second

observer recorded the behavior of the other member. This procedure resulted in a total of 128 observations. Five trained observers, naive as to the purpose of the study, were assigned approximately equivalent numbers of types of dyads (AA, UU, AU, UA). Each observation session was 10 min in length.

Data Collection and Statistical Analyses

Data were collected with a categorical observational system (Table 1) described by Gottfried and Seay (1973). This observational system was developed to permit meaningful comparison between cross-cultural and cross-species data and consequently is relatively free from high-level inference during the data collection process. The score for each category is the number of 15-sec intervals within which the defined behavior occurred. A specific category is recorded only once per 15-sec interval. One-third of the observations were monitored for reliability and interobserver reliabilities for the various categories ranged from $\rho = .74$ to $\rho = .99$, mean $\rho = .89$.

For purposes of data analysis, the individual behavior categories were grouped into classes of behaviors based on the a priori conceptual relatedness of the categories. These four major classes of behavior were (a) affiliative behaviors, including proximity, touch, eye contact, talk, and smile; (b) aggressive behavior, including fighting and hitting with objects; (c) high-activity play, including transport toys, throw toys, stand, walk/run, play with riding truck, play with ball, ride on truck, approach, and withdraw; and (d) low-activity play, including crawl, sit, play with puzzles, play with blocks, play with dolls, and groom.

RESULTS

Affiliative Behaviors

It can be seen in Table 2 that children paired with another child of the *same* level of attractiveness (AA or UU dyads) exhibited more affiliative behaviors than children paired with a peer of a different level of attractiveness (AU or UA dyads). Subsequent analyses showed that the variables contributing most strongly to the overall interaction effect were smiling and touching. In addition, 5-year-olds consistently engaged in significantly more affiliative behaviors than 3-year-olds.

Table 1 Behavior Categories

Category	Description	Spearman ρ Reliability coefficient	Factor loading
Affiliative behaviors			
Proximity	Being within 2 feet (0.61 m) of peer	.90	.83
Touch	Nonaccidental physical contact	.92	.86
Smile	Smile or laugh directed toward peer	.84	.58
Eye contact	Open eyes directed toward peer	.85	.85
Talk	Word or word approximation directed toward peer	.94	.82
Aggressive behaviors			
Fight	Hit, bite, kick, push, or scratch peer in nonplay context	.74	.67
Hit with object .	Hit with, push with, or throw an object directly at peer in nonplay context	.94	.53
High-activity play behaviors			
Approach	Movement from beyond to within 2 feet (0.61 m) or peer	.86	.52
Withdraw	Movement from within to beyond 2 feet (0.61 m) or peer	.79	.52
Stand	Standing with erect posture	.94	.88
Walk/run	Erect movement of 2 feet (0.61 m)	.87	.91
Transport toy . .	Movement of body and toy of 2 feet (0.61 m) or more	.74	.76
Throw toy	Throw or propel toy in play context	.97	.84
Play with riding truck	Contact with and manipulation of large riding truck	.83	.70[a]
Ride on truck . .	Movement of 2 feet (0.61 m) or more on truck	.98	.76[a]
Play with ball . .	Contact with and manipulation of ball	.88	.75
Low-activity play behaviors			
Sit	Rest haunches on floor	.99	.65
Crawl	Movement of 2 feet (0.61 m) or more on all four limbs	.87	.87
Groom	Fine-finger manipulation of own body or clothing	.87	.65[b]
Play with puzzle	Contact with and manipulation of wooden puzzle	.99	.58
Play with doll . .	Contact with and manipulation of doll	.85	.71[b]
Play with blocks	Contact with and manipulation of colored blocks	.92	.79

[a]Loading on factor labeled masculine sex-stereotyped play.
[b]Loading on factor labeled feminine sex-stereotyped play.

Table 2   Mean Frequency of Intervals for Interaction of Subject Attractiveness × Peer Attractiveness for Affiliative Behaviors

	Mean frequency of intervals for AA dyads	Mean frequency of intervals for AU dyads	Mean frequency of intervals for UA dyads	Mean frequency of intervals for UU dyads
Affiliative behaviors[a]	166.69	142.01	147.38	179.83
Smile	25.06	15.25	17.81	33.88
Touch	14.44	8.88	10.19	16.39
Talk	36.06	27.88	27.75	28.50
Proximity	46.44	46.94	50.19	54.50
Eye contact	44.69	43.06	41.44	46.56

Note—AA = attractive subject, attractive peer; AU = attractive subject, unattractive peer; UA = unattractive subject, attractive peer; UU =unattractive subject, unattractive peer.
[a]Summed mean frequency of intervals of occurrence for the behaviors comprising the behavior class.

Aggressive Behaviors

Table 3 indicated that the highest amounts of aggressive behaviors were seen in 5-year-old male dyads in which at least one member of the pair was unattractive. The lowest level of aggression for these 5-year-old boys was found in AA dyads. Further, aggressive behaviors were observed twice as often in 5-year-old female UU dyads than in any other type of 5-year-old female dyad. In contrast, the 3-year-olds of both sexes showed low amounts of aggressive behavior, and no clear differences based on attractiveness were evident. The age and sex main effects were consistent with the interaction effect and showed that boys exhibited more aggressive behaviors than girls and 5-year-olds more than 3-year-olds.

High-activity Play

Table 4 shows that unattractive girls paired with either attractive or unattractive partners showed higher levels of these play behaviors than attractive girls. Moreover, these unattractive girls exhibited high-activity play behaviors at about the same high frequency as did all boys.

Five-year-olds generally exhibited more high-activity play behaviors than 3-year-olds. This effect was produced primarily by the categories ride on truck, approach, and withdraw. Boys generally engage in more high-activity play behaviors than girls.

Low-activity Play

The means in Table 4 show that compared with other dyadic compositions 3- and 5-year-old girls in AA dyads and 5-year-old boys in these dyads

showed the highest amounts of low-activity play (i.e., were least active). Three-year-old boys in AA dyads, however, showed the lowest levels of low-activity play (i.e., were most active). Behavior categories contributing most heavily to this interaction effect were sit, play with blocks, and groom.

There were higher frequencies of low-activity play among attractive than unattractive children and among children with attractive rather than unattractive peers. Playing with blocks, sitting, and grooming contributed most strongly to the pattern for these two main effects. Finally, 3-year-olds were less active than 5-year-olds and that girls were less active than boys.

DISCUSSION

An overview of the effects due to attractiveness reveals that behavioral differences between attractive and unattractive children were found among aggressive behaviors, activity level, and sex-stereotyped behaviors but not in affiliative behaviors.

The findings for both aggressive behavior and activity level extend the results of attributional research indicating that unattractive children are perceived and expected to behave antisocially (e.g., Dion 1973). Negative evaluations of unattractive children seem to be a reflection of the actual tendency for these children to be aggressive. The higher activity level of unattractive children may lead them to be associated with more disturbances

Table 3 Mean Frequency of Intervals for Four-Way Interaction Effect for Aggressive, Low-activity Play, and Feminine Sex-stereotyped Behaviors

	Mean frequency of intervals for 3-year-old boys				Mean frequency of intervals for 3-year-old girls				Mean frequency of intervals for 5-year-old boys				Mean frequency of intervals for 5-year-old girls			
	AA dyads	AU dyads	UA dyads	UU dyads	AA dyads	AU dyads	UA dyads	UU dyads	AA dyads	AU dyads	UA dyads	UU dyads	AA dyads	AU dyads	UA dyads	UU dyads
Aggressive behaviors[a]	6.75	5.50	2.50	7.00	.25	1.50	2.75	1.50	1.25	17.25	18.00	12.75	4.75	1.25	1.50	12.00
Fight	.25	.25	1.75	3.50	.25	.50	.50	.25	.25	1.75	4.25	.50	.50	.00	.00	3.50
Hit with object	6.50	5.25	.75	3.50	.00	1.00	2.25	1.25	1.00	15.50	13.75	12.25	4.25	1.25	1.50	8.50
Low-activity play behaviors[a]	51.50	110.75	101.00	74.00	172.00	130.75	70.50	130.00	137.00	64.50	37.50	64.00	126.75	91.00	108.50	70.00
Sit on floor	25.00	49.00	46.25	36.25	76.50	59.50	29.00	55.75	62.25	28.75	15.25	31.50	56.75	42.25	47.25	33.50
Crawl	1.25	4.00	1.00	2.75	3.75	.75	3.25	2.75	4.50	4.25	1.25	7.50	3.00	1.50	3.50	2.00
Play with blocks	2.25	13.75	9.75	6.50	12.50	3.75	17.25	14.75	41.25	15.50	8.75	11.50	23.00	11.25	28.75	7.75
Play with dolls	.50	.25	.00	.50	16.25	5.50	3.00	1.75	.25	3.25	2.00	3.00	18.50	.25	1.25	2.75
Play with puzzles	16.75	31.50	39.25	21.00	45.50	52.25	12.75	39.25	19.75	10.00	5.25	5.00	15.00	28.00	14.25	19.50
Groom	5.75	12.25	4.75	7.00	17.50	9.00	5.25	15.75	9.00	2.75	5.00	5.50	10.50	7.75	13.50	4.50
Feminine sex-stereotyped behaviors[a,b]	6.25	12.50	4.75	7.50	33.75	14.50	8.25	17.50	9.25	6.00	7.00	8.50	29.00	8.00	14.75	7.25

Note—AA = attractive subject, attractive peer; AU = attractive subject, unattractive peer; UA = unattractive subject, attractive peer; UU = unattractive subject, unattractive peer.
[a] Summed mean frequency of intervals of occurrence for the behaviors comprising the behavior class.
[b] Univariate means for play with dolls and groom are found with low-activity play behaviors.

Table 4   Mean Frequency of Intervals for Interaction of Sex × Subject Attractiveness × Peer Attractiveness for High-Activity Play

	Mean frequency of intervals for boys				Mean frequency of intervals for girls			
	AA dyads	AU dayds	UA dyads	UU dyads	AA dyads	AU dyads	UA dyads	UU dyads
High-activity play[a]	153.65	170.15	147.76	155.15	63.27	86.91	141.78	137.88
Transport object	5.50	10.38	7.25	4.88	5.75	.63	5.63	6.25
Throw object ...	19.50	18.13	11.38	13.50	5.13	3.38	5.63	11.75
Walk/run	26.13	26.38	16.50	19.25	9.38	11.63	18.88	24.00
Stand	30.63	30.25	22.88	29.63	12.50	19.25	23.63	28.25
Play with ball ...	16.63	13.50	6.00	11.38	2.25	4.13	8.13	8.75
Play with truck ..	12.13	14.38	13.25	19.13	5.88	8.13	13.75	10.00
Ride on truck ...	18.75	25.00	39.50	30.00	10.00	22.63	35.25	20.25
Approach peer ..	12.63	17.38	15.00	13.88	6.63	8.75	15.63	15.00
Withdraw from peer	11.75	14.75	16.00	13.50	5.75	8.38	15.25	13.63

Note—AA = attractive subject, attractive peer; AU = attractive subject, unattractive peer; UA = unattractive subject, attractive peer; UU = unattractive subject, unattractive peer.
[a]Summed mean frequency of intervals of occurrence for the behaviors comprising the behavior class.

and become perceived as "troublemakers." If these activity level and aggression differences generalize to the classroom, they might account for the attribution of desirable characteristics to attractive children, since teachers seem to prefer nonaggressive and low-activity behaviors in children (Fagot & Patterson 1969).

The differential levels of aggression exhibited in 5-year-olds as a function of their physical attractiveness and the lack of such differences in younger children suggest that expectations for attractive and unattractive children may set a self-fulfilling prophecy into motion: unattractive children may be labeled as such and learn over time the stereotypes and behaviors associated with unattractiveness. Consequently, older children may exhibit aggressive behaviors consistent with others' expectations of them (e.g., Synder, Tanke, & Berscheid 1977). This finding has important implications for social development and clearly warrants additional research attention.

While the findings for aggression were predictable from previous attributional research, those for activity level and sex-stereotyped behaviors were unanticipated. The activity-level differences are, however, consistent with the positive correlation between high levels of activity and minor physical anomalies reported by Halverson and Waldrop

(1976). The slight physical anomalies of these children (Waldrop & Halverson 1971) were quite similar to physical characteristics commonly found in unattractive children (e.g., slight deviations with respect to features such as the eyes, mouth, and ears). The fact that unattractive children played actively with a stereotypically masculine toy is also consistent with evidence that unattractive children are rated by teachers as exhibiting more masculine play behavior than attractive children (LaVoie & Andrews 1976).

The activity-level and toy-preference differences obtained in this study also help explicate the findings of previous work (Styczynski & Langlois 1977, Note 1) in which attractive boys were generally disliked by acquainted peers. In the context of day-to-day interactions, the "prettier" and less active boys may be perceived more negatively and as less desirable as friends when children, particularly other boys, actually play with the toys and engage in the active, rough-and-tumble games characteristic of these ages.

The pattern of results for affiliative behaviors is generally inconsistent with previous research based on children's and adults' attributions of behavior. In those studies, attractive children were perceived to be more friendly and prosocial than less attractive children (Dion 1972, 1973), while in the present study no differences were observed in the affiliative behaviors of attractive and unattractive children when each child's level of attractiveness was individually examined. Clear differences were apparent, however, when the attractiveness of *both* the child and his or her peer was considered; both attractive and unattractive children tended to exhibit affiliative behaviors toward peers who were similar to themselves in attractiveness.

Several explanations seem possible for this inconsistency. First, there may simply be no relationship between positive behavioral expectations and the actual affiliative behaviors exhibited by children. The lack of such a relationship may be the case since attributions of behavior are presumably extracted from what a target child is believed to be like across a wide variety of situations while actual behavior may vary across situations (Mischel 1973). Moreover, ratings or attributions which reflect inferred behavioral or personality characteristics ignore the role that social agents, such as peers, play as elicitors of specific behaviors in specific contexts (e.g., Snyder et al. 1977). Finally, it may be that the behaviors selected to index affiliative or positive interactions in this study tap a different dimension of social behavior than has been investigated in attribution research. For example, there may not be a tight link between behaviors such as smiling, talking, and touching and attributions of friendliness and niceness.

An explanation for the pattern of data obtained for affiliative behaviors follows from Kohlberg's (1966) analysis of the development of conceptions of gender, namely, children's *self*-categorizations as attractive or unattractive may have an important impact on interactions with peers. Since children show an early awareness of physical-appearance differences and make differential attributions based on attractiveness, they should also categorize their own level of attractiveness. Once such self-categorizations of attractiveness are made, children would be expected to value behaviors, activities, and *peers* similar to and consistent with the self. The child would thus be expected to exhibit more affiliative behaviors when playing with peers whose attractiveness is consistent with the self-categorization. This explanation rests on the assumption that physical attractiveness is an important component of the self-concept. Recent evidence

does seem to support this assumption, at least among elementary school children (Montemayor & Eisen 1977). Regardless of the explanatory mechanism, these findings indicate that the frequency of affiliative behavior is not simply a function of the child's level of attractiveness as suggested by previous research, but rather that these behaviors are a function of the physical attractiveness of *both* the child and his or her playmate. The importance of considering the attractiveness of both members of an interacting dyad is also demonstrated by the results for activity level and toy preferences. For example, attractive girls were more likely than unattractive girls to engage in low-activity play and feminine sex-stereotyped play behaviors, but they engaged in these behaviors even more when paired with other attractive girls.

The results of the present investigation raise a number of issues to be addressed in order to fully understand the role of physical attractiveness in social and personality development. Explication of the processes underlying the emergence of behavioral differences as a function of appearance seems to warrant the first priority of future research. Investigations of the role of appearance in the developing self-concept are also necessary. Finally, social-situational factors mediating the impact of physical attractiveness require further study since degree of acquaintance, setting, and the age, sex, and physical attractiveness of both the child and his or her playmate all appear to influence behaviors emitted by attractive and unattractive children. Although many such interesting questions remain, it now seems clear that differences between attractive and unattractive children are indeed behavioral realities and do not merely exist in the eye of the beholder.

REFERENCE NOTE

1 Styczynski, L. E., & Langlois, J. H. The effects of physical attractiveness on the development of behavioral attributions and peer preferences in acquainted children. Unpublished manuscript. University of Texas at Austin, 1977.

REFERENCES

Berscheid, E., & Walster, E. Physical attractiveness. In L. Berkowitz (Ed.), *Advances in experimental social psychology.* New York: Academic Press, 1973.

Bronfenbrenner, U. Toward an experimental ecology of human development. *American Psychologist,* 1977, **32,** 513–531.

Cavior, N., & Dokecki, P. Physical attractiveness, perceived attitude similarity, and academic achievement as contributors to interpersonal attraction among adolescents. *Developmental Psychology,* 1973, **9,** 44–54.

Clifford, M. M., & Walster, E. The effects of physical attractiveness on teacher expectations. *Sociology of Education,* 1973, **46,** 248–258.

Dion, K. Physical attractiveness and evaluations of children's transgressions. *Journal of Personality and Social Psychology,* 1972, **24,** 207–213.

Dion, K. Young children's stereotyping of facial attractiveness. *Developmental Psychology,* 1973, **9,** 183–188.

Dion, K. The incentive value of physical attractiveness for young children. *Personality and Social Psychology Bulletin,* 1977, **3,** 67–70.

Dion, K., & Berscheid, E. Physical attractiveness and peer perception. *Sociometry,* 1974, **37,** 1–12.

Dion, K., Berscheid, E., & Walster, E. What is beautiful is good. *Journal of Personality and Social Psychology,* 1972, **24,** 285–290.

Fagot, B. I., & Patterson, G. R. An in vivo analysis of reinforcing contingencies for sex-role behaviors in the preschool child. *Developmental Psychology,* 1969, **1,** 563–568.

Gottfried, N. W., & Seay, B. An observational technique for preschool children. *Journal of Genetic Psychology,* 1973, **122,** 263–268.

Halverson, C. F., & Waldrop, M. F. Relations between preschool activity and aspects of intellectual and social behavior at age 7½. *Developmental Psychology,* 1976, **12,** 107–112.

Harris, R. J. *A primer of multivariate statistics.* New York: Academic Press, 1975.

Kleck, R., Richardson, S., & Ronald, L. Physical appearance cues and interpersonal attraction in children. *Child Development,* 1974, **45,** 305–310.

Kohlberg, L. A cognitive-developmental analysis of children's sex-role concepts and attitudes. In E. M. Maccoby (Ed.), *The development of sex differences.* Stanford, Calif.: Stanford University Press, 1966.

Langlois, J. H., & Stephen, C. The effects of physical attractiveness and ethnicity on children's behavioral attributions and peer preferences. *Child Development,* 1977, **48,** 1694–1698.

LaVoie, J. C., & Andrews, R. Facial attractiveness, physique, and sex role identity in young children. *Developmental Psychology,* 1976, **12,** 550–551.

Lerner, R. M., & Lerner, J. V. Effects of age, sex, and physical attractiveness on child-peer relations, academic performance, and elementary school adjustment. *Developmental Psychology,* 1977, **13,** 585–590.

Lewis, M., Young, G., Brooks, J., & Michalson, L. The beginning of friendship. In M. Lewis & L. A. Rosenblum (Eds.), *Friendship and peer relations.* New York: Wiley, 1975.

Mischel, W. Toward a cognitive social learning reconceptualization of personality. *Psychological Review,* 1973, **80,** 252–283.

Montemayor, R., & Eisen, M. The development of self-conceptions from childhood to adolescence. *Developmental Psychology,* 1977, **12,** 314–319.

Styczynski, L. E., & Langlois, J. H. The effects of familiarity on behavioral stereotypes associated with physical attractiveness in young children. *Child Development,* 1977, **48,** 1137–1141.

Synder, M., Tanke, E. D., & Berscheid, E. Social perception and interpersonal behavior: on the self-fulfilling nature of social stereotypes. *Journal of Personality and Social Psychology,* 1977, **35,** 656–666.

Waldrop, M. F., & Halverson, C. F. Minor physical anomalies and hyperactive behavior in young children. In J. Hellmuth (Ed.), *Exceptional infant.* Vol. **2.** New York: Brunner/Mazel, 1971.

Reading 34

Rehabilitation of Socially Withdrawn Preschool Children through Mixed-Age and Same-Age Socialization

Wyndol Furman
Donald F. Rahe
Willard W. Hartup

Mixed-age socialization serves children in many ways that same-age socialization does not. For example, aggression occurs more frequently among age mates than among non–age mates, but nurturance occurs more commonly in interaction with younger children (Whiting & Whiting 1975). Verbal communication also varies in amount and appropriateness across same- and mixed-age situations— even among very young children. (Lougee, Grueneich, & Hartup 1977; Shatz & Gelman 1973). Social adaptations would seem to require skills learned in both contexts.

Same-age situations require accommodations between individuals of equivalent developmental status while mixed-age situations require accommodations between individuals whose developmental status differs. Both types of accommodations may require role-taking skill and the capacity to synchronize one's actions with the actions of others. A small literature shows mixed-age accommodations to be expressed in various ways: (*a*) older children are more effective models than younger children (Peifer, Note 1); (*b*) reciprocal imitation is more characteristic of children's interactions with older children than with younger children (Thelen & Kirkland 1976); (*c*) children prefer to be taught by children older than themselves (Allen & Feldman 1976); and (*d*) under certain conditions, social reinforcement is more effective when delivered by *either* an older or a younger child than when delivered by an age mate (Ferguson, Note 2).

The long-term consequences of same- and mixed-

This study was designed and conducted under grant no. 5PO 1 05027, National Institute of Child Health and Human Development (Willard W. Hartup, principal investigator). The study is based on a thesis submitted by Wyndol Furman to the Graduate School, University of Minnesota, in partial fulfillment of the requirements for the Ph.D. degree. The authors wish to acknowledge the technical assistance of Craig Binger, Christine Richardson, and Lee Rosén.

age interaction have not been studied extensively. Do such experiences contribute to the development of individual differences in social competence? Our answer must be speculative. Variations in the opportunity to engage in rough-and-tumble interactions with age mates would seem to be linked to variations in the acquisition of an appropriately regulated aggressive repertoire. By the same token, variations in the chance to interact with younger children (especially infants) would seem to contribute to individual differences in prosocial proclivities. Few studies, however, bear on this issue.

Suomi and Harlow (1972) used a mixed-age situation to ameliorate the effects of social isolation in young rhesus monkeys. Over the years, this research team tested numerous methods for restoring normal social activity in the withdrawn, depressed animals produced by social and sensory isolation. Exposure to adult animals or to age mates failed to restore social activity (Harlow, Dodsworth, & Harlow 1965; Pratt, Note 3). But, using four experimental animals that had spent their first 6 months in isolation, the investigators tried exposure to normal infant monkeys who were only 3 months old (i.e., 3 months younger than the subjects). The initial overtures by the normal animals consisted of clinging to the isolate, thus preventing the stereotypic activity. Unable to rock, huddle, or clasp themselves, the isolate monkeys began to locomote, explore, and engage in social play. After a few weeks, the rate of stereotypic behavior had decreased significantly and, after 6 months of treatment, the social deficits of the isolate monkeys were virtually eradicated. These results contrast markedly with the isolates' behavior with age mates. In those instances, the isolates were attacked, did not reciprocate, and remained the victims of frequent aggression (Harlow et al. 1965).

These comparative studies suggest the more general

hypothesis that the social contacts most readily available to children (i.e., with age mates) may not benefit everyone equally. Accordingly, a primary objective of the present investigation was to extend our knowledge concerning the contributions of mixed- and same-age interactions to the growth of social competencies in young children. A second objective was to devise a model intervention that would have broad applicability to the rehabilitation of socially withdrawn children.

Our intervention resembled a technique employed earlier by Koch (1935). In that study, seven "distinctly unsocial children" were selected for treatment, along with seven others who were studied as matched controls. For 30 min every day for 20 days, each "experimental" child was removed from the nursery along with one sociable child (presumably the subject's own age) and surrounded by play materials believed to stimulate cooperative play. The children were "thrown upon each other" as much as possible, meaning that the adult experimenter did not direct their activity. Observations conducted when the children had returned to the nursery were used to establish the time spent in cooperative play, the frequency of conflict, and the amount of conversation. The published report is incomplete, but "changes in the direction of increased sociability were cumulative throughout the investigation" (Page 1936, p. 10).

In our case, isolated children were selected on the basis of observations conducted in seven day-care centers. Some isolate children were placed together with nonisolate children of the same chronological age; others were exposed to nonisolates who were much younger. A no-treatment control group was included. It was predicted that the outcomes of this experiment would conform to the model established by Suomi and Harlow (1972), namely, that gains in sociability would be greater for the isolates exposed to younger therapists than the gains among isolates exposed to same-age therapists or the controls. Such results were expected as a consequence of the better match in number of social overtures occurring between the isolate and younger children (cf., Charlesworth & Hartup 1967) and the provision of more frequent opportunities to practice certain social skills (e.g., ascendant behavior) in which the isolated child is deficient.

METHOD

Subjects

Observations were conducted on 262 children ranging in chronological age from 30 to 79 months ($M =$ 52.8) who were enrolled in 19 classrooms in seven day care centers serving mainly white, middle-class children. Thirty three-interval observations were made on each child (see below).

Children who engaged in peer interaction during less than 33% of the observations and whose scores were more than 10 percentage points below their class means were considered to be social isolates. Twenty-four children, ranging between 48 and 68 months ($M = 57.4$), met these criteria. All isolates had attended school for more than 3 weeks; none was described by the teachers as mentally retarded or emotionally disturbed. Mean rate of peer interaction for the isolates was 26.2%.

Design

Eight isolates were assigned randomly to younger partners (group Y); eight were assigned to same-age partners (group S); eight were assigned to a no-treatment control condition (group C). Each group consisted of five girls and three boys.

The 16 isolates in groups Y and S were each assigned to two same-sex companions. The compansions were selected randomly except with respect to their ages. Younger partners were 12–20 months younger than their isolate partners ($M = 15.4$ months), while same-age partners were between 3 months younger and 3 months older than their companions. The isolates and their companions knew one another through opportunities to interact daily in school. Mean rate of peer interaction during the observations prior to treatment was 41.5% for the younger partners and 49.9% for the older partners.

Pretreatment Observations

An observational procedure was adapted from a system originated by Furman and Masters (Note 4). Children were observed in random order for 30 observations, each consisting of three 6-sec "on" intervals alternated with comparable "off" intervals. Between 5 and 8 weeks were required to conduct the observations in each class. Observers (two graduate students and two undergraduates) recorded initially the presence or absence of social interaction within each interval. Next, the child's actions were coded using three categories.

Reinforcement Help giving, guidance, praise, affection, reassurance, protection, gift giving, compliance, acceptance of directions and gifts, warm greetings, smiling and laughing, invitation to plan, permission, giving status, cooperative play, and promises of reward.

Punishment Noncompliance, disapproval, rejection, blaming, teasing, insults, quarreling, yelling, ignoring, taking or damaging property, physical attack, and threats.

Neutral Acts All behaviors not coded as reinforcement or punishment. This category included most instances of visual attention, conversation, and associative play. Validity and coding criteria are discussed elsewhere (Furman, Masters, Rahe, & Binger 1978; Furman & Masters, Note 4).

The observers received intensive training over a period of 2–4 weeks. Interrater agreement was calculated during the last 5 days of training (an average of 434 observation intervals for each pair of observers). Agreement on the presence/absence of peer interaction was 99%, while agreement based on the individual categories ranged from 95% to 99% ($M = 98\%$).

Treatment Sessions

Each isolate and his/her partner participated in 10 play sessions scheduled over a period of 4–6 weeks. The isolates were paired with two partners—one during the first five sessions and the other during the second five sessions. Play sessions were conducted in a small room separate from the classroom. During each session, the children had an opportunity to play with two toys for approximately 20 min. The toys, designed to maximize the frequency of positive social interaction, included blocks, puppets, felt and cardboard figures, dress-up clothing, and train sets. New toys were available in each of the first five sessions, then were reused.

The experimenter (a male graduate student) sat in a corner and conducted observations of the children with a procedure similar to the one used in the classroom. Interactions with the children were kept to a minimum. To ensure that various dyads were not treated differently, the experimenter's interactions with the children were tape recorded and transcribed. Two naive raters analyzed these transcripts; these did not differ significantly between group Y and group S. In each play session, 90 successive 6-sec "on" observations were obtained separated by comparable "off" intervals.

Posttreatment Observations

Following the treatment sessions, 30 observations, in sets of three, were conducted on every child in each day-care class. Observations were made on 256 children, including the isolates, requiring 4–5 weeks. The observers did not know the identities of the isolates or their partners. Interrater agreement was checked at various times during the posttreatment observations. An average of 433 observations was made by the various pairs of observers with agreement on presence/absence of peer interaction equaling 98% and a range from 96% to 99% ($M = 98\%$) on individual categories.

The teachers were not informed that some children had been designated as isolates or that the extraclass sessions were designed to modify rates of peer interaction. They were only told that the experiment concerned the behavior of children in small groups. At the end of the posttreatment phase, the experimenter asked the teachers to complete an information questionnaire to determine whether they had remained unaware of the study's purpose. This instrument consisted of a series of six multiple-choice questions assessing the teacher's knowledge about the observations, the selection of subjects, the structure and purpose of the treatment sessions, and the reason for the posttreatment observations. The questionnaire was also administered, for comparison, to the center directors, who knew the purposes of the experiment from the beginning.

RESULTS AND DISCUSSION

It can be seen in Figure 1 that social contact in a one-on-one situation, particularly with younger children, was found to increase the social activity of isolate children in their classrooms. Dyadic contact with other children produced higher rates of peer interaction after treatment than before treatment. Improvement among the isolate children who were

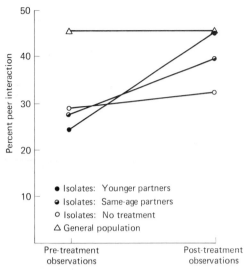

Figure 1 Peer interaction rates before and after mixed- and same-age socialization.

exposed to younger children was so marked that posttreatment interaction was almost twice as frequent as pretreatment interaction—essentially at the same level as the social interaction of the nonisolate children.

Differences between the two treatment conditions (group Y and group S) were not as striking as the differences between the treatment conditions and the control condition (group C). Nevertheless, isolates exposed to younger children gained more than those assigned to same-aged children: (*a*) The difference between posttreatment scores in group Y and group S was in the predicted direction, even though not statistically significant. (*b*) Subjects who participated in the play sessions with a younger child differed significantly from subjects assigned to the control condition while those exposed to same-age interaction did not. (*c*) Inspection of individual scores reveals that almost every child in group Y improved substantially (seven of the eight children increased their peer interaction rates by 50% or more), whereas the experimental effects in group S were more variable (only three of the eight children improved by this same amount).

The main consequence of the intervention was to alter reinforcement rates—not to change such social actions as neutral acts or punishments. Reinforcement rates were tripled among the subjects who

interacted with younger children and doubled among subjects in the same-age condition; rates among the control children were unchanged. The specificity of these changes established that the effects of the treatment were beneficial. Most of the positive reinforcements entailed some form of prosocial behavior (e.g., helping, giving, or sharing) or required social coordination (e.g., cooperative play or accepting guidance and suggestions). Since prosocial activity, coordinated effort, and social reinforcement have all been found to increase with age (see Hartup 1970), the peer intervention seems to have increased the maturity of the social activity among the isolates.

What mechanisms were responsible for the behavior changes induced by the peer interaction? The results cannot be attributed to either teacher or observer bias. The teachers were unaware of the purposes of the study. Similarly, the observers who conducted the posttreatment observations were naive with respect to the identities of the target children. Neither could the experimental outcomes derive from the fact that certain isolates were singled out for special sessions while the remaining ones were not. Being chosen for the play sessions was not noteworthy in these classes since every child participated in several testing sessions in connection with related research. Besides, a Hawthorne Effect (Roethlisberger & Dickson 1939) would not account for the differences between the children in groups Y and S, or the pattern of correlations between the play-session scores and the posttreatment observations. Also, if a Hawthorne Effect were present, the social behavior of the partners would have changed as well as the social behavior of the isolates. This was not the case.

Instead, the play sessions themselves seem responsible for the observed changes. There was a high rate of social activity occurring in these sessions. With both same-age and younger partners, the isolates' mean rates of interaction were over 60%. Interaction rates remained relatively constant across sessions; the mean rate in the first session was as great as that in the tenth session. Thus, the one-on-one nature of the play sessions seems to have been responsible for the differences between social activity in the playroom and in the classroom.

The absence of a gradual increase in sociability

across sessions is inconsistent with the notion that the treatment effects stemmed from a general "shaping" of social activity. The correlations between playroom interaction and classroom outcome also are not consistent with this notion. Shaping would result in positive correlations between reinforcement rates in the play sessions and sociability of the target children in the posttreatment observations. In point of fact, these correlations were negative.

The play sessions must have provided the isolates with experiences that occurred infrequently in the classroom. We believe these experiences included the opportunity to be socially assertive (i.e., to direct social activity). Previous research suggests that social isolates are deficient in leadership skills (Kohn & Rosman 1972). Such children are responsive to the social overtures of other children but do not readily elicit reactions to them (Staley & Gottman, Note 2). The play sessions may have fostered increased peer interaction because they provided situations in which assertive behaviors met with a higher probability of success than in the classroom. Experiences with younger children, as contrasted with experiences with age mates, would provide the isolate with the most opportunities to initiate and direct social activity.

There were negative correlations between the interaction rates in the play sessions and in the classroom following treatment that are consistent with this "leadership deficit" theory. Play sessions marked by high rates of interaction (as occurred with the same-age partners) would be sessions in which the *partner* is very active and directs most of the play. Lower rates of interaction (e.g., with younger partners) would provide the *isolate* with more opportunities to display initiative and to direct play successfully. Since assertive actions were not directly measured, however, this hypothesis must be examined in future research.

The intervention strategies assessed in this study were remarkably strong clinical treatments. In just over 3 hours of therapeutic contact with younger children, the mean rate of interaction among socially withdrawn children almost doubled—to the same level as their classmates. The results attest to the unique consequences of mixed-age socialization, as compared with same-age socialization, and provide

a treatment model that is efficient, effective, and easily implemented.

This investigation illustrates the value of comparative models for understanding human development. While the analogue between this study and the animal model on which it was based can easily be overstated, the findings indicate that our conceptualizations of developmental processes should not be limited to individual species. Like the growing body of research in human ethology (Blurton Jones 1972), this study underscores the importance of evolutionary origins in understanding human development.

REFERENCE NOTES

1 Peifer, M. R. The effects of varying age-grade status of models on the imitative behavior of six-year-old boys. Unpublished doctoral dissertation, University of Delaware, 1971.

2 Ferguson, N. Peers as social agents. Unpublished master's thesis, University of Minnesota, 1965.

3 Pratt, C. L. The developmental consequences of variations in early social stimulation. Unpublished doctoral dissertation. University of Wisconsin, 1969.

4 Furman, W., & Masters, J. C. Social learning constructs of reinforcement and punishment and their affective consequences. Manuscript submitted for publication, 1978.

5 Staley, C. B., & Gottman, J. M. Popularity, social structure and social interaction in children. Manuscript submitted for publication, 1976.

REFERENCES

Allen, V. L., & Feldman, R. S. Studies on the role of tutor. In V. L. Allen (Ed.), *Children as tutors*. New York: Academic Press, 1976.

Blurton Jones, N. (Ed.). *Ethological studies of child behavior*. London: Cambridge University Press, 1972.

Charlesworth, R., & Hartup, W. W. Positive social reinforcement in the nursery school peer group. *Child Development*, 1967, **38**, 993–1002.

Cohen, J. A coefficient of agreement for nominal scales. *Educational and Psychological Measurement*, 1960, **20**, 37–46.

Furman, W., & Masters, J. C., in collaboration with Rahe, D. F., & Binger, C. *An observational system for coding reinforcing, neutral and punishing interactions among children*. Minneapolis: Institute of Child Development, 1978.

Harlow, H. F., Dodsworth, R. O., & Harlow, M. K. Total social isolation in monkeys. *Proceedings of the National Academy of Sciences*, 1965, **54**, 90–96.

Hartup, W. W. Peer interaction and social organization. In P. H. Mussen (Ed.), *Carmichael's manual of child psychology.* (3d ed.). Vol. **2.** New York: Wiley, 1970.

Koch, H. The modification of unsocialness in preschool children. *Psychological Bulletin*, 1935, **32**, 700–701.

Kohn, M., & Rosman, B. L. A social competence scale and symptom checklist for the preschool child: factor dimensions, their cross-instrument generality, and longitudinal persistence. *Developmental Psychology,* 1972, **6**, 445–452.

Lougee, M. D., Grueneich, R., & Hartup, W. W. Social interaction in same- and mixed-age dyads of preschool children. *Child Development,* 1977, **48**, 1353–1361.

Page, M. L. The modification of ascendant behavior in preschool children. *University of Iowa Studies in Child Welfare,* 1936, **12**, No. 3.

Roethlisberger, R. J., & Dickson, W. J. *Management and the worker.* Cambridge, Mass.: Harvard University Press, 1939.

Shatz, M., & Gelman, R. The development of communication skills: modification in the speech of young children as a function of listener. *Monographs of the Society for Research in Child Development,* 1973, **38** (Whole No. 152).

Suomi, S. J., & Harlow, H. F. Social rehabilitation of isolate-reared monkeys. *Development Psychology,* 1972, **6**, 487–496.

Thelen, M. H., & Kirkland, D. K. On status and being imitated: effects on reciprocal imitation and attraction. *Journal of Personality and Social Psychology,* 1976, **33**, 691–697.

Whiting, B. B., & Whiting, J. W. M. *Children of six cultures: a psychocultural analysis.* Cambridge, Mass.: Harvard University Press, 1975.

Reading 35

Pretend Play: New Perspectives

Greta G. Fein

Children's pretend play is a familiar phenomenon to early childhood educators. But it is only recently that its origins, forms, and implications for development have received systematic attention (see Fein 1979 for an extensive review of the research literture). A variety of terms are used, often interchangeably, to refer to this type of play. *Fantasy play, imaginative play, make-believe play,* and *pretend play* are typically used as generic terms for play that has an "as if" quality, and these terms will be used in a similar fashion in this discussion. By contrast, the terms *symbolic play* and *sociodramatic play* are used to designate particular forms of pretend play that appear at different stages of development. *Symbolic play* will be used to refer to solitary play in which the child represents one thing as if it were another with no attempt to develop or coordinate pretend activities with a partner, and *sociodramatic play* will be used for pretense that is shared or coordinated with a partner. Although this distinction can be viewed as a convenient way of classifying a complex form of behavior, there are empirical grounds for believing children shift from solitary to social pretense, and that this shift marks a developmental accomplishment of considerable importance.

SYMBOLIC PLAY

At about 12 months of age, a new behavior emerges in the young child's repertoire. Prior to this time, the baby eats when hungry, sleeps when tired, and cries when distressed; objects such as bottles, cups, spoons, pillows, and blankets are used either to manipulate or to obtain nourishment and rest. Then, with apparent suddenness, the meaning of these objects subtly changes. Seemingly sated, the baby pretends to eat and, seemingly rested, the baby pretends to sleep. Although these behaviors were noted by others, Piaget (1962) was the first to offer a theoretical framework for understanding their developmental significance. According to Piaget, these behaviors mark the beginnings of representational thought, the first sign that the child is beginning to construct mental symbols and images of the real world of substances, objects, and actions.

According to Piaget and others who have subsequently extended and refined these observations, early pretend behaviors become more stable and elaborated during the second year of life (Inhelder, Lezine, Sinclair, and Stambak 1972; Nicolich 1977; Fein and Apfel 1979). By about 18 months, the child discovers that a doll can be fed or put to bed as if it were a baby. But at this age, the doll must be doll-like and the cup must be cuplike if they are to be used this way. Between 18 and 24 months, the requirement of likeness becomes relaxed. In Vygotsky's terms, dissimilar objects (a hank of wool, a piece of wood, a shell, a fist) can substitute for lifelike objects and, gradually, an immediately present object is not needed for pretending. Over the next few months, symbolic play becomes increasingly elaborate and well-formed until, by about 30 months, it can become a collaborative effort undertaken with others.

Piaget and Vygotsky agree that symbolic play reflects the child's mastery of mental symbols, elements of thought that permit the child to detach ideas about the world from the influence of objects in the immediate environment. Vygotsky (1967) views the acquisition of stimulus-free mental symbols as a gradual process in which the requirement of likeness is relaxed by degrees. Recent research supports this idea. When two-year-olds are given a realistic cup and a realistic toy horse to pretend feeding with, they have no difficulty. If a less realistic object is substituted for one of these, pretense drops slightly. If less realistic substitutes are provided for both objects, pretense decreases markedly (Fein 1975). It is as if at this age, the symbol system is too fragile to operate without firm anchors in the immediate setting. Studies of preschool children suggest that the child's liberation from the immediate situation continues to develop over the next two years (Elder and Pederson 1978; Golomb 1977). But even five-year-olds have difficulty substituting one object for another under certain circumstances (e.g., a hairbrush for food to feed a hungry baby in Golomb's study).

These and other studies suggest that symbolic play is influenced by the play materials available to the child. In young children, play is enhanced by realistic materials and realistic toy props. With age, the need for realistic materials diminishes and, according to some researchers (Pulaski 1973), less realistic toys might even enhance the imaginativeness of play in older children. Although sleek, abstract forms are appealing to adults, their play value for children seems to depend on the age of the child.

SOCIODRAMATIC PLAY

Sociodramatic play can be viewed as a reorganization of solitary symbolic play that takes into account the symbolic representations of a partner. In a sense, solitary pretense rests primarily on the child's ability or desire to imagine familiar, novel, or even bizarre events. Sociodramatic play requires, in addition, the ability to respond to the imagination of another person. Evidence from a classic study by Parten (1933) suggested that cooperative sociodramatic activities of this type do not appear until children are about three years of age.

Recent play episodes, taken from a current Merrill-Palmer Institute study of peer interactions in children between the ages of two and six years, seem to confirm Parten's observations. In the Merrill-Palmer study, well-acquainted children come in pairs to a playroom where their behavior is videotaped through a one-way mirror. The playroom is equipped with two sets of toys. Each child is videotaped playing with different peers in four 15-minute sessions. The data illustrate some general features of the pretend play behavior of children within this age range. First, sociodramatic episodes become more frequent and sustained with age. At two years these episodes are rare, but by five years it is not unusual for sociodramatic episodes to occupy an entire 15-minute period. Second, the content of the play changes from simple imitative motor actions (such as one child feeding another) to enactment of full blown social roles (such as the parent).

Two verbatim episodes from the Merrill-Palmer data follow. The first involves an exchange between two unusually sophisticated two-and-a-half-year-olds, a boy named Herman (H) and a girl named Sally (S). Herman begins the action.

H: (Takes the baby bottle and the spoon) "Take your medicine, OK?"

S: "OK, put it on my spoon."

H: (Puts it on her spoon and says,) "It's not medicine, it's for your nose. Hey, you know what?"

S: "Yeah, put it in my nose."

H: "I put it in your nose OK?" (S. bends head back. H. brings spoon to her nose.)

S: "OK" (She continues to comb her hair.)

H: "Drink some of that."

S: "OK" (S. pretends to drink what H. is feeding her.)

H: "You feed me, OK?" (H. puts down the bottle and the spoon.)

S: "OK" (S. picks up the bottle and the spoon and feeds H.) "It's medicine. It's medicine. Look, it's medicine."

H: "It's mine." (takes the bottle from S.)

S: "OK. Where's my bottle?"

H: (Looks in her carriage.) "Your bottle is down there."

S: "Oh thank you."

H: "I'll show you, OK? (Pause.) "Where's the spoon?" (H. takes the spoon from S.)

S: "No!" (S. reaches for the spoon. H. turns around and pours from the bottle to the spoon.)

H: "This is for your nose, OK? This is for your nose."

S: "OK."

H: "You're gonna be alright."

S: "I'll be alright." (Pause.) "Come here. Give me your medicine, I'll feed you, OK? What me to feed you?"

H: "You want me to feed you?"

S: "No, I'll feed you."

H: "Unh, unh."

S: "Yeah."

H: "No" (H. leaves.)

S: (Sweetly.) "It's medicine. You will be OK."

H: "Unh, unh."

S: (Sweetly and insistently.) "Come here, it's medicine. You will be OK." (S. takes a taste of it.) "It's Kool-Aid, you want some Kool-Aid?"

H: Nods yes, drinks from the spoon, and smiles.

S: (Smiling back.) "Oh, it's good."

Note that Herman and Sally are preoccupied with the concrete, sensorimotor roles of "giver" and "taker." They are able to negotiate role reversals, and Sally is even able to employ successfully the adult ruse of presenting medicine as Kool-Aid. And yet, although the play lasted for almost 10 minutes, the children never extended either by gesture, clothing, or verbal labeling the sensorimotor roles of "giver" and "taker" to the social roles of parent and child, or doctor and patient.

The second episode involves two five-year-olds, a girl named Lil (L) and a boy named Jim (J). As the action begins, Jim is playing with a fire truck and miniature people while Lil is walking back and forth with a broom.

L: "Are you the father or the son?"

J: "I'm the big brother."

L: "OK, then I'll be the big sister."

J: "Cause fathers don't even play with toys."

L: "Well, I'm the big girl, I'm the big sister. Anyway, Mom told me to take care of the two babies, our little brother and sister and you better not touch them or I'm gonna tell Mom on you."

J: "You're not gonna tell anybody on me."

L: "Huh! I'm gonna tell somone on you, don't

you think I'm not. So brother if you want to say something keep it to your own self."

J: "You know I'm bigger than you."

L: "Huh, you're not bigger than anybody."

J: "Hey, I'm bigger than you—you're just nine. So you better watch it!"

L: "You're the biggest cause you're just twelve years old. You're even bigger than me."

J: "You're just. . . ."

L: "If you want to fight just go fight yourself."

J: "You think I'm bigger than you cause I'm twelve years old. You, you're just nine. Hey, hey, you better watch it cause I'm babysitting for you all."

L: "You mean us three?"

J: "Yeah."

L: "One, two, three."

J: "There, just. . . ."

L: "One, two, three, four, and your own self. You're a baby: your own self."

J: "Hey, I ain't no baby girl, what goes and tattles on you."

Jim and Lil begin to whisper.

L: "You better watch it cause they're waking, brother."

J: "Shut up."

L: "Well make me."

J: "Shut up before you make me wake the babies up."

L: "Then I'll really tell Mom on you."

J: "Hey you can't, you cannot tell Mom on me. I'll. . . ."

L: "Then I'll tell Dad on you. Let me tell you; you be the dad and. . . ."

J: "Uh uh, I ain't playing no dad and I'm certain not no daddy."

L: "And I'm certain not no mommy."

J: "If you wanna find a daddy, if you wanna find a daddy, ask John" (the children's teacher).

Note that action roles preoccupy Herman and Sally, whereas social roles are of central importance to Lil and Jim. Father, son, brother, mother, sister, baby, along with the obligations, responsibilities, and privileges that accompany these roles are major issues for older children in defining the boundaries of the play that is to occur. Jim is quite explicit in rejecting the father role because it would not permit him to play with the toys. But as big brother, he retains some authority even though as the play unfolds, it becomes clear that this authority must be vigilantly asserted and defended.

As Garvey and Berndt (1977) have noted, two

forms of communication characterize sociodramatic episodes. Meta communications (italicized in the transcripts) are communications *about* the play. In these exchanges, the children retain their own identities, and as themselves, talk about the roles and scenes being performed. By contrast, pretend communications are exchanges held *within* the play mode. In these exchanges, the children relate to one another in the roles they have agreed to perform. For the younger children, Herman and Sally, communication boundaries are more evident in tone of voice, gestures, and supplementary props than in the words themselves. For the older children, the boundaries are sharper. Having decided to play brother and sister, Lil and Jim can pretend to fight about the things brothers and sisters often fight about, such as status and the ultimate authority. By contrast, Sally and Herman have difficulty managing conflict until Sally, in an inspired move, manages to commandeer the play role of medicine-giver.

THE CONTRIBUTION OF PRETEND PLAY TO SOCIAL AND COGNITIVE DEVELOPMENT

Early childhood educators have long believed that pretend play was beneficial for young children. Until recently, however, there was little evidence to support this belief. Studies by Rosen (1974), Saltz and Johnson (1974), Saltz, Dixon, and Johnson (1977), and Golomb and Cornelius (1977) report changes in children's social and cognitive ability as a function of training in sociodramatic and fantasy play.

Rosen (1974) gave two groups of kindergarten children 40 days of instruction and practice in sociodramatic play during their free play time. This intervention produced a significant increase in socio-dramatic play. In order to examine whether increases in sociodramatic play would have an impact on nonplay abilities, the children were assessed before and after intervention on several abilities thought to benefit from such play. For example, sociodramatic play might enhance children's sensitivity to the point of view of others. In one of the tasks assessing this ability, children were asked to choose from a set of objects (woman's hose, man's necktie, toy truck, doll, and adult book) the birthday gift he or she would choose if they were a father, a mother, a brother, a sister, or themselves. The children who received sociodramatic play training improved significantly in their ability to choose a gift appropriate for another person. In another task, small groups of

children were asked to work together as a team in constructing an object out of blocks. Children who received sociodramatic play training showed significant improvement in facilitative group behaviors (planning, cooperating, and group reference behaviors). These results confirm the findings of other investigators indicating that sociodramatic play enhances children's social skills.

There is additional evidence to suggest that fantasy activities might enhance children's performance on IQ tests (Saltz, Dixon, and Johnson 1977) and on Piagetian tests of conservation (Golomb and Cornelius 1977). In the latter study, nonconserving four-year-olds were assigned to special symbolic play sessions in which the adult first joined the child's pretend play and then challenged the child to explain how an object could be both itself and a make-believe something else. Experimental and control children (those who did not participate in the special play sessions) were given four tasks assessing conservation of quantity. On one task, for example, the children were shown two identical glass beakers containing the same amount of pink liquid. The contents of one beaker was then poured into a narrower and taller beaker, and the children were asked whether the amount of liquid in the two beakers was the same or different. On these tasks, children who judged that the amount of liquid was different after it had been poured were considered nonconservers. On the conservation tests, the symbolic training group produced more correct conservation judgments than did children in the control group. According to Golomb, symbolic play facilitates children's ability to maintain the identity of an object in spite of its transformation. In symbolic play the transformation is imaginary, whereas in conservation the transformation is perceptual.

ENHANCING PLAY

If recent research is beginning to clarify the ways children benefit from play, it is also clarifying the ways adults can enhance play. In an earlier section, evidence was presented that well-chosen materials can enhance play. Play can be encouraged in other ways as well. Properly chosen materials, realistic toys for toddlers and more abstract toys for preschoolers, can facilitate pretense. Encouragement from parents and teachers can enhance the play and its benefits.

Smilansky (1968) describes in detail a method for recording on a daily basis the pretend play of individual children. Then, for children who pretend infrequently, the teacher can suggest how a toy can be used more imaginatively or how a pretend game can be elaborated by the addition of new roles or changing scenes. Several studies using such procedures have demonstrated striking changes in the richness and complexity of sociodramatic activities (Smilansky 1968; Rosen 1974).

CONCLUSION

Pretend play seems to be an important activity for young children. Recent research has begin to document its contribution to children's social and cognitive development. The capacity for pretend play seems to be acquired without special toys or tutelage. Yet some children do not use this ability as much as others. Especially in the case of sociodramatic play, a combination of social and communication skills seems necessary for the play to happen. But once the basic skills are available and sociodramatic play occurs, the evidence suggests that these skills are refined and consolidated. New areas of cooperation and social sensitivity then emerge in children's nonplay activities. Play and nonplay seem to be related in such a way that accomplishments in one domain feed into the other.

As increasing numbers of young children spend increasing amounts of time in group care settings, the functions of play, and techniques for supporting it, will become increasingly important areas of study in early childhood research.

REFERENCES

Elder, J. L., and Pederson, D. R. "Preschool Children's Use of Objects in Symbolic Play." *Child Development* 49 (1978): 500–504.

Fein, G. "A Transformational Analysis of Pretending." *Developmental Psychology* 11 (1975): 291–296.

Fein, G. G. "Play and the Acquisition of Symbols." In *Current Topics in Early Childhood Education,* ed. L. Katz. Norwood, N.J.: Ablex, 1979.

Fein, G. G., and Apfel, N. "Some Preliminary Observations on Knowing and Pretending." In *Symbolic Functioning in Childhood,* ed. N. Smith and M. B. Franklin. Hillsdale, N.J.: Erlbaum, 1979.

Garvey, K., and Berndt, R. "Organization of Pretend Play." *Catalogue of Selected Documents in Psychology* 7 (1977): no. 1589, American Psychological Association.

Golomb, C. "Symbolic Play: The Role of Substitutions in Pretense and Puzzle Games." *British Journal of Educational Psychology* 47 (1977): 175–186.

Golomb, C., and Cornelius, C. B. "Symbolic Play and Its Cognitive Significance." *Developmental Psychology* 13 (1977): 246–252.

Inhelder, B., Lezine, I., Sinclair, H., and Stambak, M. "Les Debut de la Function Symbolique." *Archives de Psychologie* 41 (1972): 187–243.

Nicolich, L. "Beyond Sensorimotor Intelligence: Assessment of Symbolic Maturity Through Analysis of Pretend Play." *Merrill-Palmer Quarterly* 23, no. 2(1977): 89–99.

Parten, M. B. "Social Participation in Preschool Children." *Journal of Abnormal Social Psychology* 28 (1933): 136–147.

Piaget, J. *Play, Dreams and Imitation in Childhood.* New York: Norton, 1962.

Pulaski, M. A. "Toys and Imaginative Play." In *The Child's World of Make-Believe,* ed. J. L. Singer. New York: Academic Press, 1973.

Rosen, C. E. "The Effects of Sociodramatic Play on Problem-Solving Behavior among Culturally Disadvantaged Preschool Children." *Child Development* 45 (1974): 920–927.

Saltz, E., and Johnson, J. "Training for Thematic-Fantasy Play in Culturally Disadvantaged Children: Preliminary Results." *Journal of Educational Psychology* 66 (1974): 623–630.

Saltz, E., Dixon, D., and Johnson, J. "Training Disadvantaged Preschoolers on Various Fantasy Activities: Effects on Cognitive Functioning and Impulse Control." *Child Development* 48 (1977): 367–380.

Smilansky, S. *The Effects of Sociodramatic Play on Disadvantaged Preschool Children.* New York: Wiley, 1968.

Vygotsky, L. S. "Play and Its Role in the Mental Development of the Child." *Soviet Psychology* 5, no. 3 (1967): 6–18.

Chapter Nine

The School

Although contact with the family and peers precedes that with the school, once the child attains school age, the child spends much of his or her waking hours in the school or in school-related tasks or activities. How salutary the school experience will be depends not only on formal educational programs but on the structure of the school, on the characteristics of the teacher and the child, and on the interface between the home and the school.

The research presented by Gump indicates that the experience of children attending a large school is very different than that of children in a small school. Children in a large school identify with the school but are more likely to be passive than active participants in school activities. In contrast, in small schools more children participate in school activities, and it is perhaps because of this more active involvement that there are fewer dropouts in small schools.

It is frequently stated that schools are inhospitable places for males, minority groups, and lower-class children since our schools tend to be dominated by middle-class white female teachers. It is argued that these teachers have negative expectancies for such children and treat them in ways that are damaging to their social and cognitive development. Some evidence for this position is presented in the paper by Rubovits and Maehr. Rubovits and Maehr note the differential effects of teacher expectations on the achievement of black and white children.

In their paper, Garber and Heber present the results of the Milwaukee Project, a highly successful intervention program to prevent mental retardation in high-risk disadvantaged children. It shares with other successful programs the training and involvement of both the mothers and the children in the intervention procedures. Programs which have focused solely on the child and school have been less successful than those in which the mothers and their children are the targets of the study.

In the final paper, Aronson and Bridgeman address the issue of desegregation and present a new approach that may produce more positive outcomes in desegregated classrooms. In contrast to classroom competitiveness, these investigators recommend cooperation in pursuit of common goals as a means of improving relationships among students in desegregated classrooms. The implication of this work is that desegregation may not only be a legal reality, but it may have positive benefits for students as well.

Reading 36

Big Schools—Small Schools

Paul V. Gump

Today many forces are pressing small communities to merge their schools into larger systems. These communities are resisting the pressures. Claims and counterclaims are raised but there is little appeal to suitable evidence. Much evidence that is cited bears on only one side of a necessarily two-sided issue. Such evidence pertains to facilities and curriculums; it usually does not deal with the other side of the picture: the question of what are the effects of various kinds of schools upon the students. No one knows how life is different for the young persons who pass through the doors of the large and small high schools. Most evidence being offered does not tell us which educational arrangements produce more learning in English, more development of social skills, more enthusiasm for productive activity. Any research on how well institutions do their job must include the results of the institutions' efforts, not just a survey of their offerings.

The research to be reported here provides evidence on one kind of results produced by large and small schools. The research was designed to answer a question of importance to social science. This is the question of the effects of size upon institutions and upon their inhabitants. The research was not devised to answer political and educational issues; however, its results do have implication for such issues.

It must also be clearly stated that the evidence to be presented is not sufficient to answer all important questions regarding the effects of large and small schools. The evidence relates primarily to the effects of size upon: (1) variety of instruction, (2) variety of extra-curricular offerings and (3) the amount and kind of students' participation in school affairs and (4) the effects of participation upon the students.

Do Larger Schools Offer More Varied Instruction?

The simple and direct answer to this question is "yes." Like other simple answers, it is true only with important qualifications.

The research investigated 13 schools in eastern Kansas which varied in enrollments from 35 to 2287. There were a total of 34 kinds of academic and commercial classes in these schools. (Kinds do not refer to "units" but to what is ordinarily thought of as clear differences in subject matter. For example, English for freshman and English for sophomores were included in one kind of class; English and Public Speaking were categorized as two kinds of subjects; Algebra I and Algebra II were in classes of one kind. Algebra I and Geometry I were two kinds of classes.)

It was possible to arrange eleven of these schools in size groups so that each group was approximately double the size of the preceding group. One can then see how much variety of instruction increases as schools become larger. Figure 1 below displays this arrangement. The fact that as schools get bigger they also offer more is clear from Figure 1. It is equally clear from Figure 1 that it takes a lot of bigness to get a little added variety. On the average, a 100 percent increase in size yielded only a 17 percent increase in variety. Since size increase, by itself, pays relatively poor dividends, it might be well for educational planners to consider other maneuvers for increasing the richness of the small school's curriculum.

A second qualification to the assertion that larger schools offer more variety bears on the implications of the word "offer." One is likely to think that because the school has more different kinds of courses, the average student in it takes a wider range of courses. But there is real doubt about this. For a particular semester, students in four small schools actually averaged slightly more kinds of classes than did students in the largest school. It is misleading to go directly from what an organization offers to what participants experience. Not all parts of a large organization are equally available to all inhabitants; furthermore large segments of these inhabitants may not use what is theoretically available. Certain students become "specialists" and find more opportunities for their specialty in the largest school. This was true, for example of some students particularly interested in music in the large school. It would also be true for students interested in mathematics or art. The answer to "which is better" depends on what one seeks: more opportunity for "specialists"

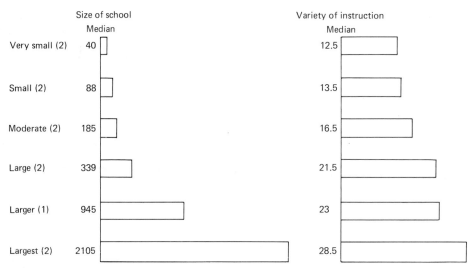

Figure 1   Does increasing school size produce a corresponding increase in variety of instruction?

or breadth of academic experience for the general student body.

Do Larger Schools Offer More Out-of-Class Activities or Settings?

This question may appear irrelevant to those who insist that out-of-class activities are unfortunate interferences with the "real business" of education. But such affairs are not irrelevant to the students. And other research suggests that engagement in school affairs is one excellent predictor of whether students stay on to finish high school. A school's athletic events, its plays and concerts, its money raising drives, its clubs, and its library and cafeteria are all part of the institution even if they are out-of-class. Within such settings a variety of participation and leadership experiences are possible. Later on the meaning of participation in this nonclass area of school will be illustrated.

Since a careful examination of participation opportunity and of actual participation requires a good deal of effort, this study focused upon the Junior classes of one large school (enrollment 2387) and four small schools (enrollment average 110). Investigators made a complete inventory of all nonclass settings in each school. Perhaps some flavor of this area can be conveyed by a short list of such settings:

Student Council Meetings
Basketball Games at Home
Varsity Dance
Junior Red Cross Rummage Sale

Cheerleader Tryouts
Library
Junior Class Play
Band Concert
Principal's Office
Scholarship Assembly
Christmas Assembly
Cafeteria

For the three-month period under test the large school provided 189 such settings open to Juniors, the small schools averaged 48.5. Again it is clear that more is offered at the large school. However, one must look at the results of the offerings; how much were these offerings used and by whom?

Do Students from the Large or Small Schools Participate More in Out-of-Class Settings?

After the investigators had made complete lists of all the schools' settings they asked the Junior students to indicate which of these they had attended over the previous three months. The number of participants was slightly larger in the big school; the variety of participation was clearly larger in the small schools. For example, the large school students would go to more affairs but they often were of the same kind. The large school students might go to a number of musical settings; the small school student to fewer musical settings but also to athletic settings. A second finding was that the large school developed a sizable minority who attended very few affairs, often only the required ones such as assemblies. This tendency of the big school to have a definite proportion of students who do little or nothing in their school's activities appears in other places in the study and will be referred to again.

Do Students from the Large or Small Schools Get More Experience in Important, Essential, or Leadership Participation?

This question is perhaps more crucial than any other in the investigation. It is important to know what students did in these settings not just whether they were there or not. It surely makes a difference whether one is an audience member or an actor at a play, a member or a chairman at a meeting, a customer or a salesman for a money-raising enterprise.

Almost every setting has positions for people who help make it go, who are relatively essential for its existence. In this research such people have been labelled *performers*. Student performers at an athletic event are the players, the cheerleaders, the concession sellers, and so forth; members sit in the stands and watch. In a library those who advise readers, keep books and records are performers; those who read and study are members. Although performers in a setting may have different degrees of importance, any performer is very likely to have responsibility, to be important in the activity of that setting. Performers are needed. If a member drops out of a setting is usually is not too damaging; if a performer quits, some readjustment is necessary. It is important to note that "being needed" when one is a performer is a fact of life in the activity; it is not simply a good feeling one may get because people are nice to one. One could predict that performers get different satisfactions from their participation than do members; that performers feel a sense of worth and obligation. Furthermore, since performers are likely to be in the center of action, they may experience more challenge than do members.

What are the chances in large and small schools that students will become performers in their schools' settings? The large school had 794 Juniors and provided 189 settings; the small schools averaged 23 Juniors and 48.5 settings. There are fewer settings per student in the large school; one might expect the large school settings to be relatively crowded, the small school settings to have fewer students. This expectation is correct: in the large school there were 36 Juniors in the middlemost setting; in the small school were 11.

In any setting, if there are many people, the chances of any one becoming a performer are less

than if there are only a few. If there are 300 Juniors at a class play, the chances of any one being an actor are less than if there are 23. In the latter case, all will be actors, (or musicians and stagehands). In the 300-person setting, perhaps 50 or 75 will be taken care of as performers and the rest will watch.

Since each student reported on what he did in each setting, it was possible to check the prediction that more small school students would become frequent performers. Results were clear cut:

During the first three months of school the average large school Junior was a performer in 3.5 settings.

For the same time period the average small school Junior was a performer in 8.6 settings.

Perhaps almost as impressive was the fact that 29 percent of the large school Juniors had not been a performer in any setting. Only two percent of the small school Juniors were non-performers. Again the large school tended to produce that sizeable minority of students who experienced much less benefit from their school offerings; these were the "outsiders."

Knowledgeable and sensitive people in the big schools are aware of this problem: they have tried various measures to counteract the effects of big populations. However, the effects of size are coercive, one is working against powerful arithmetic. If there are many people in an institution, there are likely to be many people in its settings. These many people must share a limited number of performance opportunities. The way this works can be seen looking at Figure 2 below:

From Figure 2 it can be seen that if a great many students are available for comparatively few set-

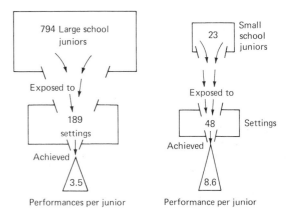

Figure 2 Relation of enrollment size to number of settings to performances per student.

tings, the average performance rate is low; when few students are available for comparatively many settings, the average performance rate is high. (It might also be added that this trend is true for large and small schools which are not so extremely different in size; performance differences are not so extensive but they are quite clear.)

Do Juniors from Large and Small Schools Get Different Kinds of Satisfaction from Their Out-of-Class Experiences in School?

It has been established that the small school yields markedly more performance experiences than does the large school. It has been suggested that being a performer is a significantly different experience than being a member. Therefore one might expect Juniors in the small schools to report different satisfactions for these nonclass experiences than do Juniors from the large school. Accordingly, this investigation measured student satisfactions. Essentially students were asked:

"What did your experiences in the good settings mean to you—what did you get out of your participation?"

Students responded with gratifying rich and frank statements of their experiences. Their answers were categorized and tabulated. As would be expected there were certain kinds of satisfactions which were frequent in schools of both sizes. For example, the out-of-class satisfactions often mentioned by both groups were related to opportunities to "learn about" such matters as: debate, parliamentary procedure, topics discussed in clubs, places and people contacted on field trips, etc.

Both groups also mentioned satisfactions having to do with novel experience or "change of pace." Students enjoyed banquets which helped them meet new people, plays in which they could "be somebody else for a change," and so forth. The richness and frequency of such answers created the conviction that these out-of-class events were important parts of life in both the large and small schools. Differences in satisfactions were also prominent; the small school students mentioned the following types of satisfactions significantly more often than did the large school students.

Increase in Competence

Examples: "Football gets you into good physical shape." "Acting in the play gave me more confidence." "Going on trips with the team helps you learn how to adjust yourself to different surroundings." "I learned how to get along with other people better."

Challenge, Competition, and Success

Examples: "This magazine subscription sale gave me a chance to see whether or not I'm a good salesman. I now believe that I am." "I like tough hard competition and in basketball I usually get it!" "It was a lot of work organizing the dance, but we all thought it was worth it."

Belonging to an Action Group

Examples: "In the play our class worked together as a group which I enjoyed very much." "I like being active with a group of fellow students." Satisfactions more common with large school students were the following:

Vicarious or "Secondary" Pleasures

Examples: "I like to watch a good, suspenseful game." "It was very interesting to hear the ideas and arguments of the debaters." "I enjoyed listening to the orchestra at the dance."

Belonging to Crowd or School

Examples: "I like the 'companionship' of mingling with a crowd at games." "Pep rallies give you a feeling of school spirit."

From the above sample of findings one senses that satisfactions in the small schools are more related to improvement of one's capacity, to challenge and action, to close cooperation among peers, and to "being important." Large school satisfactions tended to be more passive; that is, they were derived from somebody else's action. These satisfactions were also connected with belonging to "something big."

With the data it was also possible to determine why the patterns of satisfactions differed in the two sizes of schools. It was demonstrated that most of the differences came about because the small school student had many more performance experiences. When students in the large school were able to perform, they achieved many of the same satisfactions as did the performers in the small school.

Unfortunately the "facts of life" in the large school do not allow for nearly as many performance experiences per student.

Do Large or Small School Students Feel More Obligation to Support Their Schools' Activities and Affairs?

To answer this question, Mr. Ed Willems, one of the staff, interviewed two kinds of students: the "regular" and the "marginal." The word "marginal" here means those youth whose capacity, knowledge and background make them relatively unsuited for academic success. This group does poorly on IQ tests, has low grades, and their mothers and fathers often did not finish high school. The "dropout rate" for such students is often quite high. The word "regular" here simply means students with fewer such academic handicaps. Both classes of students in both sizes of school were interviewed. Mr. Willems asked what might cause them to participate in various out-of-class settings. A frequent element in their response was that of responsibility or obligation. Students would often say that they would participate because they were needed, that they had a job to do, that friends or teachers were depending upon them.

Two types of comparisons were made for this responsibility element:

1 Regulars and Marginals were combined together and then small school replies were compared to large school replies.
    Result: Small school students averaged 5.5 responsibility answers. Large school students averaged 2.0 responsibility answers.
2 Regular and Marginal students within each school were compared.
    Result: Marginal students in the small schools gave just as many responsibility answers as did Regular students. Marginal students in the large school gave only one-fourth as many responsibility answers as did Regular students.

When one thinks about "instilling a sense of civic responsibility" in our youth, these results should be considered. Here is evidence that the small schools, with their real need for students' participation, are offering experiences that may be quite valuable. This is responsibility learned in action, not out of books. It may also be significant that whether one is marginal in the sense of being involved in the enterprises around him depends not only on his talent and background but also on how much he is needed by these enterprises. The large school again

seems to have produced its group of "outsiders." Its academically marginal students are also socially marginal. This did not happen in the small school. The investigators do not want to be misunderstood. The large school personnel is not to blame for this. Conscientious administrators and teachers worked diligently to include the marginal student. And there was no campaign afoot among the students to see that large groups of marginal students were left out. The problem is more difficult and basic than this. The problem is that as institutions get larger, "selection into" and "selection out of" begins to work automatically.

If the schools are to benefit the students, they are going to have to keep them. There is accumulating evidence that the drop-out rate in the larger schools is significantly higher than in the small ones. And this tendency for people to drop out or to be absent as institutions get larger seems to be true for institutions besides the high school. It is true for Rotary Clubs, for mining crews, for textile workers, for airline workers, etc. The old saying, "The bigger the better!" is of dubious worth.

What, then, are some major findings of this investigation?

1 The larger the school the more the variety of instruction offered. However it takes an average of 100 percent increase in school size to yield a 17 percent increase in variety. Furthermore, there is no clear evidence that the greater variety in the large school results in the average student experiencing a broader range of academic classes.
2 Students in the larger school participate in a few more out-of-class activities than do students in the small school. On the other hand, students in the smaller school participate in more different kinds of settings.
3 Students in the small school participate in over double the number of performances of students in the large school. The chance to be essential, to gain the active or demanding role in activity comes much more often to the average small school student.
4 Students in the smaller schools experience different kinds of satisfaction in their out-of-class activity than do large school students. The small school yields satisfactions of developing competence, of meeting challenges, of close cooperation with peers. The large school yields more satisfactions which are vicarious and which are connected to being a part of an imposing institution.
5 Students from the small schools report more sense of responsibility to their school's affairs. Furthermore, academically marginal students in the large school are particularly lacking in reported

sense of obligation to their schools' enterprises. They appear to be social "outsiders." The marginal students in the small school, however, are just as likely to reveal responsibility attitudes as are the regular students.

Problems of school size cannot be solved by this or by any other single program of research studies. However, it seems clear that the small high school has advantages for one important phase of high school life. The large school may offer a great deal but the offering tends to be used by only part of the students. Although opportunities in the large school seem great, it is the small school that does a better job of translating opportunities into actual experiences for the total student body.

If the small school has some advantages, how can the relative disadvantage of limited instruction offerings be overcome? Up until now the major solution has seemed to be: make the small school larger by consolidation. What this comes down to is the movement, by bus, of many bodies to one central spot. This may be an unnecessary and even old-fashioned solution. Today a veritable revolution in educational practices is occurring: there are taped courses, TV lectures and demonstrations, traveling teacher specialists, and self-instructional machines and programmed books. Once we free ourselves of old molds and assumptions, it might be possible sometimes to bring education to students instead of always bringing students to education.

Finally, we need more "two-sided" research; one side on what schools are like and one side on what students are getting out of their schools. Such investigation is admittedly more costly and more difficult but it is the only kind that answers the crucial questions; questions which must be answered if we are to use research to improve education.

Reading 37

Pygmalion Black and White

Pamela C. Rubovits
Martin L. Maehr

It is not surprising that research on experimenter expectancies (Rosenthal, 1966; Rosenthal & Fode, 1963; Rosenthal & Lawson, 1964) has been quickly applied to the classroom, with some studies finding that students perform in line with their teachers' expectations for them (Meichenbaum, Bowers, & Ross, 1969; Rosenthal & Jacobson, 1968). These findings, controversial though they may be (Claiborne, 1969; Elashoff & Snow, 1970; Rosenthal, 1969; Snow, 1969; Thorndike, 1968, 1969), provide a perspective on a problem of major concern: the teaching of black students by white teachers. Black students have been found to believe that their white teachers have low estimates of their ability and worth (Brown, 1968; Davidson & Lang, 1960). It has also been well documented that white teachers expect less of lower-class children than they do of middle-class children (Becker, 1952; Deutsch, 1963; Warner, Havighurst, & Loeb, 1944; Wilson, 1963). In line with Rosenthal and Jacobson's proposal (1968) that teacher expectations affect teacher behavior in such a way that it is highly likely that student performance is in turn affected, it would seem probable that differential teacher expectation for black students and white students is related to differential school achievement. Few, if any, studies have, however, directly observed and compared teacher-expectancy effects on black students and white students. The present study was designed to do just that, and it yielded surprising results—results that can be interpreted as a paradigmatic instance of "white racism."

The present study is a replication and extension of a previous study (Rubovits & Maehr, 1971) that involved the systematic observation of teacher behavior following the experimental manipulation of expectations. The teachers, college undergraduates with limited classroom experience, each met with four students who had been randomly identified for the teacher as being "gifted" or "nongifted." The teachers did not differentiate in the amount of attention given to allegedly gifted and nongifted students; however, the pattern of attention did differ: Gifted students were called on and praised more than nongifted students. Thus, in this first study, teacher expectations were found to be related to teacher behavior in such a way that gifted students appeared to be encouraged and average students discouraged by their teachers.

The present study replicated the above procedure with one new dimension. Whereas the previous study looked at interaction of white teachers with white students, this study considered the interaction of white teachers with white students and black students; one of the students labeled gifted and one of the students labeled nongifted were black. The provided an opportunity to investigate whether or not white teachers interact differently with white students and black students, both bright and average, in ways that would differentially affect their school performance. In addition, the study attempted to identify what kind of teacher would most likely be affected by race and label. Each teacher's level of dogmatism was, therefore, assessed under the assumption that high and low-dogmatism teachers would react differently to the stereotyping effects of race and label.

METHOD

Subjects

Two different groups of subjects participated in the study. The group referred to as teachers was composed of 66 white female undergraduates enrolled in a teacher training course. All teachers had expressed interest in teaching, but not all were enrolled in an education curriculum, and none had yet had teaching experience. All teachers were volunteers; however, they were given course credit for participating in this project. The teachers knew nothing of the experimental manipulations; they simply thought they were taking advantage of a micro-teaching experience provided for them.

The group referred to as students was comprised of 264 seventh and eighth graders attending three junior high schools in a small midwestern city. These students were randomly selected within ability groups and given no instruction as to how they were to behave.

Measurement Procedures

In order to index the quality of teacher-student interaction, an instrument especially developed for this series of studies on teacher expectancy was employed. Although a more detailed description

including reliability data may be found elsewhere (Rubovits, 1970; Rubovits & Maehr, 1971), the major features of this instrument should be noted. Briefly, the instrument is an observational schedule that requires a trained observer to record the incidence of six different behaviors: (a) teacher *attention* to students' statements, subdivided into attention to requested statements and attention to spontaneous student statements; (b) teacher *encouragement* of students' statements; (c) teacher *elaboration* of students' statements; (d) teacher *ignoring* of students' statements; (e) teacher *praise* of students' statements; and (f) teacher *criticism* of students' statements.

The Rokeach Dogmatism Scale (Rokeach, 1960) was used to measure the teachers' authoritarianism. In addition, a questionnaire was given to each teacher in order to check the credibility of the experimental manipulations and to obtain some information on the teachers' perception of the students and the interpretations they gave to each student's behavior.

Experimental Procedure

One week before teaching, each teacher was given a lesson plan which outlined the topic to be taught and specified major points to be covered. As in the previous study, a lesson plan on the topic of television was employed. This topic and plan prompted considerable involvement on the part of both teacher and student. All students were found to be quite interested in discussing television and actively participated. The teachers had little or no difficulty in starting and sustaining a discussion on the topic and generally seemed at ease, improvising a great deal, adding and omitting points from the lesson plan, and using many original samples.

Attached to each teacher's lesson plan was a brief general description of the students she would be meeting. The teachers were told that an attempt would be made to have them teach as heterogeneous a group of students as possible. The teachers were also reminded that this was to be a learning experience for them, so they should be particularly alert to the differences between their students in terms of verbal ability, interest, quality of comments, etc.

The teachers were given no more information until just right before their teaching sessions, when each teacher was given a seating chart. This chart had on it each student's first name and also, under each name, an IQ score and a label indicating whether that student had been selected from the school's gifted program or from the regular track. The IQ score and a label had been *randomly* assigned to each student and did not necessarily bear any relation to the student's actual ability or track assignment.

For each teacher, a different group of four students was randomly selected from the same-ability-grouped class unit. Besides selecting from the same-ability units, one other restriction was placed on the selection of students; each session required two black students and two white students. One black student and one white student were randomly assigned a high IQ (between 130 and 135) and the label gifted. The other black student and the other white student were given lower IQs (between 98 and 102) and the label nongifted.

Each teacher was given the seating chart before the students arrived and was told to familiarize herself with the names and to examine closely the IQ scores and labels under each name. When the students arrived, the teacher was instructed to ask each student to sit in the seat designated on the chart. The teacher was further instructed before beginning the lession to look at each student and read again, to herself, the IQ score and label of each child. The necessity for doing this was emphasized to the teacher and justified by explaining that being aware of each student's ability level could help a teacher to deal with that student during the session. The teacher then introduced herself and explained that she had come from the University of Illinois to try out some new teaching materials. In the meantime, an observer seated herself two rows behind the students. The observer began categorizing the teacher's behavior as soon as the teacher had introduced herself and continued tallying behavior for 40 minutes. It must be emphasized that the observer did not know what label had been assigned to each student.

After the teaching session, the observer and the teacher discussed what had transpired, with the observer attempting to start the teacher thinking about each student's performance in relation to his reported intelligence. The teacher then filled out a questionnaire and two personality inventories. After all of the teachers had participated, the experimenters went to the two classes from which teachers had been recruited and explained the study in detail, discussing with them the results and implications of the study.

RESULTS

Interaction Analysis

Frequency counts were collected on each teacher for each of eight categories. Each teacher met with four different kinds of students: gifted black, nongifted black, gifted white, and nongifted white. For each category, therefore, every teacher received four scores, with each score indicating her interaction with one kind of student. These scores were treated as repeated measures on the same individual.

Student Variables: Race of Student

Each teacher met with two white students and two black students. Table 1 presents the mean number of teacher responses to black students and white students. . . .

Table 1 Mean Teacher Interactions with Gifted and Nongifted Black Students and White Students

Category	Black	White	Combined
1—Total attention			
Gifted	29.59	36.08	32.83
Nongifted	30.32	32.33	31.32
Combined	29.95	34.20	
1a—Attention to unsolicited statements			
Gifted	26.39	26.79	26.59
Nongifted	26.30	26.03	26.17
Combined	26.35	26.41	
1b—Attention to requested statements			
Gifted	3.88	10.64	7.70
Nongifted	4.77	5.67	5.22
Combined	4.32	8.15	
2—Encouragement			
Gifted	5.47	6.18	5.82
Nongifted	5.32	6.32	5.82
Combined	5.39	6.25	
3—Elaboration			
Gifted	2.09	2.08	2.08
Nongifted	2.44	2.15	2.30
Combined	2.26	2.11	
4—Ignoring			
Gifted	6.92	5.09	6.01
Nongifted	6.86	4.56	5.71
Combined	6.89	4.82	
5—Praise			
Gifted	.58	2.02	1.30
Nongifted	1.56	1.29	1.42
Combined	1.07	1.65	
6—Criticism			
Gifted	1.86	.77	1.32
Nongifted	.86	.68	.77
Combined	1.36	.73	

The analysis of variance for Category 1 (total attention) shows a significant difference in *quantity* of attention, with white students receiving far more attention from teachers than black students. This interpretation should be qualified in light of a Race × Label interaction and subsequent comparison of gifted and nongifted black and white means (see Table 1 and Figure 1). Such a consideration would suggest that the significant main effect in this case is almost entirely attributable to the great amount of attention given the gifted whites. . . . It can be seen that treatment of black students and white students differed most on the dimensions of ignoring, praise, attention to requested statements, and criticism. Across all teachers and also across labels, a pattern can be seen in the way teachers treated black students and white students. The directions of this pattern can be seen from the means in Table 1. Fewer statements were requested of blacks than of whites. More statements of blacks than of whites were ignored. Possibly most interesting of all, black students were praised less and criticized more.

Three dependent variables contributed little to the difference in treatment of black and white

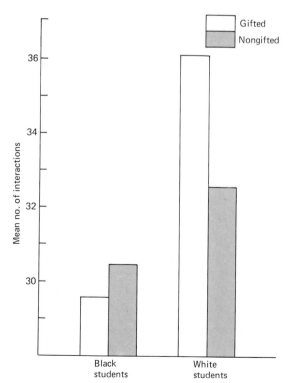

Figure 1 Teacher interaction with gifted and nongifted black and white students (Category 1: Total attention).

students. For one of these (Category 1a), it had been expected that little effect would be found. This category measures the amount of student initiated interaction. Since little effect for this category was found this would allow for the inference that there was no difference in the spontaneity of the students. . . . Thus it can be assumed that black students and white students were not treated differently by teachers because of differences in their verbosity.

Student Variables: Label of Student

Two students taught by each teacher, one black and one white, had been randomly given the label "gifted," and two, one black and one white, the label "nongifted." Table 1 presents the mean number of teacher responses in each category to gifted and nongifted students. . . .

There was no significant difference in total amount of attention to gifted and nongifted students. No differences had been expected for this category, as it was hypothesized that the *amount* of interaction between the teacher and the students would be fairly similar regardless of the student's label and that the crucial variable would be the *quality* of the interaction.

. . . However, there were differences in teacher interaction with gifted and nongifted students. . . . Two variables accounted for almost all of the difference in treatment of gifted and nongifted students. These two variables are Categories 1b (attention to requested statements) and 6 (criticism). From the means in Table 1, it can be seen that the significance occurs because more statements were requested of gifted than of nongifted students and also that gifted students were criticized more than nongifted students.

Once again, Category 1a contributed little to the total difference. . . . This allows for the inference that gifted students were not called upon more often simply because they volunteered less.

Student Variables: Interaction of Race × Label

A prime consideration of this study was any difference in the effect of label depending on the race of the student. . . . Gifted white students received more attention than nongifted white students with a reverse tendency occurring in the case of black students.

A significant . . . interaction of Race × Label was found. This difference was mostly attributable to Category 5 (praise) with Category 1b (attention to requested statements) also contributing toward the difference. In addition, Categories 1a (attention to unsolicited statements), 2 (encouragement), 4 (ignoring), and 6 (criticism) all contributed to the differences in treatment of differently labeled students of different races. . . . Category 6 (criticism) contributed little to the overall interaction effect. . . .

The direction of these interactions can be ascertained from Table 1. In the case of Categories 1, 1b, and 5, the interactions are also portrayed in Figures 1, 2, and 3. Considering these interactions collectively, a pattern begins to emerge in which the expectation of giftedness is associated with a generally positive response of teachers—*if* the student is white. For black students, if anything, a reverse tendency is evident in which the expectation of giftedness is associated with *less* positive treatment.

Teacher Variables: Level of Dogmatism

It had been hypothesized that level of dogmatism might affect susceptibility to racial and labeling effects (see Table 2). Regardless of interaction with either student variable, level of dogmatism itself was found to affect overall teacher behavior. There were . . . no quantitative differences in the attention given students by teachers high and low in dogmatism. . . . However, teachers higher in dogmatism ignored many more statements than teachers lower in dogmatism. Some of the overall differ-

ence can also be attributed to Category 6 (criticism) with teachers higher in dogmatism criticizing more statements than teachers lower in dogmatism.

Interaction of Teacher and Student Variables: Dogmatism × Race

Of particular interest in this study was whether or not teachers with different levels of dogmatism would respond differently to black students and white students. No significant interaction was found for Category 1 (total attention). . . . However . . . from Figure 4 it can be seen that dogmatism is associated with the encouraging of white rather than black students. Complementing the result is the finding that dogmatism was also associated with a tendency to ignore the statements of black students (see Figure 5). . . .

Credibility of Experimental Situation

A postexperiment questionnaire and an interview were given in order to check whether or not teachers accepted the experimental situation. No teacher expressed any suspicion of the experimental hypotheses. The teachers also showed great agreement with the assigned labels. One hundred and thirty-two students had been labeled gifted and 132 nongifted. Only in the case of 14 gifted students and 13 of the nongifted students did teachers express any reservations about accepting these labels as true indicants of the students' ability levels. These reports of the teachers, as well as clinical observations during the postexperimental interviews, suggest that the teachers not only accepted the situation as

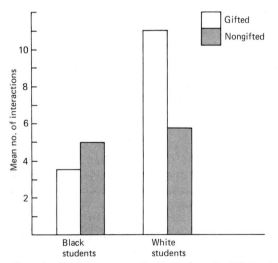

Figure 2 Teacher interaction with gifted and nongifted black and white students (Category 1*b*: Attention to requested statements).

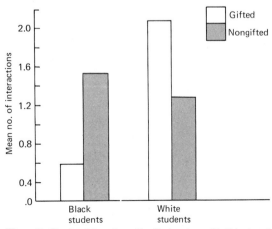

Figure 3 Teacher interaction with gifted and nongifted black and white students (Category 5: Praise).

Table 2   Mean Interaction with Gifted and Nongifted Black and White Students × Teachers High and Low in Dogmatism

Category	Black	White	Combined	Gifted	Nongifted
1—Total attention					
High dogmatism	29.94	35.68	32.81	34.54	31.08
Low dogmatism	29.97	32.73	31.35	31.12	31.58
1a—Attention to unsolicited statements					
High dogmatism	26.06	26.67	26.36	27.27	25.45
Low dogmatism	26.64	26.15	26.39	25.91	26.88
1b—Attention to requested statements					
High dogmatism	5.47	8.82	7.14	8.85	5.44
Low dogmatism	3.18	7.48	5.33	6.56	4.11
2—Encouragement					
High dogmatism	4.44	7.17	5.80	5.88	5.73
Low dogmatism	6.35	5.33	5.84	5.77	5.91
3—Elaboration					
High dogmatism	2.50	2.53	2.52	2.53	2.50
Low dogmatism	2.03	1.70	1.86	1.64	2.09
4—Ignoring					
High dogmatism	9.39	6.14	7.76	8.29	7.24
Low dogmatism	4.39	3.52	3.95	3.73	4.18
5—Praise					
High dogmatism	1.06	1.48	1.27	1.20	1.35
Low dogmatism	1.08	1.82	1.45	1.39	1.50
6—Criticism					
High dogmatism	1.86	1.02	1.44	1.76	1.12
Low dogmatism	.86	.44	.65	.88	.42

presented to them, but they also viewed each student in terms of the label assigned him.

DISCUSSION

As in a previous study (Rubovits & Maehr, 1971), teachers were found to treat students labeled gifted different from students described as average. There was no difference in the *amount* of attention given to the supposedly different-ability groups, but there were differences in the *quality* of attention. Gifted students were called on more, thus replicating a previous finding (Rubovits & Maehr, 1971). Gifted

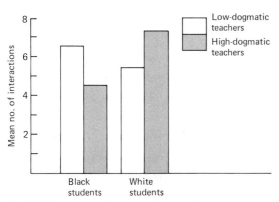

Figure 4   Interaction patterns of high- and low-dogmatic teachers (Category 2: Encourage).

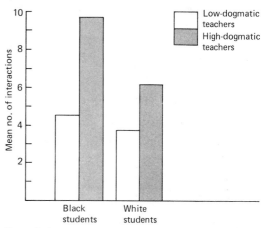

Figure 5   Interaction patterns of high- and low-dogmatic teachers (Category 4: Ignore).

students were also criticized more, but this difference may have been caused by the inclusion of black students in the gifted group as they were the recipients of almost all the criticism.

Considering the differences due to label for whites only, it can be seen that the gifted white student was given more attention than his nongifted counterpart, called on more, praised more, and also criticized a bit more. It is interesting, incidentally, that in the informal interviews with teachers the gifted white student was also chosen most frequently as the most liked student, the brightest student, and the certain leader of the class.

Of special interest, of course, are the comparisons of teacher interaction with black students and white students. In this regard, the present study provides what appears to be a disturbing instance of white racism. Black students were given less attention, ignored more, praised less and criticized more. More startling perhaps are the Race × Label interactions that suggest that it is the gifted black who is given the least attention, is the least praised, and the most criticized, even when comparing him to his nongifted black counterpart.

It is important to stress that these results are not easily attributable to an experimental artifact of some kind. There is no reason to suppose that the expectancy communication varied for race. Moreover, it cannot be argued that teachers were responding to any actual intellectual differences between black students and white students or to any incongruity between label and actual potential. Recall that students were specifically selected so as to be of equivalent intellectual ability regardless of race.

An obvious question, of course, is whether the expectancy resided in the observer or in the teacher. It is impossible to rule out observer expectancy effects completely. While the observer could not know which students were labeled gifted or average, it is obvious that she would know black from white. However, it is difficult to see how such knowledge might have determined the pattern of results that were obtained. First, the observational instrument is reasonably objective in nature, allowing for minimal judgment on the part of the observer (Rubovits, 1970). Second, the present authors in fact had no clear and obvious basis for postulating the results that did indeed occur. For example, it would have been equally logical to argue before the fact that young, idealistic teachers, most of whom expressed liberal beliefs, would make a special attempt to ingratiate themselves to blacks. Finally, the fact that high-dogmatic teachers were more inclined toward a prejudicial pattern than low-dogmatic teachers further suggests that the reported interactions were not just a figment of the observer's expectancy. If the observer were, in fact, the responsible agent, it would be difficult to see how, not knowing the dogmatism scores, she could have effected a generally predictable pattern for high and low dogmatists as well as the overall pattern. A bias leading toward differential observation of teacher-student interaction in the case of blacks and whites would presumably operate across all teachers regardless of dogmatism, thereby making it virtually impossible to obtain any meaningful Dogmatism × Race interaction. In brief, the most logical explanation of the results is that the teachers were indeed exhibiting the negative pattern toward blacks that the reported interactions indicate.

It is important to emphasize that this prejudicial pattern was not exhibited by all teachers. Teachers higher in dogmatism seemed to differentiate more in their treatment of blacks and whites. Moreover, one may wonder about the degree to which the patterns observed are unique to young, inexperienced teachers. After all, these teachers not only had little teaching experience but, as the questionnaire data would indicate, little experience of any kind with blacks. One might at least hope that the appropriate experience could be of benefit.

All in all, then, this study clearly suggests how teacher expectations may affect teacher behavior. Although the results must be interpreted within the limits of the study, with cautious generalization, the data do suggest answers to the question of why teachers are often able to do little to equalize the performance levels of blacks and whites.

REFERENCES

Becker, H. S. Social class variations in the teacher-pupil relationship. *Journal of Educational Sociology,* 1952, *25,* 451–465.

Brown, B. The assessment of self-concept among four-year-old Negro and white children. (Cited by H. Proshansky & P. Newton: The nature and meaning of Negro self-identity) In M. Deutsch, I. Katz, & A. R. Jensen (Eds.), *Social class, race and psychological development.* New York: Holt, Rinehart & Winston, 1968.

Claiborne, W. L. Expectancy effects in the classroom: A

failure to replicate. *Journal of Educational Psychology,* 1969, *60,* 377–383.

Davidson, H. H., & Lang, G. Children's perception of teachers' feelings toward them. *Journal of Experimental Education,* 1960, *29,* 107–118.

Deutsch, M. The disadvantaged child and the learning process. In A. H. Passow (Ed.), *Education in depressed areas.* New York: Bureau of Publications, Teachers College, Columbia University, 1963.

Elashoff, J. D., & Snow, R. E. *A case study in statistical inference: Reconsideration of the Rosenthal-Jacobson data on teacher expectancy.* (Tech. Rep. No. 15) Stanford, Calif.: Stanford Center for Research and Development in Teaching, Stanford University, 1970.

Meichenbaum, D. H., Bowers, K. S., & Ross, R. S. A behavioral analysis of teacher expectancy effect. *Journal of Personality and Social Psychology,* 1969, *13,* 306–316.

Rokeach, M. *The open and closed mind.* New York: Basic Books, 1960.

Rosenthal, R. *Experimenter effects in behavioral research.* New York: Appleton-Century-Crofts, 1966.

———. Empirical vs. decreed validation of clocks and tests. *American Educational Research Journal,* 1969, *6,* 689–691.

Rosenthal, R., & Fode, K. L. The effect of experimenter bias on the performance of albino rats. *Behavioral Science,* 1963, *8,* 183–189.

Rosenthal, R., & Jacobson, L. *Pygmalion in the class-room: Teacher expectation and pupils' intellectual development.* New York: Holt, Rinehart & Winston, 1968.

Rosenthal, R., & Lawson, R. A longitudinal study of the effects of experimenter bias on the operant learning of laboratory rats. *Journal of Psychiatric Research,* 1964, *2,* 61–72.

Rubovits, P. C. Teacher interaction with students labeled gifted and nongifted in a microteaching situation. Unpublished master's thesis, University of Illinois, 1970.

Rubovits, R. C., & Maehr, M. L. Pygmalion analyzed: Toward an explanation of the Rosenthal-Jacobson findings. *Journal of Personality and Social Psychology,* 1971, *19,* 197–203.

Snow, R. E. Unfinished pygmalion. *Contemporary Psychology,* 1969, *14,* 197–199.

Tatsuoka, M. *Multivariate analysis.* New York: Wiley, 1971.

Thorndike, R. L. Review of *Pygmalion in the classroom. American Educational Research Journal,* 1968, *5,* 708–711.

———. But do you have to know how to tell time? *American Educational Research Journal,* 1969, *6,* 692.

Warner, W. L., Havighurst, R. J., & Loeb, M. B. *Who shall be educated?* New York: Harper & Row, 1944.

Wilson, A. B. Social stratification and academic achievement. In A. H. Passow (Ed.), *Education in depressed areas.* New York: Teachers College, Columbia University, 1963.

Reading 38

The Efficacy of Early Intervention with Family Rehabilitation

Howard Garber
Rick Heber

Nationally, less than 3% of health funds are budgeted for preventive services. This is most unfortunate, not only because it reflects continued support for cure as the fundamental treatment strategy, but also because it represents a social and economic paradox. Economically, the cost of not preventing the occurrence of disease syndromes greatly exceeds the cost of prevention. For example, a recent Rand Corporation study (Kakalik, Brewer, et al., 1974) points out that the cost of administering rubella

Portions of this paper have been drawn from a forthcoming book entitled *Rehabilitation of Families at Risk: The Milwaukee Project.*

vaccine to a specified female at-risk population on an annual cohort basis would be $27,500. In contrast, the cost of educating just one child retarded because of rubella will cost about $32,000 for a special education program to age 13.

Unfortunately, such economic computations cannot be readily derived for the major portion of the mentally retarded. It is typically accepted that the majority of retarded children are retarded due to some insult to the central nervous system with an etiological referent. In point of fact, although the implications for development are just as serious, for nearly 80% of those individuals ever identified as retarded, there is no readily available etiological referent. Furthermore, because this form of mental retardation is so mild and because there is an inordinately high prevalence amongst the low SES and minority groups, mental retardation has become not only a medical and a psychoeducational problem, but a major social problem.

In the ten years since the Milwaukee Project began at the University of Wisconsin, many things have happened, but unfortunately many other things have not. In particular, there remains a lack of understanding of the social deprivation hypothesis. I would like to review with you the basis for the hypothesis that the Milwaukee Project has tested, the actual treatment phase of the study, and the evaluation of the treatment effects. Finally, I would like to place in perspective the results of our efforts at Wisconsin by suggesting not only some conclusions to be drawn from the study but its limitations as well.

To begin with, what has happened over the last ten years has been the continuation of the 'scientific' fact of genetic determinism, which still assumes that seriously disadvantaged families, especially those from disadvantaged minority groups, are of low intellectual ability. On the other hand, the sweeping acceptance of data on the other side of this issue has also blinded us to certain kinds of scientific questioning. The uncritical acceptance of either genetic or environmental determinism has dangerously misled us into condemning one or another group and one or another approach to intervention.

For us it was obvious that a necessary basis for studying the possibility of preventing mental retardation required a greater understanding of those individuals who were at high risk for retardation.

We began with an intense and comprehensive survey of such a seriously disadvantaged population which was known to have an excessively high prevalence of mental retardation. We chose an area in the inner city of Milwaukee that the United States Census Bureau (1960) data described as the most disadvantaged. The area showed the lowest median income, the lowest median educational level, the highest density of population, and the highest rate of condemned housing. It also showed the largest number of educable mentally retarded children in the city of Milwaukee, according to data published by the Milwaukee Public Schools. We began by monitoring successive live births in these contiguous tracts which I just described. We selected for interview and intelligence testing 88 consecutive

births where the mother had at least one child of the age of six. This resulted in a combined total of 586 children.

The prevalence of IQ's of 75 or below for this group (excluding the newborns) was 22%. The mean IQ was 86.3. However, upon separating the IQ's of the children into above 80 and below 80 IQ groups as a function of the mother's own IQ, we found that 45.4% of mothers who had IQ's below 80 accounted for 78.2% of the children with IQ's below 80. This distribution holds even more strongly for children above CA 6.

Our Milwaukee survey data illustrated another point with respect to the distribution within socioeconomic class groupings. In Figure 1 you see displayed the mean IQ of 586 children from these 88 families with increasing age (cross-sectional sampling).

We have plotted the IQ by age for two groups: the first is the survey children whose mothers have IQ's above 80; and the second is the group whose mothers have IQ's below 80. Note that on the early infant intelligence scale both groups score about equally well. After the infancy period, however, the children whose mothers have IQ's greater than 80 appear to maintain a fairly steady level while the children whose mothers have IQ's less than 80 exhibit a marked, progressive decline in measured IQ. Thus, it seems that it is not simply families within the low socioeconomic group that contribute heavily to the ranks of the mentally retarded; it is certain, probably specifiable families which contribute most of those who are retarded.

For us, then, these data represented a major breakthrough. Here was the key to the development of a detection procedure which would make accessible to us those individuals who were not yet retarded, but were at very high risk for retardation. If we could find a newborn child born into a seriously disadvantaged family where the maternal IQ was 75 or below, then according to our data the probability risk factor for retardation was 14 to 16 times as great as for the *average child*. For example, a mother with an IQ below 67 was found to have a roughly fourteenfold increase in the probability of having a 6-year-old child test below IQ 75, as compared with the mother whose IQ was within the average range. Our data also reveal that the IQ performance of mothers in these lower ranges is entirely consistent with the fathers' IQ, i.e., both are low.

These survey data could, at first glance, support

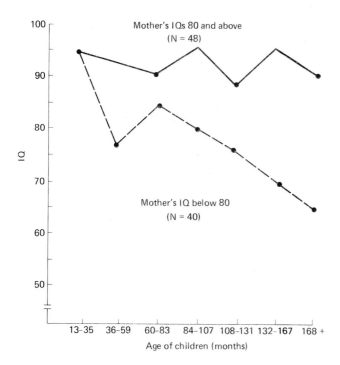

Figure 1 IQ change in the offspring of disadvantaged mothers as a function of maternal IQ.

the genetic hypothesis as to etiology of cultural-familial retardation. However, examination of these data indicates, rather, the possibility that it is the mentally retarded mother residing in the slum who creates for her offspring a social and psychological environment which is distinctly different from that created by the 'slum'-dwelling mother of normal intelligence. Furthermore, these data suggested to us that this kind of retardation associated with the "slums" of American cities is not randomly distributed but is concentrated in a small proportion of families who can be identified on the basis of maternal intelligence. In other words, the source of the excessive prevalence of mental retardation is the mentally retarded parent residing in the economically depressed inner city rather than the inner city itself.

We had then the basis for testing the hypothesis that if we could intervene with the family early in the life of this high-risk child with a comprehensive family rehabilitation program, then we could mitigate depressing environmental events and permit normal intellectual development, at least through the first year of public school.

In effect, this hypothesis is similar to those which underlie many other studies concerned with poor developmental experiences, and which can be sub-

sumed under the rubric "social deprivation hypothesis." In general, disadvantaged children—so goes the general hypothesis—could have their intellectual and social deficiencies remedied through a compensatory enriching social experience sometime in the early developmental period, and/or when such deficiencies are manifest. Of course, the major assumption of such studies is that the poor intellectual performance of disadvantaged children was directly attributable to "social deprivation" and the adverse early experience could be compensated by environmental enrichment at a later time.

In our investigation we did not examine the mutability of environmental effects on cognitive development by social and educational remediation. Rather, we tested whether or not normal children, although at high risk for mental retardation, could maintain normal intellectual development in an environment where essentially the presumed adverse or negative factors in the social environment were counteracted. Moreover, we carefully selected our population for study and carefully delineated our treatments. In general, the methodological confusion within and between other tests of the social deprivation hypothesis have invalidated or obscured interpretation.

For our study we selected 40 high-risk families

from the census tract areas previously described as the most disadvantaged. The additional criteria for selection of these families were a newborn infant with no obvious birth anomalies and a maternal IQ (WAIS) of 75 or less.

All the families chosen were Black as a cultural control in testing situations and because of the low mobility of the Black population in Milwaukee. Obviously, a longitudinal study is seriously weakened when its test sample is decimated by attrition. Using this selection procedure, we were confident that this sample of 40 families was at very high risk for mental retardation unless they received help. The 40 families were randomly assigned to an Experimental or Control condition. Twenty families were assigned to the Control group, which meant that during the next seven years they would receive only tests on a schedule prescribed for both groups. The 20 Experimental families were entered into an intense rehabilitation program with two primary emphases: (1) the educational and vocational rehabilitation of the mother, and (2) an intense, direct, personalized educational program for infants, with primary focus on language and problem-solving skills.

I would like to briefly survey some aspects of the maternal rehabilitation program and suggest some results from this phase of our study.

Shortly after contact and acceptance by the family to participate in the study, a specially trained paraprofessional teacher visited the home. Each family was assigned one special teacher whose responsibility initially was to establish rapport, gain the family's confidence, and work with both the mother and the newborn child in the home.

Once the mother trusted the infant teacher, the infant began to attend the educational center every day, from 9 until 4, five days a week, year round. The mother began her rehabilitation program when the child began participation in our infant education program, which was conducted at a carefully planned infant center.

Maternal Rehabilitation Program

One of the major purposes of the Family Rehabilitation Program was to effectively change the manner in which the low-SES, low-IQ mother operates within the home and within the community. In the past, a major obstacle to this kind of effort was the attitude of the mentally retarded mothers themselves. An attitude of hostility and suspicion towards social agencies, and a sense of despair (social and economic) pervaded their lives. Through improved employment potential, increased earnings, and self-confidence, it was hoped that positive changes in the home environment would occur.

Over the eight years of the maternal rehabilitation program, there have been five intervention stages. Initially the focus was on the mother's vocational adjustment. Since a large number of the families did not have a *stable* income-producing father, occupational training and placement was of major importance. Stage I and II were devoted to helping the mother with vocational skills. After the formal vocational training was completed, the parents were invited to attend adult education classes in the evenings. This was Stage III. By the time formal classes were no longer being given, the rapport established with the parents was strong enough for them to trust the parent worker and to call her in times of need, either on the job or in her homelife. This was Stage IV and Stage V.

The maternal rehabilitation program appeared to have been successful, although there was by no means an end to the mother's own problems or to those of her family. We evaluated the effectiveness of the maternal program by using a series of measures to provide information about the differences in home life, attitudes, self-concept, etc., between the Experimental and Control mothers, as well as a study of how these mothers interacted with their children.

The Experimental mothers showed significant changes in attitude in dealing with their children. For example, the Experimental mothers encouraged reciprocal communication between themselves and their infants. The result of this attitude change is reflected in the Experimental mothers' greater tendency to engage in verbally informative behaviors as compared to non-task-oriented physical behaviors (shown by the Control mothers and by the Experimental mothers at the beginning of the program). By contrast, the attitudes of the Control mothers showed no relationship to the behaviors observed when in interaction with their children. The Experimental mothers also showed a greater tendency to an internal locus of control, which indicated that they felt more in control of their environment. Such feelings of control are transmitted to the child, whose self-confidence is thereby enhanced.

We feel that these changes in the mothers were especially significant because they signalled an increased sensitivity to both their needs and the needs of their families, and an increased receptivity to the suggestions of respected and responsible outsiders. There was not a greater possibility that these families would make use of community resources. In other words, it seemed that as a result of the long-term family rehabilitation effort of families with retarded mothers, there had been a change in the motivation of these families to seek out, participate in, and profit from the rehabilitation resources in the community, and furthermore, to have increased sensitivity to the needs of their children in terms of nutritional and health care.

We retested all the mothers for both the Experimental and Control groups with the WAIS. The data revealed no significant change in IQ from the original testing nearly eight years before, even with a mean positive increase of about five points. However, whereas our determination of the literacy rate showed both groups to be comparable originally (35% vs. 22%), these groups are now considerably different (E at 63% and C at 37%). But both groups' mean reading levels are very low: viz., grade level, E at 4.1 and C at 3.4. Obviously there are major implications, in this regard, for the success in school of the offspring of such mothers. What is also obvious, additionally, is the tremendous help needed by such families.

The employment rate appears comparable although more Experimental than Control mothers with a child under 6 remain home, as we have hoped; their employment history is more stable, and there is also about $40 mean difference in weekly salary for the Experimental mothers.

While the actual vocational rehabilitation program occurred only during the first years of the program, we continued family support and our job counseling program throughout. In Stage V a full-time parent-coordinator maintained individual contact with the families. She counseled those families in need on nutrition, preventive medicine (e.g., inoculations), medical insurance, how to obtain assistance in legal matters or with various social problems, etc. Upon the mother's request, the parent-coordinator attended public school conferences about the older siblings, and talked to landlords and to social service workers.

Early Childhood Program

The educational program was initiated when the children were between three and six months old and continued, on a 5-day week, year-round basis, until the children were eligible for entrance to first grade at age six. The general goal of the educational program was to provide an environment and a set of experiences which would allow each child to develop to his potential intellectually, as well as socially, emotionally, and physically. The program focused heavily on the development of language and cognitive skills and on maintaining a positive and responsive learning environment for the children.

ASSESSMENT OF DEVELOPMENT

In order to assess the effects of the kind of comprehensive intervention we have made with the natural environment of the infant and his retarded mother, we undertook an intensive schedule of measurements. Our schedule of measurements for the infant included medical evaluations; standard Gesell and the Piagetian Experimental Measures of the Development of Infant Behavior; standardized tests of general intelligence, including the Stanford-Binet, the WPPSI and the WISC; an array of experimental learning tasks, including probability matching and discrimination; measures of mother-child interaction; and a variety of measures of language development, including the ITPA and several research instruments concerned with various aspects of linguistic development.

The Experimental and Control infants were on an identical measurement schedule keyed to each child's birth date. Medical data from birth and clinical examinations prior to school and after three years of school show no significant differences in height, weight, or other specific medical tests. Assessment began at 6 months and every two months thereafter until the child was 24 months old. The schedule was then changed to one session every three weeks. The particular measure administered at a given session was dependent upon the predetermined schedule of measures for that age level. Each test or task was administered to both the Experimental and Control infants by the same person. The testers, though, were not involved in any component of the children's educational program. The testers were both White and Black.

The first assessments of development were made with the Gesell Developmental Schedules. They revealed the first significant difference in performance between the two groups of children. Through the 14-month testing, the two groups responded comparably on the four schedules: Motor, Adaptive, Language, and Personal-Social. At 18 months the Control group fell three to four months below the Experimental group, although still performing close to Gesell norms. At 22 months the Experimental group scores were from four and a half to six months in advance of the Control group on all four schedules, while the Control group had fallen below the Gesell norms on the Adaptive and Language schedules.

As our children grew older we designed our assessment program to provide more comprehensive information about cognitive growth than is derived from IQ tests. In particular, IQ tests are not sensitive to the development of the various response systems in the child. We wanted information on the response patterns or behavior styles, and how a child's simple response choice may reveal his general response tendencies and his ability to select and order incoming stimulation. Furthermore, we wanted more comprehensive information about language skills than we could derive from the IQ tests or standardized language measures.

In the learning-performance tasks, such as color-form and probability matching, and oddity discrimination, the Experimental group was superior to the Control group on all testings between 2 and 8 years of age. However, the more important aspect of the differential in performance was the development of more sophisticated and more consistent response behaviors by the Experimental children. Generally, the Experimental children utilized a response strategy which demonstrated that they tend to use strategies or hypothesis-testing behavior and are sensitive to feedback information from their responses.

The Control children, on the other hand, showed a marked tendency to response stereotypy, often perseverating in their responses with no attempt to use a strategy; they also tended to be passive and unenthusiastic in their response behavior. This early learning performance has major implications for the future: for the Experimental children this approach to problem-solving should be facilitative, while the Control children's behavior style will interfere with their ability to learn and perform.

The first significant difference in language performance appeared at 18 months on the language scale of the Gesell. By 22 months the Experimental children were over four months ahead of the norm and six months ahead of the Control children. This early and dramatic trend of differential language development continued throughout the program across a wide array of measures including an analysis of free speech samples, a sentence repetition test, a grammatical comprehension test, tests of morphology, and the ITPA.

The results of our analysis of the children's spontaneous speech give a conservative estimate of the differences in language development between the two groups. There is, for example, a year's difference between the two groups in mean length of utterance, or MLU.

Our findings from the analysis of the children's free speech have been corroborated and extended by a wide variety of language tests which we gave at regular intervals over periods ranging from a year to two and one-half years. On these tests, which covered the three main aspects of language acquisition, namely comprehension (The Grammatical Comprehension Test), imitation (Sentence Repetition Tests I and II), and production (The Picture Morphology and Berko Morphology Tests), it took the Control group as long as two years to approach a level of performance that the Experimental children had demonstrated earlier. In Figure 2 we have illustrated the performance comparatively of the Experimental and Control children on three language tests administered between three and five years of age. The performance of the Experimental group (the full bar) is twice that of the Control group (the bottom portion of each bar).

We can summarize by saying that the language development of the Experimental children tended to be substantially in advance of that of the Control group agewise. For example, levels achieved by the Experimental children at age three and one-half years on the Grammatical Comprehension Test were reached by the Control children only at age five and one-half years.

We have been careful to ensure that we are not merely measuring differences resulting from different degrees of dialect usage. From our tape recordings of their conversational speech, we are certain that the children from both groups speak the same dialect, referred to as "Black English." Where there was any possibility, however, that test scores could be influenced by dialect patterns, we devised alternative scoring systems in order to reduce this possibility. One such system was used in the Sentence Repetition Tests to arrive at the "Structures Preserved" measure. This measure makes allowances for errors in repetition due to such dialect patterns as the omission of past tense and plural markers and of the copulative verb be. These omissions are recognized features of Black English.

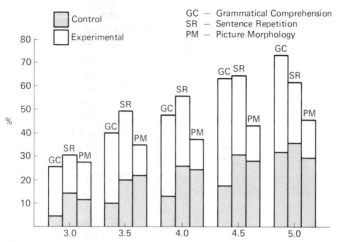

Figure 2 Comparative performance on language tests.

Our findings indicate that it is not dialect usage that underlies the difference in performance levels between the two groups, but rather a difference in the grasp of the concepts and relationships that are expressed or implied in syntactic structures.

The ITPA was administered to all children when they were four and one-half years, and again when they were six and one-half years of age. The results are consistent with our experimental measures of language. At six and one-half years, the difference between the groups found at four and one-half years had been maintained: The Experimental subjects performed six months above their mean CA while the Control subjects performed 11 months below their mean CA. The mean PLQ for the Experimental group was 108.3; that for the Control group was 86.3—a difference of 22 points.

As a group, the Experimental children showed an aptitude for language substantially greater than that of their counterparts in the control group. The readiness with which they grasped and acquired new linguistic structures appeared to be a manifestation of their readiness to learn structures in general, and suggested enhanced awareness of their surroundings and of their ability to express themselves in relation to these surroundings. What is perhaps more important is that they entered school with the language skills and aptitudes needed for further learning.

Let me briefly mention one other area of research which suggests the efficacy of intensive early cognitive stimulation. We carefully examined the

mother-child interaction by using some of the techniques of Hess and Shipman (e.g., 1968). In the mother-child interaction, most sophisticated behavior, such as the initiation of problem-solving behavior by verbal clues and verbal prods, or the organization of tasks with respect to goals in problem-solving situations, etc., is done by the mother. However, where the mother has low IQ, the interaction is often more physical and less organized, and less direction is given to the child. Indeed, while this was the case in the Control group mother-child dyads, we found that the Experimental dyads transmitted more information than the Control dyads, but this was a function of the quality of the Experimental child's verbal behavior. The Experimental children supplied more information verbally and initiated more verbal communication than the Control dyads. The children in the Experimental dyads took responsibility for guiding the flow in information, providing most of the verbal information and direction.

The mothers in both dyads showed little difference in their teaching ability during the testing session. However, in the Experimental dyads the children structured the interaction session either by their questioning or by teaching the mother. Also, the Experimental mothers appeared to be modeling some of the behaviors of their children. Consequently, they used more verbal positive reinforcement and more verbal responses. This finding suggests that the child can become the "educational engineer" in the dyad where there is a very low-IQ, low-verbal mother.

There has been a sustained differential in IQ performance from the 24 month mark until the present. At 24 months we began Cattell and Stanford-Binet testing. From 24 months to 72 months the Experimental group maintained better than a 20-point IQ difference over the Control group. When the intervention program terminated at school entry, which was at the mean age of 72 months, the Experimental group's mean IQ was 120.7 (SD = 11.2) compared to the Control group mean IQ of 87.2 (SD = 12.8), a difference of over 30 IQ points. These mean levels of IQ performance have been substantiated by an independent testing service using a "double-blind" procedure.

One should be cautioned not to over-interpret these IQ values *per se*. There is without doubt an effect of undetermined magnitude of repeated practice on the Binet under conditions of maximum motivation and where "test-taking" skills for both groups have been enhanced. What is to be viewed as of significance is the differential in performance between the two groups.

After nearly four years past intervention, we still had immediate contact with nearly 75% of our original families. At that time the Experimental children continued to show a superior level of performance. On the Metropolitan Achievement Test the Experimental group was significantly superior to the Control group on all subtests through the first two years. For the first year the distribution of the Experimental group approximated the national profile, while the performance of the Control group was markedly depressed. The performance of the group since then has further declined, first to the lower level of the city of Milwaukee, and then to the still lower one of their inner-city schools.

We have continued IQ testing of the children with the WISC, roughly one, two, three, and four years after school entry.

One major question is, of course, the extent to which the gains of intervention, if any, will be maintained as time goes on. It is apparent that up to this point, at least, the WISC differential, on the order of 20+ IQ points, has been maintained over a four-year follow-up to age ten. The Experimental group has a mean IQ of 105, as compared to the Control group mean IQ of 85.

Figure 3 shows the proportion of children who fall more than one SD below test norms at successive age levels. It can be seen that virtually no Experimental children have tested below IQ 85, while for Control children there has been a marked increase in low scores as age increases. These data are from independent testing teams, and have remained

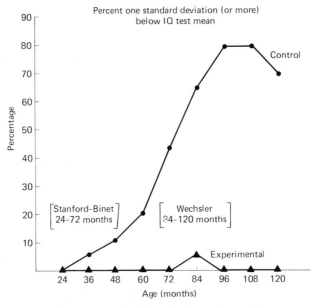

Figure 3 Percent one standard deviation (or more) below IQ test mean.

consistent and stable through 120 months of age. They give substantial indication of the difference in intellectual strength of the Experimental and Control group subjects.

Quite obviously, the Experimental children have continued to be superior in performance to the Control group of children. There has been some decline from the earlier preschool performance levels on the IQ tests, but most importantly the differential (approximately 20 points) remains between the two groups in favor of the Experimental group. Most strking, unfortunately, is that at this time (for some children, nearly four years after completion of the program), 70% of the Control group of children have IQ scores below 85, and half of these have scores below 80.

There are other tests and obviously much more data that could be presented but I think that these data on the Control children represent the status, or—perhaps a better term—the plight, of thousands of similarly disposed children. Our Experimental group at the time of school entry was considerably different in what we term intellectual strength. What there is now for these children if given the proper educational environment, is an opportunity to develop a level of competence consistent with their potential and appropriate to the challenge of life.

There is not at this time for the Controls a similar outlook.

In Figure 4 we have reproduced the original high-risk survey data and also the data from the IQ testing of all the siblings from both groups. As can be seen, all three samples show a similarly marked decline in IQ with increasing age.

We are asked repeatedly about any diffusion effects on siblings of our Experimental children. There is, in fact, a *small* but significant difference between Experimental and Control sibling IQ's in favor of the Experimentals. The Control group of siblings show the typical pattern of declining IQ as age increases (consistent with the pattern of our original survey data). And among older siblings of our research subjects there are approximately twice as many from Control families as from Experimental families who have been placed in special classes for the mentally retarded (17 of 59 vs. 9 of 68). There does seem to be a positive effect on the siblings, at least the older siblings, in those families participating in the Family Rehabilitation Program. This evidence suggests a diffusion effect, reported earlier by Klaus and Gray (1970).

What these data indicate is that there is a decreased rate of change in the declining IQ as the Experimental target child's ordinal position is ap-

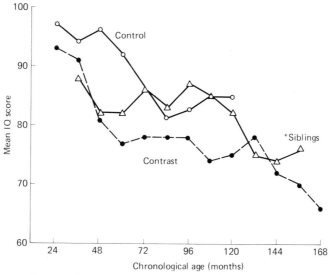

Figure 4 Mean IQ of the control, siblings and contrast groups.

△ Siblings of Experimental and
Control group subjects

proached until for those children older than the target child, the rate of change in declining IQ scores stabilizes. This does not hold true for the Control group where the change in IQ as measured by deviation from the family IQ continues to decline incrementally with increasing ages.

Taking together the data reported herein from several aspects of the family's life—e.g., behavioral and attitudinal changes in the mother; strong differential cognitive performance on the part of the treated children; and the evidence for a positive influence diffusing through the family—there is every indication that the concept of family rehabilitation effectively prevents mental retardation and improves the family process.

On the other hand, we continue to be cautious in interpreting our data because we are mindful that it has been only a small portion of time and a small portion of the experiences for these families' lives that we have influenced. Many years came before we entered their lives and many years are yet to come—certainly for the youngest, who have yet a critical part of their development to undergo. So, it must be continually kept in mind that there is yet considerable room for all members of these families to both learn and unlearn appropriate and inappropriate behaviors. We have demonstrated, at least, the ability of seriously disadvantaged families at high risk for mental retardation to respond favorably and positively to a rehabilitation treatment program effectively administered.

Let me reemphasize that early enrichment therapy intervention in the life of an individual during the first 6 years is but a brief encounter, especially when one considers the significance of their age and the learning experiences yet to come for such children and their families. Indeed, if relatively little is done to support the seriously disadvantaged at high risk for retardation after the early developmental period, there will be an increase in the risk factor again. For example, it is important to consider the nature of human learning, i.e., that it is an ongoing process, and that the kind of stimulation needed to support the growth of this process may not be available for this child either in his home or in his school. We may have recorded significant changes in the attitude and care behavior of the mother; but she remains retarded, economically distressed, and without a guiding hand in crisis situations. In effect, it is quite foolish to expect an intense direct rehabilitation effort for 6 years to be sufficient to sustain an individual and his or her family for the remainder of their lives, especially when the quality of their lives is so poor. The Milwaukee Project has demonstrated the responsiveness and potential among such people but it will require a more sustained, albeit *selective,* follow-up support program if early levels are to be sustained.

Selective follow-up is a rather important concept that I would like to explore for a moment. In part, some of the negative reaction to post-natal period compensatory programs has been based on the questionable efficacy of the approaches to date and/or what would appear to be a need for a prolonged elaborate support program for the seriously disadvantaged family.

To begin with, our use of a statistical technique to detect families at high risk for retardation ends up including a range of individual potentials. In other words, through the original selection procedure there are included some who cannot be helped to those who need little or perhaps no help. In part, subsequent research should be able to refine detection procedures so that the degree or extent of help needed can be early ascertained. We now know that mental retardation can be prevented in a high risk group; we need now to know how to make our efforst even more effective by prescribing appropriate educational procedures for each child and each family.

Neither are all children doomed to failure nor are they all capable of being successfully rehabilitated. A more thorough understanding of the differences between disadvantaged families is necessary so that we know to what extent certain families can mediate and extend the educational process of schooling, i.e., once given help to do so; and which families can not and so must have extended family support from outside.

From our own research and that of others, it appears that many families, although sharing in the common key indicator variables, such as low IQ, low socioeconomic and educational level, residential area, and schools, are quite different in family process. Therefore there will be differences in how the children from such families will sustain the benefits from early programs. Even in our Experimental group of families, there is a range of cases from total family disruption to situations in which the family process approximates the stereotype of the middle-class family.

We assessed all of the families on a high-risk

index, which was derived from several presently being used. Included are assessments of the mother and home that go beyond SES and IQ; there is also age of mother at target child's birth; an evaluation of the quality of the home environment; maternal literacy; and average spacing between children.

There is obviously some arbitrariness to the values one can assign to each risk factor and there is also some argument whether they are all indeed separate or separable items and there is some problem in the validity of some of the items— notably educational status. These problems notwithstanding we have tried to separate families according to level of high risk. In other words, assuming that all families in both the Experimental and Control groups are at high risk, we asked whether some were of a lower-high-risk status, and whether this would be reflected in the ability of the child to maintain IQ performance after intervention. Again, given the nature of the measure and the problem of justifying the assignment of value, there appears to be about a 10-point difference in IQ between the low-high-risk families and the high-high-risk families in both Experimental and Control groups. In the Experimental group the low-high-risk group is at 107 as compared to 98.5 for the high-high-risk on the WISC. In the Control group th difference is about 11 points, from 87 to 76.

On the Stanford-Binet data prior to the end of intervention, the same trend holds, only for the Control group, where the low-high-risk families are 13 points higher in average IQ than the high-high-risk. The trend does not hold for the high-high-risk Experimental families. Where the treatment program has intervened, it has offset the detrimental effect of a poor quality disruptive home. But not easily explained and most provocative is that the same Experimental children who now score lowest on the WISC were higher in IQ on the Binet than the low-high-risk children.

In other words, from pre-intervention to post-intervention performance, those children from the highest-risk families seem to have suffered the most loss in performance (as can be judged by change in within-group rank). In both cases, i.e., the Experimental and Control, it appears that fundamental to the efficacy of the intervention effort (as measured by the performance of the children) is the quality of the home environment which persists beyond intervention.

Although our maternal intervention program has been successful in the essential task of preparing the mothers for employment, which has proven to be reasonably stable, and although the mothers' verbally-stated aspirations for all of their children have been distinctly elevated as a result of their participation in the Milwaukee Project, it appears at the same time that we have been less effective in changing each mother's social patterns, her ability to remain free of conflict with her community, and most importantly, her modes of interacting with her children. Conflicts which we were able to assist in resolving through crisis aid as part of intervention now continue unabated and have perhaps increased. By these I mean social conflicts involving the mother within the family, those involving her friends outside the family, conflicts between school and parent, and conflicts involving the police and other community agencies.

For example, while children attended the intervention center, they were given breakfast, lunch and an afternoon snack. Some of the children now report going to school hungry or inappropriately dressed. Where the parent has become aware of minor school adjustment problems, she may sometimes respond by physical beatings or by threatening as, for example, in one case, "to send him South to live with his father."

Based on comments teachers have written on report cards, one third of our Experimental children are reported to have some social or behavioral difficulty in the school setting. Often these difficultues can be translated to mean "the child talks too much." The Experimental children display the same behavioral problems as the Control counterparts, but, in addition, are able to confront the teacher and their classmates verbally. Above all else, the Milwaukee Project children were given confidence, skill, and practice in the use of language as an effective tool for interacting with the adults in their lives. Whether this will be seen to be an asset or liability to the children is yet to be determined.

But we have seen genuine problems of adjustment emerge as well. With frequently poor communication between school and parent, simple problems are exaggerated to the detriment of the children. For example, notes are frequently sent home requesting a meeting and our mothers frequently do not respond; the public school teacher is inclined to believe the mother is not interested, rather than understanding that she may be unable to read or that the note's request may not be clearly stated. On the mother's part, her unquestioning attitude of "schools know best" has led to decisions of placement for the children with no parental input.

For example, one little girl of the Experimental group tested at the 96th percentile in reading on a pre-first grade achievement test. During her first two months of school she decided that she did not want to speak. Possibly she was angry about no longer being with ther preschool teachers. Her teacher had decided to place her back in kindergarten because her parents offered no support for the first grade adjustment problem she was having. Luckily, just before the change was to be made, the child walked up to the teacher's desk, opened a book and fluently read from it. A shocked teacher called her supervisor to witness the event. From then on she was a model student in her first-grade class.

Opinion has rated too high in the policy basic to the development of our nation's early education programs. Too many arguments for the inclusion of the mother in early intervention efforts are based on the emotional appeal of "the naturalness of motherhood" instead of on a careful study of the range of differences in the capacity of mothers to mediate the world for their children. It is such arguments which have made an objective analysis of the solution to the great social problem of preventing mental retardation so difficult. Interestingly, such emotional arguments come from both within and outside the scientific community.

In summary, the complexity of ordinary family life requires a multitude of extra-familial professional services—mainly in the form of medical and legal services. Many other services as may be required are either performed by the parents, e.g., educational help and/or vocational guidance, or mediated by the parents' knowledge of when and whom to ask for help. In the high-risk family, where one or both parents are retarded, most of the typical precautionary aids to family crises can not be provided, nor is the parent able to mediate between the problem and professional services for the family. High-risk parents are not always sensitive to health, nutritional or educational problems, nor are they aware of or responsive to available community resources. Coordinated services from different agencies and organizations could be utilized in support of crisis-ridden high-risk families and in support of comprehensive family rehabilitation programs. But so long as social services merely "show up on a street corner," then so long will they remain ineffective.

This evidence I have reported to you here today is what we at Wisconsin consider part of a puzzle. The puzzle is not unlike many another to which in the past the scientific method has been applied. Our data indicate the efficacy of environmental compensation properly administered to severely disadvantaged at-risk families during the early period of development of their children. But it is also only a part of the lives of such families. After the University of Wisconsin leaves, there remains for these families many social and economic crises to which the mentally retarded mother may succumb, and of course, with her, the family. In the psychological environment of the high-risk child, there remain, in addition to the mentally retarded mother, poor schools and other similarly disposed children as peers. All of these ills are exacerbated by the ills of poverty. This picture only partly depicts some of the major components of the puzzle, and our finding, that such children are amenable to help, is but one piece. However, this piece is *fundamental* to the hope that the rest of the puzzle can be resolved.

Those of us who have participated in this experience have witnessed a capacity for learning on the part of these children dramatically in excess of their epidemiologically-based expectations. At the same time, we are rapidly approaching the view that intervention and support for children reared with an intellectually inadequate parent and living in a disrupted family environment must continue throughout the child's school as well as preschool years. And our data to this point do nothing to inhibit the hope that it may indeed prove possible to prevent the high frequency of mental retardation among children reared by parents of limited intellectual competence under circumstances of severe economic deprivation.

REFERENCES

Hess, R. and Shipman, V. Maternal influences upon early learning: The cognitive environment of urban preschool chidlren. In R. D. Hess and R. M. Ball (Eds.), *Early Education*. Chicago: Aldine, 1968, pp. 91–103.

Kakalik, J., Brewer, G., Dougharty, L., Fleischauer, S., Genensky, M. and Wallen, L. *Improving Services to Handicapped Children* (R-1420-HEW, May, 1974). Santa Monica, California: Rand Corporation.

Klaus, R. and Gray, S. *Early Training Project: A Seventh Year Report.* Mimeograph, 1970.

Reading 39

Jigsaw Groups and the Desegregated Classroom: In Pursuit of Common Goals

Elliot Aronson
Diane Bridgeman

There were high hopes when the Supreme Court outlawed school segregation a quarter of a century ago. If black and white children could share classrooms and become friends, it was thought that perhaps they could develop relatively free of racial prejudice and some of the problems which accompany prejudice. The case that brought about the court's landmark decision was that of Oliver Brown *vs.* the Board of Education of Topeka, Kansas; the decision reversed the 1896 ruling (Plessy *vs.* Ferguson) which held that it was permissible to segregate racially, as long as equal facilities were provided for both races. In the Brown case, the court held that psychologically there could be no such thing as "separate but equal." The mere fact of separation implied to the minority group in question that its members were inferior to those of the majority.

The Brown decision was not only a humane interpretation of the Constitution, it was also the beginning of a profound and exciting social experiment. As Stephan (1978) has recently pointed out, the testimony of social psychologists in the Brown case, as well as in previous similar cases in state supreme courts, suggested strongly that desegregation would not only reduce prejudice but also increase the self-esteem of minority groups and improve their academic performance. Of course the social psychologists who testified never meant to imply that such benefits would accrue automatically. Certain preconditions must be met. These preconditions were most articulately stated by Gordon Allport in his classic, *The Nature of Prejudice,* published the same year as the Supreme Court decision:

> Prejudice . . . may be reduced by equal status contact between majority and minority groups in the pursuit of common goals. The effect is greatly enhanced if this contact is sanctioned by institutional supports (i.e., by law, custom or local atmosphere), and provided it is of a sort that leads to the perception of common interests and common humanity between members of the two groups. (Allport, 1954, p. 281)

THE EFFECTS OF DESEGREGATION

A quarter of a century after desegregation was begun, an assessment of its effectiveness is not encouraging. One of the most careful and thoroughgoing longitudinal studies of desegregation was the Riverside project conducted by Harold Gerard and Normam Miller (1975). They found that long after the schools were desegregated, black, white and Mexican-American children tended not to integrate but to hang together in their own ethnic clusters. Moreover, anxiety increased and remained high long after desegregation occurred. These trends are echoed in several other studies. Indeed, the most careful, scholarly reviews of the research show few, if any, benefits (see St. John, 1975; Stephan, 1978). For example, according to Stephan's review, there is no single study that shows a significant increase in the self-esteem of minority children following desegregation; in fact, in fully 25% of the studies desegregation is followed by a significant decrease in the self-esteem by young minority children. Moreover, Stephan reports that desegregation reduced the prejudice of whites toward blacks in only 13% of the school systems studied. The prejudice of blacks toward whites increased in about as many cases as it decreased. Similarly, studies of the effects of desegregation on the academic performance of minority children present a mixed and highly variable picture.

What went wrong? Let us return to Allport's prediction. Equal status contact in pursuit of common goals, sanctioned by authority will produce beneficial effects. We will look at each of these three factors separately.

1 *Sanction by authority.* In some school districts there was clear acceptance and enforcement of the ruling by responsible authority. In others the acceptance was not as clear. In still others (especially in the early years) local authorities were in open defiance of the law. Pettigrew (1961) has shown that desegregation proceeded more smoothly and with less violence in those localities where local authorities sanctioned integration. But such variables as self-esteem and the reduction of prejudice do not necessarily change for the better even where authority clearly sanctions desegregation. While sanction by authority may be necessary, it is clearly not a sufficient condition.

2 *Equal status contact.* The definition of equal status is a trifle slippery. In the case of school desegregation, we could claim that there is equal status on the grounds that all children in the fifth grade (for example) have the same "occupational" status, i.e., they are all fifth grade students. On the other hand, if the teacher is prejudiced against blacks, she/he may treat them less fairly than she/he treats whites, thus lowering their perceived status in the classroom. (See Gerard and Miller, 1975.) Moreover, if, because of an inferior education (prior to desegregation) or because of language difficulties, black or Mexican-American students perform poorly in the classroom, this could also lower their status among their peers. An interesting complication was introduced by Elizabeth Cohen (1972). While Allport (1954) predicted that positive interactions will result if cooperative equal status is achieved, expectation theory, as developed by Cohen, holds that even in such an environment biased expectations by both whites and blacks may lead to sustained white dominance. Cohen reasoned that both of these groups accept the premise that the majority group's competence results in dominance and superior achievement. She suggested that alternatives be created to reverse these often unconscious expectations. According to Cohen, at least a temporary exchange of majority and minority roles is therefore required as a prelude to equal status. In one study, for example (Cohen and Roper, 1972), black children were instructed in building radios and in how to teach this skill to others. Then a group of white children and the newly trained black children viewed a film of themselves building the radios. This was followed by some of the black children teaching the whites how to construct radios while others taught a black administrator. Then all the children came together in small groups. Equal status interactions were found in the groups where black children had taught whites how to construct the radios. The other group, however, demonstrated the usual white dominance. We will return to this point in a moment.

3 *In pursuit of common goals.* In the typical American classroom, children are almost never engaged in the pursuit of common goals. During the past several years, we and our colleagues have systematically observed scores of elementary school classrooms, and have found that, in the vast majority of these cases, the process of education is highly competitive. Children vie with one another for good grades, the respect of the teacher, etc. . . . This occurs not only during the quizzes and exams but in the informal give and take of the classroom where, typically, children learn to raise their hands (often frantically) in response to questions from the teacher, groan when someone else is called upon, revel in the failure of their classmates, etc. This pervasive competitive atmosphere unwittingly leads the children to view one another as foes to be heckled and vanquished. In a newly desegregated school, all other things being equal, this atmosphere could exacerbate whatever prejudice existed prior to desegregation.

A dramatic example of dysfunctional competition was demonstrated by Sherif, et al. (1961) in their classic "Robber's Cave" experiment. In this field experiment, the investigators encouraged intergroup competition between two teams of boys at a summer camp; this created fertile ground for anger and hostility even in previously benign, non-competitive circumstances—like watching a movie. Positive relations between the groups were ultimately achieved only after both groups were required to work cooperatively to solve a common problem.

It is our contention that the competitive process interacts with "equal status contact." That is to say, whatever differences in ability existed between minority children and white children prior to desegregation are emphasized by the competitive structure of the learning environment, and since segregated school facilities are rarely equal, minority children frequently enter the newly desegregated school at a distinct disadvantage which is made more salient by the competitive atmosphere.

It was this reasoning that led Aronson and his colleagues (1975, 1978) to develop the hypothesis that interdependent learning environments would establish the conditions necessary for the increase in self-esteem and performance and the decrease in prejudice that were expected to occur as a function of desegregation. Toward this end they developed a highly structured method of interdependent learning and systematically tested its effects in a number of elementary school classrooms. The aim of this research program was not merely to compare the effects of cooperation and competition in a classroom setting. This has been ably demonstrated by other investigators dating as early as Deutsch's (1949) experiment. Rather, the intent was to devise a cooperative classroom structure which could be utilized easily by classroom teachers on a long term sustained basis and to evaluate the effects of this intervention via a well controlled series of field experiments. In short, this project is an action research program aimed at developing and evaluating a classroom atmosphere which can be sustained by the classroom teachers long after the researchers have packed up their questionnaires and returned to the more cozy environment of the social psychological laboratory.

The method is described in detail elsewhere (Aronson, et al., 1978). Briefly, students are placed in six-person learning groups. The day's lesson is divided into six paragraphs such that each student has one and only one segment of the written material. Each student has a unique and vital part of the information which, like the pieces of a jigsaw puzzle, must be put together for any of the students to learn the whole picture. The individual must learn his/her own section and teach it to the other members of the group. The reader will note that in this method each child spends part of her time in the role of expert. Thus, the method incorporates Cohen's findings (previously discussed) within the context of an equal status contact situation.

Working with this "jigsaw" technique, children gradually learn that the old competitive behaviors are no longer appropriate. Rather, in order to learn all of the material (and thus perform well on a quiz), each child must begin to listen to the others, ask appropriate questions, etc. . . . The process opens the possibility for children to pay attention to one another and begin to appreciate one another as potentially valuable resources. It is important to emphasize that the motivation of the students is not necessarily altruistic; rather, it is primarily self-interest which, in this case, happens also to produce outcomes which are beneficial to others.

EXPERIMENTS IN THE CLASSROOM

Systematic research in the classroom has produced consistently positive results. The first experiment to investigate the effects of the jigsaw technique was conducted by Blaney, Stephan, Rosenfield, Aronson and Sikes (1977). The schools in Austin, Texas, had recently been desegregated, producing a great deal of tension and even some interracial skirmishes throughout the school system. In this tense atmosphere, the jigsaw technique was introduced in ten fifth grade classrooms in seven elementary schools. Three classes from among the same schools were also used as controls. The control classes were

taught by teachers who, while using traditional techniques, were rated very highly by their peers. The experimental classes met in jigsaw groups for about 45 minutes a day, three days a week for six weeks. The curriculum was basically the same for the experimental and control classes. Students in the jigsaw groups showed significant increases in their liking for their groupmates both within and across ethnic boundaries. Moreover, children in jigsaw groups showed a significantly greater increase in self-esteem than children in the control classrooms. This was true for Anglo children well as ethnic minorities. Anglos and blacks showed greater liking for schools in the jigsaw classrooms than in traditional classrooms. (The Mexican American students showed a tendency to like school *less* in the jigsaw classes; this will be discussed in a moment.)

These results were essentially replicated in a Ph.D. dissertation by Geffner (1978) in Watsonville, California—a community consisting of approximately 50% Anglos and 50% Mexican-Americans. As a control for the possibility of a Hawthorne effect, Geffner compared the behavior of children in classrooms using the jigsaw and other cooperative learning techniques with that of children in highly innovative (but not interdependent) classroom environments as well as with traditional classrooms. Geffner found consistent and significant gains within classrooms using jigsaw and other cooperative learning techniques. Specifically, children in these classes showed increases in self-esteem as well as increases in liking for school. Negative ethnic stereotypes were also diminished, i.e., children increased their positive general attitudes toward their own ethnic group as well as toward members of other ethnic groups—to a far greater extent than children in traditional and innovative classrooms.

Changes in academic performance were assessed in an experiment by Lucker, Rosenfield, Sikes and Aronson (1977). The subjects were 303 fifth and sixth grade students from five elementary schools in Austin, Texas. Six classrooms were taught in the jigsaw manner, while five classrooms were taught traditionally by highly competent teachers. For two weeks children were taught a unit on colonial America taken from a fifth grade textbook. All children were then given the same standardized test. The results showed that Anglo students performed just as well in jigsaw classes as they did in traditional classes (means = 66.6 and 67.3 respectively) minority children performed significantly better in jigsaw classes than in traditional classes (means = 56.5 and 49.7 respectively). The difference for minority students was highly significant. Only two weeks of jigsaw activity succeeded in narrowing the performance gap between Anglos and minorities from more than 17 percentage points to about 10 percentage points. Interestingly enough, the jigsaw method apparently does *not* work a special hardship on high ability students: students in the highest quartile in reading ability benefited just as much as students in the lowest quartile.

UNDERLYING MECHANISMS

Increased Participation

We have seen that learning in a small interdependent group leads to greater interpersonal attraction, self-esteem, liking for school, more positive interethnic and intra-ethnic perceptions and, for ethnic minorities, an improvement in academic performance. We think that some of our findings are due to more active involvement in the learning process under conditions of reduced anxiety. In jigsaw, children are required to participate. This increase in participation should enhance interest, which would result in an improvement in performance as well as an increased like for school—all other things being equal. But all other things are sometimes not equal. For example, in the study by Blaney, et al. (1977) there was some indication from our observation of the groups that many of the Mexican-American children were experiencing some anxiety as a result of being required to participate more actively. This seemed to be due to the fact that these children had difficulty with the English language which produced some embarrassment in working with a group dominated by Anglos. In a traditional classroom, it is relatively easy to "become invisible" by remaining quiet, refusing to volunteer, etc. . . . Not so in jigsaw. This observation was confirmed by the data on liking for school. Blaney, et al. found that Anglos and blacks in the jigsaw classrooms liked school better than those in the traditional classrooms, while for Mexican-Americans the reverse was true. This anxiety could be reduced if Mexican-American children were in a situation where it was not embarrassing to be more articulate in Spanish than in English. Thus, Geffner (1978), working in a situation where both the residential and school population was approximately 50% Spanish-speaking, found that Mexican-American children

(like Anglos and blacks) increased their liking for school to a greater extent in the cooperative groups than in traditional classrooms.

Increases in Empathic Role-Taking

Only a small subset of our results is attributable to increases in active participation in and of itself. We believe that people working together in an interdependent fashion increase their ability to take one another's perspective. For example, suppose that Jane and Carlos are in a jigsaw group. Carlos is reporting and Jane is having difficulty following him. She doesn't quite understand because his style of presentation is different from what she is accustomed to. Not only must she pay close attention, but in addition, she must find a way to ask questions which Carlos will understand and which will elicit the additional information that she needs. In order to accomplish this, she must get to know Carlos, put herself in his shoes, empathize.

Bridgeman (1977) tested this notion. She reasoned that taking one another's perspective is required and practiced in jigsaw learning. Accordingly, the more experience students have with the jigsaw process, the greater will their role-taking abilities become. In her experiment, Bridgeman administered a revised version of Chandler's (1973) role-taking cartoon series to 120 fifth grade students. Roughly half of the students spent eight weeks in a jigsaw learning environment while the others were taught in either traditional or in innovative small group classrooms. Each of the cartoons in the Chandler test depicts a central character caught up in a chain of psychological cause and effect, such that the character's subsequent behavior was shaped by and fully comprehensible only in terms of the events preceding them. In one of the sequences, for example, a boy who had been saddened by seeing his father off at the airport began to cry when he later received a gift of a toy airplane similar to the one which had carried his father away. Midway into each sequence, a second character is introduced in the role of a late-arriving bystander who witnessed the resultant behaviors of the principal character, but was not privy to the causal events. Thus, the subject is in a privileged position relative to the story character whose role the subject is later asked to assume. The cartoon series measures the degree to which the subject is able to set aside facts known only to him or herself and adopt a perspective measurably different from his or her own. For example, while the subject knows why the child in the above sequence cries when he receives the toy airplane, the mailman who delivered the toy is not privy to this knowledge. What happens when the subject is asked to take the mailman's perspective?

After eight weeks, students in the jigsaw classrooms were better able to put themselves in the bystander's place than students in the control classrooms. For example, when the mailman delivered the toy airplane to the little boy, students in the control classrooms tended to assume that the mailman knew the boy would cry; that is, they behaved as if they believed that the mailman knew that the boy's father had recently left town on an airplane—simply because they (the subjects) had this information. On the other hand, students who had participated in a jigsaw group were much more successful at taking the mailman's role—realizing that the mailman could not possibly understand why the boy would cry upon receiving a toy airplane.

Attributions for Success and Failure

Working together in the pursuit of common goals changes the "observer's" attributional patterns. There is some evidence to support the notion that cooperation increases the tendency for individuals to make the same kind of attributions for success and failure to their partners as they do for themselves. In an experiment by Stephan, Presser, Kennedy and Aronson (1978) it was found (as it has been in several experiments by others) that when an individual succeeds at a task he tends to attribute his success dispositionally (e.g., skill) but when he fails he tends to make a situational attribution (e.g., luck). Stephan, et al. went on to demonstrate that individuals engaged in an *interdependent* task make the same kinds of attributions to their partner's performance as they do for their own. This was not the case in competitive interactions.

Effects of Dependent Variables on One Another

It is reasonable to assume that the various consequences of interdependent learning become antecedents for one another. Just as low self-esteem can work to inhibit a child from performing well, anything that increases self-esteem is likely to produce an increase in performance among those underachievers. Conversely, as Franks and Marolla (1976) have indicated, increases in performance should bring about increases in self-esteem. Similarly, being treated with increased attention and re-

spect by one's peers (as almost inevitably happens in jigsaw groups) is another important antecedent of self-esteem according to Franks and Marolla. There is ample evidence for a two-way causal connection between performance and self-esteem (see Covington and Beery, 1976; Purkey, 1970).

OTHER COOPERATIVE TECHNIQUES

In recent years a few research teams utilizing rather different techniques for structuring cooperative behavior have produced an array of data consistent with those resulting from the jigsaw technique. For example, Stuart Cook and his colleagues at the University of Colorado (1978) have shown that interracial cooperative groups in the laboratory underwent a significant improvement in attitudes about people of other races. In subsequent field experiments, Cook and his colleagues found that interdependent groups produced more improved attitudes to members of previously disliked racial groups than was present in non-interdependent groups. It should be noted, however, that no evidence for generalization was found; i.e., the positive change was limited to the specific members of the interdependent group and did not extend to the racial group as a whole.

Working out of the University of Minnesota, Johnson and Johnson (1975) have developed the "Learning Together" model which is a general and varied approach to interdependent classroom learning. Basically, Johnson and Johnson have found evidence for greater cross-ethnic friendship ratings, self-esteem and higher motivation in their cooperative groups than in control conditions. They have not found an increase in academic performance, however.

In a different vein, Slavin (1978), DeVries (1978) and their colleagues at Johns Hopkins University have developed two highly structured techniques that combine within-group cooperation with across-group competition. These techniques, "Teams Games and Tournaments" (TGT) and "Student Teams Achievement Divisions" (STAD) have consistently produced beneficial results in lower class, multi-racial classrooms. Basically, in TGT and STAD, children form heterogeneous five-person teams; each member of a team is given a reasonably good opportunity to do well by dint of the fact that she competes against a member of a different team with similar skills to her own. Her individual performance contributes to her team's score. The results are in the same ball park as jigsaw: children participating in TGT and STAD groups show a greater increase in sociometric, cross-racial friendship choices and more observed cross-racial interactions than control conditions. They also show more satisfaction with school than the controls do. Similarly, TGT and STAD produces greater learning effectiveness among racial minorities than the control groups.

It is interesting to note that the basic results of TGT and STAD are similar to those of the jigsaw technique in spite of one major difference in procedure: while the jigsaw technique makes an overt attempt to minimize competition, TGT and STAD actually promote competitiveness and utilize it across teams—within the context of intrateam cooperation. We believe that this difference is more apparent than real. In most classrooms where jigsaw has been utilized the students are in jigsaw groups for less than two hours per day. The rest of the class time is spent in a myriad of process activities, many of which are competitive in nature. Thus, what seems important in both techniques is that *some* specific time is structured around cooperativeness. Whether the beneficial results are produced *in spite* of a surrounding atmosphere of competitiveness or *because* of it—is the task of future research to determine.

CONCLUSIONS

We are not suggesting that jigsaw learning or any other cooperative method constitutes the solution to our interethnic problems. What we have shown is that beneficial effects occur as a result of structuring the social psychological aspects of classroom learning so that children spend at least a portion of their time in pursuit of common goals. These effects are in accordance with predictions made by social scientists in their testimony favoring desegregating schools some 25 years ago. It is important to emphasize the fact that the jigsaw method has proved effective even if it is employed for as little as 20% of a child's time in the classroom. Moreover, other techniques have produced beneficial results even when interdependent learning was purposely accompanied by competitive activities. Thus, the data do not indicate the placing of a serious limit on classroom competition, or interfering with individually guided education. Interdependent learning can

and does coexist easily with almost any other method used by teachers in the classroom.

REFERENCES

Aronson, E., Blaney, N., Sikes, J., Stephan, C., and Snapp, M. Busing and racial tension: The jigsaw route to learning and liking, *Psychology Today,* 1975, *8,* 43–59.

Aronson, E., Stephan, C., Sikes, J., Blaney, N., and Snapp, M. *The Jigsaw Classroom,* Sage Publications, Inc., Beverly Hills, California, 1978.

Aronson, E., Bridgeman, D. L., and Geffner, R. The effects of a cooperative classroom structure on students' behavior and attitudes. In D. Bar-Tal and L. Saxe (Eds.) *Social Psychology of Education: Theory and Research,* Washington, D.C.: Hemisphere, 1978.

Blaney, N. T., Stephan, C., Rosenfield, D., Aronson, E., and Sikes, J. Interdependence in the classroom: A field study, *Journal of Educational Psychology,* 1977, *69,* 139–146.

Bridgeman, D. L. The influence of cooperative, interdependent learning on role taking and moral reasoning: A theoretical and empirical field study with fifth grade students. Unpublished Doctoral Dissertation, University of California, Santa Cruz, 1977.

Chandler, M. J. Egocentrism and antisocial behavior: The assessment and training of social perspective-taking skills, *Developmental Psychology,* 1973, *9,* 326–332.

Cohen, E. Interracial interaction disability, *Human Relations,* 1972, *25,* (1), 9–24.

Cohen, E. and Roper, S. Modification of interracial interractions disability: An application of status characteristics theory, *American Sociological Review,* 1972, *6,* 643–657.

Cook, S. W. Interpersonal and attitudinal outcomes in cooperating interracial groups, *Journal of Research and Development in Education,* 1978, *12,* 97–113.

Covington, M. V. and Beery, R. G. *Self-worth and School Learning,* New York: Holt, Rinehart and Winston, 1976.

Deutsch, M. An experimental study of the effects of cooperation and competition upon group process, *Human Relations,* 1949, *2,* 199–231.

DeVries, D. L., Edwards, K. J., and Slavin, R. E. Bi-racial learning teams and race relations in the classroom: Four field experiments on Teams-Games-Tournament, *Journal of Educational Psychology,* 1978, *70,* 356–362.

Franks, D. D. and Marolla, J. Efficacious action and social approval as interacting dimensions of self-esteem: A tentative formulation through construct validation, *Sociometry,* 1976, *39,* 324–341.

Geffner, R. A. The effects of interdependent learning on self-esteem, inter-ethnic relations, and intra-ethnic attitudes of elementary school children: A field experiment. Unpublished Doctoral Dissertation, University of California, Santa Cruz, 1978.

Gerard, H. and Miller, N. *School Desegregation,* New York: Plenum, 1975.

Johnson, D. W. and Johnson, R. T. *Learning Together and Alone.* Englewood Cliffs, New Jersey: Prentice-Hall, Inc., 1975.

Lucker, G. W., Rosenfield, D., Sikes, J., and Aronson, E. Performance in the interdependent classroom: A field study, *American Educational Research Journal,* 1977, *13,* 115–123.

Pettigrew, T. Social psychology and desegregation research, *American Psychologist,* 1961, *15,* 61–71.

Purkey, W. W. *Self-Concept and School Achievement.* Englewood Cliffs, New Jersey: Prentice-Hall, 1970.

Sherif, M., Harvey, O. J., White, J., Hood, W., and Sherif, C. *Intergroup Conflict and Cooperation: The Robber's Cave Experiment.* Norman, Oklahoma: University of Oklahoma Institute of Intergroup Relations, 1961.

Slavin, R. E. Student teams and achievement divisions, *Journal of Research and Development in Education,* 1978, *12,* 39–49.

Stephan, C., Presser, N. R., Kennedy, J. C., and Aronson, E. Attributions to success and failure in cooperative, competitive and interdependent interactions, *European Journal of Social Psychology,* 1978, *8,* 269–274.

Stephan, W. G. School desegregation: An evaluation of predictions made in Brown vs. The Board of Education, *Psychological Bulletin,* 1978, *85,* 217–238.

St. John, N. *School Desegregation: Outcomes for Children.* New York: John Wiley and Sons, 1975.

Targets of Socialization: Sex Typing, Self-Control, Moral Development, Aggression, and Achievement

The beliefs, values, and attitudes which guide socialization, and the means of inculcating standards and developing desired behavior in children vary among cultures. The social norms and skills regarded as appropriate differ for members of an isolated Eskimo village, for nomadic desert Berber families, or for the recently discovered people of the primitive Tasaday tribe living in the jungles of the Philippines. Even within a culture such as that of the United States there are wide subcultural variations in social standards and socialization practices. Behavior, regarded as desirable in Appalachian mountain hollows, in a black rural Southern village, in a New York Puerto Rican ghetto, or in a Midwest farming community differ.

In spite of these disparities in social standards there are certain classes of behaviors that are targets of socialization in almost every culture. In every society children are expected to become increasingly independent and able to care for themselves. They are encouraged to set and attain some achievement goals whether it is learning to read and write, to be a skilled hunter with a bow and arrow, to be a nuclear physicist, or to brew fine fermented beer. In each society members are expected to develop some degree of self-control, to inhibit or express aggression in a socially acceptable manner, to delay gratification of needs until an appropriate situation arises, and to restrain themselves from performing grossly antisocial behaviors. In addition, not only are individuals expected to exhibit self-control but they are socialized to perform prosocial behaviors such as sharing, helping, cooperation, and expressions of sympathy.

In many, but not all cultures, the norms and modes of expression of social standards vary for men and women. There may be different expectations and goals for the training of independence, achievement, self-control, and prosocial behavior in the socialization of boys and girls. Across a broad range of cultures including that of the dominant American culture these sex-role standards take the form of what Parsons has called an "expressive" role for females and an "instrumental" role for males (Parsons, 1970). Women are expected to be more sensitive and skilled in interpersonal relations, more dependent and nurturant and freer to express tender emotions than are men. Men should be more aggressive, competitive, independent, able to solve problems, and to inhibit expression of affect that might be interpreted as weakness. It can well be asked if either of these stereotypes is descriptive of a fully competent, well-adjusted individual. Aggressiveness may have had some adaptive evolutionary value for primitive man and nurturance for females but in contemporary society surely a well-functioning individual of either sex should be able to feel and express affection and care for others, be able to solve problems, and be moderately assertive and self-sufficient. This has led to the position that rather than being socialized in accord with sex-role standards children should be socialized in an androgenous fashion which aims for the same goals of competence in men and women.

In selecting papers for this section we attempted to include articles that cover behaviors that are the major targets of socialization. The first paper presents Erik Erikson's theory of the progressive sequence of developmental tasks that must be learned as individuals proceed through the eight stages of social development from birth to old age. Then Carol Dweck presents a framework for studying children's cognition and behavior in achievement situations. Hoffman discusses the development of moral thought, feeling, and behavior. Mischel talks about strategies children can use to increase self control and postpone pleasure. The issue of sex typing and sex role development in children is dealt with in the papers by Ehrhardt and Baker, Feldman, Nash and Cutrona, and Johnson. In the controversy about the role of biological factors in sex differences in behavior it has frequently been argued that hormones play an important role in the development of sex differences and that women are in some way biologically predisposed to be more interested in babies and the nurturing of the young. Ehrhardt and Baker in their study of fetally androgenized children conclude that the specific behavior exhibited by these children will depend to a large extent on the interaction between prenatal hormone levels and the child's environment. Feldman, Nash, and Cutrona report that sex differences in attending and responsiveness to babies do not appear until adolescence and are probably related to the increased concern of adolescents with sex role stereotypes. In the final paper on sex typing, Miriam Johnson presents a provocative theory arguing that the role of family structure and particularly the role of the father are salient in shaping sex-typed behavior in sons and daughters. Research studies in sex-role development have fairly consistently demonstrated that fathers are more concerned than are mothers with maintaining stereotypical sex-typed behaviors in their children, especially in their sons. Johnson examines the sex-differentiating principles introduced by fathers and their role in enhancing sex differences in development.

The last paper in this section by Eli Rubinstein on the effects of television on the young viewer cuts across many of the other topics and could as easily have been included in the section labeled agents of socialization as in targets of socialization. Television viewing is one of the most frequent activities of young people. Because of wide variations in the use of television it is difficult to offer a meaningful statement about the average time spent watching television, but it has been reported that by the age of 18 a child will have spent more time watching television than doing anything else except sleeping. Rubinstein reviews some of the positive and negative effects of television: the effectiveness of Sesame Street as an educational program, the relation between television violence and aggressive behavior in children and issues involved in sex and advertising on television.

Again we urge the student to think of the outcomes of socialization being associated with a network of interacting factors. Sex typing, aggression, self-control, and achievement are not shaped by parents alone, or by peers alone, or by schools or mass media. They are shaped to some extent by all the factors with some agents having more impact in certain situations and at certain times in the life span. In addition, although by now it must sound rather like an old record to the reader, children are active participants in the socialization process. They are not passive recipients of the demands and behavior of others. They shape the world and people about them, they interpret and process social information, and they respond in an individualistic fashion.

REFERENCES

Parsons, T. *Social structure and personality*. New York: Free Press, 1970.

Reading 40

Erik Erikson's Eight Ages Of Man

David Elkind

At a recent faculty reception I happened to join a small group in which a young mother was talking about her "identity crisis." She and her husband, she said, had decided not to have any more children and she was depressed at the thought of being past the child-bearing stage. It was as if, she continued, she had been robbed of some part of herself and now needed to find a new function to replace the old one.

When I remarked that her story sounded like a case history from a book by Erik Erikson, she replied, "Who's Erikson?" It is a reflection on the intellectual modesty and literary decorum of Erik H. Erikson, psychoanalyst and professor of developmental psychology at Harvard, that so few of the many people who today talk about the "identity crisis" know anything of the man who pointed out its pervasiveness as a problem in contemporary society two decades ago.

Erikson has, however, contributed more to social science than his delineation of identity problems in modern man. His descriptions of the stages of the life cycle, for example, have advanced psychoanalytic theory to the point where it can now describe the development of the healthy personality on its own terms and not merely as the opposite of a sick one. Likewise, Erikson's emphasis upon the problems unique to adolescents and adults living in today's society has helped to rectify the one-sided emphasis on childhood as the beginning and end of personality development.

Finally, in his biographical studies, such as "Young Man Luther" and "Gandhi's Truth" (which has just won a National Book Award in philosophy and religion), Erikson emphasizes the inherent strengths of the human personality by showing how individuals can use their neurotic symptoms and conflicts for creative and constructive social purposes while healing themselves in the process.

It is important to emphasize that Erikson's contributions are genuine advances in psychoanalysis in the sense that Erikson accepts and builds upon many of the basic tenets of Freudian theory. In this regard, Erikson differs from Freud's early co-workers such as Jung and Adler who, when they broke with Freud, rejected his theories and substituted their own.

Likewise, Erikson also differs from the so-called neo-Freudians such as Horney, Kardiner and Sullivan who (mistakenly, as it turned out) assumed that Freudian theory had nothing to say about man's relation to reality and to his culture. While it is true that Freud emphasized, even mythologized, sexuality, he did so to counteract the rigid sexual taboos of his time, which, at that point in history, were frequently the cause of neuroses. In his later writings, however, Freud began to concern himself with the executive agency of the personality, namely the ego, which is also the repository of the individual's attitudes and concepts about himself and his world.

It is with the psychosocial development of the ego that Erikson's observations and theoretical constructions are primarily concerned. Erikson has thus been able to introduce innovations into psychoanalytic theory without either rejecting or ignoring Freud's monumental contribution.

The man who has accomplished this notable feat is a handsome Dane, whose white hair, mustache, resonant accent and gentle manner are reminiscent of actors like Jean Hersholt and Paul Muni. Although he is warm and outgoing with friends, Erikson is a rather shy man who is uncomfortable in the spotlight of public recognition. This trait, together with his ethical reservations about making public even disguised case material, may help to account for Erikson's reluctance to publish his observations and conceptions (his first book appeared in 1950, when he was 48).

In recent years this reluctance to publish has diminished and he has been appearing in print at an increasing pace. Since 1960 he has published three books, "Insight and Responsibility," "Identity: Youth and Crisis" and "Gandhi's Truth," as well as editing a fourth, "Youth: Change and Challenge." Despite the accolades and recognition these books have won for him, both in America and abroad, Erikson is still surprised at the popular interest they have generated and is a little troubled about the possibility of being misunderstood and misinterpreted. While he would prefer that his books spoke for themselves and that he was left out of the picture, he has had to accede to popular demand for more information about himself and his work.

The course of Erikson's professional career has been as diverse as it has been unconventional. He was born in Frankfurt, Germany, in 1902 of Danish parents. Not long after his birth his father died, and his mother later married the pediatrician who had cured her son of a childhood illness. Erikson's stepfather urged him to become a physician, but the boy declined and became an artist instead—an artist who did portraits of children. Erikson says of his post-adolescent years, "I was an artist then, which in Europe is a euphemism for a young man with some talent and nowhere to go." During this period he settled in Vienna and worked as a tutor in a family friendly with Freud's. He met Freud on informal occasions when the families went on outings together.

These encounters may have been the impetus to accept a teaching appointment at an American school in Vienna founded by Dorothy Burlingham and directed by Peter Blos (both now well known on the American psychiatric scene). During these years (the late nineteen-twenties) he also undertook and completed psychoanalytic training with Anna Freud and August Aichhorn. Even at the outset of his career, Erikson gave evidence of the breadth of his interests and activities by being trained and certified as a Montessori teacher. Not surprisingly, in view of that training, Erikson's first articles dealt with psychoanalysis and education.

It was while in Vienna that Erikson met and married Joan Mowat Serson, an American artist of Canadian descent. They came to America in 1933, when Erikson was invited to practice and teach in Boston. Erikson was, in fact, one of the first if not the first child-analyst in the Boston area. During the next two decades he held clinical and academic appointments at Harvard, Yale and Berkeley. In 1951 he joined a group of psychiatrists and psychologists who moved to Stockbridge, Mass., to start a new program at the Austen Riggs Center, a private residential treatment center for disturbed young people. Erikson remained at Riggs until 1961, when he was appointed professor of human development and lecturer on psychiatry at Harvard. Throughout his career he has always held two or three appointments simultaneously and has traveled extensively.

Perhaps because he had been an artist first, Erikson has never been a conventional psychoana-

lyst. When he was treating children, for example, he always insisted on visiting his young patients' homes and on having dinner with the families. Likewise in the nineteen-thirties, when anthropological investigation was described to him by his friends Scudder McKeel, Alfred Kroeber and Margaret Mead, he decided to do field work on an Indian reservation. "When I realized that Sioux is the name which we [in Europe] pronounced "See us" and which for us was *the* American Indian, I could not resist." Erikson thus antedated the anthropologists who swept over the Indian reservations in the post-Depression years. (So numerous were the field workers at that time that the stock joke was that an Indian family could be defined as a mother, a father, children and an anthropologist.)

Erikson did field work not only with the Oglala Sioux of Pine Ridge, S.D. (the tribe that slew Custer and was in turn slaughtered at the Battle of Wounded Knee), but also with the salmon-fishing Yurok of Northern California. His reports on these experiences revealed his special gift for sensing and entering into the world views and modes of thinking of cultures other than his own.

It was while he was working with the Indians that Erikson began to note syndromes which he could not explain within the confines of traditional psychoanalytic theory. Central to many an adult Indian's emotional problems seemed to be his sense of uprootedness and lack of continuity between his present life-style and that portrayed in tribal history. Not only did the Indian sense a break with the past, but he could not identify with a future requiring assimilation of the white culture's values. The problems faced by such men, Erikson recognized, had to do with the ego and with culture and only incidentally with sexual drives.

The impressions Erikson gained on the reservations were reinforced during World War II when he worked at a veterans' rehabilitation center at Mount Zion Hospital in San Francisco. Many of the soldiers he and his colleagues saw seemed not to fit the traditional "shell shock" or "malingerer" cases of World War I. Rather, it seemed to Erikson that many of these men had lost the sense of who and what they were. They were having trouble reconciling their activities, attitudes and feelings as soldiers with the activities, attitudes and feelings they had known before the war. Accordingly, while these men may well have had difficulties with repressed or conflicted drives, their main problem seemed to be, as Erikson came to speak of it at the time, "identity confusion."

It was almost a decade before Erikson set forth the implications of his clinical observations in "Childhood and Society." In that book, the summation and integration of 15 years of research, he made three major contributions to the study of the human ego. He posited (1) that, side by side with the stages of psychosexual development described by Freud (the oral, anal, phallic, genital, Oedipal and pubertal), were psychosocial stages of ego development, in which the individual had to establish new basic orientations to himself and his social world; (2) that personality development continued throughout the whole life cycle; and (3) that each stage had a positive *as well* as a negative component.

Much about these contributions—and about Erikson's way of thinking—can be understood by looking at his scheme of life stages. Erikson identifies eight stages in the human life cycle, in each of which a new dimension of "social interaction" becomes possible—that is, a new dimension in a person's interaction with himself, and with his social environment.

TRUST VS. MISTRUST

The first stage corresponds to the oral stage in classical psychoanalytic theory and usually extends through the first year of life. In Erikson's view, the new dimension of social interaction that emerges during this period involves basic *trust* at the one extreme, and *mistrust* at the other. The degree to which the child comes to trust the world, other people and himself depends to a considerable extent upon the quality of the care that he receives. The infant whose needs are met when they arise, whose discomforts are quickly removed, who is cuddled, fondled, played with and talked to, develops a sense of the world as a safe place to be and of people as helpful and dependable. When, however, the care is inconsistent, inadequate and rejecting, it fosters a basic mistrust, an attitude of fear and suspicion on the part of the infant toward the world in general and people in particular that will carry through to later stages of development.

It should be said at this point that the problem of basic trust-versus-mistrust (as is true for all the later dimensions) is not resolved once and for all during the first year of life; it arises again at each successive stage of development. There is both hope and danger in this. The child who enters school with a sense of mistrust may come to trust a particular teacher who has taken the trouble to make herself trustworthy; with this second chance, he overcomes his early mistrust. On the other hand, the child who comes through infancy with a vital sense of trust can still have his sense of mistrust activated at a later stage if, say, his parents are divorced and separated under acrimonious circumstances.

This point was brought home to me in a very direct way by a 4-year-old patient I saw in a court clinic. He was being seen at the court clinic because his adoptive parents, who had had him for six months, now wanted to give him back to the agency. They claimed that he was cold and unloving, took things and could not be trusted. He was indeed a cold and apathetic boy, but with good reason. About a year after his illegitimate birth, he was taken away from his mother, who had a drinking problem, and was shunted back and forth among several foster homes. Initially he had tried to relate to the persons in the foster homes, but the relationships never had a chance to develop because he was moved at just the wrong times. In the end he gave up trying to reach out to others, because the inevitable separations hurt too much.

Like the burned child who dreads the flame, this emotionally burned child shunned the pain of emotional involvement. He had trusted his mother, but now he trusted no one. Only years of devoted care and patience could now undo the damage that had been done to this child's sense of trust.

AUTONOMY VS. DOUBT

Stage Two spans the second and third years of life, the period which Freudian theory calls the anal stage. Erikson sees here the emergence of *autonomy*. This autonomy dimension builds upon the child's new motor and mental abilities. At this stage the child can not only walk but also climb, open and close, drop, push and pull, hold and let go. The child takes pride in these new accomplishments and wants to do everything himself, whether it be pulling the wrapper off a piece of candy, selecting the vitamin out of the bottle or flushing the toilet. If parents recognize the young child's need to do what he is capable of doing at his own pace and in his own time, then he develops a sense that he is able to control his muscles, his impulses, himself and, not insignificantly, his environment—the sense of autonomy.

When, however, his caretakers are impatient and do for him what he is capable of doing himself, they reinforce a sense of shame and doubt. To be sure, every parent has rushed a child at times and children are hardy enough to endure such lapses. It is only when caretaking is consistently overprotective and criticism of "accidents" (whether these be wetting, soiling, spilling or breaking things) is harsh and unthinking that the child develops an excessive sense of shame with respect to other people and an excessive sense of doubt about own abilities to control his world and himself.

If the child leaves this stage with less autonomy than shame or doubt, he will be handicapped in his attempts to achieve autonomy in adolescence and adulthood. Contrariwise, the child who moves through this stage with his sense of autonomy buoyantly outbalancing his feelings of shame and doubt is well prepared to be autonomous at later phases in the life cycle. Again, however, the balance of autonomy to shame and doubt set up during this period can be changed in either positive or negative directions by later events.

It might be well to note, in addition, that too much autonomy can be as harmful as too little. I have in mind a patient of 7 who had a heart condition. He had learned very quickly how terrified his parents were of any signs in him of cardiac difficulty. With the psychological acuity given to children, he soon ruled the household. The family could not go shopping, or for a drive, or on a holiday if he did not approve. On those rare occasions when the parents had had enough and defied him, he would get angry and his purple hue and gagging would frighten them into submission.

Actually, this boy was frightened of this power (as all children would be) and was really eager to give it up. When the parents and the boy came to realize this, and to recognize that a little shame and doubt were a healthy counterpoise to an inflated sense of autonomy, the three of them could once again assume their normal roles.

INITIATIVE VS. GUILT

In this stage (the genital stage of classical psychoanalysis) the child, age 4 to 5, is pretty much master of his body and can ride a tricycle, run, cut and hit. He can thus initiate motor activities of various sorts on his own and no longer merely responds to or imitates the actions of other children. The same holds true for his language and fantasy activities. Accordingly, Erikson argues that the social dimension that appears at this stage has *initiative* at one of its poles and *guilt* at the other.

Whether the child will leave this stage with his sense of initiative far outbalancing his sense of guilt depends to a considerable extent upon how parents respond to his self-initiated activities. Children who are given much freedom and opportunity to initiate motor play such as running, bike riding, sliding, skating, tussling and wrestling have their sense of initiative reinforced. Initiative is also reinforced when parents answer their children's questions (intellectual initiative) and do not deride or inhibit fantasy or play activity. On the other hand, if the child is made to feel that his motor activity is bad, that his questions are a nuisance and that his play is silly and stupid, then he may develop a sense of guilt over self-initiated activities in general that will persist through later life stages.

INDUSTRY VS. INFERIORITY

Stage Four is the age period from 6 to 11, the elementary school years (described by classical psychoanalysis as the *latency phase*). It is a time during which the child's love for the parent of the opposite sex and rivalry with the same sexed parent (elements in the so-called family romance) are quiescent. It is also a period during which the child becomes capable of deductive reasoning, and of playing and learning by rules. It is not until this period, for example, that children can really play marbles, checkers and other "take turn" games that require obedience to rules. Erikson argues that the psychosocial dimension that emerges during this period has a sense of *industry* at one extreme and a sense of *inferiority* at the other.

The term industry nicely captures a dominant theme of this period during which the concern with how things are made, how they work and what they do predominates. It is the Robinson Crusoe age in the sense that the enthusiasm and minute detail with which Crusoe describes his activities appeals to the child's own budding sense of industry. When children are encouraged in their efforts to make, do, or build practical things (whether it be to construct creepy crawlers, tree houses, or airplane models—or to cook, bake or sew), are allowed to finish their products, and are praised and rewarded for the results, then the sense of industry is enhanced. But parents who see their children's efforts at making and doing as "mischief," and as simply "making a mess," help to encourage in children a sense of inferiority.

During these elementary-school years, however, the child's world includes more than the home. Now social institutions other than the family come to play a central role in the developmental crisis of the individual. (Here Erikson introduced still another advance in psychoanalytic theory, which heretofore concerned itself only with the effects of the parents' behavior upon the child's development.)

A child's school experiences affect his industry-inferiority balance. The child, for example, with an I.Q. of 80 to 90 has a particularly traumatic school experience, even when his sense of industry is rewarded and encouraged at home. He is "too bright" to be in special classes, but "too slow" to compete with children of average ability. Consequently he experiences constant failures in his academic efforts that reinforce a sense of inferiority.

On the other hand, the child who had his sense of industry derogated at home can have it revitalized at school through the offices of a sensitive and committed teacher. Whether the child develops a sense of industry or inferiority, therefore, no longer depends solely on the caretaking efforts of the parents but on the actions and offices of other adults as well.

IDENTITY VS. ROLE CONFUSION

When the child moves into adolescence (Stage Five—roughly the ages 12–18), he encounters, according to traditional psychoanalytic theory, a reawakening of the family-romance problem of early childhood. His means of resolving the problem is to seek and find a romantic partner of his own generation. While Erikson does not deny this aspect of adolescence, he points out that there are other problems as well. The adolescent matures mentally as well as physiologically and, in addition to the new feelings, sensations and desires he experiences as a result of changes in his body, he develops a multitude of new ways of looking at and thinking about the world. Among other things, those in adoles-

cence can now think about other people's thinking and wonder about what other people think of them. They can also conceive of ideal families, religions and societies which they then compare with the imperfect families, religions and societies of their own experience. Finally, adolescents become capable of constructing theories and philosophies designed to bring all the varied and conflicting aspects of society into a working, harmonious and peaceful whole. The adolescent, in a word, is an impatient idealist who believes that it is as easy to realize an ideal as it is to imagine it.

Erikson believes that the new interpersonal dimension which emerges during this period has to do with a sense of *ego identity* at the positive end and a sense of *role confusion* at the negative end. That is to say, given the adolescent's newfound integrative abilities, his task is to bring together all of the things he has learned about himself as a son, student, athlete, friend, Scout, newspaper boy, and so on, and integrate these different images of himself into a whole that makes sense and that shows continuity with the past while preparing for the future. To the extent that the young person succeeds in this endeavor, he arrives at a sense of psychosocial identity, a sense of who he is, where he has been and where he is going.

In contrast to the earlier stages, where parents play a more or less direct role in the determination of the result of the developmental crises, the influence of parents during this stage is much more indirect. If the young person reaches adolescence with, thanks to his parents, a vital sense of trust, autonomy, initiative and industry, then his chances of arriving at a meaningful sense of ego identity are much enhanced. The reverse, of course, holds true for the young person who enters adolescence with considerable mistrust, shame, doubt, guilt and inferiority. Preparation for a successful adolescence, and the attainment of an integrated psychosocial identity must, therefore, begin in the cradle.

Over and above what the individual brings with him from his childhood, the attainment of a sense of personal identity depends upon the social milieu in which he or she grows up. For example, in a society where women are to some extent second-class citizens, it may be harder for females to arrive at a sense of psychosocial identity. Likewise at times, such as the present, when rapid social and technological change breaks down many traditional values, it may be more difficult for young people to find continuity between what they learned and experienced as adolescents. At such times young people often seek causes that give their lives meaning and direction. The activism of the current generation of young people may well stem, in part at least, from this search.

When the young person cannot attain a sense of personal identity, either because of an unfortunate childhood or difficult social circumstances, he shows a certain amount of *role confusion*—a sense of not knowing what he is, where he belongs or whom he belongs to. Such confusion is a frequent symptom in delinquent young people. Promiscuous adolescent girls, for example, often seem to have a fragmented sense of ego identity. Some young people seek a "negative identity," an identity opposite to the one prescribed for them by their family and friends. Having an identity as a "delinquent," or as a "hippie," or even as an "acid head," may sometimes be preferable to having no identity at all.

In some cases young people do not seek a negative identity so much as they have it thrust upon them. I remember another court case in which the defendant was an attractive 16-year-old girl who had been found "tricking it" in a trailer located just outside the grounds of an Air Force base. From about the age of 12, her mother had encouraged her to dress seductively and to go out with boys. When she returned from dates, her sexually frustrated mother demanded a kiss-by-kiss, caress-by-caress description of the evening's activities. After the mother had vicariously satisfied her sexual needs, she proceeded to call her daughter a "whore" and a "dirty tramp." As the girl told me, "Hell, I have the name, so I might as well play the role."

Failure to establish a clear sense of personal identity at adolescence does not guarantee perpetual failure. And the person who attains a working sense of ego identity in adolescence will of necessity encounter challenges and threats to that identity as he moves through life. Erikson, perhaps more than any other personality theorist, has emphasized that life is constant change and that confronting problems at one stage in life is not a guarantee against the reappearance of these problems at later stages, or against the finding of new solutions to them.

INTIMACY VS. ISOLATION

Stage Six in the life cycle is young adulthood; roughly the period of courtship and early family life that extends from late adolescence till early middle age. For this stage, and the stages described hereafter, classical psychoanalysis has nothing new or major to say. For Erikson, however, the previous attainment of a sense of personal identity and the engagement in productive work that marks this period gives rise to a new interpersonal dimension of *intimacy* at the one extreme and *isolation* at the other.

When Erikson speaks of intimacy he means much more than love-making alone; he means the ability to share with and care about another person without fear of losing oneself in the process. In the case of intimacy, as in the case of identity, success or failure no longer depends directly upon the parents but only indirectly as they have contributed to the individual's success or failure at the earlier stages. Here, too, as in the case of identity, social conditions may help or hinder the establishment of a sense of intimacy. Likewise, intimacy need not involve sexuality; it includes the relationship between friends. Soldiers who have served together under the most dangerous circumstances often develop a sense of commitment to one another that exemplifies intimacy in its broadest sense. If a sense of intimacy is not established with friends or a marriage partner, the result, in Erikson's view, is a sense of isolation—of being alone without anyone to share with or care for.

GENERATIVITY VS. SELF-ABSORPTION

This stage—middle age—brings with it what Erikson speaks of as either *generativity or self-absorption,* and stagnation. What Erikson means by generativity is that the person begins to be concerned with others beyond his immediate family, with future generations and the nature of the society and world in which those generations will live. Generativity does not reside only in parents; it can be found in any individual who actively concerns himself with the welfare of young people and with making the world a better place for them to live and to work.

Those who fail to establish a sense of generativity fall into a state of self-absorption in which their personal needs and comforts are of predominant concern. A fictional case of self-absorption is Dickens's Scrooge in "A Christmas Carol." In his one-sided concern with money and in his disregard for the interest and welfare of his young employee, Bob Cratchit, Scrooge exemplifies the self-absorbed, embittered (the two often go together) old man.

Dickens also illustrated, however, what Erikson points out: namely, that unhappy solutions to life's crises are not irreversible. Scrooge, at the end of the tale, manifested both a sense of generativity and of intimacy which he had not experienced before.

INTEGRITY VS. DESPAIR

Stage Eight in the Eriksonian scheme corresponds roughly to the period when the individual's major efforts are nearing completion and when there is time for reflection—and for the enjoyment of grandchildren, if any. The psychosocial dimension that comes into prominence now has *integrity* on one hand and *despair* on the other.

The sense of integrity arises from the individual's ability to look back on his life with satisfaction. At the other extreme is the individual who looks back upon his life as a series of missed opportunities and missed directions; now in the twilight years he realies that it is too late to start again. For such a person the inevitable result is a sense of despair at what might have been.

These, then, are the major stages in the life cycle as described by Erikson. Their presentation, for one thing, frees the clinician to treat adult emotional problems as failures (in part at least) to solve genuinely adult personality crises and not, as heretofore, as mere residuals of infantile frustrations and conflicts. This view of personality growth, moreover, takes some of the onus off parents and takes account of the role which society and the person himself play in the formation of an individual personality. Finally, Erikson has offered hope for us all by demonstrating that each phase of growth has its strengths as well as its weaknesses and that failures at one stage of development can be rectified by successes at later stages.

The reason that these ideas, which sound so agreeable to "common sense," are in fact so revolutionary has a lot to do with the state of psychoanalysis in America. As formulated by Freud, psychoanalysis encompassed a theory of personality development, a method of studying the human mind and, finally, procedures for treating troubled and unhappy people. Freud viewed this system as a scientific one, open to revision as new facts and observations accumulated.

The system was, however, so vehemently attacked that Freud's followers were constantly in the position of having to defend Freud's views. Perhaps because of this situation, Freud's system became, in the hands of some of his followers and defenders, a dogma upon which all theoretical innovation, clinical observation and therapeutic practice had to be grounded. That this attitude persists is evidenced in the recent remark by a psychoanalyst that he believed psychotic patients could not be treated by psychoanalysis because "Freud said so." Such attitudes, in which Freud's authority rather than observation and data is the basis of deciding what is true and what is false, has contributed to the disrepute in which psychoanalysis is widely held today.

Erik Erikson has broken out of this scholasticism and has had the courage to say that Freud's discoveries and practices were the start and not the end of the study and treatment of the human personality. In addition to advocating the modifications of psychoanalytic theory outlined above, Erikson has also suggested modifications in therapeutic practice, particularly in the treatment of young patients. "Young people in severe trouble are not fit for the couch," he writes. "They want to face you, and they want you to face them, not a facsimile of a parent, or wearing the mask of a professional helper, but as a kind of over-all individual a young person can live with or despair of."

Erikson has had the boldness to remark on some of the negative effects that distorted notions of psychoanalysis have had on society at large. Psychoanalysis, he says, has contributed to a widespread fatalism—"even as we were trying to devise, with scientific determinism, a therapy for the few, we were led to promote an ethical disease among the many."

Perhaps Erikson's innovations in psychoanalytic theory are best exemplified in his psycho-historical writings, in which he combines psychoanalytic insight with a true historical imagination. After the publication of "Childhood and Society," Erikson undertook the application of his scheme of the human life cycle to the study of historical persons. He wrote a series of brilliant essays on men as varied as Maxim Gorky, George Bernard Shaw and Freud himself. These studies were not narrow case histories but rather reflected Erikson's remarkable grasp of Europe's social and political history, as well as of its literature. (His mastery of American folklore, history and literature is equally remarkable.)

While Erikson's major biographical studies were yet to come, these early essays already revealed his unique psychohistory method. For one thing, Erikson always chose men whose lives fascinated him in one way or another, perhaps because of some conscious or unconscious affinity with them. Erikson thus had a sense of community with his subjects which he adroitly used (he calls it *disciplined subjectivity*) to take his subject's point of view and to experience the world as that person might.

Secondly, Erikson chose to elaborate a particular crisis or episode in the individual's life which seemed to crystallize a life-theme that united the activities of his past and gave direction to his activities for the future. Then, much as an artist might, Erikson proceeded to fill in the background of the episode and add social and historical perspective. In a very real sense Erikson's biographical sketches are like paintings which direct the viewer's gaze from a focal point of attention to background and back again, so that one's appreciation of the focal area is enriched by having pursued the picture in its entirety.

This method was given its first major test in Erikson's study of "Young Man Luther." Originally, Erikson planned only a brief study of Luther, but "Luther proved too bulky a man to be merely a chapter in a book." Erikson's involvement with Luther dated from his youth, when, as a wandering artist, he happened to hear the Lord's Prayer in Luther's German. "Never knowingly having heard it, I had the experience, as seldom before or after, of a wholeness captured in a few simple words, of poetry fusing the esthetic and the moral; those who have suddenly 'heard' the Gettysburg Address will know what I mean."

Erikson's interest in Luther may have had other roots as well. In some ways, Luther's unhappiness with the papal intermediaries of Christianity resembled on a grand scale Erikson's own dissatisfaction with the intermediaries of Freud's system. In both cases some of the intermediaries had so distorted the original teachings that what was being preached in the name of the master came close to being the opposite of what he had himself proclaimed. While it is not possible to describe Erikson's treatment of Luther here, one can get some feeling for Erikson's brand of historical analysis from his sketch of Luther:

"Luther was a very troubled and a very gifted young man who had to create his own cause on which to focus his fidelity in the Roman Catholic world as it was then. . . . He first became a monk and tried to solve his scruples by being an exceptionally good monk. But even his superiors thought that he tried much too hard. He felt himself to be such a sinner that he began to lose faith in the charity of God and his superiors told him, 'Look, God doesn't hate you, you hate God or else you would trust Him to accept your prayer.' But I would like to make it clear that someone like Luther becomes a historical person only because he also has an acute understanding of historical actuality and knows how to 'speak to the condition' of his times. Only then do inner struggles become representative of those of a large number of vigorous and sincere young people—and begin to interest some troublemakers and hangers-on."

After Erikson's study of "Young Man Luther" (1958), he turned his attention to "middle-aged" Gandhi. As did Luther, Gandhi evoked for Erikson childhood memories. Gandhi led his first nonviolent protest in India in 1918 on behalf of some mill workers, and Erikson, then a young man of 16, had read glowing accounts of the event. Almost a half a century later Erikson was invited to Ahmedabad, an industrial city in western India, to give a seminar on the human life cycle. Erikson discovered that Ahmedabad was the city in which Gandhi had led the demonstration about which Erikson had read as a youth. Indeed, Erikson's host was none other than Ambalal Sarabahai, the benevolent industrialist who had been Gandhi's host—as well as antagonist—in the 1918 wage dispute. Throughout his stay in Ahmedabad, Erikson continued to encounter people and places that were related to Gandhi's initial experiments with nonviolent techniques.

The more Erikson learned about the event at Ahmedabad, the more intrigued he became with its pivotal importance in Gandhi's career. It seemed to be the historical moment upon which all the earlier events of Gandhi's life converged and from which diverged all of his later endeavors. So captured was Erikson by the event at Ahmedabad, that he returned the following year to research a book on Gandhi in which the event would serve as a fulcrum.

At least part of Erikson's interest in Gandhi may have stemmed from certain parallels in their lives. The 1918 event marked Gandhi's emergence as a national political leader. He was 48 at the time, and had become involved reluctantly, not so much out of a need for power or fame as out of a genuine conviction that something had to be done about the disintegration of Indian culture. Coincidentally, Erikson's book "Childhood and Society," appeared in 1950 when Erikson was 48, and it is that book which brought him national prominence in the mental health field. Like Gandhi, too, Erikson reluctantly did what he felt he had to do (namely, publish his observations and conclusions) for the benefit of his ailing profession and for the patients treated by its practitioners. So while Erikson's affinity with Luther seemed to derive from comparable professional identity crises, his affinity for Gandhi appears to derive from a parallel crisis of generativity. A passage from "Gandhi's Truth" (from a chapter wherein Erikson addresses himself directly to his subject) helps to convey Erikson's feeling for his subject.

"So far, I have followed you through the loneliness of your childhood and through the experiments and the scruples of your youth. I have affirmed my belief in your ceaseless endeavor to perfect yourself as a man who came to feel that he was the only one available to reverse India's fate. You experimented with what to you were debilitating temptations and you did gain vigor and agility from your victories over yourself. Your identity could be no less than that of universal man, although you had to become an Indian—and one close to the masses—first."

The following passage speaks to Erikson's belief in the general significance of Gandhi's efforts:

We have seen in Gandhi's development the strong attraction of one of those more inclusive identities: that of an enlightened citizen of the British Empire. In proving himself willing neither to abandon vital ties to his native tradition nor to sacrifice lightly a Western education which eventually contributed to his ability to help defeat British hegemony—in all of these seeming contradictions Gandhi showed himself on intimate terms with the actualities of his era. For in all parts of the world, the struggle now is for *the anticipatory development of more inclusive identities*. . . . I submit then, that Gandhi, in his immense intuition for historical actuality and his capacity to assume leadership in 'truth in action,' may have created a ritualization through which men, equipped with both realism and strength, can face each other with mutual confidence.

There is now more and more teaching of Erikson's concepts in psychiatry, psychology, education and social work in America and in other parts of the world. His description of the stages of life cycle are summarized in major textbooks in all of these fields and clinicians are increasingly looking at their cases in Eriksonian terms.

Research investigators have, however, found Erikson's formulations somewhat difficult to test. This is not surprising, inasmuch as Erikson's conceptions, like Freud's, take into account the infinite complexity of the human personality. Current research methodologies are, by and large, still not able to deal with these complexities at their own level, and distortions are inevitable when such concepts as "identity" come to be defined in terms of responses to a questionnaire.

Likewise, although Erikson's life-stages have an intuitive "rightness" about them, not everyone agrees with his formulations. Douvan and Adelson in their book, "The Adolescent Experience," argue that while his identity theory may hold true for boys, it doesn't for girls. This argument is based on findings which suggest that girls postpone identity consolidation until after marriage (and intimacy) have been established. Such postponement occurs, says Douvan and Adelson, because a woman's identity is partially defined by the identity of the man whom she marries. This view does not really contradict Erikson's, since he recognizes that later events, such as marriage, can help to resolve both current and past developmental crises. For the woman, but not for the man, the problems of identity and intimacy may be solved concurrently.

Objections to Erikson's formulations have come from other directions as well. Robert W. White, Erikson's good friend and colleague at Harvard, has a long standing (and warm-hearted) debate with Erikson over his life-stages. White believes that his own theory of "competence motivation," a theory which has received wide recognition, can account for the phenomena of ego development much more economically than can Erikson's stages. Erikson has, however, little interest in debating the validity of the stages he has described. As an artist he recognizes that there are many different ways to view one and the same phenomenon and that a perspective that is congenial to one person will be repugnant to another. He offers his stage-wise description of the life cycle for those who find such perspectives congenial and not as a world view that everyone should adopt.

It is this lack of dogmatism and sensitivity to the diversity and complexity of the human personality which help to account for the growing recognition of Erikson's contribution within as well as without the helping professions. Indeed, his psycho-historical investigations have originated a whole new field of study which has caught the interest of historians and political scientists alike. (It has also intrigued his wife, Joan, who has published pieces on Eleanor

Roosevelt and who has a book on Saint Francis in press.) A recent issue of Daedalus, the journal for the American Academy of Arts and Sciences, was entirely devoted to psycho-historical and psycho-political investigations of creative leaders by authors from diverse disciplines who have been stimulated by Erikson's work.

Now in his 68th year, Erikson maintains the pattern of multiple activities and appointments which has characterized his entire career. He spends the fall in Cambridge, Mass., where he teaches a large course on "the human life cycle" for Harvard seniors. The spring semester is spent at his home in Stockbridge, Mass., where he participates in case conferences and staff seminars at the Austen Riggs Center. His summers are spent on Cape Cod. Although Erikson's major commitment these days is to his psycho-historical investigation, he is embarking on a study of preschool children's play constructions in different settings and countries, a follow-up of some research he conducted with preadolescents more than a quarter-century ago. He is also planning to review other early observations in the light of contemporary change. In his approach to his work, Erikson appears neither drawn nor driven, but rather to be following an inner schedule as natural as the life cycle itself.

Although Erikson, during his decade of college teaching, has not seen any patients or taught at psychoanalytic institutes, he maintains his dedication to psychoanalysis and views his psycho-historical investigations as an applied branch of that discipline. While some older analysts continue to ignore Erikson's work, there is increasing evidence (including a recent poll of psychiatrists and psycho-analysts) that he is having a rejuvenating influence upon a discipline which many regard as dead or dying. Young analysts are today proclaiming a "new freedom" to see Freud in historical perspective—which reflects the Eriksonian view that one can recognize Freud's greatness without bowing to conceptual precedent.

Accordingly, the reports of the demise of psycho-analysis may have been somewhat premature. In the work of Erik Erikson, at any rate, psychoanalysis lives and continues to beget life.

FREUD'S "AGES OF MAN"

Erik Erikson's definition of the "eight ages of man" is a work of synthesis and insight by a psychoanaly-ti-cally trained and worldly mind. Sigmund Freud's description of human phases stems from his epic psychological discoveries and centers almost exclusively on the early years of life. A brief summary of the phases posited by Freud:

Oral Stage Roughly the first year of life, the period during which the mouth region provides the greatest sensual satisfaction. Some derivative behavioral traits which may be seen at this time are *incorporativeness* (first six months of life) and *aggressiveness* (second six months of life).

Anal Stage Roughly the second and third years of life. During this period the site of greatest sensual pleasure shifts to the anal and urethral areas. Derivative behavioral traits are *retentiveness* and *expulsiveness*.

Phallic Stage Roughly the third and fourth years of life. The site of greatest sensual pleasure during this stage is the genital region. Behavior traits derived from this period include *intrusiveness* (male) and *receptiveness* (female).

Oedipal Stage Roughly the fourth and fifth years of life. At this stage the young person takes the parent of the opposite sex as the object or provider of sensual satisfaction and regards the same-sexed parent as a rival. (The "family romance.") Behavior traits originating in this period are *seductiveness* and *competitiveness*.

Latency Stage Roughly the years from age 6 to 11. The child resolves the Oedipus conflict by identifying with the parent of the opposite sex and by so doing satisfies sensual needs vicariously. Behavior traits developed during this period include *conscience* (or the internalization of parental moral and ethical demands).

Puberty Stage Roughly 11 to 14. During this period there is an integration and subordination of oral, anal and phallic sensuality to an overriding and unitary genital *sexuality*. The genital sexuality of puberty has another young person of the opposite sex as its object, and discharge (at least for boys) as its aim. Derivative behavior traits (associated with the control and regulation of genital sexuality) are *intellectualization* and *estheticism*.

Reading 41

Learned Helplessness and Negative Evaluation

Carol S. Dweck

Learned helplessness exists when a child believes failure to be insurmountable. This belief is accompanied by deterioration in performance, and in many cases, the child becomes virtually incapable of solving the same problems that, prior to failure, he could solve with ease. On a somewhat intuitive basis, one would expect failure feedback to prove most disruptive to children who display less ability and who, perhaps, encounter discouraging outcomes regularly. This is not the case.

Our work with grade school children has shown rather conclusively that deterioration in quality of intellectual problem-solving performance is generally independent of proficiency at the task (Diener & Dweck, 1976; Dweck, 1975; Dweck & Bush, 1976; Dweck & Reppucci, 1973). Children who show impaired problem solving after they receive failure feedback are just as good at solving the problems before they experience failure as are those who show no impairment and those who show actual improvement. This article will delineate and discuss the cognitive-motivational differences between children who respond to negative evaluation with decreased persistence and those who respond with increased persistence. First, we will examine the nature and the extent of performance changes under failure. Then we will examine the findings relating to the cognitive-motivational basis of the differences in response to failure, looking also at sex differences in the tendency to experience helplessness. Next we will identify some of the means by which these differences in response to failure can be learned, with particular emphasis on patterns of classroom evaluative feedback that can promote the various tendencies. Finally, we will explore ways in which negative feedback can be used by evaluators to optimize its impact on children's present and future performance in learning situations.

As we will see, negative evaluation has both postdictive and predictive value: it carries implications about things past (such as the adequacy of performance, the nature of any inadequacies, and

Portions of this research were supported by Grant NE G-00-3-088 from the National Institute of Education and by Grant HD 00244 from the U.S. Public Health Service.

the reasons for the inadequacy), but it may also have implications for what is likely to occur in the future—success or more failure. While some of the implications may be inherent in the feedback, others may be in the eye of the perceiver. Optimal negative evaluation teaches the child to use the information inherent in the feedback and to draw implications from the feedback that facilitate the occurrence of desired outcomes.

LEARNED HELPLESSNESS: VIEWING FAILURE AS INSURMOUNTABLE

Our research has documented two clear, divergent responses to failure feedback in an intellectual problem-solving situation. In one study (Dweck & Reppucci, 1973), children were given novel block design pules to work on by two different experimenters. Problems from the two were interspersed. However, one experimenter gave problems that all children could solve fairly quickly, while the other gave problems that were insoluble, though not obviously so. After both experimenters had administered a certain number of their problems, those from the "failure" experimenter became soluble; she administered the same problems that children had solved from the "success" experimenter shortly before. Some children solved them instantly, but others failed to solve them at all. Even though they were motivated to earn tokens, even though they had solved virtually the same problem just before, even though they had a generous time limit, and even though they "looked" as though they were attempting to reach a solution, their attempts were grossly inadequate.

In another study, Diener and Dweck (1976) examined performance following failure on a discrimination learning task. One purpose of the study was to determine more precisely the nature of the deterioration in performance following failure. Do children whose performance deteriorates under failure simply withdraw as soon as it occurs and begin to respond randomly? Do they try a number of sophisticated alternative solutions, but abandon them more quickly than the persistent children? Or does the sophistication and effectiveness of their problem-solving strategy gradually erode as they experience successive failures? To answer these questions, children were trained on a series of eight soluble discrimination-learning problems. For each problem they were shown pictures on cards, two at a time, that differed in three respects—the shape of the form depicted (e.g., triangle or square), the color of the form (red or blue), and the symbol that appeared in the middle of the form (e.g., star or dot). One aspect of the stimuli (e.g., triangle) was correct for the whole problem and the child's task was to discover which was correct by utilizing the feedback following each choice. All children in the study were able to employ problem-solving strategies that were successful in reaching correct solutions on the training problems. However, children clearly differed in their problem-solving strategies following failure. Some children showed *more* sophisticated approaches following failure than they had in training—that is, they became more mature developmentally in their hypothesis-testing strategies. Other children, however, showed progressive declines in their problem-solving ability under failure. Their approach became increasingly less mature, approximating the behavior of younger and younger children, until most of them were using tactics that could never lead to solutions or were guessing randomly. Again, despite equivalent initial performance, these two groups of children showed remarkably different levels of performance once they encountered failure. As failure continued, the levels of performance became increasingly disparate.

In other studies with other tasks, the same patterns emerged—some children became literally incompetent following failure feedback, while others rose to the challenge, persisted, and maintained or improved their performance in the face of failure. If level of ability does not distinguish these two types of children, then what does? Our research has shown that the variable that consistently predicts response to failure is the child's interpretation of failure—what he thinks caused it and whether he views it as surmountable (see Weiner, 1972; 1974; cf. Brickman, Linsenmeier, & McCareins, 1976). Children who persist in the face of failure tend to see failures as resulting from insufficient motivation and tend to see the remedy as well within their control. That is, despite the occurrence of failure, these children believe that some modification of their

behavior will reverse the outcome, and they rarely seem to doubt their ability to attain success ultimately. In sharp contrast, the children whose performance deteriorates under failure feedback do not emphasize effort as an important cause of their failures and, instead, will often view failure as indicating a lack of ability. This discouraging interpretation—that they lack sufficient intelligence or skill to succeed—is accompanied by the belief that their failures are insurmountable and will continue regardless of any efforts they might display. They seem to embrace this belief even when it is contradicted by their past successes. One might think that a history of success on the task would constitute irrefutable evidence of their ability to perform that task. As we will see, however, once failure occurs, past success is not sufficient to maintain their belief in their ability to reverse failure.

After documenting the relationship between attributions for failure and performance change in the face of failure, we set out to determine whether it was possible to alter helpless children's response to failure by teaching them to interpret it differently (Dweck, 1975). We reasoned that if persistent children tend to attribute their failure to lack of effort then perhaps if helpless children were taught to make the same attribution, they would confront failure more adaptively. A number of children were identified whose performance underwent serious deterioration following failure and whose pattern of attributions were indicative of helplessness. We assessed their reactions to failure by establishing stable baselines of responding on math problems over a number of days. A mild failure experience was then programmed and its effect on their problem solving was evaluated. These children's performance on problems they had been solving daily was severely disrupted by the occurrence of mild failure, even though it occurred within the context of predominantly success experiences. Some of the children did not recover their baseline performance for several days. Following this assessment of their reactions to failure, these children were given one of two treatment procedures in a different situation. Half the children received only success experiences in the treatment situation—a procedure which was designed to "bolster" their confidence in their abilities, their expectancy of success and, according to the claims of some, to inoculate them against the effects of failure. The other half of the children received attribution retraining. They were given several failure trials each day. On the occasions when failure occurred, the experimenter attributed their failure to insufficient effort. (For full details of the training procedure, the reader is referred to Dweck, 1975.) The training was carried out for a total of 25 days. At the middle and the end of training the children were returned to the original situation and the effects of failure on their performance were again assessed. Almost none of the children who had been given only success experiences in training showed any evidence of improved reaction to failure. Prolonged experience with success had not altered their interpretation of failure and did not enable them to cope more effectively with it. In contrast, the children who had received attribution retraining showed significant improvement by the mid-training assessment and, by the end of training, they showed no adverse reaction to failure. In fact, most of these children now showed *improvement* in their problem-solving performance following failure. They had indeed begun to see failure as a cue to try harder. Informal interviews with the teachers, who did not know which children were given which treatment, revealed some interesting information. Teachers reported that certain children in the study had begun to display a different attitude toward their work in the classroom. For example, they were more persistent with new material than they had previously been and, when they were unable to complete a task, they would seek help rather than withdraw. Some would ask for more or harder work. All of the children that the teachers singled out for such changes in classroom behavior had been in the attribution retraining treatment.

These studies provide strong support for the role of cognitive-motivational factors such as attributions in determining children's reactions to feedback. A child who sees failure feedback as indicative of a lack of ability is also likely to see that failure as insurmountable. Thus when he encounters failure feedback, it has a doubly negative impact; it represents a public condemnation of his competence and a signal that failure will continue regardless of what he does. A child who tends to emphasize effort, on the other hand, tends to view failure as surmountable. He is more likely to key on the information in the feedback that will help him to regulate his behavior in a way that will make success more probable. It has few apparent negative implications for his competence and little suggestion of long-term negative outcomes.

Some of our more recent work (Diener & Dweck, 1976) is indicating that not only do these two types of children tend to make different types of attributions when a clear failure has occurred, but also that they have different likelihoods of perceiving failure and making attributions. It appears to be the helpless children who quickly define their "mistakes" as failure, identify the cause as lack of ability, and soon cease to display active problem-solving attempts. It appears that the persistent children are less apt to dwell on the causes of failure. They are instead more remedy-oriented and tend to engage in self-instructional and self-monitoring activities directed at overcoming failures and reaching the solution.

SEX DIFFERENCES IN LEARNED HELPLESSNESS

Much of our research has shown that learned helplessness in the face of failure feedback delivered by adult evaluators is more prevalent among a certain group of children—girls. Girls are more likely to attribute failure feedback from adults to a lack of ability than boys are, while boys are more apt to see such feedback as indicative of their effort (Dweck & Bush, 1976; Dweck & Reppucci, 1973; Nicholls, 1975). As one would expect, this difference is accompanied by sex differences in behavior under failure (Butterfield, 1965; Crandall & Rabson, 1960; Veroff, 1969). However, it also occurs under the threat of failure in an important area and even under increases in evaluative pressure (Dweck & Gilliard, 1975; Nicholls, 1975). Under these conditions, girls are more likely than boys to show deterioration of performance and decreased persistence. As will be discussed below, girls are also more likely to generalize a failure experience to a new situation.

In a sense it is highly paradoxical that girls are more apt to indict their abilities when they receive failure feedback. In the elementary school years girls receive the consistently higher grades (Achenback, 1970; Dweck, Goet, & Strauss, 1976), and they are more highly regarded by adults on almost every conceivable attribute (Coopersmith, 1967; Digman, 1963; Stevenson, Hale, Klein, & Miller, 1968). Thus the feedback that girls receive from adults in both the academic-intellectual sphere and in the social sphere is telling them that they possess ability. Why, then, are they so quick to doubt themselves and give up when failure occurs? A good deal of our recent research has attempted to answer this question and to explore the implications of our answer.

For years, many have claimed that girls' greater disruption by failure feedback is perfectly understandable when one considers that they are trained to be dependent on others, while boys are trained to be independent and to formulate their own standards against which to evaluate their performance (Crandall, 1963; Crandall, Dewey, Katkovsky, & Preston, 1964; Veroff, 1969). According to this view, then, girls would automatically accept others' feedback as indicative of their ability while boys would be able to weigh the feedback against their own opinion and put it in perspective. However, some of our findings contradict this position. When *peers,* instead of adults deliver the failure feedback, it is the boys and not the girls whose performance suffers (Dweck & Bush, 1976). The boys attribute failure feedback from peers to lack of ability and show impaired problem-solving; the girls cope with peer feedback quite adaptively. They see it as indicative of effort and improve their performance when they receive it. This means that boys and girls have *not* learned one meaning for failure and one response to it; rather the impact of the failure varies according to the person by whom it is delivered. Although boys may appear to be more successful in surmounting their failures in situations with adults, they are extremely sensitive to criticism from peers, who by the late grade school years are the more important social agents for them (Bronfenbrenner, 1967; 1970; Hollander & Marcia, 1970). This is not to say that girls do not also value peer opinions. It is simply that they tend not to see peer criticism on a problem-solving task as indicating that they lack ability.

The facts that girls' greater tendency toward helplessness is not general across agents does not imply that their response to failure feedback from adults is not an important concern. In virtually all academic environments adults are the major evaluators. We therefore sought to understand how children's interactions with their teachers might teach the two sexes different interpretations for teachers' failure feedback (Dweck, Davidson, Nelson & Enna, 1976). Observers in fourth- and fifth-grade classrooms coded every instance of evaluative feedback to children during academic subjects. They noted whether the feedback was positive or negative and recorded the class of behavior for which the feedback was given—either conduct, nonintellectual aspects of academic work (e.g., neatness), or intellectual aspects of academic work (e.g., correctness of answer). Observers also noted when teachers made explicit attributions for children's successes or failures and coded them as attributions to ability, motivation, or external factors.

The results have helped to resolve the paradox of how the more favorable treatment of girls can lead to denigration of their competence, and to helplessness and inability to cope with failure. The results also show how boys can learn to discount failures or see them as unrelated to their abilities. First, negative feedback given to boys was, overall, far more frequent, perhaps conveying information about the teacher's attitude.[*] Second, it was used in a more diffuse and a more ambiguous fashion via-à-vis the intellectual quality of boys' work. Past research has clearly shown that feedback used in non-specific manner to refer to a wide variety of nonintellectual behaviors comes to lose its meaning as an assessment of the intellectual quality of the child's work (Cairns, 1970; Eisenberger, Kaplan, & Singer, 1974; Warren & Cairns, 1972). In fact, negative feedback for boys was used more often for conduct and nonintellectual aspects than it was for the intellectual quality of their academic performance. Even if conduct is excluded from the analysis and we look only at work-related feedback, 45% of the feedback for boys' work referred to intellectually irrelevant aspects of their performance. That means that almost half of the criticism that boys got for their work had nothing to do with its intellectual adequacy. Instead, this feedback referred to such things as neatness, instruction-following, style of response delivery—to form rather than to content. In striking contrast, almost all of the negative feedback girls received for their work referred specifically to its intellectual aspects. Looking at the explicit attributions teachers made for children's intellectual failures, we find that teachers attributed boys' failures to lack of motivation eight times as often as they did girls! In short, when boys are given failure feedback by adults they can easily see it as reflecting something about the evaluators' attitude

[*]Boys and girls did not differ in the proportions of their answers that received positive or negative feedback for correctness, although they differed widely in the proportion of their positive and negative feedback that this correctness feedback constituted.

toward them or as being based on an assessment of some nonintellectual aspect of their work. When they do see it as referring to the intellectual quality of their work, they can attribute this failure to lack of motivation. Girls, on the other hand, are directed toward other explanations. First, the teacher is generally positive toward girls—girls get far less criticism and more praise than boys—and so girls are less apt to see criticism as reflecting a negative attitude toward them in general. Second, feedback is used for them in a very specific fashion for intellectual aspects of work, and so girls are not as likely to see the assessment as being based on an evaluation of nonintellectual qualities. Finally, to the extent that teachers see girls as highly motivated and girls also see themselves as trying their best, they cannot attribute their failure to lack of motivation. Thus, they may have little choice but to attribute their intellectual failures to lack of ability.

Are teachers simply reacting to the different behavior of the two sexes or are they instead reacting differently to similar behavior from the two sexes? The answer is probably a "bit of both." While it is clear that boys are often more disruptive, less neat in their work, and less motivated to perform well in the elementary school years, there is also some evidence that they tend to be scolded more often and more severely than girls for similar transgressions (Etaugh & Harlow, 1973). In terms of trying to understand how the use of negative feedback determines its meaning for boys and girls, however, it may not be critical whether boys' criticisms are entirely justified. We have shown (Dweck, Davidson, Nelson, & Enna, 1976) that any child exposed to the contingencies that boys and girls are exposed to in the classroom will interpret the feedback accordingly. These contingencies can serve as direct and powerful causes of children's attributions. We have taken the "teacher-girl" and the "teacher-boy" contingencies of negative feedback that we observed in the classroom and have programmed them in an experimental situation. Specifically, on an initial task, children got negative feedback that either (a) referred exclusively to the correctness of their answers (like girls in the classroom), or (b) referred sometimes to correctness and sometimes to neatness (like boys in the classroom). On a subsequent task with the same agent, children who had experienced the teacher-girl contingency, regardless of their actual sex, saw failure feedback as indicative of their ability. Almost no children in

the teacher-boy condition saw failure as indicative of their competence.

What are some of the long-term implications of these differences in attributions for failure? We have conducted several studies of generalization of failure experiences across situations (Dweck, Goetz, & Strauss, 1976). It appears that while boys who blame teachers for the failure feedback they receive may show lowered motivation in that situation, they maintain the belief in their ability to succeed in the future, for example, with different teachers. Girls, however, who tend to see their past failures as indicative of their ability, are more likely to carry the effects of their failure experiences across situations with similar tasks and across school years.

IMPLICATIONS FOR THE EVALUATOR

As we have seen, children's responses to failure feedback are guided by the manner in which they interpret that feedback. For different children failure has different postdictive and predictive value. Helpless children often view failure as conveying information about their abilities and as signalling continued failure. Persistent, mastery-oriented children view failure as carrying information about specific aspects of their performance that are modifiable. Furthermore, they tend to remain optimistic about future success, since they believe that their alternative strategies will yield results. Thus while failure for helpless children represents a condemnation of their abilities, for persistent children it represents a step on the way to the solution and contains helpful information about how to alter behavior appropriately.

What can evaluators do to enable children to use the information inherent in negative feedback most constructively? One clear implication of our research is that evaluators should teach children to emphasize the role of effort in determining outcomes. While many teachers verbally stress the importance of effort ("If at first you don't succeed . . ."), not many teachers provide *direct* demonstrations to students following a failure experience. For example, if a child gives an incorrect answer in class, the teacher can either give clues, prods, and additional response opportunities or go on to another child (see Brophy & Good, 1970). The former conveys an attribution of the failure to lack of effort and gives the child the chance to turn the failure into a success. The latter conveys to the child that further time attempting to extract the correct response would be ill spent. In general explaining to a child how his answer is wrong, where his strategy went astray, and guiding him or her toward the correct solution may help to prevent inferences of incompetence on the part of the child. Merely paying "lip service" to persistence and not providing empirical evidence of its benefits may well backfire by allowing the child to try, fail, and thereby reject effort as a relevant variable.

Of course, despite attempts to give school children only material that they are capable of mastering, children sometimes do fail because they lack the necessary ability to perform the task. Moverover, when a task is beyond the child's capabilities, we would hardly consider unlimited persistence to be desirable (see Brickman, & Bulman, 1976). In these cases, continued belief that variations in effort or strategy will lead to success would be maladaptive. Yet the child need not conclude from such experiences that he is incompetent. A good evaluator will encourage children to distinguish between a temporary or specific skill deficit and a generalized, more permanent lack of intelligence and to consider such instances as indicative of the former.

What do the findings on classroom feedback and sex differences suggest? The moral of these studies is certainly not that teachers should abandon codes of conduct and standards of neatness so that boys will view teachers as unbiased evaluators of the intellectual quality of their work. The moral is not that teachers should begin to criticize girls for a wider variety of behaviors so that they will not be so quick to see negative evaluation as a condemnation of their abilities. The aim of negative evaluation for the child's work should be to bring about improvements in performance. In order for this to occur, the basis for and the referent of the feedback should be unambiguous. Equally or even more important, however, is to provide children with the belief that their intellectual failures are surmountable and to arm them with strategies for surmounting them.

REFERENCES

Achenbach, T. M. Standardization of a research instrument for identifying associative responding in children. *Developmental Psychology*, 1970, *2*, 283–291.

Brickman, P., & Bulman, R. J. Persistence by people who expect success: Adaptive, maladaptive, or irrelevant? Unpublished manuscript, Northwestern University, 1976.

Brickman, P., Linsenmeier, J. A. W., & McCareins, A. Performance enhancement by relevant success and irrelevant failure. *Journal of Personality and Social Psychology*, 1976, *33*, 149–160.

Bronfenbrenner, U. Response to pressure from peers versus adults among Soviet and American school children. *International Journal of Psychology*, 1967, *2*, 199–207.

Bronfenbrenner, U. Reactions to social pressure from adults versus peers among Soviet day school and boarding school pupils in the perspective of an American sample. *Journal of Personality and Social Psychology*, 1970, *15*, 179–189.

Brophy, J. E., & Good, T. L. Teachers' communication of differential expectations for children's classroom performance. Some behavioral data. *Journal of Educational Psychology*, 1970, *61*, 365–374.

Butterfield, E. C. The role of competence motivation in interrupted task recall and repetition choice. *Journal of Experimental Child Psychology*, 1965, *2*, 354–370.

Cairns, R. B. Meaning and attention as determinants of social reinforcer effectiveness. *Child Development*, 1970, *41*, 1067–1082.

Coopersmith, S. *The antecedents of self-esteem.* San Francisco: W. H. Freeman, 1967.

Crandall, V. J. Achievement. In H. W. Stevenson (Ed.), *Child Psychology.* The sixty-second yearbook of the National Society for the Study of Education. Chicago: NSSE, 1963.

Crandall, V. J., Dewey, R., Katkovsky, W., & Preston, A. Parents' attitudes and behaviors and grade school children's academic achievements. *Journal of Genetic Psychology*, 1964, *104*, 53–66.

Crandall, V. J., & Rabson, A. Children's repetition choices in an intellectual achievement situation following success and failure. *Journal of Genetic Psychology*, 1960, *97*, 161–168.

Diener, C. I., & Dweck, C. S. An analysis of learned helplessness: Ongoing changes in performance, strategy, and achievement cognitions following failure. Unpublished manuscript, University of Illinois, 1976.

Digman, J. M. Principal dimensions of child personality as inferred from teachers' judgments. *Child Development*, 1963, *34*, 43–60.

Dweck, C. S. The role of expectations and attributions in the alleviation of learned helplessness. *Journal of Personality and Social Psychology*, 1975, *31*, 674–685.

Dweck, C. S., & Bush, E. S. Sex differences in learned helplessness: (I) Differential debilitation with peer and adult evaluators. *Developmental Psychology*, 1976, *12*, 147–156.

Dweck, C. S., Davidson, W., Nelson, S., & Enna, B. Sex differences in learned helplessness: (II) The contingencies of evaluative feedback in the classroom & (III) An experimental analysis. Manuscript submitted for publication, 1976.

Dweck, C. S., & Gilliard, D. Expectancy statements as determinants of reactions to failure: Sex differences in persistence and expectancy change. *Journal of Personality and Social Psychology,* 1975, *32,* 1077–1084.

Dweck, C. S., Goetz, T. E., & Strauss, N. Sex differences in learned helplessness: (IV) An experimental and naturalistic study of failure generalization and its mediators. Unpublished manuscript, University of Illinois, 1976.

Dweck, C. S., & Reppucci, N. D. Learned helplessness and reinforcement responsibility in children. *Journal of Personality and Social Psychology,* 1973, *25,* 109–116.

Eisenberger, R., Kaplan, R. M., & Singer, R. D. Decremental and nondecremental effects of noncontingent social approval. *Journal of Personality and Social Psychology,* 1974, *30,* 716–722.

Etaugh, C., & Harlow, H. School attitudes and performance of elementary school children as related to teacher's sex and behavior. Paper presented at the meeting of the Society for Research in Child Development, Philadelphia, March, 1973.

Hollander, E. P., & Marcia, J. E. Parental determinants of peer-orientation and self-orientation among preadolescents. *Developmental Psychology,* 1970, *2,* 293–302.

Nicholls, J. G. Causal attributions and other achievement-related cognitions: Effects of task outcomes, attainment value, and sex. *Journal of Personality and Social Psychology,* 1975, *31,* 379–389.

Stevenson, H. W., Hale, G. A., Klein, R. E., & Miller, L. K. Interrelations and correlates in children's learning and problem solving. *Monographs of the Society for Research in Child Development,* 1968, *33* (7), Serial No. 123.

Veroff, J. Social comparison and the development of achievement motivation in C. P. Smith (Ed.), *Achievement-related motives in children.* New York: Russell Sage, 1969.

Warren, V. L., & Cairns, R. B. Social reinforcement satiation: An outcome of frequency or ambiguity? *Journal of Experimental Child Psychology,* 1972, *13,* 249–260.

Weiner, B. *Achievement motivation and attribution theory.* Morristown, N.J.: General Learning Press, 1974.

Weiner, B. *Theories of motivation.* Chicago: Markham, 1972.

Reading 42

Development of Moral Thought, Feeling, and Behavior

Martin L. Hoffman

Research on moral development has proceeded without letup for over half a century. One reason for the sustained interest is the topic's obvious social significance in an urban industrialized society characterized by increasing crime, declining religious involvement, and events like Watergate, Jonestown, and the Kitty Genovese murder, which are brought home by the mass media. More fundamentally, morality is the part of personality that pinpoints the individual's very link to society, and moral development epitomizes the existential problem of how humans come to manage the inevitable conflict between personal needs and social obligations.

The legacy of Freud and Durkheim is the agreement among social scientists that most people do not go through life viewing society's moral norms (e.g., honesty, justice, fair play) as external, coercively imposed pressures. Though initially external and often in conflict with one's desires, the norms eventually become part of one's motive system and affect behavior even in the absence of external authority. The challenge is to discover what types of experience foster this internalization. The research, which initially focused on the role of parents, has now expanded to include peers and the mass media as well as cognitive development and arousal of affects such as empathy and guilt. The aim here is to pull together relevant findings and theories, drawing heavily from previous critical reviews (Hoffman, 1977, 1978, 1980).

CHILD-REARING PRACTICES AND MORAL INTERNALIZATION

Since the parent is the most significant figure in the child's life, every facet of the parent's role—disciplinarian, affection giver, model—has been studied.

Discipline and Affection

Moral internalization implies that a person is motivated to weigh his or her desires against the moral requirements of a situation. Since one's earliest experience in handling this type of conflict occurs in discipline encounters with parents, and since discipline encounters occur often in the early years—about 5–6 times per hour (see, e.g., Wright, 1967)—it seems reasonable that the types of discipline used by parents will affect the child's moral development. Affection is important because it may make the child more receptive to discipline, more likely to emulate the parent, and emotionally secure enough to be open to the needs of others.

A large body of research done mainly in the 1950s and 1960s dealt with correlations between types of discipline and moral indices such as resisting temptation and feeling guilty over violating a moral norm. The findings (reviewed by Hoffman, 1977) suggest that moral internalization is fostered by (a) the parent's frequent use of inductive discipline techniques, which point up the harmful consequences of the child's behavior for others, and (b) the parent's frequent expression of affection outside the discipline encounter. A morality based on fear of external punishment, on the other hand, is associated with excessive power-assertive discipline, for example, physical punishment, deprivation of privileges, or the threat of these. There is also evidence that under certain conditions—when the child is openly and unreasonably defiant—the occasional use of power assertion by parents who typically use induction may contribute positively to moral internalization (Hoffman, 1970a).

The mid-1960s saw a shift from correlational to experimental research. In the most frequently used paradigm the child is first trained, or "socialized," by being presented with several toys. When the child handles the most attractive one, he or she is punished (e.g., by an unpleasant noise, the intensity and timing of which varies). The child is then left alone and observed surreptitiously. Resistance-to-temptation scores are based on whether or not, how soon after the experimenter left, and for how long the child plays with the forbidden toy. Recently, a verbal component had been added—a simple prohibition or a complex, inductionlike reason. The general findings are that (a) with no verbal component, intensity and timing of punishment operate as they do in animals—the child deviates less when training consists of intense punishment applied at the onset of the act; (b) with a verbal component, these effects are reduced; and (c) the verbal component is more effective with mild than severe punishment and with older than younger children.

Both types of research are limited. Thus it may seem as plausible to infer from the correlations that the child's moral internalization contributes to the parent's use of inductions as it is to infer the reverse. I have argued, however, that although causality cannot automatically be inferred from correlations, in this case the evidence warrants doing so (Hoffman, 1975a), at least until the critical research employing appropriate (e.g., cross-lagged longitudinal) designs has been done. The experimental research, on the other hand, lacks ecological validity, since the socialization process is telescoped. In addition, the distinction between moral action and compliance with an arbitrary request is blurred, since compliance is used as the moral index. Compliance is also a questionable index in light of Milgram's finding that it may at times lead to immoral action. Despite these flaws, the experiments are useful because they may tell something about the child's immediate response to discipline, and as such, the findings are compatible with the correlational research (Hoffman, 1977).

I recently proposed a theoretical explanation of the findings (Hoffman, Note 1). Briefly, it consists of the following points: (a) Most discipline techniques have power-assertive and love-withdrawing properties, which comprise the motive-arousal component needed to get the child to stop and pay attention to the inductive component that may also be present. (b) The child may be influenced cognitively and affectively, through arousal of empathy and guilt, by the information in the inductive component and may thus experience a reduced sense of opposition between desires and external demands. (c) Too little arousal and the child may ignore the parent; too much, and the resulting fear or resentment may prevent effective processing of the inductive content. Techniques having a salient inductive component ordinarily achieve the best balance. (d) The ideas in inductions (and the associated empathy and guilt) are encoded in "semantic" memory and are retained for a long time, whereas the details of the setting in which they originated are encoded in "episodic" memory and are soon forgotten. (e) Eventually, lacking a clear external referent to which to attribute the ideas, they may be experienced by the child as originating in the self.

Parent as a Model

It has been assumed since Freud that children identify and thus adopt the parents' ways of evaluating one's own behavior. The intriguing question is, Why does the child do this? Psychoanalytic writers stress anxiety over physical attack or loss of the parent's love. To reduce anxiety, the child tries to be like the parent—to adopt the parent's behavioral mannerisms, thoughts, feelings, and even the capacity to punish oneself and experience guilt over violating a moral standard. For other writers, the child identifies to acquire desirable parent characteristics (e.g., privileges, control of resources, power over the child).

The research, which is sparse, suggests that identification may contribute to aspects of morality reflected in the parent's words and deeds (e.g., type of moral reasoning, helping others). It may not contribute to feeling guilty after violating moral standards (Hoffman, 1971), however, perhaps because parents rarely communicate their own guilt feelings to the child, children lack the cognitive skills needed to infer guilt feelings from overt behavior, and children's motives to identify are not strong enough to overcome the pain of self-criticism.

In the early 1960s Bandura suggested that identification is too complex a concept; imitation is simpler, more amenable to research, yet equally powerful as an explanatory concept. Numerous experiments followed. Those studying the effects of adult models on moral judgment and resistance to temptation in children (reviewed by Hoffman, 1970b) are especially pertinent. The results are that (a) children will readily imitate an adult model who yields to temptation (e.g., leaves an assigned task to watch a movie), as though the model serves to legitimize the deviant behavior, but they are less likely to imitate a model who resists temptation. (b) When a child who makes moral judgments of others on the basis of consequences of their acts is exposed to an adult model who judges acts on the basis of intentions, the child shows an increased understanding of the principle of intentions, and the effect may last up to a year.

It thus appears that identification may contribute to the adoption of visible moral attributes requiring little self-denial, which may become internalized in the sense that the child uses them as criteria of right and wrong in judging others, but it may not contribute to the use of moral standards as an evaluative perspective for examining his or her own behavior.

PEER INFLUENCE

Despite the interest, there is little theorizing and still less research on the effects of peers. The theories boil down to three somewhat contradictory views about the effects of unsupervised peer interaction: (1) Since gross power differentials do not exist, it allows everyone the kind of experiences (role taking, rule making, rule enforcing) needed to develop a morality based on mutual consent and cooperation among equals (Piaget, 1932). (2) It may release inhibitions and undermine the effects of prior socialization—a view reflected in Golding's novel *Lord of the Flies* and Le Bon's (1895/1960) notions about collective behavior. (3) Both 1 and 2 are possible, and which one prevails depends, among other things, on the hidden role of adults (Hoffman, 1980). For example, 1 may operate when the children come from homes characterized by frequent affection and inductive discipline. Parents may also play a more direct, "coaching" role, as when they do not just take their child's side in an argument with a peer but sometimes provide perspective on the other child's point of view.

The research indicates that parental influence wanes and peer groups become more influential as children get older (Devereux, 1970). The direction of the influence is less clear. Some studies report broad areas of agreement between peer and adult values (e.g., Langworthy, 1959). Others show disagreement—radical disagreement, as in the finding by Sherif et al. (1961) that newly formed unsupervised groups of preadolescent boys may undermine the preexisting morality of some members, or modest differences in emphasis, as in high school subcultures stressing athletics and popularity rather than academic achievement (see, e.g., Coleman, 1961). There is no evidence that children are more apt to endorse peer-sponsored misbehavior as they get older, and that this may reflect a growing disillusionment with the good will of adults rather than an increasing loyalty to peers, whose credibility may actually decline (Bixenstine, DeCorte, & Bixenstine, 1976). Finally, the peer-model research (reviewed by Hoffman, 1970b) suggests that exposure to a peer who behaves aggressively or yields to temptation and is not punished increases the likelihood that a child will do the same; if the model is punished, the subject behaves as though there were no model. These findings suggest that if children deviate from adult moral norms without punishment, as often happens outside the home, this may stimulate a child to deviate; if they are punished, however, this may not serve as a deterrent. The immediate impact of peer behavior may thus be more likely to weaken than to strengthen one's inhibitions, at least in our society.

SEX-ROLE SOCIALIZATION AND MORAL INTERNALIZATION

Contrary to Freud and others, females appear to be more morally internalized than males, and their moral values are also more humanistic (Hoffman, 1975b). The difference may be due partly to the fact that parents of girls more often use inductive discipline and express affection (Zussman, 1978). More broadly, since females have traditionally been socialized into the "expressive" role (Johnson, 1963)—to give and receive affection and to be responsive to other people's needs—they are well equipped to acquire humanistic moral concerns. Boys are also socialized this way, but as they get older they are increasingly instructed in the "instrumental" character traits and skills needed for occupational success, which may often conflict with humanistic moral concerns (e.g., Burton, Note 2, found that under high achievement pressure, parents may communicate that it is more important to succeed than to be honest). Since females may now be receiving more instrumental socialization than formerly, the sex difference in morality may soon diminish.

TELEVISION

The burgeoning work on effects of television on aggression and helping is tangential to mainstream research on moral development, but any assessment of social influences would be incomplete without reference to it. It may also be useful to provide an alternative to the frequent assumption that important effects have been demonstrated (see, e.g., Murray, 1973; Stein & Friedrich, 1975). To begin, the correlations between watching violent television programs and behaving aggressively are inconclusive because the causality is unclear. The one study that used a cross-lagged design and found that a childhood preference for violent programs relates to aggressive behavior in adolescence (Eron, Huesmann, Lefkowitz, & Walder, 1972) may have serious flaws (see, e.g., Kaplan, 1972).

Numerous experiments done mainly in the 1960s showed that children exposed to a live or filmed model behaving aggressively—or helping or sharing—are apt to behave like the model shortly afterward. It thus appeared that the content of television programs might affect children's moral development. To demonstrate this convincingly, however, may require controlling the television viewing of children and observing their social behavior over an extended time in a natural setting. This has been done in four studies. I will summarize one (Friedrich & Stein, 1973). For four weeks, children in a summer nursery school watched three 20-minute episodes per week of an aggressive (*Batman* or *Superman*), neutral, or prosocial (*Mister Rogers' Neighborhood*) program. Measures of interpersonal aggression (physical and verbal) and prosocial behavior (cooperation and nurturance) were based on observations made during free play for two weeks before, during, and following the exposures. The only expected effect found in the postexposure period was a decline in prosocial behavior by middle-class children who saw the aggressive film. It was also found, however, contrary to expectations, that lower-class girls who saw the aggressive film showed an increase in prosocial behavior, and the total sample showed an increase in aggression when exposed to either the aggressive or prosocial film. It is difficult to make sense of these findings, as well as those obtained in the other three studies (see review by Hoffman, Note 3). Further research is needed, perhaps using more subtle measures of aggression and prosocial behavior. It is possible, however, that even the most sophisticated designs may not reveal long-term effects because the effects may be overridden by one's overall television experience (including newscast violence), not to mention one's actual socialization experiences as well as other pressures and frustrations to which one is exposed, which may be impossible to control. The measurable effects of television on behavior may thus be largely momentary.

COGNITIVE DEVELOPMENT AND MORAL THOUGHT

Piaget's view that cognitive development contributes to moral development continues to stimulate research. Children's moral judgment, for example, has been found to relate positively to their cognitive level, as shown in solving mathematics and physics problems, and to their ability to take the role of others (Kurdek, 1978).

Piaget thought that children under 7 or 8 years of age are egocentric and thus often miss crucial aspects of moral action (e.g., intentions). Recent research that minimizes the cognitive and linguistic demands on subjects, however, shows that even 4-year-olds consider intentions when the amount of damage is controlled (Keasey, 1978). They can also allocate rewards in a way that coordinates other children's needs and contributions in simple group tasks (Anderson & Butzin, 1978). And they recognize that norms about the human consequences of action are more important than social conventions; for example, they resist attempts to convince them that it would be all right to hit someone if the rules said so, but they are more flexible about dress codes (Turiel, 1978).

Kohlberg (1969) saw morality as developing in a series of six stages, beginning with a premoral one in which the child obeys to avoid punishment and ending with a universal sense of justice or concern for reciprocity among individuals. Each stage is a homogenous, value-free, moral cognitive structure or reasoning strategy; moral reasoning within a stage is consistent across different problems, situations, and values. Each stage builds on, reorganizes, and encompasses the preceding one and provides new perspectives and criteria for making moral evaluations. People in all cultures move through the stages in the same order, varying only in how quickly and how far they progress. The impetus for movement comes from exposure to moral structures slightly more advanced than one's own. The resulting cognitive conflict is resolved by integrating one's previous structure with the new one.

Kohlberg's theory has been criticized as follows (Hoffman, 1970b, 1980; Kurtines & Greif, 1974): The stages do not appear to be homogeneous or to form an invariant sequence. There is no evidence that exposure to appropriate levels of moral reasoning inevitably leads to forward movement through the stages or that it leads to "structural" rather than value conflict. Though low positive correlations exist between moral reasoning and moral behavior, the stages are not associated with distinctive patterns of behavior. These problems may be due to the manner of scoring moral reasoning, and future research with the new scoring system (Kohlberg, Colby, Speicher-Dubin, & Lieberman, Note 4) may produce different results. The theory has also been criticized for neglecting motivation which may be needed to translate abstract moral concepts into action (Peters, 1971), and for having a western, a male, and a "romantic individualistic" bias (Hogan, 1975; Samson, 1978; Simpson, 1974).

Cognitive conflict may underlie the previously noted finding that adult models affect children's moral judgments (see "Parent as Model" section above). Since the subjects' understanding of intentions was increased and the effect lasted long, they were not mindlessly imitating the model. Rather, they probably knew the difference between accidental and intended action initially (as noted, even 4-year-olds know this) but were influenced by the more severe consequences in the accident stories. Exposure to adults who repeatedly assign more weight to intentions despite the disparity in consequences must therefore have produced cognitive conflict, which may have led the subjects to change their minds. This interpretation does not assume that cognitive conflict always leads to progressive change, since models who espouse consequences, the less mature response, might have similar effects.

Whether or not cognitive-conflict theory is confirmed, it has called attention to people's active efforts to draw meaning from experience. It has also led to a new approach to moral education (Kohlberg, 1973): Different moral stages are assumed to be represented in the classroom; in discussing moral dilemmas lower-stage children are thus exposed to higher-stage reasoning, and in the course of handling the resulting conflict their moral levels advance. This approach appeals to educators partly because they are not expected to make moral judgments or state their values. They need only present moral dilemmas, foster discussion, and occasionally clarify a child's statement. In actual practice, the children are also encouraged to participate in decisions about making rules and assigning punishments for violating them. Should the program be effective, it will therefore still remain for research to determine whether cognitive conflict is necessary.

EMPATHY AND PROSOCIAL BEHAVIOR

Empathy, the vicarious emotional response to another person, has long interested social thinkers. Philosophers like David Hume and Adam Smith and early personality theorists like Stern, Sheler, and McDougall all saw its significance for social life. Despite the interest, there has been little theory or research. The topic is discussed below in some detail, nevertheless, because it bears on the affective side of morality, which has long been neglected. The focus thus far has been on the response to someone in distress, since this seems central to morality. A brief summary of a developmental theory of empathic distress (Hoffman, 1975c, 1978) follows.

When emphathically aroused, older children and adults know that they are responding to something happening to someone else, and they have a sense of what the other is feeling. At the other extreme, infants may be empathically aroused without these cognitions. Thus, the experience of empathy depends on the level at which one cognizes others. The research suggests at least four stages in the development of a cognitive sense of others: for most of the first year, a fusion of self and other; by 11–12 months, "person permanence," or awareness of others as distinct physical entities; by 2–3 years, a rudimentary awareness that others have independent inner states—the first step in role taking; by 8–12 years, awareness that others have personal identities and life experiences beyond the immediate situation.

Empathy thus has a vicarious affective component that is given increasingly complex meaning as the child progresses through these four stages. I now describe four levels of empathic distress that may result from this coalescence of empathic affect and the cognitive sense of the other: (1) The infant's empathic response lacks an awareness of who is actually in distress (e.g., an 11-month-old girl, on seeing a child fall and cry, looked like she was about to cry herself and then put her thumb in her mouth and buried her head in her mother's lap, which is what she does when she is hurt). (2) With person permanence, one is aware that another person and not the self is in distress, but the other's inner states are unknown and may be assumed to be the same as one's own (e.g., an 18-month-old boy fetched his own mother to comfort a crying friend, although the friend's mother was also present). (3) With the beginning of role taking, empathy becomes an increasingly veridical response to the other's feelings in the situation. (4) By late childhood, owing to the emerging conception of self and other as continuous persons with separate histories and identities, one becomes aware that others feel pleasure and pain not only in the situation but also in their larger life experience. Consequently, though one may still respond empathically to another's immediate distress, one's empathic response is intensified when the distress is not transitory but chronic. This stage thus combines empathically aroused affect with a mental representation of another's general level of distress or deprivation. If this representation falls short of the observer's standard of well-being, an empathic distress response may result even if contradicted by the other's apparent momentary state, that is, the representation may override contradictory situational cues.

With further cognitive development, one can comprehend the plight of an entire class of people (e.g., poor, oppressed, retarded). Though one's distress experience differs from theirs, all distress has a common affective core that allows for a generalized empathic distress capability. Empathic affect combined with the perceived plight of an unfortunate group may be the most advanced form of empathic distress.

These levels of empathic response are assumed to form the basis of a motive to help others; hence their relevance to moral development. A summary of the research follows: (a) Very young children (2–4 years) typically react empathically to a hurt child, although they sometimes do nothing or act inappropriately (Murphy, 1937; Zahn-Waxler, Radke-Yarrow, & King, 1979). (b) Older children and adults react empathically too, but this is usually followed by appropriate helping behavior (see, e.g., Leiman, Note 5; Sawin, Note 6). (c) The level of empathic arousal and the speed of a helping act increase with the number and intensity of distress cues from the victim (see, e.g., Geer & Jarmecky, 1973). (d) The level of arousal drops following a helping act but continues if there is no attempt to help (see, e.g., Darley & Latané, 1968).

These findings fit the hypothesis that empathic distress is a prosocial motive. Some may call it an egoistic motive because one feels better after helping. The evidence suggests, however, that feeling better is usually not the *aim* of helping (see, e.g., Darley & Latané, 1968). Regardless, any motive for which the arousal condition, aim of ensuing action, and basis for gratification in the actor are all contingent on someone else's welfare must be distinguished from obvious self-serving motives like approval, success, and material gain. It thus seems legitimate to call empathic distress a prosocial motive, with perhaps a quasi-egoistic dimension.

Qualifications are in order. First, though helping increases with intensity of empathic distress, beyond a certain point empathic distress may become so aversive that one's attention is directed to the self, not the victim. Second, empathic distress and helping are positively related to perceived similarity between observer and victim: Children respond more empathically to others of the same race or sex and, with cognitive development, to others perceived as similar in abstract terms (e.g., similar "personality traits"). These findings suggest that empathic morality may be particularistic, applied mainly to one's group, but they also suggest that moral education programs which point up the similarities among people, at the appropriate level of abstraction, may help foster a universalistic morality.

Despite the qualifications, a human attribute like empathy that can transform another's misfortune into distress in the self demands the attention of social scientists and educators for its relevance both to moral development and to bridging the gap between the individual and society.

GUILT

The reemergence of interest in affective and motivational aspects of morality includes a revived interest in guilt. I have suggested a relation between guilt and empathy (Hoffman, 1976), summarized as follows: The attribution research suggests a human tendency to make causal inferences about events. One can thus be expected to make inferences about the cause of a victim's distress, which serve as additional inputs in shaping one's affective empathic response. If one is the cause of the distress, one's awareness of this may combine with the empathic affect aroused to produce a feeling of guilt (not the Freudian guilt which results when repressed impulses enter consciousness).

I have been constructing a developmental theory of guilt that highlights the importance of empathic distress and causal attribution (Hoffman, in press-b). Space permits mentioning only that the guilt stages correspond roughly to the empathy stages described above and that some gaps in the theory reflect a lack of research on certain aspects of cognitive development such as the awareness that one has choice over one's actions and that one's actions have an impact on others, as well as the ability to contemplate or imagine an action and its effects (necessary for anticipatory guilt and guilt over omission).

A summary of the findings follows: (a) A full guilt response appears in children as young as 6 years (Thompson & Hoffman, in press), and a rudimentary one appears in some 2-year-olds (Zahn-Waxler et al., 1979). (b) As noted earlier, discipline that points up the effects of the child's behavior on others contributes to guilt feelings. (c) Arousal of empathic distress appears to intensify guilt feelings (Thompson & Hoffman, in press). (d) Guilt arousal is usually followed by a reparative act toward the victim or toward others (see, e.g., Regan, 1971) or, when neither is possible, a prolongation of the guilt. (e) Guilt arousal sometimes triggers a process of self-examination and reordering of values, as well as a resolution to act less selfishly in the future (Hoffman, 1975b). It is interesting that this response, which should contribute to moral development, might be missing in children who are too "good" to transgress and thus may not have the experience of guilt. The findings suggest, somewhat paradoxically, that guilt, which results from immoral action, may operate as a moral motive.

CONCLUDING REMARKS

To pull together the findings and most promising concepts, I suggest three somewhat independent moral internalization processes, each with its own experiential base:

1 People often assume that their acts are under surveillance. This fear of ubiquitous authority may lead them to behave morally even when alone. The socialization experiences leading to this orientation may include frequent power-assertive and perhaps love-withdrawing discipline, which results in painful anxiety states becoming associated with deviant behavior. Subsequently, kinesthetic and other cues produced by the deviant act may arouse anxiety, which is avoided by inhibiting the act. When the anxiety becomes diffuse and detached from conscious fears of detection, this inhibition of deviant action may be viewed as reflecting a primitive form of internalization (perhaps analogous to the Freudian superego).

2 The human capacity for empathy may combine with the cognitive awareness of others and how others are affected by one's behavior, resulting in an internal motive to consider others. As contributing socialization experiences, the research suggests exposure to inductive discipline by parents who also provide adequate affection and serve as models of prosocial moral action (e.g., they help and show empathic concern for others rather than blame them for their plight). Reciprocal role taking, especially with peers, may also heighten the individual's sensitivity to the inner states aroused in others by one's behavior; having been in the other's place helps one know how the other feels in response to one's behavior.

3 People may cognitively process information at variance with their preexisting moral conceptions and construct new views that resolve the contradiction. When they do this, they will very likely feel a special commitment to—and in this sense internalize—the moral concepts they have actively constructed.

These processes are not stages. The first, in one

form or another (e.g., anxiety over retribution by God), may be pervasive in all ages and most cultural groups. The second may also occur in all ages, though primarily in humanistically oriented groups. The third may be true mainly among adolescents in groups for whom intellectually attained values are important.

The three processes may develop independently, since their presumed socialization antecedents differ. They may sometimes complement one another, as when the rudimentary moral sense originating in the child's early capacity for empathy and in discipline encounters contributes direction for resolving moral conflicts in adolescence. They may sometimes be noncomplementary, as when an early, anxiety-based inhibition prevents a nonmoral behavior from occurring later, when its control might be acquired through moral conflict resolution. Perhaps the processes are best viewed as three components of a moral orientation, with people varying as to which one predominates, and individual differences being due to cognitive abilities and socialization. A mature orientation in our society would then be based predominantly on empathic and cognitive processes, and minimally on anxiety. The challenge is to find ways to foster this morality. Whether this is possible in the context of the prevailing competitive-individualistic ethic is problematic. The finding by Burton (Note 2) noted earlier highlights the dilemma confronting parents who want to socialize children for both morality and achievement.

To test hypotheses implicit in the processes suggested above and to gain new knowledge as well may require complex designs including close observations of children's behavioral, cognitive, and affective responses to a socialization agent. A longitudinal dimension will also be needed to permit cross-lagged or other analyses for assessing causality and finding out which of the agent's actions are responsible for the child's moral growth. To do all this in a single study is a tall order, but it should be feasible with the aid of new procedures such as Zahn-Waxler et al.'s (1979) method of observing children's behavior in and out of discipline encounters, over long periods of time, Cheyne and Walters' (1969) use of telemetered heart-rate data to assess children's emotional responses to simulated discipline techniques, and Leiman's (Note 5) use of videotaped facial expression to tap empathic arousal. If techniques like these were appropriately combined and modified for use in naturalistic or laboratory settings as needed, I would anticipate

new levels of knowledge about how affect and cognition interact in moral development.

REFERENCE NOTES

1 Hoffman, M. L. *Parental discipline and moral internalization: A theoretical analysis* (Developmental Report 85). Ann Arbor: University of Michigan, 1976.

2 Burton, R. V. *Cheating related to maternal pressures for achievement.* Unpublished manuscript, State University of New York at Buffalo, Department of Psychology, 1972.

3 Hoffman, M. L. *Imitation and identification in children.* Unpublished manuscript, University of Michigan, Department of Psychology, 1978.

4 Kohlberg, L., Colby, A., Speicher-Dubin, B., & Lieberman, M. *Standard form scoring manual.* Unpublished manuscript, Harvard University, Moral Education Research Foundation, 1975.

5 Leiman, B. *Affective empathy and subsequent altruism in kindergartners and first graders.* Paper presented at the meeting of the American Psychological Association, Toronto, September 1978.

6 Sawin, D. B. *Assessing empathy in children: A search for an elusive construct.* Paper presented at the meeting of the Society for Research in Child Development, San Francisco, March 1979.

REFERENCES

Anderson, N. H., & Butzin, C. A. Integration theory applied to children's judgments of equity. *Developmental Psychology,* 1978, *14,* 593–606.

Bixenstine, E. V., DeCorte, M. S., & Bixenstine, B. A. Conformity to peer-sponsored misconduct at four grade levels. *Developmental Psychology,* 1976, *12,* 226–236.

Cheyne, J. A., & Walters, R. H. Intensity of punishment, timing of punishment, and cognitive structure as determinants of response inhibition. *Journal of Experimental Child Psychology,* 1969, *7,* 231–244.

Coleman, J. S. *The adolescent society.* New York: Free Press of Glencoe, 1961.

Darley, J. M., & Latané, B. Bystander intervention in emergencies: Diffusion of responsibility. *Journal of Personality and Social Psychology,* 1968, *8,* 377–383.

Devereux, E. C. The role of peer-group experience in moral development. In J. P. Hill (Ed.), *Minnesota symposia on child psychology* (Vol. 4). Minneapolis: University of Minnesota Press, 1970.

Eron, L. D., Huesmann, L. R., Lefkowitz, M. M., & Walder, L. O. Does television violence cause aggression? *American Psychologist,* 1972, *27,* 253–263.

Friedrich, L. K., & Stein, A. H. Aggressive and prosocial television programs and the natural behavior of preschool children. *Monographs of the Society for Research in Child Development,* 1973, *38*(4, Serial No. 151).

Geer, J. H., & Jarmecky, L. The effect of being responsible for reducing another's pain on subject's response and arousal. *Journal of Personality and Social Psychology,* 1973, *26,* 232–237.

Hoffman, M. L. Conscience, personality, and socialization techniques. *Human Development,* 1970, *13,* 90–126. (a)

Hoffman, M. L. Moral development. In P. H. Mussen (Ed.), *Carmichael's handbook of child psychology* (Vol. 2). New York: Wiley, 1970. (b)

Hoffman, M. L. Identification and conscience development. *Child Development,* 1971, *42,* 1071–1082.

Hoffman, M. L. Developmental synthesis of affect and cognition and its implications for altruistic motivation. *Developmental Psychology,* 1975, *11,* 607–622. (a)

Hoffman, M. L. Moral internalization, parental power, and the nature of parent-child interaction. *Developmental Psychology,* 1975, *11,* 228–239. (b)

Hoffman, M. L. Sex differences in moral internalization. *Journal of Personality and Social Psychology,* 1975, *32,* 720–729. (c)

Hoffman, M. L. Empathy, role-taking, guilt, and development of altruistic motives. In T. Likona (Ed.), *Moral development: Current theory and research.* New York: Holt, Rinehart & Winston, 1976.

Hoffman, M. L. Moral internalization: Current theory and research. In L. Berkowitz (Ed.), *Advances in experimental social psychology* (Vol. 10). New York: Academic Press, 1977.

Hoffman, M. L. Empathy, its development and prosocial implications. In C. B. Keasey (Ed.), *Nebraska symposium on motivation* (Vol. 25). Lincoln: University of Nebraska Press, 1978.

Hoffman, M. L. Adolescent morality in developmental perspective. In J. Adelson (Ed.), *Handbook of adolescent psychology.* New York: Wiley-Interscience, 1980.

Hoffman, M. L. Empathy, guilt, and social cognition. In W. Overton (Ed.), *Relation between social and cognitive development.* Hillsdale, N.J.: Erlbaum, in press. (b)

Hogan, R. Theoretical egocentrism and the problem of compliance. *American Psychologist,* 1975, *30,* 533–540.

Johnson, M. J. Sex role learning in the nuclear family. *Child Development,* 1963, *34,* 319–333.

Kaplan, R. M. On television as a cause of aggression. *American Psychologist,* 1972, *27,* 968–969. (Comment)

Keasey, C. B. Children's developing awareness and usage of intentionality and motives. In C. B. Keasey (Ed.), *Nebraska symposium on motivation* (Vol. 25). Lincoln: University of Nebraska Press, 1978.

Kohlberg, L. The cognitive-developmental approach. In D. A. Goslin (Ed.), *Handbook of socialization theory and research.* Chicago: Rand McNally, 1969.

Kohlberg, L. The contribution of developmental psychology to education—Examples from moral education. *Educational Psychologist,* 1973, *10*(1), 2–14.

Kurdek, L. A. Perspective-taking as the cognitive basis of children's moral development: A review of the literature. *Merrill-Palmer Quarterly,* 1978, *24,* 3–28.

Kurtines, W., & Greif, E. B. The development of moral thought: Review and evaluation of Kohlberg's approach. *Psychological Bulletin,* 1974, *31,* 453–470.

Langworthy, R. L. Community status and influence in a high school. *American Sociological Review,* 1959, *24,* 537–539.

Le Bon, G. *The crowd: A study of the popular mind.* New York: Viking Press, 1960. (Originally published, 1895).

Murphy, L. B. *Social behavior and child personality.* New York: Columbia University Press, 1937.

Murray, J. P. Television and violence: Implications of the Surgeon General's research program. *American Psychologist,* 1973, *28,* 472–478.

Peters, R. S. Moral development: A plea for pluralism. In T. Mischel (Ed.), *Cognitive development and epistemology.* New York: Academic Press, 1971.

Piaget, J. *The moral judgment of the child.* New York: Harcourt, 1932.

Regan, J. W. Guilt, perceived injustice, and altruistic behavior. *Journal of Personality and Social Psychology,* 1971, *18,* 124–132.

Samson, E. E. Scientific paradigms and social values: Wanted—A scientific revolution. *Journal of Personality and Social Psychology,* 1978, *36,* 1332–1343.

Sherif, M., Harvey, O. J., White, B. J., Hood, W. R., & Sherif, C. *Intergroup conflict and cooperation: The Robber's Cave Experiment.* Norman, Okla.: University Book Exchange, 1961.

Simpson, E. L. Moral development research: A case study of scientific cultural bias. *Human Development,* 1974, *17,* 81–106.

Stein, A. H., & Friedrich, L. K. The impact of television on children and youth. In E. M. Hetherington, J. W. Hagen, R. Kron, & A. H. Stein (Eds.), *Review of child development research* (Vol. 5). Chicago: University of Chicago Press, 1975.

Thompson, R., & Hoffman, M. L. Empathic arousal and guilt feelings in children. *Developmental Psychology,* in press.

Turiel, E. Distinct conceptual and developmental domains: Social convention and morality. In C. B. Keasey (Ed.), *Nebraska symposium on motivation* (Vol. 25). Lincoln: University of Nebraska Press, 1978.

Wright, H. F. *Recording and analyzing child behavior.* New York: Harper & Row, 1967.

Zahn-Waxler, C., Radke-Yarrow, M., & King, R. M. Childrearing and children's prosocial initiations toward victims of distress. *Child Development,* 1979, *50,* 319–330.

Zussman, J. U. Relationship of demographic factors to parental discipline techniques. *Developmental Psychology,* 1978, *14,* 685–686.

Reading 43

How Children Postpone Pleasure

Walter Mischel

The child who manages to survive the long pre-Christmas wait without unwrapping one of the beckoning gifts when mother's back is turned has obviously developed some kind of will power. If he or she tears off the ribbon and paper and enjoys momentary possession of the glittering prize, it might be lost forever when the transgression is discovered. The choice, of course, is made easier by the child's knowledge that to succumb to temptation might mean losing the prize—and being punished as well.

But children are not born with the ability to wait for pleasures, and unless they learn to tolerate delay they will have a difficult time coping with frustration. Without the basic ability to postpone immediate gratification for the sake of eventual rewards, people could not plan for the future, work for distant goals, or sacrifice personal indulgences for the good of the group. Because of its importance, the origins and components of the ability—or inability—to delay gratification for future payoffs have been studied by many researchers all over the world, with children and adults from different economic, racial, and cultural groups, such as the Baganda of Africa, Palestinian refugees, French schoolchildren, East Indian and black children in Trinidad, and the predominantly middle-class children who attend the Bing Nursery School at Stanford University.

Thus far we have found that the ability to postpone pleasure for the sake of later gain is not a general predisposition that transcends all situations. Delay of gratification is a complex process that depends as much on the nature of the waiting situation and the particular goal as on any general characteristic or disposition of the individual.

Our current understanding of how children acquire will power integrates processes of mental development with elements of social-learning theory (focusing on the child's history of rewards or punishment together with the consequences he sees others reap for their actions and those he expects for his own). In our research we have tried to discover the processes through which delay of gratification becomes possible and the ways that children talk and think themselves into exerting will power. We find that what a child thinks and what he is able to understand play a major role in determining whether self-control will be excruciatingly difficult or trivially easy.

Infants, as every parent knows, have little capacity to delay anything. When they are hungry, cold, hot, sleepy, or cross, they make their needs known to all within earshot. Slowly, with experience and as the mind matures, the child begins to comprehend that not everything can go his way; he must learn to tolerate a gap between his wishes and their realization. Such toleration requires fairly complex mental skills.

As one measure of the progress of a child's ability to delay gratification, we ask the child to choose between a small treat or present now and a bigger or better one later. We can vary the kind of reward, the length of the delay (from a few minutes to a few weeks), what happens during the delay, and so on. Before each experiment, we determine that our rewards—cookies, pretzels, marbles, toys, small prizes—really do appeal to the children. They then choose between the immediate possession of something that had moderate appeal (a small notebook, one marshmallow) and the later gift with greater appeal (a bigger and better notebook, two marshmallows).

Although these rewards sometimes seem trivial to adults, they are carefully selected to be meaningful and desirable for the particular samples of children we study. The immediate and delayed rewards also are close enough in value so that a conflict is created and children are faced with a genuine dilemma: Should they continue to wait for the prize they prefer or settle now for a less preferred but immediately available satisfaction?

What mental activities help a child to go on waiting? There has been much speculation about how attention to delayed but desired rewards affects a child's ability to wait for them. Most theorists have suggested that attention to the rewards during delay enhances the ability to continue waiting, for example, by allowing the child somehow to "bind time," or by encouraging "anticipatory gratification" as the child imagines vividly how pleasant the delayed reward will be. This extensive theorizing, however, until recently was not based on actual research. Therefore E. B. Ebbesen and I tried to find out how attention to the rewards involved really affects a child's ability to wait.

We taught preschool children a game in which they could summon an adult by using a signal. To start the game, the experimenter lifted a cake tin, revealing two sets of rewards lying there (two cookies and five small pretzels). The experimenter asked the child which of the two rewards he liked better, and after the child chose, she explained carefully that she would have to leave for a while but the child could signal at any time for her return. If the child signaled he would get the less desirable treat at once, but if he waited without signaling until the adult returned "by herself" he would get the treat he preferred. Children in one group waited with both treats facing them. Another group of children had no treats in front of them during the delay. Youngsters in a third and fourth group waited with either the immediate but less desirable reward or the delayed treat they preferred in front of them. Each child always waited alone while the experimenter observed through a one-way mirror.

The results were the opposite of what most theories had predicted. When both sets of rewards were in front of them, the nursery-school children were able to restrain themselves for only about one minute before calling the adult. With no treats in view, they waited an average of 11 minutes. In the other situations they waited an intermediate amount of time. Similar results have been found in other studies with other groups of children and other types of rewards: Voluntary (self-imposed) delay is easier when the rewards are out of sight.

To find out why, we observed other preschoolers in what had proved to be the worst situation—with both the immediate reward and the delayed one directly in front of them. To get insight into their thoughts we created Mr. Talk Box, a tape recorder and microphone that cheerfully introduced itself to the children. "Hi," it said, "I have big ears and I love it when children fill them with all the things they think and feel, no matter what." Thereafter, Mr. Talk Box adopted a permissive attitude and made approving but noncommittal noises to whatever a child said. Children loved this game and proceeded to reveal to Mr. Talk Box some of their strategies for coping with delay.

The preschoolers who waited the longest in the face of temptation were those who could transform the frustration of postponement into a pleasurable time. They did anything but look at the treats on the table. Some covered their eyes with their hands, rested their heads on their arms, or generated their own diversions. Some talked to themselves or made up little songs ("This is such a pretty day, hurray"). Some invented games with their hands and feet or fiddled teasingly with the signal bell. One child, after obviously finding it unpleasant to wait, avoided further frustration by falling into a deep sleep in front of the signal bell. (These strategies will undoubtedly be familiar to any adult who has been trapped at a boring lecture.)

Once we had discovered that even young children may convert frustrating delay into a tolerable wait through self-distraction, we wondered whether it would be possible to teach children who had trouble waiting how to distract themselves pleasantly, to increase the length of time they would be able to wait for a desired but delayed goal. We soon realized that preschoolers were perfectly able to follow our direct invitations to imagine "fun things" while waiting. These three- and four-year-olds gave us many elaborate examples of things that made them feel happy—like finding frogs, or singing, or being on a swing with mommy pushing.

So Ebbesen, Antonette Zeiss, and I asked some children to think about those fun things while they waited alone for their preferred treat (a marshmallow or a pretzel). We asked others to think about the treat itself; another group had no instructions. Some children waited with the treats facing them while others waited with the treats covered. Whether the treat was in front of the children or not, *thinking* about it made them want to eat it right away. "Thinking about fun things," however, worked effectively to distract the children and increased the time they were able to wait.

Although thinking about desired outcomes generally makes it hard for young children to wait, there are important and instructive exceptions. We began to learn this when Bert Moore and I gave preschoolers the chance to see life-size pictures of rewards (two marshmallows or a pretzel for half the group; two pennies or a token for the rest) while they were waiting for them. Other children saw pictures of irrelevant items while waiting. Although the *actual* rewards had made waiting so difficult, *pictures* of them helped the children to wait. Young children

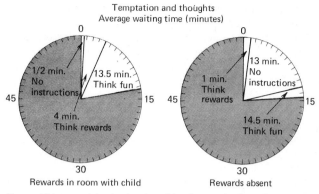

Temptation and thoughts
Average waiting time (minutes)

Rewards in room with child

Rewards absent

Young children can tolerate almost no delay if a promised treat is before them—unless they can distract themselves with pleasant thoughts.

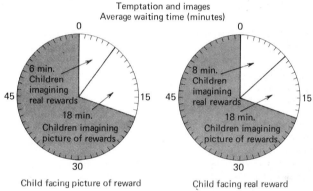

Temptation and images
Average waiting time (minutes)

Child facing picture of reward

Child facing real reward

Whether children are confronted with a promised treat or a picture of it, they can wait longest if they imagine the reward as a picture.

cannot delay when the frustration-inducing objects are right in front of them, but a symbolic reminder of what they will get if they wait seems to be highly effective—sometimes even more effective than simple distraction.

Moore, Zeiss, and I repeated this experiment with a significant variation. Children chose between two marshmallows and a pretzel. Children in one group saw a slide of the alternatives (the one they preferred and would get if they managed to wait, and the less preferred one they would get if they could not wait); children in another group waited with both sets of actual rewards in front of them. Then, regardless of what was physically facing them, we asked half of the children in each group to imagine a *picture* of the rewards. For instance, we said: "Close your eyes. In your head try to see a picture of the marshmallows and the pretzel. Make a color picture

of them; put a frame around them. The marshmallows and pretzel aren't real; it's just a picture. When I'm gone remember to see the picture in front of you."

Using comparably phrased instructions, we asked the children in each of the other situations to imagine that the *real* rewards were actually present in front of them while waiting. The results indicated that the crucial determinant of the length of time children waited was a child's mental representation, regardless of what was actually in front of the child. Twenty minutes was the maximum length of time any child had to wait. When imagining the rewards as a picture, the average delay was almost 18 minutes, regardless of whether the real rewards or a picture of them faced the child. But when the rewards were represented mentally as if they were real, the child's delay was significantly and very substantially lower, regardless of whether the picture or the actual rewards were in front of them.

Apparently the exact way that children represent the rewards in their minds affects their ability to wait for them more than the rewards' physical presence or absence. We were observing a process that may be at the root of the adult custom of transforming a goal into an abstract image, the better to work and wait for it.

The results of these and related experiments suggest a curious pattern in what helps very young children who are just beginning to develop symbolic skills postpone small pleasures. If the *actual* reward is in front of them, they can wait barely a minute before having to eat it or play with it. If they *think* about the actual reward and all of its attractive attributes, they are as frustrated as if it were actually in front of them. But a *picture* of the reward—whether literally in view or figuratively created in imagination—works like an abstract symbol that prolongs the child's ability to delay gratification and to wait for the desired reward.

As a result of follow-up experiments, we have been able to specify just what kind of thoughts about a goal or reward help children to delay gratification or make the wait difficult. If they must think about a delayed reward, they will find the wait easier if they concentrate on the reward's "cool" or abstract qualities ("marshmallows are puffy, like clouds") than if they imagine its "hot" or arousing qualities ("marshmallows taste yummy and chewy"). Indeed, abstract or cool thoughts about desired outcomes may help them wait even better than do interesting distractions. On the other hand, children who think "hot" about what they want but cannot have, dwelling on the desirable, consummatory qualities of blocked outcomes (what fun it would be to play with the shiny marbles, how sweet and crunchy the cookies taste), increase their own frustration and short-circuit effective delay of gratification.

A major lesson of the experiments at this juncture was that the same young children who could not wait because they thought about delayed rewards the wrong way (too "hot") could easily do so if encouraged to think differently ("cool" thoughts) or to distract themselves from the rewards and the dilemma of continual choice.

Of course, clarifying the conditions that help or hinder a young child's ability to delay gratification does not tell us about the child's own knowledge of these conditions. In the course of development, people generally discover the rules for effective delay, but the insights require a certain degree of mental maturity. To trace the development of children's natural understanding of how they can postpone pleasure, Harriet Nerlove Mischel and I designed another series of studies. In one study, we compared preschoolers, third graders, and sixth graders from middle- and upper-middle-class homes in Stanford, California. All the children were given the same kind of choice: for example, two marshmallows if they waited for our return, one if they rang a bell to signal that they could not wait. We asked the children what would help them wait for the two marshmallows—leaving them in view, or covering them with a cake tin—and we asked them what they could say to themselves to help them wait when the marshmallows were in front of them. (In other studies we used other treats and rewards with similar results.)

We found a clear progression in the children's expressed awareness that it helps not to attend to desired but unavailable outcomes while waiting for them. The youngest preschoolers tended to want the rewards kept in full view; by third grade, children advocated getting temptation out of the way—a strategy that was most marked among the sixth graders.

How children deal with temptation

Number who want marshmallows in view

14   10   8

Preschool Third grade Sixth grade

Number who want marshmallows covered

10   23   27

Preschool Third grade Sixth grade

Older children deal with temptation by getting it out of sight.

To see how children talk themselves into delaying gratification, we asked them, "What can you say to yourself that will help you wait?" (assuming the marshmallows, or pretzels, or other treats are in full view).

Most of the preschoolers said, "I don't know," or did not answer. Only two children under the age of five volunteered distraction as a method: "I guess I'll go into outer space. . . . (Anything else?) "I think I'll take a bath," said one who was four years and four months old. The other one (aged three years and nine months) volunteered: "I'd go over there and read. . . . I'd say 'I think I want my daddy to come home' . . . or cover it up." But they were unusual in their ability to articulate such strategies.

The third and sixth graders, in contrast, could easily specify one of several ways to maintain delay. Some said they would focus on the requirements:

"If you wait you get two marshmallows. . . . If you don't you only get one. . . . I would say it at least five times." (eight years, five months)

"Boy, Jenna, if you ring the bell you only get one. . . . Better wait for the grownup." (11 years, five months)

Other children said they would try to distract themselves:

"I wonder what I can do now . . . hum . . . I think I'll read a book until she gets back in the room." (eight years, six months)

"You can take your mind off it, and think of Christmas or something like that. . . . But the point is—think about something else." (11 years, three months)

And another popular strategy was to emulate Aesop's fox and conclude that marshmallows (or other treats in other situations) aren't all that wonderful:

"They probably don't taste very good." (eight years)

"I don't want to eat the marshmallows. . . . They're yucky." (eight years, four months)

"I'd say that the marshmallows are filled with an evil spell, and if you eat or touch it, you will be under a spell for five years." (11 years, one month)

Taken as a whole, our studies show a distinct linear progression in children's understanding of what is involved in delaying their immediate desires. Most three- and four-year-olds prefer to keep a delayed reward in full view even though seeing it makes self-control virtually impossible. Given a choice, they usually want the promised cookie right in front of them while they are waiting for it, even though the sight of the cookie is the very thing that will make waiting almost impossible. Older children begin to understand that they can resist temptation better when it is out of sight. As their symbolic capacities mature, children become able to focus on the abstract qualities of an incentive, rather than on its exciting or arousing qualities. This new ability allows them to pursue goals without constantly feeling frustrated because they are still out of reach.

Our research also suggests that the *ability* to delay gratification and the *willingness* to do so involve quite different processes. The ability requires mental maturity and the kinds of skills needed for distraction and symbolic representations of the goal to make waiting easier. The willingness to delay gratification is another matter. It is a choice that depends on specific motivations, expectations, and goals. An individual who has the capacity to delay may be unwilling to do so when the delayed outcome seems unlikely to materialize, or when it seems trivial or irrelevant. Although bigger and better marshmallows and pretzels and notebooks and erasers may be desirable for most of our young middle-class children, they may be utterly unimportant for children from other backgrounds who refuse to wait but delay readily for incentives that do matter to them.

Will power is not a simple general disposition that is exerted consistently across all circumstances. Although it depends on many things, one of its most important ingredients is the recognition that efforts at self-control succeed best when one can transform difficult situations into easier, less frustrating ones—as the mental strategies of our successful young postponers of pleasure illustrated.

For further information:

Mischel, Harriet Nerlove, Walter Mischel, and Susan Quasebarth Hood. "The Development of Knowledge about Self-control." Manuscript available from Walter Mischel at Stanford University.

Mischel, Walter. "Processes in Delay of Gratification." *Advances in Experimental Social Psychology,* Vol. 7. Academic Press, 1974.

Yates, Brian T., and Walter Mischel. "Young Children's Preferred Attentional Strategies for Delaying Gratification." *Journal of Personality and Social Psychology,* 1979, 37, 286–300.

Reading 44

Fetal Androgens, Human Central Nervous System Differentiation, and Behavior Sex Differences

Anke A. Ehrhardt
Susan W. Baker

The role of prenatal hormones in the central nervous system differentiation that mediates aspects of postnatal behavior of rats and monkeys has already been extensively reviewed. We now continue the discussion on prenatal hormone levels and their possible effects on behavior as relevant for *human* sex differences.

In the area of human behavior, evidence of fetal hormonal influences is much harder to obtain since it is impossible to design careful experiments analogous to planned animal research studies. Instead we are limited to research on spontaneously occurring clinical conditions with a known history of prenatal hormonal aberrations.

One such clinical condition will be the center of the next two chapters: the adrenogenital syndrome.

THE ADRENOGENITAL SYNDROME

The adrenogenital syndrome (AGS) is a condition in which the adrenal glands have a genetically determined defect in their function from fetal life on. The syndrome is transmitted as an autosomal recessive, which implies that both parents have to be carriers to produce one or several children with the illness. The genetic defect prevents the adrenal cortices from synthesizing cortisol. Instead the adrenal cortices release too much of another adrenal hormone that is androgenic in biological action, that is, a male sex hormone.

In the genetic female with AGS, excessive androgen production before birth masculinizes the external genitalia to varying degrees, in some cases only affecting the clitoris (enlargement) and in others also the formation of the labia (labial fusion). The masculinization of the genitalia is restricted to the external sex organs. The internal reproductive organs are differentiated as female. Postnatally, with proper endocrine management, the adrenal androgen output is regulated with life-long cortisone replacement therapy. With proper treatment, pu-

The study was supported by a grant (C1-10-CH-71) from the United Health Foundation of Western New York, the Human Growth Foundation, and the Variety Club of Buffalo, Tent No. 7.

berty, secondary sex characteristics, and female reproductive function are normal in female AGS patients, although menses tend to be of late onset (1). The masculinized external genitalia can be surgically feminized soon after birth.

The adrenogenital syndrome also occurs in genetic males, usually with no noticeable effect on the genitalia. Boys with AGS also have to be treated with cortisone; otherwise the excessive adrenal output of androgen will induce early male pubertal development. However, if corrected with early and regular cortisone replacement, boys with AGS will grow up looking like normal boys of their age.

Different subtypes of AGS occur, including one with an increased tendency to salt loss and another with hypertension. These additional traits of the clinical condition are not of particular concern here since the matter of interest in this context is the exposure to too much androgen before birth.

Genetic females with AGS are in many respects a human analogue to genetic female rats, guinea pigs, and monkeys who were experimentally exposed to androgens during the prenatal and/or neonatal critical period of central nervous system differentiation. Genetic males with AGS represent a human analogue to genetic male animals who were experimentally treated with additional amounts of androgens before and/or around birth.

Of special importance for the discussion of the effects of prenatal hormones on postnatal human behavior are those children with AGS who are regulated with cortisone at an early age, so that postnatal continuing developmental masculinization is prevented. With early regular cortisone-replacement therapy and, in the case of females, after surgical correction of the external genitalia, children with AGA grow up looking like normal boys and girls.

PURPOSE

The studies concerning the effects of prenatal hormones on behavior in human females were started at The Johns Hopkins Hospital with John Money several years ago. At that time 10 girls with progestin-induced hermaphroditism and 15 girls with early-treated AGS, between 4 and 6 years old, were evaluated and compared with matched normal control girls (2–5).* In brief, the results of these earlier studies suggested that fetally androgenized females were different from normal control girls in that they displayed a higher level of physical energy expenditure in rough outdoor play and a lesser interest in dolls and other typical female childhood rehearsal of adult female roles in fantasy and play; they were also more often identified as long-term tomboys and preferred boys over girls as playmates. The question whether the behavior modifications were related to a group difference in fetal hormone history or to any other postnatal environmental variable is difficult to answer.

The goal of our more recent studies in Buffalo was to evaluate a comparable sample of fetally androgenized genetic females at another hospital to validate or disprove the findings at Johns Hopkins. In addition, we made a change in research design. In order to have both the experimental group and control group from a social environment as similar as possible, we evaluated complete families with one or more children with AGS. We also included not only genetic females but also genetic males with AGS. Females with AGS were compared with female siblings and mothers, and males with AGS were compared with male siblings. The project has two parts: one was aimed at behavior comparisons (the subject of this chapter), the other dealt with intelligence and cognitive abilities, and will be described in Chapter 4.

As to sexually dimorphic behavior, the following group comparisons will be reported: (1) genetic AGS females versus "unaffected" female siblings (i.e., female siblings who do not manifest AGS) and their mothers; (2) genetic AGS males versus "unaffected" male siblings (i.e., male siblings who do not manifest AGS).

The hypotheses can be formulated as follows:

1 Genetic females with a known history of hgh levels of prenatal androgen have been shown in previous studies at Johns Hopkins to differ as a group from normal control girls in some aspects of gender-related behavior. If similar differences in behavior can be documented for AGS females

*Progestin-induced hermaphroditism occurred in genetic daughters of mothers who had been treated with progestinic drugs during pregnancy to prevent miscarriage. The drugs sometimes had an unexpected virilizing effect on the daughters' external genitalia.

compared with unaffected female siblings and mothers who share many aspects of their social environment, this finding is more likely also related to a difference in prenatal history, rather than solely to social environmental factors.

2 Genetic AGS males may be exposed to even higher levels of prenatal androgen than normal males. If so, they may differ from unaffected male siblings in some aspects of typically masculine behavior. The underlying (unproved) assumption is that excessive androgen for the male fetus may affect the central nervous system and be related to a pronounced pattern of postnatal masculine behavior.

METHODS

Sample Selection and Characteristics

The sample for our family study in Buffalo consists of 27 patients—17 females and 10 males. This is clearly a representative sample of the clinical population seen in the Pediatric Endocrine Clinic, considering that at the time of our study only 31 patients with AGS had been seen since the clinic's inception 10 years before. The age range was 4.3 to 19.9 years for females and 4.8 to 26.3 years for males, with most of the children in middle childhood and early adolescence. Several families had more than one child with AGS. The total unaffected sibling sample consists of 11 females and 16 males with comparable age ranges (see Table 1). Eighteen mothers and 14 fathers participated in the study. Not all siblings and parents were available for all parts of the study. The respective numbers will be indicated for each comparison. The families came from social classes II to V according to the Hollingshead index (6), with a greater number from lower than from middle and upper classes.

All patients were under corrective treatment with cortisone replacement. Fourteen of the females

Table 1   Sample Characteristics

	Sex	Patients	Parents	Siblings
N	F	17	18	11
	M	10	14	16
Age range and mean	F	4.3-19.9	28-49	6.8-24.7
		10.8	37	12.93
	M	4.8-26.3	32-52	6.8-23.7
		11.8	40.5	13.22
Race	F	25 W, 2 B	29 W, 3 B	24 W, 3 B
	M			

began receiving cortisone treatment during the first year of life, usually shortly after birth. The other three patients were started on cortisone in the second, third, and fourth year of life, respectively. Surgical correction of the external genitalia varied as follows: in six patients within the first year of life, in seven patients between ages 1 and 3 years, and in four patients later in life.

Six of the male patients began receiving cortisone treatment during the first month of life. The other four patients were started on cortisone in their fifth, sixth, seventh, and eighth year of life, respectively. The latter four patients had signs of precocious male puberty at the beginning of treatment. One of these late-treated boys was excluded from the behavior study, because both he and his mother were mentally retarded and detailed interview information could not be obtained.

Behavior Assessment

The methods and, in particular, the problems of getting good measurements of gender-related behavior are still largely the same as in the earlier studies. As in the Johns Hopkins project, we were interested in long-term childhood behavior that we could operationally define and assess in interviews with the mothers and the children themselves. These interviews were conducted with semistructured schedules. The areas included in the schedule were general developmental and play-behavior items intermixed with typical gender-related behavior.

Our interview schedule included items that are related to established sex differences in the normal population. Our choice was not influenced by a particular theory that the specific behavior item was clearly culturally determined or possibly also hormone-dependent. Our primary goal was to examine the kind of gender-related behavior that has been shown to differentiate between normal boys and girls consistently and over a wide age range. Next, we wanted to compare girls and boys with a specific atypical prenatal hormonal history to girls and boys with a presumably normal prenatal history.

One of the most consistent sex differences found in normal boys and girls has to do with rough-and-tumble play and aggression (7). From an early age on, boys tend to exert more energy in rough outdoor pursuits and become more frequently involved in fighting behavior. The results are not only remarkably consistent for our own culture but have also been

noted in several cross-cultural comparisons and in nonhuman primate observations (8, 9). Thus we wanted to know whether fetally androgenized females are different from their normal sisters and mothers in this area of gender-related behavior and more similar to normal boys. Concerning boys with AGS, the question is whether, as a group, they show a higher level of intense energy expenditure and aggression than their normal brothers.

Preference of playmates is another gender-related childhood behavior in which girls, and boys typically differ. From about age 4 on, girls consistently prefer girls and boys prefer boys if they have a choice in playmates. At about the same age, sex differences in toy preferences occur. Girls typically like dolls, doll houses, toy stoves, and the like, whereas boys prefer cars, trucks, and guns. In spite of a considerable overlap between the sexes regarding play behavior, the sex differences in typical toy preferences, play activities, and choice of playmates remain fairly consistent throughout childhood (7).

Doll play probably has a very important function in preparation for the maternal role. Actually, we know very little about the response of human children to small infants or whether and when girls and boys differ in handling and care-giving behavior. Most of our evidence comes from animal studies or indirect nurturant behavior, as in response to baby dolls. Observations of free-living nonhuman primates indicate that adolescent females show more interest in infants than do males of the same age (10, 11). Numerous studies on human subjects show that girls play more and show more care-giving behavior with dolls than do boys of the same age. However, it is by no means the case that only girls respond to dolls or infants. Boys not only have the potential but often display care-giving behavior. The difference seems to be that females manifest increased readiness to respond to the young. For example, girls were found to show significantly greater nurturant responses to a baby doll than did boys of comparable ages (12). However, when the same group of children was subdivided by sex and ordinal position in their family, it was found that girls tended to be nurturant to the baby doll irrespective of having younger siblings or not, whereas boys tended to show nurturance only if they had younger siblings at home (13). This study suggests that boys may need more exposure to small infants than do girls in order to display nurturant behavior in the presence of a baby doll. The findings are in agreement with animal studies, which also suggest that males have a longer latency phase or a higher threshold before they respond to the very young of their species.

Since the response to infants is an important area in the study of sex differences, we compared AGS girls with their sisters and mothers in doll play, their attitude toward becoming a mother, and their response to infants. The question under study is whether fetally androgenized females have less interest in any aspect of maternal behavior suggestive of a higher threshold in their response to infants.

We also compared AGS males with their normal brothers on analogous items appropriately modified for boys, to see whether boys with a history of excessive androgen before birth differ in this respect from normal boys and show behavior modification toward an even higher degree of masculinity.

Another cluster of items in our interview schedule concerned gender-role preference and more arbitrary sex differences, such as interest in appearance, clothing, jewelry, and hairdo. Concerning gender-role preference, each subject was asked whether he or she would have preferred to be a boy or a girl if there had been a choice in the beginning of life and if boys or girls had more fun and advantages in society.

Concerning clothes, jewelry, and cosmetics, we were not interested in the preferred style, which obviously changes rapidly with different fashions, but rather whether the subject showed an interest in being attractive or clearly preferred functional outfits with little or no concern about looks.

The interview schedule also included specific items for adolescents—for example, dating, erotic attractions, love affairs.

Procedure

The families were referred by the Pediatric Endocrine Clinic and were asked to cooperate in our project. We informed them that we were interested in various aspects of child development in AGS patients and in their normal siblings. Furthermore, we proposed to do an intelligence study of all family members on the basis of a battery of cognitive-ability tests. The cooperation of the families was unusually good, which probably can be largely explained by their excellent rapport with the staff of the Pediatric Endocrine Division, whom they had often known for many years.

Originally we only collected data on the children.

To obtain insight into the mothers' own developmental history and to ensure that we were not dealing with a sample of unusual mothers reinforcing their own attitudes and interests in their children, we asked the mothers to return and administered a standard interview about their own developmental history, comparable to the data we had collected on their children. We were able to collect data from 13 mothers (seven mothers of female, three mothers of male, and three mothers of both male and female patients).

The interview sessions were arranged on an individual basis and were scheduled according to the family's convenience. Data were collected over several sessions for each family. Each session lasted at least 2 to 3 hours.

Every subject and her or his mother was interviewed with the same interview schedule. The items were always consistent, although the sequence was flexible, so as to be unstilted in manner. All interviews were tape-recorded and subsequently transcribed. The transcribed interviews were rated according to coding scales, with a range from two to five verbally anchored points. Agreement between answers from mothers and from children as to the same aspect of the child's behavior has been found in the past to be very high (4), so that the answers can be pooled. Two raters tabulated the data from the transcribed interviews.

Statistical Analysis

Comparison of the patient and the various control groups were statistically tested with appropriate nonparametric tests after the rating scales for each item were dichotomized (for methodological details see ref. 4).

Data on the females are based on a comparison of the 17 patients versus the 10 mothers of females and 11 unaffected female siblings of all families in our study. Ideally we would have like to use only the sisters of female patients. However, in order to increase sample size, we used all female siblings of AGS female and male patients.

Data were analyzed with a 3×2 chi-square test (14). In case of expected frequencies less than 5, the Freeman-Halton test was applied (15).

The behavior data on the males are based on 9 patients and 11 unaffected male siblings of all families. Comparisons of the two male groups were tested with the Fisher Exact Test for fourfold tables (14).

RESULTS

Fetally Androgenized Girls versus Unaffected Female Siblings and Mothers

Activity and Aggression We found that girls with AGS were significantly more often described by mothers, sisters, brothers, fathers, and themselves as having a high level of intense physical energy expenditure in comparison with the two other groups (Fig. 1). This behavior was long-term and specific in the sense of a high degree of rough outdoor play rather than a general elevation of activity level. This kind of energetic play and sport behavior has to be differentiated from hyperactivity, which interferes with the ability to focus attention and to concentrate and which was not typical for AGS females.

Girls with AGS also differed in choice of playmates. About 50% clearly preferred boys over girls most or all of the time when a choice was available. This did not hold true for the other two groups, although some of the unaffected female siblings did play with boys and some of the mothers remembered having done so in their own childhood. However, if there was a choice, it was clearly for members of their own sex.

Our data on fighting behavior were initially quite crude and centered basically only around the question as to which member of the family usually instigated fights. There is a tendency for fetally androgenized girls to start fights more frequently than females in the other two groups, but the difference was not significant. Since fighting behavior appears to be one of the most consistent sex differences cross-culturally and in comparisons between various mammalian species, we studied this behavior again and have in the meantime obtained more detailed data on aggression (as yet unanalyzed). At this point it is not clear whether AGS females are in any way different from their sisters and mothers in respect to childhood fighting behavior.

Marriage and Maternalism The second cluster of pertinent results centers around toy preferences, response to infants, and rehearsal of adult female roles. As one can see from Figure 2, AGS girls show a conspicuously low interest in dolls. About 80% were rated as having had little or no interest in dolls at any time during their childhood, whereas this was only true for a small number of sisters and mothers. The AGS girls tended to play with cars, trucks, and blocks. They also appeared to care little for future roles as bride and mother, but were much more concerned with future job roles. Female siblings and mothers, on the other hand, were described as being interested in childhood rehearsal of wedding and marriage as well as of various career roles and were in the latter aspect not different from the patients.

Girls with AGS were also more frequently characterized as being indifferent to small infants or expressing aversion to, and dislike of, handling babies. In contrast to their mothers and female

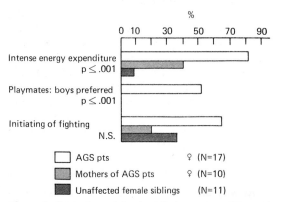

Figure 1 Comparison of female patients versus mothers and female siblings on activity and aggression. The bars represent the percentage of subjects from each group who were reported to exhibit the behavior specified by the category adjacent to the bars.

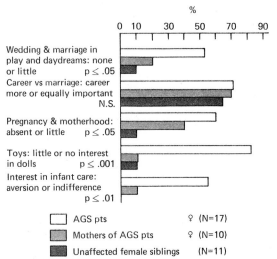

Figure 2 Comparison of female patients versus mothers and female siblings on marriage and maternalism. The bars represent the percentage of subjects from each group who were reported to exhibit the behavior specified by the category adjacent to the bars.

siblings, they often avoided caring for a baby at home and preferred not to babysit. They did not exclude the possibility of becoming a mother one day; rather their attitude was noncommittal and matter-of-fact, with little or no rehearsal in daydreams or role play about motherhood—quite in contrast to the majority of unaffected female siblings and most of their mothers during childhood.

Gender Role, Appearance, and Adolescent Dating Behavior   The next cluster of items has to do with gender-role preference and with more arbitrary sex differences, such as interest in appearance (Fig. 3). If a girl tends toward rough-and-tumble play and prefers boys and boys' toys, then she is traditionally identified as a tomboy. Fifty-nine percent of the patients were identified by themselves and others as having been tomboys during all of their childhood. This was significantly different from the sample of unaffected siblings, none of whom demonstrated this complete and long-term pattern of tomboyism. However, 27% were rated as having manifested a limited episode of some tomboyish traits during their childhood. Girls with AGS were also significantly different from the sample of mothers, only two of whom described themselves as long-term tomboys.

To the question whether it was better to be a girl or a boy, 35% of the patients were undecided or thought that they might have chosen to be a boy if such a choice had been possible. However, it is important to see these results in the proper perspective: none of the AGS girls had a conflict with her female gender identity or was unhappy about being a girl. They were generally comfortable in the female role and liked to be tomboys.

The last two items relate to clothing and appearance. More girls in the patient sample preferred functional to attractive clothing and in general were not particular about their appearance. Consistently, they were also more frequently rated as having no interest in jewelry, makeup, and hairdo than were the unaffected female siblings and the mothers during their childhood.

Our evidence on adolescent behavior is based on too few cases to make any definitive statement. Preliminary impressions tend to indicate that AGS patients are somewhat late in developing relationships with members of the opposite sex. They seem to be slow in starting to date and having their first crush on a boy. However, there is no evidence that homosexuality is increased in the patient sample. Several of the adolescent girls expressed interest in, and attraction to, boys, but were more reticent, not as eager, and possibly less skilled than the unaffected female siblings in becoming involved in a flirtatious relationship with a boy.

In summary, the comparison of female AGS patients with unaffected female siblings and mothers revealed several differences in childhood behavior. The patients tended to be long-term tomboys with a pattern of intense energy expenditure in rough-and-tumble outdoor activities, demonstrated a preference for boys over girls in peer contact, and showed little interest in clothing, hairdo, and jewelry. The patients were also less interested in playing with dolls, in taking care of small infants, and in playing bride and mother roles. They preferred trucks, cars, and building material as toys and were more concerned with the future in terms of a job or career role. They were significantly different in these respects from the other two groups. However, this behavior pattern was not considered abnormal and did not interfere in any way with the formation of a female gender identity.

Male AGS Patients versus Unaffected Male Siblings

Activity and Aggression   Boys with AGS manifested more frequently a high energy-expenditure level in sports and rough outdoor activities on a long-term basis, whereas more unaffected boys were

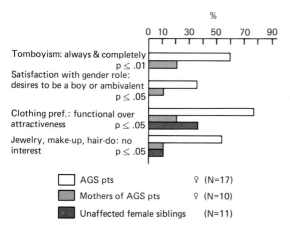

Figure 3   Comparison of female patients versus mothers and female siblings on gender-role and clothing preference. The bars represent the percentage of subjects from each group who were reported to exhibit the behavior specified by the category adjacent to the bars.

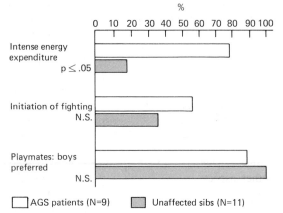

Figure 4 Comparison of male patients versus male siblings on activity and aggression. The bars represent the percentage of subjects from each group who were reported to exhibit the behavior specified by the category adjacent to the bars.

rated as having a moderate or periodic interest in sports and physical activities (Fig. 4).

There were no significant differences in fighting behavior between the two groups as judged by the criterion of initiating fights in the family and elsewhere in their environment.

Almost all boys in both groups preferred boys over girls as playmates.

Marriage and Fatherhood No significant difference was found between AGS boys and unaffected brothers in toy preferences and rehearsal of future roles of husband and father (Fig. 5). In both groups of males, very few boys were interested in dolls and other girls' toys. In both groups, some boys had thoughts and fantasies of becoming a father, although much less so than the unaffected girls who are concerned with becoming a mother. The same was true for the number of boys who liked to handle their little brothers or sisters and other small infants. The frequency was considerably lower than in the group of unaffected females, who scored 100% in the moderate and strong category.

Gender-Role Preference and Adolescent Dating Behavior The next cluster concerns satisfaction with the male gender role, which is 100% in both groups (Fig. 6). There was a total absence of effeminacy in both groups, and most of them were rated or rated themselves as extremely masculine rather than average in this regard. All boys preferred boys' clothes; approximately half in each sample had no interest in their appearance, whereas the other half had a moderate or strong interest in clothes and looking attractive. Interest in appearance *per se* is thus not specifically feminine but also a

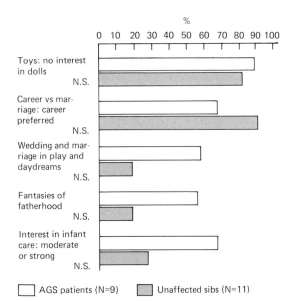

Figure 5 Comparison of male patients versus male siblings on marriage and fatherhood. The bars represent the percentage of subjects from each group who were reported to exhibit the behavior specified by the category adjacent to the bars.

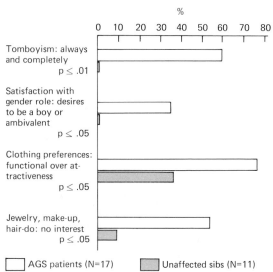

Figure 6 Comparison of male patients versus male siblings on gender-role and clothing preference. The bars represent the percentage of subjects from each group who were reported to exhibit the behavior specified by the category adjacent to the bars.

noticeable part of boys' behavior in childhood and adolescence.

The number of adolescents was too small to make a definitive statement concerning erotic attraction and dating behavior. In both groups, some boys had begun dating and had become involved in adolescent love affairs—in all cases heterosexual and with no evidence of any conflict with the male sex role.

In summary, AGS males differed from the group of unaffected male siblings in only one aspect of gender-related behavior: intense energy expenditure in outdoor play and sport activities. Otherwise, both male groups followed the typical masculine behavior pattern of our culture, with no interest in dolls, preference for boys over girls in peer contacts, some interest in the future role of husband and father, and a clear-cut preference for the masculine role.

DISCUSSION

We found that girls with AGS differed from a sample of unaffected female siblings and their mothers in certain aspects of their sexually dimorphic behavior in childhood. They were significantly more often long-term tomboys with a profile of a high energy-expenditure level in rough outdoor play, showed a preference for boys over girls in peer contact, a low interest in playing with dolls and taking care of small infants, little rehearsal of the maternal adult role as wife and mother, and little concern about the attractiveness of their appearance in clothing, hairdo, and jewelry. However, AGS girls were clearly identified in the female role, and their behavior was not considered abnormal by them, by their parents, or by their peers. Rather, they presented an acceptable pattern of tomboyish behavior in this society, not unlike tomboyism in normal females except that it occurred significantly more often in the AGS sample than in either the sibling or the mother sample.

The patients were too young to make a definitive statement concerning homosexuality. Since most of the teenage girls were already romantically interested in boys, however, it seems unlikely that we shall find a significantly higher frequency of lesbianism in girls with a history of fetal hormonal androgenization.

Our findings are in agreement with previous studies on early- and late-treated AGS females (5). Thus we have confirmed in two different hospital populations that genetic females with an exposure to endogenous masculinizing hormones after birth are different in several aspects of their sexually dimorphic behavior in childhood from a matched group of normal unrelated girls, from a sample of unaffected female siblings, and from their mothers.

The results are also comparable to findings on subhuman female primates exposed to testosterone during intrauterine development. Fetally androgenized female rhesus monkeys were found to show more rough-and-tumble play as well as more dominance behavior; they were also more similar in some other aspects of their behavior to male monkeys than to normal female monkeys (16, 17).

The consistency of results in both earlier and more recent studies suggests strongly that it is the fetal exposure to androgens that contributes to the typical profile of behavior exhibited by AGS females. This conclusion is corroborated by the fact that girls with exogenous fetal androgenization by progestinic drugs showed a very similar behavior to that of AGS girls. In the progestin-treated group the hormonal abnormality was clearly limited to the prenatal phase. In the case of AGS, however, one cannot completely rule out the possibility that postnatal hormonal abnormalities may still affect behavior development in some way, although all girls in our sample were generally well regulated on cortisone, and, in most cases, treatment was initiated shortly after birth.

Girls with the progestin-induced condition and those with the early-treated AGS have abnormalities in their external genitalia. In spite of the fact that surgical correction to normal-looking sex organs usually took place early in infancy in our previous and present studies on children with either of the two conditions, one cannot completely exclude the genital abnormality as a factor that in some way might influence subsequent behavior. One way this effect could be transmitted would be by parental attitudes toward the affected child. It is undoubtedly a traumatic experience for parents to have a baby girl born with a genital abnormality. We interviewed the parents in great depth about their reactions and any possible lurking fears. Most parents had little persistent concern about the genital abnormality at birth, especially since the appearance of their daughter's genitalia had been normal for so many years. The tomboyish behavior was not seen as related to the genital abnormality. There was usually very little parental pressure toward more femininity, which is not surprising, since the behavior in the girls with AGS was not viewed as being abnormal or masculine.

The patients typically knew that their child's medical condition was one that was affected by cortisone levels. The older girls were informed about the clitoral enlargement at birth, which usually was accepted as a minor birth defect that had been corrected. As far as the behavior was concerned, girls with AGS typically enjoyed being tomboys without any fears of being different.

In summary, from our data it is unlikely that parental or patient attitude is a significant factor modifying the particular temperamental set of behavior toward tomboyism in either sample of girls with the progestin-induced or the adrenogenital condition.

The data on AGS males suggest no difference between the patient and male sibling sample in any area assessed, except for an increase in energy level in the patient group. The even higher level of physical strength and energy in sports and play activities in the AGS sample may be related to their prenatal history of a possibly even higher level of androgens compared with normal males; in three boys it may have also been due to postnatal androgen levels before treatment was initiated. The finding in the male sample also suggests that most aspects of masculine behavior development in male childhood are not affected by the prenatal hormone abnormality in the adrenogenital condition. This result is in agreement with earlier findings by Money and Alexander (18).

If prenatal exposure to androgens modifies behavior in genetic females as in the described clinical conditions, one may assume that similar hormonal factors contribute to the development of temperamental differences between males and females in general, and finer variations of fetal hormones may also possibly influence behavior differences within the sexes. We are obviously on speculative grounds with this theory at present, but let us assume for the sake of discussion that this was a proved fact. What implications and social consequences would such a finding have? We are aware that all sex differences in human behavior are much influenced by social-environmental reinforcement of appropriate behavior for girls and boys. Thus we are not suggesting that sexually dimorphic play, toy, and peer behavior is solely determined by prenatal and/or postnatal hormone levels. We rather suggest that prenatal

androgen is one of the factors contributing to the development of temperamental differences between and within the sexes. Undoubtedly it will depend to a large extent on the interaction between prenatal hormone levels and the particular environment of the child as to what quality the specific behavior will have.

We would like to close with one other point. If prenatal hormone levels contribute to sex differences in behavior, the effects in human beings are subtle and can in no way be taken as a basis for prescribing social roles. In fact, we rather like to make an argument from the opposite point of view. If it can be documented that prenatal hormone levels are among the factors that account for the wide range of temperamental differences and role aspirations with the female, and possibly also within the male, sex, a great variety of adult roles should be available and can be adequately fulfilled by both women and men, and they should be equally acceptable and respectable for either sex.

ACKNOWLEDGMENTS

The patients in this sample were diagnosed and managed by Drs. Thomas Aceto, Jr., and Margaret MacGillivray of the Pediatric Endocrine Clinic at Children's Hospital of Buffalo, New York. Their clinical cooperation is greatly appreciated.

The data graphs were designed by the Department of Medical Illustrations, State University of New York at Buffalo.

REFERENCES

1 Jones, H. W., Jr. and B. S. Verkauf, *Am J Obstet Gynecol 109:* 292, 1971.
2 Ehrhardt, A. A. and J. Money, *J Sex Res* **3**: 83, 1967.
3 Ehrhardt, A. A., R. Epstein, and J. Money, *Johns Hopkins Med J* **122**: 160, 1968.
4 Ehrhardt, A. A., in Duhm, E. (ed.), *Praxis der Klinischen Psychologie II,* Verlag für Psychologie, Dr. C. J. Hogrefe, Göttingen, 1971, p. 94.
5 Money, J. and A. A. Ehrhardt, *Man & Woman, Boy & Girl,* Johns Hopkins University Press, Baltimore, 1972.
6 Hollingshead, A. B., *Two Factor Index of Social Position,* privately printed, New Haven, Conn., 1957.
7 Maccoby, E. E. and C. N. Jacklin, *The Psychology of Sex Differences,* Stanford University Press, Palo Alto, Calif., 1974.
8 Harlow, H., *Am Psychol* **17**: 1, 1962.

9 Harris, G. W., *Endocrinology* **75**: 627, 1964.
10 DeVore, I., in Rheingold, H. L. (ed.), *Maternal Behavior in Mammals,* Wiley, New York, 1963.
11 Jay, P., in Rheingold, H. L. (ed.), *Maternal Behavior in Mammals,* Wiley, New York, 1963.
12 Sears, R. R., L. Rau, and R. Alpert, *Identification and Child Rearing,* Stanford University Press, Stanford, Calif., 1965.
13 Maccoby, E. E. and C. N. Jacklin, *Scientific American,* in press.

14 Lienert, G. A. *Verteilungsfreie Methoden,* Anton Hain, Meisenheim am Glan, 1962, p. 88.
15 Freeman, G. H. and J. H. Halton, *Biometrika* **38**: 41, 1951.
16 Goy, R. W., *Phil Trans Roy Soc London* **259**: 149, 1970.
17 Eaton, G. G., R. W. Goy, and C. H. Phoenix, *Nature New Biol* **242**: 119, 1973.
18 Money, J. and D. Alexander, *J Nerv Ment Dis* **148**: 111, 1969.

Reading 45

The Influence of Age and Sex on Responsiveness to Babies

S. Shirley Feldman
Sharon Churnin Nash
Carolyn Cutrona

Interest in babies was assessed in 32 8–9-year-olds and 32 14–15-year-olds by 6-sec time sampling of waiting room behaviors in the presence of a live baby and by reactions to pictures of babies versus other objects. Age conferred mode differences in behavioral responsivity: adolescents made more proximal bids, 8–9-year-olds more distal bids. Males and females differed in amount of behavioral and perceptual baby interest, with girls more responsive than boys. Sex differences were virtually absent among 8–9-year-olds, but emerged during adolescence. Interpretations in terms of increased salience of sex-role stereotypes during adolescence were offered.

Sex differences, no matter what their origin, serve important social functions at the time they are manifest. However, somewhat different patterns of sex differences occur during each period of the life cycle. Within-period appraisals of behavioral sex differences help clarify the nature of the developmental tasks, while between-period comparisons provide insight into the sequence of human development.

The present research explores the emergence of sex differences in a behavior of evolutionary significance: responsivity to babies. To be viable, a society has to have enough interest in babies to nurture

them to adulthood. The infant's innate physical and behavioral characteristics are optimally designed to encourage such interest and responsivity. Despite the commonly accepted view that females more than males are attracted to infants, there is a paucity of evidence on this issue. It is not known at what ages the sexes differ in the degree or mode of their *behavioral* interest in babies.

Since responsiveness to babies is seen as stereotypically feminine, linked to childbearing and nurturing roles, we hypothesize that a sex difference in baby responsiveness will be found. The sex difference may be heightened during adolescence when uncertainty about new role demands, the salience of sexual maturation, and a heightened self-consciousness results in a retreat to the safety of stereotypes learned long ago. In middle childhood, sex roles are relatively incidental to the child's major pursuits: playing, getting along with peers, and achievement at school. Thus among younger children we predict no sex difference in responsiveness to babies.

Sixty-four middle-class subjects, equally divided by age (8–9 and 14–15 years) and sex were studied in two situations. The order of the situations was balanced across groups.

THE WAITING ROOM SITUATION

In a 6-minute episode, while awaiting a questionnaire, subjects sat in a room with two confederates:

The activities reported herein were supported by funds from Boys Town and by National Institute of Mental Health Grant 1 R03 MH28264-01. However, the opinions expressed or the policies advocated reflect only those of the authors.

a 6–10-month-old baby and its mother. Observers behind mirrors used 6-sec time sampling to score looks, smiles, funny faces/gestures, talks, gives/shows object, proximity, touch, and the target of these behaviors (adult confederate, baby). Baby's vocalizing and noisy playing were also recorded. Four scores were derived: (a) *responsiveness to baby,* a standardized composite score in which the sum of the above seven behaviors directed to the baby, plus talking to the mother about the baby are added; (b) *distal bids,* a component of the composite, equaling the sum of the number of 6-sec time intervals in which looks, smiles, shows/gives, talks, and funny face to baby is recorded; (c) *proximal bids,* a second component of the composite, is the sum of the number of 6-sec time intervals in which the subject was within 3 feet of the baby, plus the number of time intervals in which the subject touched the baby; (d) *ignores baby,* a measure of contingent responsiveness, is the sum of the 6-sec intervals in which the subject did not respond in either the same interval or the immediately following interval to the baby's vocalization or to the onset of noise from the child's toy. Interobserver reliabilities, from 36 subjects average .94.

THE PERCEPTUAL SITUATION

Subjects controlled how long each of 30 slides (of objects, babies, and people) were viewed, while an Esterline Angus recorder graphed the length of time each slide was on the screen. The order of the slides was varied for subjects according to a Latin square. From photo replicas of the slides subjects chose 5 favorites. Two measures were calculated: *picture duration,* the percentage of time spent looking at slides which was devoted to baby pictures, and *picture preference,* the number of baby pictures among the favorite 5.

For both sexes the intercorrelations among the six dependent measures were the same. Proximal and distal bids were significantly correlated with the composite measure of responsiveness to baby but did not correlate significantly with each other. Ignores baby was negatively correlated with responsiveness to baby and its component distal bids, but was unrelated to proximal bids. The perceptual measures were neither correlated with each other nor with any of the waiting room measures.

Analyses were made with Mann-Whitney tests since the assumption of normality was not met. While there were no age differences in amount of

responsiveness to baby, the two groups had different modes of relating to unfamiliar babies: More 8–9-year-olds than adolescents made distal bids to the baby while more adolescents than younger children approached the baby. In addition, more adolescents than 8–9-year-olds ignored the baby's bids for attention. No age differences were found on either of the perceptual measures. Thus, younger children appear to be inhibited in the presence of an adult. They are just as interested in the baby, but are afraid to show it overtly. Unlike the adolescents, their responsiveness is more contingent upon the baby's bids; they have less control over the situation.

For the combined age group clear sex differences emerged. Because greater responsivity to baby was predicted for girls, one-tailed tests were used. Girls were more responsive to the baby than boys. They made more distal bids and ignored the baby less. Girls also chose more baby pictures among their favorites. Although the behavioral and perceptual measures used in this study tap independent aspects of interest in babies a sex difference is consistently demonstrated. Since the inhibitory influence of the adult accompanying the infant is less likely to effect low-keyed, nonintrusive reactions to the baby, it is noteworthy that the findings are true for covert measures of interest (ignoring baby, time spent looking at the baby and the baby pictures, etc.) as well as the more overt measures.

As predicted, girls and boys 8–9-years-old were similar in the degree of interest they exhibited to a live baby, as well as to pictures of babies. However, the younger boys tended to ignore the baby more than the girls did. By adolescence, sex differences began to emerge. Girls showed a trend towards greater responsiveness to the baby, by making more distal bids. Adolescent girls chose more pictures of infants and spent a greater percentage of their time looking at baby pictures than did adolescent males.

Why should girls show this heightened interest in babies during adolescence? In our sample 5 boys and 6 girls had babysitting experience, and within each Age × Sex group none of our six measures of interest in babies was related to (self-reports of) amount of contact with or responsibility for babies. For the adolescent girl trying on new roles, at least one pathway is virtually fixed; few females at any age unequivocally decide against marriage and the nurturant role of motherhood. And although adolescent boys accept fatherhood as probable in the future, it is defined as the protector-provider role that offers little interference with career options. It appears then that by adolescence, in preparation for later roles, girls have adopted sex-sterotypic values such as baby interest into their behavioral repertoire. Are the sex differences in baby responsiveness age bound and ephemeral or do they herald the beginning of life-long sex-defined differentiation? Previous research from our laboratory suggests that clinging to this stereotypic behavior is a temporary rather than a permanent phenomenon (Feldman & Nash, in press). By adulthood, when males and females are more secure in their respective roles, there is less need to resort to stereotypic prescriptions. Being interested in babies is no longer differ-

entiated by sex among single, cohabiting, or married young adults who are nonparents, since it is not relevant to their life circumstances (as it will be in parenthood). Thus, the sex difference in responsiveness to babies found among adolescents is most likely a "crutch," a retreat to old familiar stereotypes during a period of unclear self-definition.

REFERENCES

Feldman, S. S., & Nash, S. C. The effect of family formation on responsiveness to babies. In W. Miller & L. Newman (Eds.), *The first child and family formation,* in press.

Reading 46

Fathers, Mothers, and Sex Typing

Miriam M. Johnson

In this paper the hypothesis that the father plays a more crucial and direct role than the mother in reinforcing sex typed behavior (Johnson, 1963) will be reexamined and somewhat recast in the light of further evidence. Many research findings have continued to support the conclusion that the father is important in encouraging "femininity" in females as well as "masculinity" in males. These data, many of which have been reviewed by Biller (1971) and Biller and Weiss (1970), clearly challenge the view that the degree of "femininity" in women is related to sustaining and intensifying the mother-daughter relationship and suggest instead that the father relationship is of great importance for both sexes. On the other hand, other findings indicate that mothers can by no means be discounted altogether in the sex typing process. For example, there is abundant evidence that mothers do treat male and female children differently (Kagan, 1971; Lewis, 1972) and that although "feminine" women do identify with their fathers, they do not fail to identify with their mothers (Heilbrun, 1968). Still other data seem to contradict directly the "feminizing" influence of the father on girls and suggest instead that fathers have a "masculinizing" effect (Sears, 1965; Kammeyer, 1967).

It is the purpose of this paper to specify more precisely the nature of the father's impact on sex

typing. The most important specification to be made is that there are two aspects of the feminine role—the maternal and the heterosexual. If this distinction is maintained it can be argued that while the nurturant mother role is internalized by children of both sexes, it is the paternal role that reinforces the heterosexual aspects of femininity in the girl as well as the paternal *and* heterosexual aspects of masculinity in the boy. The paternal role is being thought of here as distinctly different from the maternal role. It is not simply a male acting in the mother role.

Two hypotheses concerning the role of the father presented in the earlier paper (Johnson, 1963) will be discussed. The first hypothesis was that the father differentiates his role toward opposite sexed children more than the mother. This will be further specified along the lines that the father responds more directly to his daughter's *sexuality* than the mother does to her son's. The mother, it will be argued does differentiate her role (especially outside the middle class) toward the sexes but this differentiation is of a different sort than the sexual differentiation of the father. The second hypothesis, that the father fosters independence in both sexes, will be retained while it will be argued that this should not be equated with "masculinization." Finally, data relevant to the modified hypothesis that the father does play the pivotal role with respect to *heterosexual* behaviors in both sexes will be presented. At the end of the paper the implications of this revised theoretical model for understanding the relations between the sexes will be discussed.

The essential features of the basic model to be discussed and revised are as follows: The earliest mother relationship is primarily significant not as a focus of sex typing but rather as the basis for the establishment of "socialized" behavior in general. It is by virtue of the mother attachment that infants become "hooked into" the social system in the first place and are motivated to respond to attitudinal sanctions. The paternal role by contrast, comes into play later (in the early stages the father acts only as a substitute for the nurturant mother), is less fundamental and more specialized than that of the maternal role. It is the father who, *by differentiating his paternal role* toward opposite sexed children more than the mother, reinforces "femininity" in the girl and "masculinity" in the boy. The father promotes independence and autonomy (from the mother) in both sexes while at the same time he reinforces sex differentiated behaviors within this context. The basic elements of this model will be retained while a more precise meaning for the concepts of "masculinity," "femininity" and "differentiating behavior" will be specified.

DEFINING FEMININITY

The Significance of the Maternal Role

Essentially it has been the failure to take into account systematically the early primacy of the mother for both sexes that has made interpretation of findings regarding the father's influence on sex typing so precarious. This "primacy" derives both from the fact that she is the first object of identification[1] for both sexes and also from her being

the main socializer of both sexes during childhood. The mother's primacy can affect sex typing in several concrete respects: 1) failure to transcend the mother attachment can prevent the child from having a significant relationship with the father, 2) the mother's definition of the father and/or men would affect the child's willingness to form a solidary relationship with the father. Most importantly, however, the child's earliest relationship with the mother involves internalizing the nurturant maternal role by both sexes. In this sense it would be accurate to say that it is the maternal, not the paternal, principle which is generic and which symbolizes the common humanity of both sexes.[2]

For males, then, becoming "masculine" necessarily involves (in part at least) a rejection of the "femininity" in themselves. This view fits with the idea, most recently stressed by Chodorow (1972) in her discussion of child rearing cross-culturally, that much of learning to be "masculine" for boys involves learning *not* to be "feminine." This theory has also been an underlying theme in the work of David Lynn (1969).

1 The Maternal vs. the Heterosexual Aspects of Femininity The concept of "femininity" itself, in one sense, will be used to indicate qualities of sensitivity and responsiveness to the needs and reactions of others. Johnson, Stockard and their associates (1975) have argued that this "expressiveness"[3] need not be considered undesirable, but rather that it is a *human* characteristic par excellence which women manifest to a greater degree than men.

In order to understand the impact of the father on "femininity," however, the concept itself must be

---

[1] Parsons' (1958) definition of identification as the internalization of a reciprocal role relationship that is functional at a particular period in the child's development is being used in this paper. If one takes this view of identification, it becomes possible to postulate, as Parsons does, that the development of personality in the child involves his/her making a series of successive identifications with increasingly specialized and differentiated social roles. In this usage "being like" or "feeling like" a person and being attached to a person can both be taken as rough indices of a solidary relationship in which a system of reciprocal role expectations has been established. On the other hand, there is evidence that although felt similarity and the quality of the relationship to the parent are correlated with each other, there are considerable differences in the direction and the magnitude of their associations with measures of sex typing (Stockard, 1974).

[2] Fathers, of course, may and do participate in early child care but in so doing they are assuming the nurturant or maternal role, not what has been traditionally defined as the paternal role.

[3] In the previous paper Parsons' instrumental-expressive distinction was employed as summary terms for the social orientational differences between the sexes. In retrospect, this seems to have obscured more than it clarified because using a single dichotomy necessitated using "expressiveness" to characterize both the earliest mother-child relationship and the quite different father-daughter relationship. Further confusion was introduced because Parsons had called the mother role vis-à-vis the child "instrumental." In addition, in common sense parlance the term "instrumental orientation" is often used synonymously with "achievement orientation" or competence—a connection definitely to be avoided. Although the instrumental-expressive distinction is useful for certain purposes, especially when treated as two separate dimensions rather than as polar opposites (Johnson, Stockard, *et al.*, 1975) it needs to be carefully specified in this paper in terms of other variables.

broken down into at least two components: the nurturant or maternal component and the heterosexual component. By "heterosexual" is meant those aspects of femininity that are oriented to interaction with males in terms of their "masculinity." This would include "heterosexuality" in the specifically sexual sense but would also include general interactions with men in so far as their being "masculine" is relevant. While both the maternal and the heterosexual roles involve expressiveness the two roles are quite different with respect to power. The maternal role involves high power while the feminine heterosexual role does not. In addition the mother role is asexual while the heterosexual role is not. It is this heterosexual aspect of femininity then that the father seems to affect most.

To say that the feminine role may be broken down into maternal and heterosexual aspects is not to say, however, that "maternity" and "seduction" exhaust the possibilities of femininity. This would be as incorrect as saying that *only* mothers and fathers affect sex typing. Rather the use of these two fundamental categories reflects the basic status categories defining femininity as it develops within the family of orientation and is recapitulated in the family of procreation. Thus to make this distinction does not imply that innumerable other roles cannot be held by women.

2 Dependence vs. "Femininity" In addition to distinguishing between maternal and heterosexual aspects of "femininity" it will prove vital to avoid equating "dependency" with "femininity." Certainly it is not at all clear from the available studies on dependency that it is "normal" for women. For example, in Oetzel's summary of research on sex differences (1966) virtually all of the studies reported find girls more nurturant and affiliative than boys (pp. 330–332). On the other hand, in the summary of studies on dependency there is no consistent evidence that girls are more dependent than boys (pp. 326–327). On the basis of these and other findings, Maccoby and Masters (1970) have explicitly objected to some theorists' tendency to equate dependency with the feeling that people as people are satisfying and rewarding. In the college student study mentioned previously, Johnson, Stockard and associates (1975) were able to show that "expressive" traits in women were associated with feelings of "independence" not dependence. In fact, *among women* traits connoting "dependence" correlate

more highly with "instrumental" traits than with "expressive" traits.

Certainly much confusion in the interpretation of findings can be avoided if it is assumed that there is no inevitable connection between being psychologically self directing (autonomous) and "masculinity." If this distinction is maintained it may be seen how the father can foster *both* independence *and* sex typing in his children.

3 Non-achievement vs. "Femininity" Achievement sometimes appears to be motivated by a desire to please that may or may not arise from dependence. On the other hand, some types of achievement require high levels of independence and/or an ability to ignore what others think (Bardwick and Douvan 1971). Because of the considerations in (2) above and because of the difficulties in assessing motivation, "achievement" cannot readily be equated with "masculinity" or "femininity" *per se.*

Neither can competence be considered the prerogative of only one sex. In spite of the tendency for some men to equate incompetence with "femininity," women see themselves as being both positively expressive *and* instrumentally competent (Johnson, Stockard, *et al.,* 1975).

Especially now that women are being admitted to more and more occupational fields, the use of "choice of a 'usually masculine' job" is becoming an unreliable index of "masculinity." For all the above reasons then, the findings concerning parental antecedents of competence, ambition, careerism, etc., are at best only indirectly relevant to sex typing and therefore will not be dealt with in this paper.

4 Non-aggression vs. Femininity While positive expressive behaviors are non-aggressive, it does not follow that "aggression" can be equated with "masculinity." Rather from the present standpoint, aggression is best conceptualized as negative expressive behavior rather than as indicative of masculinity *per se.*

All of these distinctions will be utilized both implicitly and explicitly in the discussion to follow.

"THE FATHER DIFFERENTIATES MORE" HYPOTHESIS

A Middle Class Phenomenon?

It was argued previously (Johnson, 1963) that the crucial influence of the father with respect to sex typing results from his "differentiating his role" toward opposite sexed children more than the mother. The most recent findings supporting this have been reported by Block (1974). In each of four separate studies representing parents of children of four different age groups, greater paternal differentiation in child rearing orientations was found consistently. Block interprets this as indicating "the critical role of the father in encouraging sex typing and enforcing sex differences" (p. 298). On the other hand, findings which show that middle class mothers differentiate their behavior toward opposite sexed children less than working class mothers (Kagan, 1971) suggest that the mother's relative lack of differentiation may be specific to the middle class, and hence the proposition that fathers differentiate more may hold only in the middle class.

It was also argued in the earlier paper (Johnson, 1963) in connection with the proposition that the father differentiated more that there was less difference in girls' and boys' ratings of maternal behavior than in girls' and boys' ratings of paternal behavior on the nurturance-control dimension. In other words, it appeared that fathers were more nurturant toward girls and more controlling toward boys, while mothers' behavior was in the opposite direction (more nurturance for boys and control for girls) but was *much less marked*. Here too further evidence suggests that this may be more characteristic of the middle class than of the working class (Droppleman and Schaefer, 1963). It is probable that the nurturance-control dimension is too general a distinction to be related directly to sex typing. In terms of the heterosexual aspects of "femininity" the father's "nurturance" of the middle class girl may mean the same thing as the father's "control" of the lower class girl. This point will be discussed later.

Women as Objects to Men but Not Vice Versa

Although the particular findings discussed above may turn out to be specific to the middle class, there is nevertheless a precise sense in which it can be maintained that the father role does involve sex differentiating behavior more than the mother role. Furthermore this difference between the mother and the father role is very fundamental and should hold across class lines and even between cultures. In essence, the difference is that the father's role toward the girl is more directly related to control over her sexuality or is in direct response to her

sexuality than is the mother's role toward the boy. Thus the complementary role of the father to daughter is not the mirror image of that of the mother to the son. The theoretical basis for expecting this to be true derives from both psychological and social structural considerations which will be discussed in turn.

Psychological Considerations

From a psychological standpoint it may be argued that a sexual relationship between mother and child is more regressive than a sexual relationship between father and child. Precisely because of her earliest nurturing role a "seductive" mother would be a greater psychological danger to a child than a seductive father would be. Parsons (1970b) in particular has stressed the regressive implications from a psychological standpoint of mother-son incest. While the mother may want her son to be "masculine" and may "appreciate" his "manliness," even common sense observation reveals that somehow it is pathological for a mother to attempt to reinforce this by playing wife to her young son. On the other hand, it is more acceptable for a father to mildly court his daughter.

The reason a father can play "husband" to a daughter in a way that a mother cannot play "wife" to a son lies in the association of the mother relationship with dependency. The mother is the real and symbolic focus of infantile dependency needs in all cultures and a "seductive" mother would pose a threat to a child's "growing up." The "seductive" father on the other hand is not quite the same order of threat since he is "once removed" as it were from association with infantile dependency. These considerations relate to why the taboo on mother-son incest is the strongest of the incest prohibitions in all cultures and why mother-son incest is in fact much less common than father-daughter incest. All this is not to say that father-daughter incest is unpathological for the daughter, but rather to say that it is less deeply regressive than incest between son and mother is for the son.

Structural Considerations

At the structural level a basic function of the incest taboo is to force consanguineal kin groups to establish solidary relations with other kin groups by virtue of marriages between their members (Levi-Strauss, 1969; Mitchell, 1974). The rules of exchange and the acts of exchange which tie kin groups to each other are, according to Levi-Strauss, the very basis of human social organization. The important point here, however, is that it is women who are the symbolic counters in this exchange and it is men who exchange women in marriage and not vice versa. This is symbolized, for instance, in Anglo Saxon Christian marriages by the fact that it is the father who gives the bride away. It is also symbolic that white prejudice against blacks is usually phrased, "Would you want your sister to marry one?", not "Would you want your brother to marry one?" In this sense women are sexual objects or sexual property to males in the kin group in a way that men are not sexual objects or sexual property to females. In the matrilineal case it is the mother's *brother* who more often assumes the formal aspects of the father role and the mother's husband who plays the informal affective aspects. This bifuncation, while introducing complexity, does not negate the basic fact, however, that it is men who exchange women.

Levi-Strauss himself was not concerned with why it was women, not men, who were exchanged, but rather assumes it is because of male dominance or male authority which prevails in all cultures regardless of the particular roles assigned each sex. Ultimately this masculine dominance may rest on the linkage of women, through motherhood, with domesticity in all cultures. It is men, not women, who handle "external relations" and therefore "place" the children in the wider social structure. It is perhaps because of this linkage of the female with domesticity and males with *external* relations that women universally are "the second sex" at least in terms of formal power and prestige (Rosaldo, 1974).

An Illustration

The following description by Anne Parsons (1967) of the position of the daughter in a Southern Italian family reflects both the psychological and structural aspects described above. The father's (and brother's) role as defenders of "their" sexual property (to be exchanged and not consumed) as well as their own sexual responsiveness to the daughter may be seen:

> . . . The most fully institutionalized masculine role in Southern Italy, one which is defined positively and not by rebellion, is that of the protection of the honor of the women who are tabooed (p. 386). . . . Thus, the South Italian girl does not appear as inhibited or naive for

precisely the reasons that even though carefully kept away from outside men, she has in a great many indirect ways been treated as a sexual object by her father (and brothers or other male relatives) both at puberty and during the oedipal crisis (p. 387). . . . at both these points the father is highly sensitive to the daughter's femininity and the daughter is given considerable scope for exploiting this sensitivity in a very active way (p. 385).

The above described situation is generally typical of traditional societies and may be more characteristic of the working class than the middle class in the United States. As a case in point, findings in this country about the denial of freedom and punitiveness to the working class girl by her father (Droppleman and Schaefer, 1965; Elder and Bowerman, 1963) may be taken as an indication of his more traditional view of his role as protector of his daughter's sexual virtue. The lenience and nurturance toward girls found to be characteristic of the middle class father may reflect the "courtship" aspect of the same basic response to the daughter's sexuality. Thus in both cases, the paternal role affirms heterosexuality in the girl in a way that the maternal role does *not* affirm heterosexuality for the boy. The mother's *power* over the son as her child conflicts with her less powerful role as heterosexual partner.

The "Father Differentiating" Hypothesis Specified

In summary then, it appears that the hypothesis that "the father differentiates his role toward opposite sexed children more than the mother" should be amended to read that the father's role toward the girl is more directly oriented to her sexuality than is the mother's role toward the boy. The father in his relationship with the daughter both rewards and reinforces the heterosexual aspects of her "femininity"—directly by interacting with her as an "interested" male and indirectly by protecting her from "outside" males. The mother, on the other hand, does *not* play a role complementary to her son's "masculinity" in the same way the father can play to his daughter's "femininity." Her greater association with infantile dependency makes her seductiveness a psychological danger. Also her power over the son as mother conflicts with her lesser power as "wife."

The question may be raised whether the foregoing analysis would hold if fathers participated equally with mothers in infant and child care activities and mothers participated equally with fathers in non-domestic activities. Likely it would *not* hold if there literally were no sex role ascription in terms of internal and external functions. Certainly the presumption is not being made here that it would be impossible to eliminate sex role ascription. American society is moving in this direction. However, the involvement of males in early child care is proceeding considerably more slowly than the involvement of women in the labor force. So far women have remained the primary nurturers while adding external functions.

How Mothers Differentiate

Clearly it is not tenable to maintain that mothers do not behave differently toward opposite sexed children while fathers do. On the other hand, it can be maintained that even though the mother differentiates, there is a lack of symmetry between her differentiation and that made by the father. Cross-cultural and cross-class findings amply document the differential expectations and demands which mothers make on opposite sexed children (Barry, Bacon and Child, 1957; Kagan, 1971). In fact, since the mother has more to do with very early socialization in general than the father she may actually make and implement more differential demands than the father. But all this shows is that mothers and fathers share to some degree common cultural values about desirable characteristics for males and females and that mothers as primary socializers attempt to implement these values. These differential expectations held by mothers (and fathers) would essentially be irrelevant to the "father differentiating more" hypothesis as restated since it is in specific response to his children's sexuality as opposed to sex role training that he would be expected to make the distinction.

Lately too, a number of studies have appeared regarding mothers' differential treatment of male and female infants (Lewis, 1972). Here again it appears that mothers are directly reinforcing female socio-emotional orientations and masculine instrumentalness. For example, Lewis (1972) in summarizing these studies notes that one widely used method of socializing boys is to turn the infant from a face-to-face proximal position to a face-to-back position—the infant facing away from and not touching the mother. While this certainly is training for the masculine instrumental role the significant fact from our standpoint is that the mother is not

treating the male as "sex object" in a way comparable to the situation that prevails (at least potentially) between father and daughter. When the mother faces the son away from her on her lap she is not only training for instrumentalness but is symbolizing the asexual nature of the relationship. Thus although the mother is very definitely involved in sex differentiated training at a time when the father plays only a minor role, the above facts do not contradict the proposition that the mother-son relationship is a less specifically sexual one than the father-daughter relationship.

What the behavioral implications of the father's role are for the female will be discussed at a later point. First another aspect of the father role will be considered—his connection with independence from the mother for both sexes.

THE FATHER AND INDEPENDENCE FOR BOTH SEXES

In this paper the regressive consequences for the "son" of a "seductive" mother have been emphasized. Rothbart (1976) and Chodorow (1974) have stressed the regressive consequences for the daughter of the mother's favoring her as a like sexed person. To the extent that mothers tend to "identify" with their daughters more than their sons, the process of separation and individuation might be expected to be more difficult for girls than for boys. Thus from the standpoint of both males and females, the father might be expected to have an important function as a symbol of independence.

It was argued earlier (Johnson, 1963) that growing up for both sexes involves becoming emancipated from the love-dependency relationship with the mother and that the father as mother's partner, yet an outsider to the mother-child bond was in a particularly strategic position to help bring this about. In this sense, the father is seen as affecting males and females similarly—as a link with the non-domestic world. Parsons (1970a) has tended to see the father's position in a somewhat negative way, i.e., as a threat from the point of view of the child. As he puts it, the father

> constitutes the symbolic focus of the pressure from the outside world which is responsible for breaking up the 'paradise' of the child's state of blissful security with his mother (p. 40).

Firestone (1970: 53) by contrast, interprets the turn

toward the father as a positive search for power on the part of both sexes. Both would agree, however, that the breaking of the tie to the mother is equally necessary for girls as well as for boys. Forrest (1966) has also stressed the importance for the women of breaking her symbiotic ties to the mother and learning to relate to men in a non-maternal way.

There is now considerable empirical evidence that father "identification" involving both imitation and attachment does increase with age and intelligence for children of both sexes (Kohlberg and Zigler, 1967). The Kohlberg and Zigler studies appear to be yet another confirmation of the results of the numerous studies concerned with the relationship between sex of parent with whom the child is most "identified" and the child's "psychological adjustment." The most common operational definitions of "identification" in these studies are "attachment" and/or perceived or actual similarity of attitudes or traits between a child and each of his or her parents. From the present standpoint, these measures of "identification" are best understood as a rough index of the degree to which a solidary relationship exists or has existed between the identifying individual and the person identified with (see footnote 1). These studies of "identification" then have generally found that while father "identification" in males does seem to be related to psychological adjustment, mother "identification" in females does not relate at all clearly to adjustment (Johnson, 1963; Heilbrun, 1965). It would seem that the lack of correlation between adjustment and mother identification in girls may result at least in part from the dependency implications of an exclusive mother tie. Some identification in the sense of sharing a solidary relationship with the father would be expected to facilitate "growing up" which is presumably related to adjustment in both sexes.

Do Fathers "Masculinize" Women?

It is difficult to find clear cut evidence concerning the father's role in fostering feminine independence because of the general failure of most studies to distinguish "dependence" from "femininity" and within "femininity," to distinguish the maternal from the heterosexual aspects. Most empirically derived M-F tests do confound dependency with "femininity" (Johnson, Stockard et al., 1974; Lansky and McKay, 1969) and therefore findings based on them are difficult to interpret.

Much of the data purporting to show the "mascu-

linizing" influence of the father on the daughter may actually reflect the father's encouragement of the daughter's independence from the mother and concomitantly his response to her as a male. For example, Sears (1965) states that a family fearing and restricting sensual and aggressive gratification has a "feminizing" effect on both sexes. He then concludes that the intrusion of an affectionate father into the girl's rearing tends to "masculinize" her. This illustrates rather well the problem the present conceptualization would clarify. Sears is equating mothers and "morality" with "femininity" and is hence speaking of the maternal rather than the hererosexual aspect of femininity. From our standpoint the intrusion of the affectionate father certainly does not "masculinize" the girl in the sense of making her "mannish" but it may make her more independent, less emotionally restricted and at the same time more adept at interacting with males.

Other data which has been employed to argue for the masculinizing effect of males on females has come from studies of the differential effects of older male siblings on girls (Sutton-Smith et al., 1964; Kammeyer, 1967). Certainly older brothers might very well be expected to cut down on their sisters' being "little lady" types. On the other hand, overcoming emotional dependence and maternalism as well as aspiring to certain male activities should not be equated with "masculinization" in the heterosexual sense. In other words studies showing the "masculinizing" influence of the father on females might alternatively be interpreted as showing his influence in fostering independence (as well as broader interests) rather than masculinity.

The Father and Autonomy for Both Sexes—the Data

Perhaps the most clearcut evidence that father identification is related to autonomy in both males and females comes from Heilbrun (1965). He found in a study of college students that the "instrumental father" identified females were more "self-confident" than "expressive mother" identified females. The latter were more "considerate," "fearful," "gentle," "obliging," "silent," "submissive" and "trusting." As Heilbrun himself notes these traits seem clearly to be more related to passivity and dependence than to more autonomous femininity while "self-confident" is a trait suggesting "autonomy" but not necessarily "masculinity." The traits of "expressive mother" identified males also had a dependent, inhibited quality.

Studies of father absence in which "dependence" is treated as a separate variable from "femininity" also generally support the hypothesis that father absence is related to an increase in dependency in both sexes. Tiller (1971) reports the well-known Norwegian study (see also Lynn and Sawrey, 1959) that absent ships' officers' children, both boys and girls, were "in general less mature emotionally and socially and more dependent on their mothers than the children of the control group" (p. 86). Tiller also reported a study of the effects of paternal absence during puberty in which the daughters of absent whalers adopted aggressive and authoritarian attitudes and had an exaggerated idealization of the male role. He interprets these behaviors as compensatory expressions of the need for independence and freedom (p. 102).

While Santrock (1970) and Wohlford, Santrock and others (1971) in studies of black pre-schoolers found no differences in dependency among father absent and father present females, they did find that the presence of older male siblings in the home decreased dependency in female as well as male children. Hetherington (1972) in a study of father absent and father present adolescent females found that the father absent girls showed more dependency on adult females and manifested a greater feeling of anxiety and powerlessness than did the father present girls.

Although these studies do not isolate the specific mechanisms by which this greater dependency comes about (it may be maternal over-protection), they do indicate that the presence of a father or older males (as opposed to females) seems to facilitate the process of achieving independence for both sexes.

CONTRIBUTIONS OF THE FATHER RELATIONSHIP VS. CONTRIBUTIONS OF THE MOTHER RELATIONSHIP TO SEX TYPING

Much of the data relevant to parental roles and sex typing bears on the question of the relative influence of each parent on each sex. The hypothesis that the father is crucial in sex typing for both sexes has been considered by some (e.g., Sherman, 1971) to have been disconfirmed by some of these data. In this section it will be argued that if the distinction between the maternal and the heterosexual aspects of femininity is maintained the data do support the crucial role of the father for *heterosexual* behaviors.

There are a number of studies (reviewed by Johnson, 1963; Biller and Weiss, 1970; Biller, 1971) suggesting in one way or another the salience of the father in "feminizing" women. On the other hand, in many of these same studies the mother is also found to be of importance, especially for girls. For example, Mussen and Rutherford (1963) found that feminine preferences in girls were related less to the "femininity" of their mothers than to the "masculinity" of their fathers *and* the extent to which he encouraged sex typed play. (This latter has been reported more recently by Fling and Manosevit, 1972). On the other hand this same study found that while the daughter's feminine preferences are not related to the mother's "femininity" they are related to her "self-acceptance" and to her nurturance.

Again, in order to make sense of these findings it is necessary to distinguish within femininity between its maternal aspects and its heterosexual aspects. The complete findings of the Mussen and Rutherford study make sense if it is argued that liking one's mother is important to a girl's own self acceptance as a woman and to maternalism but that the mother's nurturance is not the source of "femininity" in interacting with males (the heterosexual aspect). Any test of this is difficult in this specific study since the IT Scale, which does not get at mode of interacting, was used as the measure of sex typing in the children.

This distinction between nurturance and heterosexuality must be kept in mind in interpreting studies such as that of Wright and Tuska (1966). These authors report with respect to their findings on college women's self concepts that:

> It would seem as though the 'feminine' women have experienced more nurturant, rewarding relationships with their mothers than the 'masculine' women and that through this sympathetic, influential relationship, they have been encouraged to emulate the 'feminine' role. (p. 147.)

One cannot conclude from this study that the father does *not* reinforce "feeling feminine." It simply reflects the general salience of the mother as the nurturer, and after all this *is* an important aspect of femininity. Significantly enough, almost the only and by far the largest difference with respect to the father (as opposed to the mother) that occurs between the "masculine" and "feminine" groups is that the more "feminine" feeling women (*not* the more "masculine" women) think their father has been "more successful in life" than the mother.

Father Absence and Sex Typing

The findings from father absence studies are always problematic. In the first place most children without fathers, especially in the lower class, where the nuclear unit is neither so prominent nor isolated from other kin as it is in the middle class (Schneider and Smith, 1973), often have other male relatives who play the father role. It is also possible that an "image" of a father can be as "present" and operant as the actual father's presence. Certainly too, some fathers who are present may be more psychologically absent than some physically absent fathers. In spite of these drawbacks, some of the findings from the better controlled studies of the effects of father absence, especially on females, can be useful in clarifying the argument of this paper.

The key point is that if girls (and boys) identify first with the nurturant mother then father absence would not be related to anything like a sex role reversal in girls. Rather it would leave girls (and boys) with only their primary mother identification. Father absence then would make boys seem feminine because there has been no interference with the mother identification[4] and girls appear less feminine in the sense that they have no specific heterosexual addition to the basic mother identification. In the case of girls then, father absence could be expected to affect their social interactions with peers and most especially their interactions with males. Thus studies of the effect of father absence on female sex typing should be examined in terms of which aspect of the feminine role is being tapped in the study, the maternal aspect or the heterosexual aspect.

When studies investigate more than cognitive understanding and/or sex typed preferences and get at actual social interactions, it becomes clear how father absence affects "femininity." The several studies of this type show that father absence does affect the *peer group* interactions of both males and females. For example, Thomes (1968) in a study of lower class elementary school aged children reports that the only difference she found between father absent and father present children in terms of family interaction was that girls from father present homes perceived mildly affectionate feelings coming from

the father. Although she has no observational data she does ask about interactions with peers and reports:

> In response to 'How do you usually act when you get mad at your friends?' girls from father absent homes expressed a tendency to react aggressively by 'hitting' and 'throwing things,' while most of the girls from mother-father homes said they would walk away. Mothers of the girls in the father absent homes reported that their daughters belonged to significantly fewer groups than did mothers of girls from mother-father homes. (p. 94.)

These findings suggest that the father's affectionate interaction with females does cut down on aggressive hostile behavior in girls and is related to their being more sociable than father absent girls. It would be misleading to equate "hitting" and "throwing things" with "masculinity." From the present standpoint this kind of behavior is best understood as negative "expressive" rather than "masculine" behavior and may relate both to strivings against dependency and a lack of self confidence in the father absent females.

The clearest empirical case for the present formulation concerning the effects of father absence on females comes from a study by Hetherington (1972) mentioned earlier in connection with the discussion of dependency. She found that adolescent daughters from father absent homes had not only feelings of helplessness but were socially uncomfortable and not adept in dealing with males. Girls whose fathers had died early were shy with males while girls whose fathers were absent because of divorce appeared to be overly anxious for masculine attention. In both types of cases father absence is reflected in difficulties in relating to males and dependency on females. On the other hand, Hetherington reports little deviation of father absent girls in sex typing in the sense that they did not act like men or pursue masculine activities in the recreation center where the study took place. These latter findings reflect the underlying mother identification. It is the absence of heterosexual interaction skills that characterize the father absent girls.

These studies reflect more than the fact that girls learn how to relate to men by relating to fathers. While this may indeed be true, it must be reiterated that the present theory predicts that the opposite does not seem to be as true for boys. For boys, father absence, emotional unavailability, especially

[4]For a summary of studies of the effects of father absence on boys, see Biller (1971).

in the early years, are related to *low* scores on "masculine orientation" (Biller, 1971). The present view suggests that mothers can and do influence a boy's masculinity by the way they define the father, by the way they act toward the father, etc., but they do not mediate heterosexuality for either sex.

As Hetherington (1973) has suggested, research may expect to see the effect of the father more clearly in older girls and women than in young children. This observation is borne out in the following section.

Fathers and Sexuality

While the data on father absence are at the very least consonant with the hypothesis that it is the father relationship which most affects cross-sex interactions and attitudes in both sexes, there is research indicating even more directly the pivotal role of the father with respect to heterosexual behaviors. Recently the study of the etiology of homosexuality has been criticized by many on the grounds that to study homosexuality implies that it is an "illness" to be "cured." Here a more basic question is being considered—how do parental roles foster heterosexuality?

Two studies by Eva Bené (1965a and b) are especially relevant. In one study Bené compared male homosexuals with a matched control group of married males and in a later study she compared lesbians with a matched control group of married females. All the subjects were given the Bené-Anthony Family Relations Test. With regard to males she reports that:

> the findings are consistent in suggesting that the reason why homosexuals are relatively much more attached to their mothers than to their fathers is not that they have much stronger relationships with their mothers than have heterosexuals, but that they have much poorer relationships with their fathers. (Bené, 1965 (b) p. 812.)

She found that the female homosexuals were also characterized by unrewarding father relationships. Of the 68 items which can be used to express recollected childhood feelings, 24 show significant difference between the experimental and control groups in connection with the father and only four in connection with the mother. Bené reports that the lesbians were often more hostile towards and afraid of their fathers than were the married women and they felt more often that their fathers were weak and incompetent.

Both the male and female homosexuals investigated were living "normal" productive lives and were in no sense "mental patients." Bené speculates that those investigators who found an overstrong mother attachment in male homosexuals were studying severely disturbed patients who were unlike the normal homosexuals in her sample. Bené's research then would support an important implication of the present position, namely that a disturbed maternal relationship poses a more serious threat to an individual's total personality than a disturbed paternal relationship.[5] Bené's data also support another implication of the present position, namely that sexual object choice and sex "appropriate" heterosexual behaviors are secondary and not primary human phenomena.

Obviously many factors are involved in an individual's choice of sex objects. Any simple determinism in this matter is to be avoided. But in so far as parental relationships are influential, the evidence suggests that the father relationship is of more importance in this than the mother relationship.

Another study directly concerned with sexual behavior of women using a different measure, i.e., sexual responsiveness in marital coitus, also provides support for the greater influence of the father relationship than the mother relationship. S. Fischer (1973) in a five year study using the verbal reports of 300 middle class housewives as to orgasmic frequency found that virtually the only factor which differentiated between the "low orgasm" and the "high orgasm" women was the reported quality of the woman's early relationship with her father. He found that if a woman perceives her father as not having invested serious or dependable interest in her she tends to experience orgasmic difficulties. On the other hand, he finds no correlations between orgasm consistency in marital intercourse and attitudes toward the mother.

The above studies on homosexuality and orgasmic frequency in marital coitus then seem to support the critical impact of the father relationship as opposed to the mother relationship in heterosexual behaviors. Finally, the desire as an adult to get married and have a family appears to be related to the quality of the woman's relationship to her father, not her mother.

Jean Stockard (1974) in a dissertation study based

---

[5]It is also significant in this connection that while father absent homes are relatively common, mother absent homes are very rare.

on a large sample of female undergraduates used path analysis to clarify the relationship of a number of antecedent variables, both familial and non-familial, to several different measures of adult sex role related attitudes. One of her dependent measures was the degree to which the young woman was committed to getting married and having children (regardless of her desire to work outside the home). Separate questions were asked concerning desire for marriage and desire for children but the responses were so highly correlated that they were combined into a measure of "familism." Using this measure, she found the highest path coefficient (.2144) obtained among all the variables was that between the quality of the woman's relationship with her father and "familism." Women who described their fathers as affectionate, sympathetic, interested in their activities and non-ignoring were most likely to definitely expect to get married and have a family. The woman's assessment of her relationship with her mother, however, in terms of these same variables was *not* related to "familism."

On the other hand, the next strongest path coefficient to "familism" was the degree to which the daughter felt similar to her mother (.1823). Daughters who said their habits, goals and reactions were similar to their mothers' tended to think marriage and having children were important for them. Certainly women who opt for marriage and motherhood might be expected to say they feel similar to their mothers, but from the present standpoint the striking finding is that it is the quality of the father-daughter relationship, not the quality of the mother-daughter relationship that effects "familism," the respective path coefficients being .2144 and −.0100. It is also significant that the father relationship effect operates independently of the "similarity to mother" variable.

Stockard's findings with respect to the influence of mothers and fathers on the degree to which women want to have a career (regardless of marriage and motherhood) and on the type of career (traditional or non-traditional) they want, show a *less* strong influence of the father relationship. This fits with the argument of this paper that occupational achievement and the lack of it should not be equated with sex typing. Specific occupational roles considered "appropriate" for women and men vary considerably from culture to culture and time to time. More or less invariant sex typing, including heterosexuality and familism seem to be what the father relationship most affects.

SUMMARY AND DISCUSSION

In this paper a theoretical argument made earlier (Johnson, 1963) for the crucial role of the father in promoting sex typed behavior has been specified more precisely and data examined in terms of these specifications. Although the findings used come largely from the United States, from a theoretical standpoint the ultimate concern is to determine how certain universal features of parental roles, i.e., the early primacy of the mother and the external focus of the father, may be related to the latter's being the focus of sex typing in both sexes. Precisely because of the primacy of the maternal role the mother cannot be the focus of "masculinity" in men or of non-maternal "femininity" in women. It is the father or paternal surrogate who as the focus of non-domestic relations symbolizes and promotes the adult heterosexual aspect of both male and female personalities. This suggests a specific and very basic sense in which it can be claimed that "patriarchy" (control by the father or male relative) is at the basis of the secondary status of women.

Ultimately the father's role in sex typing, heterosexuality, and the "object" status of females (but *not* in their maternal role) derives from the cultural imperative to relate kin groups to one another. This is done through the exchange of women by men from one kin group with men from other kin groups (necessitated by the incest taboo). The reason the exchange of men *by women* has never been institutionalized rests in large part on the "external" focus of the father role. This in turn seems to rest on the domestic focus of the mother role. The most parsimonious explanation for the association of the female with domesticity is simply that it is the woman who bears children and lactates. Thus the presumption would be to associate females with early child care and hence males with external functions (Rosaldo, 1974). Ultimately then it is being contended that the father controls sexuality and makes women "objects" not directly because of his own qualities but because of the association of women with the maternal role.

The foregoing speculations reflect essentially a structuralist approach represented by Kohlberg in psychology, Parsons in sociology and Levi-Strauss in anthropology. The reader will have noted that the words "reinforce," "enhance," "facilitate" and "symbolize" rather than "cause" have been used throughout the paper. This usage is deliberate and reflects the view that the actual events of a child's life impede or facilitate cognitive structuring capacities interacting with the socially defined structure of the outside world. The specific concern of this paper has been with delineating the common cultural features of the structuring of parental roles. The actual experiences of children affect them in terms of these role concepts which define expectations about what each parent "should" be like.

Feminists have had very mixed feelings concerning motherhood. Some have seen it as a burden that prevents women from participating fully as human beings in the public sphere. Others have glorified motherhood as the source of women's power par excellence, and have treated men's achievements as attempts to reproduce this power for themselves (e.g., Mead, 1955: 117). In this paper too it has been said that the maternal role is primary, generic, a focus of people's most human traits. To be "masculine" then involves a kind of "deviation" from the more androgynous maternal base line. On the other hand it has also been asserted that it is motherhood which has associated women with "domesticity" and men with "external" or "public" affairs. This in turn has made women "sex objects" to men as counters in marital exchange. In a sense then, it is the linking of motherhood with marriage, the linking of maternal role with an externally oriented paternal role, that makes women "objects."

The implications of the foregoing analysis for understanding the traditional structuring of relations between the sexes then appears to be as follows: It is incorrect to see "masculinity" and "femininity" as separate but equal principles or in any simple way as masculine first, feminine second, or vice versa. The matter is more complicated, but only slightly so. Because of the initial identification of children of both sexes with the mother[6] and because it is in connection with the mother that both sexes are inducted into "socialized" behavior, the maternal aspect of the feminine principle is seen as generic and as symbolizing the common humanity of both sexes. The sex differentiating principle is

introduced by the father. The woman's status as a sex object is related symbolically and ultimately to the father as is the male's "masculinity" (including its paternal aspects) related to the father. In this sense it can be claimed that "patriarchy" (father dominance) is at the basis of the secondary status of women. On the other hand, this secondary status of femininity in its heterosexual aspects *is* secondary to the primary status of the maternal aspect.

REFERENCES

Bardwick, J. M. and Douvan, E. 1971. "Ambivalence: The socialization of women," pp. 225–241 in V. Gornick and B. K. Moran (eds.), *Woman in Sexist Society*, N.Y.: Basic Books.

Barry, Bacon, M.K. and Child, I. L. 1957. "A cross-cultural survey of some sex differences in socialization," *Journal of Abnormal Psychology*, 55: 327, 332.

Bené, E. 1965. "On the genesis of female homosexuality," *British Journal of Psychiatry*, 3: 815–821; 1965. "On the genesis of male homosexuality," *British Journal of Psychiatry*, 3: 803–813.

Biller, H. B. 1971. *Father, Child, and Sex Role*. Lexington, Mass.: Heath Lexington Books.

Biller, H. B. and Weiss, S. 1970. "The father-daughter relationship and the personality development of the female," *Journal of Genetic Psychology*, 114: 79–93.

Block, J. H. 1974. "Conceptions of sex role: Some cross-cultural and longitudinal perspectives," in R. F. Winch and B. B. Spanier (eds.), *Selected Studies in Marriage and the Family* (4th edition). N.Y.: Holt, Rinehart and Winston.

Droppleman, L. F. and Schaefer, E. S. 1963. "Boys' and girls' reports of maternal and paternal behavior," *Journal of Abnormal and Social Psychology*, 67: 648–654.

Elder, G. and Bowerman, C. 1963. "Family structure and child-rearing patterns: the effect of family size and sex composition," *American Sociological Review*, 28: 891–905.

Firestone, S. 1971. *The Dialectic of Sex*. N.Y.: Bantam.

Fisher, S. 1973. *The Female Orgasm: Psychology, Physiology, Fantasy*. N.Y.: Basic Books.

Fling, S. and Manosevitz, M. 1972. "Sex typing in nursery school children's play interests," *Developmental Psychology*, 7: 146–152.

Forrest, T. 1966. "Paternal roots of female character development," *Contemporary Psychoanalysis*, 3: 21–38.

Heilbrun, A. B., Jr. 1968. "Sex role, instrumental-expressive behavior, and psychopathology in females," *Journal of Abnormal Psychology*, 74: 131–136.

Hetherington, E. M. 1972. "Effects of father absence on

---

[6]Recently, Stoller (1974), on the basis of his work with transsexuals has come to a similar conclusion regarding the primacy of the maternal. For Stoller, the male transsexual who feels that he is a female trapped in a male body is a kind of experimental confirmation of the initial mother identity in both sexes.

"Only if the boy . . . can comfortably separate himself from his mother's femaleness and femininity, can he then begin to develop that later, non-core gender identity we call masculinity" (p. 358).

Females on the other hand are not so threatened by gender identification problems as males precisely because they have the initial mother identification.

personality development in adolescent daughters," *Developmental Psychology,* 7: 313–326; 1973. "Girls without fathers," *Psychology Today,* 6: 46–52.

Johnson, M. M. 1963. "Sex role learning in the nuclear family," *Child Development,* 34: 319–333.

Johnson, M. M., Stockard, J., Acker, J. and Naffiger, C. 1975. "Expressiveness re-evaluated," *School Review,* 1975, *83,* 617–644.

Kagan, J. 1971. *Change and Continuity in Infancy.* N.Y.: Wiley; 1972. "The emergence of sex differences," *School Review,* 80: 217–227.

Kammeyer, K. 1967. "Sibling position and the feminine role," *Journal of Marriage and the Family,* 29: 494–499.

Kohlberg, L. 1966. "A cognitive-developmental analysis of children's sex-role concepts and attitudes," in E. E. Maccoby (ed.), *The Development of Sex Differences.* Stanford: Stanford University Press.

Kohlberg, L. and Zigler, E. 1967. "The impact of cognitive maturity on the development of sex role attitudes in the years 4 to 8." *Genetic Psychology Monographs,* 75: 89–165.

Lansky, L. M. and McKay, G. 1969. "Independence, dependence, manifest and latent masculinity-femininity: Some complex relationships among four complex variables," *Psychological Reports,* 24: 263–268.

Levi-Strauss, C. 1969. *The Elementary Structures of Kinship.* Boston: Beacon.

Lewis, M. 1972. "Parents and children: Sex role development," *School Review,* 80: 229–239.

Lynn, D. B. 1969. *Parental and Sex-role Identification.* Berkeley, Calif.: McCutchan.

Lynn, D. B. and Sawrey, W. L. 1959. "The effects of father-absence on Norwegian boys and girls," *Journal of Abnormal and Social Psychology,* 59: 258–262.

Maccoby, E. E. 1966. "Sex differences in intellectual functioning," pp. 25–55 in E. E. Maccoby (ed.), *The Development of Sex Differences.* Stanford, Calif.: Stanford University Press.

Maccoby, E. E. and Masters, J. C. 1970. "Attachment and dependency," in P. H. Mussen (ed.), *Carmichael's Manual of Child Psychology,* Vol. 2. N.Y.: Wiley.

Mead, M. 1955. *Male and Female.* N.Y.: Mentor.

Mitchell, J. 1974. "Patriarchy, kinship and women as exchange objects," *Psychoanalysis and Feminism.* N.Y.: Random House.

Mussen, P. and Rutherford, E. 1963. "Parent-child relations and parental personality in relation to young children's sex-role preferences," *Child Development,* 34: 589–607.

Parsons, A. 1967. "Is the oedipus complex universal?" In R. Hunt (ed.), *Personalities and Cultures,* Garden City, N.Y.: Natural History Press.

Parsons, T. 1970a. "The father symbol: An appraisal in the light of psycho-analytic and sociological theory," in Parsons, *Social Structure and Personality,* N.Y.: Free Press; 1970b. "The incest taboo in relation to social structure and the socialization of the child," in Parsons, *Social Structure and Personality,* N.Y.: Free Press; 1970c. "Social structure and the development of personality: Freud's contribution to the integration of psychology and sociology," *Social Structure and Personality,* N.Y.: Free Press.

Rothbart, M. K. "Sibling position and maternal involvement," in K. Reigel and J. Meacham (eds.), *The Developing Individual in a Changing World.* Vol. II. The Hague: Mouton, 1976.

Santrock, J. W. 1970. "Paternal absence, sex typing, and identification," *Developmental Psychology,* 2: 264–272.

Schneider, D. M. and Smith, R. T. 1973. *Class Differences and Sex-roles in American Kinship and Family Structure.* Englewood Cliffs, N.J.: Prentice-Hall.

Sherman, J. A. 1971. *On the Psychology of Women.* Springfield, Ill.: Chas. Thomas.

Reading 47

Television and the Young Viewer

Eli A. Rubinstein

For *some* children, under *some* conditions, *some* television is harmful. For *other* children under the same conditions, or for the same children under *other* conditions, it may be beneficial. For *most* children, under *most* conditions, *most* television is probably neither particularly harmful nor particularly beneficial. [Schramm, Lyle, and Parker 1961, p. 1]

That assessment, made in 1961 by three leading Stanford researchers, was the general conclusion of one of the first major studies of television and children. Almost two decades and about two thousand studies later, their conclusion remains a reasonably accurate evaluation of the complex and differential impact of television on its millions of young viewers. The published research since 1961 has further confirmed the harmful effects to some children of some television under some conditions. At the same time, stronger evidence for the corollary has been found: for some children, under some conditions, some television is beneficial.

It is in the differentiation between *some* children and *most* children and in the distinction between *some* television and *most* television that the scientific findings are still not clear. As in so many other instances of exposure to persuasive messages, it is the cumulative impact over extended periods of time that should be the crucial test of consequences. It seems reasonable to assume that when millions of young viewers each spend on average about a thousand hours per year watching hundreds of television programs, such time spent must have some significant effect on their social development. It is equally reasonable to assume that if the effect is so tangible there should be little difficulty in identifying its characteristics or assessing its strength. Here, however, the evidence is less than definitive—thus the continued applicability of the Schramm, Lyle, and Parker generalization.

While the total impact of television on the young viewer is still unclear, the pursuit of evidence has attracted increasing interest on the part of social scientists. In the appendix to the 1961 report by Schramm et al., 52 earlier publications dealing with television and children are annotated, and they make up a fairly complete list of relevant prior research. By 1970 (Atkin, Murray, and Nayman 1971) that list of publications had grown to a total of almost 500 citations. By 1974 a total of almost 2,400 publications were cited under the category of television and human behavior in a major review of the field by Comstock and Fisher (1975). Since 1974, research interest has continued unabated as new topics begin to be explored. The concern about televised violence has been augmented by a concern about sex on television, the persuasive power of television advertising on children, and, indeed, the effect of television on the entire socialization process of children.

Two events in the early 1970s provided the most compelling influence toward that growth of interest. One was the development of the program "Sesame Street," in which formative research was pursued in partnership with the production of the program itself. The other was the completion in 1972 of a major federally funded research program, now known as the Surgeon-General's program, to evaluate the relationship between TV violence and aggressive behavior in children.

"SESAME STREET"

"Sesame Street" provides the most extensive example of how television can be made beneficial for some children under some conditions. The story of its growth and development has been effectively told by its educational director (Lesser 1974). From the research perspective, "Sesame Street" marks a major innovation: it is the first intensive and continuing partnership between education specialists from academia and the creative and technical specialists responsible for putting television programs on the air. How that partnership evolved into not just constructive interchange but productive results is itself a lesson in formative research.

The educational goals of "Sesame Street" were developed over a series of working seminars in 1968, with participation by experts from all relevant specialties. The instructional goals were precisely formulated in a series of specific statements on five major topics: (1) social, moral, and affective development; (2) language and reading; (3) mathematical and numerical skills; (4) reasoning and problem-solving; (5) perception. The target audience was disadvantaged inner-city children.

Overall, the development of the total program toward the achievement of those goals was structured by the continuing interplay of production people and academic researchers in a feedback system involving observation of children viewing programs as they were produced. Happily, all the major participants in this innovative enterprise were completely dedicated to the larger task. Of equal good fortune was the initial allocation, from private and public sources, of $8 million for the start-up and production costs for the first eighteen months of "Sesame Street." While those three ingredients— dedicated talent, adequate start-up time, and ample funding—do not always produce success, they certainly represent a good beginning and were put to constructive use in the development of the program.

Some ten years after its introduction, "Sesame Street" has become not just a national but an international phenomenon. In addition to being the most widely viewed children's program in the United States, "Sesame Street," in both the original version and in foreign-language versions, is broadcast in more than 50 countries around the world. The Children's Television Workshop, the parent body for "Sesame Street" and all the other educational programs, cites more than 120 articles and books (Children's Television Workshop 1977) primarily on "Sesame Street" and "The Electric Company." Additional publications through early 1978 bring the total above 150 research reports. These range from studies of attention during the actual program viewing to major evaluations of both "Sesame Street" and "The Electric Company." The total literature provides an unprecedented body of research on how the entertainment appeal of television can be put to educational use.

Most, but not all, of the evaluations are positive. One major study suggests that "Sesame Street" has been less useful to disadvantaged children than advantaged children (Cook et al. 1975) because of differences in viewing interest. And, in England, for example, grave concern was initially raised that the very format of "Sesame Street" is inimical to the learning process because the program over-emphasize sheer attention-getting devices and because it links learning too closely to a commercial entertainment format. (Subsequently, "Sesame Street" was aired in Great Britain and achieved much viewer success.)

But these are issues for the educators. From the standpoint of research on television and the young viewer, the history of "Sesame Street" has been of great significance. Formative research has achieved a new status through the ongoing efforts to evaluate the progress and achievements of what Joan Ganz Cooney, the director of the entire enterprise, has called "a perpetual television experiment." The program has clearly demonstrated that television can teach children while still holding their voluntary attention as well, if not better, than conventional television programming. It is the clearest example of the positive potential of television translated into performance.

TELEVISED VIOLENCE

At about the same time that "Sesame Street" was being prepared for broadcast in 1969, a major federal research program was initiated to assess the effects of televised violence on children. The history of that research enterprise has been thoroughly described and evaluated from a variety of perspectives (Bogart 1972; Cater and Strickland 1975; Rubinstein 1975). The belief is fairly widespread that the body of research, published in five volumes of technical reports, provided a major new set of findings.

There is much less agreement about the report and conclusions of the advisory committee itself, because of the cautious language used. Even now, years after the report was published, the conclusions are debated. The debate was sparked initially because of a misleading headline in a front-page story in the *New York Times* ("TV Violence Held Unharmful to Youth") when the report was first released. A careful analysis of the subsequent press coverage revealed how influential that headline was in further confusing the interpretation of the findings (Tankard and Showalter 1977). The committee had unanimously agreed that there was some evidence of a causal relationship between televised violence and later aggressive behavior. However, the conclusion was so moderated by qualifiers that it was, and still is, criticized and misinterpreted by industry spokesmen as being too strong and by researchers as being too weak.

The effect of televised violence has been an issue of public concern almost from the inception of television in the early 1950s. Periodically, over the past 25 years, a variety of congressional inquiries as well as commissioned reports have drawn attention to the problem of televised violence. In almost every instance concern was raised about harmful effects. In all these reports, however, relatively little new research on the problem was produced. Even the prestigious Eisenhower Commission, which was asked by President Johnson in 1968 to explore the question within its total inquiry into violence in America, devoted its attention primarily to a synthesis of existing knowledge rather than to collecting new scientific information. Its conclusions—that violence on television encourages real violence— were seen as less than persuasive and were largely ignored, especially since attention was then focused on the new Surgeon-General's Committee.

The Surgeon-General's program provided the first major infusion of new monies into research on television violence, which in turn has stimulated a "second harvest," as Schramm (1976) calls it, of new work on television and social behavior. The debate on the evidence from the five volumes of research reports produced in 1972 by the Surgeon-General's program is also still lively. The essence of the debate emerges from two contrasting approaches to assessing the evidence. The Surgeon-General's advisory committee, while acknowledging flaws in many of the individual studies, held that the *convergence* of evidence was sufficient to permit a qualified conclusion indicating a causal relationship between extensive viewing of violence and later aggressive behavior. This conclusion, without the qualifications, is endorsed by a number of highly respected researchers, some of whom participated in the Surgeon-General's program and some who were not directly involved.

A different and seemingly more rigorous approach to the evidence is adopted by some other experts in the field. This contrasting view is epitomized by Kaplan and Singer (1976), who conclude that the total evidence does no more than support the null hypothesis.

A brief explanation is appropriate here about the theoretical formulations most common in the research underlying the whole question of television and aggressive behavior. Quite simply, three possibilities exist—and all have their proponents. (1) Television has no significant relationship to aggressive behavior. (2) Television reduces aggressive behavior. (3) Television causes aggressive behavior; a variant on this possibility is that both television viewing and aggressive behavior are related not to each other but to a "third variable" which mediates between the first two variables.

The Kaplan and Singer position, to give one recent example, is that the research so far has demonstrated no relationship between televised violence and later aggressive behavior. They characterize this as the "conservative" assessment of the evidence and come to that conclusion by finding no study persuasive enough in its own right to bear the burden of significant correlation, let alone causal relationship. They are not the only ones to conclude "no-effect": Singer (1971) came to the same conclusion, as did Howitt and Cumberbatch (1975).

The second point of view has been espoused primarily by Feshbach (1961). The catharsis hypothesis holds that vicarious experience of aggressive behavior, as occurs in viewing TV violence, may actually serve as a release of aggressive tensions and thereby reduce direct expression of aggressive behavior. This view has not been supported by research evidence, although it emerges time and again as a "common-sense" assessment of the relationship between vicarious viewing of violence and later behavior. Indeed, the thesis itself goes back to Aristotle, who considered dramatic presentations a vehicle for discharge of feelings by the audience. The Surgeon-General's committee, in considering this thesis, made one of their few unequivocal assessments—that there was "no evidence that would support a catharsis interpretation."

The third general conclusion, and the one now prevailing, is that there is a positive relationship between TV violence and later aggressive behavior. This facilitation of later aggression, explained primarily by social learning theory, is endorsed by a number of investigators. The basic theoretical formulation is generally credited to Bandura (Bandura and Walters 1963), who began his social learning studies in the early 1960s, when he and his students clearly demonstrated that children will imitate aggressive acts they witness in film presentations. These were the so-called "bobo doll" studies, in which children watching a bobo doll being attacked, either by a live model or a cartoon character, were more likely to imitate such behavior. These early studies were criticized both because bobo dolls, made for rough and tumble play, tend to provoke aggressive hitting and because the hostile play was only against inanimate play objects. Later studies have demonstrated that such aggression will also take place against people (Hanratty et al. 1972).

Variations on the basic social learning theory are rather numerous. Kaplan and Singer make a useful schema by incorporating three related theoretical branches under the general label of "activation hypotheses." Bandura and his students are included in the category of social learning and imitation. A second branch is represented by Berkowitz and his students, who follow a classical conditioning hypothesis, in which repeated viewing of aggressive behavior is presented to build up the probability of aggressive behavior as a conditioned response to the cues produced in the portrayal. A number of experiments by Berkowitz and his colleagues have shown that subjects viewing a violent film after being angered were more likely to show aggressive behavior than subjects, similarly angered beforehand, who saw nonaggressive films (Berkowitz 1965; Berkowitz and Geen 1966).

In still a third variation on the activation approach, Tannenbaum (1972) holds that a generalized emotional arousal is instigated by emotionally charged viewing material and that this level of arousal itself is the precursor of the subsequent behavior. Any exciting content, including erotic content, can induce this heightened arousal. The nature of response is then a function of the conditions that exist at the time the activation of behavior takes place. Thus, according to this theory, it is not so much the violent content per se that induces later aggressive behavior as it is the level of arousal evoked. Subsequent circumstances may channel the heightened arousal in the direction of aggressive behavior.

In an important examination of the utility of these various formulations, Watt and Krull (1977) reanalyzed data on 597 adolescents from three prior studies, involving both programming attributes (such as perceived violent content) and viewer attributes (such as viewing exposure and aggressive behavior) through a series of correlations. They contrasted three models, which they labeled catharsis model, arousal model, and facilitation model. The first two models are essentially as described above. The facilitation model is identified as a general social-learning model without regard to whether the process is primarily imitation, cueing, or legitimization of aggressive behavior. Thus, the Bandura and Berkowitz studies both fall into the facilitation model.

Through a series of partial correlations, Watt and Krull found (1) no support for the catharsis model; (2) support for a combination of the facilitation and arousal models; and (3) some differences due to age and/or sex, with the arousal model a somewhat better explanation for female adolescents, whereas the facilitation model better described the data for males. (Sex differences in results in many studies of television and behavior are quite common. One of the major studies in the field, by Lefkowitz et al., 1972, found significant correlations between TV violence and later aggressive behavior with boys but not with girls.)

What are the implications in this continuing controversy about the effects of television violence on aggressive behavior? As in so many other social science issues it depends on what you are looking for. The dilemma is neatly characterized in a legal case in Florida in October 1977, in which the defense argued that an adolescent boy, who admittedly killed an elderly woman, was suffering from "involuntary subliminal television intoxication." (This term, which appears nowhere in the scientific literature, was introduced by the defense attorney.) In trying to show that the scientific evidence on television's effects on behavior was not directly pertinent to this murder trial, the prosecuting attorney asked an expert witness if any scientific studies indicated that a viewer had ever been induced to commit a serious crime following the viewing of TV violence. The (correct) answer to that question was "no." The judge thereby ruled that expert testimony on the effects of televised violence would be inadmissible and brought back the jury, which had been sequestered during the interrogation of the expert witness. On the basis of the evidence presented to it, the jury found the defendant guilty of murder and rejected the plea of temporary insanity by virtue of "involuntary subliminal television intoxication."

While there is indeed no *scientific* evidence that excessive viewing of televised violence can or does provoke violent crime in any one individual, it is clear that the bulk of the studies show that if large groups of children watch a great deal of televised violence they will be more prone to behave aggressively than similar groups of children who do not watch such TV violence. The argument simply follows from the basic premise that children learn from all aspects of their environment. To the extent that one or another environmental agent occupies a significant proportion of a child's daily activity, that agent becomes a component of influence on his or her behavior. In a recent comprehensive review of all the evidence on the effects of television on children, Comstock et al. (1978) conclude that television should be considered a major agent of socialization in the lives of children.

An important confirmation of the more general

influence of television on the young viewers derives from research on the so-called "prosocial" effects of television. Stimulated by the findings of the Surgeon-General's program, a number of researchers began in 1972 to explore the corollary question: If TV violence can induce aggressive behavior, can TV prosocial programming stimulate positive behavior? By 1975, this question was of highest interest to active researchers in the field, according to a national survey (Comstock and Lindsey 1975).

A significant body of literature has now been generated to confirm these prosocial effects (Rubinstein et al. 1974; Stein and Friedrich 1975). Research by network scientists (CBS Broadcast Group 1977) has confirmed that children learn from the prosocial messages included in programs designed to impart such messages. Because the effect of prosocial program content is so clearly similar in process to the effect of TV violence, confirmation of the former effect adds strength to the validity of the latter effect.

In all the intensive analysis of the effects of TV violence, perhaps the one scientific issue most strongly argued against by the network officials has been the definition and assessment of levels of violent content. The single continuing source of such definition and assessment has been the work of Gerbner and his associates (Gerbner 1972). Beginning in 1969 and continuing annually, Gerbner has been publishing a violence index which has charted the levels of violence among the three networks on prime time. The decline in violence over the entire decade has been negligible until the 1977–78 season (Gerbner et al. 1978), following an intensive public campaign against TV violence by both the American Medical Association and the Parent-Teacher Association.

Gerbner's definition of violence is specific and yet inclusive—"the overt expression of physical force against others or self, or compelling action against one's will on pain of being hurt or killed or actually hurting or killing." Despite criticism by the industry, the Gerbner index has been widely accepted by other researchers. An extensive effort by a Committee on Television and Social Behavior, organized by the Social Science Research Council to develop a more comprehensive violence index, ended up essentially endorsing Gerbner's approach (Social Science Research Council 1975).

Perhaps of more theoretical interest than his violence index is Gerbner's present thesis that television is a "cultural indicator." He argues that television content reinforces beliefs about various cultural themes—the social realities of life are modified in the mind of the viewer by the images portrayed on the television screen. To the extent that the television world differs from the real world, some portion of that difference influences the perception of the viewer about the world in which he or she lives. Thus, Gerbner has found that heavy viewers see the world in a much more sinister light than individuals who do not watch as much television. Gerbner argues that excessive portrayals of violence on television inculcate feelings of fear among heavy viewers, which may be as important an effect as the findings of increased aggressive behavior. Some confirmation of this feeling of fear was found in a national survey of children (Zill 1977): children who were heavy viewers were reported significantly more likely to be more fearful in general than children who watched less television.

TV ADVERTISING

An area of research that has been increasing in importance since the work of the Surgeon-General's program has been concerned with the effects of advertising on children. One of the technical reports in the Surgeon-General's program described a series of studies on this topic by Ward (1972), which was among the first major published studies in which children's reactions to television advertising were examined in their relationship to cognitive development. That report provided preliminary findings on (1) how children's responses to television advertising become increasingly differentiated and complex with age; (2) the development of cynicism and suspicion about television messages by the fourth grade; (3) mothers' perceptions about how television influences their children; and (4) how television advertising influences consumer socialization among adolescents.

The entire field of research on effects of television advertising—at least academic published research—has only begun to develop in the 1970s. A major review of the published literature in the field was sponsored and published by the National Science Foundation in 1977 (Adler 1977). It is noteworthy that only 21 studies, all published between 1971 and 1976, were considered significant enough to be singled out for inclusion in the review's annotated appendix. The total body of evidence is still so small that no major theoretical formulations have yet emerged. Instead, the research follows the general social-learning model inherent in the earlier research on televised violence.

Despite the lack of extensive research findings on the effects of television advertising on children, formal concern about possible effects began to emerge in the early 1960s. Self-regulatory guidelines were adopted by the National Association of Broadcasters in 1961 to define acceptable toy advertising practices to children. Subsequently, published NAB guidelines were expanded to include all advertising directed primarily to children. An entire mechanism has been established within the industry, under the responsibility of the NAB Television Code Authority, through which guidelines on children's advertising—as well as other broadcast standards—are enforced. In addition, in 1974 the National Advertising Division of the Council of Better Business Bureaus established a Children's Advertising Review Unit to help in the self-regulation of advertising directed to children aged eleven and under. That organization, with the assistance of a panel of social science advisors, developed and issued its own set of guidelines for children's advertising.

The role of research in helping to make those guidelines on children's advertising more meaningful is only now receiving some attention, thanks in part to the NSF review cited above. Two recent events have highlighted both the paucity and the relevance of research in this field. In 1975, the Attorney General of Massachusetts, in collaboration with Attorneys General of other states, petitioned the Federal Communications Commission to ban all drug advertising between 9 A.M. and 9 P.M., on the ground that such advertising was harmful to children. After a series of hearings in May 1976, at which researchers and scientists testified, the petition was denied for lack of scientific evidence to support the claim.

In 1978, the Federal Trade Commission formally considered petitions requesting "the promulgation of a trade rule regulating television advertising of candy and other sugared products to children." A comprehensive staff report on television advertising to children (Ratner et al. 1978) made recommendations to the FTC, citing much of the relevant scientific literature on advertising to children as evidence supporting the need for such a trade rule. At the time of this writing, the entire matter was still under active consideration.

What does the existing research in this area demonstrate? It is clear that children are exposed to a large number of television commercials. The statistics themselves are significant. Annually, on average, children between two and eleven years of age are now exposed to more than 20,000 television commercials. Children in this age group watch an average of about 25 hours of television per week all through the year. The most clichéd statistic quoted is that, by the time a child graduates from high school today, he or she will have spent more time in front of a television set (17,000 hours) than in a formal classroom (11,000 hours). Indeed, all the statistics on television viewing from earliest childhood through age eighteen show that no other daily activity, with the exception of sleeping, is so clearly dominant.

Just as was shown in the earlier research examining the effects of programming content, even the limited research now available on television commercials documents that children learn from watching these commercials. Whether it is the sheer recall of products and product attributes (Atkin 1975) or the singing of commercial jingles (Lyle and Hoffman 1972), the evidence is positive that children learn. More important, children and their parents are influenced by the intent of these commercials. One study (Lyle and Hoffman 1972) showed that nine out of ten preschool children asked for food items and toys they saw advertised on television.

A number of studies have also revealed various unintended effects of television advertising. While a vast majority of the advertisements adhere to the guidelines that attempt to protect children against exploitative practices, a number of studies have shown that, over time, children begin to distrust the accuracy of the commercial message. By the sixth grade, children are generally cynical about the truthfulness of the ads. A recent educational film by Consumers Union, on some of the excessive claims in TV advertising, highlights the problem of disbelief (Consumers Union 1976). There have also been a number of surveys in which parents have indicated negative reactions to children's commercials. In one study (Ward, Wackman, and Wartella 1975) 75% of the parents had such negative reactions.

In the survey of the literature evaluated in the 1977 NSF review, the evidence is examined against some of the major policy concerns that have emerged in the development of appropriate guidelines on children's advertising. These concerns can be grouped into four categories: (1) modes of advertising; (2) content of advertising; (3) products advertised; and (4) general effects of advertising.

Studies of "modes of advertising" show, for example, that separation of program and commercial is not well understood by children under eight years of age. While these younger children receive and retain the commercial messages, they are less able to discriminate the persuasive intent of the commercial and are more likely to perceive the message as truthful and to want to buy the product (Robertson and Rossiter 1974).

The format and the use of various audio-visual techniques also influence the children's perceptions of the message. This influence is clearly acknowledged by the advertisers and the broadcasters, who have included explicit instructions in the guidelines, especially for toy products, to ensure that audio and video production techniques do not misrepresent the product. What little research there is on this entire aspect of format is still far from definitive. What is clear is that attention, especially among young children, is increased by active movement, animation, lively music, and visual changes. (All of this, and more, is well understood by the advertising agencies and those who develop the ads, and they keep such knowledge confidential, much as a trade secret.)

One other relatively clear finding on audio-visual technique relates to the understanding of "disclaimers"—special statements about the product that may not be clear from the commercial itself, such as "batteries not included." A study of disclaimer wording and comprehension (Liebert et al. 1977) revealed that a standard disclaimer ("some assembly required") was less well understood by 6- and 8-year-olds than a modification ("You have to put it together"). The obvious conclusion—that wording should be appropriate to the child's ability to understand—is just one of the many ways in which this research can play a role in refining guidelines.

Studies on the content of advertising have shown that the appearance of a particular character with the product can modify the child's evaluation of the product, either positively or negatively, depending on the child's evaluation of the character. It is also clear that children are affected in a positive way by presenters of their own sex and race (Adler 1977). On a more general level, sexual stereotypes in advertising probably influence children in the same way they do in the program content.

Although there is relatively little significant research on the effects of classes of products, two such classes have been under intense public scrutiny in recent years: proprietary drug advertising and certain categories of food advertising. Governmental regulatory agencies are currently considering what kind of controls should be placed on such advertising to children.

Concerning the more general effects of advertising targeted to children, surveys suggest that parents have predominantly negative attitudes about such advertising because they believe it causes stress in the parent-child relationship. Studies on questions such as this, and on the larger issue of how such advertising leads to consumer socialization, are now being pursued. Ward and his associates (Ward, Wackman, and Wartella 1975) have been examining the entire question of how children learn to buy. The highly sophisticated techniques used by advertisers to give a 30-second or 60-second commercial strong impact on the child viewer make these commercials excellent study material for examining the entire process of consumer socialization. Much important research still remains to be done on this topic.

SEX ON TV

Of the many public concerns about television and its potentially harmful effects on children, the issue of sex on television is at present among the most visible and the least understood. If research on the effects of advertising is still in its early development, research on sex on television has hardly begun.

It has been found that children who watch large amounts of television (25 hours or more per week) are more likely to reveal stereotypic sex role attitudes than children who watch 10 hours or less per week (Frueh and McGhee 1975). Research has documented the stereotyping on television of women as passive and rule-abiding, while men are shown as aggressive, powerful, and smarter than women. Also, youth and attractiveness are stressed more for females than males. This evidence of stereotyping was included as one part of an argument by the U.S. Commission on Civil Rights that the Federal Communications Commission should conduct an inquiry into the portrayal of minorities and women in commercial and public television drama and should propose rules to correct the problem (U.S. Commission on Civil Rights 1977). Program content in 1977 and 1978 has given increased emphasis to so-called "sex on television," at the same time that violence on television is decreasing (Gerbner et al. 1978).

Despite all the public concern and attention, including cover stories in major newsweeklies, relatively little academic research has been done on sex on TV. Two studies reported in 1977 provided information on the level of physical intimacy portrayed on television (Franzblau et al. 1977 and Fernandez-Collado and Greenberg 1977). Franzblau, Sprafkin, and Rubinstein analyzed 61 prime-time programs shown on all three networks during a full week in early October 1975. Results showed that, while there was considerable casual intimacy such as kissing and embracing and much verbal innuendo on sexual activity, actual physical intimacy such as intercourse, rape, and homosexual behavior was absent in explicit form.

Fernandez-Collado and Greenberg examined 77 programs aired in prime time during the 1976–77 season and concluded that intimate sexual acts did occur on commercial television, with "the predominant act being sexual intercourse between heterosexuals unmarried to each other." An examination of the data, however, reveals that in this study, verbal statements—identified as verbal innuendo in the study by Franzblau et al.—served as the basis for the conclusion reached. In fact, explicit sexual acts such as identify and R- or an X-rated movie do not occur on prime-time network television.

Even though few published studies have so far examined the question of sex on television, at least two important issues have been highlighted by the two studies mentioned above. The most obvious point is the difference in interpretation of the data by the two reports—unfortunately not an uncommon occurrence in social science research. Labeling and defining the phenomena under examination, let alone drawing conclusions from results, show variations from investigator to investigator. While this kind of difference is not unique to the social sciences, the more complex the data and the less standard the measurement—qualities often inherent in social science studies—the more likely these individual differences of interpretation.

The second point illustrated by these two studies of sex on TV is more intrinsic to the subject matter itself. The public concern about sex on TV suggests that the general reaction is much in keeping with the substitution of behavior for verbal statements, as is found in the study by Fernandez-Collado and Greenberg. And, in fact, there are no scientific data to indicate that verbal innuendo may not affect the young viewer as much—or as little—as explicitly revealed behavior. What is important here is that we do not know the effects of either the verbal description or the explicit depiction on the young viewer. Research findings of the Commission on Obscenity and Pornography in 1970 suggest that exposure to explicit sexuality seems harmless. Nevertheless, public sensitivities are clearly high; whether those sensitivities are justified by the facts still remains an open question. At the very least, studies should be undertaken to give some objective answers to these questions.

One such effort is a recent content analysis by Rubinstein and his colleagues (Silverman et al. 1978), which confirms the absence of explicit sex in network programs aired in the 1977–78 season but documents a continued increase in sexual innuendos. Furthermore, sexual intercourse, which was never even contextually implied in the 1975–76 analysis by Franzblau et al. (1977), was so implied fifteen times during the week of programs analyzed in the 1977–78 report. Clearly the current decrease in violent content is partially offset by added emphasis on sexual content.

ISSUES OF POLICY

What are the policy implications of research on television and social behavior? Perhaps the most fundamental point to be made is that even with fairly clear research findings, the policy to be followed rarely emerges as a direct result of the research.

The history of the Surgeon-General's program provides a useful case study of the complexities of this issue. When the Surgeon-General's program of research was initiated, the advisory committee was charged by the Secretary of HEW, Robert Finch, with the responsibility for answering the question originally raised by Senator John Pastore, Chairman of the Senate Subcommittee on Communications: Does the viewing of TV violence stimulate aggressive behavior on the part of young children? The committee was specifically enjoined from making policy recommendations, since the HEW has no regulatory responsibility in this area. Thus, when the committee report was issued in 1972, there was no discussion of direct policy implications, nor were there any specific policy recommendations in that final document.

Senator Pastore, on receiving the report in January 1972, was sufficiently concerned, both about the cautious wording of the conclusion and the absence of policy recommendations, to call another set of hearings in March 1972 to clarify the interpretation of the results and to ask the committee members for their policy recommendations now that they were no longer under official constraints. What Senator Pastore learned at those hearings is now a familiar characteristic of scientists speaking out on public policy: their scientific expertise affords them little advantage in the public policy arena. There were relatively few workable and concrete policy recommendations forthcoming. Indeed, the most specific recommendation came from the Senator himself: a

request to the Secretary of HEW and the FCC that an annual violence index be published that would measure the amount of televised violence entering American homes. No such official index has ever emerged, although Gerbner has annually produced such a measure, as a continuation of his ongoing research program.

What is clear from an examination of the Surgeon-General's program in retrospect is that the advisory committee was correctly confined to the examination of the research question. But the next step was not taken—to set up a different committee, to develop policy recommendations on the basis of that research and in keeping with legal constraints and operational feasibility. Indeed, it might well have taken more time and care to examine the complexities of social policy in order to come to realistic and useful conclusions about a social course of action than it took to evaluate the research findings.

Attempts at policy formation concerning sexual content on TV will bring the complexities of social science research to public attention. For example, as Dienstbier (1977) has pointed out, the conclusions of the Surgeon-General's committee affirm the social learning model. The Commission on Obscenity and Pornography, on the other hand, concluded in 1970 that exposure to explicit sexuality seemed harmless. Aside from the fact that the differences in these two sets of conclusions may be partly a reflection of liberal versus conservative value judgments relating to aggression and sex (Berkowitz 1971), there are some intriguing implications for social policy in other differences between the portrayal on television of violence and physical intimacy. Dienstbier suggests that increased portrayal of sex on television may become an important substitute for extensive sex education programs. While such an assertion may provoke considerable debate among social scientists, let alone the public at large, it is worthy of further consideration, as still another pertinent research question.

Difficulties in arriving at policy guidelines for advertising to children are equally apparent. In connection with the current FTC examination of the merits of a trade rule to regulate television advertising of candy and other sugared products to children, the scientific evidence, primarily derived from the NSF report (Adler 1977) and from the interpretation of that evidence by the FTC (Ratner et al. 1978), is the source of much debate. Some of the scientists who contributed to the literature are publicly complaining that their findings are misinterpreted in the FTC staff report (Schaar 1978).

It is a minor irony that researchers are just as quick to take issue with interpretations—which they say go beyond the data—designed to support some change in policy on television advertising as their colleagues were in 1972 to take issue with interpretations by the Suregon-General's committee which they felt did not go as far as their data indicated. The correct generalization may well be that social scientists find it difficult to accept someone else's interpretation of their findings regardless of the direction of the policy implications.

In all the present examination of research on television and social behavior and its implications for social policy there are a number of important issues to consider. One point that bears repeating is that the research does not by itself identify the policy direction. Nor, for that matter, does the research to date satisfactorily deal with the many research questions that are relevant to the policy directions. At a major conference on priorities for research on television and children held in Reston, Virginia, in 1975 (Ford Foundation 1976), an entire agenda for future research was developed. Topics and methodology recommended ranged from simple experiments to identify effects of disclaimers and warnings in television advertising to long-range studies, including cross-national studies, to study the effects of television on political and social beliefs.

However, except for the Surgeon-General's program of research, plus a new program supported by the NSF in 1976 following the 1975 Reston conference, no major federal program of research exists. Time and again over the past twenty years, following various congressional hearings dealing with the effects of television, recommendations have been made for a "television research center." In early 1978, Senator Wendell Anderson of Minnesota began exploring the feasibility of legislation to develop a "Television Impact Assessment Act," but to date no final draft bill has materialized.

The three major networks, primarily responding to the pressures from the Surgeon-General's program,

have expended since 1970 approximately $3 million, primarily on the issue of televised violence. The American television industry seems much less willing to examine the need for a major program of research than does the British Broadcasting Corporation, which, in 1976, commissioned an eminent sociologist, Elihu Katz, to develop a comprehensive set of recommendations for a program of social research (Katz 1977). With the American television industry operating at about a $10 billion annual budget, even one-tenth of one percent devoted to social research would amount to $10 million a year. What Katz has recommended to the BBC would serve well both the American television industry and the public: a comprehensive program of research under the auspices of a new foundation funded by a variety of sources, including the broadcasting industry.

What is critical in such an endeavor is that it be seen as a long-term program. In an earlier paper (Rubinstein 1976) I proposed such a long-term instrumentality that would include studying ways of enhancing the value of television to the child viewer. It is likely that important findings still to be uncovered may provide guidelines for making television a more useful agent of socialization than it is at present.

A whole series of new populations of television viewers await the benefits of a constructive examination of the way television influences our lives. The evidence is already clear that older people watch increasing amounts of television. Organizations of older individuals have begun to criticize the televised stereotypes of the helpless and infirm elderly. Recent public broadcast programming such as "Over Easy," directed to an older audience, has shown how television can be of specific interest and benefit to this population.

Another group worthy of special attention includes the institutionalized mental patients, who, in public mental hospitals, watch a large amount of commercial television in their day rooms (Rubinstein et al. 1977). Careful study may provide insights into how this leisure-time activity can be converted into a more meaningful part of the total therapeutic program of the institution. Rubinstein and his colleagues have been studying the effects of TV on institutionalized children (Kochnower et al. 1978).

A BRIDGE BETWEEN RESEARCH AND POLICY

What was initially a narrow focus on the presumed harmful effects of televised violence has begun to broaden into other areas that may have even more extensive and important policy implications. Social scientists can make important contributions to policy determinations, but there are important constraints that must be understood and accepted. In a persuasive argument, Bevan (1977) makes a case for the role of the scientist in contributing to the policy process. He stresses the need for scientists to "seek active roles in policy-making both in the public and in the private sectors." Fundamental to taking such a role is the need to recognize the difference between the world of the scientist and the world of the public official. There is a basic dichotomy between an emphasis on scientific inquiry and an emphasis on action and decision-making. That dichotomy is just as real between the social scientist looking at television and its effects on the viewer and the television officials who have the daily responsibility for deciding what does or does not go on the air.

All too often the social scientist venturing into television policy considerations makes naively sweeping recommendations with no understanding of the enormous complexity of responding to all the pressures and necessities of production. At the same time, some responsible members of the television industry take refuge in a defensive posture about the implications of the research findings. In this context, a variation on Bevan's recommendation that scientists engage in the policy process would be that the social scientists and the television industry officials engage in a continuing dialogue on how the research on television and children can be more effectively utilized.

Fortunately, some efforts in this direction are already under way. All three networks have a variety of activities in which outside research consultants meet with television personnel on programming for children. Special conferences and workshops on research have been sponsored in recent years by foundations, by the industry, by citizen action groups, and by professional organizations.

Perhaps the most compelling reason for more collaboration among all sectors—industry, researchers,

the viewing public, foundations, and government agencies—is the common objectives held. Television is now a dominant voice in American life. It is a formidable teacher of children. Its healthy future should be the interest and responsibility of all of us.

REFERENCES

Adler, R. 1977. *The Effects of Television Advertising on Children.* NSF.

Atkin, C. 1975. *Effects of Television Advertising on Children: First Year Experimental Evidence.* Report #1, Mich. State Univ.

Atkin, C. K., J. P. Murray, and O. B. Nayman, ed. 1971. *Television and Social Behavior. The Effects of Television on Children and Youth: An Annotated Bibliography of Research.* U.S. Government Printing Office.

Bandura, A., and R. H. Walters. 1963. *Social Learning and Personality Development.* Holt, Rinehart and Winston.

Berkowitz, L. 1965. Some aspects of observed aggression. *J. Pers. and Soc. Psych.* 2: 359–69.

———. 1971. Sex and violence: We can't have it both ways. *Psych. Today,* Dec. 1971.

Berkowitz, L., and R. Geen. 1966. Film violence and the cue properties of available targets. *J. Pers. and Soc. Psych.* 3:525–30.

Bevan, W. 1977. Science in the penultimate age. *Am. Sci.* 65:538–46.

Bogart, L. 1972. Warning, the Surgeon General has determined that TV violence is moderately dangerous to your child's mental health. *Pub. Opin. Quart.* 36:491–521. Cater, D., and S. Strickland. 1975. *TV Violence and the Child: The Evolution and Fate of the Surgeon General's Report.* New York: Russell Sage Foundation.

CBS Broadcast Group. 1977. *Learning While They Laugh: Studies of Five Children's Programs on the CBS Television Network.* New York: CBS Broadcast Group.

Children's Television Workshop. 1977. *CTW Research Bibliography.* New York.

Comstock, G., S. Chaffee, N. Katman, M. McCombs, and D. Roberts. 1978. *Television and Human Behavior.* Columbia University Press.

Comstock, G., and M. Fisher. 1975. *Television and Human Behavior: A Guide to the Pertinent Scientific Literature.* Santa Monica, CA: Rand Corporation.

Comstock, G., and G. Lindsey. 1975. *Television and Human Behavior: The Research Horion, Future and Present.* Santa Monica, CA: Rand Corporation.

Consumers Union. 1976. *The Six Billion Dollar Sell.* Mount Vernon, NY.

Cook, T. D., H. Appleton, R. F. Conner, A. Shaffer, G. Tomkin, and S. J. Weber. 1975. *Sesame Street Revisited.* New York: Russell Sage Foundation.

Dienstbier, R. A. 1977. Sex and violence: Can research have it both ways? *J. Communication* 27:176–88.

Fernandez-Collado, C., and B. S. Greenberg. 1977. *Substance Use and Sexual Intimacy on Commercial Television.* Report #5, Mich. State Univ.

Feshbach, S. 1961. The stimulating versus cathartic effects of a vicarious aggressive activity. *J. Abnormal and Soc. Psych.* 63:381–85.

Ford Foundation. 1976. *Television and Children: Priorities for Research.* New York.

Franzblau, S., J. N. Sprafkin, and E. A. Rubinstein. 1977. Sex on TV: A content analysis. *J. Communication* 27:164–70.

Frueh, T., and P. E. McGhee. 1975. Traditional sex-role development and amount of time spent watching television. *Devel. Psych.* 11:109.

Gerbner, G. 1972. Violence in television drama: Trends and symbolic functions. In *Television and Social Behavior,* vol. 1. *Media Content and Control,* ed. G. A. Comstock and E. A. Rubinstein. U.S. Government Printing Office.

Gerbner, G., L. Gross, M. Jackson-Beeck, A. Jeffries-Fox, and N. Signorielli. 1978. *Violence Profile No. 9.* Univ. of Pennsylvania Press.

Hanratty, M. A., E. O'Neal, and J. L. Sulzer. 1972. Effect of frustration upon imitation of aggression. *J. Pers. and Soc. Psych.* 21:30–34.

Howitt, D., and G. Cumberbatch. 1975. *Mass Media Violence and Society.* Wiley.

Kaplan, R. M., and R. D. Singer. 1976. Television violence and viewer aggression: A reexamination of the evidence. *J. Soc. Issues* 32:37–70.

Katz, E. 1977. *Social Research on Broadcasting: Proposals for Further Development. A Report to the British Broadcasting Corporation.* British Broadcasting Corporation.

Kochnower, J. M., J. F. Fracchia, E. A. Rubinstein, and J. N. Sprafkin. 1978. *Television Viewing Behaviors of Emotionally Disturbed Children: An Interview Study.* New York: Brookdale International Institute.

Lefkowitz, M. M., L. D. Eron, L. O. Walder, and L. R. Huesmann. 1972. Television violence and child aggression: A follow-up study. In *Television and Social Behavior,* vol. 3. *Television and Adolescent Aggressiveness,* ed G. A. Comstock and E. A. Rubinstein. U.S. Gov. Printing Office.

Lesser, G. S. 1974. *Children and Television: Lessons from "Sesame Street."* Random House.

Liebert, D. E., R. M. Liebert, J. N. Sprafkin, and E. A. Rubinstein. 1977. Effects of television commercial disclaimers on the product expectations of children. *J. Communication* 27:118–24.

Lyle, J., and H. Hoffman. 1972. Children's use of television and other media. In *Television and Social Behavior,* vol. 5. *Television in Day-to-Day Life: Patterns of Use,*

ed. E. A. Rubinstein, G. A. Comstock, and J. P. Murray. U.S. Government Printing Office.

Ratner, E. M., et al. 1978. *FTC Staff Report on Television Advertising to Children.* Washington, DC: Federal Trade Commission.

Robertson, T. S., and J. R. Rossiter. 1974. Children and commercial persuasion: An attribution theory analysis. *J. Consumer Research* 1:13–20.

Rubinstein, E. A. 1975. Social science and media policy. *J. Communication* 25:194–200.

———. 1976. Warning: The Surgeon General's research program may be dangerous to preconceived notions. *J. Soc. Issues* 32:18–34.

Rubinstein, E. A., J. F. Fracchia, J. M. Kochnower, and J. N. Sprafkin. 1977. *Television Viewing Behaviors of Mental Patients: A Survey of Psychiatric Centers in New York State.* New York: Brookdale International Institute.

Rubinstein, E. A., R. M. Liebert, J. M. Neale, and R. W. Poulos. 1974. *Assessing Television's Influence on Children's Prosocial Behavior.* New York: Brookdale International Institute.

Schaar, K. 1978. TV ad probe snags on Hill, researcher ire. *APA Monitor* vol. 9, no. 6, 1.

Schramm, W. 1976. The second harvest of two research-producing events: The Surgeon General's inquiry and "Sesame Street." *Proc. Nat. Acad. Educ.,* vol. 3.

Schramm, W., J. Lyle, and E. B. Parker. 1961. *Television in the Lives of our Children.* Stanford Univ. Press.

Silverman, L. T., J. N. Sprafkin, and E. A. Rubinstein. 1978. *Sex on Television: A Content Analysis of the 1977–78 Prime-Time Programs.* New York: Brookdale International Institute.

Singer, J. L., ed. 1971. *The Control of Aggression and Violence.* Academic Press.

Social Science Research Council. 1975. *A Profile of Televised Violence.* New York.

Stein, A. H., and L. K. Friedrich. 1975. *Impact of Television on Children and Youth.* Univ. of Chicago Press.

Surgeon-General's Scientific Advisory Committee on Television and Social Behavior. 1972. *Television and Growing Up: The Impact of Televised Violence.* U.S. Government Printing Office.

Tankard, J. W., and S. W. Showalter. 1977. Press coverage of the 1972 report on television and social behavior. *Journalism Quart.* 54:293–306.

Tannenbaum, P. H. 1972. Studies in film- and television-mediated arousal and aggression: A progress report. In *Television and Social Behavior,* vol. 5. *Television Effects: Further Explorations,* ed. G. A. Comstock, E. A. Rubinstein, and J. P. Murray. U.S. Government Printing Office.

U.S. Commission on Civil Rights. 1977. *Window Dressing on the Set: Women and Minorities in Television.* Washington, DC.

Ward, S. 1972. Effects of television advertising on children and adolescents. In *Television and Social Behavior,* vol. 5. *Television in Day-to-Day Life: Patterns of Use,* ed. E. A. Rubinstein, G. A. Comstock, and J. P. Murray. U.S. Government Printing Office.

Ward, S., D. B. Wackman, and E. Wartella. 1975. *Children Learning to Buy: The Development of Con-sumer Information Processing Skills.* Cambridge, MA: Marketing Science Institute.

Watt, J. H., and R. Krull. 1977. An examination of three models of television viewing and aggression. *Human Communications Research* 3:99–112.

Zill, N. 1977. *National Survey of Children: Preliminary Results.* New York: Foundation for Child Development.

Acknowledgments

Chapter 1

A. Rosenfeld, "If Oedipus' parents had only known." *Saturday Review/World,* September 7, 1974. Copyright © 1974 *Saturday Review/World.* Reprinted with permission of A. Rosenfeld.

Daniel G. Freedman, "Ethnic differences in babies." *Human Nature,* January 1979. Copyright © 1978 by Human Nature, Inc. Reprinted with permission of the author and publisher.

Susan Goldberg, "Premature birth: consequences for the parent-infant relationship." From *American Scientist 67,* March 1979. Reprinted with permission of the *American Scientist, Journal of Sigma Xi,* The Scientific Research Society, and the author.

H. Ricciuti, "Developmental consequences of malnutrition in early childhood" (shortened version). From *The Uncommon Child: Genesis of Behavior,* Vol. 3, 1980. Reprinted with permission of the publisher, Plenum Publishing Corporation.

Chapter 2

Aidan MacFarlane, "What a baby knows." From Aidan MacFarlane, *The Psychology of Childbirth.* Copyright © 1977, Harvard University Press (USA) and Fontana Paperbacks (London, U.K.).

Leslie B. Cohen, "Our developing knowledge of infant perception and cognition." *American Psychologist,* 1979, *34,* pp. 894–899. Copyright © 1979 by the American Psychological Association. Reprinted with permission of the author and publisher.

Lewis P. Lipsitt, "Critical conditions in infancy: a psychological perspective." *American Psychologist,* 1979, *34,* pp. 973–980. Copyright © 1979 by the American Psychological Association. Reprinted with permission of the author and publisher.

Jerome Kagan and Robert E. Klein, "Cross-cultural perspectives on early development." *American Psychologist,* 1973, *28,* pp. 947–961. Copyright © 1973 by the American Psychological Association. Reprinted with permission of the author and publisher.

Chapter 3

Selma Fraiberg, "The development of human attachments in blind and sighted infants." From Selma Fraiberg, *Insights from the blind.* New York, Basic Books, Inc., Publishers, 1977, pp. 113–139; 145–146. Reprinted with permission of the author and publisher.

Michael Lewis and Jeanne Brooks-Gunn, "Self, other, and fear: the reaction of infants to people." Reprinted with permission of the authors.

Megan R. Gunnar-VonGnechten, "Changing a frightening toy into a pleasant toy by allowing the infant to control its actions." *Developmental Psychology*, 1978, *14*, pp. 157–162. Copyright © 1978 by the American Psychological Association. Reprinted with permission of the author and publisher.

Barbara G. Melamed and Lawrence J. Siegel, "Reduction of anxiety in children facing hospitalization and surgery by use of filmed modeling." *Journal of Consulting and Clinical Psychology*, 1975, *43*, pp. 511–521. Copyright © 1975 by the American Psychological Association. Reprinted with permission of the authors and the publisher.

Chapter 4

Jerome S. Bruner, "Learning the mother tongue." *Human Nature*, September 1978. Copyright © 1978 by Human Nature, Inc. Reprinted with permission of the author and publisher.

Dan I. Slobin, "Children and language: They learn the same way all around the world." *Psychology Today*, July, 1972. Copyright © 1972 Ziff-Davis Publishing Company. Reprinted with permission of *Psychology Today* and the author.

Kathryn P. Meadow, "Language development in deaf children." From E. M. Hetherington (Ed.), *Review of Child Development Research*, Vol. 5, pp. 450–459, 466–467, 1975. Reprinted with permission of The University of Chicago Press and the author.

Jean Berko Gleason, "Code switching in children's language." From T. E. Moore (Ed.), *Cognitive development and the acquisition of language*, pp. 159–167. Copyright © 1973 by Academic Press, Inc. Reprinted with permission of the author and the publisher.

Barry Silverstein and Ronald Krate, "Cognitive-linguistic development." From *Children of the Dark Ghetto: A Developmental Psychology* by Barry Silverstein and Ronald Krate. Copyright © 1975 by Praeger Publishers, Inc. Reprinted by permission of Holt, Rinehart, and Winston.

Chapter 5

David Elkind, "Giant in the nursery—Jean Piaget." *The New York Times Magazine*, May 26, 1968. Copyright © 1968 by The New York Times Company. Reprinted with permission of the author and publisher.

Rochel Gelman, "Preschool thought." *American Psychologist*, 1979, *34*, pp. 900–905. Copyright © 1979 by the American Psychological Association. Reprinted with permission of the author and publisher.

John H. Flavell, "Metacognition and cognitive monitoring: A new area of cognitive–developmental inquiry." *American Psychologist*, 1979, *34*, pp. 906–911. Copyright © 1979 by the American Psychological Association. Reprinted with permission of the author and publisher.

Alexander W. Siegel and Margaret Schadler, "The development of young children's spatial representations of their classrooms." *Child Development*, 1977, *48*, pp. 388–394. Copyright © 1977 by The Society for Research in Child Development, Inc. Reprinted with permission of the publisher and author.

Ross D. Parke, "Some effects of punishment on children's behavior—revisited." Reprinted by permission from *Young Children*, Vol. XXIV, No. 4 (March 1969). Copyright © 1969, National Association for the Education of Young Children, 1834 Connecticut Avenue, N.W., Washington, D.C. 20009. [Revised and updated for the 1981 edition of this volume.]

Chapter 6

Sandra Scarr-Salapatek, "Unknowns in the IQ equation." *Science*, Vol. 174, pp. 1223–1228, December 17, 1971. Copyright © 1971 by the American Association for the Advancement of Science. Reprinted with permission of the author and publisher.

Sandra Scarr-Salapatek and Richard A. Weinberg, "The war over race and IQ: When black children grow up in white homes. . . ." *Psychology Today*, December 1975. Copyright © 1975 Ziff-Davis Publishing Company. Reprinted with permission of *Psychology Today* and the authors.

Robert B. Zajonc, "Family configuration and intelligence." *Science*, Vol. 192, pp. 227–236, April 16, 1976. Copyright © 1976 by the American Association for the Advancement of Science. Reprinted with permission of the author and publisher.

Eleanor E. Maccoby, Charles H. Doering, Carol Nagy Jacklin and Helena Kraemer, "Concentrations of sex hormones in umbilical cord blood: Their relation to sex and birth order of infants. *Child Development*, 1979, *50*, pp. 632–642. Copyright © 1979 by The Society for Research in Child Development, Inc. Reprinted with permission of the publisher and authors.

Chapter 7

Ross D. Parke and Douglas B. Sawin, "Father-infant interaction in the newborn period: A re-evaluation of some current myths." Reprinted with permission of the authors.

E. Mavis Hetherington, Martha Cox and Roger Cox, "The aftermath of divorce." From J. H. Stevens, Jr. and Marilyn Matthews (Eds.), *Mother-child, father-child relations*. Washington, D.C.: National Association for the Education of Young Children, 1978. Reprinted with permission of the authors.

Carol George and Mary Main, "Social interactions of young abused children: Approach, avoidance and aggression." *Child Development*, 1979, *50*, pp. 306–318. Copyright © 1979 by The Society for Research in Child Development, Inc. Reprinted with permission of the publisher and authors.

Jay Belsky and Laurence D. Steinberg, "What does research teach us about day care?: A follow-up report." *Children Today,* July–August, 1979, *8,* pp. 21–26. Reprinted with permission of the authors and publisher.

David B. Lynn, "Cultural experiments in restructuring the family." From D. B. Lynn, *The father: His role in child development,* pp. 45–61. Copyright © 1974 by Wadsworth Publishing Company, Inc. Reprinted with permission of the publisher, Brooks/Cole Publishing Company, Monterey, California, and the author.

Chapter 8

Steven R. Asher, Sherri L. Oden and John Gottman, "Children's friendships in school settings." From L. Katz, et al. (Eds.), *Current topics in early childhood education,* Vol. 1. Norwood, N.J.: Ablex Publishing Corporation, 1977. Reprinted with permission of the publisher and authors.

Judith H. Langlois and A. Chris Downs, "Peer relations as a function of physical attractiveness: The eye of the bolder or behavioral reality?" *Child Development,* 1979, *50* pp. 409–418. Copyright © 1979 by The Society for Research in Child Development, Inc. Reprinted with permission of the authors and publisher.

Wyndol Furman, Donald F. Rahe, and Willard W. Hartup, "Rehabilitation of socially withdrawn preschool children through mixed-age and same-age socialization." *Child Development,* 1979, *50,* pp. 915–922. Copyright © 1979 by The Society for Research in Child Development, Inc. Reprinted with permission of the publisher and authors.

Greta G. Fein, "Pretend play: New Perspectives." Reprinted by permission from *Young Children,* Vol. 34, No. 5 (July 1979), pp. 61–66. Copyright © 1979, National Association for the Education of Young Children, 1834 Connecticut Avenue, N.W., Washington, D.C. 20009. Reprinted with permission of the author and publisher.

Chapter 9

Paul V. Gump, "Big schools—small schools." *Issues in Social Ecology,* 1965–66, pp. 276–285. Reprinted with permission of Mayfield Publishing Company, Palo Alto, California, and the author.

Pamela C. Rubovits and Martin L. Maehr, "Pygmalion black and white." *Journal of Personality and Social Psychology,* 1973, Vol. 25, No. 2, pp. 210–218. Copyright © 1973 by the American Psychological Association. Reprinted with permission of the authors and publisher.

Howard Garber and Rick Heber, "The efficacy of early intervention with family rehabilitation" in Begab, M.; Garber H.; and Haywood, H. C. (Eds.) *Psychological Influences in Retarded Performance for Improving Competence,* Vol. 2, Baltimore: University Park Press, 1981. Reprinted with permission of the publisher and the authors.

Chapter 10

David Elkind, "Erik Erickson's eight ages of man." *The New York Times Magazine,* April 5, 1970. Copyright © 1970 by The New York Times Company. Reprinted with permission of the author and publisher.

Carol S. Dweck, "Learned helplessness and negative evaluation." *UCLA Educator,* 1977, *19,* pp. 44–49. Reprinted with permission of the publisher and author.

Martin L. Hoffman, "Development of moral thought, feeling, and behavior." *American Psychologist,* 1979, *34,* pp. 958–966. Copyright © 1979 by the American Psychological Association. Reprinted with permission of the author and publisher.

Walter Mischel, "How children postpone pleasure." From *Human Nature,* December 1978. Copyright © 1978 by Human Nature, Inc. Reprinted with permission of the publisher and author.

Anke A. Ehrhardt and Susan W. Baker, "Fetal androgens, human central nervous system differentiation, and behavior sex differences." From Richart, Friedman, and Vande Wiele (Eds.), *Sex differences in behavior,* pp. 33–51. Copyright © 1974 by John Wiley and Sons, Inc. Reprinted with permission of the publisher and authors.

S. Shirley Feldman, Sharon Churnin Nash, and Carolyn Cutrona, "The influence of age and sex on responsiveness to babies." *Developmental Psychology,* 1977, *13,* pp. 675–676. Copyright © 1977 by the American Psychological Association. Reprinted with permission of the publisher and authors.

Miriam M. Johnson, "Fathers, mothers, and sex typing." *Sociological Inquiry,* 1975, *45,* pp. 15–26. Reprinted with permission of the publisher and author.

Eli A. Rubinstein, "Television and the young viewer." *American Scientist,* 66, November 1978. Reprinted with permission of *American Scientist,* journal of Sigma Xi, The Scientific Research Society, and the author.